The Blackwell Guide to

American Philosophy

Blackwell Philosophy Guides

Series Editor: Steven M. Cahn, City University of New York Graduate School

Written by an international assembly of distinguished philosophers, the *Blackwell Philosophy Guides* create a groundbreaking student resource – a complete critical survey of the central themes and issues of philosophy today. Focusing and advancing key arguments throughout, each essay incorporates essential background material serving to clarify the history and logic of the relevant topic. Accordingly, these volumes will be a valuable resource for a broad range of students and readers, including professional philosophers.

1 The Blackwell Guide to EPISTEMOLOGY
Edited by John Greco and Ernest Sosa

2 The Blackwell Guide to ETHICAL THEORY
Edited by Hugh LaFollette

3 The Blackwell Guide to the MODERN PHILOSOPHERS
Edited by Steven M. Emmanuel

4 The Blackwell Guide to PHILOSOPHICAL LOGIC
Edited by Lou Goble

5 The Blackwell Guide to SOCIAL AND POLITICAL PHILOSOPHY
Edited by Robert L. Simon

6 The Blackwell Guide to BUSINESS ETHICS
Edited by Norman E. Bowie

7 The Blackwell Guide to the PHILOSOPHY OF SCIENCE
Edited by Peter Machamer and Michael Silberstein

8 The Blackwell Guide to METAPHYSICS
Edited by Richard M. Gale

9 The Blackwell Guide to the PHILOSOPHY OF EDUCATION
Edited by Nigel Blake, Paul Smeyers, Richard Smith, and Paul Standish

10 The Blackwell Guide to PHILOSOPHY OF MIND
Edited by Stephen P. Stich and Ted A. Warfield

11 The Blackwell Guide to the PHILOSOPHY OF THE SOCIAL SCIENCES
Edited by Stephen P. Turner and Paul A. Roth

12 The Blackwell Guide to CONTINENTAL PHILOSOPHY
Edited by Robert C. Solomon and David Sherman

13 The Blackwell Guide to ANCIENT PHILOSOPHY
Edited by Christopher Shields

14 The Blackwell Guide to the PHILOSOPHY OF COMPUTING AND INFORMATION
Edited by Luciano Floridi

15 The Blackwell Guide to AESTHETICS
Edited by Peter Kivy

16 The Blackwell Guide to AMERICAN PHILOSOPHY
Edited by Armen T. Marsoobian and John Ryder

17 The Blackwell Guide to PHILOSOPHY OF RELIGION
Edited by William E. Mann

The Blackwell Guide to American Philosophy

Edited by

Armen T. Marsoobian and John Ryder

BLACKWELL PUBLISHING
350 Main Street, Malden, MA 02148-5020, USA
108 Cowley Road, Oxford OX4 1JF, UK
550 Swanston Street, Carlton, Victoria 3053, Australia

First published 2004 by Blackwell Publishing Ltd

Library of Congress Cataloging-in-Publication Data

The Blackwell guide to American philosophy / edited by Armen T. Marsoobian and John Ryder.
p. cm. — (Blackwell philosophy guides ; 16)
Includes bibliographical references and index.
ISBN 0-631-21622-7 (hardcover : alk. paper) — ISBN 0-631-21623-5 (pbk. : alk. paper)
1. Philosophy, American. I. Marsoobian, Armen. II. Ryder, John, 1951– III. Series.

B851.B49 2004
191—dc22
2003020353

A catalogue record for this title is available from the British Library.

Set in 10/13pt Galliard
by SNP Best-set Typesetter Ltd., Hong Kong
Printed and bound in the United Kingdom
by TJ International Ltd, Padstow, Cornwall

For further information on
Blackwell Publishing, visit our website:
http://www.blackwellpublishing.com

Contents

Notes on Contributors

Mitchell Aboulafia is Professor and Head of Philosophy at the Pennsylvania State University. He is the author of *The Cosmopolitan Self: George Herbert Mead and Continental Philosophy*, *The Mediating Self: Mead, Sartre, and Self-Determination*, *The Self-Winding Circle: A Study of Hegel's System*, and of articles in social theory, American philosophy, and Continental thought. He is the editor of *Philosophy, Social Theory, and the Thought of George Herbert Mead* and co-editor of *Habermas and Pragmatism*.

Douglas Anderson teaches in the Philosophy Department at the Pennsylvania State University and is a past recipient of the University's Eisenhower Teaching Award. He focuses on American philosophy and the history of philosophy, and is author of two books and numerous essays dealing with issues in American philosophy and culture.

Nicholas C. Burbules is Grayce Wicall Gauthier Professor in the Department of Educational Policy Studies at the University of Illinois, Urbana/Champaign. He has published widely in the areas of philosophy of education, technology and education, and critical social and political theory. He is also the current editor of *Educational Theory*. His forthcoming books include *Pragmatism and Educational Research* (with Gert Biesta) and *Poststructuralism and Educational Research* (with Michael Peters), both due to be published by Rowman and Littlefield in 2004.

James Campbell was educated at Temple University and the State University of New York at Stony Brook, and is currently Distinguished University Professor at the University of Toledo. He has been a Fulbright Lecturer at the University of Innsbruck (1990–1), and the University of Munich (2003–4). He is editor of *Selected Writings of James Hayden Tufts* (Southern Illinois University Press), and author of *The Community Reconstructs: The Meaning of Pragmatic Social Thought* (University of Illinois Press), *Understanding John Dewey: Nature and Cooperative Intelligence* (Open Court), and *Recovering Benjamin Franklin: An Exploration of a Life of Science and Service* (Open Court).

Vincent Colapietro is Professor of Philosophy at Pennsylvania State University (University Park Campus). His main areas of historical research are classical American philosophy and Continental European philosophy from the late nineteenth century until the present. His areas of systematic interest include metaphysics, aesthetics, semiotics, and political philosophy. He is the author of *Peirce's Approach to the Self* (1989), *Glossary of Semiotics* (1993), and *Fateful Shapes of Human Freedom: John William Miller and the Crises of Modernity* (2003). He is currently working on a book exploring the affinities and differences between pragmatism and psychoanalysis.

William D. Dean is professor of Constructive Theology at the Iliff School of Theology. Specializing in the distinctively American tradition of religious thought, his books include: *American Religious Empiricism* (1986), *History Making History* (1988), *The American Spiritual Culture* (2002), and *The Religious Critic in American Culture* (1994), which received the American Academy of Religion Award for Excellence. He earned the B.A. from Carleton College and the Ph.D. from The University of Chicago.

Michael Eldridge teaches philosophy at the University of North Carolina at Charlotte. His *Transforming Experience: John Dewey's Cultural Instrumentalism* (Vanderbilt University Press, 1998) considered Dewey's proposal to intelligize practice in social and political life. He was the 1999 Center for Dewey Studies' Democracy and Education Fellow, and he wrote the introduction for the second volume (1919–39) of the Dewey correspondence (published by InteLex Corp. on CD-ROM; 2001).

William J. Gavin is Professor of Philosophy at the University of Southern Maine, where he has taught for the past 34 years. He has also been Guest Professor at the Institute of Philosophy, Katholeik Universiteit Leuven, Belgium, and Visiting Faculty Fellow at the National University of Ireland, Galway. He is the editor of two books on American Philosophy: *Context Over Foundation: Dewey and Marx*, and, most recently, *In Dewey's Wake: Unfinished Work of Pragmatic Reconstruction*. He is the author of two books: *William James and the Reinstatement of the Vague*, and *Cuttin' the Body Loose: Historical, Biological, and Personal Approaches to Death and Dying.*

Leonard Harris is Professor of Philosophy at Purdue University, where he is also a graduate faculty member of the Philosophy Department, the English and Philosophy Department Program, Communications and Philosophy Department Programs, and former director of African American Studies. He was William Paterson University Visiting Distinguished Professor, 2002–3, and is a non-resident Fellow of Harvard University. He is the editor of *Philosophy Born of Struggle: Anthology of Afro-American Philosophy from 1917* (1983), *The Critical Pragmatism of Alain Locke* (1999), *The Philosophy of Alain Locke: Harlem Renaissance and*

Beyond (1989), *Children in Chaos: A Philosophy for Children's Experience* (1991), co-editor with S. Pratt and A. Waters of *American Philosophies* (2002), and with A. Zegeye and J. Maxted of *Exploitation and Exclusion: Race and Class* (1991), as well as editor of the *Newsletter on Philosophy and the Black Experience.*

Richard E. Hart is Cyrus H. Holley Professor of Applied Ethics and Professor of Philosophy at Bloomfield College in New Jersey. He is the editor or co-editor of three books in the areas of environmental ethics, American philosophy, and Plato studies. He has lectured and written numerous articles and reviews on such American figures as John Dewey, Justus Buchler, Susanne Langer, and John Steinbeck. He has served on the Boards of the American Association of Philosophy Teachers, the Long Island Philosophical Society, and the Executive Committee of the Society for the Advancement of American Philosophy. He is a member of the editorial boards of *The Personalist Forum, Aitia*, and *Metaphilosophy.*

Larry A. Hickman is Director of the Center for Dewey Studies and Professor of Philosophy at Southern Illinois University, Carbondale. He is the author of *Modern Theories of Higher Predicates* (1980), *John Dewey's Pragmatic Technology* (1990), and *Philosophical Tools for Technological Culture* (2001), as well as editor of *Technology as a Human Affair* (1990), *Reading Dewey* (1998), *The Essential Dewey* (with Thomas Alexander, 1998), and *The Correspondence of John Dewey* (1999 and 2001).

Scott Johnston has just completed his Ph.D. in the philosophy of education program in the Department of Educational Policy Studies at the University of Illinois, Urbana/Champaign.

John W. Lango is Professor of Philosophy at Hunter College of the City University of New York and author of *Whitehead's Ontology* and various articles about Whitehead (and other subjects), most recently, "Whitehead's Category of Contrasts" and "Relational Particulars and Whitehead's Metaphysics."

Peter T. Manicas has written books and many articles on the philosophy of social science, American naturalism and pragmatism, and social theory. For many years in the Department of Philosophy at Queens College, CUNY, he is currently Director of Liberal Studies at the University of Hawaii at Manoa and Professor of Sociology.

Joseph Margolis is Laura H. Carnell Professor of Philosophy at Temple University. He has published more than 30 books and is the author, most recently, of *Selves and Other Texts: The Case for Cultural Realism, What, After All, Is a Work of Art? Lectures in the Philosophy of Art*, and *Reinventing Pragmatism: American*

Philosophy at the End of the Twentieth Century. Appearing soon is his latest book, *The Unraveling of Scientism: American Philosophy at the End of the Twentieth Century*.

Armen T. Marsoobian is Professor of Philosophy at Southern Connecticut State University. His primary areas of research are American philosophy, aesthetics, Peircean semiotics, and metaphysics. His articles on Dewey, Peirce, Buchler, Emerson, and aesthetics have appeared in a variety of journals and anthologies. He has co-edited two books in systematic metaphysics, Justus Buchler's *Metaphysics of Natural Complexes* and *Nature's Perspectives: Prospects for Ordinal Metaphysics*. Most recently he has edited a volume of essays entitled *The Philosophical Challenge of September 11*. He is editor-in-chief of the philosophical journal *Metaphilosophy*. Currently he is working on a manuscript on aesthetic meaning and opera.

John J. McDermott is University Distinguished Professor of Philosophy, Texas A&M University. He is one of the pre-eminent philosophers active on the American scene. He has written hundreds of essays and authored two books: *The Culture of Experience: Philosophical Essays in the American Grain* (1976) and *Streams of Experience: Reflections on the History and Philosophy of American Culture* (1986). He has edited the writings of William James, Josiah Royce, and John Dewey. Most recently he has been editing the multi-volume edition of *The Correspondence of William James* (University of Virginia Press).

Timothy McDonough is a doctoral student in the philosophy of education program in the Department of Educational Policy Studies at the University of Illinois, Urbana/Champaign.

Frank M. Oppenheim, SJ, received the Ph.D. in philosophy from St. Louis University in 1962, and has taught philosophy at Xavier University, Cincinnati, Ohio, for more than 40 years. Currently, he is serving as a research professor in philosophy at Xavier, continuing his specialization in Josiah Royce, American philosopher of community (1855–1916). He has published three books and more than 20 articles on Royce and looks forward to the spring 2004 publication by the University of Notre Dame Press of his life's opus magnum: *Reverence for the Relations of Life: Re-imagining Pragmatism via Josiah Royce's Interactions with Peirce, James, and Dewey*.

Scott L. Pratt is Associate Professor and Head of the Philosophy Department at the University of Oregon. He received his B.A. in philosophy from Beloit College (Wisconsin) and his Ph.D. from the University of Minnesota. He teaches courses in American philosophy, epistemology, philosophies of culture and race, and the history of modern European philosophy. He is the author of numerous articles on topics in American philosophy and pragmatism, and of the recent book, *Native Pragmatism: Rethinking the Roots of American Philosophy* (Indiana University Press). He is also co-editor of *The Philosophical Writings of Cadwallader Colden* (Humanity Books) and *American Philosophies: An Anthology* (Blackwell).

Sandra B. Rosenthal is Provost Eminent Professor of Philosophy at Loyola University, New Orleans. She has published 11 books and more than 200 articles on pragmatism and on its relation to other areas of philosophy. She has given formal lecture series on pragmatism in China, Germany, and Poland; delivered more than 200 papers/lectures at conferences and universities in the US and abroad; served as president of several major philosophical societies; and is a member of numerous editorial boards of journals and book series. Her publications include *Speculative Pragmatism, Charles Peirce's Pragmatic Pluralism*, and *Time, Continuity and Indeterminacy.*

John Ryder is Professor of Philosophy, Director of the Office of International Programs, and Academic Director of the Center on Russia and the United States at the State University of New York. His articles have been published in a wide range of journals, and have been translated into several foreign languages. He is editor of a special issue of the journal *Metaphilosophy* on philosophy in Eastern Europe. He is author of *Interpreting America: Russian and Soviet Studies of the History of American Thought* (1999), editor of *American Philosophic Naturalism in the Twentieth Century* (1994), and co-editor of *The Philosophical Writings of Cadwallader Colden* (2002) and *Pragmatism and Values* (2003). He is the co-founder and co-chair of the Central European Pragmatist Forum, and in 2002 became president of the Alliance of Universities for Democracy.

Herman J. Saatkamp, Jr. is President of The Richard Stockton College of New Jersey. Previously, he was Dean of the School of Liberal Arts at Indiana University and Purdue University in Indianapolis, holding appointments in the Indiana University's School of Medicine as Professor of Medical and Molecular Genetics and as Professor of Medical Humanities. He received his Ph.D. from Vanderbilt University in 1972. He was the General Editor of *The Works of George Santayana* (1977–2003). Medical ethics, American philosophy, ethical theory, and genetic explanations of complex animal behavior are his research fields of expertise and interests. His publications include 9 books and more than 50 articles.

Charlene Haddock Seigfried is a Professor of Philosophy and American Studies and a member of the Women's Studies Committee and the Philosophy and Literature Program at Purdue University. She is past president of the Society for the Advancement of American Philosophy, was the John Dewey Lecturer for 1998, and is currently Vice-President of the William James Society and a member of the executive board of the Society for the Study of Women Philosophers. Recent works include *Pragmatism and Feminism, Feminist Interpretations of John Dewey* (ed.), and introductions for the University of Illinois Press editions of Jane Addams, *Democracy and Social Ethics* and *The Long Road of Woman's Memory.*

Shannon Sullivan is Associate Professor of Philosophy and Women's Studies at Penn State University. She teaches and writes in the intersections of feminist theory, American pragmatism, Continental philosophy, and critical race theory. She recently published *Living Across and Through Skins: Transactional Bodies, Pragmatism, and Feminism* (Indiana University Press) and currently is finishing a book tentatively entitled *Hearts of Darkness: Unconscious Habits of White Privilege.*

Bryan Warnick is a doctoral student in the philosophy of education program in the Department of Educational Policy Studies at the University of Illinois, Urbana/Champaign.

Kathleen Wallace is Professor of Philosophy at Hofstra University. She is co-editor of the second, expanded edition of Justus Buchler's *Metaphysics of Natural Complexes* (SUNY Press) and of *Nature's Perspectives: Prospects for Ordinal Metaphysics* (SUNY Press). She is also the author of numerous articles on ordinal metaphysics, Santayana, Hume, and feminist philosophy.

Preface

This *Guide* is the culmination of many years of effort on the part of the editors. Early in the process we received invaluable guidance from John J. McDermott, who strongly believed in the book's importance given the then prevalent amnesia surrounding the history of American philosophy. The Society for the Advancement of American Philosophy has provided an intellectually nourishing community for many of the scholars who have contributed to this volume. Creating this volume would have been a much more difficult task without this society. The editors would also like to acknowledge a strong philosophical debt to Justus Buchler. It was in Buchler's seminars at State University of New York at Stony Brook that the editors had their first significant exposure to the rich diversity of thought that marks the American philosophical tradition. We dedicate this volume to the memory of Justus Buchler.

Heartfelt gratitude must go to Erin K. Carter who contributed much toward making the diverse chapters of this volume stylistically consistent and eminently readable. Thanks also goes to Alex Larson, a student assistant, who helped manage many aspects of this project. Finally, Connecticut State University is gratefully acknowledged for the financial support that helped make this project possible.

Editors' Introduction

This book is a guide to American philosophy, not to philosophy in America. The distinction is an important one. Beginning roughly after the end of the Second World War, as John McDermott points out in the Epilogue to this book, American philosophers turned to various European philosophical movements then current for their inspiration. For most of the latter half of the twentieth century philosophy in America concerned itself primarily with the issues and developments in logical and linguistic analysis that stemmed from the influence of the Vienna Circle and from the work of Bertrand Russell and Ludwig Wittgenstein in the UK. To a lesser extent, some philosophers in America turned their attention to the work in phenomenology and existentialism that had its primary home in Germany and France.

But American philosophy, with which all of the chapters in this book deal, is something else. Above all, it means the philosophical studies undertaken by what are often called the "classical American philosophers" of the later nineteenth and early twentieth centuries. This was the period of Charles Sanders Peirce, William James, John Dewey, George Herbert Mead, George Santayana, Josiah Royce, Alfred North Whitehead, and many others; this was the period during which philosophical pragmatism was born, first in the work of Peirce, and soon after to be developed in novel directions by James and Dewey. It was also the period in which American philosophical naturalism developed a sense of itself as a distinctive philosophical perspective. Santayana was a naturalist philosopher, as was his contemporary John Dewey, and building on the work of Dewey and his colleague F. J. E. Woodbridge, a school of philosophical naturalism developed at Columbia University that prospered into the 1960s.

American philosophy of the classical period of course did not create itself *ex nihilo*. No philosophical perspective ever does. Peirce, James, Dewey and their colleagues knew and valued the work of many of the philosophers in America who had preceded them. Chief among them were the earlier nineteenth-century idealists, including of course the Transcendentalists Emerson and Thoreau. James, in addition, had greater intimacy with many European ideas as a result of his frequent trips to Germany and France. Peirce and Dewey especially had their philosophical training in the broadly idealistic intellectual milieu of the mid-nineteenth century, under the influence of both Emersonian Transcendentalism and the Hegelianism of recent German immigrants.

But then American idealism was not spun out of whole cloth either. In fact, not surprisingly, the story of American philosophy begins in the early years of the North American colonies, to which brilliant colonial figures brought their European intellectual traditions, which they in turn used in their confrontation with conditions peculiar to their new home. The social and political theory of the seventeenth-century Puritans is a case in point – in fact the entire Puritan intellectual edifice is an example. Puritan philosophy reached its apex in the early eighteenth century in the work first of Cotton Mather and then, most famously, in the person of Jonathan Edwards. At the same time other factors were at work, expressed in one direction by the Anglican philosopher Samuel Johnson, and in a more practical, and ultimately political direction by Benjamin Franklin, Thomas Jefferson, James Madison, and the entire revolutionary generation. American idealism of the nineteenth century developed as an extension of certain of these trends and as a reaction against others. In the latter half of the nineteenth century, the impact of Darwinism and other evolutionary theories had a telling impact on this idealism and set the stage for the naturalism and scientism of the decades to follow. The point, however, is that there is a continuous story of the development of American philosophy from its Puritan origins through the classical period of the pragmatists and naturalists, to contemporary writings by a number of philosophers who work in the broadly defined pragmatist and naturalist traditions. The chapters in this volume tell that story.

Organization

A word is in order first about the organization of the book, and then about the principles of selection of the individual chapters. The volume is divided into three sections plus an Epilogue. The three sections cover the historical background, the major figures in American philosophy, and the major themes in the tradition. The essays in Part I provide a broad overview of the historical trajectory of American philosophy from the colonial period through nineteenth- and twentieth-century idealism to the pragmatism and naturalism that have dominated the tradition from the late nineteenth century to the present.

Part II, which constitutes the bulk of the volume, consists of individual essays on the major figures in the tradition, as well as those who have particular interest in contemporary circumstances. There is invariably a certain degree of overlap between essays in the first and second sections. Some of the ground covered in chapter 3, on pragmatism, reappears in the essays in Part II on the major pragmatists. While this inevitable fact presented certain editorial challenges, we came to realize that the respects in which these chapters overlap are in fact a virtue. The reader interested in pragmatism may turn first to chapter 3 for an overview, and then to chapters 5, 6, 9, and 10, and others, for a deeper study of the ways pragmatism was developed by individual thinkers, in this case by Peirce, James, Dewey, and Mead. The same reader may also wish to look at other chapters on individual thinkers to see the ways in which many of the pragmatist insights and conceptual commitments were used by such figures as Jane Addams, C. I. Lewis, W. E. B. Du Bois, and Susanne Langer. The same suggestion applies to those interested in American idealism. Chapter 2 will provide the general background, while chapter 7 explores in detail the work of Josiah Royce, the greatest of the twentieth-century American idealist philosophers. And with respect to naturalism, the background is in chapter 4, many of the themes of which can be explored more deeply in chapters 8, 9, 16, and 18, on Santayana, Dewey, W. V. O. Quine, and Justus Buchler respectively.

Part III consists of essays devoted to the major themes in the American philosophical tradition. The reader who is interested in education, or religion, or aesthetics, or social and political thought, or in the traditional concerns of epistemology, may turn to those chapters for an overview of the ways those themes have been treated in the tradition. Again, there is inevitably a certain degree of overlap between these chapters and some of the preceding ones, but it is also the case that the overlap is advantageous for the reader because it will enable him to better select those chapters that are likely to interest him most.

John McDermott's "The Renascence of American Philosophy," which constitutes the Epilogue, is an overview of the study of American philosophy in American universities over the past several decades. It is also a survey of the available primary texts of the major figures in the tradition. That survey is itself supplemented by a list of suggested readings, both primary and secondary, that follows each of the chapters. Taken together, the lists of suggested readings constitute an up-to-date bibliography of the primary works available and the best of the secondary literature on the whole range of American philosophy.

Selection

One of the most difficult problems editors of a volume of this sort face is selecting the topics to be covered, or, more seriously, the individual philosophers to be included. With respect to the topics, it is obvious enough that there must be chapters on pragmatism, idealism, naturalism, community, and experience, since these intellectual movements and topics are at the heart of the American philosophical tradition. With respect to the individual thinkers to be included, it is also obvious enough that there must be chapters on Peirce, James, Royce, Santayana, Dewey, Mead, and Whitehead. Beyond these major figures, the principles of selection become murkier. Because this, like any volume, is constrained by space, it was necessary to leave out many figures for whom a plausible case for inclusion could easily be made.

First, we decided not to include any essays on figures before the "classical" period, which we regard to have begun with Peirce. Readers interested in the work of Edwards, Franklin, Thoreau, or Emerson may turn especially to the historical chapters in Part I. Second, a collection like this might rightly include, for example, essays on such classical or post-classical period figures as F. J. E. Woodbridge, Roy Wood Sellars, John Herman Randall, Jr., Ernest Nagel, or Sidney Hook, and we could mention many others. In the end, we decided that we would include representative figures who developed the classical tradition in interesting or influential ways. Thus there are chapters devoted to C. I. Lewis, W. V. O. Quine, and Justus Buchler.

We also decided that in the section on major figures we would not include any who are currently writing. That is not because there are no interesting or important philosophers currently at work in the American stream, but because the tradition itself is so rich that, given the space constraints, it was impossible to do justice to both its historical depth and its current vitality. Some of the essays in the sections on historical background and major themes, however, do address contemporary work, so the reader may look there to obtain a sense of the work currently being done. It is in those essays that the insights of Richard Rorty, for example, and John Lachs, as well as some of the contributors to the volume itself, for example Joseph Margolis and John McDermott, are discussed. Thanks to these individuals, and many others, the American philosophical tradition is not only alive, but currently in the midst of a robust reawakening.

Finally, we would like to point out that there are essays here that we can say with confidence would not have appeared in a comparable volume twenty or even fewer years ago. This is due to the view we have taken of the nature of a literary canon. As a general point, history, including literary and intellectual history, lives in the present. That is to say that it is in the present that history has meaning, and power. This means, among other things, that the significance of historical developments, and again this includes the literary and the intellectual, is to some important degree determined not simply by past events but as importantly by present problems and concerns. Within the past two decades, attention among scholars interested in American philosophy has extended to areas it had not inhabited before, particularly with respect to questions of race and gender. That this should happen is particularly appropriate in the context of the study of American philosophy, since it is one of the hallmarks of the American tradition, stated powerfully by Dewey and others, that if philosophy is to have significance it cannot restrict itself to the problems of the past, but it must turn its attention to the problems of the present. This is the heart of what Dewey meant by the phrase "reconstruction in philosophy." In that spirit, scholars of American philosophy have in recent years paid increasing attention both to African American and women philosophers in the tradition, and to the bearing their work and insights may have in contemporary circumstances. Thus we have included chapters on four figures who, though well known before, have only recently taken up an appropriate place among the central thinkers in the history of American philosophy. The chapters on W. E. B. Du Bois, Alain Locke, Jane Addams, and Susanne Langer describe both the character and power of their thought, as well as the direction of current scholarship in the study and application of their work.

It is our hope that the collection of essays included in this volume, written by the best scholars in the field, can contribute to the current renascence of American philosophy. As Dewey might have put it, we are today sorely in need of intellectual insight and an intelligent approach to the problems of individual and social life. As these essays indicate, there is a wealth of such insight and intellectual guidance in the American philosophical tradition.

Part I

Historical Traditions

Chapter 1

Early American Philosophy

John Ryder

Introduction: The Span of Early American Philosophy

The term "early American philosophy" refers to philosophy in the British colonies of North America, in particular the colonies that would later become the United States of America, from the middle years of the seventeenth century until the early nineteenth century, a span of almost two hundred years. That span of time includes as its major stages orthodox Puritanism as it developed in the colonies, the period in the early eighteenth century when Puritanism confronted the then modern scientific and philosophical work of Isaac Newton and John Locke, the social and natural philosophy of the revolutionary period, and the emerging philosophical idealism of the early nineteenth century.

A number of outstanding philosophers and scientists lived and worked in the colonies during this period. Among the more important Puritan thinkers of the seventeenth century were John Cotton, John Winthrop, and Increase Mather, all of whom represented orthodox Puritanism. At the same time there were several important Puritan dissenters, notably Anne Hutchinson and Roger Williams. By the early eighteenth century Puritanism needed to confront the new work of Newton and Locke. Some early attempts were undertaken by Cotton Mather, and later by the most profound thinker American Puritanism ever produced, Jonathan Edwards. At the same time, other Puritan thinkers began to mix traditional Puritan thought with emerging social ideas of popular sovereignty and even natural rights. In the early eighteenth century the most important of these was the preacher John Wise, and in mid-century Jonathan Mayhew began to mix Puritanism with more secular, almost revolutionary thought.

By the eighteenth century other thinkers, who either broke away from Puritanism or who grew out of other theological traditions altogether, began to engage European philosophy in an American colonial context. One of these was Samuel Johnson, an Anglican minister who became Bishop Berkeley's most influential representative in the colonies. Johnson, following Berkeley, was a philosophical idealist, but at the same time as he wrote, which was in the first half of the eighteenth century, a materialist tradition began to develop. The most influential materialist philosopher at this time was the Edinburgh-educated physician Cadwallader Colden, whose fascinating career included philosophical writings on materialism, important contacts with and writings about the Iroquois Confederacy in the New York colony, and serving for 16 years as Lieutenant Governor of the Province of New York. Colden's career spanned most of the first three-quarters of the eighteenth century, since he died in 1776. Among his contemporaries in what might be called the early American Enlightenment was the much more well-known philosopher, scientist, inventor, entrepreneur, ambassador, and political revolutionary Benjamin Franklin.

By the time of Colden's death, American philosophy entered a new stage, one that was dominated by the revolutionary break from England and the efforts to forge a new nation, a new government, and in some respects a new kind of society. Not surprisingly, the intellectual emphasis at this time to a certain extent turned away from the theological concerns of the Puritans and the more abstract interests of people like Colden to the social and political issues generated by the Revolution and the subsequent birth of the United States. The most outstanding philosophical figures at this time were Thomas Jefferson, Thomas Paine, and James Madison, whose work provided the theoretical background to and the substance of the social and political events of the revolutionary years and the period of the development of the Federal Constitution in the 1770s and 1780s. As important as social and political philosophy was during these years, however, American philosophers did continue to attend to more theoretical questions of natural philosophy. Among the more important of these people were Thomas Jefferson, Benjamin Rush, and Thomas Cooper.

By the end of the eighteenth and beginning of the nineteenth centuries there was a turn away from the natural philosophy, materialism, and revolutionary social thought of the Enlightenment to a more pronounced philosophical idealism, which corresponded to a religious revival that sprang up around the country. One result of the rejection of the early interest in natural philosophy and materialism, coupled with the increasing influence of religion, was the rise of Transcendentalism, a philosophical and literary movement that dominated American thought, particularly in New England.

The Context of Early American Thought

No philosophical thinking ever occurs in a vacuum, in the sense that it appropriates certain intellectual traditions and it addresses issues and problems that are conditioned by the intellectual milieu and by the economic, social, and political contexts of its time. This is certainly true of American philosophy in the colonial and revolutionary periods. The Puritans of New England brought with them from England a number of philosophical and religious conceptions. They were strongly Calvinist, which means among other things that they regarded the world as fully determined by the will of God, and this included the destinies of human beings both during their lives and for eternity. Their Calvinism was influenced by the sixteenth-century Dutch theologian Ramus, himself a Reformation era heir to the Platonism and Aristotelianism of the later Middle Ages. Puritans' thinking, consequently, took as a given the view that God was fully in control of the world and human destinies, the truth of certain Platonist and Aristotelian conceptions of the relation of nature and human beings to God, and the belief that their role in creating a society in the New World reflected God's will.

One of the most important assumptions of the Puritans, in fact the one that compelled them to leave England for the New World, was what came to be called Congregationalism. This is the view that social communities are to be constructed on religious principles, one of which is that social and political authority should reside with the religious leaders chosen by the congregation. As a result of these assumptions, Puritan thinking, even about social and political matters, was thoroughly theological. Puritan communities were theocratic, and their philosophical investigations inevitably reflect that fact.

In the early years of the New England colonies Puritan thinking concerned primarily the details of the ways their theocratic assumptions could best be put into practice. They had to decide how to structure their new societies, how to understand the relation between religious authority and secular problems, how to understand themselves, chosen as they were to do God's will in the New World, in relation to the native inhabitants of the areas they colonized, and not least importantly the extent of the congregation's authority in relation to that of the leadership. These were precisely the questions that caused Anne Hutchinson, Roger Williams, and others to dissent from the decisions of the authorities, and ultimately to strike out on their own. The problem was that the Puritans, and similar groups such as the Pilgrims, had left England in search of the freedom to pursue their own religious goals. They did not, however, hold that religious freedom was a good in itself. In America that view belongs to the late eighteenth century. The Puritans searched for the freedom to pursue their religious life not because religious freedom is paramount but because they believed that their view was the truth. It took a good deal of theoretical and practical struggle before religious freedom became a good in itself.

As time went on, the intellectual, economic, and political contexts began to change. By the end of the seventeenth century, for example, the English Crown had reasserted its control over the Puritan colonies, which compelled the Puritan intellectuals to reconsider the place of their congregations in new political contexts. Furthermore, the Puritans, still thinking themselves special in God's eyes, began to feel threatened by the French Catholics in nearby Quebec, a threat that they saw in religious terms as the encroachment of evil on the kingdom of God's elect. Again, Puritan thinking began to take a new turn, as it had to address its problems in a new light. Most importantly of all, however, was the appearance in the New World of the work of Isaac Newton and John Locke in the early eighteenth century. The most astute of the Puritan thinkers, Jonathan Edwards the greatest among them, realized that the world-view expressed in Newton's physics and mathematics, and the conception of human nature and political relations developed by Locke, were fundamental challenges to their understanding of the world. Edwards attempted to adjust his Calvinism to accommodate them, but he was to fail. Other Puritan thinkers, such as John Wise and Jonathan Mayhew, responded to the new ideas, and to new social and political realities, by adopting new conceptions. For Wise it was a somewhat democratic impulse based on Puritanism's initial Congregationalism, and for Mayhew it was the conception of natural rights.

By the middle of the eighteenth century the colonial economic situation had changed so thoroughly that to many people the older social and political relations, especially the relationship between the colonies and Great Britain, seemed no longer to work. In this context it is not surprising that a new emphasis on social and political theory arose. As the break with Great Britain approached, it became clear to its leaders that a theoretical justification would need to be developed, the result of which was the appropriation of English and French political theory to support the concepts of natural rights and popular sovereignty, most profoundly and succinctly expressed in Jefferson's Declaration of Independence, but in other documents as well. Similarly, the rise in sophisticated political theory, the greatest practitioner of which was James Madison, came itself as a response to the demands of the American political situation in the years after the revolutionary war. Madison, Alexander Hamilton, and others rose to the occasion to create the theoretical underpinnings of the new, secular republic.

History did not end with the creation of the Constitution in 1789, however. The country continued to expand, creating new economic opportunities and problems, and associated social developments. Furthermore, religious thought began to take a different tack, even in the older settled regions of the eastern seaboard that had accommodated themselves to the secularism that underwrote revolutionary social and political thinking. As a result, in both the new settlements in the "west," and in older communities in the east, theologians, philosophers, and literary figures began to explore more spiritually oriented intellectual possibilities.

The Trajectory of Early American Philosophy

It can be dangerous to attempt to generalize about a philosophical period, especially one as complex as the nearly two centuries that are under consideration here. The danger of course is over-simplification, not to mention the risk of too selective an emphasis. With that danger in mind, though, it is advantageous to consider several themes that appear in early American thought which have been exceptionally influential throughout American history. If their emphasis is selective, it is because they scream to be selected.

The overriding theme is that of building a new world. From their earliest settlements, the Puritans saw themselves as creating something new, something unique, something special, something particularly delightful in God's eyes. They referred to themselves as constructing the New Canaan, or the City on a Hill. Their new world would embody God's will in a way that no other had done before. In this very Puritan conception is the seed of what would come to be called American exceptionalism, the view that for one reason or another America holds a unique place among nations, and that it has a special mission. On the one hand, this view has been the source of great hope for Americans. We are, it is sometimes said, an optimistic people, and it is certainly easier to be optimistic if one believes that one is special, or in a certain sense chosen, or at least that one's society is the light to which all others look for hope. On the other hand, the belief that one has a special mission or destiny can be tragically dangerous. The Puritan City on a Hill grew into the nineteenth-century notion of Manifest Destiny, which itself was used to justify the ruthless destruction of Native Americans and their societies. It was also the justification of the beginnings of American imperialism at the turn of the twentieth century. And later in the twentieth century it sustained the American leadership, and much of the American population, through the Cold War, sometimes to devastating effect in such places as Vietnam. Even Ronald Reagan would appeal to the Puritan's own language, as he did in a speech proclaiming again that America was and remains the City on a Hill.

The shortcomings of these consequences of early American thought, however, should not obscure its virtues. The same theme of building a new world that was expressed in Puritanism reappeared in the revolutionary thought of the eighteenth century. The Puritans may have tried to construct a New Canaan, but the revolutionary leaders from 1776 through 1789 succeeded in constructing a new republic. Though that republic was not then, nor is it now, the model of pure virtue that many of its most vocal supporters assert, it is nonetheless a positive historical development of extreme importance. Jefferson, Paine, Madison, and others legitimated, in a way no one else had been able to do, the concepts of rights, of sovereignty, of popular government, of republicanism, of religious freedom, and of democracy. The philosophical and practical uses to which those concepts were put gave them a new currency, and they have continued to inspire social activists and political visionaries to this day.

Seventeenth-Century Puritanism

The Puritans were members of one of the many religious sects that developed in England and Scotland during the course of the sixteenth-century Reformation. By the end of the century, with the reign of Elizabeth I, the Church of England had assumed the position of the established church in the realm. For many Christians, however, the Church of England had not distanced itself sufficiently from the theology and practices of Rome, and so a number of other traditions developed, many of which were influenced by the Calvinism that had become prominent in several places on the continent. The Puritans were one such group. Since the concept of religious freedom was not well established in any of the religious traditions of the time, however, the Church of England was not tolerant of the many dissenting sects. In the early years of the seventeenth century many of the Puritans, who felt that they would never be able to pursue their religious beliefs and practices freely in England, left first for Holland and then for the New World. In North America they settled in several colonies in what became, collectivity, the Massachusetts Bay Colony. By the 1640s the Puritans in England had became much stronger, and in fact they were able, as the leading force in the parliamentary rebellion against the Stuart monarchy, to gain power in England and establish the Puritan Commonwealth, a regime that survived until the Restoration of the monarchy in the early 1660s.

In North America, the Puritan settlers developed their own intellectual, social, and political traditions in response to their unique circumstances and needs. As we have seen, they brought with them the Calvinism, itself heavily Augustinian in orientation, of their home communities in England. In their version of Augustinianism, the history of humankind since the Fall is a history of the battle between good and evil. In the end, because God is in absolute, that is to say complete and fully determined, control of events, and since God is all good, history is the stage on which good progressively triumphs over evil. In that struggle, however, people play a crucial role as instruments of either good or evil. One of the most profound features of Calvinism is its belief in predestination, which is the view that the destiny of any given individual is fully determined by God independently of anything the individual does in life. Any other view would be inconsistent with God's omnipotence. Since one's eternal destiny is predetermined, it became important to Puritans to live such lives as would provide "signs" that one is among the chosen, the elect. To be among the elect, and to carry on one's life in the context of the battle of good with evil, defined the theological atmosphere in which Puritan thought addressed its problems, the most crucial of which were social and political.

The three concepts most central to Puritan social and political theory were the distinction between the visible and the invisible "churches," covenant theory, and Congregationalism. In the mid-seventeenth century the Puritan leader John Cotton developed his conception of the unity of the visible and invisible churches. As the colonies developed and proliferated, it became necessary to develop an understanding of the relations among them and of their essential unity. Cotton did this by arguing that the "visible" churches, by which he meant the many distinct Puritan communities, all had a single, "invisible" source, and so they were unified as distinct expressions of a single foundation. The invisible ground of the earthly communities was of course God's will and power, and the distinct communities, as expressions of that source, took on the single obligation to express and effect God's will. The political authorities of the communities, then, were themselves understood to be the guardians of God's will, and they in turn assumed the responsibility to ensure that God's will and purposes were manifested in the social life of the communities and protected from the threats posed by the ever present forces of evil. In such a community, there was no room for dissent.

The question of the nature of freedom was also important for the Puritans to consider. John Winthrop developed the theory of the distinction between natural and civil or moral freedom. Natural freedom is the capacity to do as one wills, which includes and even allows the capacity to do evil. Natural freedom, or doing as one wills, is to be contrasted with civil or moral freedom which, according to the divine law, places limits and constraints on the exercise of natural freedom. Natural freedom, as the capacity to sin, is an instrument of evil. Civil and moral freedom, by contrast, represent law as it flows from the will of God, law that provides the conditions necessary for a spiritually informed life.

Civil and moral freedom, and the relation between the visible and the invisible church, were secured through what the Puritans called the Covenant. Many later American commentators have regarded Puritan covenant theory as an early expression of what was in the eighteenth century to become social contract theory, one of the most important theoretical foundations of the concept of popular sovereignty and constitutionalism. The Puritan Covenant was an agreement between the members of the community and God, the most famous example of which was the Pilgrims' Mayflower Compact. Agreements or covenants like this one served as the foundation of Puritan communities, combining as they did the fledgling democracy of Puritan congregations, in the form of a limited popular sovereignty, and the Calvinist commitment to ground society in God's will.

The incipiently democratic character of Puritan communities, their Congregationalism, was the third significant feature of Puritan social and political theory and practice. One of the objections maintained by those who dissented from the Church of Rome, and subsequently the Church of England, was that too much religious authority was concentrated in the central hierarchy of the church. As an alternative, the Puritans developed an organizational structure whereby individual religious communities, or congregations, would maintain and govern their own religious and social life. On the one hand, this decentralized structure created a problem, since despite its virtues there remained a practical and theoretical need for unity among the congregations. As we have seen, the concept of the "invisible church" was an attempt at the theoretical level to develop the necessary unity. On the other hand, Puritan Congregationalism served over time as a soil in which the seeds of democracy could sprout. Despite its theocratic and what we would probably now consider to be narrow-minded understanding of the world, the legitimation of local, decentralized authority in Puritan Congregationalism made it possible for the eighteenth-century concepts of individual rights and popular sovereignty to break through the tradition of aristocratic privilege and the absolute authority of the monarch.

None of this happened easily or smoothly, however. The Puritan commitment to its own version of the truth, and its subsequent intolerance of alternative views, directly contradicted its tendency toward individual or at least local religious and social autonomy. The contradiction would be overcome in time, but only through the struggle and sacrifice of many members of the community. The seventeenth century saw several such "dissenters" from Puritan orthodoxy whose opposition to the theocratic establishment had important theoretical and practical consequences. The three most influential were Anne Hutchinson, Thomas Hooker, and Roger Williams. Hutchinson and Hooker objected primarily to the structure of the Puritan congregations, which is to say to the inordinate power of the theocratic leaders which they took to be inconsistent with congregationalist principles. Tolerance not being a strong suit of the Puritan divines, Hutchinson and Hooker both found themselves and their followers exiled from the Massachusetts Bay Colony. The same fate befell Roger Williams, whose dissent from Puritan orthodoxy was in many ways far more thoroughgoing than that of Hutchinson or Hooker. Williams not only objected to the concentration of authority in the leadership, but he also advanced a number of progressive ideas that would only gain more common currency in the eighteenth century. He rejected the divine origin of government, he advocated what would later be called inalienable natural rights, he defended freedom of religious thought and the separation of church and state, and he argued for the rights of native peoples and blacks. In light of the importance of these ideas in the eighteenth and subsequent centuries, Williams appears in retrospect to be the most forward-looking of the seventeenth-century Puritan figures.

Puritanism in the late seventeenth century is best understood as a response to a series of critical challenges. The first of these was political. Earlier in the century, as the Massachusetts Bay and other colonies were established, they were left largely on their own. By late in the century, however, the Crown began to exert its control more directly over all the North American colonies. In 1684 the British government annulled the Massachusetts Charter, and in 1691 it appointed a colonial governor, answerable directly to London. These measures effectively ended the political authority of the Puritan oligarchy. At the same time, the Puritan communities began to feel themselves besieged by a growing Catholic presence as a result of immigration from Quebec. From an orthodox Calvinist point of view, such pressure from representatives of the Church of Rome was a threat to the religious convictions of the Puritans and to their mission in the New World. When we add to all this an economic recession that occurred in Massachusetts in 1690, we can begin to understand how to the Puritan leadership at the time it may have appeared that their world was falling apart.

The second set of challenges to orthodox Puritanism was intellectual, and their sources, as we have already seen, were primarily the work of Isaac Newton and John Locke. Both of these influential English scholars were working in the latter years of the seventeenth and the early years of the eighteenth centuries, and they were both largely responsible for articulating a view of the world and of human nature and society that was diametrically opposed to that of the Puritans. In his physics, optics, and mathematics, Newton had described and justified a view of the world in which natural phenomena are understood as mechanistic processes governed by natural law. Furthermore, particularly through his mathematics he had made it clear that the processes of nature can be understood through rational inquiry and analysis. Newton's work was so compelling that the traditional Aristotelianism of the Calvinist world-view, and its reliance on revelation as the source of knowledge of the world, became increasingly untenable.

John Locke's work in psychology, or what we might call philosophical anthropology, his empiricist approach to knowledge, and his political writings had a comparable effect. Locke had argued that human beings are the products of environments; we develop as we do, and learn what we know, as a result of our experience. This general perspective served to "naturalize" our understanding of human being just as Newton, following many scientists and mathematicians before him, had "naturalized" our understanding of nature. In Locke's case he went further to apply the same rational and naturalist principles to the study of human society and politics. By doing so he developed a conception of social and political relations, and specific prescriptions for political organization, that had no place for God's will and divine revelation. By doing so as forcefully and compellingly as he did, Locke effectively undermined the foundations of Puritan theocracy. At the turn of the eighteenth century, Newton and Locke more than any others defined the modern conception of nature, knowledge, and human being. The modernist perspective posed a critical challenge for Puritanism.

Early Eighteenth Century

Two men with powerful intellects rose to the occasion to attempt to sustain orthodox Puritanism in the face of the challenges of modernity. The first of them was Cotton Mather, whose life and work spanned the turn of the eighteenth century. Mather, like the other influential Puritan thinkers, was a clergyman and a representative of the Puritan theocracy. In an attempt to maintain orthodox principles, but contrary to the spirit of Congregationalism, Mather was among those who at the end of the seventeenth century tried to unite the congregations into a single system. Unlike his contemporaries, however, Mather was also interested in making use of current learning in the service of traditional Calvinism. Mather is perhaps most famous as the figure who supervised, indeed encouraged, the hysteria of the witch trials in Salem in the 1680s. In fact, while this does represent one important aspect of Mather's thinking and activities, it was also Mather who, in his book *The Christian Philosopher*, incorporated into his theology much of the Newtonian view of the world and the experimental methods of contemporary science. Newton's mechanistic model of nature left open the question of creation, purpose, and guidance of the world. While many Newtonians concluded that the "machine" of nature must have a maker, they did so by positing a God who creates the world and then leaves it to natural law to elaborate the details. For Mather, the creator of the machine was the traditional God of Calvinism, and he interpreted natural laws as God's means of influencing the progress of the world. There were limits, however, to the extent to which Newtonianism and Calvinism could be united, one of the most striking of which is that if God uses natural law to pursue his own ends then there is no way to account for predictability, one of the most significant features of nature according to Newtonian science.

As interesting as Mather's attempt to accommodate modern knowledge was, the most brilliant of the late Puritan thinkers was the early seventeenth-century clergyman Jonathan Edwards. Like Mather, Edwards is most well known for aspects of his fundamentalist Calvinism, in his case in the form of the fire and brimstone preacher. Edwards delivered what is still one of the most famous sermons in American history, "Sinners in the Hands of an Angry God." But also like Mather, Edwards was a thoughtful, careful philosopher who used a rigorous logic in the attempt to sustain Calvinist principles.

While he was a young student at Yale, Edwards had the opportunity, which at the time could be had nowhere else in the colonies, to read the latest works of Newton, Locke, and other prominent scientists and philosophers of the time. This exposure led Edwards early in his career to attempt to synthesize his Ramist Calvinism with Cartesianism, Lockean empiricism, and Newtonian physics. He never abandoned his devout Calvinism, though, and he became famous not long after for his leading role in the religious enthusiasm known as the Great Awakening. He retained a deep religious pietism throughout his life. But he also retained his serious attention to the science and philosophy of his time. He accepted Newtonian atomism as well as central aspects of Locke's psychology, though he gave both his own theological twist. Not surprisingly, though, he was not a slavish adherent of either Newton or Locke. He could not, for example, accept the concept of a void, because the reality of non-being, of nothingness, would be a limitation of the absolute power of God.

Edwards's most famous philosophical work was his objection to free will and defense of strict determinism. As an orthodox Calvinist he might have defended determinism on scriptural or at least theological grounds, but it is an indication of the degree to which he absorbed the tenor of his times that he went to considerable lengths to develop his defense of a traditional Calvinist point of view in largely rational terms. Employing elements of contemporary psychology, as well as a conception of natural causation, Edwards argued that no act of the will can be regarded as free, or uncaused. His arguments for determinism are complex and sophisticated, and they indicate how far Puritan thought had come from its earlier scriptural dogmatism.

If Mather and Edwards tried to confront modernity in the defense of Puritan orthodoxy, there were other representatives of the Puritan tradition who were inclined to develop strains of Puritan theory and practice in directions that brought them into contact with the more secular trends of colonial social and political thought. John Wise and Jonathan Mayhew were the most outstanding examples of this trend in Puritanism. John Wise, the earlier of the two, was a staunch defender of congregationalist principles at the turn of the eighteenth century. Among the other challenges that faced Puritanism during these years, the congregations of New England found themselves in a struggle with both the Puritan oligarchy which was trying to unite the churches under a single synod, and the English Church and government, which were attempting to exert control over them. Wise defended the congregations and their traditional autonomy, and in doing so he advanced social ideas that anticipated later eighteenth-century secular social principles. In response to the threat of subordination to the English, for example, he argued in general against the Crown's infringement of colonists' rights. In the process he also argued for the "natural freedom" and innate sociality of humankind. Congregationalist, essentially democratic principles fulfill this "natural freedom," he argued, and furthermore democracy follows from the "social disposition" of human beings. The line of descent from theological Congregationalism to secular democratic theory becomes more clearly evident in Wise than it had been in any earlier thinker, with the possible exception of Roger Williams.

The last of the traditional Puritan theologians who can also be regarded as a proto-Enlightenment thinker was Jonathan Mayhew, who lived during the early and central decades of the eighteenth century, dying just ten years before the Declaration of Independence. Like Wise, Mayhew was dealing primarily with church matters, but the terms in which he made his arguments prefigured many of the central tenets of the revolutionary period. For example, he argued that the church leadership has an obligation to conduct the affairs of the church in certain ways, and if the leadership does not fulfill its responsibilities in that regard it is a duty of the membership to rebel against it. A similar argument for the right to revolution, though in a purely secular context, is the central feature of the Declaration of Independence. In addition to the right to revolution, Mayhew also found himself defending other features of what was to become American revolutionary theory, specifically the separation of church and state, popular sovereignty, the view that government is grounded in the consent of the governed, and that the primary purpose of government is to secure the safety and happiness of the people.

As important as Puritan theory was, in both its orthodox and dissenting forms, there was in the first half of the eighteenth century other significant philosophical activity that would prove far more important for the subsequent development of American intellectual culture and society. The three most important philosophers during this period, each for his own reasons, were Samuel Johnson, Cadwallader Colden, and Benjamin Franklin.

Samuel Johnson received much the same philosophical education as did Jonathan Edwards. Like Edwards, he was a student at Yale, where he received a traditional Puritan education, and where he also came into contact with current trends in science and philosophy. Unlike Edwards, Johnson's experience led him to reject much of his Calvinist upbringing and join the Anglican Church. It was

Johnson among others who argued for the importance of free will, and against whom Edwards wrote his defense of determinism. Johnson is perhaps most well known, however, for having been the most prominent supporter in the colonies of the philosophical idealism of George Berkeley. Johnson was convinced that Berkeley's immaterialism was the most appropriate philosophical interpretation of the new learning that developed from Newton and Locke, and that it accorded perfectly with the theological mainstream of Anglican thinking at the time.

There were problems with Berkeley's ideas, though, and Johnson attempted to address them in his own writings. In his 1752 book *Elementa Philosophica* Johnson drew on his own Platonistic, Calvinist upbringing to give immaterialism more of a Platonist treatment than Berkeley had. Johnson was concerned that Berkeley's famous principle *esse est percipi*, to be is to be perceived, risked reducing the existence of things to individual perception, which in turn runs the risk of solipsism. To avoid this conclusion Johnson argued that the existence of objects of perception and perceiving minds is rooted in divine forms, and that knowledge of the forms is possible through an intellectual intuition that resembled Descartes' "light of reason." Johnson's metaphysics, however, was probably less influential than his ethics, which he developed in Part II of the same book. Here, surprisingly for someone raised in the heart of orthodox Puritanism, Johnson argued that ethics is the inquiry into the "highest happiness."

Johnson was also party to one of the most intriguing philosophical correspondences in early American thought. He was of course on familiar terms with other leading intellectuals of the time, one of whom was Cadwallader Colden, and he and Colden exchanged letters over more than two decades in which they debated the sort of Berkeleyan immaterialism that Johnson sought to defend. For his part Colden was a staunch advocate of materialism, a point of view which he developed in what for the time were new directions. Colden was educated in medicine at Edinburgh University in Scotland, and he emigrated to the colonies in the early years of the eighteenth century. By the time of his death he had become one of the most prominent figures in the colonies in science, philosophy, and mathematics. He also served as Lieutenant Governor of the Province of New York, and he was an important representative of the Crown to the Iroquois Confederacy in upstate New York. Colden was in fact the author of the first history of the Five Nations of the Iroquois.

Colden could not follow Berkeley's idealistic treatment of Newtonianism. It was clear to Colden that not only did Newton's work imply the independent existence of matter, but that matter was to be understood as active. This was a startling idea for eighteenth-century science and philosophy, since it was taken for granted, as it had been for the two thousand years since Aristotle, that matter was passive. In Newton's version, a material particle at rest would stay at rest until acted upon from the outside, and the reason was that matter had no active principle of its own. By contrast, in his most important work, *The First Principles of Action in Matter*, Colden argued that in fact matter is active in three distinct senses. There is, he said, the power of resistance, the power of motion, and the power that enables bodies to act on one another at a distance. Underneath these notions is an idea that Colden emphasized throughout his work, which is that the nature of anything is its effects, what it does, and therefore because the nature of material bodies is in their effects, they must be inherently active. It is significant that with this point of view Colden is striking what would, more than a century later, become a distinctly pragmatist note.

The final important figure of this period, arguably the most influential, can also with the benefit of hindsight be read as a precursor, or perhaps even an originator, of an American pragmatist perspective. In fact, recent scholarship on Benjamin Franklin has done just that. Franklin was born and raised in Boston in the early years of the eighteenth century, but he made his mark as a printer, publisher, and political figure in Philadelphia, where he lived for most of his life. He was also by all accounts one of the leading scientists of his day, and later in his life the most well-known American intellectual and political figure in Europe. Franklin is most famous for his work in the sciences, particularly his studies of electricity, later for his advocacy of a revolutionary break from England, and for his contributions to that cause, primarily as colonial ambassador to France during the revolutionary war. It is only recently that Franklin is being appreciated more as a philosopher in his own right.

To see the significance of Franklin as a philosopher one has to be prepared to accept a broad conception of philosophy not simply as the pursuit of technical questions in epistemology, metaphysics, and logic, but as the rational, systematic consideration of the questions and difficulties generated by the human situation. Franklin had little or no interest in the former, but a great deal in the latter. His expressly philosophical writings, which span nearly the whole of his long life, deal primarily with questions of ethics. And all of his writings on the problems of people, the civic issues faced in Philadelphia, and the social, economic, and political challenges of his time, express a general assumption that the ideas that matter are the ideas that make a difference somewhere, that are capable of effecting change, of solving problems. Read from this point of view, Franklin, even more than Colden, embodied, to some extent defined, American cultural notions of practicality and a pragmatist intellectual character.

Later Eighteenth Century

The same broad understanding of philosophy that allows us to understand the philosophical importance of Franklin also lends philosophical significance to the social and political insights that dominated the latter half of the eighteenth century in America, during what is sometimes called the American Enlightenment. As was true for the Puritan thinkers of the earlier years of the century, American social and political thinking of the latter half was strongly influenced by European philosophers. The first among these was again John Locke.

Locke had been active in the largely peaceful, so-called Glorious Revolution in England in 1689, when James II (and the Stuart monarchy) was deposed, and William of Orange was invited by Parliament to assume the English Crown, an event that was the birth of England's constitutional monarchy. That experience was a profound influence on Locke, who at the turn of the eighteenth century wrote his *Two Treatises on Government*, in which he worked out among other things the concept of the separation of powers in government. In France in the first half of the eighteenth century a follower of Locke, the Baron de Montesquieu, developed his principle of the separation of powers even further. Locke and Montesquieu were well read by the American leaders of the Revolution, as were the more radical French *philosophes*, probably including Rousseau, who had developed in great detail the concept of the social contract, following Locke and Thomas Hobbes before him. The ideas of these political philosophers, as well as those of the Scotsman David Hume and others, can be traced in the writings of James Madison, John Adams, Thomas Jefferson, Alexander Hamilton, Thomas Paine, and many others who led the American Revolution and the subsequent creation of the American state. Montesquieu and the British writers tended to have a greater influence on the more conservative group among the Americans, those who would later be known as the Federalists, while the thinking of Rousseau and the French radicals appears in the more radical wing of the American revolutionary movement, especially in Paine, Jefferson, and their followers.

The American Revolution had its roots in very practical, in fact economic, concerns. The colonial leaders opposed several of the taxes being imposed on them by the English Parliament, and more generally they resented the mercantilist policies followed by London. Parliament's habit of granting state monopolies to certain companies effectively squeezed colonial merchants out of important markets, with the eventual result of a growing desire on the part of colonists to divorce themselves from London's control and develop their own independent policies. The sentiment grew among the colonists for self government, which in turn raised in very practical and clear terms the need to determine the principles on which such government would rest. The result of that process was of course the American Revolution, but the philosophical effect was the development of powerful new social and political theory. In constructing their political concepts the Americans drew on their own experience, on English and French sources, as well as to a certain extent on the experience of Native Americans, who in the Iroquois Confederation for example had a rich store of practical experience in the construction of complex political organizations.

The American Enlightenment developed few ideas that had not been expressed before. Its importance lies in the fact that its leaders understood those ideas carefully enough to apply them, and by succeeding as well as they did, they contributed to the power and influence those ideas have had to the present day. One of the most important concepts of the period was the notion of natural rights. In most of Europe, even the more "progressive" nations like England, it was taken for granted that what rights people had were a consequence primarily of noble birth or of accumulated wealth. The circumstances of one's birth and the amount of wealth one commanded were even more powerful determinants of any rights one could expect in the more traditional regimes of France, the German States, the Hapsburg Empire, the Russian Empire, and the other traditional monarchies of Europe. The idea that people had rights by nature rather than by social convention or circumstance was a radical challenge to the prevailing social structures. Precisely what rights those are, and who actually has them, were matters of disagreement even among their proponents. In the Declaration of Independence, for example, Jefferson asserted the rights of life, liberty, and the pursuit of happiness, while a decade later the framers of the Constitution, following John Locke, thought more in terms of a natural right to the pursuit and accumulation of property. With respect to those who should be regarded as having such rights, most American writers of the time believed that they applied for the most part only to free white men of property. Whichever way one saw it, the idea of natural rights had serious ramifications as it began to be more widely held.

There were two critical political concepts that followed from the notion of natural rights. The first was the idea of popular sovereignty, which is to say that the ultimate source of political authority is a nation's citizenry. Again, this is a profound challenge to the commonly held view that the nobly born and the wealthy are the natural rulers of society and the source of a government's legitimacy. Once one asserts that a broader segment of the population is the real "sovereign" rather than the monarch or the nobility, one must take a different approach to the structure and ends of government. With respect to its structure, the result is an electoral system whereby the citizenry, or that segment of it that is able to secure the right of suffrage, chooses its leaders. With respect to the ends of government, there emerged the second profound implication of the concept of natural rights, which was that the purpose of government is to protect the rights of its citizens. Precisely what this means in practice will depend on which rights the citizenry is regarded as having. For example, if we accept the view that the most fundamental right is the pursuit and accumulation of property, as many of the American revolutionary leaders did, then it will naturally follow that the role of government is to protect citizens' access to that pursuit and their property if and when they succeed in accumulating any. On the other hand, if we hold in a more Jeffersonian spirit that something like the pursuit of happiness is a fundamental right, then it will more likely follow that the role of government is to ensure that the citizenry has access to the necessary conditions of happiness, whether that might be land, or education, or gainful employment, or housing, or some other social good. Jefferson took the first two of these quite seriously, and he developed plans for both the distribution of land to all free, white men, and a system of universal public education. The question of which rights a government is to secure for its people remains a contested one today, but there is broad agreement with the Enlightenment view that it is the responsibility of government to protect those rights.

With the victory of the Revolution and the inadequacy of the Articles of Confederation, many practical and theoretical questions came to the fore. The result was the writing and eventual adoption in 1789 of the Constitution of the United States, which today is by far the oldest political constitution still in effect. The Constitution's insights were many, most of them at the practical level of the development of political structures that allowed for the formation of a national organization and a national identity. At the theoretical level the Constitution reflects many of the disagreements between the more conservative and the more radical segments of the American social and intellectual leadership. The most glaring example, aside from the compromises about slavery, was the fact that the Constitution as it was originally drafted embodied the view of the vast majority of those working on it that the primary role of government was the protection of property rights, no matter how disproportionately property, and therefore wealth, was distributed. In other words, there was little in the original draft of the Constitution that spoke to the interests or rights of the vast majority of the population. This was rectified somewhat by the insistence of many of the more radical political leaders around the country that the Bill of Rights be appended to the original document. The Bill, which consisted of the first ten amendments to the Constitution, included a number of rights that ordinary citizens could claim against the power of the government.

One of the most significant amendments in the Bill of Rights, because it has had lasting ramifications for the character of American society and because it reflected an important trait of the intellectual temper of the times, was the one that prohibited the government from establishing any religion as the state religion and which granted freedom of and from religion to all citizens. This was as revolutionary a concept at the time as were natural rights or popular sovereignty, because it had been assumed that no society could survive, let alone flourish, without a religious establishment that had the authority of the state behind it. Such a view was certainly taken for granted in all the major states of Europe. By prohibiting the establishment of a state religion, and by recognizing the right of citizens to hold and practice religious beliefs, or not, as they chose, the Constitution took a giant step in the direction of the modern, secular state.

The fact that the disestablishment clause of the First Amendment was even possible reflects a significant feature of the philosophical temper of the Enlightenment, in America and Europe. The more radical of European and American intellectuals had been arguing for decades against the power of the church, whichever one it might happen to have been, and the corresponding social, economic, and political power of the clergy. Related to this quite practical criticism of existing societies was the growing inclination to view the world in general in more secular terms. This was made possible by both the social critique of the church and the advances in science, mathematics, and philosophy represented by Newton, Locke, and others. Newton's insights were so profound, and so compelling, that they allowed others to begin to see the world or the universe not in theistic terms, as the Puritans and everyone else until then had, but rather as a vast machine, a mechanism that operated on principles that were discoverable empirically and explainable mathematically without recourse to a divine being.

The latter claim is actually a bit of an exaggeration. The mechanical universe as it was understood in the eighteenth century could be explained in natural rather than supernatural terms, except for its origin. As long as matter was understood passively, as it was by most people, then the mechanical process of nature could be explained scientifically, but not its origin. Scientists and philosophers for the most part continued to believe that a divine being had created the machine, but had then left it to run its course on its own natural principles. This view was called deism, and it was very common among late eighteenth-century intellectuals. In America such intellectually influential leaders as Thomas Jefferson, Thomas Paine, and Ethan Allen, among others, could be identified as deists. One of the distinctive characteristics of deistic thought was that while it recognized a creator God, it was a God that had lost its personal nature. The deists' God was not a loving father or vengeful lord, as more traditional theologians postulated, but was more of a mechanical principle necessitated by the prevailing scientific and philosophical ideas. The deists' God was also not the source of salvation, so deism had no need of churches, ceremonies, and clergy. It was not in any traditional sense a religion. It was, rather, an intellectual nod in the direction of religion while endorsing a largely secular, naturalist, and humanist understanding of the world and society.

For some of the leading philosophers of the time, Jefferson again among them, it was even possible to make the bold intellectual step, following somewhat the lead of Colden earlier in the century, to materialism in their understanding of the world. As the explanatory power of the idea of spirit began to wane, as it would in a deist's approach to nature, it became increasingly tempting to abandon it altogether and endorse the idea that nature, including human being and all the complexity of its psychological make-up and social expression, is to be understood entirely in material terms. Jefferson, for example, would say in a letter to John Adams that "to think of anything non-material is to think of nothing." There were other notable materialists of the day as well, including Thomas Cooper, a young devotee of Jefferson. Despite its increasing frequency, however, materialism and materialists were still regarded with great suspicion by the mainstream of the population, or that segment of the mainstream that attended to such matters. The reaction to Cooper's views in fact would continue to be a problem for him well into the nineteenth century.

Conclusion

One of the reasons Cooper and other materialists would find little support in the nineteenth century is that the materialism and naturalism of the previous decades fell into disfavor. Perhaps it was the normal swing of the intellectual pendulum, or perhaps it was the fact that many of the more progressive social and political promises of the revolutionary period remained unfulfilled as the nineteenth century dawned. Whatever the reason, the early nineteenth century saw a resurgence of interest in religion and in philosophical idealism. As more people began to move inland from the coastal cities, there was a religious revival in what was still the "western" regions of the country. In the east, particularly in Boston and nearby areas of New England, Enlightenment deism and naturalism were merged with the older Puritan and congregationalist traditions to produce Unitarianism, which in turn proved to be fertile ground for the development of American thought. It was primarily within the Unitarian context that in the early decades of the nineteenth century American romanticism found expression in New England Transcendentalism.

Despite the turn to romanticism and idealism, though, it could be argued that the early centuries of American philosophy had a significant impact on the future of American thought. This is especially true with respect to the two most important developments in American philosophy in subsequent years: pragmatism and naturalism. We have seen that there was a distinctly pragmatist strain in the work of both Cadwallader Colden and Benjamin Franklin. While it is true that the philosophers who would develop the pragmatist line of thought, primarily Charles Sanders Peirce, William James, and John Dewey, did not turn to either Colden or Franklin, one can in retrospect see that their pragmatist inclinations serve as the beginning of a distinctly pragmatist trajectory in American thought. If one adds Emerson, which is entirely plausible given his emphasis on action, the path from Colden and Franklin to Dewey and contemporary pragmatist philosophers becomes clearer still. Similar observations can be made about the secular, naturalist character of Enlightenment thought and its relation to the naturalism that played such an important role in twentieth-century American thought.

Arguably, however, the influence of early American philosophy was far greater on American culture in general than on the development of technical philosophy. The Puritanism of the seventeenth century laid the foundation for the persistent American view of the uniqueness of the American experience, for American exceptionalism, with all its achievements and shortcomings. The eighteenth century, especially in the period of the Revolution and its aftermath, gave currency to the importance and continuing influence of natural, human rights, popular sovereignty, and to a constitutionalism that has persisted to the present day.

Suggested reading

Bailyn, Bernard, *The Ideological Origins of the American Revolution* (Cambridge, MA: Harvard University Press, 1967).

Campbell, James, *Recovering Benjamin Franklin* (La Salle, IL: Open Court, 1999).

Conklin, Paul, *Puritans and Pragmatists* (Bloomington: Indiana University Press, 1968).

Faust, Clarence H. and Thomas H. Johnson, *Jonathan Edwards: Representative Selections* (New York: Hill and Wang, 1962).

Flower, Elizabeth and Murray G. Murphy, *Philosophy in America*, vol. I (New York: Capricorn Books, 1977).

Kuklick, Bruce, *Churchmen and Philosophers* (New Haven, CT: Yale University Press, 1985).

Lemay, J. A. Leo and Paul M. Zall, eds., *The Autobiography of Benjamin Franklin: A Genetic Text* (Knoxville: University of Tennessee Press, 1981).

Miller, Perry, *The Life of the Mind in America* (New York: Harcourt Brace Jovanovich, 1965).

Parrington, Vernon L., *Main Currents in American Thought*. Vol. I: *The Colonial Mind* (New York: Harcourt, Brace & World, Inc., 1954).

Pratt, Scott and John Ryder, *Philosophical Writings of Cadwallader Colden* (Amherst, NY: Prometheus Books, 2002).

Ryder, John, *Interpreting America: Russian and Soviet Studies of the History of American Thought*, pt. I (Nashville, TN: Vanderbilt University Press, 1999).

Schneider, Herbert, *A History of American Philosophy* (New York: Columbia University Press, 1963).

Smith, John, *Jonathan Edwards* (Notre Dame, IN: University of Notre Dame Press, 1992).

Waller, George M., ed., *Puritanism in Early America* (Boston, MA: D. C. Heath and Company, 1950).

Walters, Kerry S., *The American Deists* (Lawrence, KS: University of Kansas Press, 1992).

White, Morton, *Philosophy, The Federalist, and the Constitution* (New York: Oxford University Press, 1987).

Wills, Gary, *Explaining America* (New York: Penguin Books, 1981).

—— *Inventing America* (New York: Vintage Books, 1979).

Chapter 2

Idealism in American Thought

Douglas Anderson

Introduction

American soil was initially fertile for the growth of idealism, and during the eighteenth and nineteenth centuries a variety of idealistic philosophies flourished. Traces of these idealisms remain in contemporary philosophical thought in the United States. Both subjective and objective idealisms have found their way into the fabric of American culture at various times. Subjective idealism has usually appeared as a corollary to other philosophical perspectives, such as skepticism or critical philosophy, as in the recent phenomenon of neo-pragmatism. In this chapter, I focus on objective idealism, which, following nineteenth-century practice, I define roughly as the belief that the cosmos is essentially mind-like. Secondarily, I attend to the "social idealism" – the effort to realize ideals in human practice – that often accompanied idealistic metaphysics in the American tradition.

Objective idealism arrived on the shores of New England unannounced, embedded in the culture of Calvinism. Jonathan Edwards stands out as its most forceful and persuasive proponent in the early years of the colonial era. Edwards did not identify himself as an idealist, but his Calvinism bore with it a metaphysical foundation that was thoroughly idealist in character.

Edwards's idealism is revealed as early as 1730 in his "Notes on the Mind." The dual influences of Bishop George Berkeley and Isaac Newton are readily apparent. From Berkeley, Edwards borrowed the conception of God as creator and sustainer of all being:

> And indeed the secret lies here: That, which truly is the Substance of all Bodies, is *the infinitely exact, and precise, and perfectly stable Idea, in God's mind*, together with his stable Will, that the same shall gradually be communicated to us, And to other minds, according to certain fixed and exact established Methods and Laws.[1]

Insofar as God's ideas are constitutive of the real, Edwards followed Berkeley in a corollarial conception of "truth." "Truth, in the general, may be defined, after the most strict and metaphysical manner, *The consistency and agreement of our ideas, with the ideas of God*."[2] Newton's influence is found in the way God's ideas are organized. The laws of nature are writ large as the lawful development of God's ideas. The upshot of this for Edwards is a kind of steady-state universe in which causal relations are constrained by the order of the whole. As Edwards puts it: "The existence and motion of every Atom, has influence, more or less, on the motion of all other bodies in the Universe, great or small, as is most demonstrable from the Laws of Gravity and Motion."[3]

The practical effects of Edwards's Calvinistic idealism can be found throughout his sermons and writings. For Edwards, we are finite beings attendant on a sovereign God. In his 1734 essay "A Divine and Supernatural Light," he discloses human dependence on this God for our epistemic and moral insights. Through "God's light" we are able to apprehend His ideas and thus achieve truth: "God is the author of all knowledge and understanding whatsoever. He is the author of the knowledge that is obtained by human learning: he is the author of all moral prudence, and of the knowledge and skill that men have in their secular business."[4]

The idealism of Edwards's Calvinism was indeed a creative synthesis of the ideas available to him to make sense of the content of his faith. But for many in New England, there was a more intuitive, habitual, and naive grasp of this idealistic outlook. The world was indeed God's idea or plan, and it was their purpose to fulfill some small role in the unfolding of this plan. Edwards laid this out clearly in his treatise on the freedom of the will; our freedom was to be found only in following the path God laid out for us. Yet, as habitual as this belief was in eighteenth-century New England, it was challenged experientially by the entrepreneurial lifestyles enabled by the opportunities of the New World. The likes of Benjamin Franklin could not easily settle for the closure and constraints of Calvinistic idealism. Consequently, other idealisms began to emerge that championed personal freedom over the neat, deterministic ontology of Edwards's universe.

Perhaps most notable among these was that of Samuel Johnson. Johnson (1696–1772) was a Congregationalist minister who converted to the Anglican Church. Early on he taught at Yale University and, later, was, for nine years, president of King's College (which later became Columbia University). Johnson corresponded with Bishop Berkeley, and his own version of idealism reveals a significant debt to Berkeley's work.

Using our experience of the human mind as the ground of his metaphysics, Johnson argued that the universe was the work of a "Great Supreme Intelligence," which he defined as "an *infinite Mind or Spirit, or a Being infinitely intelligent and active*."[5] This infinite mind, in Platonic fashion, he considered the keeper of the Ideas or Archetypes from which all particular existents are derived. It is best construed as a creative agent who conditions and sustains our being in the world, but who does not determine all the details.

The ethical dimension of Johnson's idealism was clearly distinct from that of Edwards. For Johnson, God is the author of our moral truths and grants us access to them through a moral sense, "a kind of quick and almost intuitive sense of right and wrong."[6] However, we are free to turn our backs on our moral sense; agreeing with the Arminians whom Edwards resisted, Johnson granted persons a limited but free agency. As he saw it, "*Moral good* must therefore consist in freely chusing [sic] and acting conformable to the *truth* and *Nature of Things*."[7]

Transcendentalism

Both Edwards and Johnson tried to provide full and clear descriptions of their theistic worlds, showing the role of persons within the larger framework. During and after the American Revolution, the philosophical emphasis shifted from systematic metaphysics to the practical and the political. Thus, when idealism reappeared in a new guise, that of the New England transcendentalists, it did so as a result of issues concerning the conduct of life. Specifically, the transcendentalists sought to revise their conceptions of religious experience and morality. The constraints of Calvinist and Anglican church doctrines were for the most part left behind, to be replaced by a transcendentalist ontology that was considerably more amorphous than the idealisms of Edwards and Johnson.

The transcendentalist movement of the first half of the nineteenth century included Ralph Waldo Emerson, Margaret Fuller, Henry Thoreau, Bronson Alcott, and Elizabeth Peabody, among others. On the whole, the transcendentalists were not oriented toward systematic philosophy or technical metaphysics. Rather, as romantics, they were responding to the cool rationality of Enlightenment materialism and deism, and to the coldness and blandness of Calvinism and Unitarianism. In addressing these experiential issues, however, the transcendentalists also rejected the Lockean empiricism or "sensualism" that had given impetus to both Calvinism and Unitarianism in New England. Their critique of their contemporary scene was underwritten by an implicit idealistic metaphysics. In his essay "The Transcendentalist," Emerson described this metaphysics and its origin:

> It is well known to most of my audience, that the Idealism of the present day acquired the name of Transcendental, from the use of that term by Immanuel Kant, of Konigsberg, who replied to the skeptical philosophy of Locke, which insisted that there was nothing in the intellect which was not previously in the senses, by showing that there was a very important class of ideas, or imperative forms, which did not come by experience, but through which experience was acquired; that these were intuitions of the mind itself; and he denominated them *Transcendental* forms.[8]

The influence of German idealism was initially indirect, arriving in the New World via the writings of Samuel Taylor Coleridge. Coleridge worked under the influence of Kant, Fichte, and Schelling. He focused on the efficacy of "Reason," a faculty of the human mind that provided direct insight without the use of the senses. Later, in the late 1840s, Frederick Henry Hedge introduced his translations of a number of German writers, including Goethe and Hegel. In concert with this ongoing importation of German idealism there was in New England a rekindled interest in Platonism. Emerson and Alcott in particular were fond of the suggestions of the power of intuition to be found both in Plato and a number of Plato's interpreters. The pay-off of these conspiring influences was a focus among the transcendentalists on autonomy, moral liberty, universal harmony, and the intuitive capacities of the human mind. The idealism of the transcendentalists hinged on the existence of an independent divinity and on a divinity of the human mind itself.

For the transcendentalists, our Reason provided a direct access to some moral and aesthetic truths, even if these were only dimly seen. Nature too became something more than a well-oiled machine; it was, for transcendentalism, shot through with meaning. Nature was the vehicle of God's or the "Over-soul's" thought and will. It served as a moral and aesthetic measure of our character; it became that to which we aspire. Emerson and Margaret Fuller gave articulation to this feature of their idealism in addressing the readers of *The Dial*:

> We do not wish to say pretty or curious things, or to reiterate a few propositions in varied forms, but, if we can, to give expression to that spirit which lifts men to a higher platform, restores to them the religious sentiment, brings them worthy aims and pure pleasures, purges the inward eye, makes life less desultory, and, through raising man to the level of nature, takes away its melancholy from the landscape, and reconciles the practical and the speculative powers.[9]

And inasmuch as we are lifted to higher platforms, we ally ourselves with the divine, for "the soul's communication of truth is the highest event in nature."[10]

The systematic philosophical work of the transcendentalists was sporadic at most; their interest was indeed on reconciling the speculative and the practical. Their adoption of an idealistic world-view clearly came to underwrite their moral perfectionism. This effect of transcendentalist idealism was widely evident. Various communes and schools were created to try to bring about an ideal lifestyle on a small scale. Reform movements also developed. However, nowhere was the practical side of transcendentalism more forcefully revealed than in Thoreau's appeal to moral certainty in "Civil Disobedience" and in Fuller's defense of the worth of women to society and the universe. Of all the things accomplished by the transcendentalist movement, these practical proclamations have had the most lasting appeal in American culture.

Idealism in the Midwest

While the fire of transcendentalism's romantic idealism was still burning in New England, another brand of American idealism began to take shape at two separate locations in the developing Midwest – in southern Ohio and in St. Louis. In this frontier setting, experiment and self-reliance were not only intellectual themes but matters of fact. The grand experiment of these Midwestern thinkers was to bring the philosophy of G. W. F. Hegel to bear on the American experience. Although they did have some intellectual commerce with the eastern transcendentalists, the Ohio and St. Louis Hegelians worked out their own versions of idealism. Loyd Easton identifies four men as the "Ohio Hegelians": J. B. Stallo, Peter Kaufmann, Moncure Conway, and August Willich. Among these four, it was Stallo who attended most closely to a systematic defense of idealism. In his early years he wrote and published *The General Principles of the Philosophy of Nature* (1848). In it he reviewed the work of Kant, Fichte, and Schelling in light of Hegel's thought. Hegel's commitment to idealism was forthright:

> The fundamental principle upon which, according to my conviction, all true philosophy of nature rests, is, that the different manifestations of the vitality which bursts forth in nature's phenomena are comprehensively united, centered in the mind; that the implacable rigor of cosmic laws, which sways *extensive matter*, is identical with the eternal freedom of *mind in its infinite intensity*.[11]

Although Stallo later distanced himself from his youthful enchantment with Hegel, he did not relinquish his fundamentally idealistic outlook.

Stallo's book brought a fresh assessment of Hegel to Emerson and others in the east, causing them to begin to incorporate elements of Hegel's thought into their own. Meanwhile, Stallo himself turned to the practice of law and employed his idealism in the defense of the freedom of conscience in America. The other Ohio Hegelians likewise brought Hegel's thought to bear in their efforts at social reform. As Easton points out, the social, economic, and religious tensions in Ohio in the 1850s were a good setting for the mediating effect of Hegelianism: "Hegel's dialectic could help his followers assimilate the struggles and conflicts taking place around them."[12] To this end, Kaufmann engaged in Christian labor reform and Willich, who was also influenced by Marx and Feuerbach, worked hard to promote socialism among laborers in Cincinnati. Furthermore, Hegel's idealism allowed for the study of science in conjunction with the maintenance of religious belief; thus Stallo's later writings focused on new developments in science and Conway's central project was the articulation of a Hegelian-style religious naturalism.

In St. Louis in the 1850s and 1860s another Hegelian movement emerged. This one was inspired by one Henry C. Brokmeyer, a German immigrant and jack-of-all-trades, who studied philosophy briefly at several American colleges before coming to work in a foundry in St. Louis.[13] In 1866, together with Denton Snider, William Torrey Harris, Thomas Davidson, and George Holmes Howison, Brokmeyer formed the St. Louis Philosophical Society, which gathered regularly to study the work of Kant and Hegel. The influence of this small group on American philosophy and American culture was substantial.

Brokmeyer (1828–1906), the charismatic leader, lived a multifaceted life. From 1875 to 1885 he maintained an active political career and in 1876–7 he was acting Governor of Missouri. He spent his later years alternately living in the Oklahoma Territory among the Creek and in St. Louis. Brokmeyer spent many years translating Hegel's *Logic* for his colleagues in the Philosophical Society. However, the overly literal translation was never published and Brokmeyer never came to have any direct impact on American thought outside of St. Louis. The same was true of his friend Snider, who spent most of his energies as an essayist. Although his idealism informed his essays, his influence in philosophy was negligible. Harris and Howison, however, both left marks on American thought and culture as a result of learning Hegel under the tutelage of Brokmeyer.

Harris (1835–1909), a native New Englander, initially worked as a teacher and school principal in St. Louis. In 1868 he became Superintendent of the city's system of schools. His educational practices were heavily influenced by German thought. He took seriously Hegel's claim that individuals could only realize themselves insofar as they realized their communities. Among other things, Harris introduced kindergartens to St. Louis schools. In 1889, after his return to New England, Harris was appointed as the fourth Commissioner of Education for the United States. In the last years of the nineteenth century he wrote a number of works on philosophy and education, but none of them made a significant impact. Nevertheless, his educational policies were effective and they bore the mark of his Hegelianism. In this way American culture was again influenced by idealism.

Perhaps more importantly, in 1867 Harris created the *Journal of Speculative Philosophy*, the first strictly philosophical journal in the United States. The journal carried translations and interpretations of the work of Hegel, Fichte, and Schelling, thereby disseminating idealism to a wider audience. Harris also published early works by John Dewey, Charles S. Peirce, William James, and Josiah Royce. In this way German idealism became directly and indirectly involved with the inception of pragmatism.

Howison (1834–1916) exerted an influence on the development of American idealism primarily as a teacher. He was trained as a mathematician, and his interest in philosophy developed through his participation in the Philosophical Society. After leaving St. Louis he wound up in California, where he started the philosophy program at the University of California at Berkeley. Many of his students became teachers at colleges and universities around the country. In 1901 Howison published a small book entitled *The Limits of Evolution and Other Essays Illustrating the Metaphysical Theory of Personal Idealism*. In it he gave voice to his reservations concerning Hegelianism and absolute idealism generally.

Howison argued that absolute idealism, just as thoroughly as materialism, dismissed the autonomy and moral responsibility of the individual person. To preserve the integrity of the individual, Howison argued for a creative, developmental teleology in which individuals have a hand in the evolutionary process. Furthermore, he maintained that absolute idealism made a priori consciousness a function only of the absolute mind which controlled its dissemination to finite minds

– in short, persons are merely modes of the absolute mind. In response, Howison claimed that "the proper interpretation of a priori consciousness, at the juncture where it is established, is at most, and at next hand, as a human, not a divine, original consciousness, and, indeed, as a consciousness interior to the individual mind."[14] His was an idealism in which the aboriginal truths were distributed among finite minds, thus preserving some measure of autonomy for them.

Howison's written work did not have a major impact on the history of American philosophy, but it is representative of a general concern over absolute idealism's diminution of the importance of individual persons. With the advent of pragmatism, naturalism, and positivism, wholesale rejections of idealism began to claim philosophical ground in American institutions. From the 1880s into the first decade of the next century, the trajectory of idealism itself took a turn toward more pluralistically oriented idealisms. Josiah Royce, America's best-known and most systematic idealist, retained his absolutist stance, but made concerted efforts to find room for individual autonomy within his system. Others, such as Borden Bowne, took Howison's angle of rejecting the monism implicit in absolute idealism.

Royce and his Influence

The history of idealism in America reached its zenith in the work of Royce, a colleague and close friend of William James at Harvard. Royce openly constructed and defended his idealism in a series of important books, and his work played a significant role in shaping twentieth-century thought in the United States. Although Royce's idealism is sometimes caricatured as a straightforward Americanization of Hegel, this picture does not do justice either to the more central German influences of Kant, Lotze, Schelling, and Schopenhauer, or to the originality of Royce's thinking.

Having been raised in the mining community of Grass Valley, California, Royce's early thought had a strongly pragmatic flavor that he never completely abandoned. His idealism first took shape in *The Religious Aspect of Philosophy*. There he used the actual possibility of error as the ground for establishing an absolute perspective as the judge of all truth claims. He thus committed himself to a triadic structure of inquiry. If there are two competing views, they must be able to be judged by a third that stands outside of but includes both. Thus, to avoid relativism, Royce posited God or absolute thought as the thought that contained all other thought. God, as an absolute judge, became the guarantor of the possibility of error and truth. Although he later became interested in developing the role of the individual within his system, Royce never strayed from his central insight. In *The World and the Individual* he developed his systematic account in greater detail. In it he established his well-known suggestion that one infinite series may contain other infinite series, thus providing a mathematical analogy for his own conception of an absolute mind that encompasses other minds.

In the late 1880s and the 1890s Royce encountered the work of Charles S. Peirce.[15] Peirce's work in logic and, especially, his suggestion that truth was established developmentally through a community of inquirers, had an important impact on Royce's thought. In *The Problem of Christianity* Royce began to conceive his absolute judge in light of a community of believers. He did not relinquish his idealism, but Peirce's ideas allowed him to revise it in a direction that retained more of the experiential power of his early thinking. Borrowing creatively from Peirce's logic, Royce developed a theory of semiotic interpretation that conceived of the world as containing its own interpretive activity. The aim of existence was no longer merely to merge with the absolute but to establish a universal community through the practice of interpretation.

Despite the abstractness of his philosophical work, Royce never backed away from his insistence that philosophy should have practical effects. In a 1904 talk entitled "The Eternal and the Practical," Royce reminded the pragmatists of his outlook:

> Whatever may be our interest in theory or in the Absolute, we are all accustomed to lay stress upon practical considerations as having a fundamental, even if not the most fundamental, importance for philosophy; and so in a general, and, as I admit, in a very large and loose sense of the term, we are all alike more or less pragmatists.[16]

This point was not lost on those who were close students of Royce's work.

In the twentieth century Royce's influence can be seen in the work of several important thinkers: William Ernest Hocking, John William Miller, and John E. Smith. Hocking, a student of Royce and James at Harvard who subsequently taught at Harvard, took Royce's interest in the practical effects of idealist thought a step further in *The Meaning of God in Human Experience.* His summation of idealism's aim is instructive:

> It might seem that the idealist more than any other should appreciate the function of the positive and authoritative in religion; should know (as Hegel knew) that only the concrete can breed the concrete; should know (as Royce knew) that only the individual can breed the individual; should know, then, that only the historic can bear fruit in history, so that when the pragmatic test comes, a religion which is but a religion-in-general, a religion universal but not particular, a religion of idea, not organically rooted in passion, fact, and institutional life, must fail.[17]

Hocking's focus on the reciprocal nature of philosophy and practice led him to write on a wide range of subjects, from education to contemporary physics. Much of his work still seems seminal, though its actual influence has been sporadic at best. Perhaps the most notable disciple of Hocking's work was the French philosopher Gabriel Marcel.

John William Miller, a student of Hocking who taught at Williams College from the 1930s to the 1970s, quietly created an extremely original historical idealism that focuses on the possibilities and achievements of the human mind. His writings focus on the role of the idea in human history as a condition for meaning, for providing both a context for understanding and a possibility of authority in knowing. In a quite novel way, Miller takes up Royce's concern for the possibility of error; where there is not authority, there can be no error. Unfortunately, Miller found himself in a philosophical environment that was essentially hostile to what he had to say, so most of his writings were not published until recently.

John E. Smith (1921–), Clark Professor at Yale University, has kept alive the spirit of Roycean idealism in his own work. Like Miller, however, Smith is an original thinker. His idealism begins by emphasizing the will of the individual and its importance for religious and moral experience. Smith complements idealism with a pragmatic emphasis on human experience, turning his discussions of community, meaning, and purpose to bear on the social conditions and problems of the late twentieth century. The focus of Smith's earliest books was religious experience, and he remains an important interpreter of the history of American philosophy. However, the originality of his pragmatic idealism is perhaps best seen in *Purpose and Thought* and in the essays of *America's Philosophical Vision.*

Personalism

While Royce was developing his absolute idealism, another idealistic philosophy emerged across the river in Boston. This was the personalism of Borden Parker Bowne (1847–1910). Bowne, working under the influence of Berkeley, Leibniz, and Lotze, was exploring ways of making Protestant theism compatible not only with new developments in science but with the developing concern for social issues such as poverty and peace among church members. Bowne was both a Methodist minister and a professor of philosophy at Boston University.

The central thesis of Bowne's personalism was that God is best conceived as a supreme person. Thus, the world is the creative unfolding of God's purpose. However, unlike traditional theisms, in which God's purpose is fully articulate and specified at the outset of creation, Bowne's theism hinges on a developmental teleology in which God's purpose must develop and adapt as the universe itself develops. This shift had two important consequences. First, it left room for discussion of new developments in the sciences. For Bowne, evolution was something to be understood within the context of his theism, not something to be dismissed out of hand. Second, it made an opening for the freedom and responsibility of finite persons in helping define and fulfill God's purpose. Thus, for Bowne, "Man is making, he is not yet made."[18]

Bowne's idealism was both critical and systematic. Much of his work was aimed at undermining three opposing philosophical positions: mechanism, scientism, and conservative theism. Although his criticisms of these outlooks were thoroughly rational, they were launched experientially. That is, Bowne believed these views to run counter to ordinary human experience. Mechanism, in defining persons as physical automata, was forced to explain away human experiences of freedom, creativity, and morality. As a student of physics, Bowne believed Christianity needed to incorporate the findings of the sciences. However, he found scientism unreasonable insofar as it turned science from a process of inquiry into a set of dogmatic beliefs. In short, he argued that scientism was, at root, unscientific: "The only thing that is forbidden by our general view is science as a dogmatic system, which, however, is not science, but merely a species of philosophy without foundation."[19] Finally, Bowne's resistance to traditional Protestant theism was its inflexibility in the moral realm. Instead of acknowledging and incorporating the new social concerns of an industrial and international setting, traditional theism rested on outmoded and stagnant interpretations of Christian morality.

Bowne's personalism thus upheld the idealist tradition of balancing theory and practice. A survey of his writings shows that Bowne wrote essays dealing directly with practical social and moral issues as well as those dealing with metaphysics and ethical theory. It was perhaps because of this social and moral dimension of his work that Bowne's personalism took on a life of its own. Young church members and intellectuals found in personalism a satisfying avenue for bringing their intellectual, religious, and social interests together in a unified life.

After Bowne, personalism was carried on as a tradition at Boston University and at other schools where Bowne's students found employment. Edgar S. Brightman took Bowne's place at Boston University and carried out his line of thinking in several directions, writing extensively on the nature and implications of personalist idealism. Others, such as Peter Bertocci, provided new perspectives on personalist thought well into the second half of the twentieth century. On the practical side of personalism's legacy are Martin Luther King and a host of professional philosophers and church activists who were fully engaged in the civil rights and peace movements of the 1960s and '70s. Although Bowne's original idealism was highly systematic, its historical importance for American culture is to be found more in its adoption as a philosophy of life than in its influence as an academic "school of thought."

Brand Blanshard

Apart from the developments in personalism and the work of Hocking, Miller, and Smith, idealism in the twentieth-century United States was all but eliminated in substantial, systematic form. The one exception was the work of Brand Blanshard (1892–1987). At first glance, one is tempted to include Blanshard among those who recovered and revised the Roycean perspective. But a longer look reveals that his idealism has a distinctly non-Roycean flavor. Blanshard is something of a renegade who managed to hold his own ground at a time when Deweyan pragmatism and logical analysis dominated the philosophical scene.

Blanshard was more likely to call himself a "rationalist" than an idealist, but there is no mistaking his idealistic tendencies. Smith refers to Blanshard as a "rationalistic idealist" and the phrase seems apt.

Blanshard was a student of both John Dewey and the British idealist F. H. Bradley. The structure and eye for detail of Bradley and the down-to-earth tone of Dewey both inform his work. He arrived at his idealism through long, argumentative engagements with the history of philosophy and with contemporary philosophers of note. His books, such as his two-volume *The Nature of Thought*, are lengthy and detailed precisely because he required himself to mark out his own views in conjunction with his criticisms of the likes of Spinoza, Plato, Wittgenstein, and Dewey. He displayed both range and precision of thought.

Blanshard's rationalistic idealism is fairly straightforward. He began with what he called "the faith of the rationalist" – a belief that "the world is a place that we can learn about by rational thought."[20] His faith required him to examine the nature of thought and idea, which he did at length. He arrived at the Kant-like position that finite minds are constrained by the systematic structure of ideas, that "the universals appearing in consciousness do make a difference to the course of thought, that they exercise some constraint on what we say and do."[21]

Seen from the outside, Blanshard's world is a processional system of relations and entailments in which particulars are only fully realized when the whole system is completed. Like Berkeley and Bradley, he maintains what Peirce called a "Platonic nominalism" in which the universe itself is, ultimately, the only particular. Blanshard put the point as follows: "Fully to define what one means by this individual thing one must pursue its specification till thought attains its immanent end. That end is attained when ambiguity is supplanted by full determinateness. Such determinateness can be arrived at only by traveling to its terminus the road of universals."[22]

Blanshard carried over his system of logical entailment to his discussions of ethics and aesthetics. The necessitarianism of his metaphysics meant that there must be necessity in the moral realm as well as in human creativity. For example, he maintained that an artist was under an aesthetic necessity in choosing the elements of his or her work of art: only particular elements could serve the aim of the whole work. Likewise, moral laws act as effective constraints in developing human nature toward a fuller self-realization.

Thus, like other idealists, Blanshard brings the true, the good, and the beautiful into a relation of identity. "I hold with all deliberateness," he commented, "that to be moral is to be rational, and to be rational is to be moral."[23] Thought in its completion is both ideal measure and ideal judge. Unlike many earlier idealists, however, Blanshard refused to identify his idealist universe with a traditional, personalized God. For him, "God" is the ideal outcome of thought's activity, not an already existent being who is manipulating the ways of the world. Although Blanshard's work is largely neglected now, it has a freshness, clarity, and temper of rebelliousness that in the long run will make it a point of interest for those studying the development of philosophy in America.

Idealism as an explicit philosophical point of view has not enjoyed a great deal of popularity in recent years. Nevertheless, traces of its influence remain deeply embedded in much that goes on in American philosophy. It is easy to argue that idealism is outmoded and has simply seen its day. However, some of its experiential intuitions remain intact and given the fact that idealism has enjoyed a number of revivals in the history of human thought, it may be premature to preclude its putting in another appearance on the American philosophical scene.

Notes

1 Walter Muelder and Laurence Sears, *The Development of American Philosophy* (Boston: Houghton Mifflin Company, 1940), p. 12. From Edwards, "Notes on the Mind," in *The Works of President Edwards, Volume 1* (New York, 1829–30).
2 Ibid., p. 13.
3 Ibid., p. 11.
4 Harold Simonsen, *Selected Writings of Jonathan Edwards* (New York: Ungar, 1970), p. 66.
5 Muelder and Sears, *The Development of American Philosophy*, p. 43. From Johnson, *Elementa Philosophica* (Philadelphia: Press of Benjamin Franklin, 1752).
6 Ibid., p. 48.
7 Ibid., p. 47.
8 Ralph Waldo Emerson, *Nature: Addresses, and Lectures* (Philadelphia: David McKay, 1885), pp. 298–9.
9 George Hochfeld, *Selected Writings of the American Transcendentalists* (New York: The New American Library, 1966), p. 295.
10 Ralph Waldo Emerson, *Essays: First Series* (Boston: Houghton Mifflin Company, 1883), p. 263.
11 J. B. Stallo, *General Principles of the Philosophy of Nature* (Boston: Crosby and Nichols, 1848), pp. vii–viii.
12 Lloyd D. Easton, *Hegel's First American Followers* (Athens: Ohio University Press, 1966), p. 25.
13 Brokmeyer is also spelled "Brockmeyer." I have chosen the more common spelling.
14 George Holmes Howison, *The Limits of Evolution and Other Essays Illustrating the Metaphysical Theory of Personal Idealism* (New York: Macmillan, 1901), p. 45.
15 Peirce occasionally declared himself to be an "objective idealist." However, because he is the founder of pragmatism and pragmaticism, his work is discussed in more detail in the chapter on pragmatism.
16 Josiah Royce, "The Eternal and the Practical," *The Philosophical Review*, XIII (March 1904): 115.
17 William Ernest Hocking, *The Meaning of God in Human Experience* (New Haven, CT: Yale University Press, 1912), p. xii.
18 Borden Parker Bowne, *Personalism* (Boston: Houghton Mifflin Company, 1908), p. 301.
19 Ibid., p. 304.
20 Paul A. Schilpp, *The Philosophy of Brand Blanshard* (La Salle, IL: Open Court, 1980), p. 159.

21 Ibid., p. 144.
22 Brand Blanshard, *The Nature of Thought*, vol. I (London: George Allen and Unwin, 1939), p. 505.
23 Schilpp, *The Philosophy of Brand Blanshard*, p. 295.

Suggested reading

Anderson, Paul R. and Max H. Fisch, *Philosophy in America* (New York: D. Appleton-Century Company, 1939).

Blanshard, Brand, *The Nature of Thought*, 2 vols. (London: George Allen and Unwin, 1939).

Bowne, Borden Parker, *Studies in Theism* (New York: Phillips and Hunt, 1879).

Emerson, Ralph Waldo, *The Collected Works of Ralph Waldo Emerson*, ed. A. R. Ferguson (Cambridge, MA: Harvard University Press, 1971–9).

Miller, John William, *The Paradox of Cause* (New York: Norton, 1974).

Royce, Josiah, *The Problem of Christianity*, 2 vols. (New York: The Macmillan Company, 1913).

—— *The World and the Individual*, 2 vols. (New York: The Macmillan Company, 1899, 1901).

Schneider, Herbert, *A History of American Philosophy* (New York: Columbia University Press, 1946).

Chapter 3

The First Pragmatists

Joseph Margolis

Uncertain Beginnings

In a recent, well-received attempt to picture the historical setting in which American pragmatism arose, Louis Menand offers the arresting suggestion that the Civil War (1861–5), which preceded the advent of pragmatism by a handful of years, produced an intellectual vacuum of sorts in which the ethos of the slave economy of the South and the then-current advanced thinking of the North – let us say, both political and philosophical – were rendered irrelevant or effectively dismissed.[1] By a series of converging developments, the War prepared the way, it seems, for "modern" America; and the leading members of a rather obscure, academically minded conversation group prone to philosophical dispute, which may or may not have seriously called itself The Metaphysical Club, met informally and irregularly, in a period of about nine months, from January 1872, in Cambridge, until events affecting the reorganization of Harvard University and the scattering special interests of the nominal members of the Club led to its dissolution.

In that interval, William James, Charles Sanders Peirce, and Oliver Wendell Holmes came to know one another and one another's ideas through the Club (as far as we can tell); they "formed" (if that is the right word) the nexus of those converging philosophical themes which were later to be called "pragmatism" and which, still later and from entirely different sources, attracted John Dewey, who would have been a mere 23 years old at the Club's inception – Peirce being already 33 and James 30 – but who eventually became the quintessential pragmatist, as that "doctrine" came to be understood by the end of the 1940s, when its remarkable popularity appeared to have been exhausted. Menand claims that "Holmes, James, Peirce, and Dewey were the first modern thinkers in the United States,"[2] an intriguing judgment from a customarily careful author, ranging over a period of about 125 years. What, one wants to ask, was so original and promising about pragmatism?

The rise of pragmatism to its first prominence in America was a very improbable process on every count. Its acknowledged founder, Charles Sanders Peirce (1839–1914), was unsuccessful in nearly everything he touched, both in his professional and personal undertakings. He was unable to secure an academic post. He was widely disliked (though secretly envied for his undoubted brilliance) for his arrogance and difficult personal manner and unorthodox views. He seems to have suffered greatly from what is now called trigeminal neuralgia, or "neuralgia of the face," with accompanying manic-depressive symptoms, which undoubtedly explains in some measure the misperception of his not infrequently extreme behavior. He was reduced to poverty and even beggary in his later years. Some believe there was a sort of conspiracy against publishing his work, even his "Lowell" lectures of 1903 (which William James made possible, though he apparently opposed their publication). He had a steady stream of physical ailments throughout his life; took several bad falls about the time of the Lowell lectures; was often incapacitated though he worked prodigiously when he was able to work; seriously considered suicide; and, as his biographer, Joseph Brent, observes, "was profoundly confused about himself," even "found himself mysterious."[3]

No wonder! For he thought of himself, in the middle of his unprovoked disasters, as a logician of the highest rank. He says, in the draft of a letter he seems never to have sent: "the only writers known to me who are in the same rank as I are Aristotle, Duns Scotus, and Leibniz, the three greatest logicians in [my] estimation, although some of the more important points [about logic] escaped each."[4] Not only does he say this, but it would not have been unreasonable for any knowledgeable logician to have thought so as well. How then to account for his doomed life?

It was not until William James (1842–1919), lecturing in 1898 at the University of California, generously identified the all-but-unknown Peirce as the originator of the pragmatist doctrines he (that is, James) was advocating in his lecture – themes James says he found in Peirce's early paper, "How To Make Our Ideas Clear" (1897), published 20 years before and all but forgotten, or gained from unrecorded discussions at the Metaphysical Club, which seems to have met more irregularly and more informally than Peirce recalls: it was only through these slim means – that the name and doctrine of pragmatism began to take hold.[5]

The question of the actual origination of the pragmatist "doctrine" became a matter of importance for Peirce when James Baldwin, the editor of the *Dictionary of Philosophy and Psychology*, invited Peirce (in 1900) to help formulate, for the *Dictionary*, the definitions of important philosophical terms. Peirce wrote to James directly to ask who actually "originated the term . . . I or you?" James wrote back to say that it was he, Peirce, as he (James) had already acknowledged in his California lecture (1898 [1907]), copies of which James had evidently sent Peirce, who never acknowledged their receipt.

There's a great deal of to-and-fro about this in Peirce's mind. But James's biographer, Ralph Barton Perry, offers the last word on this now minor matter, made major only because of Peirce's sinking fortunes and his posthumous prominence:

"the idea [Perry says] that pragmatism originated with Peirce was originated by James."[6] The apparent absence of the use of the term by Peirce before 1900 is somewhat telling, though not altogether, if one were inclined to dispute the matter.

Peirce may have used the very term "pragmatism" (which has a use in Kant) in a paper, in the 1870s, presented to the Metaphysical Club, but now lost. More to the point, he seems to have been struck, in some meetings of the Club, by the published views of the British philosopher, Alexander Bain (1875), a so-called phenomenalist, who hit on a kind of proto-pragmatism – which Peirce reports in a short draft of a paper, "Pragmatism Made Easy" (*c.*1906) – to the effect that "what a man really believes is what he would be ready to act upon, and risk much upon."[7] Bain's idea permitted Peirce to join, indissolubly, his (Peirce's) "pragmatic maxim" and the prevailing evolutionism of the day. The "maxim" (there were a number of different formulations) makes its first appearance in "How To Make Our Ideas Clear" (1875). (The subtitle of a part of the paper, "The Pragmatic Maxim," was supplied by the editors of the *Collected Papers.*)

But the point of the exchange between Peirce and James is that the exchange itself implicitly acknowledges the uneasiness of each man regarding the "pragmatism" of the other. James had no real interest in Peirce's extreme subtleties and grand system, and Peirce seems to have thought James rather muddleheaded. In particular, James had little interest in Peirce's idealism and Peirce was clearly chagrined by James's foray into the theory of truth.

Furthermore, the essential nerve of the pragmatic maxim – of the various versions of the maxim – is to treat the explication of *meaning* (the meaning of "hard," as predicated of a diamond, in Peirce's most famous example) in terms of how a thing behaves under the condition of how we might use it or act pertinently on it, believing it to be such (as by attempting to scratch a diamond). Here, apart from the inevitable complications of such a difficult conjecture (for instance, the meaning of the subjunctive formulation of the sense of "hard"), Peirce fixes once and for all the thesis that, in its most critical form, the "clearness of ideas," linked to belief and intelligent action informed by belief – Peirce's "third grade" of clearness, a deliberate challenge to Descartes' criteria – casts our understanding of an idea in terms of its issue in action believed or imagined to be pertinent, given practical desires and interests. It is not, however, intended as a definition or criterion of meaning itself, in any respect that might be thought to anticipate the views of the Vienna Circle. In a deep sense, this rough-hewn theme of the practical grasp of meanings for an active agent simply engaged, here and now, with the question of what to do remains the essential pragmatist theme, at once a challenge to the Cartesian notion of "clear and distinct" ideas, the novel focus of pragmatism, and the clarification of realism in the pragmatist account.

James thought the term ("pragmatism") appears in "How To Make Our Ideas Clear," but it does not. (Perhaps James was aware of the fact.) But it was James's considerable fame, assured almost instantly with the reception of his *Principles of Psychology* (1890), that gave pragmatism a prominence and an audience Peirce could never have attracted. Even today, Peirce is more honored than read (where he is known at all), through no more than a half-dozen papers of the same vintage or at least the same orientation as the one James featured.

A good part (but by no means all) of Peirce's voluminous, largely unpublished journals and articles became available for the first time in the edition of his *Collected Papers* (1931–66), the first six volumes of which were published in the 1930s. From then on to the present, Peirce's work has steadily gained in importance and reputation. He is now regarded as a philosopher who belongs to the first rank worldwide. But it is still rather rare to find even professional readers familiar with his technical work beyond the half-dozen or so more-or-less pop pieces for which he is publicly and justifiably admired. It is his innovations in the theory of signs (semiotics), in the very beginnings of modern formal logic (particularly, the logic of relations), in his ingenious account of the relationship between chance (tychism) and law in the context of the continuity and regularities of nature itself (so-called synechism), largely unknown beyond the academy, that have secured his reputation. The power and distinction of Peirce's work can hardly be guessed from James's reference to his early papers or from the rest of James's own work (which is never technical or specialized or even academic); or, for that matter, from John Dewey's entirely different entry, very much later, into pragmatism's ranks. Nevertheless, Peirce's technical contributions are inseparable from his own form of pragmatism.

Peirce was aware that he had profoundly influenced the leading pragmatists of the era: most notably James and Josiah Royce (1855–1916), whose philosophical views (Royce's, that is) most clearly resemble his own, though they cannot easily be called pragmatist. In fact, Peirce taught Royce how to master the intricacies of logic, which led Royce to believe (not accurately) that Peirce had proved that the "dialectical triadic process" attributed to G. W. F. Hegel (reckoned as one of the greatest philosophers of the Western world, undoubtedly the greatest of the early nineteenth century) was no more than a special (and obviously informal) instance of Peirce's more rigorous and more general triadic schema! Peirce's influence, mediated in various ways, spread to a larger circle of the "first" (English-language) pragmatists, which included, most prominently, John Dewey, G. H. Mead, the British humanist F. C. S. Schiller (1864–1937) and, primarily through Royce, the logician C. I. Lewis. But none of these can be said to have been primarily influenced by Peirce more than, say, by James, except those who, like Charles Morris and C. I. Lewis, had a special interest in semiotics and logic. Mead is the most important of the somewhat later pragmatists, associated with Dewey almost entirely.

Lewis (1883–1964) is an important contributor here. He reads Peirce in good part through Royce's reading of Peirce, that is, through viewing formal logic in terms of the continuum of social experience within which, alone, a full account of legitimate inference in existential circumstances may be articulated (which Russell and Whitehead's *Principia Mathematica* (1910) could not capture: most notoriously, as in their notion of "material implication,"[8] which Lewis sought to displace by an account of "strict implication"). He is best known (among the pragmatists) for his attempt to explicate a "pragmatic" account of the a priori confined to the analytic.[9] As a logician, Lewis addresses an essential question broached by Peirce and Dewey as well, but addressed by them in very different ways: namely, that of the relationship between formal logic and "existential" (human) inquiry. (Hegel had already broached a similar query.)

Oliver Wendell Holmes (1841–1935), who was an original member of the Metaphysical Club, did exhibit pragmatist leanings in his conception of the law, but he is not a central figure in the movement. The only other major American pragmatist, George Herbert Mead (1863–1931) is primarily a social psychologist known for his theory of the social construction of the self[10] and an incipient interest in the question of historicity (which is relatively undeveloped), as it is also, surprisingly, in Dewey. Mead has some interest in Hegel: indeed, his treatment of the self may in some measure be Hegelian in inspiration. He is almost exclusively associated with Dewey (at the University of Chicago).

When we pass beyond this second circle, the term "pragmatist" becomes rather muddy and strained, as it plainly does when we add the names of W. V. O. Quine, Nelson Goodman, or, even, more problematically, Martin Heidegger, Ludwig Wittgenstein, Thomas Kuhn, Donald Davidson, or, in Peirce's own day, Oliver Wendell Holmes and Ralph Waldo Emerson – not to mention the Italian and French pragmatists.

Pragmatism is a uniquely American phenomenon, then. It was widely ridiculed in Britain in its first reception, in its Jamesian and Deweyan versions – notoriously in Bertrand Russell's widely known, somewhat malicious review of James's attempt to explain the pragmatist conception of truth[11] and an unsympathetic reading of Dewey's account of the rigors of logic in terms of the informalities of practical life.[12] There is some justice in Russell's broadsides, although Russell himself was unduly unsympathetic (at least at first), possibly because he sensed (correctly) the resurgence of a "Hegelian" (or idealist) theme he and G. E. Moore had worked so hard (and successfully) to eliminate in England at the start of the twentieth century. It is also true that Russell, precisely in formalizing an uninterpreted logic, separated from the context of human experience and action, actually contributes to the original provocation of the pragmatists against the adequacy of any such logic. (That was, of course, the motivation of Peirce's, Royce's, and Lewis's views of logic – as well as Dewey's, which was inevitably slimmer on technical details than the others' – of course, it was also the motivation for Hegel's logic.)

Yet, strange though it may be, James actually improved his account of truth under Russell's goading and thereby gave pragmatism a clearer focus; furthermore, the deeper validity of Dewey's conception of the "origins" of logic began to dawn on a more receptive readership, despite the enormous differences between Peirce's and his own competence in logic. Neither development could have been anticipated.

Actually, Peirce is hardly mentioned in the earliest discussions of pragmatism, being so little known. So pragmatism made its way into the circles of informed public discussion chiefly as James's doctrine and, later, as Dewey's. In fact, already in his extremely successful and widely acclaimed *Pragmatism* (1907), James indicates his own reliance on the more "up-to-date" formulations of Dewey and Schiller, to whom he explicitly defers. You may begin to see in this a source of consternation on Peirce's part, since Peirce realized that the possibility of holding on to the opening fame (and fortune!) James made possible was slipping from his control. Events were moving too quickly for Peirce: there is no compelling evidence of his ever having fixed (for attribution), at an early date, the meaning and use of the term "pragmatism" itself.

More than that, it is probably true that Peirce's version of pragmatism – his original theory of meaning meant to offset Descartes' "clear and distinct ideas," hence a doctrine at once semantic and epistemological – was never quite so central in his own mature philosophical vision as it proved to be for James's. Peirce made an almost comic effort to retrieve his exclusive authorship by coining the deliberately ugly term "pragmaticism"[13] to save his doctrine from being subsumed under the misinterpretation (as he conceived matters) of James's formulations in *Pragmatism*. Once again, Perry catches the irony of the situation: "the modern movement known as pragmatism is largely the result of James's misunderstanding of Peirce."[14] Well, perhaps not quite a misunderstanding: certainly, a new emphasis (though, frankly, never very skillfully pursued).

Here, we begin to see more clearly how improbable the unity of pragmatism is and was when we turn to actual substantive doctrines. For the truth is: *James* sensed, more than he explicitly realized, that Peirce's treatment of the "clearness" of ideas actually ran counter (in some measure) to his own (Peirce's) elaboration in "How To Make Our Ideas Clear." In any case, it may be fairly argued that Peirce's "original" pragmatist conception was better served by James's initial fumbling on the meaning of "truth" than by his own theory of truth; and that James's eventual correction of how to understand the doctrine was essential for Dewey's later formulation of *his* brand of pragmatism, which gained its clearer focus partly by correcting James's treatment. The whole affair is a marvelous patchwork. But you must not look for a settled agreement between Peirce, James, and Dewey on the principal questions. There is none – or, what there is is largely idealized in retrospect, when, that is, what we take a "proper" pragmatism to be is already cast in Dewey's way.

Dewey (1859–1952) seems to have been a student in one of Peirce's classes at Johns Hopkins University. There is very little sense, however, of Dewey's ever having been directly influenced by Peirce, until at least, say, the time of writing his *Logic* (1938)[15] – fully 50 years into his career – which, even so, shows remarkably little influence of Peirce's technical work, very little more in fact than a perfunctory (but not irrelevant) reference to the great progenitor. Dewey reviewed Peirce's *Collected Papers* in the 1930s (when the first six volumes were published by Harvard University Press), which may rightly explain why Dewey would have come to his own version of pragmatism more or less independently of Peirce – unless *via* James. The evidence tends to show that Dewey was influenced more by James's *Principles of Psychology* than by James's *Pragmatism.* In fact, as already remarked, James sought out Schiller's and Dewey's own views on truth, rather than the other way around.

Dewey was born in 1859, the same year Darwin published *On the Origin of Species.* Even there, there is an immense difference to be made out between Peirce's and Dewey's evolutionary views. Though both were much attracted to post-Kantian "idealism," Peirce actually strengthens his ties to post-Kantian thought in his maturity; whereas Dewey sheds all such ties nearly completely – and deliberately. Peirce was a true evolutionist – with a distinct touch of the teleologism of the evolutionary doctrine (muted, it must be said, by his formulation of what he offered as an improvement on Kant: the rational ideal of evolutionary "Hope," never an actual constituent or transcendental ingredient in the structuring of knowledge itself); whereas Dewey was not an evolution*ist* in the doctrinal sense at all, though he was, effectively, a Darwinian. (Darwinism, of course, is explicitly – indeed, unalterably – opposed to any evolutionary *telos.*)

Dewey had already completed nearly a lifetime of work as a pragmatist before he turned to examine Peirce in any detail. There is a rather pretty (though entirely indirect) bit of evidence of Dewey's independence. Very early in his career, Dewey attacks Alexander Bain's *The Senses and the Intellect* (1855) as an arch-specimen of "Subjective Idealism" (or "phenomenalism") – a variant of the "Cartesian" doctrines the original pragmatists were bound to oppose in their different ways) – that is, as not capturing (as Dewey says) "the [ontological limitation of the] psychological standpoint applied to the relation of subject and object."[16] At this time, Dewey was not drawn to the proto-pragmatist stance Peirce found so appealing in Bain; he was wrestling instead (as an idealist: more "British" than "German") with the post-Kantian question (*a*) of making provision for the non-reducibility of the objective world to subjective consciousness, while at the same time (*b*) opposing any epistemic disjunction between the known world and our capacity to know it. (This *is* "idealism's" principal theme, read in either its British or German versions: that is, the sense in which idealism *is not* a form of metaphysical idealism.)

Dewey achieves his final resolution on this matter by broadly Darwinian means, which frees him from post-Kantian idealism and profoundly colors his own brand of pragmatism. But there is no evidence that he was led to this idea, which is similar in some regards to Peirce's own developing account, by Peirce himself. To state the matter paradoxically: the idealist theme draws Peirce further and further away from his original pragmatist intuition about "meaning" in the here and now; in Dewey, it seems to have been a useful preamble that led him to pragmatism itself. Peirce and Dewey continue to drift apart, largely because Dewey (but not Peirce) sheds his early idealist orientation.

Peirce's "post-Kantian" tendencies (which he himself sometimes terms "Schillingian" rather than "Hegelian" and explicitly construed as idealist) simply strengthen as his philosophy matures. The bearing of "Kantian," "post-Kantian," "Hegelian," and "idealist" themes on both Peirce and Dewey plays an important part in getting clear about the distinction of pragmatism itself. But the linkages are not entirely clear. For instance: in "How To Make Our Ideas Clear," Peirce plainly means to reconcile a robust realism and an ingenious idealism. As we discover in his later writings, Peirce does not oppose matter and mind in principle, and when he speaks of a seemingly "panpsychic" dimension in nature he apparently means no more than the self-regularizing "habits" of natural processes that appear to congeal as laws of nature – what, in one incarnation, Peirce terms "Thirdness." (Matter, he says, "is effete mind."[17])

You see how difficult it would be to produce a unified doctrine that Peirce and James and Dewey might actually share. There would have been no large pragmatist "movement" at all had it not been for the late recovery of Peirce's philosophical originality. You realize, of course, that, if that is so, then the doctrinal range of what we now call pragmatism is largely reconstructed and idealized (and delimited) from the 1930s on – when Peirce's work was effectively first made public (a considerable time after his own death). Prior to that moment, pragmatism appeared to be James's invention (however improbably), for it seems unlikely that James would have hit on the term or would have had the patience (or competence) for the technical distinctions Peirce developed. Furthermore, since James "misunderstood" Peirce, and since James himself had no sustained interest in pressing pragmatism in a systematic way, the "movement" would have been confined to James's admittedly attractive but limited direction. Pragmatism "had" to be interpreted in Peirce's or Dewey's way – or by a combination of the two – if it was ever to become a movement of the amplitude and vigor that it eventually could claim.

It is also true that Peirce's systematic philosophy was really somewhat at odds with the original nerve of the pragmatism he set off – the theme he found so attractive in Bain. Also, James, drawn to the same pragmatist theme, never followed Peirce's grander system. That is perhaps the key to the most important benefit of James's theory of truth, which Peirce took to be a mistaken rendering of his own doctrine. It was never simply that, however; it was, rather, a convincing turn toward what a fully worked-out pragmatism was bound to require. James made the adjustment spontaneously – possibly in part for the wrong reasons. Peirce's original emphasis on the "clearness" of our conceptions (the "meaning" of our "ideas": the central theme of his various pragmatic "maxims") required a proper link with the theory of truth (a remarkably prescient hit by James). James found the right clue *in* Peirce's paper all right, the one already mentioned; but he also sensed that Peirce had somehow gone astray in what *he says there* about truth and reality – *if*, that is, Peirce meant to adhere to the pragmatism *James* admired and adopted, or, even further afield, to adhere to something like the very different pragmatism Dewey eventually produced.

The fact is, Peirce must have regarded his first "pragmatist" theme as no more than a small part of his larger systematic speculations, which are indeed enormously inventive and arresting. But they are also stalemated in a post-Kantian trance, so to say, while James had no real patience for their subtleties and Dewey was already committed to a more forward-looking conception (working free of both the

Kantian and post-Kantian formulations). Both Peirce and Dewey meant to save objective science and knowledge, of course – though not (according to Dewey) at the price of an "idealism" that muddied the relationship between "subjects" and "objects."

This marks a later stage of the same concern that led Dewey (even when he was a kind of "idealist") to reject Bain's "subjective idealism" as confused. Dewey resolves the matter well before the publication of *Experience and Nature* (1925 [1929]),[18] which counts as his most ambitious and systematic effort at metaphysics and epistemology – well before the publication, remember, of Peirce's *Collected Papers.*

Nevertheless, it is at least partly Peirce's eminence as a metaphysician-logician-philosopher of science that gradually lends the gathering pragmatist movement a recognizable air of competence in a "full service" sense (as one says of banks and gas stations) that helped consolidate pragmatism's standing in the philosophical lists. James veered off in the direction of his interests in religion and the existential concerns of personal life, which, however engaging, could never have been counted on to hold the entire movement together in a lively enough way – that is, beyond James's personal success. And Dewey's demanding interests in psychological, educational, and moral and political matters would also not have held the philosophical movement together had it not been for his own impressive resolution of the problems collected in *Experience and Nature* (in effect, the master problems of a viable realism), increasingly linked (in pragmatism's public and professional reception) to a somewhat inaccurate impression of the full role (within pragmatism) of Peirce's mastery of topics that neither James nor Dewey could rightly claim.

The irony is that Peirce's reputation as the shadowy source of pragmatism was much more important to pragmatism's forceful flowering than his actual "post-Kantian" speculations, which were largely unknown and clearly not of any sustained interest to either James or Dewey. It was also James's graceful and immediately intelligible style in popularizing pragmatism *à la* Peirce (if that is what James did), together with the very important – productive – "error" he made in promoting Peirce, when he alone was sufficiently famous, that held the philosophical world's attention long enough for Peirce to be recovered at least a little and for Dewey to fulfill the promise of a systematic vision that is now more or less what we understand by pragmatism.

Peirce hardly knew Dewey's work, though James refers, in *Pragmatism*, to his and Schiller's conception of truth; Dewey hardly knew Peirce in any detail before he had already fashioned the main themes of his own doctrine; and James never got beyond a very suggestive formulation – by far the best known – that could not have sustained (beyond, perhaps, his intuitions about truth) the interest of the philosophical community in the problems that Peirce and Dewey separately addressed.

James's interest in the problem of truth veered off too quickly in the direction of supporting the "truth" of religious faith, somehow abetted by the "truth" of science. James construed the formula, "true is a species of good" – that is, the idea that what is true is what is good in the way of belief – as serving science and religion equally well, even reconciling them with one another. James's own use of the formula encouraged critics, both fair-minded and malicious, to wonder aloud whether James actually meant that whatever is "good to believe" *is*, for that reason, true! Fortunately, James saw the worry and "corrected" his pragmatist formula, never very reliably but well enough to make it clear that "good in the way of belief" was not a criterion of truth at all but a way of drawing attention to the practical role that truth (and ascriptions of truth) play in the general economy of life. In this important sense, James provided the proper mate to Peirce's conception of meaning.

James spent an inordinate amount of time, however, trying to show how the notion of truth bridges the seemingly opposed interests of science and religion, which clearly embarrassed the more careful pragmatists. What James seems to have intended (which collects in a way his own neurotic and depressive tendencies) was to say that there was room enough, in practical life, to "believe-true" what no counterevidence would ever falsify: for instance, that it was "good to believe" that there was a God (to treat the belief as true). In his best moments, James did not mean that it might be good to believe what the relevant evidence might (or actually would) falsify. But you can see how James's fumbling put pragmatism in a very poor light.

Common Tendencies

Pragmatism was, then, a patchwork from the start, an excellent and fortunate patchwork as it happens, but the outcome, nevertheless, of improvizations from three disparate sources – Peirce, James, and Dewey – that have very little overlap in terms of the bulk of the characteristic inquiries each favored. In the main, they would not have been sympathetic to one another's principal themes, though one can make a reasonable case for the convergence between James and Dewey on the early topics James found in Peirce himself. Peirce rejected James's reading of the would-be common theme he presumably shared with James, insofar, that is, as James went beyond merely reporting Peirce's doctrine regarding "making our ideas clear." James yielded generously to Schiller and Dewey on the meaning of "truth," though, understandably, Dewey found it necessary to correct James (in Dewey's own favor) along lines that, in effect, conceded the validity of Russell's objection to James's early formulations (of what "truth" meant in the pragmatist idiom). Dewey explicitly remarks that James's "pragmatism" had rather little influence on him – that it hardly compared with the influence of his *Psychology*.

Peirce remains within the Kantian and post-Kantian fold; indeed, he appears increasingly as a transatlantic cousin of the first generation of post-Kantians that included Schelling and Hegel particularly. Peirce has the same sort of appetite for metaphysical grandeur that they do; although his account is cast in a distinctly American mold, he relives and rethinks the Kantian and post-Kantian attack on the "Cartesian" philosophies spanning Descartes and Kant himself. Peirce seems to have been more knowledgeable about Kant than about Hegel, and more favorably disposed to Kant, even though he makes it clear that he means to supersede Kant. Furthermore, he was able to claim a command of the materials of logic and mathematics and science and the philosophy of science that was the equal of anyone then current in American thought and even, not unreasonably, of the best philosophical work of the entire Eurocentric tradition of his day.

James's writing veers off in the direction of what he came to call his "radical empiricism," which he himself believed could be reasonably separated from his pragmatism. What James offers in the "empiricist" spirit, which he shares to some extent with Dewey (and almost not at all with Peirce), pretty well comes to this: a distinctly labile use of the term "experience" that joins a psychological *and a non-psychological sense*, by which, at a great remove, James approximates (in an empiricist idiom) to the principal lesson of the post-Kantian critique of the "Cartesians": namely, that, on pain of paradox and contradiction, we cannot concede an epistemic discontinuity between "subjects" and "objects."

What James offers here would doubtless have been viewed as primitive by both Peirce and Dewey, if they had bothered to address the details of his doctrine. In Peirce, a more mysterious counterpart notion, meant to serve a purpose formally similar to that of "experience," is cast in terms of what Peirce calls "Thirdness,"[19] in a sense that cannot be construed, in nature at large, as psychological at all; although the specific forms of "Thirdness" manifested in human intelligence or interpretation or explanation *are*, Peirce believes, instantiations of the other. This theme, it would be fair to say, has affinities with cognate notions bridging the mental and the physical, the cognitive and the intelligible, the regular in the way of causality and the significant, the factual and the normative – which appear among the post-Kantians, particularly Schelling and Hegel and, in America, Emerson.

It is in fact an important version of what we now mean by the principal theme of the post-Kantian idealists, which Peirce increasingly strengthened as the central doctrine of his own systematic philosophy. Peirce recognized that his own theory *was* an idealism of sorts; whereas Dewey regarded his idealist roots as vestiges of a faulty philosophy *he* labored to excise. To say, however, that the mature views of Peirce and Dewey were both genuinely "pragmatic" is to stumble over an obvious embarrassment. History has come to favor Dewey's final conception over Peirce's, yet Peirce's original vision marks the true beginning of the movement.

To allow the standard verdict is to concede that Peirce turned away in important regards from what we now view as pragmatism; it also confirms that James was right to have reoriented Peirce's account of meaning in favor of a specifically "pragmatist" account of truth, which Peirce found completely unacceptable. In fact, the pragmatist account of truth is, very nearly, the single most important alternative to the recently fashionable analytic accounts of "true" (so-called "deflationary" accounts) that treat "true" in semantic terms alone, somehow detached from epistemic and realist concerns. One ought not ignore the irony that Rorty, writing as a pragmatist, completely misinterprets James's contribution in the deflationary way, in attempting to bridge the difference between pragmatism and analytic philosophy.[20]

Yet to draw the standard verdict discounts too quickly the intriguing and subtle complexities of Peirce's mature philosophy, which found a way of embracing the idealist themes Dewey thought essential to abandon, without violating any of the usual "canonical" marks of pragmatism as we now construe the theory – for instance, as denying any realist teleology in nature and any supernatural governance of nature itself. It may be that, in pragmatism, we have the advantage of two and a half quite different sources of a viable doctrine, one source of seminal inspiration (Peirce), two decidedly divergent but comparably mature systems (Peirce and Dewey), and "a half" of an incompletely worked-out correction that bridges the essential continuity of the two systems that survive (James).

James appears increasingly as an apologist for religion, risking the promise of his own pragmatist account of truth in his overly generous effort to address the human condition. Neither Peirce nor Dewey favored any such extension. Dewey, however, never completely abandoned the double use of "experience" that linked him to the British idealists, if not to the German idealists.

For his part, Peirce went a considerable distance in attenuating the objectionable features of idealism, but he saw no need to reject the "doctrine" altogether. It is very nearly a question of fashionable and unfashionable labels: "Thirdness" (in Peirce) might be said to designate what remains of the *metaphor* of a greater "Mind" in nature, in terms of cosmic order, evolution, the continuity of human minds and bodies, and the continuity between their analogues in nature at large.

"Habit" is the metaphor Peirce prefers, by which he means the generally observed regularities of nature, suggesting a deeper lawful order not yet clearly perceived or clearly realized in nature that might explain the phenomenal order that confronts us. Perhaps it signifies no more than that: perhaps it introduces nothing strange or unheard-of, at all. Is that idealism? Peirce's transcendental Hope permits the use of a telic metaphor as a way of guessing at a deeper source of order underlying familiar regularities. It makes no claims about the constitutive structures of reality itself. In a curious way, as in so many other matters, it affords an alternative idiom to Dewey's pared-down instrumentalism, cast in the idealist's heuristic imagery.

Philosophically, Dewey was the sparest of the three, the youngest of the original pragmatists, and the one who reaches deepest into the ambient philosophical, social, political world closest to our own. Dewey is also the only one of the three who could be said to have been chiefly occupied with the formulation of a systematic pragmatism (or instrumentalism, as he was increasingly tempted to label his doctrine), risking the full thrust of the realism that marks *Experience and Nature*. He clearly does not favor James's extravagance (on the matter of truth), and he is perhaps closest to the spirit of Peirce's logic of abduction, which is itself a remarkably attractive refinement of a Hegelian theme. That is an important feature of his own *Logic* (in which, in a footnote, he acknowledges the influence of Peirce's seminal studies).

Dewey's own view of logic was influenced more by his instruction (in effect) in Hegelian thought, perhaps even more by the logic of the British idealists (Bernard Bosanquet and F. H. Bradley and T. H. Green) interpreted through the perception of George Morris, one of Dewey's philosophy teachers at Johns Hopkins and, later, a colleague at the University of Michigan. It was largely through Morris's congenial influence that Dewey first identified himself as an "idealist" and, even later, after abandoning idealism, remained loyal to the idealists' critique of the "Cartesians" and Kant. It is in the same spirit that Dewey acknowledges the influence of James's psychology (more than James's pragmatism), for he found in G. Stanley Hall, another of his teachers of philosophy at Hopkins, an influential voice (very different from Morris's) that introduced him to Wilhelm Wundt's scientific psychology, which counteracted the idealism he first favored. Peirce, of course, was his third instructor in philosophy: though there is no evidence of any influence there.

Dewey seems to have begun to read Peirce seriously somewhat before the 1920s. On the matter of his alternative conception of logic, it must be said in all fairness that Dewey never quite reconciled his own intuition that logic must follow the actual process of human inquiry (the actual course of practical life) and his willingness to accept the settled formalisms of canonical logic. The result, as far as the *Logic* book is concerned, is a valiant but unsuccessful union of the concrete processes of inquiry and the abstract fixities of academic logic. All this contributes to pragmatism's initial scatter. And yet a clear and justifiable sense of the gathering focus of the movement begins to make itself felt. It is true that Peirce's and Dewey's accounts of formal logic could not be more different, both in detail and in their metaphysical associations. But, in general terms, both support the idea that an adequate account of the formal features of inference must *follow* the evolving processes of practical inquiry. They surely agree on that important pragmatist (and, in an obvious sense, Hegelian) theme.

What can we say, then, about pragmatism's growing unity that will not seem too improbable or too elementary or too much skewed in favor of the eventual pre-eminence of Dewey's formulation? Perhaps some of the distinctions that follow will serve as a fair first pass, even though they may be found in other figures and other movements – not quite joined in the characteristic way that marks the work of the original pragmatists.

First of all, they view the achievement of human knowledge – in particular, the achievement of science – as arising out of the most elementary animal abilities (ranging, in an evolutionary sense, from, say, the amoeba, or protoplasm itself, to the life of conscious creatures that lack language and human conceptual powers to the *sui generis* abilities of human agents). This is emphasized in the profoundest way by both Peirce and Dewey; independently, on Dewey's part, as much as on Peirce's.

Peirce's treatment of the idea, which ramifies through his entire system, is linked in an important way to a distinctive thesis known as "fallibilism" (often misunderstood or conflated with Dewey's version), which has had considerable influence in the theory of knowledge (bearing particularly on questions of scientific discovery and certitude) and the meaning of truth and reality. You will find its most explicit influence in Karl Popper's (1972) paper, "Of Clouds and Clocks,"[21] which is itself central to the development of Popper's quite different doctrine ("falsificationism") which he offered as an alternative to the positivism championed by Rudolf Carnap and Moritz Schlick. Dewey's treatment of fallibilism is significantly different from Peirce's, though the irony is that its germ can be found in Peirce himself, in fact in the "How To Make Our Ideas Clear" paper, which James had (in a "fortunate" way) mismanaged.

The upshot of both Peirce's and Dewey's treatment of the "animal" (or, in Peirce's sense, the "protoplasmic") source of all knowledge – a fortiori, science – leads us to hold, as a second dictum, against canonical philosophies like Aristotle's, Descartes', and Kant's, that knowledge, thought, intelligence, reason, language itself are all primarily practical, biologically generated aptitudes (originally lacking concepts or categories of "thought"), that are naturally addressed (along an evolutionary continuum) to the resolution of "real" doubts (Peirce) or, more elaborately, "a problematic [or 'indeterminate'] situation" (Dewey). These notions are plainly anthropomorphized but are meant to range over the subhuman as well. It suggests, once again, the meaning, for Peirce, of "habit" in nature at large, and of course the various metaphors of idealism. But the difference between Peirce's and Dewey's versions of fallibilism rests with the fact that Dewey's leads to the determinate resolution of a "problematic situation," whereas Peircean inquiry is infinitely and endlessly extended. Accordingly, their conceptions of truth (at the end of inquiry) diverge as well.

The Darwinian theme has the immediate consequence of subsuming so-called "theoretical reason" under "practical reason" (or under some suitable animal surrogate). The traditional view had held that "reason" (or what, among our perceptual or related abilities) actually discerns, in a neutral way, what is true or real regarding the independent world is a cognitive *faculty* (or family of faculties) that operates best apart from any practical or interested or perspectived concerns. So the pragmatist emphasis on the animal origins of human science (one must stress "origins" rather than "mode of functioning") was a distinctly heterodox qualification. It is, in fact, the decisive key to understanding the pragmatist objection to Cartesianism – and, accordingly, the relevance of Peirce's attack on the doctrine of "clear and distinct ideas." For Descartes expressly relies on a facultative power and Peirce calls that power into question by his pragmatist treatment of the semantics of language and conception.

The upshot collects two important notions: one, that we must abandon the purely "facultative" reading of reason and perception and thought in favor of a way of acting effectively in matters of "doubt" or "indeterminacy," informed (at a more advanced level among humans) by the habituated (evolved) skills of reasoning and perceiving that serve our practical needs; the other, that there are, therefore, no foundational or privileged cognitive resources to rely on, by which to account for the specific success of an objective and valid science, and that there is no biological discontinuity between animal and human abilities in the resolution of practical impasses. It should be clear that the facultative and pragmatist views can both claim Darwinian support, though they are incompatible with one another. It is also worth remarking, though it is puzzling, that Richard Rorty and Robert Brandom, speaking recently as pragmatists, explicitly oppose the idea of a strong continuity between animal and human intelligence along Darwinian lines, precisely because they restrict the possession of concepts to linguistic competence.[22]

A convenient way of putting the point, in a sense reasonably close to what both Peirce and Dewey favor (though not a formula either specifically endorses), suggests that science is a refined and notably rigorous development of the evolving practical know-how (*savoir-faire*) that animal survival manifests, rather than the result of exercising the specific cognizing faculties of objective knowing (*savoir*) that traditional theorists had insisted on. Both Peirce and Dewey were prepared to admit that "scientific method" – a notion both favored – is bound to have its own distinctive rigor well beyond the resolution of specifically animal needs. Hence, Peirce would admit that even original human "doubt" in the barest practical matters could not account satisfactorily for the special work of the advanced sciences; and Dewey would concur in terms of his own idea of an "indeterminate situation" (which is featured particularly in *Logic* and *Experience and Nature*). Both, of course, see in this a radical departure from canonical realisms.

One is inclined to say that this last theme is as close as we are likely to come to what is most original and commanding in the pragmatist resolution of the realism question. Both Peirce and Dewey obviously grasp the strategic importance of two notions (still neglected today) that should be incorporated in every successful realism: one, that the deliberate cognitive powers invoked in every viable science must have evolved from (without being confined to) biological or animal dispositions that cannot themselves be assigned cognitive standing except when compared with (and interpreted in terms of) the human paradigm; the other, that it is in virtue of the embedding of our cognitive powers in the material origins of life itself that the realist standing of the sciences can be finally explained without residual paradox. There, by a single stroke, the principal Cartesian puzzles can be completely resolved – particularly mind/body dualism and the "inner"/"outer" disjunction of representationalism.

Dewey construed these gains in Darwinian terms; Peirce addresses them also as an evolutionist, though his evolutionism is actually broader than the specifically Darwinian themes he favors. The fact remains that Hegel had already sketched (in his extraordinarily involuted way) an anticipation of the general argument, in the *Phenomenology* well before the publication of Darwin's *Origin of Species.*[23] This may provide the most convincing (oblique) evidence that both Peirce and Dewey were "Hegelians," in however attenuated a way. But it is precisely in Dewey's

Experience and Nature that the leanest and most satisfactory pragmatist resolution of the realist question is provided, along Darwinian and Hegelian lines.

It is but a step from this to a further dictum: namely, that knowledge and science are essentially open-ended, improvizational, subject to change as a result of evolving societal experience, evolutionary in fact, incapable of any unconditional or necessarily changeless findings, hence opposed to fixed invariances, universalities, essences, necessities in knowledge or in reason or in nature. In this sense, all the pragmatists effectively agreed to a further and final dictum, namely, that nature is a "flux," which is to say, not a "chaos" but a space of changing processes that still permits the detection of reasonably regular structures, none of which is assuredly invariant against all possibility of change.

Notes

1 L. Menand, *The Metaphysical Club* (New York: Farrar, Straus and Giroux, 2001).
2 Ibid., p. xi.
3 J. Brent, *Charles Sanders Peirce: A Life* (Bloomington: Indiana University Press, 1993), pp. xviii, 323.
4 Ibid., p. 325.
5 W. James, *The Works of William James*, ed. Frederick H. Burkhardt, 19 vols. (Cambridge, MA: Harvard University Press, 1975–88).
6 R. B. Perry, *The Thought and Character of William James*, 2 vols. (Boston: Little, Brown, 1935), ii, p. 407 nn.5–6.
7 Brent, *Charles Sanders Peirce*; C. S. Peirce, *The Collected Papers of Charles Sanders Peirce* (hereafter *CP*), ed. Charles Hartshorne, Paul Weiss, and Arthur Burks, 8 vols. (Cambridge: Harvard University Press, 1931–66), 5.12.
8 B. Russell and A. N. Whitehead, *Principia Mathematica*, vol. 1 (Cambridge: Cambridge University Press, 1910; 2nd edn. 1925).
9 C. I. Lewis, *Collected Papers of Clarence Irving Lewis*, ed. John D. Goheen and John L. Mothershead, Jr. (Stanford: Stanford University Press, 1970).
10 G. H. Mead, *Mind, Self and Society*, ed. Charles W. Morris (Chicago: University of Chicago Press, 1934).
11 B. Russell, "William James's Concept of Truth," in *Philosophical Essays* (London: Longmans, Green, 1910).
12 B. Russell, "Dewey's New Logic," in P. A. Schilpp, ed., *The Philosophy of Bertrand Russell* (New York: Tudor, 1939; 2nd edn. 1951).
13 *CP* 5.414.
14 Perry, *The Thought and Character of William James*, p. 409.
15 J. Dewey, *The Later Works, 1925–1953* (hereafter *LW*), ed. Jo Ann Boydston, 17 vols. (Carbondale: Southern Illinois University Press, 1981–90).
16 J. Dewey, *The Early Works, 1882–1898* (hereafter *EW*), ed. Jo Ann Boydston, 5 vols. (Carbondale: Southern Illinois University Press, 1967–72), 1.133.
17 *CP* 6.25.
18 Dewey, *LW*.
19 *CP* 1, Bk. III.

20 R. Rorty, "Pragmatism, Davidson and Truth," in Ernest Lepore, ed., *Truth and Interpretation: Perspectives on the Philosophy of Donald Davidson* (Oxford: Basil Blackwell, 1986).

21 K. R. Popper, "Of Clouds and Clocks," in *Objective Knowledge: An Evolutionary Approach* (Oxford: Clarendon Press, 1972).

22 R. Rorty, "Robert Brandom on Social Practices and Representations," in *Philosophical Papers*, vol. 3 (Cambridge: Cambridge University Press, 1998); R. B. Brandom, *Articulating Reasons: An Introduction to Inferentialism* (Cambridge, MA: Harvard University Press, 2000).

23 G. W. F. Hegel, *Hegel's Phenomenology of Spirit*, trans. A. V. Miller (Oxford: Clarendon Press, 1977 [1807]), §§ 166–78.

Suggested reading

Brent, Joseph, *Charles Sanders Peirce: A Life*, revised and enlarged edn. (Bloomington: Indiana University Press, 1998).

Dewey, John, *The Early Works, 1882–1898*, ed. Jo Ann Boydston, 5 vols. (Carbondale: Southern Illinois University Press, 1967–72).

Dewey, John, *The Middle Works, 1899–1924*, ed. Jo Ann Boydston, 15 Vols. (Carbondale: Southern Illinois University Press, 1976–83).

Dewey, John, *The Later Works, 1925–1953*, ed. Jo Ann Boydston, 17 vols. (Carbondale: Southern Illinois University Press, 1981–90).

James, William, *The Works of William James*, ed. Frederick H. Burkhardt, 19 vols. (Cambridge, MA: Harvard University Press, 1975–88).

Kuklick, Bruce, *The Rise of American Philosophy: Cambridge, Massachusetts, 1860–1930* (New Haven, CT: Yale University Press, 1977).

Lewis, Clarence I., *Collected Papers of Clarence Irving Lewis*, ed. John D. Goheen and John L. Mothershead, Jr. (Stanford, CA: Stanford University Press, 1970).

Mead, George H., *Mind, Self and Society*, ed. Charles W. Morris (Chicago: University of Chicago Press, 1934).

Menand, Louis, *The Metaphysical Club* (New York: Farrar, Straus and Giroux, 2001).

Peirce, Charles S., *Collected Papers of Charles Sanders Peirce*, ed. Charles Hartshorne, Paul Weiss, and Arthur Burks, 8 vols. (Cambridge, MA: Harvard University Press, 1931–66).

—— *Writings of Charles S. Peirce: A Chronological Edition*, vols. 1–6, eds. Max H. Fisch, Edward C. Moore, Christian J. W. Kloesel, and Nathan Houser (Bloomington: Indiana University Press, 1982–99).

Perry, Ralph Barton, *The Thought and Character of William James*, 2 vols. (Boston: Little, Brown, 1935).

Rorty, Richard, *The Consequences of Pragmatism* (Minneapolis: University of Minnesota Press, 1982).

Seigfried, Charlene Haddock, *Pragmatism and Feminism* (Chicago: University of Chicago Press, 1996).

Thayer, H. Standish, *Meaning and Action: A Critical History of Pragmatism*, 2nd edn. (Indianaopolis, IN: Hackett Publishing, 1997).

Chapter 4

Naturalism

Michael Eldridge

Introduction

God has ceased to be an explanatory principle for philosophers. For some, such as David Hume, this occurred in the eighteenth century; for others, say, Friedrich Nietzsche, it was the late nineteenth century. But certainly by the end of the twentieth century it was the case for almost all.[1] This secular outcome is what philosophic naturalism attempts to understand and advocate. But just exactly what philosophical naturalism is, is not easily specified. John Lachs, who delivered the fourth Romanell Lecture, once declared that "naturalism is as elusive as it is important."[2] Charles Sanders Peirce and George Santayana, about whom Lachs was writing, were naturalists in that each agreed that "the world, with whatever magnitude of order it displays, is a single system which articulates itself in space and time. This system is governed by its own laws, which diligent inquiry may disclose. Man is in some fashion continuous with the natural world and may find his fulfillment within it."[3] Less hesitantly and more directly, Roy Wood Sellars, in one of the classics of the American philosophical naturalist tradition, wrote:

> Naturalism stands for the self-sufficiency and intelligibility of the world of space and time. Supernaturalism maintains that this realm is not self-sufficient and that it can be understood only as the field of operation of a spiritual reality outside itself. Historically and logically, naturalism is associated with science, while supernaturalism finds expression in an ethical metaphysics, the *rule* of God."[4]

In these two statements we see some of the recurring themes: opposition to supernaturalism, association with science, and humanity as fully a part of nature. In short, nature, which is inclusive of humanity, is all there is, and that's okay. The problem comes, however, as we shall see, when a particular philosopher attempts to work out systematically the details of what I have just too breezily articulated. Note, for instance, that Sellars speaks forthrightly of "science" and Lachs speaks more circumspectly of "diligent inquiry." Lachs's language is not accidental; his more general formulation reflects a tension within the movement regarding the role of science in "diligent inquiry." Naturalism is, as Lachs notes, an elusive world-view. Consequently, tracing its history is a problem. Moreover, it is an under-studied phenomenon, and there is not a full, critical history.[5]

Given its significance, this is surprising. We have now reached the point that Robert Audi, in the entry on naturalism in the authoritative 1996 *Supplement* to *The Encyclopedia of Philosophy*, can observe, "Naturalism is more often presupposed than stated."[6] This may be due, as Audi argues, to the inability of naturalists, at least thus far, to formulate their position clearly and coherently. But it may also be the case that naturalism is the unexamined background belief of philosophers in general.[7] Not personally or even professionally unexamined, for academic philosophers in introductory courses regularly deal with the assumptions and arguments of those who reject an external cosmic agent. And a philosopher is, if anybody is, one who is aware of the implications of what she is talking about. But naturalism as the systematic working out of a non-theistic world-view is not the focus of very many professional philosophers' work.

This has not always been the case. Early in the twentieth century a varied group of American philosophers identified themselves as naturalists and sought to develop the implications of their position. For a time, toward the middle of the century, they were even considered to be the dominant philosophical tendency in America. There is, of course, no official beginning, but many of the new naturalists pointed to the early work of George Santayana, a not fully American philosopher who taught at Harvard at the turn of the century before returning to Europe. There was then a sustained period of self-identified naturalism that was at the center of discussion in the American philosophic community in the 1920s, '30s, and '40s. The philosophical deliberations of these naturalists will be what will occupy our attention in this chapter. Eventually, we will come to a messy ending. Books and articles continue to be produced by philosophers working within this tradition, but the most visible work is in specific fields – epistemology, philosophy of mind, philosophy of language, and ethics. This fragmented discussion is not carried on as if it were part of a whole or the successor to a wider perspective, and the self-identified heirs of the earlier new naturalism are often dismissive of the efforts of, say, those doing "naturalized epistemology." The heirs claim that the latter phenomenon, in its allegedly exclusive reliance on science, is reductionist and undeserving of the naturalist name. Isolation, obscurity, and alienation are hardly the desirable conclusion to what many earlier in the twentieth century looked forward to as a noble development in the history of philosophy. But it is a part of the ending at which we will arrive.

Santayana: American Naturalism's Early Role Model

Naturalism in the nineteenth century was associated with materialism and empiricism, and contrasted with idealism, the leading philosophical tendency of the century. Peirce's friend and Santayana's teacher, William James, contrasted the two in *Pragmatism* (1907) and finally moved away from idealism because he could not accept its monistic world-view. But he clearly wanted to find a way to be religious, to have some of the features of tender-mindedness that he associated with idealism. He wanted something more than the tough-minded empiricism to which he seemed to be driven by his embrace of science and specifically Darwinian biology. For James, the leading American philosopher at the turn of the century, it was by a force of will and some imprecision that he was able to overcome the stand-off between the dominant idealism and the emerging materialism of the nineteenth century. It was left to his brilliant students to inaugurate what came to be called "the new naturalism."

Lachs observed, succinctly and ironically, that Santayana's early five-volume *The Life of Reason* (1905–6) was "used as a bible by American naturalists."[8] Philosophical naturalists, of course, had no need either of the supernatural or of an authoritative guide, but they did need a way to bring together the tough and the tender, the empirical and the spiritual. What they got from Santayana, according to John Herman Randall, Jr., was a well-developed protest against the opposing philosophic tendencies of the previous century, a protest that would shape their own distinctive efforts. Santayana, drawing on his immense knowledge of the history of philosophy, but particularly Plato and Aristotle, developed an alternative to nineteenth-century materialism and its non-naturalistic opponents – supernaturalism and transcendental idealism. "These five volumes, especially the latter four," wrote Randall, "have become a classic document of the new naturalism."[9]

Why Randall exempted the first volume is interesting, and a consideration of his reason will foreshadow the first major confrontation that I want to examine. Randall found in the first volume "seeds" of a new "dualism" that would bring together modern "materialism and mechanism" with a Platonic realm of timeless and nonexistent essences. This post-*Life of Reason* dualism "brought the not-undeserved charge that his professed naturalism of those days is now 'broken-backed'."[10] Randall here used the phrase that John Dewey had employed in his exchanges in the late 1920s with Santayana. In a review of Dewey's *Experience and Nature*, one of the landmarks in naturalistic metaphysics, Santayana accused Dewey of being "half-hearted" in his naturalism – to which Dewey then replied that Santayana's naturalism was "broken-backed." This is not just a matter of charge and countercharge. As we shall see, their disagreement, which also manifested itself in a review written by Dewey of Santayana's *The Realm of Essence*, reflects a deep tension in naturalism regarding the role of humans in the scheme of things.[11]

But Randall's reservation benefited from hindsight. At the time of their formation as philosophers, several of the naturalists were reading *The Life of Reason* as a suggestive working out of what they desired – a way to be naturalistic without being reductive. This is the hallmark of the new naturalists. They wanted their ideals to have a natural basis. On this point Santayana was clear. Note, for example, the following passage:

> Spiritual unity is a natural product. There are those who see a great mystery in the presence of eternal values and impersonal ideals in a moving and animal world, and think to solve that dualism, as they call it, by denying that nature can have spiritual functions or spirit a natural cause; but nothing can be simpler if we make, as we should, existence the test of possibility.[12]

Clearly, Santayana wanted the world science describes *and* the ideals articulated in poetry, morality, and religion. It is significant that Santayana devoted two of the five volumes to art and religion and only one to science. This is a naturalism that is pluralistic in method and inclusive in its concerns; there is no reductive move here. It is what the later naturalists found attractive. What they came to have reservations about, as I have indicated, is just how integrated Santayana's naturalism was.

Some Episodes in the History of the New Naturalism

The commonalities are such that we can group the new naturalists together, but some identifiable differences did surface and indeed crystalize into distinctive traditions. These are the Aristotelian orientation of F. J. E. Woodbridge and his prominent student, John Herman Randall, Jr., the pragmatic naturalism of John Dewey, and the non-pragmatic (or refusal to privilege the human) approaches of Santayana and Morris Raphael Cohen. The naturalism of Justus Buchler and the materialism of Roy Wood Sellars are not so easy to classify. Buchler's inclusive approach has important continuities with his Columbia University teachers and colleagues, but is a distinctive contribution. Sellars, like Santayana, called himself a materialist and has some commonality with the pragmatists. Where he differs from the latter is interesting. Sellars thought it important to continue to work in some of the traditional philosophic areas, such as epistemology and metaphysics, about which the pragmatists were ambivalent or even dismissive. I will illustrate these commonalities and differences by looking at several discussions. The first, to which I have already alluded, is an exchange in the 1920s and '30s between Santayana and Dewey. The second is Randall's criticism of Dewey's failure to appreciate the role of religious institutions. The third is the discussion initiated by the manifesto of the Columbia naturalists, *Naturalism and the Human Spirit*.

The Dewey–Santayana exchange

In 1925 John Dewey published *Experience and Nature*, a naturalistic account of mind, nature, art, and philosophic method. Santayana reviewed it in the *Journal of Philosophy*, the journal published by the Department of Philosophy at Columbia University, with which Dewey was long associated. Santayana recognized Dewey's naturalist intent, but he questioned the success of his effort. At one point in the review Santayana wondered about the lack of a cosmology in Dewey's metaphysics and then answers his own question: "This question, which is the crux of the whole system, may be answered, I think, in a single phrase: *the dominance of the foreground*." For Santayana, naturalism entailed a cosmic view of nature, in which "there is no foreground or background, no here, no now, no moral cathedra, no center so really central as to reduce all other things to mere margins and mere perspectives." But for the pragmatist Dewey our theories are tools we have constructed to deal with the problems at hand. This situatedness was unacceptable to Santayana. So much so that Santayana denied that Dewey was a naturalist after all: "If such a foreground becomes dominant in a philosophy naturalism is abandoned." True naturalists are those, such as "the old Ionians or the Stoics or Spinoza, or like those many mystics, Indian, Jewish, or Mohammedan, who, heartily despising the foreground, have fallen in love with the greatness of nature and have sunk speechless before the infinite." Thus Dewey's "naturalism is half-hearted and short-winded." It lacks the scope of the non-centered naturalism with which Santayana is enthralled; it is too particular in its orientation.[13]

In his reply two years later in the *Journal of Philosophy*, "Half-Hearted Naturalism," Dewey quickly charged Santayana with dualism, one of the most serious offenses that a philosopher can commit from a Deweyan perspective: "In short, his presupposition is a break between nature and man; man in the sense of anything more than a physically extended body, man as institutions, culture, 'experience'."[14] In *Experience and Nature*, he reports later in his reply, he "tried to bring together on a naturalistic basis the mind and matter that Santayana kept worlds apart." Hence when Santayana made a distinction between matter and mind, even developing an ontology of essence, matter, spirit, and truth and speaking of them as distinct realms, Dewey was quick to suspect, as he says, something "reminiscent of supernatural beliefs." Santayana's naturalism lacked the continuity that Dewey prized; hence his charge that it was "broken-backed."[15]

It is not my task to adjudicate this disagreement. Rather I am attempting to identify the various forms of the new naturalism. Thus, in this instance, we see that despite their common antipathy to older forms of materialism and nineteenth-century idealism and their common commitment to nature as the inclusive category *in some sense*, they represent two distinct orientations within naturalism. Santayana took a more cosmic view, refusing to privilege the human or the social. Dewey was a pragmatist and took human interest as central. Yet he thought that he had successfully integrated mind, including collective intelligence or culture, and nature, or at least thought such an integration was possible. It is not surprising then that Santayana's world-view played itself out, in Lachs's phrase, in a "spectator theory of fulfillment." Lachs wrote:

> Santayana's interest in the spiritual transcendence of the flux intensified with his advancing years. Between the two wars he lived out of a suitcase or two, traveling in Europe from city to city. He had obviously given up the attempt to lead the life of reason in a social setting: he was isolated in every way but intellectually.[16]

Dewey, in contrast, was deeply embedded in the life of his family, university, profession, city, and nation, and his metaphysics reflects this situatedness. He expected intelligence generally and philosophy in particular to make a difference in the world, to be a tool for the improvement of our practices. Consequently, his metaphysics is a working out of certain implications of his commitment to philosophy as a criticism of our cultural practices. It describes the general conditions that make this situated life and its improvement possible.

The disagreement between these two naturalists was not an isolated affair. It reflected an ongoing tension. For instance, Morris Raphael Cohen criticized Dewey in 1939 in a way reminiscent of Santayana. The title of his essay indicates the affinity with Santayana's approach: "Some Difficulties in Dewey's Anthropocentric Naturalism."[17] But I am getting ahead of the story.

Aristotelian pluralism and its reaction to pragmatic naturalism

Another member of the first generation of new naturalists was Frederick J. E. Woodbridge, a colleague of Dewey's at Columbia, who arrived two years before Dewey in 1902. Woodbridge, a founder of the *Journal of Philosophy* and a long-time graduate dean at Columbia, was not as prolific a writer as Santayana and Dewey and was less well known outside academic circles. But he certainly wielded influence as a teacher and editor. I will focus attention on one of his very visible students shortly, but first I want to draw out the connections with Santayana and Dewey.

In his contribution to *Contemporary American Philosophy*, a collection of autobiographical essays by prominent American philosophers published in 1930, Woodbridge makes clear his "indebtedness to Santayana" (and Aristotle). He describes Santayana's *Life of Reason* as "a book I wish I could have written myself." Woodbridge's reaction to one statement from that book is worth quoting in full, for it brings out the character of his naturalism:

> When I read, "With Aristotle the conception of human life is perfectly sound, for with him everything ideal has a natural basis and everything natural an ideal fulfilment" – when I read this, not only did the disorderly writings of the Stagerite combine together to produce one impressive effect, but what I myself had been clum-

> sily feeling for received a clarified and satisfactory expression. In that one sentence was revealed what certainly seems to be one of the major tasks of philosophy: to exhibit the passage from the natural to the ideal; from common sense to reason; from animal love to ideal love; from gregarious association to free society; from practice and invention to liberal art; from mythology to enlightened religion; and from crude cosmologies to that impersonal objectivity found in science. In that one sentence, too, I found an acceptable standard of criticism, for it seemed to me that ideals are significant as they round out and complete some natural function, and that the natural, when cut off from the ideal, must not be looked upon as affording by itself any standard of conduct or reason for its existence; it is brutally impersonal.[18]

Woodbridge firmly located ideals within nature, but just as firmly insisted that nature is incomplete without human development. Moreover, science is but one of the ways in which we fulfill nature. It is this pluralism, with its appreciation for the past, that brought Woodbridge and his student, Randall, into conflict with Dewey.

In his own autobiographical account, John Herman Randall, Jr. made clear his several obligations to his teachers at Columbia, but he singled out Woodbridge and Dewey. He notes that many assume that Dewey was the primary influence on him, and he acknowledges that they have much in common. Of Dewey's writings, Randall said, "My experience with them has always been that after painfully working out a problem for myself I have then found that he had reached my solution beforehand. But never by my path. And it has always taken quite an effort to follow his own course in reaching our common truth. I fear I have never been able to think like Dewey." He then added, "I should like to believe I think like Woodbridge." Indeed, he credited Woodbridge with being his "great philosophical inspiration" and "the chief factor in my philosophical development." "He has been my great teacher, along with Aristotle. He taught me how to understand the Greeks – with able assistance from [Wendell T.] Bush as to Plato. He taught me how to understand the history of philosophy. He taught me what Metaphysics is – and is not – and why it is important. He taught me the meaning of a philosophical naturalism."

Dewey could be quite disparaging of Aristotle and the direction in which he turned philosophy, a direction that needed major correction by reflection on the significant accomplishments of modern science. Yet Randall, while acknowledging the difficulty of getting others to share his view, thought Dewey and Woodbridge had much in common: "Actually, Dewey and Woodbridge were very close together philosophically, in all but their very different languages. I long ago gave up trying to explain to students the precise difference." He then offered this revealing explanation: "Woodbridge uses the language of the philosophies of being, Dewey that of the philosophies of experience – usually of Hegelian experience, not British. This confuses students today, who have forgotten the Hegelian tongue. I find the former language, that of being, more congenial myself, but I hope I can understand both. It is largely the same philosophy."[19] This is partially correct. They share a naturalism, and Woodbridge is often credited with making Dewey more appreciative of Aristotle than he was and even willing to "do metaphysics," the result being Dewey's *Experience and Nature*.[20] But there are important differences as well. Dewey was much more oriented toward science and process than Woodbridge the metaphysical realist.

To illustrate the tension between these colleagues, "close friends,"[21] and star student, I want to examine Randall's criticism of Dewey's attitude toward religion, or, more precisely, religious traditions. This is a good case for us to examine because it was the claim of the new naturalists that they were not reductive materialists. They understood themselves as offering a positive account of morality, religion, and art. The nobler things of life, they argued, are not eliminated by a naturalistic approach. Dewey, however, was sharply critical of those religions that were supernaturalistic in their orientation, which is to say, he was sharply critical of most religions. His way of fulfilling the new naturalism's project was to speak of "the religious in experience." The various traditional and conventional religions had distorted what was religiously valuable – inclusive, intense allegiances that transformed a person, making one a unified self. The better way to be religious was to be found not in the supernaturally oriented religions but in intelligent, passionate participation in society.

Randall thought that Dewey was indulging "in much loose talk about ridding religious experience of 'all historic encumbrances'." Then came the naturalist zinger: such talk was "hardly appropriate from one usually so insistent on the continuity of human institutions and cultures."[22] In contrast, Randall's naturalism embraced existing institutions. He thought there was a value in them that Dewey was overlooking. In a review of *A Common Faith*, the slim volume that contains Dewey's religious proposal, and *Art as Experience*, Dewey's expansive discussion of art and aesthetic experience, Randall was critical of Dewey's approach to religion, contrasting Dewey's sensitive appreciation of art with his external treatment of religion. Randall found the "historic religions" much richer than Dewey did, but conceded that popular religion may well be impoverished in the ways that Dewey described. It was a mistake, however, to focus on religion's failings:

> Whether this is all that religion has meant or might mean in human experience is another matter, on which he hardly touches. Above all one misses that enrichment of life through a host of immediately enjoyed and shared meanings, which religion has given, and to which Dewey is usually so sensitive. The whole esthetic side of religion, the sheer enjoyment of the practice of the cult, the entire set of human values enshrined in religious institutions, are things primarily to be emancipated from.[23]

Randall's pluralistic naturalism allowed him to take existing human practices as they were. Their existence as institutions carried with them a presumption of value. Dewey, however, thought that a significant change had occurred in the last several hundred years with the advent of scientific practice and modern democracy. Social intelligence had become explicit in the development of these institutions. One feature of these remarkable, liberating changes was their secularity. Both practices showed the possibility of human experience becoming self-directive:

> Now, old experience is used to suggest aims and method for developing a new and improved experience. Consequently experience becomes so far constructively self-regulative. . . . We do not merely have to repeat the past, or wait for accidents to force change upon us. We *use* our past experience to construct new and better ones in the future. The very fact of experience thus includes the process by which it directs itself in its own betterment.[24]

This Randall also accepts, but what he cannot accept is Dewey's resolute conviction that the historic and conventional religions are primarily to be understood as so thoroughly supernaturalistic that they detract from this self-directive impulse and method. There is more to them than their supernaturalism.

In *A Common Faith*, Dewey wrote:

> If I have said anything about religions and religion that seems harsh, I have said those things because of a firm belief that the claim on the part of religions to possess a monopoly of ideals and of the supernatural means by which alone, it is alleged, they can be furthered, stands in the way of the realization of distinctively religious values inherent in natural experience.[25]

Having turned away from these institutions, Dewey looked primarily to the nonreligious institutions of society for help in realizing a naturalistic religiosity.

Columbia naturalism's manifesto and its critics

Despite their differences, Woodbridge and Dewey and their distinguished students made common cause in the 1930s and '40s – so much so that their collaborative effort was a manifesto of what some regarded as the dominant philosophical orientation at mid-century. The collaboration of the various naturalists in the volume edited by Yervant Krikorian was not contrived. In the epilogue, Randall contended that the essays "exhibit much unity of thought." Indeed, "the reader has surely found . . . a community of temper, of method, and even of general outlook, rather remarkable in any group of writers so crotchety and individualistic as professional philosophers." The "general outlook" is the familiar one to students of the new naturalism: "Nature" is an inclusive term; it is not to be used in contrast with "supernature" to designate reality. There is nothing over and beyond nature; nor need there be. Nature is all-inclusive and sufficient. The method which unites them is the scientific one. It is not that naturalists restrict themselves to the techniques of the various sciences. Rather, their method is consonant with those of the sciences and thus is appropriately designated "scientific." Randall, having noted that the new naturalists had understood humanity to be fully a part of nature, summarized the program:

> Viewed in this extended perspective, and in the light of the great intellectual movements of the nineteenth century, contemporary naturalism thus represents at once the culmination of the idealistic criticism, and of the natural sciences of man and human culture. It carries on the idealistic emphasis that man is united to his world by a logical and social experience. But it rephrases the idealistic scheme of man's activities and environment in biological and anthropological categories. While like the idealists it makes them all amenable to a single intellectual method, it reformulates that method in experimental terms. At the same time, contemporary naturalism is rooted in the natural sciences, extending their content and scope, and expanding and rendering more flexible their methods to include a treatment of even those human activities formerly set apart as "spiritual".[26]

Hence the title of the volume, *Naturalism and the Human Spirit.* Far from being reductionistic, naturalism was able to show that a suitably enhanced science, or experimental or empirical method, could address the full range of human experience and the world which humanity inhabits.

Some of the 15 contributors to Krikorian's volume sought to do this by addressing specific areas that some thought lay outside the scope of this method: religion (Sterling Lamprecht), democracy (Sidney Hook), ethics (Abraham Edel), aesthetics (Eliseo Vivas), logic (Ernest Nagel), mind (Yervant Krikorian), metaphysics (William R. Dennes). Others dealt with history (George Boas and Edward W. Strong) and sociology (Thelma Z. Lavine), areas that had come to be regarded as social sciences. Dewey wrote the lead essay, drawing the contrast between naturalism and anti-naturalism quite sharply. Representing the other great Columbia influence on naturalism was an essay by Harry Todd Costello on Woodbridge, who had died in 1940, four years prior to publication of this volume. Honored not by an essay but by the book's dedication was Morris Raphael Cohen. Not fitting easily into the overall scheme of the book is an essay by Herbert Schneider which provides a naturalistic account of "the unnatural" and a warning against identifying "the natural" with "the good." It is thus at once an essay in value theory and a metaphysical statement. Harold Larrabee meets a real need in providing a history of naturalism in America, surveying some 250 years and considering not just intellectual developments but also their economic and cultural contexts. Not surprisingly, the volume was attacked by W. H. Sheldon as having failed in its attempt to describe a naturalism that dealt successfully with non-material matters: "Their naturalism is just materialism over again under a softer name." They may deny that theirs is a reductive materialism, but they limit themselves to the scientific method, and in so doing they restrict themselves to what such a method can investigate – the physical. Thus, "the creed has no longer two articles: nature and method. It has only one: method."[27] And this method cannot investigate non-material matters. This attack, of course, denies what the naturalists claimed to have achieved. Whether or not it is successful would require an assessment of Sheldon's critiques of the specific attempts to do what he denies can be done. What is interesting about Dewey, Hook, and Nagel's response to Sheldon is not just their replies to the specifics but also their collective embrace of a non-reductive materialism.[28] Often the new naturalists, in their efforts to mediate nineteenth-century disputes, had distanced themselves from the materialists. Santayana and Roy Wood Sellars had distinguished themselves in their willingness to call themselves materialists. Indeed, Sellars noted in his review of *Naturalism and the Human Spirit* that an essay by Donald Williams that articulated a "materialistic naturalism" that was present in the "manuscript stage" was "omitted" from the book as published.[29] Moreover, two years earlier, Sellars had asked in an essay, "Dewey on Materialism," why Dewey had been unwilling to embrace the sort of "reformed materialism" that Sellars advocated.[30] Then, in the preceding year, 1944, Sellars had taken Hook to task for "his rather cavalier treatment of materialism": "It is as though materialism was to be robbed of its name, pushed to one side with scarcely concealed scorn, and witness that name appropriated by naturalism. In short, the thesis seems to be that the only defensible meaning assignable to materialism is that of naturalism."[31] Clearly, by 1945 Dewey and Hook were willing to call themselves materialists of a sort that would seem to include Sellars.

The dispute with Sellars was not just about the naturalist's embrace of a reformed materialism. There was more to it than that. Both Sellars and Arthur Murphy in their reviews criticized the Columbia naturalists for failing to be as philosophical as they should. Sellars, like his fellow naturalists, applauded "the extension of scientific method to the social sciences and even to the analysis of the arts and aesthetic experience." But he thought there was still work for the philosopher to do, work that was peculiarly the philosophers' to do: "To me the weakness in all this is the neglect of epistemology and ontology." As he had made clear two years before in "Is Naturalism Enough?", Sellars thought "pragmatic naturalism" lacked a clearly defined ontology, such as his own "physical realism," and an appropriately "analytic" epistemology, one that inserted "consciousness in the organic self."[32] The pragmatists, of course, had at times been disdainful of the need for either an ontology or an epistemology, but Dewey had nevertheless published what could serve as their equivalents in his *Experience and Nature* and *Quest for Certainty*. Moreover, many of the essays in *Naturalism and the Human Spirit* had been openly metaphysical, notably Dennes's "The Categories of Naturalism."

It is this latter essay on which Murphy ultimately concentrated his attack. Throughout his lengthy review he searched for a clear statement of just what naturalism is. Finally, he came to Dennes's contribution, which he regarded as "the most important," but one that begged the question, in that Dennes did not supply a philosophical justification for his naturalistic categories of event, quality, and relation, relying instead on science for these positive findings. Dennes claimed that philosophy is a form of criticism, having no positive theses: "contemporary naturalism recognizes much more clearly than did the tradition from which it stems that its distinction from other philosophical positions lies in the postulates and procedures which it criticizes and rejects rather than in any positive tenets of its own about the cosmos."[33] Yet, according to Murphy, naturalism's criticism of "time-transcending substances" rests on its unjustified adoption of a "metaphysics of events, relation, and quality" as "the constituents of all that exists."[34]

Whether Murphy is correct or not is not something I want to determine here. I cite the criticisms of Sellars and Murphy because they were two respected philosophers who had much in common with both pragmatism and naturalism yet criticized the Columbia naturalists for not being *philosophical* enough. They had failed to offer arguments that would engage philosophers who valued the scientific method but thought that philosophy was more than, or other than, this.

Naturalism in the Last Half of the Twentieth Century

Several of the Columbia naturalists we have already mentioned were prominent in the third quarter of the twentieth century, a period in which the new naturalism was eclipsed by other movements in American philosophy. I look briefly at their work and then examine Quine's influence, closing with just a glimpse of a current heir of the Columbia naturalists.

Three prominent Columbia naturalists at mid-century

Sidney Hook had been closely associated with John Dewey in the last several decades of Dewey's life, initially as a student then later as one who assisted him with publications, involved him in public advocacy, and defended his pragmatic naturalism. Although Hook taught for several decades at New York University, because of his association with Dewey, his graduate school affiliation, and, above all, his views, he can be classified as a Columbia naturalist. Although Hook's dissertation, *The Metaphysics of Pragmatism* (1927), written under Dewey, is well regarded, Hook became disenchanted with metaphysics, turning more and more to issues of public policy. Science and democracy are the themes that recur in Hook's work. Perhaps more than any other Deweyan, Hook came to represent the side of Dewey that some would regard as scientistic. He certainly was an advocate of the scientific method and even defined naturalism at one point as "the systematization of what is involved in the scientific method of inquiry."[35]

Ernest Nagel, Hook's fellow student and long-time friend, was also skeptical of what the editors of the volume of essays dedicated to Nagel call "the value of detached metaphysical speculation."[36] The title of his contribution to the Krikorian volume, "Logic without Ontology," expresses well his interest. But the piece on which I want to focus is his 1954 American Philosophical Association (Eastern Division) presidential address, "Naturalism Reconsidered."[37] There he was willing to "run the risk of becoming involved in futile polemics" in order to defend naturalism against two criticisms: (1) naturalism begs the question against supernaturalism and (2) naturalism, "in committing itself to the logic of scientific proof," is "analogous to religious belief in resting on unsupported and indemonstrable faith." Earlier, he had declared his intention to avoid system building and his desire for philosophy to emulate science. It was his hope that progress could be made through specialization and careful analysis. Thus he was faced with a problem – how to engage in refutation without engaging in the same sort of endeavor that he was criticizing. His response, similar to what he had argued in "Logic without Ontology," was to point out that naturalism made no appeal to experience-transcending principles, such as "the uniformity of nature." Thus it differed from religious belief in its approach. I cite Nagel's response to make two points. First, Nagel, Hook, and other naturalists move easily from a methodological to a substantive naturalism. But many of their critics think that one can make full use of the scientific method without committing oneself to a naturalistic metaphysics. The two are independent of one another. Second, naturalism's coherence was clearly under attack at mid-century and beyond, and many were turning to alternatives.

One Columbia naturalist, Justus Buchler, explicitly moved away from a scientific methodological orientation. Beth Singer has commented that "Buchler has a strong interest in science and scientific method. But, like [Alfred North] Whitehead, he views the perspective of science as but one among a number of alternative ways of judging the world, each of which has its own validity."[38] Long associated with Columbia as a student and professor, before finishing his career at the State University of New York at Stony Brook, Buchler wrote his dissertation on Charles Sanders Peirce under the direction of Nagel and collaborated with Randall on an introduction to philosophy. But his major contribution was in the development of an original naturalism that was frankly metaphysical, and in inspiring several students who continue to work in the naturalistic tradition.[39] Central to Buchler's work is not only an engagement with various traditions of the new naturalism, but also an attempt to take, as the collaborative volume about his work attests in its title, "nature's perspectives." Thus neither in method nor in cosmic context does he privilege science or human activity. He aspired, as did Santayana, to, in Sidney Gelber's phrase, a "radical naturalism," yet he avoided the dualism to which his older Columbia colleagues thought Santayana had succumbed.[40] Also of interest is Gelber's explanation of why Buchler left Columbia for Stony Brook:

> In spite of the rich, impressive accomplishments of Columbia as a university, and the distinctive history of the Department of Philosophy in the shaping of American thought, Buchler had become increasingly disturbed by the overall changes in the University's intellectual climate and the quality of its commitments to general education. In addition, the serious diminution of philosophical pluralism in the Department of Philosophy threatened a decline in its intellectual vitality. The profession as a whole typified what he encountered at Columbia.[41]

What the profession was becoming was analytic in orientation.

Quine and pervasive niche naturalism

Current naturalisms, such as what one finds in discussions of epistemology, philosophy of mind, and ethics, over the last few decades simultaneously reflect the older new naturalists' scientific orientation and Sellars and Murphy's metaphysical and epistemological concerns. But these current naturalists, unlike Sellars and Murphy, are largely unaware of the earlier naturalists and many of them, even more than Hook and Nagel, are frankly scientistic in their approach. But there are also continuing efforts in the new naturalism traditions identified in this chapter, ones that attempt to come to terms with the insistence that naturalism must make its case on philosophical grounds.

The charitable view of why many current naturalist projects are restricted in scope and method is suggested by an observation of Tyler Burge. In his survey article, "Philosophy of Language and Mind: 1950–1990,"[42] Burge called attention to the "strong orientation" of positivism "toward the methods of science," an orientation that has "fueled the acceptance of materialism in the philosophy of mind" and other areas of philosophy. Yet, "the main direction of philosophy during" the last several decades "has been toward a broader-based, more eclectic, less ideological approach to philosophical problems" and more "interplay between modern philosophy and the history of philosophy." Then he noted that "this broadening seems not to have seriously undermined the standards of rigor, clarity, and openness to communal check bequeathed by such figures as Frege, Russell, Carnap, Hempel, Gödel, Church, and Quine." It is this last observation that suggests to me the charitable interpretation. Analytic philosophy may have broadened its concerns somewhat, but it is still oriented toward dealing with manageable problems in a careful way. It is not an approach that is conducive to grand schemes. Someone working in the analytic tradition will be most comfortable dealing with an issue within the philosophy of mind, epistemology, ethics, or some other field of philosophy rather than presenting a comprehensive philosophy.

Another positivist legacy, according to Burge, has been "the emergence of philosophical community" through open interchanges in conferences, journals, and books. "Philosophy is not," in Burge's opinion, "and never will be a science," but "it has taken on this much of the spirit of science." So although the mainstream of philosophy during much of the latter part of the twentieth century was most comfortable in narrowly defined problem areas, there was nevertheless a scientific orientation. It is not that philosophers became scientists, but the tug is from the side that takes "empirical science as the paradigm of synthetic knowledge."[43]

All of this is illustrated by W. V. O. Quine, arguably America's most influential philosopher in the last half of the twentieth century. His scientific orientation is clear but his influence has primarily been wielded through carefully crafted articles. For instance, his essay "Epistemology Naturalized" is often the point of reference for current discussions of naturalism in epistemology.[44] The essay is one of the "other essays" in his 1969 work, *Ontological Relativity and Other Essays.*

In the title essay, which was originally presented as the inaugural John Dewey Lectures in 1968, Quine associated his work with Dewey:

> Philosophically I am bound to Dewey by the naturalism that dominated his last three decades. With Dewey I hold that knowledge, mind, and meaning are part of the same world that they have to do with, and that they are to be studied in the same empirical spirit that animates natural science. There is no place for a priori philosophy.[45]

Yet clearly Quine is more scientistic than Dewey, as this often-quoted statement from "Epistemology Naturalized" illustrates: "But I think that at this point it may be more useful to say rather that epistemology still goes on, though in a new setting and a clarified status. Epistemology, or something like it, simply falls into place as a chapter of psychology and hence of natural science." This "strong version of the replacement thesis," as Kornblith labels it, threatens to replace epistemology with psychology. Of course, in actual practice, epistemology has continued unabated; one could even argue that Quine's radical thesis has given it new life. But Quine has not always been as provocative as this. Some 20 years later he declared: "The naturalistic philosopher begins his reasoning within the inherited world theory as a going concern. He tentatively believes all of it, but believes also that some unidentified portions are wrong. He tries to improve, clarify and understand the system from within."[46] Such a remark places Quine squarely within the new naturalist tradition of the first part of the twentieth century. What separates him is his post-positivist orientation. Quine came of age philosophically not only during the heyday of American philosophical naturalism but also logical positivism, whose work he has often engaged in critique.

Columbia naturalism's heirs

Not as prominent as Quine but even more engaged with the new naturalists are several philosophers who never took the logical positivists seriously.[47] They find Quine's naturalism to be reductionistic. The challenge for these historically minded and methodologically pluralistic naturalists is to show the relevance of the earlier naturalists to the issues discussed currently and in a suitably careful and rigorous way.[48]

One prominent philosopher doing this is Kai Nielsen. Although his inheritance is broader than that of Peirce and Dewey – including, notably, Marx – what distinguishes him from other naturalists, both the mainstream field-specific ones and the other heirs of the Columbia naturalists, is his advocacy of a comprehensive naturalism that engages the work of a broad range of well-known philosophers. Nielsen has put forth a "nonscientistic, contextualist and historicist naturalism" in several books, but notably in *Naturalism Without Foundations: The Prometheus Lectures.*[49] Moreover, he engages the arguments of Quine, John Rawls, Alasdair MacIntyre, Richard Rorty, Michel Foucault, Jürgen Habermas, Hilary Putnam,

Alvin Plantinga, and others. His naturalism is unrestricted in scope, conversant with past and current naturalisms, and dialectically engaged with prominent contemporary philosophy.

Thus naturalism at the beginning of the twenty-first century is alive and well, if not as clearly identifiable as it was at mid-century. In some ways it is just as prominent, but the "it," while never a simple, unitary movement, is even more diverse, even disjointed, today. Many naturalists are not engaged with one another's work. Some, particularly the self-conscious heirs of the Columbia naturalists, are even contemptuous of Quinean naturalism. Many are publicly naturalistic in only very narrowly defined ways and most of them are seemingly unaware of their American antecedents. Yet naturalism broadly defined is an actively pursued philosophical program. Or, perhaps more accurately, various naturalisms are energetically being pursued by a great many, if not the majority of, philosophers today. Roy Wood Sellars's assertion in the preface to *Evolutionary Naturalism* was an overstatement, but it is even more true now than it was then:

> We are all naturalists now. But, even so, this common naturalism is of a very vague and general sort, capable of covering an immense diversity of opinion. It is an admission of a direction more than a clearly formulated belief. It is less a philosophical system than a recognition of the impressive implications of the physical and the biological sciences. And, not to be outdone, psychology has swelled the chorus by pointing out the organic roots of behavior and of consciousness.

Not all philosophers were naturalists then and not all are naturalists now. But the discussion over the last century has shifted in a naturalist direction. For some, this is an inclusive, pluralist naturalism that looks to the new naturalists featured in this chapter (Santyana and the Columbia naturalists). For others, this is philosophy carried out in close association with science, with little reference to a comprehensive program. The latter are now more prominent. But for both, as well as those who identify themselves as non-naturalists, the discussion is conducted without appeal to the supernatural. Non-naturalism is no longer taken automatically to mean supernaturalism. Thus naturalism as it was understood in the earlier part of the twentieth century has become the background belief of contemporary philosophers. Accordingly, as a comprehensive world-view it has ceased to be the research program of those who are now considered to be naturalists. The cosmic question, if not settled, is at least sufficiently resolved that naturalism is now tacitly assumed. The debate now seems to be over the details of this naturalist world-view.

Notes

1 Barry Stroud, "The Charm of Naturalism," *Proceedings and Addresses of the American Philosophical Association* 70 (November 1996): 43–5, has observed, "Most philoso-

phers for a least one hundred years have been naturalists in the non-supernaturalist sense." But the Society of Christian Philosophers, through its meetings and its journal, *Faith and Philosophy*, and the Catholic Philosophical Association provide visible, populous alternatives to the secular orientation of the mainstream of professional philosophy.

2 The Romanell lectures are made possible by a gift of Patrick Romanell and are to be "on topics related to philosophical naturalism" (*Proceedings and Addresses of the American Philosophical Association*, 60 (June 1987): 822). Romanell was the author of *Toward a Critical Naturalism: Reflections on Contemporary American Philosophy* (New York: The Macmillan Company, 1958). Romanell's book and the lectures that bear his name reveal much about the direction of American philosophical naturalism, but this is a story that cannot be told here.

3 John Lachs, "Peirce, Santayana, and the Large Facts," *Transactions of the Charles S. Peirce Society*, 16 (1980): 4.

4 Roy Wood Sellars, *Evolutionary Naturalism* (New York: Russell & Russell; originally published in 1922, reissued in 1969), p. 2.

5 The best single source is an anthology by one of the co-editors of this volume. In *American Philosophic Naturalism in the Twentieth Century* (Amherst, NY: Prometheus Books, 1994), John Ryder has assembled a wide array of readings and capably introduced them. But Ryder's introductions are expository; they are not critical in the sense of reviewing the relevant secondary literature and rival interpretations and then providing the reader with an informed judgment on the contested issues. Nor is Ryder's book a history. Ironically, the two fuller treatments are by a Russian scholar and an American religious studies professor whose book is the result of his having "wrestled" with the naturalism of his Columbia University teachers. See Anyur M. Karimsky, "American Naturalism from a Non-American Perspective," *Transactions of the Charles S. Peirce Society*, 28 (1992): 645–65, and William M. Shea, *The Naturalists and the Supernatural: Studies in Horizon and an American Philosophy of Religion* (Macon, GA: Mercer University Press, 1984). See also "Idealism, Realism and Naturalism," in Ryder, *Interpreting America: Russian and Soviet Studies of the History of American Thought* (Nashville: Vanderbilt University Press, 1999), ch. 5.

6 Donald M. Borchert, ed., *The Encyclopedia of Philosophy Supplement* (New York: Macmillan Reference USA, 1996), p. 372.

7 Richard Foley, in "Quine and Naturalized Epistemology," observes, "Movements to naturalize are dominant in almost every area of contemporary philosophy" (*Midwest Studies in Philosophy* 19 (1994): 243).

8 John Lachs, *George Santayana* (Boston: Twayne Publishers, 1988), p. 6. In "Some Gleanings from *The Life of Reason*" (*Journal of Philosophy*, 51 (January 21, 1954): 46–9), Ernest Nagel recalls the influence of Santayana on his generation, providing evidence for Lachs's observation.

9 "Epilogue: The Nature of Naturalism," in Yervant H. Krikorian, *Naturalism and the Human Spirit* (New York: Columbia University Press, 1944), p. 363. This volume is a major event in the history of naturalism and will be discussed below.

10 Ibid.

11 John Dewey, *LW* 3:287–93. References to Dewey's works are to the critical edition edited by Jo Ann Boydston and published by the Southern Illinois University Press at Carbondale. There are 37 volumes in three series: *The Early Works* (*EW*), *The Middle*

Works (*MW*), and *The Later Works* (*LW*). Therefore the citation *LW* 3:287–93 is to vol. 3, pp. 287–93 of *The Later Works.*

12 George Santayana, *The Life of Reason* (New York: Charles Scribner's Sons, 1906), 1:282.

13 George Santayana, "Dewey's Naturalistic Metaphysics," *Journal of Philosophy*, 22 (1925): 378–80; reprinted as Appendix 1 in *LW* 3:373–5. My account of this interchange is influenced by David Sidorsky's fuller treatment in the introduction to this *LW* volume of the later works, 3:x–xxi. Sidorsky not only describes the exchange but places it in the context of philosophy generally in the first few decades of the twentieth century. For a critical assessment of the debate that defends Dewey's naturalism as a "whole-hearted" one, see John J. Stuhr, "Santayana's Unnatural Naturalism," in Peter Caws, ed., *Two Centuries of Philosophy in America* (Totowa, NJ: Rowman and Littlefield, 1980), pp. 144–50. Those not familiar with Santayana's subtle ontology can consult Lachs, *George Santayana*, ch. 4. While the differences between Santayana and Dewey are real and significant, they may not be as stark and seemingly incommensurable as their criticisms of one another suggest.

14 *Journal of Philosophy*, 24/58; *LW* 3:74.

15 *LW* 3:74; *LW* 3:79.

16 Lachs, *George Santayana*, pp. 147, 24.

17 *Philosophical Review*, 49 (1940): 196–228; reprinted in *LW* 14:379–410.

18 Frederick J. E. Woodbridge, "Confessions," in George P. Adams and William Pepperell Montague, eds., *Contemporary American Philosophy: Personal Statements* (New York: Russell & Russell, 1962), 2:415f.

19 John Herman Randall, Jr., "Towards a Functional Naturalism," in *Contemporary American Philosophy: Second Series* (London: George Allen & Unwin, Ltd, 1970), pp. 59–61.

20 See the biography of Dewey edited by his daughter, Jane, in Paul Arthur Schilpp, *The Philosophy of John Dewey* (Evanston, IL: Northwestern University Press, 1939), pp. 35f.

21 Harry Todd Costello's characterization in "The Naturalism of Woodbridge," in Krikorian, *Naturalism and the Human Spirit*, p. 296.

22 John Herman Randall, "The Religion of Shared Experience," in Sidney Ratner, ed., *The Philosopher of the Common Man: Essays in Honor of John Dewey to Celebrate His Eightieth Birthday* (New York: G. P. Putnam's Sons, 1940), p. 137. This is an important essay in understanding Dewey's religious proposal. The best account of the development of Dewey's own faith is Steven C. Rockefeller, *John Dewey: Religious Faith and Democratic Humanism* (New York: Columbia University Press, 1991). My criticisms of Randall and Rockefeller can be found in *Transforming Experience: John Dewey's Cultural Instrumentalism* (Nashville: Vanderbilt University Press, 1998), chs. 5 and 6.

23 John Herman Randall, "Art and Religion as Education," *Social Frontier*, 2 (1936): 111. Some of the arguments and language of this review are repeated in the fuller "Religion of Shared Experience."

24 *Reconstruction of Philosophy*, *MW* 12:134.

25 *LW* 9:19f.

26 In Krikorian, *Naturalism and the Human Spirit*, pp. 355, 373f.

27 W. H. Sheldon, "Critique of Naturalism," *Journal of Philosophy*, 42 (May 10, 1945): 254, 275.

28 John Dewey, Sidney Hook, and Ernest Nagel, "Comments and Criticisms: Are Naturalists Materialists?" *Journal of Philosophy*, 42 (1945): 520.

29 "Reviews," *Philosophy and Phenomenological Research*, 6 (1945–6): 438.

30 "Dewey on Materialism," *Philosophy and Phenomenological Research*, 3 (1943): 381–92.

31 "Is Naturalism Enough?" *Journal of Philosophy*, 41 (1944): 533. Hook replied in the same issue, "Is Physical Realism Sufficient?" (pp. 545–51), to which Sellars responded, "Does Naturalism Need Ontology?" (pp. 686–94).

32 "Reviews," *Journal of Philosophy*, 42 (1945): 401–17.

33 In Krikorian, *Naturalism and the Human Spirit*, pp. 270–94.

34 Book Review, *Journal of Philosophy*, 42 (1945): 411.

35 Sidney Hook, *The Quest for Being* (Buffalo, NY: Prometheus Books, 1991: originally published in 1961 as *The Quest for Being and Other Studies in Naturalism and Humanism*), p. 173.

36 Sidney Morgenbesser, Patrick Suppes, and Morton White, eds., *Philosophy, Science, and Method* (New York: St. Martin's Press, 1969), p. v.

37 *Proceedings and Addresses of the American Philosophical Association 1954–55*, 28 (October 1955): 5–17.

38 *Ordinal Naturalism: An Introduction to the Philosophy of Justus Buchler* (Lewisburg, PA: Bucknell University Press, 1983), p. 47.

39 See Armen Marsoobian, Kathleen Wallace, and Robert S. Corrington, eds., *Nature's Perspectives: Prospects for Ordinal Metaphysics* (Albany: SUNY Press, 1991).

40 In addition to her contribution to this volume, see Kathleen Wallace, "Ontological Parity and/or Ordinality," *Metaphilosophy*, 30 (October 1999): 302–18, particularly pp. 305–10, for a clear, concise explanation of Buchler's key notions of ontological parity and ordinality.

41 "Notes and Reflections on Justus Buchler," in Marsoobian et al., eds., *Nature's Perspectives*, p. 12. The irony was that the move away from pluralism on the part of the Department of Philosophy at Columbia was determined in no small part by the influence of Nagel, Buchler's dissertation advisor.

42 *Philosophical Review*, 101 (1992): 3–51. This article is one of four "essays on contemporary philosophy" that comprise the centennial issue. The essay, "The Naturalists Return," by Philip Kitcher, pp. 53–114, is a very good account of the resurgence of naturalism understood from the contemporary perspective that is seemingly unaware of the new naturalism or Columbia naturalism that is the focus of this chapter.

43 Burge, "Philosophy of Language and Mind," pp. 50f.

44 In Hilary Kornblith, ed., *Naturalizing Epistemology*, 2nd edn. (Cambridge, MA: MIT Press, 1994). See also the essays by Richard Foley, Peter Hylton, Laurence BonJour, Alvin I. Goldman, Richard Fumerton, Richard E. Grandy, and Mark Kaplan, in Peter A. French, Theodore E. Uehling, Jr., and Howard K. Wettstein, eds., *Midwest Studies in Philosophy*. Vol. XIX: *Philosophical Naturalism* (Notre Dame: University of Notre Dame Press, 1994).

45 (New York: Columbia University Press, 1969), p. 27.

46 *Theories and Things* (Cambridge, MA: Harvard University Press, 1981), p. 72.

47 Many of these are active in the Society for the Advancement of American Philosophy and often publish in the *Transactions of the Charles S. Peirce Society*.

48 See, for instance, John Capps, "Dewey, Quine and Pragmatic Naturalized Epistemology," *Transactions of the Charles S. Peirce Society*, 32 (1996): 634–67. Capps,

whose paper was originally read at the 1996 annual meeting of the Society for the Advancement of American Philosophy, declared his intention to be that of "undercut[ting] many of the commitments of contemporary naturalized epistemology, while at the same time arguing for the centrality of the Deweyan version to debates in this area" (p. 634). See also Capps, "Naturalism, Pragmatism and Design," *The Journal of Speculative Philosophy*, 14 (2000): 161–78, in which Capps distinguishes three kinds of naturalism and uses a modest version, pragmatic naturalism, to respond to some of the claims of the intelligent design theorists.

49 Kai Nielsen, *Naturalism Without Foundations* (Buffalo, NY: Prometheus, 1996), p. 25.

Suggested reading

Capps, John, "Naturalism, Pragmatism and Design," *The Journal of Speculative Philosophy*, 14 (2000): 161–78.

French, Peter A., Theodore E. Uehling, Jr., and Howard K. Wettstein, eds., *Midwest Studies in Philosophy*. Vol. XIX: *Philosophical Naturalism* (Notre Dame, IN: University of Notre Dame Press, 1994).

Karimsky, Anyur M., "American Naturalism from a Non-American Perspective," *Transactions of the Charles S. Peirce Society*, 28 (1992): 645–65.

Kitcher, Philip, "The Naturalists Return," *The Philosophical Review*, 101 (1992): 53–114.

Kornblith, Hilary, ed., *Naturalizing Epistemology*, 2nd edn. (Cambridge, MA: MIT Press, 1994).

Krikorian, Yervant H., ed., *Naturalism and the Human Spirit* (New York: Columbia University Press, 1944).

Romanell, Patrick, *Toward a Critical Naturalism: Reflections on Contemporary American Philosophy* (New York: The Macmillan Company, 1958).

Ryder, John, ed., *American Philosophic Naturalism in the Twentieth Century* (Amherst, NY: Prometheus Books, 1994).

Sellars, Roy Wood, Review of Krikorian, *Naturalism and the Human Spirit*, in *Philosophy and Phenomenological Research*, 6 (1945–6): 436–9.

Shea, William M., *The Naturalists and the Supernatural: Studies in Horizon and an American Philosophy of Religion* (Macon, GA: Mercer University Press, 1984).

Part II

Major Figures in American Philosophy

Chapter 5

C. S. Peirce, 1839–1914

Vincent Colapietro

Charles Sanders Peirce – Scientist, Logician, and Philosopher

In 1839, C. S. Peirce was born into advantageous circumstances but, in 1914, died in poverty and isolation.[1] He graduated from Harvard College in 1859, the year in which Charles Darwin's *Origin of Species* was published. His father (in the judgment of the son, "a man of remarkable force of character and intellect" [MS 1606, 1])[2] was one of the foremost mathematicians in the United States in the nineteenth century, enjoying a distinguished career as a professor at Harvard and a scientist with the US Coast & Geodetic Survey. Charles worked as a scientist with this agency for three decades, beginning in 1861. As a young man, he also held a position at the Harvard Observatory. During his lifetime, his only authored book was *Photometric Researches* (1878), a scientific treatise growing out his work in this capacity. Undeniably tragic in some respects, his life can hardly be counted a failure.[3] For his published writings "run to approximately twelve thousand pages," whereas we have eighty thousand pages of his unpublished manuscripts.[4] The latter perhaps even more than the former provide unmistakable evidence that Charles Peirce was a philosophical genius. Though he tended to make a mess of his life (incurring foolish debts, alienating generous friends, and squandering exceptional opportunities), he made much of his genius and even more of his passion to find things out. Ernest Nagel's judgment is far from idiosyncratic: "Charles Sanders Peirce remains the most original, versatile, and comprehensive philosophical mind this country has yet produced."[5]

Peirce's philosophical contribution is of a piece with his scientific training: he not only came to philosophy from science but also pursued philosophical questions largely for the sake of articulating a normative theory of objective investigation. He did manifest an intrinsic interest in substantive philosophical questions, but methodological concerns were never far from his persistent attempts to address in a straightforward manner these substantive issues. Early in his career he gave a series of lectures on "The Logic of Science." His lifelong concern to disclose the logic of science resulted, in the end, in a transformation of his understanding of logic. He came to envision logic as a theory of inquiry.

Peirce refused to define philosophy in opposition to science in the modern sense. In order to understand his conception of philosophy, it is necessary to consider the place of philosophy in his classification of the sciences and also simply his view of science. He drew a sharp distinction between practical and theoretical investigation. Since many theoretical sciences have evolved out of practical pursuits, the arts are hardly irrelevant to an understanding of science, especially since Peirce stresses the importance of the history of the sciences for a comprehension of their nature (see, e.g., EP 2:38).[6] But *theoria* has transcended its origin, such that a large number of purely theoretical investigations have emerged in their own right. The vitality of these investigations crucially depends on pursuing them for their own sake, apart from any concern with what practical benefits might accrue to theoretical discoveries. Philosophical investigation was, in Peirce's judgment, a theoretical science,[7] though one disfigured almost beyond recognition by too intimate association with seminary-trained philosophers (1.620; 6.3).[8]

Taken together, Peirce classified the distinct branches of philosophical inquiry as one of the three broadest divisions of theoretical knowledge. He located philosophy between mathematics, the rubric under which he subsumed the most abstract branches of theoretical inquiry, and (using a term borrowed from Jeremy Bentham) idioscopy, the least abstract ones (e.g., physics, chemistry, biology, and psychology). He supposed, like all other sciences, the branches of philosophy drew upon mathematics for important principles and conceptions, not the least of these pertaining to relationships of an exceeding abstract character. He also supposed that less abstract sciences such as physics and psychology drew upon not only mathematics but also philosophy for some of their most basic principles and conceptions. In this threefold classification of theoretical science, he was indebted to Auguste Comte's principle of classification ("one science depends upon another for fundamental principles, but does not furnish such principles to that other" (1.180)). A thoroughly naturalistic account of scientific intelligence, however, undergirds this formal classification of the theoretical sciences. Moreover, a historical sensitivity informed Peirce's numerous attempts to offer a detailed classification of our scientific pursuits.[9]

Scientific Intelligence and Theoretical Knowledge

He took science to be "a living thing" (1.234; cf. 1.232), preoccupied with "conjectures, which are either getting framed or getting tested" (1.234). It is nothing less than a mode of life; more fully, "a mode of life whose single animating purpose is to find out the real truth, which pursues this purpose by a well-considered method, founded on thorough acquaintance with such scientific results already ascertained by others as may be available, and which seeks cooperation in the hope that the truth may be found" (7.55).[10]

He stressed repeatedly that scientific inquiry is essentially a communal endeavor. Reliance on others is here a necessity. The appeal to the observations and assessments of others is constitutive of science, at least in Peirce's sense, a sense he took to be faithful to what the successful practices of experimental inquiry manifest about themselves in their actual development. His definition of reality as what the community of inquirers *would* discover, given adequate resources and time, reflected his training as a scientist. His antipathy to much of modern philosophy was a reaction to the prevalent tendency of inquirers during this epoch to exhibit "an absurd disregard for other's opinions" (W 2:313).[11] His identification with modern science was of a piece with his commitment to communal inquiry.

The passionate pursuit of theoretical knowledge was, for Peirce, intrinsically worthwhile and intelligible. In one sense, he traced the origin of our knowledge to our instincts, in another, simply to the dynamic conjunction of human intelligence and cosmic intelligibility. He supposed, "all that science has done [thus far] is to study those relations . . . brought into prominence [by] . . . two instincts – the instinct of *feeding*, which brought with it elementary knowledge of mechanical forces, space, etc., and the instinct of *breeding*, which brought with it elementary knowledge of psychical motives, of time, etc." (1.118; cf. 5.591). In general, he was convinced that humans are able to divine something of the principles of nature because they have evolved as part of nature and, therefore, under the influence of these principles (7.46). Humans partake of the world they know: the ways of the cosmos are not utterly foreign to the propensities of our minds, otherwise they would be forever unknown and we long since extinct (see, e.g., 7.38). "Our faculty of guessing," Peirce contended, "corresponds to a bird's musical and aeronautic powers; that is, it is to us, as those are to them, the loftiest of our merely instinctive powers" (7.48) or inherited dispositions. Here is a robust affirmation of biological continuity without any reductive implications. For, whatever its origin, countless individuals throughout human history have been animated by, above all else, the pursuit of knowledge for its own sake. The intelligence of human beings and the intelligibility of their circumambient world are, in another sense, sufficient to explain why we inquire (2.13). The lure of intelligibility proves to be irresistible to an intelligence disposed simply to wonder why, say, an event occurred or our expectations were contravened (7.189). At least some humans conduct investigations simply to find out whatever truth might be discovered by a painstaking, persistent, and systematic inquiry. Aristotle was one such person, Peirce another.

It may not be oxymoronic to speak of instinctual intelligence, if only to facilitate a contrast with scientific intelligence. The ingenuity and, in a sense, intelligence with which bees, by means of instinctual complex movements, indicate the direction and distance of honey – or beavers by means of intricate actions construct a dam – are too obvious to deny. The dispositions by which these feats are performed appear to be largely innate or instinctual. At least something akin to intelligence appears to be operative in the accomplishment of such complex tasks, securing some obvious advantage.

Human intelligence is, however, predominantly scientific intelligence in its most rudimentary form; for it is "an intelligence capable of learning by experience" (2.227). In accord with Peirce's own principle of continuity, we should not suppose that there is an absolutely sharp dichotomy between instinctual and scientific (or experiential) intelligence, for (as we have already seen) our very capacity to learn from experience attests to the beneficial operation of instinctual tendencies. Scientific intelligence is rooted in our instinctual drives. Our capacity to learn from experience is closely connected with our capacity to subject our conceptions, assertions, and inferences to criticism. Peirce proposed that "'rational' means self-criticizing, self-controlling and self-controlled, and therefore open to incessant question" (7.77; cf. 5.440). In light of this definition, it is clear that *scientific* and *rational* intelligence, though apparently different in meaning, inescapably overlap in fact; for we can most effectively learn from experience only by an ongoing process of complex interrogation in which our suppositions, conceptions, claims, and conclusions are all subjected to self-criticism. Peirce was aware of "man's stupendous power of shutting his eyes to plain facts,"[12] but he was confident in the *force majeure* of human experience: "Experience may be defined as the sum of ideas [and beliefs] which have been irresistibly borne in upon us, overwhelming all free-play of thought, by the tenor of our lives. The authority of experience consists in the fact that its power cannot be resisted; it is a flood against which nothing can stand" (7.437; cf. 5.50).

The pursuit of theoretical knowledge entails the cultivation of scientific intelligence and, in turn, the cultivation of such intelligence is also the cultivation of instinctual intelligence in its distinctively human form (for what human instincts facilitate above all else is the acquisition of habits other than the ones with which we were born). Human rationality is, in the first instance, "an Unmatured Instinctive Mind." As such, phylogeny is merely ancillary to ontogeny: the history of the species is, in effect, taken up into that of the individual and, as the inheritor also of vast cultural resources, the individual becomes a self-determining and, to some extent, even a self-defining agent (see, e.g., 5.533; 1.591). The instinctual mind of human beings requires a development beyond that of the evolutionary history in which it took shape and proved itself viable; the "prolonged childhood" of human beings proves as much, as does the "childlike character" of the instinctual mind itself. In humans and to some extent perhaps also in other species (ones especially adapted to learning from experience), "Instinct is a weak, uncertain Instinct." This allows it to be "infinitely plastic"; and this underwrites alterability and hence the possibility of intellectual growth (growth in intelligence, the capacity to learn ever more effectively from experience). "Uncertain tendencies, unstable states of equilibrium[,] are conditions *sine qua non* for the manifestation of Mind" (7.381). The general disposition to acquire novel dispositions entails a plasticity itself entailing a susceptibility to disequilibria. Doubt is one name for the instability into which an agent is thrown when the dispositions of that agent prove ineffective in a given situation; for doubt is at bottom the arrest, or disruption, of a belief or habit.

Philosophy Within the Limits of Experience Alone

Despite his indebtedness to Kant, Peirce did not make theoretical philosophy into an essentially critical discipline charged with the task of defining the intrinsic limits of human knowledge. Like Kant, he did insist that the limits of experience define the limits of knowledge ("all our knowledge is, and forever must be, relative to human experience and to the nature of the human mind" (6.95)), but he conceived experience in such a way as to be capable of aiding us in discovering to some degree the way things are (not simply the way they appear to us). He refused to sever appearance from reality, and also our experience of things from their status and properties apart from our experience. If we rigorously adhere to experience, not granting that things completely separable from our experience are even conceivable, we are forced to jettison Kant's concept of the thing-in-itself: "The *Ding an sich* . . . can neither be indicated nor found [in any *possible* experience]. Consequently no proposition can refer to it, and nothing true or false can be predicated of it. Therefore, all references to it must be thrown out as meaningless surplusage" (5.525). Whereas Kant maintained that things in themselves are conceivable but unknowable (since we are able to think them without contradiction but not able to know them by recourse to any experience), Peirce argued they were incognizable, meaning that they are not even conceivable (see, e.g., 5.255). Given that "all our conceptions are obtained by abstractions and combinations of cognitions first occurring in judgments of experience" (5.255; also W 2:208), their significance is totally bound up with the junction of such judgments. At any rate, Peirce held that the limits of experience define not only those of knowledge but also those of meaning itself: human beings are so completely hemmed in by the bounds of their possible practical experience, their minds are so restricted to being instruments of their needs and desires, they cannot in the least *mean* anything transcending those bounds (5.536). Our experience of our selves and of even our most adequate theories attests to a cosmos far outstripping our comprehension: "The experience of ignorance, or of error, which we have, and which we gain by correcting our errors, or enlarging our knowledge, does enable us to experience and [thereby] conceive something which is independent of our own limited views" (7.345). "Over against any cognition, there is an unknown but knowable reality; but over against all possible cognition, there is only the self-contradictory" (5.527; also W 2:208). Peirce concluded that *being* and *cognizability* are synonymous (5.257; also W 2:208): whatever else we might mean by being, we must mean that which in some manner and measure is, in principle, accessible to our minds via our experience. He went so far as to affirm, in the colloquial (not Kantian) sense: "we have *direct experience of things in themselves.* Nothing can be more completely false than that we can experience only our own ideas" (6.95). However superficial, fragmentary, and even distorted is the knowledge based on such experience, it cannot be gainsaid: what we have experimentally derived from our encounters with reality warrants the title of knowledge. Though emphatically a fallibilist, Peirce was hardly a skeptic. Indeed, he took his commitment to the doctrine of fallibilism (namely, "the doctrine that our knowledge is never absolute but always swims . . . in a continuum of uncertainty and of indeterminacy" (1.171)) to be inseparable from his faith in the reality of knowledge. He stressed, "only a deep sense that one is miserably ignorant . . . can spur one on in the toilsome path of learning" (5.583). Further, he claimed, "no blight can so surely arrest all intellectual growth as the blight of cocksureness" (1.13). Yet Peirce had at once a "high faith" in knowledge *and* an acute sense of fallibility. He took our knowledge to be nothing more than a fabric of conjectures, based on a patchwork of experience, but he insisted that even in this form it is highly valuable. He took the pursuit of knowledge, in his own case at least, to be nothing less than an act of worship (8.136 n.3).

His philosophical interests were both methodological and substantive; they were shaped by his scientific training and work. He reported: "I came to philosophy not for its teaching about God, Freedom, and Immortality, but intensely curious about Cosmology and Psychology" (4.2). His curiosity about the cosmos tended to outstrip that about the psyche, though he did outline a theory of consciousness, mind, and self. Peirce went so far as to describe his philosophy as "the attempt of a physicist to make such conjecture as to the constitution of the universe as the methods of science may permit, with the aid of all that has been done by previous philosophers" (1.7).

He worked tirelessly to transform philosophy into such a scientific inquiry and, hence, a communal undertaking, insisting: "We individually cannot reasonably hope to attain the ultimate philosophy which we pursue; we can only seek it, therefore, for the *community* of philosophers" (5.265). In a letter to William James, he proclaimed, "philosophy is either a science or is balderdash."[13] The task of the philosopher is to join all those who are devoted to discovering whatever truth about the world might be derived from our experience of the world. In this endeavor, philosophers are distinguished from other scientists by relying solely on ordinary experience. The field of their observations does not require instruments such as telescopes or microscopes, travel to faraway places, or even much special training, but is that provided by the everyday encounters with environing affairs to virtually every normal person during every waking hour of that person's life.

Peirce supposed: "We naturally make all our distinctions too absolute" (7.438). The tendency to sunder humans from other animals (5.534), self from other (7.571), mind from matter, the conscious regions of mind from its unconscious depths, perception from abduction (the process by which hypotheses are generated), and appearance from reality would be examples of this tendency. In opposition to the marked dualistic tendency so prominent in traditional Western philosophy, Peirce championed *synechism*, a doctrine disposing him to search for the respects in which things are continuous (see, e.g., 6.169).[14] Though he accorded (under the rubric of secondness) great importance to opposition, otherness, disruption, and a host of allied phenomena, he stressed (as instances of thirdness) continuity, mediation, intelligibility, and other kindred phenomena. His doctrine of the categories of firstness, secondness, and thirdness was crafted as a way of dealing with any imaginable reality. The category of firstness highlighted the qualitative immediacy characteristic of anything whatsoever (what anything is, *in itself*, apart from all else), while that of secondness underscored brute opposition, irreducible alterity, and that of thirdness the network of *connections* in and through which any reality acquires its defining properties. Hence, his doctrine of synechism was of a piece with his emphasis on thirdness.

For an understanding of Peirce's conception of philosophy, we must appreciate his insistence on appearance being intrinsically connected to reality: the way things appear, including the way they manifest themselves in ordinary experience, is indicative of the way things are; in turn, the reality of anything to which we can meaningfully refer is such that it possesses the capacity, in some circumstances however remote or rare, to disclose itself (cf. 5.313). The reality with which philosophy deals is nothing more recondite than the readily accessible objects and events of our direct experience. (Even so, these objects and events might provide evidence for "One Incomprehensible but Personal God" (5.496).) The manner in which philosophy investigates these objects and events is nothing other than that of painstaking observation, conceptual generalization, and controlled conjecture. For Peirce, this obviously meant that philosophy must abandon the pretension of being able to attain demonstrative knowledge of transcendent reality ("The demonstrations of the metaphysicians are all moonshine" (1.7)), contenting itself rather with conjectural knowledge of the empirical world.

This also meant strict adherence to technical terms: "if philosophy is ever to stand in the ranks of the sciences, literary elegance must be sacrificed – like the soldier's old brilliant uniforms – to the stern requirements of efficiency" and, thus, the philosopher must be required "to coin new terms to express such new scientific conceptions as he may discover, just as his chemical and biological brethren are expected to do" (5.13). Of course, ordinary language is of immense importance to the philosophical investigator. Peirce stressed, "a language is a thing to be reverenced; and I protest that a man who does not reverence a given language is not in the proper frame of mind to undertake its improvements" (MS 279). Moreover, the "case of philosophy is peculiar in that it has positive need of popular words in their popular senses – not as its own language (as it has too usually used those words), but as objects of its study" (EP 2:264–5; cf. 8.112). Painstaking attention to ordinary usage is, thus, an important part of philosophical investigation (see, however, 2.67, 2.70, and 2.211). But it is important mainly insofar as it facilitates a critical appeal to everyday experience. The appeal to ordinary usage is, for Peirce, bound up with an appeal to *everyday* experience; and the appeal to such experience provides the guidance requisite for carrying forward the work of philosophy.

Herein lies its main difference from such special sciences as physics, chemistry, and biology. In contrast to such special (or idioscopic) sciences, the distinct branches of philosophical inquiry are *cœnoscopic.* For philosophy "contents itself with so much of experience as pours in upon every man during every hour of his waking life" (5.13 n.1; cf. 1.241). "Experience," Peirce asserted, "may be defined as the sum of ideas [and beliefs] which have been irresistibly borne in upon us, overwhelming all free-play of thought, by the tenor of our lives. The authority of experience consists in the fact that its power cannot be resisted; it is a flood against which nothing can stand" (7.437; cf. 5.50).

Since the observations afforded by such experience are common to virtually all humans, without the benefit of special training or instruments, Peirce appropriated Jeremy Bentham's term *cœnoscopic* to designate the disciplines contenting themselves with such observations. He was aware that he was using *experience* "in a much broader sense than it carries in the special sciences"; for in them it is set in contrast to interpretation, whereas for philosophy "experience can only mean the total cognitive result of living, and includes interpretations quite as truly as matters of sense" (7.538). In other contexts, he acknowledges that what counts in science as observation cannot be severed from ratiocination and, thus, presumably from interpretation (see, e.g., 1.34–5). Even so, the experience to which we appeal in philosophy is not the observations consequent upon controlled circumstances or obtainable solely by special means; it is, rather, what the course of life forces upon us willy-nilly (7.391; 1.426).

The Conduct of Inquiry

Armed with an interior understanding of scientific inquiry, Peirce offered a normative account of objective investigation. His pragmatism was central to this account. It grew out of conversations in the Metaphysical Club (an informal group involving Chauncey Wright, Oliver Wendell Holmes, Jr., William James, and a handful of others) and was formulated, though not named as such, in "How to Make Our Ideas Clear" (1878). He originally conceived this essay as part of a series entitled "Illustrations of the Logic of Science" though eventually envisioned it as part of his 1893 "Search for a Method." Despite his deep, multifaceted opposition to Descartes, the full title to one of his predecessor's main works can be borrowed to identify an overarching goal of Peirce's philosophical project: Discourse on the method for rightly conducting one's reason and for seeking truth in the sciences. "The Fixation of Belief" and "How to Make Our Ideas Clear" are important articulations of Peirce's discourse on method, even though he came to be critical of some aspects of these essays. In the former, he defines the method of science in contrast to three other ways of fixing belief; in the latter, he enunciates a maxim by which anyone adhering to the method of science can render clearer the ideas (or signs) on which investigations turn.

A conception of intelligence underlies Peirce's pragmatism. He maintained, "one, at least, of the functions of intelligence is to adapt conduct to circumstances, so as to subserve desire" (5.548). Of course, such adaptation might involve modification of circumstances; hence, it does not mean conformity to the world simply as it happens to be: adapting conduct to circumstances might mean altering them in accord with desire. The function of intelligence drives toward the recognition of facts and the discovery of laws, but with equal force it drives toward the modification of virtually whatever in the course of experience proves to be malleable. This includes intelligence itself. Peirce was convinced "intelligence does not consist in feeling in a certain way, but in acting in a certain way" (6.286). Action must not be limited to physical exertions in the outward world of actuality but must be stretched to include inward actions, imagined endeavors taking place solely in the inward world of fancy (6.286; cf. 5.496). Humans are far from the only animals exhibiting intelligence, though the crucial role of imaginary action and (closely allied to this) the effects of symbolization make of human intelligence something quite unique. Human intelligence is a biologically evolved function encompassing a vast array of instinctual tendencies, almost all of which bear upon action broadly conceived. Most of these tendencies are directed not to outward bodily motions but rather to inward imaginary actions, their "theatre" being "the plastic inner world" of human fancy (MS 318, 44).[15] The products of these actions are symbols by which the scope of imagination is dramatically expanded. But "it is only out of symbols that a new symbol can grow. *Omne symbolum de symbolo*" (2.302). Thus, the imaginary operations by which novel symbols are generated must already involve symbols or, at least, proto-symbols. The image serving as a sign of one's dead ancestor or as a sign of the distant place from which one has just returned qualifies to serve this role. By this means, the absent structures thought and informs action. Just as our intelligence is instinctively imaginative, so our imagination is irrepressibly symbolific.[16]

The conduct of inquiry involves, for Peirce, the struggle to overcome doubt and, in the context of this struggle, the need to clarify the meanings of our terms. The two following subsections address these topics.

Overcoming doubt

Our intelligence is linked as intimately to action as to imagination. Peirce noted, "the greater part of intelligent actions are directed toward causing the cessation of some irritation" (6.282). These irritations are often simply somatic (e.g., hunger). But an important type of irritation is, however, bound up with bodily dissatisfaction (see, e.g., 5.372), of a somewhat different character, for it directly concerns the arrest of intelligence. This type of irritation signals nothing less than the failure of intelligence; it goads the organism to regain its equilibrium, by acting (either outwardly or imaginatively) in such a way as to establish an effective response to this irritant and all analogous ones. This means establishing a *general* way of acting (in a word, a habit). Whatever else our beliefs might be, they are such habits of action. This is, indeed, mainly what they are. Doubt is, in its least eviscerated sense, hesitancy in action signaling the dissolution of belief. Whereas habits are states tending toward their own perpetuation, doubts are ones driving toward their own cessation (5.372; also W 3:247). "The irritation of doubt causes a struggle to attain a state of belief" (5.374; also W 3:247)), a struggle Peirce called *inquiry*.

Efforts to overcome doubt and attain a state of belief may take a variety of forms. By the method of tenacity, we cling tenaciously to any belief threatened by doubt, aggressively excluding from consideration any factor counting against this belief. This purely individual manner of fixing (or securing) belief, however, cannot sustain itself in practice; for the "social impulse is against it" (5.378; also W 3:250). The testimony of others can have the power to convince a person he or she is insane (5.233; also W 2:202), such is the strength of this impulse. Of more immediate relevance, Peirce claimed: "No matter how strong and well-rooted in habit any rational convictions of ours may be, we no sooner find that another equally well-informed person doubts it, than we begin to doubt it ourselves" (2.160). The anger we so often feel toward those who induce us to doubt such convictions is a sign of our susceptibility to the authority of others (ibid.). What others believe cannot but influence what we ourselves believe, not least of all because their contrary beliefs have the capacity to generate genuine doubt; such is the potential strength of the social impulse in human beings (5.378). Accordingly, we need a communal way of fixing beliefs. The method of authority provides just this. This method consists in instituting an authority with the power to establish – and enforce – what everyone within the jurisdiction of this authority must believe. But this method, too, cannot sustain itself in practice; for in the most priest-ridden or police-controlled states (5.381; also W 3:251), there will always be some persons who, prompted (again) by the social impulse instinctive to human beings, cannot help supposing that the differing beliefs of those from different cultures or ages may, in principle, be true (i.e., worthy of espousal). A finite, fixed authority is insufficiently communal; nothing less than an infinite, evolving community can offer the epistemic authority needed to fix beliefs, at least for social beings such as human inquirers always are.

In contesting the brutality of external authority, it seems natural to turn toward the deliverances of an internal authority with which rational inquirers are inclined to identify themselves (e.g., the *cogito*). To accept these deliverances entails no violation of one's nature; much rather, it means accepting whatever proves to be agreeable to one's own reason, i.e., one's own innermost self. Whereas the institutional authority of the Catholic Church during the Middle Ages provided Peirce with his paradigm of the method of authority, he saw in Descartes' appeal to the apodictic certainties of his own individual rationality a historical example of this third method (the a priori method). But, "what if our *internal* authority should meet the same fate, in the history of opinions, as that external authority has met?" (5.215). Peirce was convinced that, in his own day, the signs of individual consciousness having suffered this fate were discernible (5.383). For it "makes of inquiry something similar to the development of taste; but taste . . . is always more or less a matter of fashion" (ibid.). Hence, rather than eliminating the "accidental and capricious element" in the process of fixing beliefs, it has enthroned this element as sovereign. In this and other respects, the method of apriority "does not differ in a very essential way from that of authority" (5.383).

In order for us as embodied, social agents to overcome doubt, we need a communal method grounded in the hypothesis that there are real things to which experiential appeals can be made in the ongoing course of genuine investigation. "Such is the method of science" (5.384). "This is the only one of the four methods which presents any distinction of a right and a wrong way" (5.385). This distinction is, for example, collapsed by the method of authority, since the dicta of instituted authority are, by definition, true: there can, in principle, be no distinction between what it dictates and what is so. This implies that self-criticism and, thus, self-correction are precluded. To institute a communal method for fixing beliefs committed to the realistic hypothesis means, in contrast, that even the most securely established beliefs of any finite community at any actual stage of its ongoing history are open to revision: what the members of such a community hold and what reality holds can never be identified, except provisionally. The possibility of detecting and correcting errors requires the hypothesis that the properties of things may, in principle, be other than those ascribed to them by us. We require a general method within which it is always apposite to distinguish between our specific strategies of inquiry and the most reliable procedures (between "a right and a wrong way" or between our way and a better one). The method of science alone secures this distinction.

Clarifying meaning

In connection with his doubt-belief theory of inquiry, Peirce formulated a heuristic maxim designed to help scientific inquirers clarify the meaning of certain ideas pivotal to objective inquiry. In a later manuscript, he stressed: "I understand pragmatism to be a method of ascertaining the meanings, not of all ideas, but only of what I call 'intellectual concepts,'" such concepts being "those upon the structure of which, arguments concerning objective fact may hinge" (5.467). He took his pragmatism to be neither a theory of truth nor even a theory of meaning (for his account of meaning, the student of Peirce must look to his general theory of signs and, in particular, his extensive discussions of the interpretants of signs), but only a maxim by which inquirers can become clearer about the meanings of the terms used in their endeavors to discover truths pertaining to facts and especially laws. He stressed it has nothing to do with the qualities of feelings except insofar as these are indicative of the properties of things; in other words, it has nothing to do with feelings in themselves but only as signs, as subjective determinations bearing upon objective affairs. The *hardness* of an object can of course be felt, but the meaning of this predicate concerns not the qualitative immediacy of feeling but its implied bearing on conduct. It concerns how objects under this description *would act* on things other than themselves. What is true of predicates like hardness here is true of all other "intellectual concepts": they "essentially carry some implication concerning the general behavior either of some conscious being or of some inanimate object, and so convey more, not merely than any feeling, but more too, than, any existential fact, namely, the 'would-acts,' 'would-dos' of habitual behavior" (5.467). To say that an object is *hard* is, thus, to imply something about how it would act; what we mean by this term is, at least in context of inquiry, inseparable from such implications. Peirce went so far as to assert that, according to his pragmatism, "the *total* meaning of the predication of an intellectual concept is contained in the affirmation that, under all conceivable circumstances of a given kind . . . the subject of the predication would behave in a certain general way" (5.467).

First Grade of Clearness: tacit familiarity In order to make our ideas clear, some kind of translation of signs is necessary (5.427). But this presupposes an intimate familiarity with signs derived from our ability to utter and interpret them effectively in countless situations. At the most rudimentary level, for example, we might know how properly to use the term *real*, without being able to define it abstractly. This minimal level of semiotic competency is of no trifling importance; all higher levels presuppose the tacit familiarity of human agents with countless types of sign-use.

Second Grade of Clearness: abstract definition For the sake of clarity, however, it is often helpful to translate this tacit familiarity into an explicit definition, often of an abstract character. Returning to our example, by probing the difference between the *real* and the *fictive*, we may (following Peirce himself) arrive at this definition: the *real* is that whose status and properties are independent of what anybody may take them to be, sufficiently independent to secure the possibility of anybody being mistaken.

Third Grade of Clearness: pragmatic clarification But "we must be on our guard against the deceptions of abstract definitions" (7.362). More generally, Peirce thought that the conceptual clarification achieved by means of abstract definitions was inadequate for the purposes of experimental inquiry. Simply translating a concept into other concepts is insufficient; ultimately translating concepts into habits of conduct is requisite. Such is the main import of Peirce's pragmatic maxim: "Consider what effects, that might conceivably have practical bearings, we conceive the object of our conception to have. Then, our conception of these effects is the whole of our conception of the object" (5.402). The pragmatic clarification of *reality* pushes beyond the abstract definition of this term, by identifying the effects implied in ascribing this property to anything. "The only effect which real things have is to cause belief" (5.406; also W 3:271) or to contribute to the formation of belief principally by the capacity of reality to generate doubt (to challenge presently fixed belief) and to provide the means for overcoming doubt (to fix provisionally superior beliefs). In other words, doubt, inquiry conceived as the struggle to overcome doubt, and the recovery of belief as the immanent goal of any genuine inquiry are the marks by which inquirers experientially know and pragmatically define the *real.* The real is that to which the community of inquirers would be led by the course of experience, if only this experience were of sufficient duration and these inquirers were truly animated by a love of truth and, hence, effectively oriented by the results of self-criticism. The "very origin of the conception of reality shows that this conception essentially involves the notion of a COMMUNITY, without definite limits, and capable of a definite increase in knowledge" (5.311; also W 2:239; cf. 5.354; 2.645). The conceivable practical effects implied in the predicate "real" are ones pertaining directly to belief, doubt, and inquiry.

In this connection, *practical* is thus not to be understood in any narrow sense, especially one set in sharp contrast to *theoretical.* Peirce did not subordinate theory to practice but rather insisted upon seeing theory itself as a mode of practice quite distinct from other modes. The "practical" bearings to which his pragmatic maxim refers are, thus, ones pertaining to the conduct of inquirers qua inquirers. In a letter to the British pragmatist F. C. S. Schiller, Peirce is explicit about how he understood the term *practical*: By it, "I mean apt to affect conduct; and by conduct, voluntary action that is self-controlled, i.e., controlled by adequate deliberation" (8.322). Those effects having "conceivable practical bearings" are, hence, ones apt to affect the comportment of theoretical inquirers in this distinctive role.

The Scope of Philosophy

Throughout his life, Peirce was devoted to an intense study of philosophical authors. Accordingly, his efforts to transform philosophy into a science exhibited not only the imprint of his scientific bent but also the influence of his philosophical reading (see, e.g., 1.3–6). While he refused to define philosophy in opposition to science, his vision of philosophy vis-à-vis the history of this discipline cannot be so univocally expressed. Insofar as philosophy in its classical sense was identified with a discipline aiming *directly* at rectifying the conduct of oneself and others (1.618), he differentiated his own understanding of this enterprise from that of the classical philosophers. But insofar as one could find in Aristotle and other such forerunners an uncompromising defense of theoretical philosophy, he identified his view with theirs. Though he was confident that a devotion to *theoria* would slowly and indirectly exert a beneficent influence on the character of the theoretical inquirer (1.648), he was fearful that tying theoretical investigation too closely to moral discipline would be disastrous for both *theoria* and *praxis.* He was convinced that "the two masters, *theory* and *practice*, you cannot serve. The perfect balance of attention which is requisite for observing the system of things is utterly lost if human desires intervene, and all the more so the higher and holier those desires may be" (1.642). He did recognize that: "The most vital factors in the method of modern science have not been the following of this or that logical prescription . . . but they have been the moral factors" (7.87), above all, the genuine love of theoretical truth for its own sake. But the virtues demanded of inquirers are ordinarily not the immediate object of their deliberate pursuit; they are formed in a largely unconscious and indirect manner, consequent upon single-minded devotion to the overarching goal of theoretical discovery. The love of truths not yet known is the seed from which the science in Peirce's sense is destined to grow. The scientific method was, in his judgment, "a historic attainment" (6.428); the lives of scientists such as Copernicus, Kepler, Galileo and their far distant precursors scattered throughout ancient history were themselves so many experiments regarding the efficacy of this method of inquiry (4.31). Even this method was, however, not "essential to the beginnings of science"; the scientific spirit, what Peirce also calls "scientific *Eros*" (1.620), is sufficient to account for the origin of this undertaking: "To science once enthroned in this sense, among any people, science in every other is heir apparent" (6.428).

In spirit and aspiration, Peirce was as close to Aristotle as he was to any other figure in the history of philosophy. This is nowhere more evident than in the manner he combined a deep respect for everyday experience (hence, for ordinary language) and a theoretical curiosity of boundless scope. Like Aristotle, Peirce took philosophy to be a systematic pursuit of theoretical knowledge wherein philosophers must be deliberately attentive to the most reliable methods and procedures for conducting this search. Allied with this understanding, he conceived logic to be an *organon* or tool crafted by investigators for the sake of facilitating investigation, though he stressed methods for generating fruitful hypotheses as much as ones for assessing epistemic claims. The philosopher consequently cannot help but be a logician, for responsible inquiry requires of theoretical inquirers, philosophical or otherwise, critical attention to the specific strategies, tools, and procedures by which they conduct their inquiries. But, in addition, the philosopher cannot avoid metaphysics, any more than can any other human being: "Whether we have an anti-metaphysical metaphysics or a pro-metaphysical metaphysics, a metaphysics we are sure to have. And the less pains we take with it the more crudely metaphysical it will be" (EP 1:108).[17] The positivists who jeer at metaphysicians are, by their systematic blindness to their own metaphysical commitments, the ones most likely to have their positions thoroughly vitiated by the crude and unexamined metaphysics with which these positions are packed (1.129).

Peirce took philosophy to encompass more than logic and metaphysics. He came to see that logic, precisely as a normative theory of theoretical investigation, did not stand alone, but was intimately connected to two other normative sciences. Logic might be characterized as a normative account of self-controlled inquiry, at the center of which is a normative account of reasoning in its proper sense (a term taken by Peirce to mean self-criticized and self-controlled inference).

Logic in a narrow sense provides us with the resources to assess the strength of various types of reasoning; in a wider sense, it provides guidance on how to conduct an investigation. So understood, logic focuses on a species of self-controlled conduct. Accordingly, it presupposes a more general normative theory of self-controlled (or deliberate) conduct. There is nothing strained or idiosyncratic in using *ethics* to designate this theory. Logic presupposes ethics, in the sense that a normative theory of self-controlled inquiry presupposes a normative theory of self-controlled conduct and self-cultivated character. If conduct is to be thoroughly deliberate, it must be deeply critical, extending to the very ideals by which agents ultimately judge their conduct, character, and even feelings.[18] One might assume that critical reflection upon rival candidates for ultimate ends falls within the scope of ethics. Yet Peirce came to distinguish such reflection from ethics, apparently since we might offer a normative account of deliberate conduct in provisional abstraction from whatever ultimate ideal happens to be espoused by an ethical agent. Ultimately, a formal, systematic inquiry into rival conceptions of the ultimate aim of human conduct, for the purpose of identifying what alone might be intrinsically admirable (or adorable in its original sense of worthy of adoration), is necessary. For reasons not altogether clear, Peirce allotted this task to a distinct normative science, one he called *esthetics.* Instead of "a silly science of Esthetics" aiming at the enjoyment of sensuous beauty, he asserted that what we need is a sustained reflection on what is admirable or lovable in itself, apart from all else (EP 2:460). He identified the continuous growth of concrete reasonableness as what alone deserves to be espoused as the *summum bonum* (see, e.g., 5.433). "In general, the good is the attractive – not to everybody, but to the sufficiently matured agent; and the evil is the repulsive to the same" (5.552). The sufficiently mature agent is the one who has conscientiously undertaken a critical reflection on the ultimate ideal from which specific evaluations draw their force and authority. Self-controlled conduct ultimately draws upon a self-cultivated sensitivity attuned to the creative development of concrete reasonableness. Peirce is explicit that this unending process involves nothing less than the concrete embodiment of a transpersonal Reason in our habits and artifacts, including our institutions and practices, our scientific inquiries and artistic achievements (1.615). The possibility of self-controlled conduct ultimately rests on the guidance of a self-cultivated sensitivity attuned to the growth of such reasonableness (or Reason). Because of this and other affinities, Peirce acknowledged: "My philosophy resuscitates Hegel, though in a strange costume" (1.42).[19] However this may be, the main point here concerns the interconnections among the normative sciences. Just as logic as a normative theory of self-controlled inquiry presupposes ethics as a normative theory of self-controlled conduct, in its turn, ethics presupposes esthetics as the discipline to which the task of identifying the ultimate end falls but also the one in which the cultivation of feelings responsive to the lure of this ideal takes place (1.574; 1.594).

Philosophical inquiry encompasses, then, at least metaphysics and three normative sciences bound together in an intimate union. But it also includes phenomenology, conceived not simply as a descriptive discourse. For the task of the phenomenologist is, at least, as much generalization as description. The phenomenologist does need the ability characteristic of artists, "the rare faculty of seeing what stares one in the face, just as it presents itself, unreplaced by any interpretation" (5.42). But, for the task Peirce assigns to phenomenology (that of identifying and articulating a doctrine of categories), the phenomenologist also needs "the generalizing power of the mathematician who produces the abstract formula that comprehends the very essence of the feature under examination purified from all admixture of extraneous and irrelevant accompaniments" (5.42). As a doctrine of categories, phenomenological inquiry is for Peirce *prima philosophia*, since it provides an integrated set of heuristic clues by which philosophical investigators dealing with metaphysical or normative questions are goaded and guided in their undertakings. Quite simply, phenomenology in Peirce's ordering of the branches of philosophy comes first. It comes first by virtue of being charged with the task of providing a systematic articulation of the most general conceptions by which any other philosophical investigation can be conducted. The categories are more than distillations of the generalizations of the phenomenologist; they are also suggestions and directives for inquiry in all other fields. Without such conceptions, philosophy would be an instance of utterly blind groping; with them, it is equipped not only with eyes but also sources of illumination. Peirce designed his doctrine of categories to serve as a *lanterna pedibus* (cf. EP 2:399), a light by which to guide the steps of inquirers. As a doctrine of categories, phenomenology principally concerns what *might be* the case. What his categories do, and what they are limited to doing, is simply to call attention to features of whatever one is investigating. "They suggest a way of thinking" (1.351), a manner of approaching the matter at hand. "This is all the categories pretend to do" (1.351). The doctrine of categories opens an array of possibilities and, in light of these possibilities, suggests paths of inquiry. In contrast, the normative sciences of logic, ethics, and esthetics concern what *ought to be* the case, whereas metaphysics tries to ascertain what truly *is* the case. It turns out, however, that being is not reducible to actuality or existence. Hence, Peirce in his metaphysics recognizes three modes of being.

Philosophy is, in the first instance, a phenomenological discourse geared toward the systematic articulation of the most general conceptions imaginable. In the second, philosophy is a normative discourse proximately concerned with offering a normative account of objective inquiry (the sort of investigation in which a commitment to the discovery of truth for its own sake animates and sustains a community of inquirers, because such truth is glimpsed, however partially and uncertainly); at this level, it is ultimately concerned with identifying what a sufficiently mature agent *would* perceive to be the ultimate end worthy of our unconditional espousal. But, at a third level, philosophy drives toward a metaphysics inclusively envisioned, a discourse embracing a cosmology as well as ontology (an account of the cosmos no less than of the modes of being).

The Theory of Signs

But Peirce identified himself as a logician more often than as a physicist; and his conception of logic encompassed a general theory of signs, in order to offer an adequate account of inquiry.[20] His interest in methods of inquiry was never far from the center of his concern, even when directly engaged in an investigation bearing upon "the constitution of the universe." He alleged that, from his first encounter with logic at the age of twelve, he never studied anything ("mathematics, ethics, metaphysics, gravitation, thermodynamics, optics, chemistry, comparative anatomy, astronomy, psychology, phonetics, economics, the history of science, whist, men and women, wine, metrology") except as a study of signs ("semeiotic" in his preferred spelling or semiotics in ours). Intertwined with his interest in a broad range of substantive topics and in the successful procedures for investigating these diverse subjects, thus, was a fascination with signs in their myriad forms. He was convinced that "the woof and warp of all thought and all research is symbols, and the life of thought and science is the life inherent in symbols" (2.220). But, strictly speaking, he took signs of quite different forms rather than just symbols to be the indispensable media of our cognitive processes and epistemic practices. The life of thought and inquiry is that inherent in signs of diverse species. For this and other reasons Peirce thought it would be extremely useful, "for those who have both a talent and a passion for eliciting the truth about such matters, to institute a cooperative cenoscopic attack upon the problems of the nature, properties, and varieties of Signs" (EP 2:462). He himself devoted intense effort and countless pages to such an endeavor. But, regarding his "life-long study of the nature of signs," he acknowledged: "I am, as far as I know, a pioneer, or rather a backwoodsman, in the work of clearing and opening up what I call semiotic, that is, the doctrine of the essential nature and fundamental varieties of possible semiosis; and I find the field too vast, the labor too great, for a first-comer" (EP 2:413). Nonetheless, his accomplishments in this field are of fundamental importance. In sum, Peirce characteristically identified himself as a logician and, in turn, eventually identified logic with the study of signs.[21] The life-long student of reasoning felt compelled to undertake a life-long study of signs. This study yielded the resources for illuminating reasoning but also much else.

Three convictions especially guided Peirce's investigation of signs. First, he was convinced that "thinking always proceeds in the form of a dialogue" (4.6), ordinarily between different phases of the ego (e.g., the critical self of a later moment calling into question the supposition guiding the conjectural self of just a moment before). Signs are thus the indispensable media of not only interpersonal but also reflexive communication: they are instruments as much of thought as of conversation, since thought itself is, as Plato noted, an inner conversation or "a silent speech of the soul will itself" (W 2:172). If this dialogical conception of thinking is accepted, "immense consequences follow" (EP 2:172). Peirce devoted care to tracing out these consequences of this position, one he identified as *tuism* (the "doctrine that all thought is addressed to a second person, or to one's future self as to a second person" (W 1:xxix)). His theory of science no less than his account of the self reveals as much.

Second, he was convinced that thought could not be severed from its modes of expression. Of course, a thought expressed in one way almost always can be expressed in other ways, though not infrequently this results in a depletion or distortion of meaning. But Peirce rejected the supposition that thought is something apart from its possibility of expression or articulation. The particular signs used on any actual occasion are not themselves the thought; at least they cannot be unqualifiedly identified with the thought being expressed: "Oh, no; no whit more than the skins of an onion are the onion. (And about as much so, however.)" It was evident to Peirce that: "One selfsame thought may be carried upon the vehicle of English, German, Greek, or Gaelic; in diagrams, or in equations, or in graphs: all these are but so many skins of the onion, its inessential accidents" (4.6). No less manifest was that anything properly designated as "thought should have *some* possible expression for some possible interpreter." He took this possibility to be "the very being of its being" (4.6). Hence, he insisted, "all that we know of thought is but a reflection on what we know of its expression" (2.466 n.1). The logician in the narrow sense of a critic of the forms of reasoning, hence, must be a logician in the broader or semiotic sense of a student of signs in general (including of course linguistic signs).

Third, Peirce was convinced that at least "every symbol is a living thing, in a very strict sense that is no mere figure of speech" (2.222). Neither consciousness nor mind endows signs with life; rather, the actions of signs are themselves signs of vitality, however rudimentary. Peirce was aware that such a claim is likely to strike many people as "stark madness, or mysticism, or something equally devoid of reason and good sense" (MS 290, 58). But he supposed a blindness rooted in something close to perversity prompted such a judgment (see, e.g., 1.349). The "great truth of the immanent power" of living signs was one championed by Peirce.

The signs with which we are most directly and intimately familiar are ones closely associated with consciousness or, at least, mind (Peirce emphatically refused to identify mind with consciousness, since he was convinced that most of our mental processes are unconscious). This inclines us to suppose that there is an essential connection between semiosis and mind: the interpretive acts of a mental agent or mindful being are often supposed by us to constitute the sole source of significance. Apart from these acts, allegedly nothing would count as a sign. To Ludwig Wittgenstein's question ("Every sign *by itself* seems dead. What gives it life?"[22]), then, the answer appears to be some interpreter; and mind is that which equips any being with the capacity to fulfill this function. Peirce was, however, opposed to this mentalist account of signs, putting forth alternatively a semiotic account of mind. Mind is here not so much a principle of explanation as a phenomenon calling for explanation. There is hardly any question that the human mind is (in Susanne Langer's telling expression) symbolific;[23] this mind is adapted not only to acquire diverse modes of symbolization but also to craft new symbols from its inheritance. We are symbol-making as well as sign-using animals. The key to mind is the use of signs, whereas that to the distinctive character of the human mind is the capacity to use inherited signs in innovative ways and, more dramatically, to fashion novel signs. An indication of this is the role of metaphor in our use of language. Rather than tracing signs to their alleged origin in mind, Peirce explained mind by its manifest reliance on signs.

Peirce's definition of semiosis (or sign-action) is at the center of his theory of signs. Semiosis is a paradigm of his category of thirdness, for it involves an irreducibly triadic relationship. So too is an act of giving. In such an act, a giver, gift, and recipient are essentially related to another one: divestiture (the giver relinquishes possession of an object) and acquisition (the recipient acquires possession of this same object) are, in giving, not accidentally related, but rather bound together in a single act. In semiosis, an *object*, *sign*, and *interpretant* are likewise bound together in a single process, though not necessarily by the intention of any agent. If a person knocks on a door, the sound generated by this action is a sign of someone being there (or one soliciting the recognition of anyone on the other side). The knocker is the object, whereas the response to the sound would be the interpretant. But semiosis is, in principle, an open-ended process, for the interpretant very frequently serves as a sign generating yet another interpretant. The *immediate* object of semiosis is the way the object is represented by a sign or series of signs, whereas the *dynamical* object is whatever has determined or, at least, the capacity to determine, a sign or series of signs. The dynamic object is that which has the capacity to constrain a process of representation and, thus, to enable the recognition of misinterpretation. It is the object as potentially other than its representation.

Peirce's categories guided his investigation of signs. This is evident in his various classifications of interpretants and also his elaborate classifications of signs, virtually all of which are explicitly based upon categoreal considerations. His two most important classifications of interpretants clearly indicate this. In one, emotional, energetic, and logical interpretants are distinguished from one another. Some signs generate feelings and have no other interpretants than the emotions they generate. Other signs generate actions (e.g., the action of soldiers in response to the command "Ground arms!" issued by the officer of their troop). The actions themselves are the energetic interpretants of the sign. Still other signs are not only inherently general but also (by virtue of their generality) play a crucial role in some rational process (e.g., experimental inquiry or political deliberation). Concepts would be examples of such logical interpretants. But so too would habits. In fact, Peirce holds that only habits can serve as the ultimate logical interpretants of signs, a claim central to his reformulation of pragmatism. In another important classification of interpretants, immediate, dynamic, and final are distinguished from one another. First, there must be something inherent in any sign that renders it interpretable in a determinative way, such that something would count as a misinterpretation. The immediate interpretant of any sign is, then, its grounded interpretability; it signifies a possibility, but not an utterly abstract one. Second, there is often some actual effect generated by the action of a sign. The dynamic interpretant is any effect actually produced by a sign as such. Finally, there is the final interpretant, "the effect that would be produced on the mind by the Sign after sufficient development of thought" (EP 2:482). The relationship between these two classifications of interpretants is but one thorny question confronting anyone who is seriously interested in exploring the details of Peirce's semeiotic.

Peirce also offered elaborate classifications of signs based upon the application of his categories to this field of inquiry. Let us briefly consider one of these, involving three trichotomies. First, a sign considered in itself, apart from either its object or interpretant, (i.e., a sign as a first) is either a quality or event or law. This yields the trichotomy of *qualisign* (a quality serving as a sign), *sinsign*, and *legisign*. Second, a sign considered in relation to its dynamical object yields Peirce's most famous trichotomy of signs – that of *icon*, *index*, and *symbol*. In an icon, a sign is related to its dynamical object by virtue of some inherent similarity the sign bears to its object. A photograph of you signifies you (partly) by virtue of such a similarity. In an index, a sign is related to its dynamical object by virtue of a causal connection between the sign and its object. The weathervane signifies the direction of the wind by virtue of its object causing it to point in this direction. Hence, it is an indexical sign. But, in a certain respect, so too is a photograph, for the photographic image of anything signifies that thing by virtue of a causal connection between itself and its object. This suggests that it is best to conceive of icon, index, and symbol not as separable signs but as potentially interwoven sign functions. In a symbol, a sign is related to its dynamic object by virtue of a habitual connection, either naturally or conventionally established. A commonplace misunderstanding of the Peircean conception of symbol is to suppose that, for him, a symbol is based on a conventional relationship between symbol and symbolized. But the disposition of bees to interpret the dance of other members of their species as *indicative* of the direction and distance of honey would be an example of a symbol based on a habitual connection of a natural (rather than conventional) character. In this example, it is perhaps possible to discern symbolic, indexical, and even iconic functions interwoven in such a way as to produce a remarkably effective instance of semiosis. In the instances of semiosis of greatest interest to Peirce, the mutually supportive operations of iconic, indexical, and symbolic signs were paramount. Third, a sign may be considered in relationship to its interpretant. Such consideration would yield the trichotomy of what (leaving aside Peirce's forbidding terminology in this case) roughly corresponds to concepts, propositions, and arguments.

Underlying these elaborate classifications the sympathetic reader can catch what, at bottom, is animating Peirce's inquiry into the nature and varieties of semiosis. It is inseparable from his pragmatism. Peirce once noted that, in him, pragmatism "is a sort of instinctive attraction to living facts" (5.64). His theory of signs reveals nothing less than an intense, sustained attraction to the life inherent in signs, especially insofar as they are crucial to the conduct of inquiry.

The Conjecture of a Physicist: Absolute Chance, Brute Reaction, and Evolving Law

Peirce's normative account of objective inquiry, doctrine of categories, and theory of signs are among his most important contributions to philosophical investigation. His guess at the riddle of the universe is arguably of less importance, perhaps even of dubious merit.[24] Yet we as philosophers should be hesitant to dismiss too hastily a cosmology that is apparently "in the general line of the growth of scientific ideas" (1.7).[25] At the center of Peirce's cosmology are, at least, three claims. The first concerns chance, the second actuality, and the third the evolution of laws. These three claims are intimately connected to one another. First, there is Peirce's doctrine of *tychism* (derived from the Greek word for chance). The cosmos is such by virtue of an evolution out of chaos. The possibility of such an evolution presupposes the objectivity of chance. Chance is not solely a function of our ignorance, such that if we knew fully enough the laws operating in nature we would be able to predict virtually every natural event; rather, it is a feature of reality. The natural world is a scene of chance occurrences: randomness is real. Second, brute actuality plays as important a role in the constitution of the universe as does objective chance. Third, the supposition of immutable laws seems to be in contradiction to the evolution of the cosmos itself. For Peirce, "philosophy requires thorough-going evolutionism or none" (6.14). This means that we need to take seriously the hypothesis that the laws of nature have themselves evolved: "To suppose universal laws of nature capable of being apprehended by the mind and yet having no reason for their special forms, but standing inexplicable and irrational, is hardly a justified position" (6.12). The laws by which we explain some phenomena are themselves phenomena and, as such, call for explanation. The only way of explaining them involves supposing a process by which they were generated; and the only condition allowing for such a process is an original condition of absolute chance virtually indistinguishable from complete nullity.

Interwoven with Peirce's evolutionary cosmology are a number of distinctive views, three of which especially merit mention here. First, there is his doctrine of evolutionary love (6.287–317). The pragmaticist[26] "does not make the *summum bonum* to consist in action," but in that process of evolution whereby existents come to embody more fully generals that are themselves becoming more harmoniously integrated (5.433). "In its higher stages, evolution takes place more and more largely through self-control" (ibid.); and the deliberate cultivation of self-control ultimately involves an uncompromising commitment to concrete reasonableness, involving the surrender of our finite selves to an infinite ideal (5.356–7;

8.262).[27] Peirce identified this with *agapé*. The higher stages in the growth of concrete reasonableness require nothing less.

Second, habits, laws, and what Peirce calls generals are no less real than existents, actualities, and individuals. Strictly speaking, they are alone real, while existents are actual. In opposition to the nominalist, for whom only individuals are real, Peirce argued for scholastic realism, contending that an adequate account of science requires a robust affirmation of generals (principally the irreducibly general laws pervading nature). Third, this affirmation is part of his insistence on there being three modes of being (see, e.g., 1.21–3; 1.515; 8.305) – possibility, actuality, and reality (what might be called habituality, since the would-do of habits is the exemplar of this mode of being). Peirce's metaphysics includes an ontology as well as cosmology, an explication of the senses of being as well as a conjecture regarding the constitution of the universe. In addition to actuality or existence (the mode of being characteristic of individuals), there is that of might-be and would-be.

The actual universe disclosed in our everyday experience is inexplicable on egoistic, nominalistic, and other often highly fashionable yet severely reductivist assumptions. Thus, alternative hypotheses must be seriously considered. This is nowhere more manifest than in Peirce's metaphysics.

Conclusion

Paradoxically, Peirce was at once far more than a pragmatist and more of a pragmatist in all areas of investigation than even many of his most insightful interpreters appear to appreciate. He was committed to the continuous growth of concrete reasonableness, envisioned as a cosmic process in which biological evolution, cultural development, and personal striving are enveloped. For him, this meant the deliberate cultivation of habits of self-criticism and self-correction. Though he sharply distinguished theoretical inquiry from practical affairs, he fully realized that scientific investigation is a moral undertaking, depending essentially upon purified motives, conscientious decisions, and distinctively moral virtues (see, e.g., 7.87). It was for him also something akin to religion. "To believe in a god at all, is not that to believe that man's reason is allied to the originating principle of the universe?" – and further is it not also to believe that this origin is, however vaguely, analogous to our own rationality?

Peirce's philosophy provides the resources for a naturalistic account of human intelligence and, more generally, human existence, while at the same time arguing for the need to open ourselves to the lure of ideals intimating the presence of "One Incomprehensible but Personal God" (5.496).[28] He tried to establish his theism in the same manner as he did all of his other philosophical doctrines, from within the limits of experience alone. Whatever one thinks of this or any other specific doctrine advanced by Peirce, the quality and depth of his reflections cannot be gainsaid. If philosophy is a science,[29] in turn "science consists in *inquiry*, not in 'doctrine.'"[30] Whatever conclusions reached or doctrines defended by Peirce, the approach articulated and exemplified by him as a scientist, logician, and philosopher, investigating a staggering array of topics, is itself worthy of continuing inquiry. An international community of scholars intensely interested in this American philosopher testifies to this.

Notes

1 For an informed, insightful, engaging account of Peirce's life, see Joseph Brent, *Charles Sanders Peirce: A Life*, revised and enlarged edn. (Bloomington and Indianapolis, IN: Indiana University Press, 1998). Also see Douglas R. Anderson, *Strands of System: The Philosophy of Charles Peirce* (West Lafayette, IN: Purdue University Press, 1995), ch. 1. Finally, it is advisable to consult "A Brief Intellectual Autobiography by Charles Sanders Peirce," ed. and annotated by Kenneth Laine Ketner, *American Journal of Semiotics*, 2/1–2 (1983): 61–83.

2 All references to Peirce's writings will be given in the body of this text, in accord with the standard form of scholarly citation. In this instance "MS" refers to an unpublished manuscript, and the number to that established to identify it by Richard S. Robin in *Annotated Catalogue of the Papers of Charles S. Peirce* (Amherst, MA: University of Massachusetts Press, 1967). Hence, "MS 1601" refers to what Robin identifies as an Autobiographical Fragment. Here Peirce wrote: "Although I was not a precocious child, at the age of 8 I took up of my own accord the study of chemistry, to which the following year I added natural philosophy."

3 Kenneth Laine Ketner effectively argues in "Peirce as an Interesting Failure?" against the thesis that Peirce was a failure: *Proceedings of the C. S. Peirce Bicentennial International Congress*, ed. K. L. Ketner et al. (Lubbock, TX: Texas Tech University Press, 1981), pp. 55–8.

4 Edward C. Moore, "Preface" to *Writings of Charles S. Peirce: A Chronological Edition*, vol. 1 (1857–66) (Bloomington, IN: Indiana University Press, 1982), p. xi.

5 Ernest Nagel, *Scientific America*, 200 (1959): 185. Cited by Edward C. Moore in his "Preface" to *Writings of Charles S. Peirce: A Chronological Edition*, vol. 2 (1867–71) (Bloomington, IN: Indiana University Press, 1984), p. xi.

6 "EP 2" refers to *The Essential Peirce: Selected Philosophical Writings*, vol. 2 (1893–1913) (Bloomington and Indianapolis, IN: Indiana University Press, 1998), edited by the Peirce Edition Project.

7 See my "Transforming Philosophy Into a Science," *American Catholic Philosophic Quarterly*, LXXII/2 (Spring 1998): 245–78; also my "Peirce the Concrete Fallibilist, Convinced Pragmaticist, and Critical Commonsensist," *Semiotica*, 111/1–2 (1996): 75–101.

8 Citations such as these are to *The Collected Papers of Charles Sanders Peirce* (Cambridge, MA: The Belknap Press of Harvard University Press, 1931–66), vols. 1–6, ed. Charles Hartshorne and Paul Weiss; vols. 7 and 8, ed. Arthur W. Burks. "1.620" refers to vol. 1, paragraph 620 of Peirce's *Collected Papers*, "6.3" to vol. 6, paragraph 3. In accord with standard practice, paragraph (rather than page) numbers are cited.

9 For a detailed, informed account of Peirce's classification of the sciences, see Beverley Kent, *Charles S. Peirce: Logic and the Classification of the Sciences* (Kingston and Montreal: McGill-Queen's University Press, 1987). Also see Anderson, *Strands of System*, ch. 2.

10 For an excellent account of Peirce's account of scientific inquiry, see C. F. Delaney, *Science, Knowledge, and Mind: A Study in the Philosophy of C. S. Peirce* (Notre Dame, IN: University of Notre Dame Press, 1993), ch. 2.

11 In 1982, the first volume of a critical edition of Peirce's most important writings appeared. These volumes are entitled *Writings of Charles S. Peirce: A Chronological Edition* and cited simply as "W." "W 2:313" refers to vol. 2, p. 313 of this critical edition.

12 *Charles Sanders Peirce: Contributions to the Nation* (Lubbock, TX: Texas Tech University Press, 1978), ed. Kenneth Laine Ketner and James Edward Cook, Part II (1894–1900), p. 99. In Peirce's contributions to *The Nation*, one finds a wealth of material still insufficiently mined.

13 Quoted in Ralph Barton Perry, *The Thought and Character of William James* (Boston: Little Brown & Co., 1993), vol. 2, p. 438.

14 In an insightful and suggestive study, *The Continuity of Peirce's Thought* (Nashville, TN: Vanderbilt University Press, 1998), Kelly A. Parker argues that the principle of continuity is itself the thread by which Peirce wove together apparently disparate doctrines into a coherent system.

15 In *The Quest for Certainty*, vol. 4 of *The Later Works of John Dewey* (1925–53) (Carbondale and Edwardsville, IL: Southern Illinois University Press, 1988), Dewey makes substantially the same point: "By means of symbols . . . we act without acting. That is we perform experiments by means of symbols which have results which are themselves only symbolized, and which do not therefore commit us to actual or existential consequences. . . . The invention or discovery of symbols is doubtless by far the single greatest event in the history of man. Without them, no intellectual advance is possible; with them, there is no limit set to intellectual development except inherent stupidity" (LW 4:121).

16 Cf. Susanne K. Langer, *Philosophy in a New Key: A Study in the Symbolism of Reason, Rite, and Art* (Cambridge, MA: Harvard University Press, 1957), p. 51.

17 *The Essential Peirce: Selected Philosophical Writings*, vol. 1 (Bloomington and Indianapolis, IN: Indiana University Press, 1992), ed. Nathan Houser and Christian Kloesel.

18 See Richard J. Bernstein, "Action, Conduct, and Self-Control," in Bernstein, ed., *Perspectives on Peirce: Critical Essays on Charles Sanders Peirce* (New Haven, CT: Yale University Press, 1965), pp. 66–91; also his "The Lure of the Ideal," in Roberta Kevelson, ed., *Peirce and Law: Issues in Pragmatism, Legal Realism, and Semiotics* (New York: Peter Lang, 1991), pp. 30–43; finally Vincent Colapietro, *Peirce's Approach to the Self* (Albany, NY: SUNY Press, 1989), ch. 5.

19 For Peirce's relationship to Hegel, see Max H. Fisch, "Hegel and Peirce," in *Peirce, Semeiotic, and Pragmatism* (Bloomington, IN: Indiana University Press), pp. 261–82.

20 For helpful overviews of Peirce's general theory of signs, see David Savan, *An Introduction to C. S. Peirce's Full System of Semeiotic* (Toronto: Toronto Semiotic Circle, 1987–8); Michael Shapiro, *The Sense of Grammar: Language as Semeiotic* (Bloomington, IN: Indiana University Press, 1983); and James Jakób Liszka, *A General Intro-*

duction to the Semeiotic of Charles Sanders Peirce (Bloomington and Indianapolis: Indiana University Press, 1996).

21 See chs. 17, 18, and 20 (especially pp. 389–97) of Fisch's *Peirce, Semeiotic, and Pragmatism.*

22 Ludwig Wittgenstein, *Philosophical Investigations*, trans. G. E. M. Anscombe (New York: Macmillan, 1958), Part I, p. 432.

23 Langer, *Philosophy in a New Key*, p. 51.

24 See, e.g., W. B. Gallie, *Peirce and Pragmatism* (New York: Dover Publications, 1966), ch. 9. Cf. Christopher Hookway, *Peirce* (London and New York: Routledge, 1985), pp. 262–3.

25 See, e.g., Ilya Prigogine and Isabelle Stengers, *Order Out of Chaos: Man's New Dialogue with Nature* (New York: Bantam Books, 1984). Prigogine won the Nobel Prize in 1977 for his work on the thermodynamics of non-equilibrium systems. After quoting one of Peirce's cosmological essays from *The Monist*, the authors note: "Peirce's metaphysics was considered as one more example of a philosophy alienated from reality. But, in fact, today Peirce's work appears to be a pioneering step toward understanding the pluralism involved in physical laws" (p. 303). In a more recent work by a theoretical physicist, Lee Smolin's *The Life of the Cosmos* (New York: Oxford University Press, 1997), it would be impossible for anyone acquainted with Peirce's cosmology not to hear echoes of his thoroughgoing evolutionism in Smolin's own conjecture about the constitution of the universe. This is all the more remarkable since Peirce is not mentioned.

26 Peirce coined this word after William James's "Philosophical Conceptions and Practical Results" (1898) had thrust Peirce's ideas into notoriety, though in ways often at odds with his understanding. He bemoaned "the merciless way that words have to expect when they fall into literary clutches"; and finding his "bantling 'pragmatism' " mercilessly treated by litterateurs, he announced: "it is time to kiss his child good-by and relinquish it to its higher destiny; while to serve the precise purpose of expressing the original definition, he begs to announce the birth of the word 'pragmaticism,' which is ugly enough to be safe from kidnappers"! (5.414).

27 Peirce, *Charles Sanders Peirce: Contributions to the Nation,* Part I, pp. 188–9. Cf. Colapietro, *Peirce's Approach to the Self*, pp. 95–7.

28 See Donna Orange, *Peirce's Conception of God* (Bloomington, IN: Indiana University Press, 1984); Michael Raposa, *Peirce's Philosophy of Religion* (Bloomington, IN: Indiana University Press, 1989); Anderson, *Strands of System*; and Vincent G. Potter, *Peirce's Philosophical Perspectives* (New York: Fordham University Press, 1996).

29 For a criticism of this thoroughgoing identification, see Colapietro, "Transforming Philosophy Into a Science," especially pp. 274–8.

30 Charles Sanders Peirce and Victoria Lady Welby, *Semiotic and Significs: The Correspondence between Charles S. Peirce and Victoria Lady Welby*, ed. Charles S. Hardwick (Bloomington, IN: Indiana University Press, 1977), p. 79. Cf. 1.11.

Suggested reading

Primary sources

Peirce, Charles S., *Charles S. Peirce: Selected Writing*, ed. Philip P. Wiener (New York: Dover Publications, 1980).

Peirce, Charles S., *Collected Papers of Charles Sanders Peirce*, eds. Charles Hartshorne, Paul Weiss, and Arthur Burks, 8 vols. (Cambridge, MA: Harvard University Press, 1931–66).

—— *The Essential Peirce*, eds. Nathan Houser and Christian Kloesel, 2 vols. (Bloomington: Indiana University Press, 1992).

—— *Philosophical Writings of Peirce*, ed., Justus Buchler (New York: Dover Publications, 1986).

—— *Writings of Charles S. Peirce: A Chronological Edition*, vols. 1–6, eds. Max H. Fisch, Edward C. Moore, Christian J. W. Kloesel, and Nathan Houser (Bloomington: Indiana University Press, 1982–9).

Secondary sources

Anderson, Douglas R., *Strands of System: The Philosophy of Charles S. Peirce* (West Lafayette, IN: Purdue University Press, 1995).

Apel, Karl-Otto, *Charles S. Peirce: From Pragmatism to Pragmaticism* (Amherst, MA: University of Massachusetts Press, 1981).

Brent, Joseph, *Charles Sanders Peirce: A Life*, revised and enlarged edn. (Bloomington and Indianapolis: Indiana University Press, 1998).

Buchler, Justus, *Charles Peirce's Empiricism* (New York: Harcourt, Brace, 1939).

Colapietro, Vincent M., *Peirce's Approach to the Self* (Albany, NY: SUNY Press, 1989).

Delaney, C. F., *Science, Knowledge, and Mind: A Study in the Philosophy of C. S. Peirce* (Notre Dame, IN: University of Notre Dame Press, 1993).

Esposito, Joseph, *Evolutionary Metaphysics: The Development of Peirce's Theory of Categories* (Athens, OH: University of Ohio Press, 1980).

Fisch, Max H., *Peirce, Semeiotic, and Pragmatism: Essays by Max H. Fisch, Kenneth Laine Ketner, and Christian J. W. Kloesel* (Bloomington: Indiana University Press, 1986).

Gallie, W. B., *Peirce and Pragmatism* (Harmondsworth: Penguin, 1952).

Goudge, Thomas A., *The Thought of C. S. Peirce* (Toronto: University of Toronto Press, 1950).

Hausman, Carl R., *Charles S. Peirce's Evolutionary Philosophy* (New York: Cambridge University Press, 1993).

Hookway, Christopher, *Peirce* (London and New York: Routledge, 1985).

Misak, C. J., *Truth and the End of Inquiry: A Peircean Account of Truth* (Oxford: Clarendon Press, 1991).

Murphey, Murray G., *The Development of Peirce's Philosophy* (Indianapolis, IN: Hackett, 1993).

Potter, Vincent G., *Charles S. Peirce: On Norms and Ideals* (New York: Fordham University Press, 1997).

—— *Peirce's Philosophical Perspectives* (New York: Fordham University Press, 1996).

Rosenthal, Sandra B., *Charles Peirce's Pragmatic Pluralism* (Albany, NY: SUNY Press, 1994).

Thompson, Manley, *The Pragmatic Philosophy of Charles S. Peirce* (Chicago: University of Chicago Press, 1953).

Chapter 6

William James, 1842–1910

William J. Gavin

James's Personal Life – Vagueness and Commitment

For the first three decades of his existence, William James had a unique, pampered, but slightly unusual lifestyle. Born in New York City in 1842, he traveled back and forth to Europe several times with his family before he was 21, being placed in and removed from several educational contexts by his somewhat doting father. He was fluent in French at 14 and German at 18. He turned initially to painting as a vocation, gave that up for a career in science, and ultimately entered Harvard Medical School, from which he obtained an M.D. in 1869. Moreover, James's health at this time was not robust – he lost the use of his eyesight twice, suffered from insomnia and weakness of the back, and had "gastrointestinal disturbances and periodic exhaustion."[1] His afflictions were also of a psychological nature, leading to deep depression and to a feeling that his will was inefficacious and paralyzed. Having gone to Europe to take the "sulphur baths" for his various illnesses, he writes to his father from Berlin on September 5, 1867: "Although I cannot exactly say that I got low-spirited, yet thoughts of the pistol, the dagger and the bowl began to usurp an unduly large part of my attention, and I began to think that some change, even if a hazardous one, was necessary."[2] This personal conflict with nihilism and subsequent temptation to commit suicide continued into 1870, when James writes in his diary: "Today I about touched bottom, and perceive plainly that I must face the choice with open eyes: I shall *frankly* throw the moral business overboard, as one unsuited to my innate aptitudes, or shall I follow it, and it alone, making everything else merely stuff for it?"[3] The "moral business" referred to here is that of a meaningful life, and specifically the question of whether one can act efficaciously in pursuing chosen goals.

By April 30, 1870, a definite change has come over James, through reading the works of the French philosopher Charles Renouvier. James writes in a notebook:

> I think that yesterday was a crisis in my life. I finished the first part of Renouvier's second "Essais" and see no reason why his definition of Free Will – "the sustaining of a thought *because I choose to* when I might have other thoughts" – need be the definition of an illusion . . . My first act of free will shall be to believe in free will . . . Not in maxims, not in *Anschauungen* [contemplative views], but in accumulated *acts* of thought lies salvation . . . Hitherto, when I have felt like taking a free initiative, like daring to act originally, without carefully waiting for contemplation of the external world to determine all for me, suicide seemed the most manly form to put my daring into; now, I will go a step further with my will, not only act with it, but believe as well; believe in my individual reality and creative power. My belief, to be sure, *can't* be optimistic – but I will posit life (the real, the good) in the self-governing *resistance* of the ego to the world. Life shall [be built in] doing and suffering and creating.[4]

We know how important this moment in James's life was from a letter he wrote in 1909, the year before he died, to James Ward. He says: "I think the center of my whole *Anschauung*, since years ago I read Renouvier, has been the belief that something is doing in the universe, and that *novelty* is real."[5]

What James realized in this instance is that what one might abstractly term the philosophical issue of freedom versus determinism cannot be solved on exclusively logical grounds or by appeal to neutral empirical data. That is, one could construct a coherent argument for determinism, that we are the victims of our circumstances, and bolster it by showing that it corresponded to data – in this case, primarily the data of James's physical disorders. One could also construct an argument that the human self is free and able to act creatively and efficaciously; this argument too could be bolstered by appeal to corresponding empirical data, in this case, for example, James's successful pursuit of a medical degree. But ultimately, the arguments are inconclusive, indeterminate. Two competing hypotheses, of equal worth – equally strong – can be put forth, both passing the traditional criteria of logical coherence and confirmation through correspondence with empirical "facts." The issue is that complicated – that thick or rich in possibilities. Further, the issue is, as James would put it later, "forced, living, and momentous." That is, we cannot decide, the alternatives are understood, and equally powerful, and the issue is not trivial. In such situations, and there are many of them, James argued later that we have the right to select one option over another for sentimental reasons. Differently stated, we have the right to engage in the "will to believe" – because there is quite simply nothing else left.[6] "Our passional nature not only lawfully may, but must, decide an option between propositions, whenever it is a genuine option that cannot by its nature be decided on intellectual grounds; for to say, under such circumstances, 'Do not decide, but leave the question open,' is itself a passional decision – just like deciding yes or no – and is attended with the same risk of losing the truth."[7]

In brief, what James realized in 1870 is, first, that the issue of freedom versus determinism was ambiguous or vague, and, second, that this vagueness is what is important about it. In a vague situation like this, one is forced to react, to anticipate, and the participation itself becomes a constituent part of the outcome. The issue of James's own freedom versus determinism was richer, more subtle, than what could be completely captured in linguistic or conceptual categories and, as such, it forced James to live life intensely, or zestfully.

This biographical snapshot of an important moment in James's life, seen as amorphous and hence demanding personal participation, can be used as a wedge into his writings in general. This chapter will employ it as a unifying theme for James's writings in psychology, religion, metaphysics, and epistemology.

Vagueness in the Principles of Psychology

James's first major work, *The Principles of Psychology*, was 12 years in the making. Published in 1890, it earned for him the title, "father of American psychology." In the famous ninth chapter, entitled "The Stream of Thought," James gives the reader a portrait of human consciousness as an unfinished stream, with five general characteristics. Three of these characteristics – consciousness as personal, intentional, and selective – emphasize the zest, the efficacy involved in human awareness.[8] Two of the characteristics – consciousness as continuous and consciousness as changing – emphasize the richness of human awareness. Let us look briefly at each of these two groupings.

In calling all thoughts "personal," James immediately stresses involvement on the part of each of us. There are no impartial thoughts existing as transcendental spectators, impartially viewing the game of life. Every thought is "*owned*."[9] The fourth characteristic stresses this same lack of impartiality; consciousness, as found by the psychologist, appears to deal with or "intends" an object. There is no such thing as simply being aware; one is always aware *of* something, whether or not that something actually exists. Consciousness, in this sense, is always creative.

It is the fifth characteristic of consciousness that emphasizes its being interested more in one part of its object than another, and its welcoming and rejecting, or choosing, all the while it thinks. The senses, for example, are nothing but selective organs that pick out, from among all the movements of experience, those which fall within certain limits of velocity. The barest perception possible is a focalization. We see *this* as opposed to *that*, or, in James's own words: "Out of what is in itself an undistinguishable, swarming *continuum*, devoid of distinction or emphasis, our senses make for us, by attending to this motion and ignoring that, a world full of contrasts, of sharp accents, of abrupt changes of picturesque light and shade."[10]

Two insights can be gleaned here. First of all, James is again emphasizing the active role of consciousness. Life is intense because by our choices we are molding or creating it. So called "things" from this point of view, are not separate impartial entities, but, rather, "special groups of sensible qualities, which happen practically or aesthetically to interest us, to which we therefore give substantive names, and which we exalt to [the] . . . exclusive status of independence and dignity."[11]

Second, it is only because the simplest sensation is richer than we have heretofore acknowledged that selection is possible. For example, what we hear is not simply thunder, but, rather, thunder-preceded-by-silence. We shall return to this example when discussing the second group of characteristics. For the present, let us note simply that selectivity makes consciousness intense, but one must select *from* something. It is only because the present moment of consciousness is ongoing, has *more* to it than we have noticed, that selection can take place. Focalization, in brief, depends on a fringe. This fringe is the unfinished continuum in which we find ourselves involved, and in response to which we create ourselves by our selective choices.

Not only do sensations select (e.g., a given velocity of sound waves to "hear"), but from the sensations we do have, we select some to call "true" and some to call "false." Thus, for example, I select the view of my tabletop as square to be the "true" one, relegating other possibilities, such as two acute and two obtuse angles, to the status of "perspectival." In two senses, then, perception is selective. Reasoning proper is even more selective, consisting as it does in a choice of one aspect of an object as the "essence" and a subsuming of the object, now properly labeled, into its proper conceptual frameworks.[12] Logically speaking, there are many such frameworks, and we simply select that one which is most suitable to our present needs. Consciousness then is selective at all levels:

> [C]onsciousness is at all times a *selecting agency*. Whether we take it in the lowest sphere of sense, or in the highest of intellection, we find it always doing one thing, choosing one out of several of the materials so presented to its notice, emphasizing and accentuating that and suppressing as far as possible all the rest. The item emphasized is always in close connection with some *interest* felt by consciousness to be paramount at the time.[13]

We are always aware, then, of our needs and interests. To be conscious at all is to be partial. Awareness is intense because each of us is involved with its making. Jacques Barzun realized the connection between ambiguity and creativity in James. He says:

> [In *The Principles*] James struck a deathblow at Realism [in aesthetics]. The then prevailing views of the mind were that it copied reality like a photographic plate, that it received and assembled the elements of experience like a machine, that it combined ideas like a chemist. For this "scientist" mind, James substituted one that was a born artist – a wayward, creative mind impelled by inner wants, fringed with mystery, and capable of infinitely subtle, unrecordable nuances.[14]

But this is only half the story. James's defense of the efficacy of consciousness is part and parcel of his view that consciousness is richer than we have realized, that it has substantive and transitive parts which overlap. These are discussed under the second and third characteristics of consciousness, namely that within each personal consciousness, thought is always changing, and that thought is sensibly continuous.[15]

The first of these two aspects asserts that change is a definite element in consciousness and must be dealt with as such. No single state of consciousness, once it has gone, can recur and be identical with what it was before. Something has occurred in between these two appearances; these interim occurrences cannot be ignored, save by arbitrary whim. At the very least the *time* of the two appearances is different. Furthermore, the second of the two must take the first one into account, in terms of the present context. Each present state of consciousness, then, is partly determined by the nature of the entire past succession. As James says: "Experience is remoulding us every moment, and our mental reaction on every given thing is really a resultant of our experience of the whole world up to that date."[16]

Not only does consciousness change, but the changing is an ongoing process. As an unfinished continuum, consciousness has both substantive and transitive parts. The transitions between two substantive moments of consciousness are as real as the substantive moments themselves. Conscious states, in other words, are continuous, because they are connected by transitional fringes. Recall the example where James asks that we consider what a conscious awareness of thunder would be like: "Into the awareness of the thunder itself the awareness of the previous silence creeps and continues; for what we hear when the thunder crashes is not thunder *pure*, but thunder-breaking-upon-silence-and-contrasting-with-it."[17] These transitive elements are represented in language by such words as "of," "and," "but," etc. These are all contrast words. We are aware of this *and not* that, this part *of* that, etc. Once again, we are reminded that consciousness, as selective, is forced to mold experience. On the other hand, the experience in and through which the molding takes place presents itself as a continuum, or in James's words, a stream. "Consciousness . . . does not appear to itself as chopped up in bits. Such words as 'chain' or 'train' do not describe it fitly as it presents itself in the first instance. It is nothing jointed; it flows. A 'river' or a 'stream' are the metaphors by which it is most naturally described."[18]

It is precisely because consciousness is an ongoing continuum, in which even a simple sensation is impossible, that we have to be selective. Since the sensible present has duration, and is characterized in terms of a coming-to-be-and-a-passing-away, we are always focalizing on one part of it. The richness of consciousness demands its selectivity, and vice versa. James himself found it difficult to articulate both of these notions with a single word. But his closest attempt, the word "vagueness," is found in the stream of consciousness chapter as an attempted summary: "It is, in short, the reinstatement of the vague to its proper place in our mental life which I am so anxious to press on the attention."[19] Conscious experience is vague, in the sense of being richer than any abstract formula. It is unfinished, and here also could be called vague. Finally, it is as vague that consciousness demands selectivity.

The Religious Experience as Vague

One area, among many, where the importance of the vague is apparent is that of religion. In 1902 James was invited to give the prestigious Gifford Lectures at Edinburgh University, subsequently published as *The Varieties of Religious Experience.* In this work James specifically rejects rationalistic a priori systems; he opts instead for a view of religion that sees the human person as becoming coterminous with a vague "more" existing on the periphery of consciousness. The very title gives us a clue to James's intent. The book itself is one long plea that religious experience is pervasive. Taking his examples from all areas of organized religion, James again and again ostensively makes this point – there is simply no ignoring the amount of "evidence" for religious experience. For the same reason – that is, the pervasiveness of religion – no finished formula is available. "The word 'religion' cannot stand for any single principle or essence, but is rather a collective name."[20] This plea for the richness of religious experience is negatively expressed in James's harsh critiques against vicious intellectualism in religion: "The intellectualism in religion which I wish to discredit . . . assumes to construct religious objects out of logical reason alone . . . it reaches [its conclusions] in an *a priori* way." And again, "In all sad sincerity I think we must conclude that the attempt to demonstrate by purely intellectual processes the truth of the deliverances of direct religious experience is absolutely hopeless."[21]

There was, in James's opinion, no one formula that could contain the whole of religious experience. Any such dogmatic statement would have been diametrically opposed to his unfinished universe. In the final chapters of this work, James offers a justification as to why one should opt for religious experience. We believe that the justification is made in terms of vagueness, that is, richness and intensity, and we will confine our present analysis of *The Varieties* to these two aspects.

The pervasiveness of religious experience is indicated early in *The Varieties*, as is seen in the following attempt to define religion: "Religion, whatever it is, is a man's total reaction upon life, so why not say that any total reaction upon life is a religion?"[22] Here we can see clearly the "extensity" of religious experience. I must react, for the same reason I am forced to make moral decisions – there is no possibility of being neutral. A total reaction, for James, would be "religious." And the criteria used to measure total reactions are richness and intensity.

Acting as a psychologist interested in the religious experience of a person rather than in any organized religion, James continually connects this religious experience with the subliminal area of consciousness:

> [W]e cannot, I think, avoid the conclusion that in religion we have a department of human nature with unusually close relations to the transmarginal or subliminal region

> . . . that the [subliminal region] . . . is obviously the larger part of each of us, for it is the abode of everything that is latent and the reservoir of everything that passes unrecorded or unobserved. . . . Experiences making their entrance through . . . [this] door have had emphatic influence in shaping religious history.[23]

We are reminded here of the development of the stream of consciousness in terms of an ongoing focus–fringe continuum. James's interest in religion is partially based on the fact that the religious person is constantly striving to acknowledge this peripheral aspect of his or her consciousness. In religion a person becomes conscious that this "higher part is coterminous and continuous with a MORE of the same quality, which is operative in the universe outside him, and which he can keep in working touch with, and in a fashion get on board of and save himself when all his lower being has gone to pieces in the wreck."[24]

In brief, one reason why James finds religious experience so worthwhile is that it consistently remains open to the richness of experience. As a psychologist, he expressed this in terms of a religious consciousness dealing with the subliminal. Consciousness is fringed by a more; religion deals with that "more." As a result, religious experience enables one to build a richer experience. "Among the buildings out of religion that the mind spontaneously indulges in, the aesthetic motive must never be forgotten. . . . Although some persons aim most at intellectual purity and simplification, for others, *richness* is the supreme imaginative requirement."[25]

But this again is only half the story. Not only is richness to be found in religious experience, but intensity is also found. Elsewhere, James states that the "universe is no longer a mere It to us, but a Thou, if we are religious." A human being, in responding to the presence of a Thou, lives life intensely. The emotion encountered in a religious experience "overcomes temperamental melancholy and imparts endurance to the Subject, or a zest, or a meaning, or an enchantment and glory to the common objects of life."[26] Precisely because the religious experience deals with the marginal, the fringe, the more, etc., it is demanding. The religious person, whose reaction to life is "total," is necessarily taking a chance. She is "betting on" the ideal impulses that come from her subliminal region. She is willing to chance giving up a present moment for a vaguely held ideal. "A man's conscious wit and will, so far as they strain toward the ideal, are aiming at something only dimly and inaccurately imagined." Again we notice that the concept of "vagueness" – so useful in describing the richness of religious experience in terms of the subliminal – also serves to denote the necessity of taking a chance. Religion for James includes "a new zest, which adds itself like a gift to life."[27] In describing a religious virtue like charity, we find the notion of risk at the very center of its possible realization: "If things are ever to move upward, someone must be ready to take the first step, and assume the risk of it. No one who is not willing to try charity, to try non-resistance as the saint who is always willing, can tell whether these methods will or will not succeed."[28]

The importance of risk, zest, intensity as a common element in all truly religious experiences constitutes the second reason James opted for rather than against it. Religious experience is risk-filled; here it is that one can reach the heights of satisfaction or fall to the depths of despair. "Here if anywhere," James says, "is the genuinely strenuous life."

At a preliminary level *The Varieties of Religious Experience* makes three very significant points:

1 In approaching religious experience psychologically, it reminds us that James's criteria here will be the same as in *The Principles of Psychology* – richness and intensity.
2 In terms of the first of these, religious experience is valuable because it is continually open, groping for a richer, more integrated experience.
3 In terms of intensity, religious experience continually demands involvement, zest, chance on the part of each of us.

This emphasis upon vagueness, richness, and intensity is mainly of a descriptive nature in *The Principles*, and the emphasis tends to be on a descriptive account of the personal in *The Varieties*. But his position here becomes more universal and self-reflective, more aware of its own presuppositions as James turns toward metaphysics.

James's Metaphysics: "The Really Real" as Opaque

James's metaphysics is primarily contained in two texts. *Essays in Radical Empiricism*, published posthumously in 1912, consists of a series of papers published by James mainly in 1904–5, and virtually selected by him as the content of this volume. The second text is *A Pluralistic Universe*, published in 1909 as the outcome of the Hibbert Lectures given at Oxford University in 1908. In the preface to *The Meaning of Truth* he offers the following definition of his metaphysical outlook – which he termed "radical empiricism":

> Radical empiricism consists first of a postulate, next of a statement of fact, and finally of a generalized conclusion.
>
> The postulate is that the only things that shall be debatable among philosophers shall be things definable in terms of drawn from experience.
>
> The statement of fact is that the relations between things, conjunctive as well as disjunctive, are just as much matters of direct particular experience, neither more so nor less so, than the things themselves.
>
> The generalized conclusion is that therefore the parts of experience hold together from next to next by relations that are themselves parts of experience. The directly apprehended universe needs, in short, no extraneous trans-empirical connective support, but possesses in its own right a concatenated or continuous structure.[29]

Here James advocates a view of reality as a rich, concatenated process, neither totally unified nor wholly divided. Traditional metaphysics had continuously emphasized the importance of permanent substances, and the relative non-importance of change – the latter being termed merely accidental. But in a Jamesian outlook, as one scholar has noted, the static "subject–object duality is no longer to the point, for at both ends these terms are but abstract statements of actually dynamic processes."[30] In other words, the human self is not given as an original item in this process, but rather develops through time, via a series of interactions with experience. The present moment is vague, in the sense that it is not yet distinguished into the conscious self vis-à-vis the object which the self is conscious of. James tells the reader:

> [W]e must remember that no dualism of being represented and representing resides in the experience *per se*. In its pure state, or when isolated, there is no self-splitting of it into consciousness and what the consciousness is "of." Its subjectivity and objectivity are functional attributes solely, realized only when the experience is "taken" *i.e.*, talked-of, twice, considered along with its two differing contexts respectively, by a new retrospective experience, of which that whole past complication now forms the fresh content. The instant field of the present is at all times what I call the "pure" experience. It is only virtually or potentially either object or subject as yet.[31]

As the above quote makes evident, it is through language that the subject–object duality arises. Once arisen, however, human consciousness exhibits a curious stubbornness. The conscious self is, in a sense, embedded in language, and, to an extent, cut off from the primordial level of reality. The latter continues to evolve, with the result that all conceptual knowing, since it takes place through language, leaves something out, is incomplete, and essentially so. The "really real" is not only broader, vaguer than what is now known, it is broader than the knowable. Language, or reflection as such, cannot completely grasp the primordial, continuously exfoliating flux, which is never completely present, but always passing. To bring this out more clearly, James emphasizes the importance of the *affective* realm, where clear subject–object distinctions have not yet come into being. As he put it, experiences we term "*appreciations* . . . form an ambiguous sphere of being, belonging with emotion on the one hand, and having objective 'value' on the other, yet seeming not quite inner nor quite outer." An experience of a painful object is usually a painful experience; a perception of loneliness is a lonely perception, and so on. "Sometimes the adjective wanders as if uncertain where to fix itself. Shall we speak of seductive visions or visions of seductive things?" As we have seen, each present moment in experience, for James, as it drops into the past, is classified as consciousness or content, or both. The world of the affective or the prerational is more real, in the sense that it preserves the original given vagueness of experience. "With the affectional experiences . . . the relatively 'pure' condition lasts. In practical life no urgent need has yet arisen for deciding whether to treat them as rigorously mental or as rigorously physical facts. So they remain equivocal; and, as the world goes, their equivocality is one of their great conveniences."[32]

For James, then, the "really real" (not just consciousness anymore) is the fringe, the vague, the "more." Affectional experiences are more real than others to the extent that they preserve vagueness. Moreover, experiences do become classified as subjective or objective, conscious or content, or both. These distinctions come upon the scene, they are not primordial. They arise with and through language. This leads James to the realization that language, while necessary and important, is also limiting, when used incorrectly.

Throughout *A Pluralistic Universe* one finds indications on James's part that he thought reality more subtle than any formal system. At the very beginning he writes: "No philosophy can ever be anything but a summary sketch, a picture of the world in abridgment, a foreshortened birds-eye view of the perspective of events." And again, "A philosophy . . . must indeed be true, but that is the least of its requirements." Such a meta-theoretical outlook has an essential vagueness or open texture to it. The match-up between formal outlook and reality is not a completely neat one. There is room for possibility, for action.

> If we take the whole history of philosophy, the systems reduce themselves to a few main types which, under all the technical verbiage in which the ingenious intellect of man envelops them, are just so many visions, modes of feeling the whole push, and seeing the whole drift of life, forced on one by one's total character and experience, and on the whole *preferred* – there is no other truthful word – as one's best working attitude.[33]

In statements such as these, James has given advance notice of his metaphysical position. That position maintains that reality is not only broader than the known; it is broader than the knowable. Logic, while necessary, is not a sufficient description of reality. His rejection of the sufficiency of logic is strong and clear:

> For my own part, I have finally found myself compelled to give up the logic, fairly, squarely, and irrevocably. It has an imperishable use in human life, but that use is not to make us theoretically acquainted with the essential nature of reality. . . . Reality, life, experience, concreteness, immediacy, use what word you will, exceeds our logic, overflows and surrounds it. If you like to employ words eulogistically, as most men do, and so encourage confusion, you may say that reality obeys a higher logic, or enjoys a higher rationality. But I think that even eulogistic words should be used rather to distinguish than to commingle meanings, so I prefer bluntly to call reality if not irrational, then at least non-rational in its constitution – and by reality here I mean where things *happen*, all temporal reality without exception. I myself find no good warrant for even suspecting the existence of any reality of a higher determination than that distributed and strung-along and flowing sort of reality which we finite beings swim in. That is the sort of reality given us, and that is the sort with which logic is so incommensurable.[34]

In a more general fashion, James rejected an overly intellectual approach and held that language and concepts per se can only give us aspects of reality. They conceal in the very act of disclosing. James suggests that this overemphasis on intellectualism began as far back as Plato and Socrates, when concepts began to be used "privately as well as positively," that is, not only to define reality, but to exclude the undefinable.

In opposition to all this, he espouses a relational metaphysics. Each moment of experience is related positively and negatively, conjunctively and disjunctively, with a series of others, and indirectly with everything else. Important for our purposes here is James's clear delineation of a metaphysic wherein reality is broader than the known, and this is not simply a temporary problematic. "Thought deals . . . solely with surfaces. It can name the thickness of reality, but it cannot fathom it, and its insufficiency here is essential and permanent, not temporary." And again, "The whole process of life is due to life's violation of our logical axioms." What really exists for James "is not things made but things in the making." And this process cannot be completely grasped by language, concepts, or thought itself. Each passing moment is more complex than we have realized, more vague and multi-dimensional than our concepts can pick up. Even the very smallest pulse of experience possesses this common complexity, this vagueness.[35]

The Pragmatic Upshot

Pragmatism: A New Name for Some Old Ways of Thinking emerged as the result of a series of lectures James delivered at the Lowell Institute in Boston in 1906 and at Columbia University in 1907. In the Jamesian pragmatic theory of truth also, the concept of vagueness, with its dual aspects of richness and intensity, can serve as a focal point. To begin with, we should note that pragmatism for James was not just a theory of "meaning" as it was for Charles Sanders Peirce, but, rather, a theory of truth. There is an element of "urgency" in James's pragmatism, which includes as part of the "effect of an idea" what it will do for the person who believes it – that is, how it will actually change a person's relationship to and interaction with the unfinished universe of radical empiricism. Here it should be noted that James's epistemology is best taken as dependent upon a metaphysical system which, as we have seen, is not neutral in and of itself. Analogously, the method of pragmatism is not metaphysically neutral in nature, but rather assumes the existence of an uncertain universe, wherein meaning must still be made. The question in *Pragmatism* then is not: "Where/how does one find objectivity?" since James admits that this is not feasible. Rather, the question is, "How does one avoid subjectivity?"

What, then, is the pragmatic method, and how does it work? In *Pragmatism*, James asserts:

> To attain perfect clearness in our thought of an object . . . we need only consider what conceivable effects of a practical kind the object may involve – what sensations we are to expect from it, and what reactions we must prepare. Our conception of these effects, whether immediate or remote, is then for us the whole of our conception of the object, as far as that conception has positive significance at all.[36]

As the above quote indicates, the meaning of an idea is to be articulated operationally, in terms of its effects. An idea with no effects, or one of no consequence, would be declared meaningless. Any idea, in James's terms, must have its "cash-value" brought out; it must "make a difference." Furthermore, the fact that each and every idea is to be operationally defined asserts that a process is involved. An idea, or a theory, is a project, or hypothesis. In and of itself it is neither true nor false. It becomes true if it can be verified. "Truth," as James said, "*happens* to an idea. . . . Its verity *is* in fact an event, a process. . . . Its validity is the process of its validation."[37] Thought and action are involved together here. I do not *first* know that an idea is true *and then* act upon it. Rather, only insofar as I act on the idea as a plan do I become aware of its truth or falsity. Action, since it takes place in a context or a situation, is impossible at an exclusively private level; it must, in some sense, be public. But this is not the same as saying that all ideas must be objectively verified. Such a statement James could not make, since he constantly espoused a philosophy which maintained the efficacy of the human contribution.

On the one hand, pragmatism does emphasize the active role each of us plays in any theory of truth:

> What shall we call a thing anyhow? It seems quite arbitrary, for we carve out everything, just as we carve out constellations to suit our human purposes. . . . We break the flux of sensible reality into things . . . at our will. We create the subjects of our true as well as of our false propositions[;] . . . you can't weed out the human contribution.[38]

On the other hand, the very fact that all ideas are processes, and as such necessarily involve interpenetrant thought and action, reminds us that at the very least, ideas must be made public. Knowledge, while not objective, is more than subjective. Any private claim to truth will not be honored; only those which have been made public via action. This takes time. "Woe to him whose beliefs play fast and loose with the order which realities follow in his experience; they will lead him nowhere or else make false connections."[39]

The theory of truth advocated by James is intensive, but it is also extensive. The process of making an idea public is a continuous one and, more important, it is cumulative:

> Our knowledge grows in *spots* . . . and like grease spots, the spots spread. But we let them spread as little as possible: we keep unaltered as much of our old knowledge, as many of our old prejudices and beliefs, as we can. We patch and tinker more than

> we renew. The novelty soaks in; it stains the ancient mass; but it is also tinged by what absorbs it. Our past apperceives and co-operates; and in the new equilibrium in which each step forward in the process of learning terminates, it happens relatively seldom that the new fact is added *raw*. More usually it is embedded cooked, as one might say, or stewed down in the sauce of the old. New truths thus are resultants of new experiences and of old truths combined and mutually modifying one another.[40]

The process of making a difference, then, is not an atomistic day-to-day affair. Each and every moment of experience must take the past into account. Older truths are important; we must remain loyal to as many of them as possible. "New truth is always a go-between, a smoother-over of transitions. It marries old opinion to new fact, so as ever to show a minimum of jolt, a maximum of continuity." The picture of truth as presented in *Pragmatism* is one of an ever-shifting yet cumulative appropriation. Truth, defined as agreeable leading, "grafts itself onto previous truth, modifying it in the process." Always, however, in this vague situation, the notion of making a difference is seen as involving both extensity and intensity. The goal is to keep as much of the past as possible, while still dealing with the novelty and intensity of the present challenge.[41]

> Man's beliefs at any time are so much experience *funded*. . . . Truths emerge from facts; but they dip forward into facts again and add to them; which facts again create or reveal new truth (the word is indifferent) and so on indefinitely . . . The case is like a snowball's growth, due as it is to the distribution of the snow on the one hand, and to the successive pushes of the boys on the other, with these factors co-determining each other incessantly.[42]

In a line at the end of one of the essays in *Pragmatism*, "Pragmatism and Common Sense," James asks: "May there not after all be a possible ambiguity in truth?" Again here, as in *The Principles* and elsewhere, the importance of vagueness or ambiguity is affirmed. Truth is vaguer than any given formula because it is still in the making; as such, it receives its "final touches" via our decisions and choices. Truth involves our needs. It is vague because it is non-objective, but it remains cumulative. Pragmatism as a theory of truth is vague because it demands participation, and vague because it is still in the making.

Conclusion

As early as his 1879 essay "The Sentiment of Rationality," James tells us that the "bottom of being is logically opaque to us." Going further, he holds that we are afflicted with an "ontological wonder-sickness" such that "[o]ur mind is so wedded to the process of seeing an *other* beside every item of its experience, that when the notion of an absolute datum is presented to it, it goes through its usual procedure and remains pointing at the void beyond, as if in that lay further matter for contemplation."[43] This predilection to affirm the importance of the vague is one pervasive theme running through the life and works of this great philosopher and interdisciplinary thinker. It is to be found in his work on psychology, on religion, in metaphysics, and in epistemology. There are, no doubt, other ways to view James's thought. This one, however, gets at two cardinal aspects of his vision: the need to preserve the "thickness" or "fatness" of any given context; and the need to allow the self, fragile as it is, some minimal role to play in interacting with experience. Hopefully, this chapter will serve as a prod or "spur," inviting readers to "go beyond" and experience at first hand James's own vision of the universe.

Notes

1 Jacques Barzun, *A Stroll With William James* (New York: Harper and Row, 1983), p. 12. For an excellent biography of James, see Gay Wilson Allen, *William James* (New York: Viking Press, 1969). See also James William Anderson, "'The Worst Kind of Melancholy': William James in 1869," in Mark R. Schwehn, ed., *A William James Renaissance*, Harvard Library Bulletin, vol. XXX, no. 45, October 1982, pp. 371, 369. See also Ralph Barton Perry, *The Thought and Character of William James*, 2 vols. (Boston: Little, Brown and Company, 1935), vol. II, p. 672.

2 *The Letters of William James*, edited by his son Henry James, 2 vols. (Boston: The Atlantic Monthly Press, 1920), vol. I, pp. 95–6.

3 Perry, *The Thought and Character of William James*, vol. I, p. 322.

4 *The Letters of William James*, vol. I, pp. 147–8. Brackets indicate that the manuscript is doubtful.

5 Perry, *The Thought and Character of William James*, vol. II, p. 656.

6 William James, "The Will to Believe," in *The Will to Believe and Other Essays in Popular Philosophy* (New York: Longmans, Green and Co., 1927), pp. 3ff.

7 Ibid., p. 11.

8 William James, *The Principles of Psychology*, 2 vols. (New York: Dover Publications, 1972), vol. I, p. 225.

9 Ibid., p. 226.

10 Ibid., pp. 284–5.

11 Ibid., p. 285.

12 Ibid., pp. 285, 287.

13 Ibid., p. 139.

14 Jacques Barzun, "William James and the Clue to Art," in *The Energies of Art* (New York: Vintage Books, 1962), p. 320.

15 James, *The Principles of Psychology*, vol. I, p. 225.

16 Ibid., pp. 230ff., 234.

17 Ibid., p. 240.

18 Ibid., p. 239.

19 Ibid., p. 254.

20 William James, *The Varieties of Religious Experience* (New York: Longmans, Green and Company, 1914), p. 26. Hereafter referred to as VRE.

21 Ibid., pp. 453, 455.
22 Ibid., p. 35.
23 Ibid., pp. 483–4.
24 Ibid., p. 508.
25 Ibid., p. 459.
26 James, "The Will to Believe," p. 27. One could, of course, argue that for many people who are not religious, the universe is also a "Thou." See also VRE, p. 505.
27 VRE, pp. 209, 485.
28 Ibid., p. 358.
29 William James, *The Meaning of Truth* (Ann Arbor: University of Michigan Press, 1970), pp. xxxvi–xxxvii.
30 William James, "Essays in Radical Empiricism," in *Essays in Radical Empiricism and A Pluralistic Universe* (Gloucester, MA: Peter Smith, 1967), pp. 86ff. John J. McDermott, "To Be Human Is to Humanize: A Radically Empirical Aesthetic," in idem, *The Culture of Experience: Philosophical Essays in the American Grain* (New York: New York University Press, 1976), p. 32.
31 James, *Essays in Radical Empiricism*, p. 23.
32 Ibid., pp. 34, 35, 146.
33 William James, "A Pluralistic Universe," in *Essays in Radical Empiricism*, pp. 20–1.
34 Ibid., pp. 212–13.
35 Ibid., pp. 250, 257, 263.
36 James, *Pragmatism* (New York: Longmans, Green and Co., 1908), pp. 46–7.
37 Ibid., p. 201.
38 Ibid., pp. 253–4.
39 Ibid., p. 205.
40 Ibid., pp. 168–9.
41 Ibid., pp. 61, 241.
42 Ibid., pp. 224–6.
43 William James, "The Sentiment of Rationality," in *The Will to Believe*, p. 71.

Suggested reading

Primary sources

The Works of William James, ed. Frederick Burkhardt (Cambridge, MA: Harvard University Press, 1975–86). This critical edition includes the following texts:

Pragmatism. Introduction by H. Standish Thayer (1975).
The Meaning of Truth. Introduction by H. Standish Thayer (1975).
Essays in Radical Empiricism. Introduction by John J. McDermott (1976).
A Pluralistic Universe. Introduction by Richard Bernstein (1977).
Essays in Philosophy. Introduction by John J. McDermott (1978).
The Will to Believe. Introduction by Edward H. Madden (1979).
Some Problems of Philosophy. Introduction by Peter H. Hare (1979).
The Principles of Psychology, 3 vols. Introduction by Gerald Meyers and Rand B. Evans (1981).

Essays in Religion and Morality. Introduction by John J. McDermott (1982).
Talks to Teachers of Psychology. Introduction by Gerald E. Meyers (1983).
Essays in Psychology. Introduction by William R. Woodward (1983).
Psychology: Briefer Course. Introduction by Michael Sokal (1984).
The Varieties of Religious Experience. Introduction by John E. Smith (1985).
Essays in Physical Research. Introduction by Robert A. McDermott (1986).

The Writings of William James, ed. and with an introduction and annotated bibliography by John J. McDermott (Chicago: University of Chicago Press, 1977).

Secondary sources

Allen, Gay Wilson, *William James: A Biography* (New York: Viking Press, 1967).
Barzun, Jacques, *A Stroll With William James* (New York: Harper and Row, 1983).
Bjork, Daniel W., *William James: The Center of His Vision* (New York: Columbia University Press, 1988).
Fontinell, Eugene, *Self, God and Immortality: A Jamesian Investigation* (Philadelphia: Temple University Press, 1986).
Gavin, William J., *William James and the Reinstatement of the Vague* (Philadelphia: Temple University Press, 1992).
Myers, Gerald E., *William James: His Life and Thought* (New Haven: Yale University Press, 1986).
Perry, Ralph Barton, *The Thought and Character of William James*, 2 vols. (Boston: Little, Brown and Company, 1935).
Seigfried, Charlene Haddock, *Chaos and Context: A Study of William James* (Athens: Ohio University Press, 1978).
—— *William James's Radical Reconstruction of Philosophy* (Albany: State University of New York Press, 1990).
Simon, Linda, *Genuine Reality: A Life of William James* (New York: Harcourt Brace & Company, 1998).
Suckiel, Ellen K., *The Pragmatic Philosophy of William James* (Notre Dame: University of Notre Dame Press, 1982).
Wild, John, *The Radical Empiricism of William James* (New York, Doubleday, 1969).

Chapter 7

Josiah Royce, 1855–1916

Frank M. Oppenheim, SJ

Biography

Josiah Royce, philosopher, teacher, and public lecturer, who was born on November 20, 1855 in Grass Valley, California and died on September 14, 1916 in Cambridge, Massachusetts, strongly influenced twentieth-century philosophy in the United States. In his late career he integrated his distinctive form of idealism with a Peircean kind of realism and developed a unique religious philosophy of interpretation that pivoted upon the ideas of community, spirit, and process.

His parents, Josiah Royce, Sr., and Sarah Eleanor Bayliss Royce, were English-born immigrants to America, who became evangelical 49ers trekking to California. After being taught by his mother during childhood in Grass Valley, young Royce studied at San Francisco schools and did undergraduate work at the University of California, Berkeley. One year of literary and philosophical studies in Germany, plus two years of graduate studies at The John Hopkins University, led to his doctorate in philosophy in 1878. After teaching English composition at Berkeley for four years and marrying Katharine Head, he began in 1882 his 33-year philosophical career at Harvard. There he became a member of its "great department" in philosophy, along with William James, George Herbert Palmer, Hugo Münsterberg, and George Santayana. Royce had three sons, Christopher, Edward, and Stephen, of whom his promising first-born Christopher died as a mental invalid six years before Royce himself died.

Since Josiah Royce regarded his intellectual life as far more important than the story of his external life, a sketch of the high points in his intellectual development follows. He acknowledged his mother and three sisters as his first teachers of philosophy. As a lad and youth, he voraciously read the Bible, science, history, mathematics, literature, and philosophy. During his undergraduate years, the evolutionist Joseph LeConte and the poet Edward Rowland Sill strongly influenced him. The period from 1875 to 1883 determined his philosophical thinking. For then, his reading of J. S. Mill led him to become, as he later acknowledged, "a decidedly skeptical critical empiricist."[1] Yet his study of the German Romantic poets and of Kant, Fichte, and Schopenhauer soon counterbalanced the British influence. His Hopkins thesis, Berkeley research, and earliest teaching at Harvard gradually led him out of his pessimistic skepticism to the breakthrough that thereafter steadily oriented his philosophy. For, in January 1883, he reached his religious insight into the truth of an All-knowing Judge. He soon published this first maximal insight in *The Religious Aspect of Philosophy* (1885). In 1891, his reading of Ernst Schroeder's *Algebra der Logik* led him to a major insight that only by an infinite self-reflective series could the inner logic of the idea of reality be fittingly represented.

Thanks to George H. Howison's correction, Royce revised his notion of the individual into that of a beloved "object of exclusive interest," a notion he published in *The Conception of God* (1897). Guided by this bearing, Royce experienced Charles Peirce's Cambridge Conferences of 1898 as epoch-marking, since "they started me on such new tracks."[2] Integrating Peirce's ideas of continuity, individuality, infinity, system, and the logic of relatives into his own idea of individuality, Royce broke through to his second maximal insight, his "Fourth and Final Conception of Being." Historically, being had three previous conceptions: the extreme realists conceived being as totally independent of knowing, while mystics conceived it as totally identical with knowing, and critical rationalists conceived it as lying in the validity of true propositions. Royce synthesized the valid features of the realist, mystical, and critical rationalist conceptions of being but transcended them through his interpretation that the being of this world and of each of its individuals could only be approached through appreciating them as beloved objects of exclusive interest. As the first American to deliver a series of Gifford Lectures at Edinburgh University, Royce presented in them this second maximal insight of his intellectual career, one that was soon published in his middle-period masterpiece, *The World and the Individual* (1899–1901).

Thereafter, Royce's mind branched into two diverse but complementary interests: ethics and logic. His renewed focus on ethics blossomed in another major insight concerning *loyalty*. This he defined with emphasis as "*the Will to Believe in something eternal, and to express that belief in the practical life of a human being.*"[3] His *Philosophy of Loyalty* (1908) featured as his supreme ethical norm "being loyal to universal loyalty" – that is, being loyal to the moral growth of every human self. If loyalty reaches this "reflective" form, it becomes "an essentially self-sustaining process, that . . . becomes truly universal and truly individual."[4] Meanwhile, his renewed focus on logic led him in 1910 to create his significant *Principles of Logic*. This work featured his comprehensive "System *Sigma*" which emphasized a human self's "modes of action."

After a stroke in early February 1912, a recuperating Royce, temporarily relieved from teaching, carefully compared and contrasted the early, middle, and late published writings of "our American logician," Charles Peirce. In this way Royce grasped Peirce's theories of signs, interpretation, and his three categories far more profoundly than previously. This third maximal insight and his own creative appreciation of how the future would impact on Christianity led to his greatest masterpiece, *The Problem of Christianity* (1913). This Peircean insight also governed his later articles, "Mind," "Negation," and "Order," as well as his final *The Hope of the Great Community* (*HGC*), written amidst a deteriorating World War I. Royce acknowledged that during these final years the ideas of community and spirit were working daily in his mind, along with that of process, and increasingly taking on a new vitality and deeper significance. He wrote to a friend: "I do not believe that I ever told my tale as fully, or with the same approach to the far-off goal of saying sometime something that might prove helpful to students of idealism, as in the *Problem of Christianity*."[5] On September 14, 1916, he died in his Cambridge home.

The Issues Royce Confronted

Experience

Philosophy must start from experience. Yet in addition to its mere presence, experience possesses meaning.[6] Royce started from his early experience of error. From this base he deduced the conditions making actual error possible. Throughout his life he used illustrations in his writings, much as Charles Peirce used existential graphs, to give an experiential basis to his reflections. He also found that self-consciousness cannot arise without an experience of some other mind that offers contrasting ideas to one's own. That is, he found that no I-awareness arose without a You-awareness.

His experience with, and fervent belief in the philosophical fertility of the problem of evil led him to grapple with this problem so persistently throughout his career that it constituted a central artery in the body of his thought. Taught by misunderstandings and other tragedies in his own life, he became convinced of the urgent needs to reject evil resolutely and to dedicate oneself wholeheartedly to a genuine community and its cause as something greater than oneself. These encounters with evil taught him that one needed to open oneself affirmatively toward the unity of the whole – whether called the Absolute or God or the Universal Community – and in this way contact the *norm of genuineness.*

In his middle period, he placed co-equal primacy on an idea as a plan of action and on its external meaning. The external meaning keeps contrasting with a finite internal meaning and calls for the latter's fuller embodiment, much as one finds in one's desire to sing a melody. That experience lay both in a human self's internal yearning or purposing and in its limited finite embodiments.

Through the concrete experiences of his seminar in scientific methodology, Royce came in his final period to feel the pulse of genuine community life. Having chosen community as his ruling category, he emphasized the need to correct

William James's *Varieties of Religious Experience* from its excessively individualistic emphasis and from James's focus on only extraordinary cases of religious experience. By contrast, the emphasis of the late Royce fell on the social and the ordinary in religious experience. His late philosophy of religion grew out of his experiences of the social sources of religion *and* from that font which is the unique individual.

During World War I, Royce's experience of man's fallen state, instanced in Germany's treason against humankind, led him to prophetic utterance. His experience of atoning graces won by brave soldiers killed and innocent war victims slain led to his philosophy of hope (see *HGC*). Especially in his final period, Royce's empiricism balanced realism and idealism by transcending both in an interpretive process propelled by realistic contrast effects and guided by the logos-spirit. In all these ways Royce started from meaningful experience and strove to keep the idea central even as he strained "*to be as realistic as we can*."[7]

The religious

Philosophy, as humankind's search for wisdom, must have a religious aspect. Amid an increasingly materialistic and secularist culture, Royce was bold enough to keep witnessing that philosophy must manifest a religious aspect. While respecting his naturalistic counterparts, he held that a philosophy without God is not a striving for ultimate wisdom.

In his early period, his philosophical conversion from a critical skepticism to a religious orientation occurred as follows. By mining through the conditions for the possibility of error, Royce eventually came to see that whether one's opinion is true or false, one is here involved in a teleological situation which brings one's thought of the moment into contact with a type of consciousness which is not the merely human type. This was the late Royce's way of describing what he first found in 1883: the unavoidable truth that an all-knower lives as the real norm for all fallible human assertions. Without that actually real norm, all human assertions could be neither true nor false and, as assertions, could not even reach the level of meaningfulness. Such was Royce's main claim in *The Religious Aspect of Philosophy.*

At the turn of the century, Royce wrote that the human "Self . . . has a meaning that seeks unity with God only through the temporal attainment of goals in a series of successive deeds."[8] And this self "possesses individuality . . . in God and for God."[9] Led by the exact reasoning that underlay the modern theory of infinite assemblages, Royce found that the human self, although always finite and partial in this world, still lives in God and reflects God's life, since, as Royce emphasized, we "*need not conceive the eternal Ethical Individual, however partial he may be, as in any sense less in the grace of complication of his activity or in the multitude of his acts of will than is the Absolute*."[10] Such was the middle Royce's way of emphasizing the "union of God and man."

By 1908, Royce made clear that the human self's act of authentic loyalty created a union with God in the "religion of loyalty." By 1912, Royce proclaimed one of his distinctive themes, "the religious mission of sorrow"; namely, that if one's sufferings are interpreted transformatively as sorrows, then the sorrowing human self experiences a light whereby he or she sees the god-like glory of persevering love. The following year Royce mined Christianity's distinctive contributions to the religious aspect of philosophy. He refined the key Christian ideas of community, the lost state of the individual detached from community, of the atoning process and finally of grace. Grace integrates these "three most central ideas" of Christianity and in its nisus for fuller wisdom creates the Beloved Community.[11]

Logically, Royce based the human self's union with the logos-spirit upon the "relation of belonging" (the *epsilon* relation). Existentially, he based this union on the imperative, borrowed from the apostle Paul, to "pray to interpret," since God is the divine Spirit of Interpretation, and the divine Will to Interpret. Such prayer opens up the human self to the spirit's light and love so that it can function as a graced member in a genuine community. Little wonder, then, that Royce found that this "praying to interpret" in germ "contains the whole meaning of the office, both of philosophy (as a search for wisdom) and of religion."[12] Such praying revealed the deep divine spark in Royce, who sought in practice to live out his way of being open to the gift of divine wisdom, to the spirit of discerning spirits, and to the power of the Word of God as the "sword of the Spirit." All these diverse approaches to the religious aspect of philosophy culminated in his final year's emphasis on the religious aspect of *hope* in the Great Community (see *HGC*). Tested by the tragedies of World War I, this hope waited for the dawning of a better human community, one more purified and in closer touch with the entire processing cosmos of all minded and non-minded beings and guided by the universal logos-spirit of the universal community.

Community

For sound philosophizing, the use of the idea of community is indispensable. Royce held that the idea of community was as fundamental as the idea of any unique individual. Hence, in his metaphysics and ethics, he insisted on balancing community and individual. For him, the genuine community, although on a different level of reality and consciousness than that of individuals, is a person like the human individual, with a personal life, mind, and will of its own. Two corollaries followed: (1) his fundamental doctrine of the *two levels* of reality and of consciousness – namely: "Man the individual" and "Man the Community";[13] and (2) his late thesis that reality, truth, and knowledge are *inescapably social*.[14]

Accordingly, in his ethics he strove to balance genuine individualism with genuine loyalty and to discern the misleading spirits behind phony individualisms and phony loyalties. For instance, he insisted on this judicious balancing as follows. A community could be fittingly developed only if moral individuals reached moral maturity. On balance, however, individuals could become morally mature only to the extent that their genuine community called forth and required greater moral maturity from them. At the same time, however, the community empowered their free self-determination to strive toward greater moral maturity by becoming ever more unique individual members.

Interpretation

A contemporary theory of knowledge must recognize interpretation as humankind's most fundamental way of knowing. This requires a shift from the traditional view of knowing as a subject–object (dyadic) relationship which employs perceptions or conceptions or combinations of both to the new Peircean view of knowing presented as an interpretational (triadic) process between sign-sender, sign-mediator (or interpreter), and sign-receiver.

As a philosopher of life, Royce insisted that philosophers need to shift to interpretive knowing if they aim to deal adequately with life in a way marked by sensitivity, docility, and initiative. That is, to deal adequately with the objects of interpretation – being, the inner life of other selves, temporal process, significant deeds, signs, minds, communities, etc. – a human knower must be sensitive enough to be open to the manifold of empirical riches. Secondly, a human knower must remain open or docile to the mysterious process of this impacting sign-laden manifold, both at the lower biological level and even more so at the levels of mind and spirit. Finally, such a knower needs to exercise enough free initiative to reverence its own unique way of living and the countless, differently unique ways of action in the billions of interpreting minds around it. For this, knowing through static percepts and concepts must prove inadequate, and only the process of interpretive knowing can suffice.

Logos-spirit

In philosophy, the logos-spirit must play a fundamental role, as interpreter of the universe. The problem experienced by what religious consciousness has called the Holy Spirit became a starting point for the late Royce. For he saw that in the Fourth Gospel's doctrine of the logos-spirit "lies the really central idea of any distinctively Christian (rather than merely Greek) metaphysics."[15] So Royce mined what he called this most neglected, yet in many ways the most significant, article of the Christian creed: "I believe in the Holy Ghost, the Holy Catholic Church, the communion of saints."[16] The metaphysical gold he unearthed and purified from this ore was that this Spirit invites and calls forward all human communities and all their minded members, whether living in them or alienated from them. Moreover, Royce found no better way to conceive the divine nature than by alternately musing on it as the "Community of Interpretation" and above all as the spirit-interpreter "who interprets all to all, and each individual to the world, and the world of spirits to each individual."[17]

Developments that Royce Fostered

Merely listing a baker's dozen of such developments must here suffice.

1 By indicating the importance of Peirce's thought early on and by becoming the chief early expositor and applier of Peirce's leading ideas, Royce became the grandfather of the contemporary Peircean movement in philosophy.
2 Without downplaying religious feelings, Royce rightly counterbalanced James's excessive individualism in the *Varieties* and his bypassing of the fact that non-illusory religious experience requires reasonably reliable doctrine.
3 In relation both to John Dewey's instrumentalism and to starkly limited human selves' encounter with the dire problem of evil, Royce offered a strong counter-witness. He held that in this contest with evil, humans need even more to trust courageously and patiently in an all-knowing interpretive deliverer than primarily to rely on self-confident, social, human intelligence to control their natural and cultural environments. However much the latter holds a second-place priority, Dewey had ranked it primary.
4 Counteracting a culture of militant secularism, Royce steadily witnessed to a refined rational interpretation of the truth that the all-knower is most real.
5 He also emphasized that to philosophize adequately both a deep appreciation of the experience basic to common sense and the sciences as well as a masterful grasp of the history of philosophy are indispensable.
6 As another indispensable ingredient for philosophizing, he kept calling for a truly critical discernment of an adequate and genuine interpretation of reality, what he referred to as the "Fourth and Final Interpretation of Being."
7 He pioneered in researching the interface between formal logic and the elements of geometry.
8 He underscored the need for a harmony of logics – still mostly unachieved – among a pluralism of logics that included those of common sense, of passion, and of will in union with the logics of the Aristotelian tradition and of the many newer fields of symbolic logic.
9 He integrated the central ethical ideas of freedom, goodness, and duty into a doctrine of the ethical life which requires a loyal commitment to respect and promote genuine loyalty wherever found.
10 To reach a humanly adequate knowledge of this unique universe and of its unique individual members, he designed his distinctive "relational form of the ontological argument," quite unlike Anselm's argument.[18]
11 By his emphases on language and especially on the social functions of language, he helped seed the movement toward linguistic analysis, much as did the late Wittgenstein after him.

12 Counteracting many philosophers' tendency to disregard the Bible's hints of wisdom, Royce critically refined and spoke up for Americans' widespread, common-sense, evangelical tradition, even as he purified and simplified it.
13 Finally, by synthesizing Christianity's most central ideas with those of Peirce, he transformed traditional idealism into his distinctively unique form of idealism, open as far as possible to realism, based on a community of interpretation, and animated by the logos-spirit.

The Chief Significance of Royce's Mature Work

The philosophy of moral and religious life

The empiricist Royce based his late philosophy on commonly experienced and carefully described motives, interests, instincts, and ideals. In this way he engaged in what Peirce called "phenomenology," the first of the philosophical knowledges in the Peircean division of the sciences of research.

Royce studied the life of minded selves – their psychology, logic, and ethics – and especially either their "life in the unity of the Spirit" or their existence as "morally detached" from that unity. He focused on such conscious life at its individual and communal levels, pinpointing conditions for the development or the decline of both moral individual self-consciousness or moral community self-consciousness. The latter could grow toward ever greater genuineness or degenerate retrogressively even into a "community of hate."

As a condition for self-conscious life, Royce insisted on social and temporal consciousness. Just as there is no ego without an alter, there is no "I" without a "you." Similarly, the input of memory and expectation enriches one's present consciousness. Hence, just as there is no awareness of oneself in the here and now without some awareness of one's past and future selves, so there are never fewer than three selves in one's present awareness: one's past, present, and future selves joined in living communication with each other. Considerations like these led to Royce's late conception of every self as a dynamic community and every community as a living self or "person."

This human self – now communally structured both socially and temporally – rises to moral life through a transformation out of a state of alienation from society into authentic loyalty to a genuine community. To this self, the community's leader or some other outstanding member manifests "life in the unity of the spirit."

If this self is to reach and grow still further into religious life, it must be continuously lifted out of its self-centered aggressiveness or self-centered withdrawal from community. This requires a deliverer who, by increasing loyalty, leads this self through a patient transformation of its sufferings into truth-revealing sorrows so that it opens itself to experience a life of loving loyalty in the unity of the spirit. In this genuine community of truly loyal selves, it becomes like them, open to the call of the universal community and its guiding interpreter spirit. Such is a glimpse of Royce's philosophy of life.

Community: the ruling category of Royce's late philosophy

"Life in the unity of the spirit" lies in the flow of communication between genuinely loyal community members who are united in a generally orderly process of serially interpreting signs. This process is mediated and served by some "spirit of interpretation." Both in his *Studies in Good and Evil* and especially in *The Problem of Christianity*, Royce stressed the social rise of mind and the function of language in the genesis and development of minded beings. He not only became an advocate of a careful history of philosophy as a centuries-long community enterprise, but especially in his final years often communed with those minded beings who led this community of philosophers. Sometimes his serving of a broader community of knowers brought him mental bruises. For instance, regarding the history of the "conquest" of California, he raised the standard of historical truth against the popular Captain John Frémont. Again, regarding an accurate interpretation of Hegel, he insisted on the standard of philosophical truth against a well-meaning but quixotic Francis E. Abbot.

His explicit use of the idea of community became prominent as he closed his *Sources of Religious Insight* and especially throughout *The Problem of Christianity.* Royce's idea of a community embodying itself in companies of committed human selves supplied him with a front line of attack against widespread nominalism. It also led him in his final years to undergird his middle period's logical approach to metaphysics with his newly developed and far-reaching social approach to metaphysics. By means of the latter approach he underscored how metaphysically indispensable it was to employ a social approach to reality, knowledge, and truth.

Reality, to be reality, had to be socially related to a mind that made true judgments about it, thus forming a "community of interpretation." Knowledge, to be knowledge, had to be the fruit of at least three minds consenting truly about some shared reality. Truth, to be truth, had to arise from that community-forming, confirming contact which a finite mind has – or finite minds have – with the all-knowing mind.

From this social approach to metaphysics logically flowed the late Royce's more widely known doctrine about the growth of community consciousness and communal life. This doctrine sets down three conditions for the development of community consciousness and then three degrees of ascending quality in such consciousness.

The first condition requires a potential community member to intentionally extend his consciousness to identify with some common, idealized, past and future events, deeds or persons. This starts the creation of a "community of memory and hope." The second condition requires each member to communicate freely with other members about these common idealized past and future events, deeds or persons. The third requires that at the affective level they come to feel almost identically the same way about these shared events, deeds, or persons. Through these three steps, the first degree of their community consciousness is constituted.

Yet such communal consciousness (initiated by idealized self-extensions, based on shared communication, and appreciated in feeling almost identically by all members), can be found even in pirate bands and the Mafia. How can it be transformed into *genuine* community consciousness, the second degree? Royce replied that both the community and each member need to undergo a moral conversion which starts with a loyal commitment to "the highest loyalty . . . the cause of universal loyalty."[19] This classic Roycean maxim means that each adopts a resolute will to promote the authentic moral growth of everyone in the world, starting with oneself. Such a transformation of will, or moral conversion, requires that members be influenced by the life of a "Beloved (or graced) Community" in three basic ways. First, each member is led to a mutual understanding of the diverse and reciprocally needed roles of the community's other members. Secondly, each member identifies himself by truly recognizing other members and the community itself as "parts of their own life." Finally, each member accepts and is accepted by other members *as* members of the community – that is, as persons belonging to it. This acceptance embraces one's own and all other members' warts and wrinkles as well as their positive qualities. To maintain this mutual acceptance in a genuine way without pretense probably constitutes the most challenging requirement among these three Roycean prerequisites for the second degree of genuine community consciousness.

As communities actually grow in the number of their members, genuine understanding of so many members' diverse roles becomes impossible for limited human-minded beings. So, for Royce, the supreme prerequisite for creating the third qualitative degree of genuine community consciousness lay in a gift from above. This gift consists in a loving loyalty both toward the universe as a whole – since each human self needs to be led to "fall in love with the world"[20] – and also, upon this basis, to commit oneself practically and wholeheartedly to some particular community. The latter lives as a communal-minded being which one adopts as one's own cause. Without this gift of genuinely loving loyalty, which comes from the logos-spirit and is mediated through some beloved community, this moral transformation of oneself from a "morally detached individual" into a genuinely loving and loyal member of an authentic community cannot take place. Such then is one approach to the late Royce's view of community in which a minded interpreter operates at the communal and the individual levels.

Royce's focus on norms

Logico-mathematical norm Royce loved and revered that common-sense logic used by ordinary folk. Yet more importantly, he knew that a "logic of passion" and a "logic of the will" with their "modes of action" were needed to bring a human self to commit oneself to a community and its cause. These logics of passion and of will supplied the foundation for his doctrines of genuine loyalty and reason-guided voluntarism.

From 1902 to 1905 Royce engaged in what amounted to a tutorial in higher logic directed by Peirce via a correspondence course. Royce published the results in a 1905 article that explored the link between logic and geometry by tracing the latter's foundations in logic. Additionally, in 1908, Royce explored the informal logic at work in the three motives – subjective, instrumental, and objective – required for an adequate theory of truth. Eventually he generated a fundamental logical program called System *Sigma* and created his most significant logical work, *The Principles of Logic*, written in 1910.

More specifically, Royce's logic found its practical tool in his frequently used "Reflective Method." Developed upon a Socratic basis, this method lay in discovering performatory contradictions which reveal to an interpreter certain truths that are undeniable and absolute. By trying to deny these truths and finding that they reinstate themselves in the very process of attempting to deny them, this method uncovers only a few most basic truths. For instance, let us try to affirm that there is a final prime number, or try to deny Descartes' *Cogito, ergo sum.* If either effort is carried out searchingly, we soon experience a profound inner contradiction. Or let us try to affirm that the time-process has an end or can be reversed. Or again, try to deny that humans can make universal judgments.

Royce's 1912 "Peircean insight" transformed these studies into a logic of interpretive knowing that both employed and transcended perceptual and conceptual cognitions by using Peirce's theory of signs and his three categories. Yet in Royce's hands this theory of knowing was guided by Royce's unique interpretation of being and then applied in an original way to metaphysics and philosophy of religion in ways Peirce never attempted. Empowered with his deepened grasp of Peirce's theory of interpretation, Royce developed his logic still further to undergird his *Problem of Christianity* with a frequently unnoticed foundation, the relation of "belonging." That same year he published "An Extension of the Algebra of Logic" in the *Journal of Philosophy.* In 1914, again thanks to Peirce, Royce became even more expert in the logic of statistical reasoning – a form of logic he interwove with the logics involved in mechanical and historical reasoning.

During these final years, Royce offered his "Seminary in Logic," concerned with the comparative methods of scientific inquiry. Not just graduate students, but also Harvard professors from the various disciplines took part in these meetings to render explicit the logic of their different researches. Serving as mediator of these interchanges, Royce found here his "best concrete instance of the life of a community."[21]

Little wonder, then, that in the final year of his life he described to his colleagues his style of thinking as:

> a fondness for defining, for articulating, and for expounding the perfectly real, concrete, and literal life of what we idealists call the "spirit," in a sense which is indeed

> Pauline, but not merely mystical, super-individual; not merely romantic, difficult to understand, but perfectly capable of exact and logical statement.[22]

Unfortunately, however, Royce's work in logic and mathematics is often overlooked and has been published only partially (see *Royce's Logical Essays*). Even in its published form, Royce's logic commands attention, while in its unpublished form it constitutes what C. I. Lewis, one of Royce's students and an eminent logician himself, described as an unexplored continent of treasure hidden in Royce's logical papers in the Harvard Archives. His published work – both logical essays and works on topics other than logic – are undergirded by a surprising synthesis of informal logic, traditional formal logic, and a vast variety of the different fields of symbolic logic.

Ethical norm and Royce's ethics The final decade of Royce's moral thought, starting from his preparations for *The Philosophy of Loyalty*, only advanced his process of ever further clarification and development of his ethical ideal and ideas. His career-long employ of the ethical norms of autonomy, goodness, and duty – which he called the "three leading ethical ideas"[23] – has been detailed by me in a recent work, *Royce's Mature Ethics.*

Royce's late ethics called for a radical personal transformation, effected by the individual and the spirit of loyalty. It led one out of an exaggerated self-centeredness and into a wholehearted commitment to being "loyal to universal loyalty." This commitment called the genuinely loyal self to discern between authentic and phoney spirits of loyalty and individualism. The genuineness of this ethical life was normed by the transformed loyalist's appeal to, and confirmation by, the righteously ruling logos-spirit of the universal community of interpretation. If a human self did not belong to that spirit, if logically it lacked an *epsilon* relation to it, then a person's ethical life had to be at least crippled, if not intrinsically corrupted by unilateral self-aggressiveness or fearful withdrawal from a challenging environment.[24]

Centrally, then, genuine loyalty emphasized the *need to balance* genuine loyalty with genuine individualism. It also called one to struggle against various disloyal (or traitorous) tendencies, especially those individualisms not balanced by service to communities. Although Royce kept aware of the mysteries and dangers of loyalty at its different levels and in its various forms – whether genuine, or inadequate, or even corruptive – he focused principally on a loving loyalty toward a community and its members, made genuine by an openness to the universal community of all minded beings.

Aesthetic norm Confessing his muteness in the presence of beauty, a more than usually shy Royce never fully developed a philosophy of beauty. Yet he lived as a lover of music and poetry, grew increasingly committed to the role of aesthetics in human appreciations and choices, and recognized beauty as a source of religious insight. He asserted:

> love shows its glory as love only by its conquest over the doubts and estrangements, the absences and the misunderstandings, the griefs and the loneliness, that love glorifies with its light amidst all their tragedy. In a world where there was no such consciousness as death suggests to us mortals, love would never consciously know the wealth and the faithfulness of its own deathless meaning.[25]

Thus he found that art "in its own way often gives us brief glimpses of the eternal order" and "delights to display to us all this dignity of sorrow."[26] In brief, then, Royce was fulfilling the dying Peirce's desire to insist on the fruitfulness of reasoning by the "exaltation of *beauty, duty, or truth.*"[27]

Royce's distinctive theory of knowledge

The late Royce's theory of knowledge pivoted on his clarifications of interpretation, mind, and truth. He ranked his Peirce-inspired notion of interpretation as the fullest and most basic human way of knowing. It relied on materials supplied by perception and conception, yet entered appreciatively into minded beings and the signs they process. In this process, a sign-sending mind directs some communication, which an attuned mediator (or interpreter) modifies accurately, to fit the needs and dispositions of the sign-receiver. Unless accidentally interrupted, this process goes on indefinitely by its own nature, and grows in multiple ways.

Royce's late idea of "mind" is indispensable for an individual and community who interpret. As mentioned, he interpreted both individuals and communities as "persons" or "minds." For him a mind lives not only as an essentially social and serially developing reality, but also as a reality that is essentially both a unique individual *and* a community. Its sign-senders, sign-interpreters and sign-receivers engage in their various modes of action that constitute the process of interpretation. Accordingly, the social nature of reality ultimately lies in the process of these social interpretive actions which bring contrasting parts of truth into growing coherence, thanks to the interpreter spirit's attractive guidance. Hence, if from this progressively realized community of interpreting minded beings one were to focus exclusively upon either reality or knowledge or truth, each member of this inseparable triad would suffocate from lack of relationships to the other members and thus dwindle into insignificance. Such is the importance of Royce's social approach to mind and consequently to his theory of knowledge. For to be knowledge, knowledge has to be the fruit of three minded beings consenting truly about some shared reality.

Similarly, to be true, truth has to arise from the confirming and community-forming contact which finite minds have with the all-knowing mind. So in Royce's late theory of truth, he showed that to reach truth, one had to employ more motives than are employed by the subjectivist or mere pragmatist, although their distinctive motives are indispensable. The subjectivist is interested in truth insofar as it fits his own uniqueness. The pragmatist is interested in truth insofar as it "works" or has effective consequences. For an adequate theory of truth, however, Royce insisted on adding to these two motives a third motive: that of a thoroughgoing objectivity. This objectivity lives in a thinker's love of, and quest for, truth and in the scientific conscience of hearers disciplined by the search for a more accurate and richer approach to a fuller grasp of truth. By stressing this third motive, Royce buttressed both the operative presence of a few absolutely constant truths and the absolute objectivity of truth against subjectivists and mere pragmatists.

Royce's distinctive metaphysics

Royce insisted that one's conception (or, better, interpretation) of being reach beyond three historical conceptions: (1) beyond the extreme realists' total independence of an object from the knower; (2) beyond the philosophical mystics' total identification of the knowing subject with being; and (3) beyond the sophisticated critical rationalists' settling on the validity of verifiable propositions as the closest humans can get to this world's unique being. Instead, Royce called thinkers to a fourth and final interpretation of being that, through a loving loyalty to this world, appreciated both its unique actuality and all its unique individuals. This fourth interpretation of being was indispensable for apprehending the truth of the reality of the universe's interpreter spirit. The conditions for the possibility of actual error included an all-knowing mind which grasped and bridged the gap between the finite knower's intent of an object and his mistaken judgment about it. The all-interpreter knows both the true judgment about this object and its own judgment of this finite knower's judging as mistaken.

This often misunderstood argument to the universal consciousness became the distinctive and neuralgic point of Royce's entire philosophy. It retained its central and constant bearing throughout all his intellectual developments after 1883. For Royce kept expressing this argument via different approaches to increase both his own and others' grasp of its central nerve. Even as late as his *Metaphysics* of 1915–16, he countered those who tended to identify truth with verifiability by asking what makes a judgment true when no human verification occurs. There he also created his "relational form of the ontological argument," unlike Anselm's, to render explicit the role which a grasp of this universe's uniqueness plays in his argument to an all-knower.

Royce's maximal insights

Royce acknowledged that as a youth he had first been driven to philosophy by religious problems. His *religious insight*, a first maximal insight, intensified his early interest in religious problems and the philosophy of religion. It led him to set his early period of philosophizing first within the context of an all-knower, then, after

1892, within that of an all-experiencer (whose life throbbed with willing and feeling as well as knowing), and finally, after 1912, within the context of an universal interpreter-spirit.

This religious insight surfaced in his middle period treatment of "The Union of God and Man" in *The World and the Individual.* By 1910–11, Royce approached a general philosophy of religion from a unique perspective. For in his *Sources of Religious Insight*, he focused not on various religions' creeds, codes, or cults, but on the individual self's experiential fonts that lead to some awareness of divine deliverance. In contrast to William James's thrust in *The Varieties of Religious Experience*, such an awareness arises authentically only if one commits oneself loyally to a genuine community. For, with Royce, religion finds its central nerve in the "religion of loyalty" and culminates in the life-giving activity of atonement. Unfortunately, Royce's *Sources of Religious Insight* remains unduly neglected even though he witnessed that it "contains the whole sense of me in a brief compass."

He soon applied both his religious insight, as freshly interpreted in the *Sources*, and Peirce's principles of interpretation to the specific religion of Christianity. The result was his late masterpiece, *The Problem of Christianity.* Theoretically, it produced a new triadic theory of knowing that employed interpretation and a "Community of Interpretation" as its hallmarks. Practically, it produced powerful resources for Christian ecumenism and interreligious dialogue.

Royce's middle period maximal insight into *individuality* and *individuation*, viewed as ethical realities, consisted in recognizing that individuals are "affective objects of exclusive interest," a "beloved this and no other." This interest creates and individuates an object so that the resulting individual exists only in a social situation. For the two decades stretching from the dawn of this second maximal insight in 1896 until his death, Royce continued to refine and sharpen its contours. He was convinced that individuality arises only through some subject's social relationship of valuation toward some other.

Individuality lay for Royce not in a metaphysical category (as in Aquinas and Scotus) but in an ethical reality which required the morally fitting affective and social ingredients. Royce's thesis that "in our present form of human consciousness, the true Self of any individual man is not a datum, but an ideal" may strike many as odd on first hearing it.[28] Yet Royce, concurring with Peirce, held that finite human knowers approach this ideal but never fully comprehend its mysterious reality. One must persistently emphasize this ideal to avoid slipping into various kinds of pseudo-selves. These latter keep a human self from further realizing her own unique plan of life which should guide the never-completed creation of her true self in the present life.

Royce crystalized his view through three statements.[29] To be genuine, one's ideal self must possess "true rationality of aim"; namely, "the purpose to find for your self just your own place in God's world, and to fill that place, as nobody else can fill it." Royce emphasized his sole ground for asserting this; namely, that "*precisely in so far as you know the world as one world, and intend your place in that one world to be unique, God's will is consciously expressed.*" Accordingly, Royce stated that his "theory of the Self assigns to it [the Self] the character of the Free Individual but maintains that this character belongs to it in its true relation to God." Here Royce transmuted his indispensable relation of belonging (the *epsilon* relation) into an ethico-religious requisite for true individuality. So, his theory disallows two things: that any authentic human self be hermetically sealed off from God, and that it pretend to live in total independence from Him. The latter theory would propose a radically false view of the human self and thus violate one's genuine individuality. Instead, Royce asserted:

> Individuality is a category of the satisfied will. . . . [Yet] for us creatures of fragmentary consciousness, and of dissatisfied will, as we here in the temporal order are, the individuality of all things remains a postulate, constitutes the central mystery of Being, and is rather the object that our exclusive affections seek, that our ethical consciousness demands, that love presupposes, than any object which we in our finitude ever attain.[30]

The late Royce's insight into *community* constituted his third maximal insight. For him, community is a living and life-giving process of triadic interpretation whose life is animated and guided by a "spirit of interpretation" and whose unique turning points are interpreting minded beings. Hence, he insisted that "the generalized theory of an ideal society," or of community as an interpretive process of minded beings, had to be the metaphysical system needed to define the real world of interpretation.

Royce found the idea of community dawning more clearly in his thought during his final years. His consequent choice of community as the ruling category of his late philosophy can be integrated into a wider context by saying that while the late Royce's ruling category was community, his ruling process was temporal continuity, and his ruling dynamism or life-source was the logos-spirit. With community as his ruling category, the late Royce developed his social approach to metaphysics, as already indicated.

Notes

1 *Metaphysics* (*Metaph.*) – stenographic report of Royce's last course in metaphysics, 1915–16 (Albany: SUNY Press, 1998), p. 80.
2 *The Letters of Josiah Royce* (*LJR*), ed. John Clendenning (Chicago: University of Chicago Press, 1970), p. 422.
3 *The Philosophy of Loyalty* (*PL*) (New York: Macmillan, 1908), p. 357.
4 *LJR*, p. 533.
5 Ibid., p. 647.
6 *The World and the Individual* (*WI*), 2 vols. (New York: Macmillan, 1899–1901), vol. 1, pp. 285–8.
7 *Metaph.*, p. 255.
8 *WI*, 2: 428.

9 Ibid., p. 433.
10 Ibid., pp. 451–2.
11 *The Problem of Christianity* (*PC*), 2 vols. (New York: Macmillan, 1913). Single-volume paperback reprint with John E. Smith's introduction and Frank M. Oppenheim's foreword and revised indices (Washington, DC: The Catholic University of America Press, 2001), p. 70.
12 Ibid., p. 319.
13 Ibid., pp. 218–20.
14 *Metaph.*, pp. 7–90.
15 *PC*, p. 235.
16 Ibid., p. 233.
17 Ibid., p. 318.
18 *Metaph.*, pp. 115–41.
19 *PL*, p. 192.
20 *PC*, p. 270.
21 *The Basic Writings of Josiah Royce* (*BWJR*), 2 vols., ed. John J. McDermott (Chicago: University of Chicago Press, 1969), including an annotated bibliography by Ignas Skrupskelis, vol. 1, p. 35.
22 Ibid.
23 *Josiah Royce's Late Writings: A Collection of Unpublished and Scattered Works* (*JRLW*), 2 vols. (Bristol, UK: Thoemmes Press, 2001), vol. 2, p. 93.
24 *PC*, pp. 351–7.
25 *WI*, 2: 409–10.
26 Ibid., p. 410.
27 Peirce to Royce, June 30, 1913, published in *Transactions of the Charles S. Peirce Society* 26 (1990): 142.
28 *WI*, 2: 287.
29 Ibid., p. 294.
30 Ibid., pp. 432–3.

Suggested reading

Major primary sources, with abbreviations used in internal references

The Basic Writings of Josiah Royce (*BWJR*), 2 vols., ed. John J. McDermott (Chicago: University of Chicago Press, 1969), including an annotated bibliography by Ignas Skrupskelis.

The Letters of Josiah Royce (*LJR*), ed. John Clendenning (Chicago: University of Chicago Press, 1970).

Royce's Logical Essays: Collected Logical Essays of Josiah Royce (*RLE*), ed. Daniel S. Robinson (Dubuque, IA: William C. Brown Co., 1951).

The Religious Aspect of Philosophy (Boston: Houghton Mifflin, 1885).

The Spirit of Modern Philosophy (Boston: Houghton Mifflin, 1892).

The World and the Individual (*WI*), 2 vols. (New York: Macmillan, 1899–1901).

The Philosophy of Loyalty (*PL*) (New York: Macmillan, 1908).

The Sources of Religious Insight (New York: C. Scribner's Sons, 1912). (Paperback reprint with introduction and index by Frank M. Oppenheim (Washington, DC: The Catholic University of America Press, 2001).)

"The Principles of Logic," in *Logic: Encyclopedia of the Philosophical Sciences*, vol. 1, pp. 67–135 (London: Macmillan, 1913; repr. New York: Wisdom Library, *c.*1961).

The Problem of Christianity (*PC*), 2 vols. (New York: Macmillan, 1913). (Single-vol paperback reprint with John E. Smith's introduction and Frank M. Oppenheim's foreword and revised indices (Washington, DC: The Catholic University of America Press, 2001).)

Metaphysics (*Metaph.*). Stenographic report of Royce's last course in metaphysics, 1915–16 (Albany: SUNY Press, 1998).

The Hope of the Great Community (New York: Macmillan, 1916).

Josiah Royce's Late Writings: A Collection of Unpublished and Scattered Works (JRLW), 2 vols. (Bristol, UK: Thoemmes Press, 2001).

Secondary sources

Clendenning, John, *The Life and Thought of Josiah Royce*, rev. and expanded edn. (Nashville, TN: Vanderbilt University Press, 1999).

Hocking, William. E., "On Royce's Empiricism," *Journal of Philosophy*, 53 (1956): 57–63.

Kegley, Jacquelyn Ann, *Genuine Individuals and Genuine Communities: A Roycean Public Philosophy* (Nashville, TN: Vanderbilt University Press, 1997).

Oppenheim, Frank M., *Royce's Mature Ethics* (Notre Dame, IN: University of Notre Dame Press, 1993).

——*Royce's Mature Philosophy of Religion* (Notre Dame, IN: University of Notre Dame Press, 1987).

Chapter 8

George Santayana, 1863–1952

Herman J. Saatkamp, Jr.

Introduction

Philosopher, poet, literary and cultural critic, George Santayana is a towering figure in the era of classical American philosophy whose significance rivals that of John Dewey, William James, and Charles Sanders Peirce. Beyond philosophy, his literary production may be matched only by Ralph Waldo Emerson. As a public figure, he appeared on the front cover of *Time* (February 3, 1936), and his autobiography (*Persons and Places*, 1944) and only novel (*The Last Puritan*, 1936) were for months the best-selling books in the United States as Book-of-the-Month Club selections.[1] The novel was nominated for a Pulitzer Prize, and Edmund Wilson ranked *Persons and Places* among the few first-rate autobiographies, comparing it favorably to Yeats's memoirs, *The Education of Henry Adams*, and Proust's *Remembrance of Things Past*. Remarkably, Santayana achieved this stature in American thought without being an American citizen, proudly retaining his Spanish citizenship throughout his life. Yet, as he readily admitted, it is as an American that his philosophical and literary corpus must be judged. Using contemporary classifications, Santayana is the first and foremost Hispanic-American philosopher.

Santayana's philosophy is rooted in an extraordinary synthesis of European and American thought that develops two dramatic themes: naturalism and creative imagination. One is based on the material instincts of everyday life, and the other is articulated in the lyrical cry of consciousness. One is the basis for science and deliberate action, while the other is the basis for the literature of experience. One without the other loses either the determinant and wondrous heritage of existence or the rich and infinite possibilities essential to the aesthetic and moral features of life. Naturalism provides the basis for understanding the world, and consciousness makes possible celebrating and valuing the world. Some have characterized Santayana as a dualist, but Santayana claims not to be a metaphysician and insists that he is simply a naturalist, believing in only one world, and that consciousness must be seen as a natural aspect of the physical universe.

Creative imagination and naturalism interweave throughout his life and his works, making his contributions unique in American thought and powerful beyond America's boundaries. His naturalism and emphasis on constructive imagination were harbingers of important intellectual turns on both sides of the Atlantic. He was a naturalist before naturalism grew popular; he appreciated multiple perfections before multiculturalism became an issue; he thought of philosophy as literature before it became a theme in American and European scholarly circles; and he managed to naturalize Platonism, update Aristotle, fight off idealisms, and provide a striking and sensitive account of the spiritual life without being a religious believer. His Hispanic heritage, shaded by his sense of being an outsider in America, captures many qualities of American life missed by insiders, and presents views some have equaled to Tocqueville in quality and importance.

Santayana's early retirement in 1912 from Harvard University, at the age of 48, left him without graduate students and colleagues to advance his philosophical and literary work, and his influence and reputation waned following his death in 1952. During the centennial celebrations of Santayana's birth, Arthur Danto called for a revival of Santayana studies. He noted that many philosophers are recapitulating "the intellectual crisis which Santayana helped overcome," breaking through "to a view of things not dissimilar to the one [Santayana] achieved."[2] Later, Hilary Putnam echoed Danto's remarks: "If there has been less attention paid to Santayana's philosophy than to that of Royce or Peirce, this is in large part because his philosophical mood and philosophical intuitions were actually ahead of his time. In many ways he anticipated some of the dominant trends of American philosophy of the present day."[3] Since the 1960s Santayana scholarship has increased considerably, and it is hoped that this brief survey contributes to that renascence by giving some brief accounts of Santayana's life and publications, his philosophical wedding of naturalism and creative imagination, and his views of American culture.

Life and Publications

Spanish heritage

Santayana characterized his early boyhood as "a passing music of ideas, a dramatic vision, a theme for dialectical insight and laughter; and to decipher that theme, that vision, and that music was my only possible life."[4] One may describe Santayana's life as a composition of intermingling and dramatic themes that begin with his early life in Spain and lead to the deliberate actions of the mature, reflective philosopher.

Born in Madrid, Spain, on December 16, 1863, Santayana's heritage is that of the Spanish diplomatic society with its high education and familiarity with the world community. His father was Agustín Ruiz de Santayana, a retired Spanish diplomat who had traveled the world and whose last post was as governor of one of Spain's Philippine islands. His mother, Josefina Sturgis (formerly Josefina Borrás y Carbonell), was the daughter of a Spanish diplomat. She was born in Scotland, and her father died as governor of the same island that Santayana's father would later govern. After her father's death and upon the arrival of the new governor (Santayana's father), Josefina moved to Manila and married a Boston merchant, George Sturgis (d. 1857), whose early death left her alone with children in Manila. There were five children from this first marriage, three of whom survived infancy. Honoring a pledge to her first husband, Josefina Sturgis moved to Boston to raise her children.

On a holiday in Spain, Josefina and Agustín met again and were married. He was 50 years of age and she was probably 35. Santayana was christened Jorge Agustín Nicolás Ruiz de Santayana y Borrás. The melodic Hispanic-American strains are found even at birth. His half sister, Susan, insisted that he be known not by the Spanish "Jorge," but by the American "George," after her Boston father. Santayana, in turn, always referred to his sister in the Spanish, "Susana." He was a permanent resident of Spain only during 1863–72.

Santayana lived 8 years in Spain, 40 years in Boston, and 40 years in Europe. His own perspective on the phases of his life was not bound by location, as can be seen from the titles he originally suggested for the three books of his autobiography: (1) "Background," (2) "On Both Sides of the Atlantic," and (3) "All on One Side." The background (1863–86) encompasses his childhood in Spain through his undergraduate years at Harvard. The second period (1886–1912) is that of the Harvard graduate student and professor with a trans-Atlantic penchant for traveling to Europe. The third period (1912–52) is the retired professor writing and traveling in Europe and eventually establishing Rome as his center of activity.

1863–1886

Geographical and familial distances characterize Santayana's early life. The family moved from Madrid to Ávila, where Santayana spent his boyhood. But in 1869 Santayana's mother left Spain, renewing her pledge to raise the Sturgis children in Boston. Santayana lived in his father's house until 1872 when his father brought him to Boston, recognizing that the opportunities for his son were better there. However, the father found Boston inhospitable and returned alone to Ávila within a few months. Contributing factors in the decision included Agustín's poor English, the city's Protestant character, the harsh winter and hot summer, and the location of their house on the backwaters of the Charles River. The separation between father and mother was permanent. Santayana regularly corresponded with his father until Agustín's death (1893). After his first year in Harvard College,

Santayana lived with or visited his father for portions of each year. In Boston, Santayana first attended Mrs. Welchman's Kindergarten to learn English from the younger children, then he was a student at the Boston Latin School, and he completed his B.A. and Ph.D. at Harvard College (1882–9), including 18 months of study in Germany on a Walker Fellowship.

Santayana's literary career is evident early in his life. Before leaving Spain he wrote *Un matrimonio* (A Married Couple), the poem of an 8-year-old describing the trip of a newly married couple who meet the Queen of Spain. Later he wrote a poetic parody of *The Aeneid*, "A Short History of the Class of '82", and "Lines on Leaving the Bedford St. Schoolhouse." His undergraduate years at Harvard reveal an energetic student with an active social life. He was a member of 11 organizations, including *The Lampoon* (largely as a cartoonist), the *Harvard Monthly* (a founding member), the Philosophical Club (President), and the Hasty Pudding.

Several scholars conclude that Santayana led an active homosexual life from his student days on. Evidence for this conclusion is drawn largely from allusions in Santayana's early poetry supported by the known homosexual and bisexual orientations of several of Santayana's friends and associates.[5] Santayana never married, and he provides no clear indication of his sexual preferences. Attraction to both women and men seems evident in his correspondence, particularly that of his undergraduate and graduate years at Harvard. The one documented comment about his homosexuality occurred when he was 65. Following a discussion of A. E. Housman's poetry and homosexuality, Santayana remarked, "I think I must have been that way in my Harvard days – although I was unconscious of it at the time."[6]

1886–1912

Receiving his Ph.D. from Harvard in 1889, Santayana became a faculty member at Harvard University (1889–1912) and eventually a central figure in the era now known as the period of classical American philosophy. He was a highly respected and popular teacher, and his students included poets (Conrad Aiken, T. S. Eliot, Robert Frost, Wallace Stevens), journalists and writers (Walter Lippmann, Max Eastman, Van Wyck Brooks), professors (Samuel Eliot Morison, Harry Austryn Wolfson), a Supreme Court Justice (Felix Frankfurter), many diplomats (including his friend Bronson Cutting), and a university president (James B. Conant). He retired from Harvard in 1912 and lived the remainder of his life in Europe, never returning to the US nor to an academic post.

Academic life never seemed fully appealing to Santayana except in its freedom to pursue intellectual interests and curiosity. His father hoped that Santayana would return to Spain either to pursue a diplomatic career or to become an architect. Instead, Santayana became a professor, but, at first, continued to live more as a student. He found faculty meetings, committees, and governance structures largely empty and their discussions mostly partisan heat over false issues, and the general corporate and business-like adaptation of universities increasingly less conducive to intellectual curiosity, development, and growth. In a letter to a friend in 1892, Santayana expressed the hope that his academic life would be "resolutely unconventional" and noted that he could only be a professor *per accidens*, saying that "I would rather beg than be one essentially."[7]

In 1893 Santayana underwent a change of heart, a *metanoia* as he called it. He gradually altered his mode of living from that of an active student, now professor, to one focused more on the imaginative celebration of life. In doing so, he began planning for his early retirement. Three events preceded his *metanoia*: the unexpected death of a young student, witnessing his father's death, and the marriage of his sister Susana. Santayana's reflections on these events led to a festive conclusion:

> Cultivate imagination, love it, give it endless forms, but do not let it deceive you. Enjoy the world, travel over it, and learn its ways, but do not let it hold you. . . . To possess things and persons in idea is the only pure good to be got out of them; to possess them physically or legally is a burden and a snare.[8]

For Santayana, this conclusion was liberating; it was the ancient wisdom that acceptance of the tragic leads to a lyrical release.

Naturalism and the lyrical cry of human imagination became the focal points of Santayana's life and thought. Naturalism has pragmatic aspects, as we will see, but it also had many aspects antithetical to this growing dominant theme of American thought. And Santayana's more European focus on the aesthetic qualities of the worthwhile life was unique among his colleagues in the Harvard philosophy department. His naturalism had its historical roots in Aristotle and Spinoza and its contemporary background in James's pragmatism and Royce's idealism. But the focus on and celebration of creative imagination in all human endeavors (particularly in art, philosophy, religion, literature, and science) is one of Santayana's major contributions to American thought. This focus, along with his Spanish heritage, Catholic upbringing, and European suspicion of American industry, set him apart in the Harvard Yard.

The beginning of Santayana's philosophical career was "resolutely unconventional." He was unwilling to serve on university committees and expressed concern about the aim of Harvard to produce muscular intellectuals to lead America as statesmen in business and government. Were not delight and celebration also a central aspect of education? His first book was *Sonnets and Other Verses* (1894),[9] a book of poems, not philosophy. And, until the turn of the century, much of his intellectual life was directed to the writing of verse and drama. He was a principal figure in making modernism possible but was not a modernist in poetry or literature. His naturalism and emphasis on constructive imagination influenced both T. S. Eliot and Wallace Stevens. Eliot's notion of the "objective correlative" is drawn from Santayana, and Stevens follows Santayana in his refined naturalism by incorporating both Platonism and Christianity without any nostalgia for God or dogma.

As a professor he was among the leaders in transforming the American literary canon, displacing the dominant Longfellow, Lowell, Whittier, Holmes, Bryant canon. Santayana's essay "The Genteel Tradition in American Philosophy" (presented to the Philosophical Union of the University of California in 1911)[10] greatly affected Van Wyck Brooks's *America's Coming-of-Age*, a book that set the tone for modernism. Brooks drew directly on Santayana's essay, adapting Santayana's idea of two Americas to fit his notion of an America split between highbrow and lowbrow culture.

By the turn of the century Santayana's philosophical interests exceeded his poetical ones, and although he never abandoned writing poetry, he no longer considered his poetic writing his central work. Even so, the trench warfare and casualties of World War I inspired some of his most moving work: "A Premonition: Cambridge, October, 1913"; "The Undergraduate Killed in Battle: Oxford, 1915"; "Sonnet: Oxford, 1916"; and "The Darkest Hour: Oxford, 1917." Throughout his life, even near death, he recited and translated long fragments of Horace, Racine, Leopardi, and others.

His early philosophical writings during his Harvard years extended the development of his pragmatic naturalism and his concern for creative imagination. *The Sense of Beauty* (1896)[11] remains a primary source for the study of aesthetics. Philip Blair Rice wrote in the foreword to the 1955 Modern Library edition:

> To say that aesthetic theory in America reached maturity with *The Sense of Beauty* is in no way an overstatement. Only John Dewey's *Art as Experience* has competed with it in the esteem of philosophical students of aesthetics and has approached its suggestiveness for artists, critics and the public which takes a thoughtful interest in the arts.[12]

Santayana's radical approach to aesthetics is emphasized in Arthur Danto's "Introduction" to the 1988 critical edition where he notes that Santayana brings "beauty down to earth" by treating it as a subject for science and giving it a central role in human conduct, in contrast to the preceding intellectualist tradition of aesthetics. "The exaltation of emotion and the naturalization of beauty – *especially* of beauty – imply a revolutionary impulse for a book it takes a certain violent act of historical imagination to recover."[13]

The relationship between literature, philosophy, and religion is a prominent theme throughout Santayana's writings. In *Interpretations of Poetry and Religion* (1900) Santayana develops his view that religion and poetry are expressive celebrations of life. Each in its own right is of highest value, but if either is taken for science, the art of life is lost along with the beauty of poetry and religion. Science aims at explaining the natural world, while poetry and religion are festive celebrations of human life born of consciousness. Poetry and religion, at their most powerful, are identical: then "poetry loses its frivolity and ceases to demoralise, while religion surrenders its illusions and ceases to deceive."[14] His father expressed similar views in his letters to his son, providing the genesis of his son's reflections, and this conclusion is expressed as late as the 1946 publication of *The Idea of Christ in the Gospels*, where Santayana presents the idea of Christ as poetic and imaginative, contrasted with attempts at historical, factual accounts of the Christ figure. The impact of Santayana's view was significant, and Henry James (after reading *Interpretations of Poetry and Religion*) wrote that he would "crawl across London" if need be to meet Santayana.

With the publication of the five books of *The Life of Reason: Or, The Phases of Human Progress* (1905–6), Santayana became a major figure in the philosophy of the new century. Many naturalists saw the work as founding American naturalism. Woodbridge, Edman, Randall, Erskine, Cohen, and Lamont considered the work almost canonical. The five books comprise a survey of the religions, societies, arts, and sciences of the Western world, deciphering intellectual policies consistent with reasonable action. From this work comes the often-quoted warning to those who do not remember the past: they are condemned to repeat it.[15] Morris R. Cohen noted that it "is the only comprehensive, carefully articulated, philosophy of life and civilization which has been produced on these shores."[16]

Continuing his interests in philosophy and poetry, *Three Philosophical Poets* (1910) was the first volume of the Harvard Studies in Comparative Literature. Santayana's analyses are efforts at employing a naturalistic account of poetry and philosophy, attempting to combine comparative structures with as few embedded parochial assumptions as possible, while making explicit our material boundness to particular worlds and perspectives. His analyses of Lucretius, Dante, and Goethe are described by one biographer as "a classical work and one of the few written in America to be genuinely comparative in conception and execution, for its absence of national bias and its intellectual, linguistic, and aesthetic range."[17]

Santayana formally announced his retirement from Harvard in May 1911. But his noted success as a teacher, poet, philosopher, and cultural critic caused President Lowell to ask him to reconsider. In turn, Lowell agreed to any arrangement that would provide Santayana the time he desired for writing and for travel in Europe. Santayana initially assented to alternating years in Europe (at the Sorbonne) and the US, but in 1912 his resolve to retire overtook his sense of obligation to Harvard. At the age of 48, he left Harvard to become a full-time writer and to escape the academic professionalism that nurtured a university overgrown with "thistles of trivial and narrow scholarship."

1912–1952

Just after Santayana sailed from the US, his mother died, apparently of Alzheimer's disease. He visited her weekly, then daily, during his last two years at Harvard, and he made arrangements for his half sister, Josephine, to live in Spain with Susana, who was now living in Ávila and married to a wealthy businessman. An inheritance of $10,000 from his mother, coupled with his steady income from publications, made retirement easier. He arranged for his half brother, Robert, to manage his finances, just as Robert had done for their mother. Hence, in January 1912, at the age of 48, Santayana was free to write, free to travel, free to choose his residence and country, and free from the constraints of university regimen and expectations.

There were many attempts to bring him back to the United States. Harvard offered him several professorships beginning in 1917. As late as 1929 he was offered the Norton Chair in Poetry, one of Harvard's most respected chairs. In 1931 he received an invitation from Brown University, and Harvard later asked him to accept the William James Lecturer in Philosophy, a newly established honorary post. But Santayana never returned to Harvard, nor to America. Believing that the academic life was not a place for him to cultivate intellectual achievement or scholarly work, Santayana also refused academic appointments at both Oxford University and Cambridge University. In 1932 he delivered two public addresses celebrating the tercentennial of the births of Spinoza and Locke. "Ultimate Religion" was presented in The Hague, and "Locke and the Frontiers of Common Sense" was presented to the Royal Society of Literature in London.

When Santayana left the United States, he planned to reside in Europe, and during several exploratory trips to European cities, he decided on Paris. However, when World War I broke out, he was in England and unable to return to the mainland. He resided first in London and then primarily at Oxford and Cambridge. After the war, he was more of a traveling scholar, and his principal locales included Paris, Madrid, Ávila, the Riviera, Florence, and Rome. By the late 1920s, he settled principally in Rome, and during the summers he often retreated to Cortina d'Ampezzo to write and to escape the heat.

In the 1930s, he at first thought the rise of Mussolini would bring order to the chaotic Italian society, but he soon perceived the rise of a tyrant rather than a statesman. He tried to leave Italy by train for Switzerland, but at the border he discovered that he did not have the proper papers. His was a complicated case: a Spanish citizen with most of his income deriving from the US and England. Unsuccessful in his efforts to leave Rome, on October 14, 1941 he entered the Clinica della Piccola Compagna di Maria, a hospital-clinic run by a Catholic order of nuns, where he lived until his death 11 years later. This arrangement was not entirely unusual. The hospital periodically received distinguished guests and cared for them in an assisted-living environment. Santayana died of cancer on September 26, 1952. The Spanish Consulate at Rome provided the "Panteon de la Obra Pia espanola" in the Campo Verano cemetery as a suitable burial ground for the lifelong Spanish subject. Commemorating Santayana's life in his "To an Old Philosopher in Rome," Wallace Stevens wrote:

> Total grandeur of a total edifice,
> Chosen by an inquisitor of structures
> For himself. He stops upon this threshold,

As if the design of all his words takes form
And frame from thinking and is realized.

Santayana's scholarly publication record after leaving Harvard is remarkable: *Winds of Doctrine* (1913), *Egotism in German Philosophy* (1915), *Character and Opinion in the United States* (1920), *Soliloquies in England and Later Soliloquies* (1922), *Scepticism and Animal Faith* (1923), *Dialogues in Limbo* (1926), *Platonism and the Spiritual Life* (1927), the four books of *The Realms of Being* (1927, 1930, 1938, 1940), *The Genteel Tradition at Bay* (1931), *Some Turns of Thought in Modern Philosophy* (1933), *The Last Puritan* (1935), *Persons and Places* (1944), *The Middle Span* (1945), *The Idea of Christ in the Gospels* (1946), *Dominations and Powers* (1951), and *My Host the World* (1953).

Santayana's decided view that philosophy is a natural, reflective activity in the midst of animal life led him to the ancient wisdom that self-knowledge is the root of a worthwhile life and the basis for philosophical reflection. But philosophical reflections are not for everyone. They are only for those whose nature and circumstances permit this chosen path. The practical import of his philosophical reflections caused Santayana to be a public figure in American thought long after he left the American continent. The second volume of *The Library of Living Philosophers* (1940) was devoted to an examination of Santayana's thought, and his response to his critics, "Apologia Pro Menta Sua," is essential reading for anyone wishing to understand his philosophy.

In contrast to the abstractness of contemporary philosophy and to some efforts to revive pragmatic naturalism in a chameleon-like form, Santayana's philosophy focuses on the capaciousness of social and cultural practices articulated institutionally, on the unconscious physical complexity of individual and social action, on the depths of individual suffering, and on the heights of personal joy and responsible action. His is a celebrational philosophy, a chosen way of living, a festive journey that is comparable to a work of art. And he would be the first to admit that his philosophy can only be understood in the cultural context of his thought, beginning with the philosophical goal of self-knowledge.

Naturalism, Creative Imagination, and Pragmatism

Santayana's naturalism is based on the ancient Greek virtue of self-knowledge. He begins with the acceptance of human action as constrained and contoured by material forces shaping one's constitution and environment. Human life is as subject to scientific investigation and explanation as is all life. It is common sense, not metaphysics, that the human animal lives in a particular environment with a specific make-up and heritage. The task of life is to live as well as fated circumstances permit. Acceptance of one's fate leads to self-knowledge and action, not to inaction or renunciation. It makes possible the shaping of one's life based on that knowledge. Self-awareness and reason are natural products of the inchoate determinants of human life, and they provide dramatic qualities to human existence that liberate it spiritually, not materially, from its tragic predicament.

The primer to Santayana's mature philosophy is *Scepticism and Animal Faith*. With Spanish irony he structures the book after Descartes's *Meditations* while arriving at an anti-foundationalist's conclusion. Genuine doubt ends in a meaningless "solipsism of the present moment," a vacant awareness of a given without the basis for belief, knowledge, or action. Knowledge cannot be found in abstract reasoning, but only in action itself, in the middle of things (*in medias res*), where there is an instinctive, arational belief in the natural world. This natural belief is "animal faith," a tacit belief in a world that can be acted upon. Focusing on beliefs implicit in animal action, Santayana displaces privileged mentalistic accounts with his pragmatic naturalism. This challenge to American and English philosophy is carried forward in his four-volume *Realms of Being*, which explicates distinguishable characteristics of our knowledge of the world: matter, essence, spirit, and truth. Unlike many of his contemporaries, Santayana preferred classical terminology. He believed that the terminological heritage brought greater insight than mere neologisms. His preference for "essence" as opposed to "sense data" bears out his claim. His anti-foundationalism and pragmatic naturalism coupled with his emphasis on the spiritual life and his view of philosophy as literature anticipated many developments in philosophy and literary criticism that occurred in the latter half of the twentieth century, and these served as a challenge to the more humanistic naturalism of John Dewey and other American naturalists.

Reason is generated by the harmony in one's material predicaments and holds only so long as circumstances permit. Consciousness, or spirit as Santayana called it, is a celebratory offspring of the material world. Its perspective is not limited to the undramatic, uncaring, material conditions of one's own being, society, or species. Human consciousness may survey a limitless range of possibilities not existent, not requisite for action, not necessary for survival, but delightful, festive, and eternal. Santayana refers to the immediate objects of consciousness as essences. Essences considered alone are without import or intent, although in the heat of action the animal naturally takes them as symbols of entities in the world. Pure spirit, however, suspends practical judgment and delights in the immediacy of the given essence. The joint births of reason and spirit make life worthwhile, giving dramatic, festive characteristics to the undramatic and fated world.

Santayana uses the term "spirit" for consciousness or awareness, knowing that its religious and philosophical roots provide both depth and difficulty to the concept. Spirit is "precisely the voice of order in nature, the music, as full of light as of motion, of joy as of peace, that comes with an even partial and momentary perfection in some vital rhythm." Such harmony is temporary, and the disorganized that natural forces permit spirit to arise "only spasmodically, to suffer and to fail. For just as the birth of spirit is joyous, because some nascent harmony evokes it, so the rending or smothering of that harmony, if not sudden, imposes useless struggles and suffering."[18] Accepting the world's insecure equilibrium enables one to celebrate the birth of reason and spirit. Reason permits individual and social organization to prosper, and spirit leads to the delight of imagination and artistry.

Santayana's concept of the spiritual is rooted in the monastic life of the Catholic faith. But Santayana's rendering removes all religious, political, or practical underpinnings. Santayana's "spiritual life" is not a life existing over time with activities structured toward particular ends. Rather, the spiritual life is more often momentary and, when sustained, maintains a wondrous, vacant awareness, usually for short periods of time. The spiritual life occurs when in strings of conscious moments one contemplates eternal essences independent of their human significance, when conscious life has lost its drift in the natural world of means and ends, and when the expressive human life is raised beyond everyday concerns to contemplation of the conscious given. Such a spiritual life cannot last long because it would be ill-fated in a world where both action and inaction have serious consequences. The tiger in the night, or a predator in the stock market, is not concerned about its next meal's reflective life. Even so, some humans are able to attain a spiritual quality sustained in a lifestyle, mystics and poets perhaps, and Santayana admired those who could even though he said he could not count himself among them. In short, for the human animal, conscious life makes possible reflection and value, it gives meaning to life in a world shaped and guided by unconscious material forces. If one's nature is so inclined, one may attempt to order one's life so that the spiritual life is cultivated and celebrated.

Pragmatism

Santayana's account of spirit and essence may lead one to wonder how he can be included as a pragmatist, and this classification is accurate only if one includes an extended notion of pragmatic naturalism. For Santayana, explanations of human life, including reason and spirit, lie within the sciences. The nature of truth simply is correspondence with what is, but since neither humans, nor any other conscious being, is able to see beyond the determinant limits of their nature and environment, pragmatism becomes the test of truth rather than correspondence. In short, the nature of truth is correspondence, while the test of truth is pragmatic. If an explanation continues to bear fruit over the long run, then it is accepted as truth until it is replaced by a better explanation. In this, Santayana's account of pragmatic truth is more closely aligned with Peirce's conception than with that of James or Dewey, including a tripartite account of knowledge consisting of the subject, symbol, and object. Pragmatism properly is focused on scientific inquiry and explanations, and it is severely limited, even useless, in spiritual and aesthetic matters. Pragmatism is rooted in animal life, the need to know the world in a way that fosters successful action. If all life was constituted only by successful or unsuccessful activities, one's fated circumstances would govern. But consciousness makes liberation possible and brings delight and festivity in material circumstances.

Removing himself, physically and philosophically, from the American scene, Santayana increasingly came to believe that the brimstone sensibility of American pragmatism was wrong-headed. The American philosophy professor attempted to model a philosophical statesman engaged in social and cultural policy formulation. Absent such weighty considerations, the professors, it seemed, were not pulling their civic weight. This trend and model led pragmatism to belie "the genuinely expressive, poetic, meditative, and festive character of their vocation."[19] However, Santayana knew this insight was not entirely lost in American pragmatism, but he thought the pragmatic drift made it increasingly difficult for it to surface. James makes a similar point in "On a Certain Blindness in Human Beings," suggesting that the world of practical responsibility fosters a blindness to multifaceted ways of living that can only be escaped by catching sight of "the world of impersonal worths as such" – "only your mystic, your dreamer, or your insolent loafer or tramp can afford so sympathetic an occupation."[20] Whether connected or not, Santayana later came to identify himself as an intellectual vagabond, not isolated in the specific perspectives of an ideology, hosted by the world, and devoted to spiritual disciplines. One of his favorite self-characterizations was that of a philosopher on holiday.

Henry Levinson notes several formal and stylistic differences between the American pragmatic emphasis on shaping society and Santayana's festive approach to individuality:

> as he lives in Oxford during his fifties, a privileged and middle-aged bystander to combat, he finds himself clearing his philosophical voice in a new way, one that highlights *soliloquy* more than statesmanship, *festivity* or celebration more than representation, *playfulness* more than utility, *understanding* more than judgment, *comic relief* more than tragic resignation or sublime exultation, *religious discipline* more than academic enterprise, and *confession of faith* more than profession of claims intended to carry authority for everybody. These are the characteristics that lead Santayana eventually to call his philosophy "a discipline of the mind and heart, a lay religion."[21]

His common-sense approach to philosophy led to his relativism. There is truth, but we only have glimpses of it from our perspectives. Science provides the best avenue for understanding and explaining the world through its pragmatic test of truth. But all perspectives on truth and the good have their own standing in the world. None is more privileged than another, except as one may lead to more successful action than another depending on the needs and desires of the animal. There is no overarching good toward which all individual actions are aimed, and truth is not subservient to any ideal good or moral claim. This does not mean that there is no evidence for the truth of a statement or the good of an individual or society, but the evidence is based on success in action, and success is embedded in the particular needs and desires of an individual or society – it has no standing independent of these.

Santayana was unwilling to give precedence to any form of life, save to an individual form with particular aims in a specific environment with heritable traits. If it were possible to view the world from nowhere, that is, independent of one's material circumstances, all views of truth and the good would have equal standing. Of course, such a view is not possible for any living being, since existence presumes a material world. Just so, Santayana was unwilling to give any particular form of government an absolute status. Rather, the appropriate government is geared to the heritage and material prospects of its citizens, to the cultivation of forms of life that foster success and also imagination. To the dismay of his American colleagues, he recounted the many ways in which democracies, both socialistic and capitalistic, substituted homogeneity and mass life for excellence in individual life. In Santayana's approach, social life that does not enrich individual life has substituted means for ends and, having lost sight of its aim, becomes empty and worthless.

His refusal to give democracy the pre-eminent authority in governmental structures, led to conflicts with some of his American colleagues. The consistent misunderstanding between Santayana and Dewey is perhaps one of the greatest tragedies of Santayana's leaving America in 1912. His absence made it unlikely that two individuals of such different temperaments but similar philosophies could communicate easily over such long distances. Santayana characterized Dewey's naturalism as too humanistic, too wedded to the democracy associated with capitalistic enterprise, and too contained with clarifying experience rather than the material culture and heritage that shaped human action and well-being.

The tension between statesmanship and poetic spirituality provides Santayana with the prerequisites for judging liberal democracy. The twin fears of private anarchy and public uniformity are the ground for Santayana's criticisms of democracy, but if such a democracy could lessen individual suffering, heighten individual delight, respect multiplural forms of life with multiple goods, and do so without collectively forcing a uniform moralism on its citizens, then it would be appropriate for the time. Even with his considerable focus on individual suffering, his account of social justice appears lacking to many. Santayana's inattentiveness to social inequality is perhaps understandable in the context of his naturalism, where the final cause is the "authority of things." His basic contention that suffering is the worse feature of human life, not social inequality, causes him to focus more on the natural dilemmas of the individual than on social action. Coupling this contention with the view that all institutions, including governments, are inextricably rooted in their culture and background perhaps makes it understandable that he would not readily see how particular views of social inequality can be transferred readily from one culture to another. In addition, Santayana's European, and particularly Spanish, background clearly influenced his attitudes toward social action. His repeated "Latin" perspective caused him to look with considerable suspicion toward forcing Anglo-Saxon outlooks on other cultures. Santayana's stay in Oxford during the Great War led to his famous counter to Wilson's "war to end all wars": "Only the dead have seen the end of war."[22]

Santayana is decidedly a political conservative. However, throughout his long life he leaned toward a variety of socialisms, particularly those founded on some form of materialism. One may say that he believed freedom to be the result of order (natural order), not order the result of freedom: "Freedom is a result of perfect organization. The problem is so to organize ourselves as to become free."[23] His conservatism, Spanish heritage, and forced residence in Rome during World War II caused some mistakenly to believe that he sympathized with Mussolini and Hitler. Indeed, he initially found the new organization and productivity of Italy under Mussolini promising, as he did the socialistic developments in Russia. But as these political forces developed, he distinguished himself from these political figures and the form of national socialism that evolved in Germany and Italy. In 1934 the editor of *The Saturday Review of Literature*, Henry Seidel Canby, asked Santayana for an essay on fascism, but Santayana "was not especially interested in a local regimen in Italy, but in the wider political questions that he later treated in his book on *Dominations and Powers*."[24] In the resulting essay, "Alternatives to Liberalism," Santayana suggests that the liberals should not have been surprised at the rise of Lenin, Mussolini, and Hitler. They came to power as a result of public opinion and the natural need for order. But he counters this comment by noting the short-lived aspirations of political Titans. The best government "would think on the human scale, loving the beauty of the individual. If their ordinances were sometimes severe under stress of necessity, that severity would be rational, or at least amenable to reason. In such a case, holding truth by the hand, authority might become gentle and even holy."[25] But the contemporary scene is different.

> Now, on the contrary, we sometimes see the legislator posing as a Titan. Perhaps he has got wind of a proud philosophy that makes the will absolute in a nation or in mankind, recognizing no divine hindrance in circumstances or in the private recesses of the heart. Destiny is expected to march according to plan. No science, virtue, or religion is admitted beyond the prescriptions of the state. . . . Fortunately on earth nothing lasts for ever; yet a continual revulsion from tyranny to anarchy, and back again, is a disheartening process.[26]

In individual matters he was remarkably forthcoming, as when he provided financial support to numerous friends, often of quite different philosophical, literary, and political persuasions from his own. He, for example, provided Bertrand Russell (a person whose philosophical and political views hardly paralleled those of Santayana) significant funds on a yearly basis during a period when Russell was in difficult financial circumstances and unable to find a teaching post in England or the US.

Building on his naturalism, institutional pragmatism, social realism, and poetic religion, Santayana distanced himself from the role of philosophical statesman by removing the representative authority of language from the quest for a comprehensive synthesis, and by narrowing the line between literature and philosophy (as he had earlier done between religion and poetry). In addition, Santayana's pragmatic naturalism was linked to other, non-American, aspects of philosophical development. John Lachs and Michael Hodges regard Santayana as a precursor of Wittgenstein's insights into the social structures that shape human life and expression. Santayana's central contribution is to view reason as the harmonizing of diverse interests through institutions of social practice, and to recognize that knowledge is contextual and symbolic, not literal. His critical and analytical skills as a philosopher also added to his cultural criticisms, particularly his view of the United States.

America

In 1911 Santayana taught summer school at the University of California at Berkeley. He was seeing the American West before his retirement from Harvard. Reflecting on American philosophical culture, he presented his now famous "Genteel Tradition in American Philosophy" to the Philosophical Union. America is a "wise child" whose head is filled with old ideas even while the child is venturing into new waters without ideas to match: "an old head on young shoulders, always has a comic and an unpromising side."[27] He drew a distinction between the American will and intellect that became almost a slogan of the day. "The American Will inhabits the sky-scraper; the American Intellect inhabits the colonial mansion. . . . The one is all aggressive enterprise; the other is all genteel tradition."[28] Basically, he thought of American philosophy as borrowing its intellectual heritage from Europe, a heritage that did not match the aggressive, democratic enterprise of the new nation. It was like pouring old wine in a new bottle.

The background for this genteel tradition lay in Calvinism and transcendentalism. At first Americans were guided by the agonized conscience of their puritan background. "Human nature . . . is totally depraved: to have the instincts and motives that we necessarily have is a great scandal, and we must suffer for it; but that scandal is requisite, since otherwise the serious importance of being as we ought to be would not have been vindicated."[29]

This rather drab world of dominion and sin was eventually replaced by a more common notion of good will: "Good-will became the great American virtue; and a passion arose for counting heads, and square miles, and cubic feet, and minutes saved – as if there had been anything to save them for. How strange to the American now that saying of Jonathan Edwards, that men are naturally God's enemies!"[30] The development of this native outlook came about through poets (Whitman) and humorists (Mark Twain), and led to an openness in the society. The intellects may not have had their heads above the water where they could see far and wide, but they saw life as an experimental act, a vital tension in the context of events. The influence of Darwin and of science was evident in the desire for a practical adjustment to life's conditions regardless of whether there was an intellectual account suitable to those conditions.

William James exemplified a new approach and moved away from the strictures of European apprenticeship. "William James, in this genial evolutionary view of the world, has given a rude shock to the genteel tradition. What! The world a gradual improvization? Creation unpremeditated? God a sort of young poet or struggling artist?"[31] James's difference is dramatically vivid in his radical empiricism, openness to the paranormal, reduction of science to success in action, and view of the world as both young and wild and not captured by the logic of any philosophy.

In brief, Santayana suggests that American thought has moved beyond the yoke of European intellectual heritage, and American philosophers are striving to find a philosophy that matches their experience; it is an optimistic appraisal. He closes with reference to the California forests and mountains, and a clear emphasis on naturalism and creative imagination:

> When you escape, as you love to do, to your forests and your Sierras, I am sure again that you do not feel you made them, or that they were made for you. . . . In their non-human beauty and peace they stir the sub-human depths and the super-human possibilities of your own spirit . . . they give no sign of any deliberate morality seated in the world. It is rather the vanity and superficiality of all logic, the needlessness of argument, the finitude of morals, the strength of time, the fertility of matter, the variety, the unspeakable variety, of possible life.[32]

Santayana continued his assessment of American culture and persons in *Character and Opinion in the United States* (1920) and his novel *The Last Puritan* (1936). In the first, he gives an assessment of individuals and circumstances, providing intellectual portraits of some Harvard colleagues. These assessments both praise and criticize his colleagues and friends, presenting a view of American life that was, and is, difficult to discern from within. In the essays on American culture, one can find Santayana's principal reasons for leaving the US. He had learned to prize the English emphasis on social cooperation and personal integrity, and he thought these were corrupted in America so that "You must wave, you must cheer, you must push with the irresistible crowd; otherwise you will feel like a traitor, a soulless outcast, a deserted ship high and dry on the shore."[33]

His only novel, *The Last Puritan*, provides a literary setting for his view of America and the historical changes occurring during the transition from the nineteenth to the twentieth century. For Santayana, this *fin de siècle* was a transition from a Great Merchant Society to a more democratic and commercial one. Travel, communication with people in other cultures, and a cosmopolitan life were more available than at any previous time. The change brought the passing of a generation, the finale for a particular class and their ethos, the last of the puritans. The new generation owed less to their cultural parentage, had remarkably different hopes for the future, and recognized that the dimensions of a natural world were ever increasing. Santayana had a remarkable sense of the impending impact of scientific investigation on our understanding of the world and of our place in it. Although his characterization is that of a century ago, there is much that remains appropriate for the turn of the twenty-first century.

In the 1890s Santayana began a series of sketches on college life that resulted in *The Last Puritan*, a work that was compared positively with Goethe's *Wilhelm Meister*, Pater's *Marius*, and Mann's *The Magic Mountain*. Essentially, it is about the life and early death of an American youth, Oliver Alden, who is sadly restricted by his puritanism. Santayana draws a sharp contrast with the European Mario, who delights in all matters without a narrow moralism. He portrays the last puritan as bounded by habit, obligation, and activity, almost joyless. Oliver does everything he should do. He is an athlete, a scholar, a good person, but life is never festive or full of delight. He knows there are alternative ways of joyful living and has a sense of guilt about not achieving them. In contrast there is the celebratory European who, true to his heritage and in hope for the future, is free to enjoy life, to appreciate its diversity, its plural goods, and its delights. Santayana's literary approach reveals a depth to human character as well as the narrowness of American culture and its impact on quotidian life.

Conclusion

Santayana's philosophical and literary outlook seems almost timeless. He believes that classical philosophical questions arise in each century and in each country, and although they are viewed from different perspectives and times, there is a wondrous continuity in them. He believes that individual suffering, in its diverse forms, is the greatest problem facing a society, and he sees ideology and public opinion as threats to individual joy. He counsels for a clear understanding of our biological and social histories, and maintains with Socrates that self-knowledge is the basis for a worthwhile life. For faculty and students, his critical account of American universities seems exceedingly apt. In the nineteenth century he had already identified many characteristics that cast a shadow on our scholarly lives. He feared that academic professionalism would smother intellectual achievement with business-like governance and committees. He thought the scholarship of his colleagues was growing increasingly narrow and without a perspective on higher education.

With the growth of a united Europe and the development of Asia, Santayana's perspective of an outsider in America provides a unique appraisal of American character and thought. Our present circumstances highlight his concern that youthfulness and energy will not lead to the wisdom requisite for living well in a global culture. And his sense of the joy of life and its complex physical determinants stand in high relief as we enter an age of molecular genetics and galactic exploration.

Notes

1 George Santayana, *Persons and Places: The Background of My Life* (New York: Charles Scribner's Sons; London: Constable, 1944). George Santayana, *The Last Puritan: A Memoir in the Form of a Novel* (London: Constable, 1935; New York: Charles Scribner's Sons, 1936).
2 "Santayana and the Task Ahead," *The Nation* (December 21, 1963): 437–40.
3 "Santayana Restored," brochure for *The Works of George Santayana* (Cambridge, MA: The MIT Press, 1985).
4 *Persons and Places*, p. 159.
5 John McCormick, *George Santayana: A Biography* (New York: Alfred A. Knopf, 1987), pp. 49–52.
6 Daniel Cory, *Santayana: The Later Years, A Portrait with Letters* (New York: George Braziller, 1963), p. 40.
7 George Santayana in a letter to Henry Ward Abbot, written from Stoughton Hall, Harvard, February 15, 1892. Original in Rare Book and Manuscript Library, Columbia University.
8 *Persons and Places*, pp. 427–8.
9 *Sonnets and Other Verses* (Cambridge and Chicago: Stone and Kimball, 1894).
10 "The Genteel Tradition in American Philosophy," *University of California Chronicle*, 13 (1911): 357–80. (First presented to the Philosophical Union of the University of California, August 25, 1911.)
11 *The Sense of Beauty: Being the Outlines of Æsthetic Theory* (New York: Charles Scribner's Sons; London: A. and C. Black, 1896).
12 *The Sense of Beauty: Being the Outlines of Æsthetic Theory* (New York: Random House, Inc., 1955), p. ix.
13 *The Sense of Beauty: Being the Outlines of Æsthetic Theory*, critical edn. ed. William G. Holzberger and Herman J. Saatkamp, Jr. (Cambridge, MA, and London: The MIT Press, 1988), p. xxviii.
14 *Interpretations of Poetry and Religion* (New York: Charles Scribner's Sons, 1900). Critical edn. ed. William G. Holzberger and Herman J. Saatkamp, Jr. (Cambridge, MA, and London: The MIT Press, 1989), p. 172.
15 *The Life of Reason, or the Phases of Human Progress: Introduction and Reason in Common Sense* (New York: Charles Scribner's Sons, 1905), p. 284.
16 Morris R. Cohen, *American Thought: A Critical Sketch* (Glencoe, IL: Free Press, 1954), p. 311.
17 McCormick, *George Santayana*, p. 193.
18 *The Birth of Reason and Other Essays by George Santayana*, ed. Daniel Cory, with an Introduction by Herman J. Saatkamp, Jr. (New York and London: Columbia University Press, 1995), p. 53.
19 Henry Samuel Levinson, *Santayana, Pragmatism, and the Spiritual Life* (Chapel Hill and London: The University of North Carolina Press, 1992), p. 165.
20 William James, *Talks to Teachers on Psychology and to Students on Some of Life's Ideals* (New York: H. Holt, 1899), p. 141.
21 *Santayana, Pragmatism, and the Spiritual Life*, p. 193. Levinson quotes from Santayana's *Realms of Being* (New York: Charles Scribner's Sons, 1942), p. 827.

22 *Soliloquies in England and Later Soliloquies* (New York: Charles Scribner's Sons; London: Constable, 1922), p. 102.
23 *Birth of Reason*, p. 85.
24 Ibid., p. 108fn.
25 Ibid., pp. 114–15.
26 Ibid., p. 115.
27 *The Genteel Tradition: Nine Essays by George Santayana*, ed. Douglas L. Wilson (Cambridge, MA: Harvard University Press, 1967), p. 39.
28 Ibid., p. 40.
29 Ibid., p. 41.
30 Ibid., pp. 42–3.
31 Ibid., p. 59.
32 Ibid., pp. 62–3.
33 *Character and Opinion in the United States: With Reminiscences of William James and Josiah Royce and Academic Life in America* (New York: Charles Scribner's Sons, 1920), p. 211.

Suggested reading

The Works of George Santayana. Herman J. Saatkamp, Jr. (General Editor) and William G. Holzberger (Textual Editor) (Cambridge, MA, and London: The MIT Press): *Persons and Places: Fragments of Autobiography*, vol. 1 (1986); *The Sense of Beauty: Being the Outlines of Aesthetic Theory*, vol. 2 (1988); *Interpretations of Poetry and Religion*, vol. 3 (1989); *The Last Puritan: A Memoir in the Form of a Novel*, vol. 4 (1994); *The Letters of George Santayana*, vol. 5, *Book One: [1868]–1909* (2001), *Book Two: 1910–1920* (2002), *Book Three: 1921–1928* (2002).

Overheard in Seville: Bulletin of the Santayana Society, ed. Angus Kerr-Lawson and Herman J. Saatkamp, Jr. (Indianapolis: Indiana University, Purdue University Indianapolis). Published annually.

Primary sources

Character and Opinion in the United States (New York: Charles Scribner's Sons, 1920).

The Genteel Tradition: Nine Essays by George Santayana, ed. Douglas L. Wilson (Cambridge, MA: Harvard University Press, 1967).

The Life of Reason: Or, The Phases of Human Progress (New York: Charles Scribner's Sons; London: Constable): *Introduction and Reason in Common Sense* (1905), *Reason in Society* (1905), *Reason in Religion* (1905), *Reason in Art* (1905), *Reason in Science* (1906).

Realms of Being (New York: Charles Scribner's Sons; London: Constable): *The Realm of Essence: Book First* (1927), *The Realm of Matter: Book Second* (1930), *The Realm of Truth: Book Third* (1937/8), *The Realm of Spirit: Book Fourth* (1940).

Scepticism and Animal Faith: Introduction to a System of Philosophy (New York: Charles Scribner's Sons; London: Constable, 1923).

Soliloquies in England and Later Soliloquies (New York: Charles Scribner's Sons; London: Constable, 1922).

Secondary sources

Abellán, José Luis, *George Santayana, 1863–1956* [sic] (Madrid: Del Orto, 1996).

Alonso Gamo, José María, *Un español en el mundo: Santayana; poesía y poética* (Madrid: Ediciones Cultura Hispánica, 1966).

Arnett, Willard, *Santayana and the Sense of Beauty* (Bloomington: Indiana University Press; London: M. Paterson, 1955, 1984).

Cory, Daniel M., *Santayana: The Later Years, A Portrait with Letters* (New York: George Braziller, 1963).

Dawidoff, Robert, *The Genteel Tradition and the Sacred Rage* (Chapel Hill: The University of North Carolina Press, 1992).

Duron, Jacques, *La Pensée de George Santayana: Santayana en Amérique* (Paris: Nizet, 1949).

Estébanez Estébanez, Cayetano, *La Obra Literaria de George Santayana* (Valladolid: Secretariado de Publicaciones e Intercambio Editorial, Universidad de Valladolid, 2000).

García Martín, Pedro, *El sustrato abulense de Jorge Santayana* (Avila: Institución "Gran Duque de Alba" de la Excma. Diputación Provincial de Avila, 1989).

Lachs, John, *George Santayana*, Twayne's United States Authors Series (Boston: Twayne Publishers, 1988).

——and Michael Hodges, *Thinking in the Ruins: Wittgenstein and Santayana on Contingency* (Nashville, TN: Vanderbilt University Press, 1999).

Levinson, Henry Samuel, *Santayana, Pragmatism, and the Spiritual Life* (New York: Charles Scribner's Sons, 1942).

Lind, Bruno, *Vagabond Scholar: A Venture Into the Privacy of George Santayana* (New York: Bridgehead, 1962).

McCormick, John, *George Santayana: A Biography* (New York: Alfred A. Knopf, 1987).

Price, Kenneth M. and Robert C. Leitz, *Critical Essays on George Santayana* (Boston: G. K. Hall and Co., 1991).

Schilpp, Paul Arthur, *The Philosophy of George Santayana* (Evanston, IL: Northwestern University Press, 1940).

Singer, Beth, *The Rational Society* (Cleveland, OH: Press of Case Western Reserve University, 1970).

Singer, Irving, *George Santayana, Literary Philosopher* (New Haven, CT: Yale University Press, 2000).

Sprigge, Timothy, *Santayana: An Examination of his Philosophy* (London and Boston: Routledge and Kegan Paul, 1974, 1995).

Woodward, Anthony, *Living in the Eternal* (Nashville, TN: Vanderbilt University Press, 1988).

Chapter 9

John Dewey, 1859–1952

Larry A. Hickman

Early Years: Burlington, Baltimore, Ann Arbor, Chicago

John Dewey, hailed by the *New York Times* on the occasion of his ninetieth birthday as "America's Philosopher," was born in Burlington, Vermont on October 20, 1859. He died at his apartment in New York City on June 1, 1952.

During Dewey's 92 years, Americans experienced profound transformations in almost every area of their lives. At the time of his birth on the eve of the Civil War, James Buchanan was President and America was still to a great extent dependent on wind, water, and wood technologies. During his youth, steam, coal, and steel became dominant features of the American scene. By the time of his death, during the height of the Cold War and just months before the election of Dwight Eisenhower, Americans had come to depend on the atom, plastics, and the transistor.

During his decade at the University of Chicago (1894–1904), Dewey witnessed major demographic changes that included labor unrest, waves of European immigrants, and massive migration by African-Americans from the rural South to the urban North. During his years at Columbia University in New York City (1905–39), he was involved in the politics of World War I and an active participant in the New York Teachers' Union, the National Association for the Advancement of Colored People (NAACP), and the American Civil Liberties Union (ACLU). In 1937, at the age of 77, he traveled to Mexico City to chair The Commission of Inquiry into the charges made against Leon Trotsky in the Moscow Trials.

Perhaps more than any other philosopher of his time or since, Dewey understood the extent to which the institutions of industrial democracies were being transformed by science and technology. His efforts to reconstruct philosophy and education were predicated on that understanding. His ideas were – and remain – as revolutionary as the times through which he lived.

During his undergraduate years at the University of Vermont (1875–9), Dewey attended lectures on speculative and social philosophy taught by H. A. P. Torrey. Among his reading materials were progressive journals whose contributors espoused evolution, positivism, and agnosticism. After graduation in 1879, Dewey taught school in Oil City, Pennsylvania. In 1881 he returned to Burlington briefly in order to continue his study of philosophy with Torrey.

Dewey's first publication appeared in the *Journal of Speculative Philosophy* in April 1882. A few months later he began his graduate studies at Johns Hopkins University, where he attended lectures by Charles S. Peirce on logic and by G. Stanley Hall on experimental psychology. His real interest, however, was the neo-Hegelian idealism of George Sylvester Morris, which provided him with the tools to deal with what he termed the "dualism" of New England culture. In 1884 Dewey completed his Ph.D. and accepted a teaching position with Morris, who was by then head professor of philosophy at the University of Michigan.

While at Ann Arbor, Dewey met and fell in love with an intelligent, charming, and socially progressive student named Harriet Alice Chipman, who was slightly older than he. They were married on July 28, 1886. Of their seven children, two died during early childhood and one was adopted. Their marriage ended with her death in 1927. Their daughter Jane would write that "above all, things which had previously been matters of theory acquired through [Dewey's] contact with [Alice] a vital and direct human significance."

Two essays published in the British journal *Mind* in 1886 and his first major book, *Psychology* (1887), established Dewey's reputation. In those publications he attempted to integrate the neo-Hegelianism of Morris with the experimental psychology of Hall. His book was the first experimental psychology text written by an American. It was sharply criticized by William James and others, however, because of its defense of idealism and the fact that it employed "soul" as a psychological concept. During this period of his career, Dewey's ideas about religion became increasingly liberal and he began to abandon the conventional idea that concepts are metaphysical entities. He treated them instead as tools for resolving and reconstructing problematic situations. A second major book, a critique of Leibniz's *New Essays Concerning the Human Understanding* was published in 1888.

Dewey taught briefly at the University of Minnesota during 1888, but was recalled to Ann Arbor when Morris died suddenly. During his second term at Michigan he published *Outlines of a Critical Theory of Ethics* (1891) and *The Study of Ethics: A Syllabus* (1894). He abandoned the idea of a super-conscious absolute spirit that he had adopted earlier as part of the neo-Hegelian idealism he had learned from Morris. It was replaced by a constellation of ideas, some of which had been proposed by William James in his *The Principles of Psychology* (1890). These included the hypotheses that consciousness is a stream and that human beings are biological organisms in a concrete environment, therefore responsible for their own habits and, by extension, their own evolution.

In a similar vein, Dewey argued that David Hume's bifurcation of facts and values had become untenable. He even went so far as to suggest that there could be a science of ethics. The "ought," he wrote in "Moral Theory and Practice" (1891), is itself an "is." It is the "is" of action. Dewey broke stride with other areas of traditional philosophy as well. He began to argue that a science of "direct, practical truths" was possible without metaphysics. He concluded that metaphysics in the traditional sense had become unnecessary.

In 1894 Dewey accepted a position at the new University of Chicago. His department included psychology and pedagogy as well as philosophy. Pedagogy was soon established as a separate department of education and Dewey was appointed its head as well. He immediately set out to assemble a group of colleagues and students, including George Herbert Mead and A. W. Moore, who could help him develop a new school of thought.

If Dewey's thinking had been profoundly influenced by the incipient functionalism in James's *Principles of Psychology*, it was now Dewey's turn to take the lead. He published "The Reflex Arc Concept in Psychology" (1896), in which he undermined the foundations of stimulus-response psychology, thus causing irreparable damage to the structuralist/introspectionist program of E. B. Titchener. Titchener had characterized psychology as the attempt to map the structures of the mind by means of introspection. Dewey offered an alternative: a functionalist model of behavior that characterized the organism as not just reactive but interactive with respect to its environment. In this new model, the organism selected and conditioned its own stimuli. Structure and introspection were replaced in Dewey's model by function and observable behavior.

Almost a half-century later, in 1942, a committee of 70 leading psychologists selected Dewey's "Reflex Arc" essay as the most important contribution to *Psychological Review* during the first 50 years of its publication. In 1899 Dewey served a term as president of the American Psychological Association.

Dewey's private correspondence during his years at Chicago reveals a growing progressivism with respect to social values, as well as an increasing dissatisfaction with what he regarded as the anti-progressive tendencies of his own university. He became a regular participant in the affairs of Jane Addams's Hull House and a passionate advocate of educational reform, including co-education for women. In 1896 he founded the University Elementary School (also called the Dewey School and the Laboratory School). In 1899 he published *The School and Society*, a major statement of his educational theory.

Much of the educational practice during the late nineteenth century tended to be driven by one of two opposing models. The "curriculum centered" model advanced by W. T. Harris emphasized content. Children were treated as receptacles for the accumulated wisdom of civilization and therefore encouraged to learn by memorizing and reciting. The "child-centered" model advanced by G. Stanley Hall emphasized expression of the child's natural impulses, so learning was treated as equivalent to self-expression. In Dewey's view, these conflicting positions presented a false choice: the aim of pedagogy should be to correlate subject matter and impulse. One aspect of the work of the educator, he argued, was to find ways of subjecting the curriculum to the test of the child's experience. Another aspect was to find ways of helping the child reconstruct his or her experience in the light of the demands of the curriculum. The method Dewey used in this instance – isolating and abstracting the best elements of opposing viewpoints and reconstructing them into a novel alternative – became a hallmark of his wider philosophy.

Dewey's philosophy of education took account of the increasing industrialization and urbanization of American life. He was acutely aware of the many antidemocratic forces that threatened communities. He viewed the schools as places where social experimentation could be nourished and democratic practices could flourish.

During Dewey's decade at Chicago he published the first of what would be three books on logic. *Studies in Logical Theory* (1903) was written in collaboration with his students and colleagues. It presented an instrumentalist logic that owed a great deal to the functionalism that William James had developed for psychology. It emphasized the role of ideas as tools of practical inquiry. William James could hardly contain his excitement about what Dewey was accomplishing at Chicago. In 1903 he wrote to Sarah Wyman Whitman:

> Chicago University has during the past six months given birth to the fruit of its ten years of gestation under John Dewey. The result is wonderful – a real school, and real Thought. Important thought, too! Did you ever hear of such a city or such a University? Here [at Harvard] we have thought, but no school. At Yale a school, but no thought. Chicago has both.[1]

By 1904, growing differences between Dewey and University of Chicago President William Rainey Harper reached a point of no return. As a result of misunderstandings related to the funding of the Dewey School and the terms of Alice Dewey's contract as its Principal, both Deweys resigned their posts. Almost immediately, Dewey was offered a position at Columbia University in New York City. His appointment as professor of philosophy began in February 1905. He was also appointed to the graduate faculty and the faculty of Teachers College. In 1930, he was appointed Professor Emeritus of Philosophy in Residence, retaining his full salary. In 1939, at the age of 80, Dewey entered full retirement with the title of Professor Emeritus of Philosophy.

Middle Years: New York City, Japan, China

While Dewey was at Chicago, many of his arguments were directed against the objective idealists whose ideas were then in vogue. By the time he arrived at Columbia, philosophical fashion had changed. The ideas of philosophical realists were in vogue. In general terms, idealists held that reality is mind-dependent and realists held that reality is such as it is regardless of whether anyone has knowledge of it. The arguments of the realists now provided an interesting test for the instrumentalist logic that Dewey had developed as a response to the idealists.

As he had done and would continue to do, he constructed a middle position between the extremes. His instrumentalism took account of the observable fact that organisms are subjected to the pushes and pulls of their environments, and that humans make tools or instruments of many different types in an attempt to deal with such uncertainties. Some of these tools are tangible, but others are noetic or conceptual. As "reality," the facilities and constraints of life are at best inchoate and unformed. Even though most of life's uncertainties are unimportant and not worth bothering with, some of them are perceived as requiring some sort of remedial action. Humans use instruments to refine and reconstruct those portions of "reality" that they do not find satisfactory. What the realists generally regarded as mind-independent facts are fictions, Dewey argued, but so are the completely mind-constituted facts generally alleged by the idealists.

This remarkable insight required a reconstruction of what is commonly meant by the term "fact." Staking out a middle position between the idealists and the realists, Dewey located "facts" within the context of inquiry. With the idealists, he held that facts are constructed. Against the idealists, however, he argued that facts are never totally mind-dependent. They are constructed, that is, but they are not constructed out of nothing. With the realists, he accepted the idea that there are aspects of our environment that are stubborn and unavoidable. Against the realists, however, he argued that such "data" become meaningful as real facts only as they are taken up in processes of inquiry. Facts are "facts-for-inquiry," or "facts-of-a-case" – they are among the instruments that we use to effect adjustment to changing environmental conditions.

Dewey continued to expand the boundaries of his instrumentalism. He had already published two book-length studies of ethics, *Outlines of a Critical Theory of Ethics* (1891) and *The Study of Ethics* (1894), as well as a number of essays such as "Moral Theory and Practice" (1891) that dealt with the topic. His textbook *Ethics* (1908), however, written with James H. Tufts, took the unprecedented step of including discussions of current social problems. In other words, he presented his instrumentalist ethics as a set of tools for dealing with real-world conditions. One of the most significant features of this volume, and one that was intimately related to its concern with practical affairs, was its treatment of the relation of ends and means in ethical decisions. He rejected the idea that there is some end-in-itself (unless it be the general notion of growth itself) that is intrinsically valuable always and everywhere in the sense that it should determine the pattern of ethical deliberation. He argued that ethical deliberation involves a consideration of competing ends, and that new ends must be developed out of that competition. In other words, in the process of determining what is morally valuable, there must be a kind of "dramatic rehearsal" in which means are considered in relation to ends, ends are considered in relation to means, and both ends and means are adjusted to one another as appropriate. Means and ends thus become tools for deliberation instead of intractable entities. Even though it is appropriate to speak of growth as an end-in-itself, it is hardly an intractable concept in Dewey's ethics. Ideas about what constitutes growth are enlarged and enriched as ethical deliberation evolves.

In making this move, Dewey was once again demonstrating his well-honed technique of finding what was valuable and rejecting what he considered faulty in two extreme positions. He was rejecting the duty-oriented (deontological) ethics of Kant as well as the consequence-oriented calculations of British utilitarians such as Bentham. Neither ethical means, such as a good will, nor ethical ends, such as consequences to be achieved, were deemed sufficient in themselves. Dewey thought that actual living social contexts demand that there be interplay between flexible means and flexible ends, or ends-in-view.

In *How We Think* (1910), a small volume addressed to teachers, Dewey laid out the fundamentals of his instrumental logic in ways that were applicable to classroom situations. This work includes Dewey's now-famous articulation of the five logical steps that he thought are present wherever instances of good thinking are encountered. First, there is a felt difficulty. If there is no sense that there is a problem, then there is no need for inquiry. Second, the problem must be located and defined. Much of the work of solving a problem lies in the successful completion of this step. Third, there is the suggestion of a possible solution. This is the stage at which provisional hypotheses are formulated. Fourth, there is a reasoning process that attempts to work out the possible consequences of the hypotheses. In this stage of thinking, some hypotheses are discarded as impractical. By performing such thought experiments, or "dramatic rehearsals," time and energy are saved. Finally, there is the additional experimentation or observation that is required for the leading hypothesis to be either accepted or rejected. In other words, doubt has been assuaged and harmony restored. The process of inquiry is complete until another feeling of doubt ensues.

Despite the time and effort that he devoted to writing, Dewey always seemed to find time for service to his profession and his community. He served as president of the American Philosophical Association during 1905–6 and vice-president of the American Association for the Advancement of Science in 1909. He was also an active participant in the work of the Henry Street Settlement on the lower east side of Manhattan, the formation of teachers' unions, and efforts to secure the vote for women (the suffragist movement).

Dewey supported intervention by the United States in World War I because he thought that the defeat of Germany would lead to the construction of institutions that would foster lasting peace. His stance occasioned a permanent rupture of his friendship with fellow progressive Randolph S. Bourne. Even though he supported the war effort, however, he was also adamant in his defense of free speech. He was an active participant in the founding of the Teachers League of New York (1913), the American Association of University Professors (1915), and the American Civil

Liberties Union (1920). He was also a regular contributor to the progressive journal *New Republic.*

Dewey continued to develop his instrumentalist version of pragmatism. In the introduction to his second book on logic, *Essays in Experimental Logic* (1916), he portrayed knowing as a technical activity that uses tools in order to turn raw materials into finished products. Continuing his work in educational theory, he and his daughter Evelyn collaborated on *Schools of Tomorrow* (1915). In *Democracy and Education* (1916), he claimed that education has no end beyond itself, since it is synonymous with growth and improved adjustment to environing circumstances. The year it was published Dewey wrote to Horace M. Kallen that "*Democracy and Education* in spite of its title is the closest attempt I have made to sum up my entire philosophical position."

Although he thought that testing individuals in order to determine their talents and capacities was a legitimate part of education, he strongly opposed the use of test results as a means of classifying or stratifying individuals. What type of education did he think is required and fostered by a democratic society? It is one that "gives individuals a personal interest in social relationships and control, and the habits of mind which secure social changes without introducing disorder."

From 1919 to 1921, Dewey lectured in Japan and China. In 1922 he published *Human Nature and Conduct*, in which he rejected the notion of a fixed human instinct popular in some quarters. He argued instead that the plastic impulses of children and adults alike can be modified as a basis for a naturalistic ethics. In his view, impulses are released when established habits come into conflict because of novel circumstances. Habits must then be reconfigured or reconstructed. "Character" is the configuration of an individual's habits, and each individual is responsible for his or her own habits. Individuals are therefore responsible for the construction of their own characters just as they would be for any other artifact that they had made. Of course this view put Dewey at odds with proponents of psychoanalysis, who he thought tended to confuse psychic action with the results of social interaction. He also objected to the tendency of psychoanalysis to posit a psyche as a structural entity that exists prior to experience.

Experience and Nature (1925), widely regarded as Dewey's most important work, emphasized the organic, historical, and anthropological conditions of human life. Rejecting traditional metaphysical splits such as those that had divided the supernatural from the natural, attributes from modes, essence from existence, subsistence from existence, and even Bertrand Russell's attempt to partition experience into absolute necessity versus the actual world, Dewey argued that the ideal world, including its mathematical abstractions, its theological systems, its social, political, and legal institutions, and even its moral precepts, arises as humans attempt to render the facilities and constraints of an unpredictable nature more stable and dependable.

It is in *Experience and Nature* that one finds what is arguably the clearest statement of Dewey's naturalism. He treats nature not as a thing, but as an affair of beginnings and endings: an affair of affairs. Humans are characterized as being within and a part of nature, not outside of and over against it. The human organism is not separated from evolutionary history, but is instead presented as its cutting edge. One of the consequences of this view is that the roots of technology, which in Dewey's view includes the tools and methods of abstract thought as surely as it does tools and artifacts that are concrete and tangible, are located in evolutionary history and in the countless adjustments made over millions of years by plants and non-human animals. In other words, Dewey naturalizes technology. It is only with the advent of human life that nature comes to reflective consciousness: only then does nature, as he puts it, come to have a "mind of its own." Another consequence of this view is that ends are removed from their historical location in an ideal realm of transcendent values. Once naturalized, they become what Dewey calls "ends-in-view" – flexible and subject to experimentation as the need arises. Mind is treated not as a noun, but as a verb or adverb. Since it refers to behavior, mind is identified as the "instrumental method of directing natural changes."

Dewey's naturalism leads him to argue that everything that is known or knowable exists in relation to other things. There is therefore no such thing as an absolute existence or absolute value. At the level of human life, it is the business of communication (which Dewey terms the most wonderful of all affairs) to generate the meanings by which natural events are enabled to pass beyond their existence as mere occurrences and become pregnant with implications.

Dewey's dissatisfaction with the traditional philosophical treatment of "the mind–body problem" led him to coin the term "body–mind." Starting from the human organism as a whole, experiencing and interacting with its environing conditions, Dewey employed the term on the left of the hyphen to point backward to a history of evolutionary development that is continuous with the rest of non-human nature and is brought forward as instinct, structure, and habit. He employed the term to the right of the hyphen to point forward to the future development of the organism, a future that is determined by its ability to make plans and hypotheses, as well as its ability to draw implications and thus to take charge of its own evolution. By rejecting the traditional notion that body and mind are ontologically separate, as matter and spirit, Dewey was also able to reject the traditional assumption that the determination of their relation constitutes an epistemological problem.

Experience and Nature is a magnificent overview and consolidation of the work of the 66-year-old philosopher. It also contains much that was new. It presents for the first time an extensive presentation of Dewey's theory of art, for example, as well as an attempt to reconstruct the term "metaphysics." Chapter 9, for example, titled "Experience, Nature and Art," articulates themes to which Dewey would return almost a decade later in *Art as Experience*. Moreover, since Dewey had many years earlier argued that metaphysics in its traditional sense was finished, it was a matter of considerable surprise to some of his readers that the final chapter of his book revisited the subject. He characterized his reconstructed metaphysics as "a statement of the generic traits manifested by existences of all kinds without regard to their differentiation into physical and mental," and as a "ground-map of the province of criticism." Metaphysics was thus presented as a tool of inquiry, establishing "base lines" that are at once more specific than those generated by quotidian experience and more general than those that are the result of scientific experimentation.

It is a testimony to the prescience and originality of *Experience and Nature* that some of its central ideas anticipated by two decades or more some of the insights advanced by Ludwig Wittgenstein during the 1940s and 1950s that are now understood by his interpreters as key features of his later philosophy. These include Dewey's rejection of the possibility of a private language, his treatment of language as instrumental and meaning as contextual, his treatment of universals in terms of what Wittgenstein would later call "family resemblances," his criticism of the hoary quest for certainty, and his contention that belief in physical necessity is just a superstition.

Dewey continued to travel. He visited Turkey in 1924 at the request of its government in order to evaluate its educational system. In 1926 he lectured at the National University of Mexico. He also continued to be interested in the activities and institutions by means of which democracy either flourishes or fails. In his 1927 book *The Public and Its Problems* he argued that public groups must be nourished in ways that increase their ability to generate and test new ideas. He argued for more scientific social planning. In 1928 he visited schools in the Soviet Union. His reports, published in the *New Republic*, argued that the United States should recognize the Soviet Union. As a result, some conservatives branded him a "communist."

In 1929 Dewey published *The Quest For Certainty*. The aim of traditional philosophy, especially since Descartes, he argued, had been to achieve a foundation of certain knowledge. According to Dewey's instrumentalist logic, however, the test of an idea is its outcome and the test of an outcome is whether it resolves a problematic situation in a satisfactory manner. His use of the terms "satisfaction" and "satisfactory" have been the occasion for much misunderstanding on the part of his critics. He did *not* mean simply that a solution must be satisfactory with respect to some individual person or group of persons. In that event he would have committed himself to some variety of subjectivism or extreme relativism, which he did not. For Dewey it is instead an entire situation – objective social conditions which include the inquirer or inquirers as a part – that must be resolved in a satisfactory fashion. There is thus a time-dimension that must be considered when deciding whether or not an outcome is satisfactory. It does not follow from the fact that a group of persons is "satisfied" with the oppression of a minority group, for example, that the situation will be deemed satisfactory in a broader objective sense, that is, when objective cultural-historical considerations have been taken into account.

Dewey's position on this issue has been termed "objective relativism" since it holds that when a problem arises there are objective conditions that must be taken into account and that in most cases there are alternative ways of doing so. Certainty, on this view, is not only elusive but unnecessary. What we humans need, and what we can have, is the kind of fallible assurance that is achieved through scientific inquiry.

Some of Dewey's critics at the time thought that he had yielded to the temptation of scientism, or making science a test for all other forms of experience. Some of his more recent interpreters, including neo-pragmatist Richard Rorty, have taken the opposite view, namely that Dewey regarded science as a type of literature. It is probably fair to say that Dewey's own view of the matter lies somewhere between these extreme interpretations. He thought that the sciences had been highly successful in their attempts to manage the human environment, but that there were vast areas of experience in which they have no business. On the other hand, he thought that the sciences and the arts, including literature, have different tools, materials, and aims: they do different types of work.

Later Years: Retirement, Travel, Eleven More Books

His first retirement in 1930 afforded the 70-year-old Dewey even greater opportunities to channel his still-considerable energy into writing projects. The next 20 years would see the publication of some of his most important books. In *Individualism, Old and New* (1930), for example, he examined the effects of industrialization and urbanization on American life. He argued that the old frontier myths of rugged individualism that had pervaded American consciousness, especially the myths of its business practices, should be abandoned in favor of new forms of cooperation and social planning. The old social Darwinist individualism was simply no longer appropriate to changing conditions. A new, more appropriate variety of individualism would utilize emerging tools of science and technology to create the conditions under which individual talents and energies could be liberated. Industrialization was precipitating a break-up of old patterns of association and was threatening to shatter the integrity of the modern self. Now, he argued, was the time to construct new forms of association that would actively promote and enhance individualism, and not merely assume it.

Up to this point, Dewey had written very little about aesthetics. Now his retirement provided the opportunity to prepare a series of lectures on the subject. They were presented at Harvard University in 1931 as the William James Lectures and published in 1934 as *Art as Experience.* The book was dedicated to Albert C. Barnes, a long-time friend who had assembled a major collection of modern art that is now housed at the Barnes Foundation in Merion, Pennsylvania.

Dewey used this work to continue his attack on the kind of dualistic thinking that tends to split various types of experience off from one another. One of the marks of good art, he argued, is the extent to which it harmonizes means and ends. Tools, methods, and materials cooperate with one another and with the artist's ends-in-view, each interacting with and altering the other until a harmonious conclusion is reached. He argued that the traditional distinction between "fine" art, on the one hand, and "utilitarian" art on the other was not intrinsic to works of art themselves: it was instead predicated on faulty ways of thinking about what art is and what it does. He thought that what is normally termed "fine" art should also be useful in the sense of increasing significance and liberating meanings. What is normally termed "vernacular" or "utilitarian" art should also be fine in the sense of exhibiting harmonies, rhythms, and other qualities that set it apart from what is happenstance and ordinary. Some of Dewey's critics claimed that for better or worse *Art as Experience* represented a major departure from his earlier positions. Dewey replied that his aesthetic theory was merely a further development of the instrumentalist version of pragmatism that he had been developing for more than a quarter of a century.

Dewey's mother had been a staunch evangelical Christian, and he himself had held conventional religious views as a young man. After his move to Chicago in 1894 Dewey had little to say about religion. In his book *A Common Faith* (1934), however, which was written as a part of a dialogue with several theologians of the period, we have the benefit of his mature thinking on the subject. He began by pointing out the obvious fact that the term "religion" refers to many types of beliefs and cultural practices, many of which are incompatible with one another. It seemed to him, therefore, that there was no single clear and unambiguous meaning of the term. On the other hand, the term "religious" was generally used to refer to the qualities of any experience whatsoever that inspired enthusiasm and commitment. He therefore called for a "common faith" that would be able to unite the aspirations of all human beings across such traditionally difficult fault lines as class, race, and sect. Far from being the enemy of scientific technology, as some religious doctrines have historically proven themselves to be, his common faith would utilize the tools of scientific technologies to inspire action toward the common good.

Dewey's next book, *Liberalism and Social Action* (1935), was written in part as a reply to theologian Reinhold Niebuhr, who had singled Dewey out for criticism in his book *Moral Man and Immoral Society* (1932).[2] Niebuhr had argued that because of the fundamental fact of human sin, the forces of injustice were too great to be countered by reason and experimental science. If justice were to be established, then either an absolutizing moral principle such as Christian love or else force would have to be employed. Dewey had responded to the first portion of this claim in *A Common Faith*, when he argued that concepts such as "sin" were much too vague to do any real work. He compared them to the "abstract powers" that science had long since discredited.

In *Liberalism and Social Action*, Dewey took up the second part of Niebuhr's argument. After recounting the history of liberalism since the seventeenth century, he called for a new, radical form of liberalism. What he termed a "renascent" liberalism would utilize scientific methods to reform institutions that had become corrupt or obsolete. By its use of intelligence, it would provide a basis for common action in every sphere of human life where problems were encountered.

Some of his critics have accused Dewey of excessive optimism. But if optimism is the view that everything will turn out for the best, then Dewey was no optimist. He was well aware that sometimes even the most careful planning can be thwarted by unforeseen circumstances and that even the most intelligent of actions can be subverted by disaster. Two of his beloved sons, it should be recalled, died in early childhood. But if Dewey was not an optimist, he was hopeful. He thought that the only alternatives to the type of liberalism that he favored, a liberalism based on intelligence and hard work, were drift and improvisation, reliance on supernatural powers (which in his view came to much the same thing), or coercive force.

Perhaps reacting to the failure of the League of Nations and rethinking his own pro-war stance two decades earlier, Dewey argued during the 1930s that the United States should avoid involvement in the growing problems of East Asia and Europe. It was during this period that his reputation as a public philosopher soared to even greater heights, and he became widely known as "America's Philosopher." His honors during this period included honorary doctorates from the University of Paris in 1930 and Harvard University in 1932.

In the spring of 1937, at the age of 77, Dewey traveled to Mexico City to serve as chair of a commission to examine the charges brought against Leon Trotsky by Stalin during the "Moscow Trials" of 1936–7. The hearings were held in a suburb of Mexico City, where Trotsky was living in exile. The members of the commission interviewed Trotsky, examined the evidence against him, and then exonerated him of all charges. In 1928, when Dewey visited schools in Soviet Russia, American fascists had branded him a communist. Now, almost a decade later, responding to his involvement with the Trotsky hearings, American communists branded him a fascist. Of course, Dewey was neither. His political views are probably best described as similar to those of Willie Brandt, the former Social Democratic Chancellor of the Federal Republic of Germany or perhaps, as Alan Ryan has argued,[3] to those of British guild socialist G. D. H. Cole.

As war clouds gathered during the 1930s, conservative organizations in America proposed that academic freedom should be limited and that teachers should take loyalty oaths on grounds of national security. Dewey vigorously and publicly opposed such steps, as well as attempts to introduce religious instruction into the public schools. He continued to refine his educational philosophy and to reconstruct its basic ideas in the light of changing trends and fashions. In *Experience and Education* (1938), he once again attempted to articulate a position that would include the best of the two opposing camps: traditionalists on one side, and "progressives" on the other. He was particularly eager to distance himself from educators who claimed to be applying his theories under the rubric of "progressive education" but whose educational practice amounted to little more than encouraging self-expression on the part of the child. Education, he contended, must include guidance. It must take into account the developmental stages of the child and it must relate the child's experiences to his or her social-cultural milieu. Schools must be more than places of "preparation for living." Schools must foster social experimentation and ongoing educational reform.

Dewey's 1938 book *Logic: The Theory of Inquiry* has the reputation of being one of his most difficult works. There can be little doubt that this attempt to refine and advance the instrumentalist logic of his 1903 *Studies in Logical Theory* and his 1916 *Essays in Experimental Logic* ran against the grain of received logical theory. Unlike the formal logic texts published then and now, it did not begin with simple elementary (and putatively context-free) propositions and then combine them to form judgments. Further, it did not define truth in terms of a matrix of values for combinations of elementary propositions or in terms of the correspondence of those propositions to states of affairs already known. Instead, it treated propositions as something to be abstracted from contexts in which inference was attempting to move toward judgment. It treated truth pragmatically, that is, as contextual and provisional.

Dewey discarded the term "truth" because of what he considered its unfortunate connotations. In its place he proposed "warranted assertibility." The "warranted" portion of the phrase points to the past, to experimental inference already accomplished and judgments already rendered. The "assertibility" portion of the phrase points to the future, to novel conditions and tests not yet conducted. Warranted assertibility thus takes account of inquiriential work accomplished and asserts, provisionally, that its results are sufficiently general that they will be applicable to future situations. Dewey's third and final book on logic was not well received. During the last decade of the twentieth century, however, there has been growing interest in its controversial approach to the subject.

Theory of Valuation and *Freedom and Culture*, both published in 1939 by the 80-year-old Dewey, reflect his continuing interest in social criticism as well as his continuing search for new solutions to persistent problems. In *Theory of Valuation* he rejected the notion that moral judgments are merely emotive responses or subjective interpretations, as some philosophers were suggesting at the time. But he also attacked what some other philosophers regarded as the only antidote to emotivism and subjectivism, namely, the idea that moral judgments must be based on transcendental or supernatural foundations. As he had a decade earlier in *The Quest for Certainty*, he argued that moral judgments, if they are to serve as warrants, must be based on the results of experimental tests. In support of his argument he called his readers' attention to the ambiguity of the term "value." "Value" can mean either what is *valued*, or what has proven to be *valuable*. That something is valued, he pointed out, is similar to saying that something has been eaten. It indicates little more than that something has been done. But to claim that something is *valuable* is analogous to claiming that it is *edible*. In both cases it has been proven to be so as a result of objective experimental tests.

In *Freedom and Culture* Dewey examined some of the cultural factors that were reshaping the political landscape. Totalitarian governments of both left and right were in ascendancy in 1939, and it was apparent to most Americans that the world was on the eve of a great war. Some argued that threats to democratic institutions abroad could be averted only by limiting freedom at home. But Dewey replied that in its time of crisis America needed more democracy, not less. He attacked extremists of both left and right. He warned of the dangers of racial and religious prejudice. And he anticipated the dangers of what President Eisenhower would later term "the military-industrial complex." He was especially concerned about the ways in which emerging communications media were being used to manipulate public opinion. As an antidote to these threats he proposed greater emphasis upon education, and especially upon methods of scientific inquiry and cooperative action toward common goals.

Hitler's invasion of Poland in 1939 led Dewey to support the Lend-Lease Bill in 1940 and America's entry into the war in December 1941.

In 1939 Dewey and some of his colleagues founded the Committee for Cultural Freedom as a part of their attempt to expose, and oppose, the forces that threatened intellectual freedom. The Committee condemned totalitarian governments of the political right, including Germany, Italy, Japan, and Spain. But it also condemned the government of the Soviet Union, once again raising the ire of American communists. Dewey came to the aid of Bertrand Russell in 1940 when Russell's appointment at the College of the City of New York was rescinded on the grounds that he was an atheist and immoral. Dewey's eightieth birthday in October 1939 was celebrated at a conference in New York City attended by hundreds of his colleagues and friends. The first volume of *The Library of Living Philosophers*, published in 1939, was dedicated to his work. The same year his former student Sidney Hook published *John Dewey: An Intellectual Portrait.*

In 1939 Dewey entered full retirement with the title Professor Emeritus of Philosophy. During his remaining years he continued to respond to attacks on his educational theory advanced by Mortimer Adler and others. (Adler once went so far as to claim that professors of Dewey's type were a greater threat to democracy than was Hitler's nihilism, and he demanded that they be "liquidated"!) Dewey continued to oppose curbs on academic freedom and freedom of speech. He warned of the dangers of America's alliance with the Soviet Union. He publicly opposed the activities of the House Committee on Un-American Activities. Above all, however, he continued to write. The essays and reviews he published between 1939 and 1948 fill 2 of the 37 volumes of his *Collected Works.* In 1946, at the age of 87, he married Roberta Lowitz Grant, a widow 45 years his junior. The couple adopted two children.

Dewey's last major work, written in collaboration with Arthur F. Bentley, was *Knowing and the Known* (1949). It is still not entirely clear how much of the book was Dewey's contribution and how much was Bentley's. For one thing, the work seemed to undermine the Darwinian naturalism that Dewey had espoused for more than a half-century. For another, it seemed to qualify Dewey's long-held notion that science is continuous with everyday experience. Despite these and other ambiguities, however, one thing about the work is perfectly clear: it mounted a searing attack on logical positivism, which was then in its heyday. It staged a frontal assault on the positivists' commitment to the existence of atomic facts, their dualistic attempt to split the empirical off from the logical, and their foundationalism. As antidote to the doctrines of the logical positivists, Dewey and Bentley elaborated a theory of inquiry in which the transaction of an organism with its environment was a central theme.

Dewey died on June 1, 1952, at his home in New York City. An urn containing his ashes rests with another, containing the ashes of his second wife Roberta, beneath a memorial monument at the University of Vermont. In 1968 the United States Post Office honored him with a 30-cent stamp.

Legacy: Initial Eclipse, Revival of Interest, Rise of Neo-pragmatism

Although he was revered as a public philosopher, by the time of his death Dewey's accomplishments as a technical philosopher had already gone into eclipse. This was due in part to the fact that during the 1930s a wave of logical positivists, fleeing fascism in Austria and Germany, had become established within American graduate schools of philosophy. This branch of analytic philosophy, sometimes known as "ideal language philosophy," was represented by figures such as Hans Reichenbach and Rudolph Carnap. An additional factor was the rise to prominence during the 1950s in American graduate schools of another branch of analytic philosophy, sometimes known as "ordinary language philosophy," which had been developed at Cambridge and Oxford and articulated in the work of Ludwig Wittgenstein, J. L. Austin, Gilbert Ryle, and others. Finally, during the 1950s and '60s there was growing interest among American graduate students in the work of what was then loosely termed the "existentialist" philosophers of France and Germany, especially Jean-Paul Sartre and Martin Heidegger. Courses devoted to the work of Dewey and the other pragmatists all but disappeared from the curricula of American universities.

Nevertheless, some astute observers during the quarter-century following Dewey's death noticed that logical positivism, under pressure from "attenuated" pragmatists such as W. V. O. Quine, was abandoning some of its core programs in favor of positions that had previously been advanced by Dewey and his fellow pragmatists. Some of Quine's central contributions, such as the claim the traditional distinction between analytic and synthetic statements is untenable, can be found in Dewey's work. Moreover, Quine's famous insistence that "to be is to be the value of a variable"[4] may be viewed as but a special application of what Dewey termed the avoidance of "the philosophers' fallacy," namely the doctrine that an object of knowledge cannot be construed as existing in any particular manner prior to and independent of the inquiry that establishes that it exists as object of knowledge in a particular manner. As Dewey put it in his 1938 *Logic*, "When a linguistic form is separated from the contextual matter of problem-inquiry it is impossible to decide of what *logical* form it is the expression."

Moreover, careful readers of the works of Wittgenstein began to notice that during the 1930s, when he abandoned the program he had worked out and published during the 1920s, he turned to a kind of instrumentalism that Dewey had articulated several decades earlier. Some of Wittgenstein's most famous positions, including his argument against the possibility of a private language, his rejection of the idea that language "pictures" reality, his notion that language is a instrument or tool for use in articulating forms of life, and his view that necessity is logical, not existential, were anticipated by Dewey.

About the same time, knowledgeable readers of the works of Heidegger began to notice interesting similarities between his treatment of tools and artifacts in *Being and Time* (1927) and Dewey's treatment of the same issues in *Essays in Experimental Logic* (1916) and *Experience and Nature* (1925). Both philosophers made much of the distinction between tools-as-objects and tools-in-use, and both rejected the subordination of practice to theory that had been advanced as a part of the tradition of Western philosophy since Aristotle.

These and other considerations may have led Richard Rorty to offer the observation, in the introduction to his book *Consequences of Pragmatism* (1982), that Dewey and James seemed to be waiting at the end of the road which analytic philosophers, as well as certain "continental" philosophers, were traveling.

Since the 1980s, Dewey's ideas have enjoyed a remarkable resurgence of interest among philosophers, historians, political scientists, sociologists, and others. Several factors seem to have contributed to this rehabilitation. First, a standard, critical edition of Dewey's work, *The Collected Works of John Dewey, 1882–1953*, edited under the direction of Jo Ann Boydston at the Center for Dewey Studies at Southern Illinois University in Carbondale, began to be available during the 1960s. The 37-volume edition was completed in 1990. Second, Dewey's philosophy was championed by Richard Rorty, one of the most respected and influential figures among contemporary American philosophers. In December 1979 Rorty delivered his presidential address to the Eastern Division of the American Philosophical Association. He proposed that it was time for philosophers in America to revisit the pragmatism of James and Dewey, and this especially because then current (analytic) methods of doing philosophy seemed so far removed from life's concerns. Rorty's address was all the more remarkable given his impeccable credentials as an analytic philosopher and the fact that his audience consisted almost entirely of philosophers trained in analytic methods.

Rorty's address was one of the first statements of what would come to be known as his "neo-pragmatism." How does his neo-pragmatism compare to the "classical" version held by Dewey? Both versions embrace *fallibilism*, or the view that absolute truth is a myth, and that the temporal dimension of human experience renders inquiry forever unfinished. Both versions are *naturalistic* in the sense that they reject transcendental explanations and entities, including those commonly termed "supernatural." Both versions seem to hold some form of *radical empiri-*

cism (a bequest from William James), which is the view that non-cognitive experience is capable of grasping relations and that things are what they are experienced as. Both versions also advance a genetic account of human inquiry, according to which normative claims have historically arisen out of human practice.

There are several issues, however, on which Rorty's neo-pragmatism and Dewey's classical version appear to part company. Whereas Dewey viewed the sciences and the arts as having different methods and materials, as well as different social functions, Rorty has written of "rubbing out" that distinction, in effect treating science as a type of literature. Moreover, whereas Dewey was an activist among political progressives, Rorty has suggested that it may only be possible to "cope" with changing social conditions. And perhaps most importantly, Dewey was an objective relativist. He argued that even though what is *valued* is often subjective or relative to small groups or cultures, experimentation in value fields can and does lead to objective assessments with respect to what is *valuable*. Rorty, on the other hand, seems to hold a more extreme form of relativism, according to which the most one can do with respect to value judgments is to learn as much as possible from the books one reads and the people one meets. In other words, Rorty's neo-pragmatism does not seem to include one of the key elements of Dewey's version, namely his commitment to experimentalism.

Will Dewey's influence will continue to grow, or will it once again be eclipsed by new philosophical movements? It is impossible to answer this question in advance of actual events. It seems fair to conclude, however, that as long as men and women continue to concern themselves with the problems of knowing and valuing that arise from their interaction with environing conditions, Dewey's work will continue to be a source of potential insights.

Notes

1 William James to Sarah Wyman Whitman, October 29, 1903. Published in Henry James, ed., *The Letters of William James* (Boston: Atlantic Monthly Press, 1920), vol. 2, pp. 201–2.

2 Reinhold Niebuhr's *Moral Man and Immoral Society* was reprinted in 2002 (Louisville, KY: Westminster/John Knox Press).

3 Alan Ryan, *John Dewey and the High Tide of American Liberalism* (New York: W. W. Norton, 1995), p. 116.

4 W. V. O. Quine, "On What There Is," in *From a Logical Point of View* (New York: Harper and Row, 1961), p. 15.

Suggested reading

Primary sources

Dewey's collected works. Standard references to John Dewey's work are to the critical (print) edition, *The Collected Works of John Dewey, 1882–1953*, ed. Jo Ann Boydston (Carbondale and Edwardsville: Southern Illinois University Press, 1969–91), and published in three series as *The Early Works* (*EW*), *The Middle Works* (*MW*) and *The Later Works* (*LW*). Pagination of the print edition has been preserved in *The Collected Works of John Dewey, 1882–1953: The Electronic Edition*, ed. Larry A. Hickman (Charlottesville, Virginia: InteLex Corp., 1996).

Secondary sources

Selected works about Dewey. For a comprehensive bibliography of works about Dewey, see *Works about Dewey, 1886–1995*, ed. Barbara Levine (Carbondale and Edwardsville: Southern Illinois University Press, 1996). The CD-ROM edition contains a supplement to the print edition.

Alexander, Thomas M., *John Dewey's Theory of Art, Experience, and Nature: The Horizons of Feeling* (Albany: State University of New York Press, 1987).

Boisvert, Raymond D., *Dewey's Metaphysics* (New York: Fordham University Press, 1988).

Boydston, Jo Ann, ed., *Guide to the Works of John Dewey* (Carbondale and Edwardsville: Southern Illinois University Press, 1970).

Burke, Thomas, *Dewey's New Logic: A Reply to Russell* (Chicago: University of Chicago Press, 1994).

Cahn, Steven M., ed., *New Studies in the Philosophy of John Dewey* (Hanover, NH: University Press of New England, 1977).

Campbell, James, *Understanding John Dewey: Nature and Cooperative Intelligence* (Chicago and La Salle: Open Court, 1995).

Dykhuizen, George, *The Life and Mind of John Dewey* (Carbondale and Edwardsville: Southern Illinois University Press, 1973).

Garrison, Jim, ed., *The New Scholarship on Dewey* (Dordrecht: Kluwer Academic Publishers, 1995).

Gouinlock, James, *John Dewey's Philosophy of Value* (New York: Humanities Press, 1972).

Hickman, Larry A., *John Dewey's Pragmatic Technology* (Bloomington and Indianapolis: Indiana University Press, 1990).

—— *Philosophical Tools for Technological Culture* (Bloomington and Indianapolis: Indiana University Press, 2001).

——ed., *Reading Dewey: Interpretations for a Postmodern Generation* (Bloomington and Indianapolis: Indiana University Press, 1998).

Hook, Sidney, *John Dewey: An Intellectual Portrait* (New York: John Day Co., 1939).

Rockefeller, Steven C., *John Dewey: Religious Faith and Democratic Humanism* (New York: Columbia University Press, 1991).

Rorty, Richard, *Consequences of Pragmatism: (Essays: 1972–1980)* (Minneapolis: University of Minnesota Press, 1982).

Rosenthal, Sandra B., *Speculative Pragmatism* (Amherst: University of Massachusetts Press, 1986).

Rucker, Darnell, *The Chicago Pragmatists* (Minneapolis: University of Minnesota Press, 1969).

Schilpp, Paul Arthur, *The Philosophy of John Dewey*. The Library of Living Philosophers, vol. 1 (Evanston, IL: Northwestern University Press, 1939; repr. La Salle, IL: Open Court Publishing Co., 1970; 3rd edn. 1989).

Shook, John R., *Dewey's Empirical Theory of Knowledge and Reality* (Nashville, TN: Vanderbilt University Press, 2000).

Sleeper, Ralph William, *The Necessity of Pragmatism: John Dewey's Conception of Philosophy* (Urbana and Chicago: University of Illinois Press, 2001).

Welchman, Jennifer, *Dewey's Ethical Thought* (Ithaca, NY: Cornell University Press, 1995).

Westbrook, Robert B., *John Dewey and American Democracy* (Ithaca, NY: Cornell University Press, 1991).

Chapter 10

George Herbert Mead, 1863–1931

Mitchell Aboulafia

Introduction

The notion that our understanding of our selves is in large measure dependent on how others see us is an idea with a pedigree. Ancient Greek writers such as Plato and Aristotle clearly knew that we are social beings, as did a whole string of modern political, social, and economic theorists from Rousseau, to Marx, to no less a figure than the father of modern capitalism, Adam Smith. And so did George Herbert Mead, one of America's most influential social theorists and theorists of the self.

Mead was born in South Hadley, Massachusetts, in 1863, and moved with his family to Oberlin, Ohio, in 1869. Both his parents were educators, and his mother, Elizabeth Storrs Mead, would eventually serve as the president of Mount Holyoke College. Long before Mead became an important theorist of the social construction of the self, he exhibited an interest in social and political questions. As a young man, he wished to work, as it was once said, for the betterment of mankind, and he saw involvement in political activity as the proper path to accomplish this goal. Writing to his close friend Henry Castle in his twenties, Mead rather enthusiastically declared:

> We must get into politics of course – city politics above all things, because there we can begin to work at once in whatever city we settle, because city politics need men more than any other branch, and chiefly because, according to my opinion, the immediate application of principles of corporate life – of socialism in America must start from the city.[1]

Mead remained committed to progressive politics throughout his life, and he eventually came to see the transformation of society as a question of changing the conduct or behavior of individuals and social groups. His life-long desire to help transform the world was an aspiration derived in part from his religious roots, which were sunk rather deep in the Congregationalist tradition. His father, Hiram Mead, was a clergyman who moved his family to Ohio so that he could take up the chair of Sacred Rhetoric and Pastoral Theology at the Oberlin Theological Seminary,[2] and his mother was reputed to have been a religious woman. After his student years at Oberlin College, Mead found himself torn between a career teaching philosophy and Christian social work, although he recognized that his burgeoning secular sensibilities would make the latter choice quite problematic.[3] Mead eventually distanced himself from his religious heritage, but, like John Dewey, he had the aura of the secularly religious about him. He retained an optimism about the human condition until his dying day, an optimism that we often associate with religious faith, and this in spite of having lived through the inhumanity of the First World War.

Mead became an important member of the University of Chicago's distinguished philosophy department, serving on the faculty from 1893 until his death in 1931. And staying true to his early commitment to social change, he became active in the political and social life of early twentieth-century Chicago. Mead was an original thinker of considerable breadth, a philosopher whose ideas crossed the boundaries of traditional academic disciplines and which have been singularly influential in sociology and social psychology. He is often viewed as the most prominent figure in the development of what came to be called the school of symbolic interaction in sociology. John Dewey has reported, however, that Mead had little sense of the depth of his own originality, although he was quite interested in questions of novelty and creativity.[4]

If you had asked Mead about creativity, he would have pointed to the synthetic capacities of human mind, capacities that arose as the result of natural processes that were both biological and social in character. Following Mead's lead here, I would like to suggest that Mead's originality stemmed in large measure from his capacity to gather ideas from various traditions and merge them into a unique synthesis. Three important sources of Mead's ideas were empiricism, Hegelianism, and Darwinian theory. Under the influence of the pragmatic revolution in thought that had been set in motion by James and Peirce, Mead and his good friend Dewey drew on these sources to create a second generation pragmatism that was highly sensitive to the social dimension of human experience. A brief turn, then, to the thought of Hegel, Darwin, and the empirically minded Adam Smith should be of some assistance in introducing Mead's ideas.[5]

Intellectual Influences

The Smith who is most valuable for understanding Mead is the Smith of *The Theory of Moral Sentiments*, a work he completed long before *The Wealth of Nations*. Why is this work of value in understanding Mead? In it Smith develops an almost sociological account of moral development, one that has direct affinities to Mead's own social-psychological account of the development of the self and mind. According to Smith, we come to know ourselves as moral beings by appreciating how others view our actions, as opposed to, for example, becoming moral through a Platonic capacity for dialectical reasoning, one that allows us to fathom the mysteries of morality. He writes in *The Theory of Moral Sentiments*:

> [O]ur first moral criticisms are exercised upon the characters and conduct of other people; and we are all very forward to observe how each of these affects us. But we soon learn, that other people are equally frank with regard to our own. We become anxious to know how far we deserve their censure or applause, and whether to them we must necessarily appear those agreeable or disagreeable creatures which they represent us. We begin, upon this account, to examine our own passions and conduct, and to consider how these must appear to them, by considering how they would appear to us if in their situation. We suppose ourselves the spectators of our own behaviour, and endeavour to imagine what effect it would, in this light, produce upon us. This is the only looking-glass by which we can, in some measure, with the eyes of other people, scrutinize the propriety of our own conduct.[6]

For Smith, we become moral and understand morality, which entails both the operation of sympathy as well as specific sympathetic responses, through empirical observation. But it is not enough to say with Smith that our moral conduct is dependent on the evaluation of others or even the feelings of sympathy that we may have for others. To characterize us in this fashion is not to explain how others come to have this sort of impact on us, that is, it does not elucidate how we become so susceptible to the words and suggestions of others. Nor does it explain in any detail how the development and constitution of the self incorporates and requires the experiences of others, a task that occupied a good deal of the life of George Herbert Mead. To comprehend these matters requires a more thoroughgoing analysis and scientific examination of the self than we find in Smith. Yet Smith's approach in *The Theory of Moral Sentiments* is an important one, for it not only respects the social nature of individuals, it also exhibits an early modernist attempt to provide a genetic or developmental account of how the social plays a fundamental role in shaping an individual's personality and conduct. Such accounts would become rather commonplace in the twentieth century, and Mead's developmental approach would become one of the more influential ones in sociological and social psychological circles.

But we cannot move from Smith's observations and empiricist sensibilities directly to Mead's fully developed model of the social self and conduct. For in addition to the empiricist tradition, the influences of Hegel and romanticism must be considered. Mead was well aware of the importance of the latter in modern thought. He tells us that romanticism brought with it a new understanding of the relationship between history and the self. The self came to be seen as something that could change and grow, and it could do this through the roles that it assumed.

> What the Romantic period revealed, then, was not simply a past, but a past as the point of view from which to come back at the self. One has to grow into the attitude of the other, come back at the self, to realize the self; and we are discussing the means by which this was done. Here, then, we have the makings of a new philosophy, the Romantic philosophy.[7]

> It was because people in Europe, at this time, put themselves back in the earlier attitude that they could come back upon themselves. . . . As a characteristic of the romantic attitude we find this assumption of rôles.[8]

If the Enlightenment provided an appreciation for the cosmopolitan and universal, romanticism yielded a sense of the historically specific and culturally unique. Mead was a thinker intent on drawing on both these traditions, giving the particularities of experience their due while recognizing the importance of the cosmopolitan. What some romantics recognized, according to Mead, was that the challenge of appreciating cultural differences could be met through what he would come to call role-taking. We will turn to the theme of role-taking below.

Hegel was singularly important for Mead. Although Hegel is often thought of as a romantic, he actually criticized a good deal of the romantic sensibility. What Hegel did share with the romantics was an organic model of society and an interest in the diversity of cultures. For him the latter were to be understood as social systems that reflected a certain spirit in their arts, religion, and philosophy. Cultures give rise to selves that are historically specific, for the self's development is intimately tied to a *zeitgeist*, a spirit of the times. An individual growing up in ancient Greece, for example, would possess a different sort of self than one coming of age in contemporary Europe. (This is not to say that individual personality differences do not exist. It is to say that the uniqueness of individuals must be understood in the context of the cultures in which they develop.) But Hegel didn't stop at what may appear to be a version of cultural relativism. For Hegel, there is a world spirit that develops and educates itself through time. Each world culture embodies some aspect of the world spirit's self-education. Members of contemporary cultures have learned, for example, that slavery is immoral after their progenitors have passed through different stages of cultural development. So, we are who we are because of the historical development of world culture, a development that is made possible by the fact that more recent cultures have learned from the past and in a sense "contain" something of the past. In essence, we are not cut off from the past because the past has a continuing presence in the present, or, as Mead might say, the past has no real existence outside of the present (where it is now "located"). The upshot is that selves in a given culture are not isolated from their historical antecedents; rather, they require these antecedents to be what they are.

Mead wanted to understand how social groups are involved in the development of the self. And one way to approach his model is to say that he borrowed a version of Hegel's notion of spirit and applied it to social groups. Social groups have "little" spirits of their own, that is, they form comprehensible systemic wholes, which can be understood in terms of the conduct of their members. These groups do not require a notion of a world spirit in order to be understood or analyzed. Mead would come to tell us that a social group is maintained in part through the presence of a *generalized other* in individuals, a neologism that we will examine below. Mead, however, drew on something more from Hegel, his dialectic of self and other.

Hegel understood how each individual self depends on the recognition of others in order to be itself. We become who we are through the recognition of others for Hegel. This is one of the messages of Hegel's famous master and slave dialectic in the *Phenomenology of Spirit*.[9] We learn in Hegel's account that the master depends on the slave to recognize his superiority, independence, and humanity. But because the master depends on the slave to provide this recognition, he is in a bind, for he views the slave as inferior, and an inferior individual cannot recognize a superior one. Hegel's account reveals to us that we only become fully human when we live in a community of individuals who can and do recognize each other.[10] Mead would have been sympathetic with this conclusion.

One additional antecedent needs to be drawn into the picture: namely, Darwin. His approach to evolution represents, of course, a fundamental turning point in the history of Western thought. The notion that species have unchanging essences was thrown to the winds or, more properly speaking, to the vast drama of the life and death of species. Here was a model of historical or temporal transformation that was not confined to human history, as it was in the work of Hegel. But Darwin's model did something more. It provided the basis for an interpretation of nature that emphasized the importance of chance and novelty. No one knows exactly what forms of life may come into existence, for it is in principle impossible to know in advance what sorts of mutation will arise and successfully adapt. And this is not just a matter of human ignorance. It is in the nature of the process. Mead and many of the most influential pragmatists came to see novelty as part of the very fabric of the universe.

Novelty was not a theme that Hegel emphasized, but Mead's interpretation of Darwin dovetails in a rather interesting way with Hegel. For Mead, the self can only be understood as part of a social group. Social groups are systemically organized; their parts only function and make sense in relationship to one another. For Hegel, cultures are social wholes that must be approached systemically; their parts or "moments" are constituted through their relationships and must be seen as members of a larger system to be fully understood. We can find a variant of the latter systems approach in Mead's Darwinian ecological sensibility. Think of a natural environment, an ecology of a certain area. It can be viewed as a system because it is in a sense constituted by the interactions of the species that are part of the ecology. We can think of an eco-system of this sort as a "local" system, as opposed to a global or world historical one. Mead focuses on local systems, which are subject to change due to the introduction of novel events. Hegel, on the other hand, sees "local" systems as participating in a larger whole, in the development of a world spirit. The "essence" of each local spirit is part and parcel of the larger whole. Hegel's history is actually an unfolding of a "fixed" set of potentialities of the world spirit, and in this he brings to bear notions of potentiality and actuality he inherited from Aristotle.[11]

Sociality

Nature and history are clearly not fixed for Mead. Variations occur, and the transitions from one state to the another are just as real as the states themselves. Mead uses the term *sociality* to characterize these transitions. Much of life, as William James might say, is in the transitions.

> When the new [life] form has established its citizenship the botanist can exhibit the mutual adjustments that have taken place. The world has become a different world because of the advent, but to identify sociality with this result is to identify it with system merely. It is rather the stage betwixt and between the old system and the new that I am referring to. If emergence is a feature of reality this phase of adjustment, which comes between the ordered universe before the emergent has arisen and that after it has come to terms with the newcomer, must be a feature also of reality.[12]

For Mead, the betwixt and between that we find as new organisms/species come to inhabit and shape ecological niches is just as real as a given ecological system itself. These transitions give lie to the fact that systems are permanently fixed, given for all time. But notice that Mead refers to this rift in the systemic as sociality. Why does he choose such a term to denote this phenomenon? Because social life is itself a life of transitions, and Mead was first and foremost a social philosopher.

Our social life is also a life of language. Language is a necessary condition for human beings to become fully human, that is, to possess what Mead calls a self. The self for Mead is not necessarily equivalent to the personality, and it is definitely not equivalent to the totality of the organism. It is a cognitive "object," intimately related to self-consciousness, which in turn depends on language for its development. We will not be able to provide a full account of Mead's understanding of language here, but there are some important points that we can make about his approach that will be of assistance in understanding his thought.

Mead drew on Wundt's notion of the gesture in explaining the origins of human language. Gestures are made by many biological organisms, including human beings. So, for example, when a dog growls at another dog, this is a gesture. Its meaning, Mead tells us, is found in the responses of other dogs to the gesture. Dogs, however, are not aware of the meanings of their gestures. They simply respond to them. Human beings, on the other hand, can be aware of the meanings of their gestures, that is, the responses that their gestures call out in others and themselves. This capacity depends on the use of significant symbols.

The significant symbol is typically a vocal gesture, although it can also be found in hand sign languages. In using speech one hears the gesture as one is using it (or one sees it as one is using it in a sign language). In so doing one has a tendency to react to the gesture in a manner similar to the other individual hearing it. If I say "run" to you as we are walking down the street together, there is a tendency in me to run also. This tendency is what Mead refers to as an implicit response:

> Gestures become significant symbols when they implicitly arouse in an individual making them the same responses which they explicitly arouse, or are supposed to arouse, in other individuals, the individuals to whom they are addressed.[13]

Human beings internalize a great many vocal gestures, and in so doing they come to be able to respond to themselves, that is, talk to themselves. As speakers and hearers they can be both the subject and object of a conversation, that is, they can respond to their own symbolic stimuli. In other words, reflexivity is a hallmark of their experience.

One of the reasons that Mead emphasizes the vocal gesture is that it provides a source of reflexivity that he takes to be a fundamental feature of the human mind. We move from a capacity for being reflexively aware of specific symbols to being reflexively aware of social processes that are linked to symbolic life. In the reflexive awareness that is found in social life, Mead tells us, mind arises.

> It is by means of reflexiveness – the turning back of the experience of the individual upon himself – that the whole social process is thus brought into the experience of the individuals involved in it; it is by such means, which enable the individual to take the attitude of the other toward himself, that the individual is able consciously to adjust himself to that process, and to modify the resultant of that process in any given social act in terms of his adjustment to it. Reflexiveness, then, is the essential condition, within the social process, for the development of mind.[14]

The notion of taking roles is commonplace in contemporary sociological circles, and Mead did much to promote the idea. For Mead, it is because of our capacity for reflexivity that role-taking is possible for human beings. We saw earlier how Mead referred to the importance of role-taking for the romantics. But this capacity is very much a part of human life in general for Mead. For example, children role play as part of their personal development. Roles are constellations of behaviors that we find in all human communities, although they differ in number and type, and they only make sense in relationship to other constellations; for instance, one cannot play the role of doctor unless one has internalized the role of patient. The reflexivity that is entailed in the use of vocal gestures helps make possible the interaction that we call role-playing, for I can only play roles if I can anticipate the responses of others to my own actions, and then adjust my responses accordingly.

In other words, I must be able to "see" my own words and actions as others "see" them.[15]

Self and Society

Roles can be thought of as proto or quasi selves for Mead. They do not tell the whole story of the self because the self is more than just the specific roles that it plays. Roles are too limited to constitute a self. Why? Recall that for Hegel the self can be spoken of as embodying the spirit of the times. Mead would prefer to bypass the language of spirit, but he knew that the self must be more than a specific role, if only for the reason that roles are themselves imbued with larger cultural sensibilities. Although Mead did not want to accept the whole Hegelian machine – after all, he was a thinker of "little" systems that could undergo modification due to novel events – he did understand that the self is more complex than mere roles.

Mead suggested that to understand the difference between roles and the self we should contrast play with the game. When we play we do not necessarily have to become aware of larger systemic wholes. On the one hand, for example, a child can play at being a doctor, emphasizing only certain features of the doctor's role. On the other hand, when we engage in organized games we must become aware of our relationship to a number of different roles at once, as well as the rules of the game. To play baseball, for example, we must be aware of all of the positions on the field. When we do so we are not just aware of specific others, but we become aware of what Mead calls the *generalized other*.

> The organized community or social group which gives to the individual his unity of self may be called "the generalized other." The attitude of the generalized other is the attitude of the whole community. Thus, for example, in the case of such a social group as a ball team, the team is the generalized other in so far as it enters – as an organized process or social activity – into the experience of any one of the individual members of it.[16]

It is the capacity for being aware of a multiplicity of roles and the relationship between them that sets us apart from other animals.

> But the animal could never reach the goal of becoming an object to itself as a whole until it could enter into a larger system within which it could play various roles. . . . It is this development that a society whose life process is mediated by communication has made possible. It is here that mental life arises – with this continual passing from one system to another, with the occupation of both in passage and with the systematic structures that each involves. It is the realm of continual emergence.[17]

So the self, then, must be thought of as reflecting a larger social unit, be it a family or a community of some sort. These communities, in turn, are linked to other communities by sharing cultural and social spaces; they overlap and patterns of behavior that are appropriate to one community can be found in others. The self that arises in relationship to specific communities – or, more properly speaking, that arises in relationship to different generalized others that reflect the systematic connections that exist in various communities – is referred to as a "me."[18] There is, then, clearly more than one "me," for we inhabit different communities, different systems. It is worth noting that Mead highlights the passing from one system to another in the above quotation. Even if there is overlap between communities, social groups are by no means identical. Individuals must learn to navigate transitions from one social group to the next, for human beings typically participate in more than one social group. Part of being human is learning to live in the transitions.

Interactions with others and different groups actually produce new sorts of selves, that is, new selves emerge from different interactions. And very often it is one's own novel reactions that help to transform a social group and one's "me," just as in an eco-system mutations may help to modify the system in which they arose. To capture this novel, non-determined dimension of the self, Mead used the term "I," and he meant it to refer to a set of functions.[19] It can be thought of as the spontaneity of an individual, the capacity for responding in unpredictable ways, the "power" to upset the apple cart of the old "me." The self, then, is in one sense a "me," but in another it must be thought of as a combination of the "I" and "me," with the understanding that there is more than one "me" in each of us. And with the further understanding that human beings modify their environments not only due to unexpected responses, but also in methodical ways when faced with problems and difficulties. Human inventiveness in the face of difficulties draws on creative responses and prior experience, that is, on both the "I" and the "me."

Whether Mead's approach to the self can capture all of the richness of the self is open to question. But it is important to bear in mind that Mead did not argue that the self constituted all aspects of the person. By definition, it is that aspect of the person that can be brought to consciousness through symbolic means. Be this as it may, we can say that his vision of the self was very much tied to a political vision, one that had been with him from his earliest days. Mead, like many of the pragmatists, was a committed ameliorationist, one who thinks that society can be favorably reformed through human intervention. Nature is not fixed for Mead, and neither is human society. The kind of society that we can work for, and should work for, is a democratic one, one that relishes differences and allows each the opportunity to develop as many aspects of his or herself as possible.[20] Mead's vision of a malleable self is clearly commensurate with his vision of the good society, a society in which one's individuality is linked to and nurtured by one's social life.

Notes

1 Cited in Dmitri Shalin, "G. H. Mead, Socialism, and the Progressive Agenda," *American Journal of Sociology*, 93: 923. Reprinted in Mitchell Aboulafia, ed., *Philosophy, Social Theory, and the Thought of George Herbert Mead* (Albany: SUNY Press, 1991).

2 See Gary A. Cook, *George Herbert Mead, The Making of a Social Pragmatist* (Urbana: University of Illinois Press, 1993), p. 2.

3 Mead wrote to Henry Castle: "I shall have to let persons understand that I have some belief in Christianity and my praying be interpreted as a belief in God, whereas I have no doubt that now the most reasonable system of the universe can be formed to myself without a God. But notwithstanding all this I cannot go out with the world and not work for men. The spirit of a minister is strong with me and I come fairly by it." Shalin, "Progressive Agenda," pp. 920–1.

4 John Dewey, "Prefatory Remarks," to George Herbert Mead, *The Philosophy of the Present*, ed. and with an introduction by Arthur E. Murphy (Chicago: Open Court, 1932), p. xxxvi.

5 Although there is little dispute about the influence of Hegel and Darwin on Mead, further historical research would have to be done to prove the direct links between Smith and Mead. Nevertheless, there is evidence to suggest that Mead was indeed familiar with Smith's ideas. And the latter's notions provide an accessible path for introducing Mead's philosophy. See Mitchell Aboulafia, *The Cosmopolitan Self: George Herbert Mead and Continental Philosophy* (Urbana and Chicago: University of Illinois Press, 2001), ch. 2.

6 Adam Smith, *The Theory of Moral Sentiments*, ed. D. D. Raphael and A. L. Macfie (Oxford: Clarendon Press, 1976; repr. Indianapolis: Liberty Classics, 1982), p. 112.

7 *Movements of Thought in the Nineteenth Century*, ed. and with an introduction by Merritt H. Moore (Chicago: University of Chicago Press, 1936), p. 60.

8 Ibid., p. 63.

9 G. W. F. Hegel, *Phenomenology of Spirit*, tr. A. V. Miller (Oxford: Clarendon Press, 1977), pp. 111–19.

10 Mead and Hegel would have appreciated Smith's insight into intersubjectivity when he said, "We suppose ourselves the spectators of our own behavior, and endeavor to imagine what effect it would, in this light, produce upon us. This is the only looking-glass by which we can, in some measure, with the eyes of other people, scrutinize the propriety of our own conduct" (*The Theory of Moral Sentiments*, p. 112).

11 Of course, the question of how to understand the "fixed" set of potentialities is one of the million-dollar questions in Hegel scholarship. But this claim will do for the introductory purposes at hand.

12 Mead, *The Philosophy of the Present*, p. 47.

13 *Mind, Self, and Society: From the Standpoint of a Social Behaviorist*, ed. and with an introduction by Charles W. Morris (Chicago: University of Chicago Press, 1934), p. 47.

14 Ibid., p. 134.

15 There are obviously a number of issues that this account raises about the nature of self-consciousness. For Mead, there is a sense in which the use of significant symbols entails a form of self-consciousness, that is, the awareness of the meaning of symbols.

This is not to be confused with the more explicit form of self-consciousness that arises when I am aware of my self. This account also raises issues about the relationship of habitual responses to those that are more explicitly self-conscious, for example, those that occur when difficulties challenge prior expectations. A detailed treatment of these issues, however, is outside of the scope of this introductory essay. For further discussion, see Aboulafia, *The Mediating Self: Mead, Sartre, and Self-Determination* (New Haven, CT: Yale University Press, 1986), and *The Cosmopolitan Self.*

16 *Mind, Self, and Society.* p. 154.

17 *The Philosophy of the Present.* p. 85.

18 Mead gives the following as examples of groups to which individuals may belong: "Some of them are concrete social classes or subgroups, such as political parties, clubs, corporations, which are all actually functional social units, in terms of which their individual members are directly related to one another. The others are abstract social classes or subgroups, such as the class of debtors and the class of creditors, in terms of which their individual members are related to one another only more or less indirectly" (*Mind, Self, and Society*, p. 157).

19 Ibid., pp. 192–222.

20 "It is often assumed that democracy is an order of society in which those personalities which are sharply differentiated will be eliminated, that everything will be ironed down to a situation where everyone will be, as far as possible, like everyone else. But of course that is not the implication of democracy: the implication of democracy is rather that the individual can be as highly developed as lies within the possibilities of his own inheritance, and still can enter into the attitudes of the others whom he affects" (ibid., p. 326).

Suggested reading

Primary sources

The Philosophy of the Present, ed. and with an introduction by Arthur E. Murphy and prefatory remarks by John Dewey (Chicago: University of Chicago Press, 1980; originally published La Salle, IL: Open Court, 1932).

Mind, Self, and Society: From the Standpoint of a Social Behaviorist, ed. and with an introduction by Charles W. Morris (Chicago: University of Chicago Press, 1934).

Movements of Thought in the Nineteenth Century, ed. and with an introduction by Merritt H. Moore (Chicago: University of Chicago Press, 1936).

Philosophy of the Act, ed. and with an introduction by Charles W. Morris in collaboration with John M. Brewster, Albert M. Dunham, and David L. Miller (Chicago: University of Chicago Press, 1938).

Selected Writings: George Herbert Mead, ed. and with an introduction by Andrew J. Reck (Chicago: University of Chicago Press, 1981; originally published Indianapolis: Bobbs-Merrill, Library of Liberal Arts, 1964).

The Individual and the Social World: Unpublished Work of George Herbert Mead, ed. and with an introduction by David L. Miller (Chicago: University of Chicago Press, 1982).

Secondary sources

Aboulafia, Mitchell, *The Cosmopolitan Self: George Herbert Mead and Continental Philosophy* (Urbana and Chicago: University of Illinois Press, 2001).

——ed., *Philosophy, Social Theory, and the Thought of George Herbert Mead* (Albany: SUNY Press, 1991).

——*The Mediating Self: Mead, Sartre, and Self-Determination* (New Haven, CT: Yale University Press, 1986).

Cook, Gary A., *George Herbert Mead, The Making of a Social Pragmatist* (Urbana: University of Illinois Press, 1993).

Habermas, Jürgen, "Individuation through Socialization: On George Herbert Mead's Theory of Subjectivity," in *Postmetaphysical Thinking: Philosophical Essays*, tr. William Mark Hohengarten (Cambridge, MA: MIT Press, 1992), pp. 149–204.

Joas, Hans, *G. H. Mead: A Contemporary Re-Examination of His Thought*, tr. Raymond Meyer (Cambridge, MA: MIT Press, 1985).

Miller, David L., *George Herbert Mead: Self, Language, and the World* (Chicago: University of Chicago Press, 1980; originally published Austin: University of Texas Press, 1973).

Natanson, Maurice, *The Social Dynamics of George H. Mead* (The Hague: Martinus Nijhoff, 1973; originally published Washington, DC: Public Affairs Press, 1956).

Rosenthal, Sandra B. and Patrick L. Bourgeois, *Mead and Merleau-Ponty: Toward a Common Vision* (Albany: SUNY Press, 1991).

Chapter 11

Jane Addams, 1860–1935

Charlene Haddock Seigfried

Jane Addams, as much as John Dewey and George Herbert Mead, was responsible for the particular combination of philosophical theory and practice known as the Chicago School of pragmatism. Her innovative approach to social problems attracted Dewey's attention even before he moved to the University of Chicago from Michigan. He became a member of the Hull House Board of Trustees when it incorporated in 1895, six years after it was founded by Addams and Ellen Gates Starr. Dewey's contact with them and the other remarkable women residents of the settlement considerably deepened and sharpened his own ideas.[1] He credited Addams with developing the idea of democracy as a way of life, an approach that is a defining feature not only of pragmatist social and political theory, but of its ethics or value theory. Mead also worked with Addams, and William James called her book, *Democracy and Social Ethics*, "one of the great books of our time."[2] Addams is just as important in her own right, however, as she is for influencing the well-known male pragmatists.

Addams's life and work are inextricably linked to the Hull House settlement in Chicago. Settlements provided a way for socially conscious members of the new generations of college-educated women to use their recently acquired skills to alleviate the worst effects of industrialization on the waves of immigrants crowding into the inner city. The settlement movement began with the establishment of Toynbee Hall by an Anglican clergyman, Samuel Barnett, and some young Oxford men, in the East End of London in 1884. It was inspired by personal service to the poor. By 1890 three settlement houses, founded independently of each other, were in operation in Boston, New York, and Chicago. According to Mina Carson, "they saw their role as mediators between competing social and economic interests, interpreters shuttling between the alien cultures of the recent immigrants and the entrenched and defensive 'natives.'"[3] Hull House in Chicago developed a pragmatist experimental model of transaction that criticized "top-down" approaches to problem-solving in favor of working with others in a way calculated to change the attitudes and habits of both the settlement workers, who were mostly middle- and upper-class women, and members of the impoverished working class. Besides attracting the admiration and support of the Chicago School of academic pragmatists, Hull House also formed an important part of the milieu out of which the departments of sociology and of social work were later established at the University of Chicago.[4]

Working together with an unusually dedicated, creative, and effective group of women, Addams was instrumental in developing a cooperative rather than positivistic social scientific approach to the enormous problems generated by laissez-faire capitalism.[5] She helped found the first kindergarten, playground, and juvenile court system in Chicago, and was active on a wide range of social issues, from the emancipation of women to public hygiene. Among the urban social issues Addams and the first generation residents Florence Kelley, Julia Lathrop, Dr. Alice Hamilton, and Starr were concerned with were "compulsory education, child labor, mothers' pensions, parks and playgrounds, workmen's compensation, vocational education and guidance, protection of newly arrived immigrants, women's labor unions, and crusades against prostitution."[6] Sophonisba Breckinridge and Edith Abbott were the two residents with the closest ties to the sociology department of the University of Chicago, working extensively with Charles R. Henderson and Mead, but as they became dissatisfied with the direction sociology was taking, they increasingly identified with Hull House and focused their efforts toward social work and reform.[7] Addams's interests and work were enhanced and her influence multiplied due to her position as the central figure in a community of mutually supportive, intellectually astute, dynamic, and indefatigable women reformers.

Addams's crusades for social justice extended beyond her neighborhood and country.

> [She] was a member of the first executive committee of the National Association for the Advancement of Colored People, a vice-president of the National American Woman Suffrage Association, and a founder of the American Union Against Militarism, from which emerged both the Foreign Policy Association and the American Civil Liberties Union. A life-long pacifist, she was elected chairman of the Woman's Peace Party in 1915, and in 1919 became the first president of the Woman's International League for Peace and Freedom, having presided over the 1915 International Congress of Women at The Hague from which the league originated.[8]

Addams received the Nobel Peace Prize in 1931. She was an accomplished speaker and prolific author, with ten books and more than 500 articles and book chapters to her credit.[9]

Challenging the Inequality of Interdependency

The interdependency of all persons in society, from the local to the global, and the need for cooperation and mutual responsibility in order for human beings to realize their potential, are central beliefs in Addams's ethical theory.[10] In her many speeches and publications Addams frequently referred to the experiences, values, and beliefs of women of diverse ethnic backgrounds and social classes. She avoided the pitfalls of essentialism by developing a uniquely pragmatist version of feminism that recognized that women could affirm a special angle of vision, interests, and values without closing themselves off from a multiplicity of identities and coalitions. Along with other, predominantly female, members of the Hull House settlement, Addams worked with recent immigrants, both women and men, in the poorest areas of Chicago in a concerted effort to address the worst effects of laissez-faire capitalism. She not only sought to transform the oppressive relationship of factory owners to their workers, to alleviate personal suffering, and to overcome social discrimination, but she also emphasized the perspectives of the oppressed classes in her work and writings.

Besides demonstrating the relevance of pragmatism to the most serious social, political, and economic problems of her times, Addams also contributed to its theoretical development. In her life and work she demonstrated the unity of theory and practice advocated by pragmatism. She was an indefatigable social activist, a superb organizer, and a non-governmental world leader. But she was also, in the words of Christopher Lasch, "a thinker of originality and daring."[11] She made explicit the implicit gender bias in democratic appeals to the "Common Man." But she did not exempt her own beliefs from critical scrutiny. Addams was ahead of her time in her awareness of her own class and ethnic privilege, and in her insights into how such privilege subtly undermines the dignity and effectiveness of the poor and working classes and less favored ethnic groups.[12]

Harmonizing Thought and Action: *Twenty Years at Hull-House*

Addams lived her life outside academia, so neither interdisciplinary scholarly evidence nor scholarly debate were the primary forums for testing her theories. She did make original contributions to the new field of sociology but more directly than most philosophers, she exercised the pragmatic method in everyday life. Of all the classical American pragmatists, she could arguably be said to be the most completely receptive to the pragmatist ideal of developing theory *out of* practice, rather than bringing theory *to* practice.[13] This can best be demonstrated in *Twenty Years at Hull-House*, in which Addams develops her autobiography as inextricably bound up with the founding of and everyday life in a bustling settlement house in the midst of an impoverished but vibrant immigrant working-class neighborhood. There can be no doubt of her intentions, since she concludes the Preface by saying that each of her earlier books "was an attempt to set forth a thesis supported by experience, whereas this volume endeavors to trace the experiences through which various conclusions were forced upon me."[14] By recounting her life story through the developing history of a social settlement house, Addams not only gives *Twenty Years at Hull-House* an unusual autobiographical tone, but also consciously demonstrates, throughout the book, a particular philosophical approach. It is not just a chronological account loosely organized around a set of topics, as is *The Second Twenty Years at Hull-House*, nor even just a *Bildungsroman*, although it does show how Addams grew to maturity through her reflections on a series of experiences. It is also an original book on method in philosophy.

Her approach is autobiographical, contextual, pluralistic, narrative, experimentally fallibilist, and embedded in history and specific social movements. It shows how knowledge and values cannot be separated any more than theory and practice can. It also exhibits the way individual development is inextricably tied to social development and how, as a consequence, individualistic morality must give way to social morality. Addams shows how perspectivism is not neutral but rather reflects the power disparities of class, ethnicity, and gender. She brings to inquiry an awareness that persons are unequally positioned to contribute to problem-solving or even be perceived as having valid points of view, and she develops a means of working through rather than ignoring or suppressing this fact. Addams argues for a democratically grounded inclusiveness in bringing the pragmatic method to bear on social problems.

In *Twenty Years at Hull-House* Addams not only marshals the experiences that influenced and guided the theory developed in her other books, but she also demonstrates the effectiveness of her questioning unexamined assumptions and of her unflagging determination to overcome injustices. The social nature of ethics explicated in *Democracy and Social Ethics* is made more plausible through Addams's vivid accounts of inner city life, where she seeks to overcome the widespread insensitivity and indifference to the plight of those on whom the new industrial order pressed the hardest. The reminiscences of "impressive old women" who can at last clearly speak their minds eventually leads to *The Long Road of Woman's Memory*, in which the power to retain and transform past experiences is utilized for social reconstruction. The abstract principle of the importance of education gains cogency by the often tragic incidents that demonstrate the need for child labor laws. But it also undergoes revision in light of the importance of the income supplied by children to families barely subsisting on meager wages. Addams develops the intergenerational conflicts of the immigrant working classes, whose children are torn between traditional cultural values and the urban seductions of mixed sex jobs and a vibrant street culture. By taking account of the allure of urban entertainments that brought the sexes together, Addams is able in *A New Conscience and an Ancient Evil* to begin moving away from blithely condemning prostitution as a moral evil, and by recognizing the void that street gangs fill, she can reject simplistic moral judgments in *The Spirit of Youth and City Streets.* Finally, the many glimpses of the lives and work shared with the other residents in the Hull House community are expanded and commented upon in the posthumous *My Friend, Julia Lathrop.*

The Centrality of Experience

Experience, knowledge, values, and experimental method are dynamically interconnected in Addams's pragmatist philosophy. Her emphasis on the centrality of experience in understanding and the acquisition of knowledge is consistent with the pragmatist revolt against the long philosophical tradition of privileging theory at the expense of practice. It is also at the heart of her social ethics. The role of experience in Addams's philosophy can be summed up in three claims she makes in *Democracy and Social Action*: (1) we are morally obliged to choose, rather than passively receive, our experiences; (2) this obligation requires that we seek out diverse experiences; and (3) genuine experience can no more lead us astray than scientific data.

We ought to choose our experiences because our moral intuitions are a result of our cumulative life history, and we should seek out those experiences best calculated to promote a fair and just social order. Insofar as social isolation contributes to stereotyping those outside the familiar group, actively seeking to share the experiences of others can be an effective means of recognizing human solidarity. Diverse experiences are important because they are one way to escape the predispositions typical of the outlooks deriving from any particular class, ethnicity, race, sexual orientation, or other orientations outside our usual range. Experiences, like scientific data, are the raw material out of which ideas and judgments are formed, and are therefore the starting points as well as the testing grounds for transformative methods of inquiry. In the midst of any perplexity, Addams encourages us to ask "Has the experience any value?" and, by doing so, to transform what could otherwise remain an unproductive frustration into a productive method of social inquiry.[15] Dewey also emphasizes that knowledge and values are inseparably linked in pragmatist theories of experience when he says that "interest in learning from all the contacts of life is the essential moral interest."[16]

Social solutions based on abstract principles, rules, and regulations alone are sure to go wrong. The problem with principles arrived at speculatively, especially when reinforced by other like-minded people, is that they can lead to propaganda and fanaticism. The alternative is to begin with the concrete situations that exhibit the most need for intelligently guided social reconstruction. We need to understand people's lives and habits as a whole, situated in a given set of circumstances, embedded in a particular culture and suffused with various beliefs. Instead of unreflectively applying what we already know to new situations and thus risking promulgating errors or reifying prejudices, theory should be developed by working with those affected to overcome social injustices. Having those in positions of power impose solutions from above might resolve problems sooner, but such solutions are less likely to be lasting and effective than they would be if one enlists the cooperation of all those involved.

Knowledge is best acquired through what Addams calls "sympathetic understanding," and it should be tested by acting on our beliefs and evaluating the outcomes. She agrees with the pragmatist thesis of the pluralism of perspectives, which necessitates the pragmatic experimental method as a way to determine how useful any particular belief is, how far any particular perspective extends, and what changes need to be made in light of the findings of other perspectives. But Addams extends and transforms the pragmatic method by showing concretely how people are unequally situated in terms of power and access to information. Along with other marginalized pragmatist theorists like W. E. B. Du Bois and Alain Locke, she emphasizes the fact – often overlooked by the other pragmatists – that perspectives not only limit, but can distort the facts we are trying to understand. For knowledge to accurately reflect the facts of the situation and to lead to outcomes desirable for all concerned, we must listen to others and – just as importantly – work with them to overcome mutually acknowledged problems. In analyzing and setting the conditions of inquiry, perspectival limitations and distortions as well as unequal power relations must be taken into account.

Cooperative Experimental Method

Hull House itself is conceived as a cooperative experiment in scientifically gathering the evidence necessary for the solution of social and industrial problems. This emphasis on the social nature of inquiry is characteristic of pragmatist theory; what Addams contributes is the recognition that inquiry takes place among persons who participate in various hierarchies of power and influence and that this fact must be addressed in the theory itself. Addams uses the perplexity that is felt when our preconceptions are called into question by those differently situated as a way to focus attention on the power disparities that, when ignored, undermine the effectiveness of the experimental method.

Addams illustrates what she means by a social method by recalling how Hull House workers, under the guidance of a physician, worked with Italian immigrant women to help them take better care of their physically underdeveloped children.[17] The problem was not a lack of knowledge on the part of the settlement workers, but how best to communicate it to immigrants who were understandably reluctant to change traditional beliefs and patterns of conduct for alien ones. It was useless just to distribute written information concerning recently collected scientific data about the relation of poor diet and unsanitary conditions in tenement houses to such problems as childhood malnutrition and typhoid fever. The issue was not solely one of illiteracy or not understanding English, but of deep-seated cultural differences and suspicions. Rather than lecturing about nutrition or directly attacking superstitious beliefs about the evil eye causing disease, a group of Italian women and their children were invited to join the Hull House women in festive Sunday morning breakfasts and were given access to public baths at the settlement house. Knowledge was gained by both sides in the process, and Addams indicates that soon the intelligent care of children learned by this group was passed on to their other friends and neighbors in the Italian community.

Addams contrasts this successful effort with one less successful, due to the failure of a Hull House resident and temperance advocate to understand southern Italian culture. She explains how the resident's well-meaning but ineffectual efforts to address the problem of a child who kept coming to kindergarten in an intoxicated state only made matters worse when a breakfast of bread soaked in good American whiskey was substituted for the wine the mother had been using. She deliberately illustrates the inevitable mistakes and even tragedies that occur when we blindly impose upon others what we understand to be right or true, instead of working with those involved to dispel both our and their preconceptions and the limitations of the respective belief systems. Both cases were offered to illustrate the experimental method, which in pragmatist theory is always guided by an ameliorative end in view. By openly acknowledging that inquiry takes place among unequally positioned subjects, Addams begins removing the barriers to free and open communication and negotiation. She argues that – given the problem of bias – sympathetic understanding is a prerequisite for acquiring knowledge. Such sympathy does not refer to an intention to unilaterally put oneself in the place of the other, but rather signifies a desire to include representatives of those affected in any inquiry, based on the assumption that what they have to contribute is valuable and less likely to be distorted when they can speak for themselves. This includes every stage of inquiry, from the initial definition of the problem and the choice of means to the evaluation of success in reaching the desired end. Multiple perspectives are required to avoid both over-generalizing from a limited knowledge base and the harms caused by one-sided moral judgments.

Addams's experimental method is explicated through highlighting the perplexities encountered whenever different classes, sexes, generations, and ethnicities interact. She develops the way such perplexities can be utilized as steps to inquiry. A sense of bewilderment is strategically emphasized throughout *Twenty Years at Hull-House* because Addams wants to rebut the impression that she and Starr knew what they were doing when they founded a settlement house in the inner city. This false impression was a result both of the settlement house's eventual success and fame and of the popular prejudice that as members of what came to be known as the new class of "technocratic experts," they engineered social progress by simply applying a body of theory to practice. Unless this impression was squelched, Addams feared that the actual cause of their success would be lost, namely, their refusal to simply impose their own supposedly superior judgments and values on others and the willingness of the settlement workers to adopt an experimental approach.

Socializing Democracy: Addams's Social Ethics

Addams's social ethics is grounded in the democratic belief of the absolute value of each human person and is secured through affirming human solidarity. It recognizes disparities of power as barriers to full communication and cooperative behavior. Dogmatic attitudes, which are strengthened when the complications of life are forgotten, undermine a democratically social ethics, which is strengthened through attitudes of tolerance that provide a space for questioning one's own preconceptions and, alternatively, for considering alien attitudes and values. Socializing democracy means securing our own well-being by securing it for others.

The social relation that is for pragmatists the core of ethics is essentially a reciprocal one. Addams argues for consciously valuing our mutual interdependence. Since privilege does not confer a monopoly of knowledge or goodness, we should actively seek to learn from everyone we meet and from every situation in which we find ourselves, without regard to class, age, gender, religious affiliation, educational level, or ethnic background. Through this process of sharing, values eventually spread from one person or group to another, being transformed in the process, until they eventually become universal in the only sense of universal morality pragmatists recognize.

Addams's first two books were on social ethics. In *Democracy and Social Ethics* and *Newer Ideals of Peace* she criticizes the exaggerated individualism, overemphasis on autonomy, and abstract rationalism of traditional moral theory, and argues that just as persons develop through interactions with others, so also morality is social. For Addams, given the fact that human beings develop over time in a social milieu, the dignity and value of each person requires that society develop the capacity of persons to make informed decisions about the way they choose to live. Interdependence means that what we do both reflects and impacts the lives and beliefs of others. Individualistic moral theories ought therefore to be replaced with a social ethics that emphasizes mutual interdependence and encourages reciprocity in relationships and decision-making that both recognizes the limitations of personal perspectives and the reality of unequal power relations and seeks to minimize their negative effects. *Newer Ideals of Peace* not only urges the end of war between nations, but also the end of the internal wars of industrial capitalists against labor, including child labor; of class, racial, and gender exploitation; and of the exploitation of immigrants by city government. Addams argues that there would be no need for developing new experiments in better ways of living if the current relations among members and segments of society were not characterized by hostility and misunderstanding.

Democratic experience provides that corrective and guide to social morality without which only an exaggerated individual morality develops. The significance of our interactions with others must be incorporated into our own conscious experiences. Otherwise, we will think of our moral achievements as wholly personal, inviolable possessions. We will think ourselves so different from others that we will begin to make an exception for ourselves in our moral judgments and social actions. Knowing the lives of others in order to believe in their integrity is a necessary first step in the beginning development of social morality.

Addams uses perplexity as a central organizing principle in *Democracy and Social Ethics.* She introduces the word "perplexity" at strategic junctures in each chapter to identify the challenge to one's conventional attitudes, beliefs, morals, and practices that results from efforts to communicate and work across class, ethnic, gender, and generational boundaries. A particular perplexity can be an occasion for mental and moral growth or it can be an excuse for turning away from what cannot easily be accommodated to one's usual outlook and moral intuitions. A perplexity is subjectively experienced as an unpleasant or even highly disturbing emotional state at the same time that it reveals objective barriers to resolving a problematic social situation. The situations in which perplexities arise cannot be resolved without developing a new understanding of the situation and calling into question received values.[18]

Pacifism

Whereas Dewey's pacifism is moderated by his instrumentalism, so that he can reluctantly support war when no other option remains to prevent greater harm, Addams's pacifism is absolute. She never wavers from the pragmatist principle that means must be continuous with ends. Thus if peace is demonstrably a better state of affairs than war, then it ought to be pursued non-belligerently through sympathetic understanding and attempts at the mutual solution of common problems even when such efforts are one-sided. As a pragmatist, she was also committed to mediating among diverse and conflicting perspectives and values and to supporting mutually arrived at solutions to intransigent problems, even when they ran counter to her own moral intuitions. Addams never resolved to her own satisfaction the conflict of her ideal of pacifism with her ideal of reciprocity embedded in the pragmatic method of inquiry. In this case, upholding the sanctity of each person – which she understood as the fundamental value of democracy – was unalterably opposed to violent attacks on any one of them, even as a means to preventing greater violence.

In *Newer Ideals of Peace* Addams shows how militarism not only regulates relations among nations but also underlies and orders the internal relations of society. Instead of just opposing war, her prescription for a more active and dynamic ideal of peace requires replacing this military model with an enlightened industrialism. Addams examines the quality of the relations among various segments of society to make visible its hidden military assumptions and to urge instead the ideals of a genuine evolutionary democracy. In *Peace and Bread in Time of War* she argues that war cannot be prevented by the same use of political and legal force that in a more virulent form leads to war. Addams sounds an early warning against the transformation of nationalism from a hopeful sign of unity in the years leading up to the First World War into the hypernationalism that not only contributed to the outbreak of war but also threatened to fuel future conflicts. She put her faith in a younger generation more attuned to internationalism in their everyday lives to lead the way to effective international organizations designed for the peaceful resolution of problems. She reaffirms her democratic faith that ordinary persons will spontaneously recognize their common humanity despite differences. Addams draws on her Hull House experiences of cooperation across ethnic, racial, and class boundaries at the local level as one that provides the best model for effectively organizing all levels of societies and nations in cooperative ventures. She believes that by working together to overcome the misery, poverty, and ignorance that drive people to war, bonds of affiliation will be created and reinforced; these bonds will make it abhorrent for anyone to unleash the violence of war on their "neighbors," no matter how distant in space or different in beliefs, customs, and outlook. But Addams also intimates the fragility of such cooperative feelings and their susceptibility to the corrupting influence of propaganda, since she also vividly depicts the virulent animosity directed at pacifists like herself who remained true to their convictions in time of war.

Feminism

Addams has been categorized as a cultural feminist, but this judgment must be tempered by recognizing her pragmatist orientation. In the nineteenth and early twentieth centuries cultural feminists accepted the common belief that women were essentially different from men, but they denied that this difference entailed women's inferiority. They sought to remove the cultural, political, and religious barriers that unfairly prevented women's full development as persons. Because it was believed that women's nature was essentially maternal, the home was thought to be their proper sphere, and women were judged to be more nurturing, docile, generous, spiritual, and emotional than men. Rather than accepting these limitations, cultural feminists redefined women's traits as special abilities requiring greater recognition of the important social contributions women made, and justifying extending their benevolent influence into the public sphere.

Addams did believe that women and men differed in characteristic ways, and she appealed to women's maternal feelings and antipathy to violence as creating a natural affinity for pacifism. But she also understood nature in the pragmatist sense of being second nature; that is, as deep-seated habits or dispositions brought about through socialization, and therefore modifiable over time. Women were not homogenous, with the same essential nature, but were conceived in multiple ways that emphasized their diverse ethnicities, classes, religions, ages, and experiences. She sought both to develop the positive aspects of women's socialization in new ways and to criticize and remove its negative effects. She supported enfranchising women because the vote would enable them to extend their concerns with nurturing the family to the neighborhood, the country, and the world. But Addams also argued that women's roles were too restricted in the home and they had the right to seek work and alternative lifestyles outside it. Her primary affectionate relationships were with other women and her special bond with Mary Rozet Smith was not hidden, although according to contemporary categories it would be called lesbian.

Addams's feminist theory was thoroughly pragmatist, but at the same time showed where pragmatism was limited by its primarily white male origins. Her goal was not to describe women's lives, but to contextualize them in order to emphasize an emancipatory end-in-view. Her support of restricted working hours for women put her at odds with liberal feminists, but she had seen for herself the physical exhaustion and psychological stress endured by working-class women who returned from extremely long hours of physical labor outside the home to the equally demanding tasks of child care and housework in the home. Addams did not begin with abstract principles like equality, but with concrete situations that needed remedying. Her pragmatist method required working together with other women to transform oppressive situations, whether this meant inaugurating the first kindergartens or juvenile court system in Chicago or supporting the unionization of sweatshop workers. Simply by paying attention to women in her actions and writings and taking their needs seriously, Addams not only called attention to their sufferings and recognized their contributions to society, but also made their neglect in theory and practice visible.

Addams emphasizes the destabilizing and transformative power of women's memories in *The Long Road of Woman's Memory*. In doing so, she develops the pragmatic method in important new ways. Memory is not interpreted as a passive recollection of given facts, but rather as a dynamic reconstruction of the past in order to transform the present. Addams shows how selected aspects of what constitutes the background of inquiry can become explicit in women's desires to transform the pain and anguish of present experiences for the better. By relating these subjective memories to those of other women impacted by similar social, political, and economic forces, they can become the impetus for concerted actions for social justice. Addams is surely one of the earliest exponents of pragmatist feminism and its most challenging theorist.

Notes

1 George Dykhuizen, *The Life and Mind of John Dewey* (Carbondale: Southern Illinois University Press, 1973), p. 105.

2 William James, quoted in Christopher Lasch, ed., *The Social Thought of Jane Addams* (New York: Irvington, 1982), p. 62.

3 Mina Carson, *Settlement Folk: Social Thought and the American Settlement Movement, 1885–1930* (Chicago: University of Chicago Press, 1990), p. 53.

4 Settlement House information taken from Charlene Haddock Seigfried, "Socializing Democracy: Jane Addams and John Dewey," *Philosophy of the Social Sciences*, 29/2 (June 1999): 212–13. See also Seigfried, *Pragmatism and Feminism* (Chicago: University of Chicago Press, 1996), pp. 58–9, 73–9.

5 See Eleanor J. Stebner, *The Women of Hull House: A Study in Spirituality, Vocation, and Friendship* (Albany: SUNY Press, 1997); Mary Jo Deegan, *Jane Addams and the*

Men of the Chicago School, 1892–1918 (New Brunswick, NJ: Transaction Books, 1988); and Kathryn Kish Sklar, "Hull-House Maps and Papers: Social Science as Women's Work in the 1890s," in Helene Silverberg, ed., *Gender and American Social Science: The Formative Years* (Princeton, NJ: Princeton University Press, 1998).

6 Lynn D. Gordon, *Gender and Higher Education in the Progressive Era* (New Haven, NJ: Yale University Press, 1990), p. 89.

7 Deegan, *Jane Addams and the Men*, pp. 44–5.

8 Ellen Condliffe Lagemann, introduction to Jane Addams, *Jane Addams on Education* (New York: Teachers College Press, 1985), p. 30.

9 The last two paragraphs are taken from Charlene Haddock Seigfried, introduction to Jane Addams, *The Long Road of Woman's Memories* (Urbana: University of Illinois Press, 2002).

10 Dewey expressed most starkly the social nature of pragmatist ethics: "The moral and the social quality of conduct are, in the last analysis, identical with each other." *Democracy and Education*, in John Dewey, *The Middle Works of John Dewey*, vol. 9, ed. Jo Ann Boydston (Carbondale: Southern Illinois University Press, 1980), p. 368.

11 Lasch, ed., *The Social Thought of Jane Addams*, p. xv.

12 The last two paragraphs are taken from Seigfried, introduction to Jane Addams, *Democracy and Social Ethics* (Urbana: University of Illinois Press, 2002).

13 See Michael Eldridge, *Transforming Experience* (Nashville: Vanderbilt University Press, 1998); Richard Shusterman, *Practicing Philosophy* (New York: Routledge, 1997).

14 Addams, *Twenty Years at Hull-House* (New York: Penguin Group, 1981), p. xviii.

15 Addams, *Democracy and Social Ethics*, ed. Anne Firor Scott (Cambridge, MA: Belknap Press, 1964), p. 63.

16 Dewey, *Middle Works*, vol. 9, p. 370.

17 Addams, "A Function of the Social Settlement," in Lasch, ed., *The Social Thought of Jane Addams*, p. 198.

18 Perplexity as a pragmatic method of social inquiry is developed in Seigfried, introduction to Jane Addams, *Democracy and Social Ethics.*

Suggested reading

Primary sources

Democracy and Social Ethics (Urbana: University of Illinois Press, 2002 [1902]).
Newer Ideals of Peace (New York: Macmillan, 1907).
The Spirit of Youth and the City Streets (New York: Macmillan, 1909).
Twenty Years at Hull-House (New York: Penguin Group, 1981 [1910]).
A New Conscience and an Ancient Evil (New York: Macmillan, 1912).
The Long Road of Woman's Memories (Urbana: University of Illinois Press, 2002 [1916]).
Peace and Bread in Time of War (New York: Macmillan, 1922).
The Second Twenty Years at Hull House (New York: Macmillan, 1930).
The Excellent Becomes the Permanent (New York: Macmillan, 1932).
My Friend, Julia Lathrop (New York: Macmillan, 1935).
The Social Thought of Jane Addams, ed. Christopher Lasch (New York: Irvington, 1982).

Secondary sources

Carson, Mina, *Settlement Folk: Social Thought and the American Settlement Movement, 1885–1930* (Chicago: University of Chicago Press, 1990).

Deegan, Mary Jo, *Jane Addams and the Men of the Chicago School, 1892–1918* (New Brunswick, NJ: Transaction Books, 1988).

Dewey, John, "Democratic versus Coercive International Organization: The Realism of Jane Addams," in John Dewey, *The Later Works of John Dewey,* vol. 15, ed. Jo Ann Boydston (Carbondale: Southern Illinois University Press, 1989).

Fischer, Marilyn, *On Addams* (Belmont, CA: Wadsworth, 2001).

Lagemann, Ellen Condliffe, Introduction to Jane Addams, *Jane Addams on Education* (New York: Teachers College Press, 1985).

Seigfried, Charlene Haddock, *Pragmatism and Feminism* (Chicago: University of Chicago Press, 1996).

——"Socializing Democracy: Jane Addams and John Dewey," *Philosophy of the Social Sciences*, 29/2 (June 1999): 206–30.

——ed., *Feminist Interpretations of John Dewey* (University Park: Pennsylvania State University Press, 2002).

——Introduction to Jane Addams, *Democracy and Social Ethics* (Urbana: University of Illinois Press, 2002).

——Introduction to Jane Addams, *The Long Road of Woman's Memory* (Urbana: University of Illinois Press, 2002).

Stebner, Eleanor J., *The Women of Hull House: A Study in Spirituality, Vocation, and Friendship* (Albany: SUNY Press, 1997).

Chapter 12

W. E. B. Du Bois, 1868–1963

Shannon Sullivan

William Edward Burghardt Du Bois was born in Great Barrington, Massachusetts only three years after the end of the Civil War, and died in Ghana, Africa the night before Martin Luther King's historic march on Washington. The timing of this beginning and ending of a long, fruitful life seems fitting for a man who devoted himself to the study of race and the elimination of racism. While he held that "the problem of the Twentieth Century is the problem of the color-line,"[1] Du Bois was not, however, the target of much overt racial prejudice while growing up. After a childhood in a small town composed primarily of white people, Du Bois moved to Nashville, Tennessee, to attend college at Fisk University. In the South, he was delighted to find himself surrounded by a large number of other black people for the first time, but he also received there his first encounters with blatant, vigorous racism on the part of white people. After leaving Fisk, Du Bois continued his studies at Harvard University, where he worked with Josiah Royce, George Santayana, and William James. It was James who steered him away from a career in philosophy with a (non-racist) warning that it would be difficult to earn a living in the field. Du Bois therefore turned toward the study of history and social problems and, in so doing, helped create the field of sociology.

Labeling Du Bois a sociologist is somewhat misleading, however, because his work cannot be neatly contained in any one discipline. It crosses academic boundaries to include and intermingle fields such as philosophy, economics, history, psychology, and sociology. In large part, this boundary crossing occurs because Du Bois sought to understand the concrete complexities of human life, which also cannot be neatly contained in discrete compartments. For that reason, Du Bois was grateful that James "turned [him] back from the lovely but sterile land of philosophical speculation, to the social sciences as the field for gathering and interpreting that body of fact which would apply to [his] program for the Negro."[2] Du Bois asserted that what he had to create in his own work because he could not find it elsewhere was a systematic analysis of human behavior and activities. He thus conceived of a plan for "applying philosophy to an historical interpretation of race relations."[3] In doing so, Du Bois pragmatically turned to concrete questions concerning the facts and experiences of lived existence, but in such a way that extended American philosophy beyond James, Dewey, and Peirce's developments of it, to the raced and often racist characteristics of people's lives and experiences.

The Dual Vision of Black People

Du Bois claimed that most (white) Americans formed mistaken opinions about black people without any actual knowledge of their lives. To remedy this problem, he wrote *The Souls of Black Folk* (1903), which described the condition of black people to those who were not familiar with it. Part of that condition, according to Du Bois, is that black people live behind a metaphorical veil. The veil prevents white people from understanding the lives of black people, and thus the primary goal of *The Souls of Black Folk* is to allow white people a glimpse behind it. The veil is distinctive in that it does not prevent black people from clearly seeing life on the other side of it, however. Like a two-way mirror, it allows black people to observe white people unaware: the transparent side allows black people to peer across the divide into the white world, but the reflective side prevents white people from returning the gaze of the black observers on the other side.

As my analogy of the two-way mirror suggests, the double vision had by black people places them in an epistemologically superior position to white people. Black people can see clearly the lives, characters, and situations of white people, while white people cannot do the same with black people. Du Bois does not dwell on this theme in *The Souls of Black Folk*, however, perhaps because it would alienate his white audience. Instead, he attempts to get white people to see black lives sympathetically by describing the suffering generated by having double vision, or "double consciousness." The black person may be "gifted with second-sight in this American world," but what this gift of double consciousness entails is a "sense of always looking at one's self through the eyes of others, of measuring one's soul by the tape of a world that looks on in amused contempt and pity."[4] In *The Souls of Black Folk*, Du Bois makes the value of this gift seem questionable because of the bellicose split that he claims results from it: an unreconciled struggle between the black person's American and "Negro" sides. While Du Bois insists that the black person wants to retain, not erase these two sides in their merger, he makes clear that their existence is the cause of many of black people's hardships, including racist stereotypes used against them. Caught between the opposing demands of his or her American and "Negro" sides, it is small wonder, Du Bois explains, that the black person often appears to white people as indecisive, will-less, and mentally weak.

The theme of the veil continues in the first of Du Bois's three autobiographies, *Darkwater: Voices from within the Veil* (1920). In its tone, *Darkwater* stands out as Du Bois's most confrontational and defiant book. No longer concerned about offending his white readers, he extends his project of translating across the two sides of the veil by turning the spotlight from black souls to white ones. In the book's most powerful chapter, "The Souls of White Folk," Du Bois emphasizes – even gloats about – the epistemologically superior position the veil affords him. Describing himself as high in a tower peering down upon the frothing sea of human souls, Du Bois declares that, with regard to white people, he is "singularly clairvoyant" and "see[s] in and through them."[5] Exposing white souls, which mistakenly take themselves to be beautiful, Du Bois claims:

> I see these souls undressed and from the back and side. I see the workings of their entrails. I know their thoughts and they know that I know. This knowledge makes them now embarrassed, now furious. . . . My word is to them mere bitterness and my soul, pessimism. And yet as they preach and strut and shout and threaten, crouching as they clutch at rags of facts and fancies to hide their nakedness, they go twisting, flying by my tired eyes and I see them ever stripped – ugly, human.[6]

Both literally and metaphorically, black people often were in the position, as house servants and caretakers, to see the nakedness and offal of white people. Anticipating contemporary standpoint theory, which links knowledge with social location, Du Bois suggests that being on a low rung of the racial ladder in the United States enables black people to gain the best possible knowledge of those at its top.

Having stripped whiteness bare, Du Bois claims that the heart of it is ownership of other things and people. He demonstrates what he sees as the white attitude of propriety through an examination of World War I, which he explains as a war between white nations over who will be allowed to exploit darker nations. For Du Bois, colonial expansion summarized not only the war, but also the entire relationship of white European and Euro-aligned nations to the rest of the non-white world. "Bluntly put," Du Bois argues, the theory with which Euro-white nations operate is that "[i]t is the duty of white Europe to divide up the darker world and administer it for Europe's good."[7] According to Du Bois, if exploitation of others for their own gain is the fundamental principle of white nations, then the atrocities of World War I should come as no surprise. As he views it, the judgment of the world's "darker men" about World War I is right on target: "this is not Europe gone mad, this is not aberration nor insanity; this *is* Europe; this seeming Terrible is the real soul of white culture – back of all culture – stripped and visible today . . . these dark and awful depths and not the shining and ineffable heights of which it boasted."[8]

After painting such a dire picture of whiteness in 1920, Du Bois's second autobiography, *Dusk of Dawn: An Essay Toward an Autobiography of a Race Concept* (1940), mellows somewhat, written in "some more benign fluid" than the "tears and blood" than *The Souls of Black Folk* and *Darkwater* were penned.[9] Du Bois nonetheless describes "the attitude of the white world as sheer malevolence," at least as seen from the perspective of "darker races."[10] Combining portrayals of white and black souls in one book, in *Dusk of Dawn* Du Bois switches from metaphors of dual vision and double consciousness to descriptions of "The White World" as enveloping "The Colored World Within," as two key chapters are titled. Holding a mock conversation with a fictitious white friend, Du Bois turns white supremacy on its head by arguing that black people are superior to white people in all the areas that white people usually pride themselves on: beauty, intelligence and creativity, spirituality, and cultural achievement. His provocative claims ultimately are not intended to promote a reverse racism but rather to demonstrate that the allegedly objectively superior characteristics of white people are either matters of personal opinion ("I hate straight features; needles and razors may be sharp – but beautiful, never"[11]) or the source of great suffering (white intelligence, spirit, and achievement has produced horrific wars, industrial drudgery, and capitalist exploitation). As in *Darkwater,* Du Bois attempts in *Dusk of Dawn* to get white people to see themselves from the perspective of those whom they oppress in the hope that this will help eliminate racist beliefs and practices.

What should black people do, penned in as they are by such a malevolent world? Du Bois's controversial reply is that they should embrace their segregation. He argues that in his day, segregation is not optional – it is a reality imposed upon black people, whether they like it or not. It largely occurs, however, either haphazardly or through the will of white people. Black people would benefit if, instead, they thoughtfully and strategically planned their segregation, developing black churches, schools, banks, and other institutions that would improve black people's lives. The ultimate goal of these developments would be to eliminate all compulsory segregation, but it can only be reached, Du Bois thinks, if black people become more self-sufficient. "Rail if you will," he urges, "against the race segregation here involved and condoned, but take advantage of it by planting secure centers of Negro co-operative effort and particularly of economic power to make us spiritually free for initiative and creation in other and wider fields."[12]

To achieve such organization, Du Bois holds that black people will need intelligent leadership by fellow black people. As he sees it, the "Talented Tenth" of black people in the United States, who are well educated and of exemplary character, have an obligation to study the situation of black people and chart a course for their development. The perceived elitism of this suggestion generated a great deal of controversy in Du Bois's day. Indeed, Du Bois admits that as he first developed the concept of the Talented Tenth in 1903, it was tantamount to an aristocratic "flight of class from mass."[13] As Du Bois was introduced to Marxism, however, he became critical of his earlier European and imperial perspectives, which led him to modify many of his ideas. In 1940, he promoted the Tenth not as a method of flight, but as a way of lifting up black people as a whole. He realized that some would still see the Tenth as a threat to the masses of black people but nonetheless held that it was needed because leadership of the black people could not be entrusted to white people. Du Bois believed that as outsiders, white leaders inevitably would misunderstand and thus ill-serve black people, even if they had the best of intentions. Throughout his career, Du Bois maintained that the

Talented Tenth was necessary because black leadership was essential to black progress, but that a chasm between leaders and the masses could be prevented if relationships between them were nurtured.

The Status of Race and the Contributions of Black People

Contemporary philosophers have recently paid quite a bit of attention to Du Bois's 1897 address to the American Negro Academy, "The Conservation of Races." In this essay, Du Bois acknowledges that racism against black people makes it tempting for them to wish for the elimination of race, but he argues that abolishing the distinctions between races would be a damaging mistake. Before demonstrating the value of race to black people, however, Du Bois is careful to explain what he does and does not mean by the concept of race. He firmly rejects the then (and even now) commonly held notion that physical, biological characteristics neatly divide people into distinct races. As the sciences of Du Bois's day were beginning to recognize and the sciences of today confirm, these characteristics are shared among the different races. There is as much variation of skin color, hair texture, cranial capacity, and other physical characteristics within any particular race as there is between different racial groups. Physical and genetic differences between races, therefore, are insufficient to explain the distinction between races.

While this fact could lead – and, indeed, has led for some philosophers – to the declaration that race is not real, Du Bois insists on the concept's continued reality and importance because it has greatly affected and continues to affect the lives of people of all races. While races "perhaps transcend scientific definition, nevertheless, [they] are clearly defined to the eye of the historian and sociologist."[14] For Du Bois, scientific reality is only one kind of reality and does not necessarily trump other ways of understanding human existence. If the details of so-called "real life" are to be understood rather than dismissed, then the concept of race must be retained, according to Du Bois, because it is the key thread running throughout human history.

Du Bois argues that not only is race relevant to comprehending the past, it also has a valuable role to play in the future. While some races, such as the white race, have already had the opportunity to give "to civilization the full spiritual message which they are capable of giving,"[15] many races, such as the "Negro" race, have not. Disagreeing with those who think that assimilation into white America would be best for African Americans, Du Bois calls for black people to develop their own distinctive and original contribution to the world by means of black art, literature, "genius," and "spirit." The concept of race is crucial to such development, which is why abandoning it would be devastating to black people. For Du Bois, while racial distinctions admittedly help make possible racism, they also are crucial to the ability of black people to take pride in themselves. Du Bois's goal is to pry race and racism far enough apart for us to see that their connection is contingent.

In Du Bois's view, race need not be used to support pernicious practices such as racism. It can contribute to the uplifting of African Americans instead.

Du Bois did not believe that black people had not made any contributions to the world, but in 1897 he minimized them and offered only the example of ancient Egyptian civilization as at least partly "Negro" in origin. Twenty-seven years later, Du Bois modified his claims slightly by expanding his recognition of the number of contributions already made by black people, particularly in the United States. In *The Gift of Black Folk: The Negroes in the Making of America*, he asks, "Who made America?" and answers that it was "the common, ordinary, unlovely man" who was black.[16] Du Bois presents evidence that people of African descent helped explore what was to become the United States prior to the arrival of Columbus and that they brought with them many crops, such as tobacco, cotton, sweet potatoes, and peanuts, often thought to be indigenous to North America. He also argues that in addition to being explorers who helped "discover" America, black people provided much of the labor that helped the United States develop commercially and economically, and they fought as soldiers in every war to help defend an American freedom that, ironically and unjustly, was denied to them. Physical brawn was not the only gift given by black people, however. Du Bois explains that they also gave the United States its distinctive, homegrown form of music, the American folk song, and have furthered American art and literature both by influencing white art and literature and by creating art and literature of their own. But perhaps most important to Du Bois is the particular style of spirituality black people have brought to America. As he describes it, in contrast to the cool and cautious formalism of white religion that remembers every sin, black spirituality provided a sensuous, intense joyousness that is generous and forgiving. As Du Bois sees them, black people have managed to love and care for their enemies, even those who enslaved them, and they have befriended the lowly, poor, and friendless, returning kindness for ill will and truth for falsity. Du Bois declares that these loving attitudes and practices constitute the greatest of all gifts of black to white America.

One of the notable features of *The Gifts of Black Folk* – and, indeed, of much of Du Bois's work – is its acknowledgement of the particular hardships faced by and the unique contributions made by black women. Du Bois pays sorrowful tribute to the black mammy, who has been made to take on the world's burdens in a Christ-like fashion. He details how she was forced to neglect her own children in order to care for those of her masters and how she provided nourishment and thus life to the white men and women of the south that became its great leaders and wealthy ladies. Even more impressive, however, is Du Bois's recognition of the importance of black women's fight for economic independence and equality with men, something that white feminism in the United States largely did not begin to acknowledge until the end of the twentieth century. Devoting an entire chapter of *The Gifts of Black Folk* to "The Freedom of Womanhood," Du Bois explains how black women's emancipation helps provide freedom to all women, white as well as black. Because women's emancipation and equality depends on transforming the ideal of family in which women are caretakers and homemakers only and because the black woman is central to white and black families alike, "the Negro woman more than the women of any other group in America is the protagonist in the fight for an economically independent womanhood in modern countries."[17]

Another important theme developed in *The Gifts of Black Folk* is the centrality of black people to the development of democracy in the United States. In harmony with his 1897 pronouncement that race is central to world history, Du Bois claims that "the Negro is the central thread of American history" such that "[o]ne cannot think . . . of democracy in America or in the modern world without reference to the American Negro."[18] Du Bois can be seen here as giving a striking twist to the Deweyan emphasis on democracy. While democracy is a crucial concept to Dewey's pragmatism and Dewey advocated a broad definition of it as a way of life rather than a narrow understanding of it as mere political procedure, he rarely if ever explicitly discussed race in conjunction with it. For Du Bois, in contrast, democracy in the United States cannot be understood apart from race because it was the presence of black slaves in America that forced the country to ask whether it would attempt to live up to its ideal of freedom for all people:

> [I]t was the rise and growth among the slaves of a determination to be free an active part of American democracy that forced American democracy continually to look into the depths; that held the faces of American thought to the inescapable fact that as long as there was a slave in America, America could not be a free republic; and more than that: as long as there were people in America, slave or nominally free, who could not participate in government and industry and society as free, intelligent human beings, our democracy had failed of its greatest mission.[19]

Du Bois argues that democracy as initially established in the United States was never practically intended to include all people and that acceptance of this inequality made it easy for white people to think of democracy and slavery as compatible. Du Bois implies that if left to their own devices, white Americans probably never would have realized the incompatibility of the two. In his view, black people forced America to notice the incongruity between democracy and slavery, and thus it was black people who made it possible for America to strive toward becoming a genuine democracy.

Du Bois also explains that in a very "peculiar" and bittersweet way, black people's fight for freedom helped emancipate white laborers, who also have been excluded from much of America's government, industry, and society. The white leaders of industry, unions, guilds, and government began opening doors for the white lower classes because only by doing so could they summon enough white strength and solidarity to combat black emancipation. Because the white vote was needed to disenfranchise blacks, the white masses had to be enfranchised. Unions had to include all white people because without non-union white laborers, black competition was insufficient to break a strike. Thus, as Du Bois wryly notes, "[t]he

Negro is making America and the world acknowledge democracy as feasible and desirable for all white folk, for only in this way do they see any possibility of defending their world wide fear of yellow, brown and black folk."[20] Du Bois does not think this must be the end of the story, however. The question posed to America by black people remains: does American democracy mean freedom for white people only, or does it mean the inclusion of all people, regardless of their race? Du Bois asserts that by continuing to force (white) Americans to confront this question, black people's agitation contributes to the freedom of all people – black freed person and white laborer alike – toward which the emancipation of the slaves in the United States was an essential step.

Du Bois continues his examination of black contributions to America and particularly American democracy in *Black Reconstruction in America: An Essay Toward a History of the Part Which Black Folk Played in the Attempt to Reconstruct Democracy in America, 1860–1880* (1935). One of the outstanding features of this hefty volume is its subtle analysis of the ways in which race and class intertwine. In addition to documenting the important role that black people played in America in the years following the Civil War, Du Bois demonstrates how (aversion to) blackness made possible both the identification of the white lower classes specifically as white and the creation of whiteness as a unified entity that subsumed class differences. Du Bois argues that before the war, racial divisions had begun to strengthen as the system of slavery became more rigid, but it was only during war "that it became the fashion to pat the disenfranchised poor white man on the back and tell him after all he was white and that he and the planters had a common object in keeping the white man superior."[21] These reassurances became necessary because poor white Southerners noticed that slaveholders were avoiding military service, making the war a fight to benefit rich white people at the expense of the poor. Thus, Du Bois explains, in a remarkable twist of logic poor whites were told and began to believe that slavery (and thus also the war to preserve it) benefited poor whites more than it did slave-owners because slavery ensured that black people would occupy the lowest rung of the economic and social ladder.

Perhaps then the answer of poor whites to the crucial post-bellum question, as posed by Du Bois, is not very surprising: would white laborers align themselves with other, black workers, or would they bind themselves with white planters and industrialists through a supposed unity of white blood? Poor whites chose the latter. Du Bois explains that instead of joining forces with black workers to fight exploitation by capitalists, white laborers saw them as competitors and revolted against the idea of competing against black people. This revolt caused some discord between white workers, who did not want black people to be hired at all, and white planters, who were happy to profit from black labor since the terms of employment of black people could be made virtually indistinguishable from slavery. The tensions were not enough, however, to disrupt the quickly solidifying unity of white people as white. Du Bois describes a number of ways that poor whites aligned themselves with rich whites: for example, by modeling their aspirations on the exploitative life of the white planter, whom they wished to become, and by working together with rich whites in secret organizations, such as the Ku Klux Klan, to terrorize and kill black people. As Du Bois demonstrates, a combination of poor whites' racist aversion to black people and rich whites' classist stoking of the flames of racism created a unified race of white people that did not exist in a hardened way in the United States prior to the nineteenth century.

"The Negro Problem"

In *The Souls of Black Folk*, Du Bois writes that the unasked question that hovers between white and black people is that of the white person to the black, "How does it feel to be a problem?"[22] "The Negro problem," as it was called, fully developed after the Civil War, when white people wondered what was to be done about the situation of so many free black people living in the midst of white America. The implication was that merely to exist as a black person was a problem and, furthermore, that the problem only multiplied if black people thought themselves free and equal to white people. Born as "the Negro problem" was becoming acute in the United States, Du Bois significantly transformed the meaning of that problem over the 95 years of his life. His work changed the focus of the problem from one of black people to one of white America. Black people do not cause the problem, Du Bois tells us. What is (allegedly) problematic about them is, instead, that they force white people to confront the problems and failures of white ideals and institutions – especially that of democracy, the ideal that America prides itself on most of all. Such confrontation abounds in Du Bois's work. As he claims in *Dusk of Dawn*, "[m]y life had its significance and its only deep significance because it was part of a Problem; but that problem was, as I continue to think, the central problem of the greatest of the world's democracies and so the Problem of the future world."[23] We today live in Du Bois's future world, and, as he predicted, we continue to confront the problems of race prejudice and discrimination that helped shape his life.

Notes

1 W. E. B. Du Bois, *The Souls of Black Folk* (Mineola, NY: Dover Publications, Inc., 1994; originally published in 1903), p. v.

2 W. E. B. Du Bois, *The Autobiography of W. E. B. Du Bois: A Soliloquy on Viewing My Life from the Last Decade of Its First Century* (New York: International Publishers Co., Inc., 1996), p. 148.

3 Ibid.

4 Du Bois, *The Souls of Black Folk*, p. 2.

5 *Darkwater: Voices From Within the Veil* (Mineola, NY: Dover Publications, Inc., 1999; originally published in 1920), p. 17.

6 Ibid.
7 Ibid., p. 23.
8 Ibid., p. 22; emphasis in original.
9 *Dusk of Dawn: An Essay Toward an Autobiography of a Race Concept* (New York: Schocken Books, 1984; originally published in 1940), p. xxx.
10 Ibid., p. 170.
11 Ibid., p. 142.
12 Ibid., p. 215.
13 Ibid., p. 217.
14 W. E. B. Du Bois, "The Conservation of Races,' in Eric J. Sundquist, ed., *The Oxford W. E. B. Du Bois Reader* (Oxford: Oxford University Press, 1996; originally published in 1897), p. 40.
15 Ibid., p. 42.
16 *The Gift of Black Folk: The Negroes in the Making of America* (New York: Washington Square Press, 1970; originally published in 1924), p. 1.
17 Ibid., p. 142.
18 Ibid., pp. 65, 67.
19 Ibid., p. 67.
20 Ibid., p. 139.
21 *Black Reconstruction in America: An Essay Toward a History of the Part Which Black Folk Played in the Attempt to Reconstruct Democracy in America, 1860–1880* (New York: The World Publishing Company, 1962; originally published in 1935), p. 80.
22 *The Souls of Black Folk*, p. 1.
23 *Dusk of Dawn*, pp. xxiv–xxx.

Suggested reading

Anderson, Elijah, and Tukufu Zuberi, eds., *The Study of African American Problems: W. E. B. Du Bois's Agenda, Then and Now*. Vol. 568 of *The Annals of The American Academy of Political and Social Science* (Thousand Oaks, CA: Sage Publications, 2000).

Appiah, Anthony Kwame, "The Conservation of 'Race,'" *Black American Literature Forum*, 23/1 (1989): 37–60.

Bell, Bernard W., Emily R. Grosholz, and James B. Stewart, eds., *W. E. B. Du Bois on Race and Culture: Philosophy, Politics, and Poetics* (New York: Routledge, 1996).

Burks, Ben, "Unity and Diversity through Education: A Comparison of the Thought of W. E. B. Du Bois and John Dewey," *Journal of Thought*, 32/1 (1997): 99–110.

Campbell, James, "Du Bois and James," *Transactions of the Charles S. Peirce Society*, 28/3 (1992): 569–81.

De Marco, Joseph P., "The Concept of Race in the Social Thought of W. E. B. Du Bois," *Philosophical Forum*, 3/1 (1972): 227–42.

Lester, Julius, ed., *The Seventh Son: The Thought and Writings of W. E. B. Du Bois* (New York: Random House, 1971).

Lewis, David Levering, *W. E. B. Du Bois: Biography of a Race, 1868–1919* (New York: Henry Holt and Co., 1994).

—— *W. E. B. Du Bois: The Fight for Equality and the American Century 1919–1963* (New York: Henry Holt and Co., 2000).

——ed., *W. E. B. Du Bois: A Reader* (New York: Henry Holt and Co., 1995).

Outlaw, Jr., Lucius T., *On Race and Philosophy* (New York: Routledge, 1996).

West, Cornel, *The American Evasion of Philosophy: A Genealogy of Pragmatism* (Madison, WI: The University of Wisconsin Press, 1989).

Chapter 13

Alfred North Whitehead, 1861–1947

John W. Lango

Introduction

Whitehead's academic work can be divided roughly into three main periods, the first two in England, and the third in the United States: (1) mathematics and logic (at Cambridge and at University College in London), including the writing of *Principia Mathematica* with Bertrand Russell; (2) physics and philosophy of science (at the Imperial College of Science and Technology in London); and (3) philosophy (at Harvard). This volume is a guide to American philosophy, and so the focus of the present chapter is on his third period. Influenced notably by William James, his later work is part of the stream of American philosophy.

While at Harvard, he wrote a variety of philosophical books, ranging from the very accessible (e.g., *Religion in the Making* (1926)) to the extremely difficult (e.g., *Process and Reality* (1929)). *Process and Reality* is arguably a major contribution to the history of Western metaphysics. The primary goal of this chapter is to provide an introduction to it, and to indicate its relevance for current issues in philosophy.[1]

One such issue is whether mind can be explained in terms of matter. The mind–body problem is difficult, John Searle has maintained, because of four features of the mind: "consciousness, intentionality, subjectivity, and mental causation."[2] To indicate the relevance of *Process and Reality* for the mind–body problem, this chapter considers especially the feature of subjectivity.

The subtitle of *Process and Reality* is "An Essay in Cosmology." But Whitehead did not mean by "cosmology" the scientific cosmology of astronomers. Instead, what he meant can be gleaned from the following passage:

> It must be one of the motives of a complete cosmology to construct a system of ideas which brings the aesthetic, moral, and religious interests into relation with those concepts of the world which have their origin in natural science.[3]

And such a comprehensive system of ideas is, to use a more standard philosophical term, a sort of metaphysical system. In particular, his metaphysics is formulated as a system of "categories" (i.e., a "categoreal scheme").[4]

In bringing the stated human interests into relation with concepts derived from the natural sciences, his metaphysics was especially influenced by Einstein's theory of relativity.[5] Similarly, Descartes's philosophy was especially influenced by the Copernican revolution in physics and astronomy. Roughly speaking, Whitehead's categoreal scheme is a metaphysics of events in relativistic space-time. For the sake of illustration, this chapter emphasizes the relation between the feature of subjectivity and the relativistic concept of space-time.

Process and Reality is extremely difficult, and so it should not be surprising that it has been interpreted differently. In this chapter, I shall state part of my own interpretation of it.[6] But I have no space to defend my interpretation against alternative interpretations.[7] Also, for the sake of comparison, I shall sketch my construal of some views of more familiar philosophers (e.g., Descartes), again without defense. The aim is to provide a comprehensible introduction.

Subjectivity

In summarizing the feature of subjectivity, Searle said: "I see the world from my point of view; you see it from your point of view."[8] It is this aspect of the feature of subjectivity – the idea of a subjective point of view – that is integral to Whitehead's metaphysics. Common philosophical terms are used somewhat differently by different philosophers, and the term "subjectivity" is no exception. By means of some comparisons with Descartes, the purpose of this section is to introduce Whitehead's particular conception of subjectivity.

Descartes is famous for infusing the theme of subjectivity into modern philosophy. His *Meditations* was written in the first person, it was written from the point of view of the knowing subject. Let me summarize some of its main claims. Even if a malicious demon is deceiving me, even if there really is no external world, I cannot doubt that I exist, and that I have sensory perceptions that seem to be of an external world. Thus arises the problem of solipsism.

Whitehead's metaphysics "accepts Descartes' discovery that subjective experiencing is the primary metaphysical situation which is presented to metaphysics for analysis."[9] Roughly speaking, *Process and Reality* was written from the point of view of an experiencing subject. Note, however, that, influenced by American pragmatism – and, in particular, by James's notion of a stream of consciousness[10] – Whitehead's concept of experiencing is broader than Descartes's concept of thinking. Also, as will eventually become evident, his concept of subjectivity is broader.

Returning to Descartes, let me summarize some claims that are, I think, implicit in the *Meditations*. In addition to the problem of my knowledge of an external world disclosed by my sensory perceptions, there is the problem of my knowledge of a past disclosed by my memory. To make the latter problem more vivid, "I will believe that my memory tells me lies, and that none of the things that it reports ever happened."[11] Nevertheless, even if a malicious demon is deceiving me, even if I really have no past, I cannot doubt that I exist now in the present, and that I have memories that seem to be of a past. Thus arises the problem of "solipsism of the present moment."[12]

In contrast to the traditional emphasis on vision (e.g., in Descartes's philosophy), there is in Whitehead's metaphysics an emphasis on memory. A paradigm of subjective experiencing is my present experiencing of my past.

Let us consider an example. In the final chapter of *Ulysses*, James Joyce immerses us for more than 40 pages in the stream of Molly Bloom's consciousness. For example: "it was rotten cold too that winter when I was only about ten was I yes I had the big doll with all the funny clothes."[13] She remembers the cold winter when she was about 10. But we frequently question our dating of events, and so she immediately asks, "was I," and just as immediately answers, "yes." For she verifies her age by remembering her doll.

This example illustrates how we sometimes resolve doubts about our memories of remote events. It also serves to illustrate a more radical sort of question. In order to be able to ask "was I," she has to continue to remember the cold winter. Why is there this continuity between her present and her immediate past? What is the relationship between her present (when she asks "was I") and her immediate past (when she first remembers the cold winter)?

Descartes solved the problem of my knowledge of an external world in terms of an epistemological conception of representation: sufficiently clear and distinct sensory perceptions truly represent external objects. In contrast, Whitehead answered the question of the relationship between my present and my immediate past in terms of a metaphysical conception of causation: my present arises from my immediate past by means of a sort of causal process. My present experiencing of my immediate past is a sort of causal relation to it.

Let me pause to mention a source of difficulty in reading *Process and Reality*: its use of novel technical terms. Using two such terms – "actual occasion" and "physical prehension" – his answer to the question can be summarized thus: on the present (actual) occasion of my existence, I physically prehend my immediate past. An actual occasion is a sort of minimal event, and a physical prehension is a sort of causal relation. Not having been conventionally trained in philosophy, he presumably invented such unfamiliar terms in the manner of the mathematician (cf. such mathematical neologisms as "manifold" and "matrix") in order to avoid misleading connotations of traditional terms.[14]

In contrast to Descartes's mind–body dualism, Whitehead "naturalized" the mind. Human experiences are part of the natural world. My stream of consciousness is (in some sense) included in streams of brain events. My present arises by means of a sort of causal process from an immediate past that includes not just conscious mental events but also non-conscious brain events. (Let us postpone the question of whether those conscious mental events are themselves brain events.)

Accordingly, his concept of experiencing needs to be understood quite broadly. My present experiencing of my immediate past includes my non-conscious experiencing of brain events (i.e., my having a sort of causal relation to them). Since the term "experiencing" might misleadingly connote "consciousness," let me restate this point in Whitehead's technical terminology. On the present occasion of my existence, I physically prehend immediately past brain events. (A physical prehension can be conscious or non-conscious.)

In review, the example from *Ulysses* serves to illustrate this question: why is there continuity between my present and my immediate past? Descartes answered the question in terms of the traditional idea of substance: the mind is a thinking substance, and it is the nature of a substance to endure through time. But he realized that such an answer is not unproblematic. "For a lifespan can be divided into countless parts, each completely independent of the others, so that it does not follow from the fact that I existed a little while ago that I must exist now."[15]

In contrast, Whitehead rejected the idea of enduring substance. Instead, continuants are analyzed in terms of occurrents, and occurrents are understood as processes. A core idea in his metaphysics of events is the idea of process: "The elucidation of meaning involved in the phrase 'all things flow' is one chief task of metaphysics."[16] (Note that it is customary to classify him as a process philosopher.) Indeed, a lifespan can be divided into countless (actual) occasions. But, instead of being independent of the others, each such occasion arises from temporally preceding occasions by means of a sort of causal process.

What, then, is the relation between process and subjectivity? Echoing one of Heraclitus's fragments, he remarked that "no subject experiences twice."[17] All things flow, even subjectivity. Subjectivity is not attributed by his metaphysics to a continuant, an entity whose nature is to endure through time. Instead, subjectivity is attributed to an occurrent, an entity whose nature is to happen at a time. Accordingly, the question can be answered briefly thus: a present subject (an actual occasion) arises from an immediately past subject (a numerically distinct actual occasion) by means of a sort of causal process. Consequently, a major problem for his metaphysics is to justify roughly the following claim: I myself as a continuing person am derivative from a stream of occurrent subjects.

Concerning the nature of metaphysics, Strawson said that "descriptive metaphysics" aims to describe "the most general features of our conceptual structure," whereas "revisionary metaphysics" aims to revise (some of) them.[18] Clearly, Whitehead's metaphysics is revisionary. For instance, our common-sense metaphysical beliefs do not (seem to) include the above claim. In describing "our conceptual scheme as it is," Strawson maintained that material bodies and persons are the basic particulars.[19] In contrast, in Whitehead's categoreal scheme, the particulars that are the most basic are actual occasions. Material bodies and persons are (roughly speaking) streams of actual occasions. In general, his metaphysics diverges considerably from (what many philosophers take to be) "our conceptual scheme."

Why is his metaphysics so revisionary? In devising a comprehensive metaphysical system, he interrelated concepts derived from human experience and concepts derived from the natural sciences. And the natural sciences have often been revolutionary, they often have forced us to revise our understanding of nature. Among the most revolutionary was the theory of relativity, a theory that especially influenced his metaphysics. A primary reason why his metaphysics is so revisionary is that it incorporates concepts derived from the theory of relativity.

In summary, the feature of subjectivity includes the idea of a subjective point of view. The "primary metaphysical situation" is, Whitehead asserted, "subjective experiencing."[20] And fundamental to my subjective experiencing is my present experiencing of the immediate past. Moreover, my present experiencing arises from my immediate past by means of a sort of causal process. Thus, in introducing his particular conception of subjectivity, I have also introduced (however incompletely) his particular conceptions of causation and process. Actual occasions are the elements of process, and they are causally interrelated by means of physical prehensions.

Although I have only discussed part of his particular conception of subjectivity (more will emerge later), let me state briefly a key point. A subjective point of view is fundamentally a point of view on the past. And it is only secondarily a point of view on the present and the future.

There is another key point. Descartes maintained that, because the mind has as its essence thinking, it cannot have extension in space. In contrast, Whitehead held that a subjective point of view is literally spatial. More exactly, it is literally spatiotemporal. At the present moment, I am situated here in this place in space. In particular, my present experiencing is located in the space of my brain. My subjective point of view on the past is literally from the standpoint of a region of space-time.

Space-Time

To repeat, Whitehead's metaphysics was especially influenced by the theory of relativity. I want now to discuss the relation between the feature of subjectivity and the relativistic concept of space-time. For simplicity, my discussion is limited to the special theory of relativity. More precisely, it is concerned with Hermann Minkowski's geometrical interpretation of Einstein's special theory of relativity.[21]

Quine, who studied with Whitehead at Harvard, remarked that this interpretation "provided an essential impetus, certainly, to spatiotemporal thinking, which came afterward to dominate philosophical constructions in Whitehead and others."[22] But I cannot hope to summarize the content of the theory in a chapter of this brevity. Fortunately, there is no need to consider experiments or mathematical formulae. It is enough to mention some general concepts that are part of the theory.

To dramatize (what is arguably) one difference between physics and metaphysics, I shall draw upon an introduction to relativity theory by Robert Geroch.[23]

The concept of "an event" is, Geroch asserts, fundamental to the theory. Note that what he means by an "event" is an "idealized occurrence" at a space-time point – in other words, a point event. "Are [point] events real?" he asks. "What are they really like?" His answer to these questions is: "Physics does not, at least in my opinion, deal with what is 'real' or with what something is 'really like.' "

In contrast, metaphysics does deal with the question of what is real, or so Whitehead thought. Let me summarize some of his pertinent views. Indeed, point events are idealizations. In order for there to be a real occurrence (or happening), there has to be a finite lapse of time, however minimal. Accordingly, rather than the concept of a point event, what is fundamental is the concept of a minimal event that occupies a minute (but still finite) region of space-time.[24]

What are these minimal events really like? In the preceding section, I discussed mainly (actual) occasions of human experience. I want now to emphasize that his conception of actual occasion is far more general. "An actual occasion is the limiting type of an event."[25] Instead of point events, what are fundamentally real are actual occasions. Instead of being limited to a space-time point, each actual occasion occupies a minute space-time region. A chief goal of *Process and Reality* is to characterize what actual occasions are really like.

Does something happen in *every* region of space-time? Is the universe a plenum of events? The universe is for the most part empty of ordinary material bodies. Now consider a region of "empty space" approximately the size and shape of your body. If you were there, you would see countless stars. Even though the region is empty of ordinary material bodies, waves of light travel through it. (Also, virtual particles occur in it.) To generalize, we can think of (almost) every region in space-time as harboring events. Even if there were a space-time region totally devoid of physical occurrences, that nothing happens there would still constitute (vacuously) a sort of event. Accordingly, Whitehead's metaphysics includes the claim that the universe is a plenum of actual occasions.

To initiate the topic of subjectivity, I shall draw upon a different introduction to relativity theory, one by David Bohm. Relativity theory stresses "the special role of each observer."[26] Roughly speaking, each observer has at a given moment in time his own unique "point of view."[27] Note that at that moment he is located (approximately) at a particular point in space. Hence, thinking spatiotemporally, it is better to say that an observer has at (approximately) a given point in space-time his own unique point of view. From any such point of view, an observer "can only know of events that are . . . in his absolute past."[28] Each observer's unique point of view at a given space-time point is fundamentally a point of view on the past.

Whitehead's metaphysics was especially influenced by this relativistic concept of an observer's point of view. In what follows, I shall summarize how that concept can be understood in terms of Minkowski's geometrical interpretation of relativity theory. In light of this summary, I shall then sketch how the concept influenced Whitehead's metaphysics.

An observer's point of view at a space-time point can be represented geometrically in a Minkowski diagram of space-time.[29] Each point on the diagram represents a point event. Let the point *O* represent what happens to a particular observer at a particular point in space-time. From the standpoint of *O* the diagram is divided into three parts, which represent the observer's absolute past, absolute future, and absolute elsewhere. Her point of view at that space-time point is fundamentally a point of view on the point events in her absolute past.

A familiar idea from the theory of relativity is the idea of the relativity of simultaneity. Another familiar idea is that measurements of spatial lengths and measurements of lapses of time are relative to the observer. It might seem odd, then, that the term "absolute past" includes the word "absolute." However, measurements of four-dimensional space-time intervals are *not* relative to the observer. Instead, the interval between two point events in space-time is absolute (or invariant). A main reason why Minkowski theorized that space and time are combined together into a single space-time was to make such absolutes evident.

One such absolute is that a point event is in the absolute past. The pastness of a point event for an observer (at a given space-time point) is an objective fact about nature. There is no relativity about whether a point event is in her absolute past. (Similar remarks hold of her absolute future and her absolute elsewhere.)

But there is a relativity of a different sort. The absolute past of an observer at a given space-time point is *her* absolute past. Consider a different observer at a different space-time point. The absolute past of that observer at that space-time point is *his* absolute past. Either her absolute past contains point events that are not in his absolute past, or his absolute past contains point events that are not in her absolute past, or both. It is because absolute pasts are thus different that the term "point of view" is apt. (Note also that one and the same observer has different absolute pasts at different space-time points.)

Why can an observer only know of events in her absolute past? Consider an approximate example of a point event: a light bulb is turned on for a moment and then turned off.[30] (Note that this example really involves a finite volume of space and a finite lapse of time. Nonetheless, it also is only an approximate example of an actual occasion. Since it involves many electrons and many photons, it is really an example of a multiplicity of actual occasions.) The bulb flashes, and light radiates in all directions. In the theory of relativity, it is assumed that light travels with a (finite) constant velocity. Consequently, an observer can only see the flashing bulb at a later moment. At the moment when she sees it, the (approximate) point event itself (i.e., the flashing of the bulb) is in her absolute past.

To generalize, any sort of physical action that is transmitted from a point event to an observer involves a finite lapse of time. Thus, at a space-time point *P* where she experiences the transmitted physical action, the original point event is in her absolute past. (Since the rate of transmission of physical actions cannot exceed the speed of light, her absolute past is bounded by the surface of a light cone). Her absolute past (at the space-time point *P*) contains just those point events from which physical actions are, or might have been, transmitted to her (at *P*). Consequently, the only information that can be (causally) transmitted to her is information about point events in her absolute past. In this (causal) sense of the term "know," she can only know of events in her absolute past.

Similarly, her absolute future (at *P*) contains just those point events *to* which physical actions could be transmitted *from* her (at *P*). And her absolute elsewhere (at *P*) contains just those point events that are causally independent of her (at *P*). For a physical action cannot be transmitted between her (at *P*) and a point event in her absolute elsewhere (at *P*) without exceeding the speed of light.

How, then, did the concept of an observer's point of view influence Whitehead's metaphysics? The universe is almost entirely empty of observers. Nonetheless, any space-time point *might* be the locus of an observer's point of view. (There can be frames of reference at any space-time point.) Accordingly, let us generalize the concept of an observer's point of view. Let us regard *every* point event in space-time as having its own unique point of view.

This generalization can be understood as follows: Let the point *O* in the Minkowski diagram represent a point event *E* that is *not* the point of view of an observer. Again, from the standpoint of *O*, the diagram is divided into three parts, which represent *E*'s absolute past, *E*'s absolute future, and *E*'s absolute elsewhere. Any sort of physical action that is transmitted from a point event to *E* involves a finite lapse of time. Such a point event is in *E*'s absolute past. *E*'s absolute past contains just those point events from which physical actions are, or might have been, transmitted to *E*. Thus *E* has (in a generalized sense) a point of view on the point events in its absolute past.

Now consider a different point event *F*. Either there are point events from which physical actions could be transmitted to *F* but not to *E*, or there are point events from which physical actions could be transmitted to *E* but not to *F*, or both. In brief, *F*'s absolute past is different from *E*'s absolute past. It is because absolute pasts are thus different that it is appropriate to regard *every* point event in space-time as having its own unique point of view. Each point event has, so to speak, its own unique perspective on the universe of point events.

In devising his comprehensive metaphysical system, Whitehead interrelated a concept of subjectivity derived from human experience and such a generalized concept of point of view derived from the theory of relativity. To repeat, Descartes's *Meditations* was written from the point of view of a knowing subject; and, similarly, *Process and Reality* was written from the point of view of an experiencing subject. It should now be realized that Whitehead's concept of subjectivity is vastly broader.

Instead of point events, what are fundamentally real are, according to Whitehead, actual occasions. Each actual occasion *M* has its own subjective point of view. Recall that *M* is located in a minute space-time region. From the standpoint of that region, space-time is divided into three parts: *M*'s "causal past," *M*'s "causal future," and the locus of *M*'s "contemporaries."[31] By *M*'s "contemporaries" he did not mean those actual occasions that are (absolutely) simultaneous with *M*. According to the theory of relativity, simultaneity is "relative" (to the frame of reference), and so there is no absolute present state of the world. Instead, he meant that two actual occasions are contemporaries when neither can physically prehend the other (i.e., when they are causally independent of each other).

M's subjective point of view is fundamentally a point of view on the actual occasions in its causal past. Thus *every* actual occasion – not just (actual) occasions of human minds – has its own subjective point of view. Space-time contains a plenum of experiencing subjects.

Also, Whitehead's concept of experiencing is vastly broader than Descartes's concept of thinking. Just as (according to Bohm) an observer can only (causally) know of events in her absolute past, so (according to Whitehead) an actual occasion can only experience (i.e., physically prehend) actual occasions in its causal past. A physical prehension is a sort of causal relation. Physical actions are transmitted from actual occasion to actual occasion by means of physical prehensions. The causal past of each actual occasion *M* contains just those actual occasions from which physical actions are, or might have been, transmitted by means of physical prehensions to *M*. (This is why the term "causal past" includes the word "causal.") In this way, *M* arises from its causal past by means of a sort of causal process.

Let *N* be a different actual occasion. Either there are actual occasions from which physical actions could be transmitted to *N* but not to *M*, or there are actual occasions from which physical actions could be transmitted to *M* but not to *N*, or both. In short, *N*'s causal past is different from *M*'s causal past. It is (partly) because causal pasts are thus different that it is appropriate to regard *every* actual occasion as having its own subjective point of view. Each actual occasion has its own unique perspective on the universe of actual occasions.

I have been illustrating "the influence of the 'relativity theory' of modern physics" on Whitehead's metaphysics.[32] Although there is no space to discuss further illustrations, let me mention one. The relativistic concept of world line is generalized in his metaphysics as the conception of "personal order."[33] Concepts derived from relativity theory permeate his metaphysics.

In concluding, let me repeat Searle's remark about the feature of subjectivity: "I see the world from my point of view; you see it from your point of view." For the purposes of this section, the word "see" has been read in terms of geometric optics. In a literal spatiotemporal sense, each actual occasion has a subjective point of view on its causal past.

But the word "see" can be read quite differently: "I evaluate the world from my point of view; you evaluate it from your point of view." ("I have my values; you have yours.") In something like this metaphoric sense, the subjective point of view of each actual occasion also involves valuation.

Valuation

Concepts derived from human experience are interrelated in Whitehead's metaphysics with concepts derived from the natural sciences. In particular, his metaphysical concept of valuation is derived from human experience. Human beings have preferences, they make value judgments, they have purposes and aims. Accordingly, I shall first consider how the subjective point of view of an actual occasion of a human mind involves valuation. Note that I am using the word "valuation" in a general sense that should not be confused with his technical term "valuation."[34]

I shall then consider a critical problem for his metaphysics: how is this concept of valuation interrelated with the concept of point of view derived from the theory of relativity? For the theory of relativity does *not* say that point events have preferences, they make value judgments, they have purposes and aims. How can the subjective point of view of *every* actual occasion (e.g., occasions of electrons) involve valuation? To summarize with a single word, the problem is that of his (alleged) panpsychism.

Let us return to an earlier example, an actual occasion of Molly Bloom's mind, the occasion when she answers "yes": "it was rotten cold too that winter when I was only about ten was I yes I had the big doll with all the funny clothes." She remembers an event in her causal past: the rotten cold winter. And she remembers another event in her causal past: her possession of the big doll. Among the profusion of events in her causal past that she is capable of remembering – there are immensely many events in her causal past that she is incapable of remembering (e.g., non-conscious brain events) – these two events are greatly important for her, these two have special value. The main point is that her acts of remembering are acts of valuation. Her subjective point of view on her causal past involves not just a spatio-temporal standpoint but also valuation.

Her aim is to answer the question of whether she was about ten that winter. She realizes this aim by something like the following process of quick reflection: "I was about ten when I possessed the big doll, I possessed the big doll during the rotten cold winter, and so that winter I was about ten." To engage in this reflection, she has to bring the two memories together, she has to integrate (or synthesize) them in the right way. There are two key points here. This occasion when she answers "yes" arises from her causal past by means of a causal process that involves such integration. And that causal process is guided by her (subjective) aim.

In sketching this example, I have tried to illustrate Whitehead's account in *Process and Reality* of the process whereby actual occasions of a human mind arise from their causal pasts. That account includes such topics as sensory perception, belief, consciousness, and judgment. Because it is so complex, it cannot be summarized in this brief chapter. And so I want to stress that my sketch of the example is very incomplete.

But the sketch suffices, I think, to introduce (however vaguely) three metaphysical concepts: valuation, integration, and subjective aim. The metaphysical concept of an actual occasion's point of view is a generalization of the relativistic concept of an observer's point of view. Similarly, the metaphysical concepts of valuation, integration, and subjective aim are generalizations of concepts that pertain specifically to human experience. The causal process whereby *every* actual occasion arises from its causal past is guided by a subjective aim, and includes the integration of physical prehensions. And *every* actual occasion's physical prehensions of events in its causal past involve valuations of them. In short, his metaphysics is, in a broad sense of the term, teleological.

Thus we encounter the problem of his (alleged) panpsychism: how can such concepts hold of (actual occasions of) nonhuman beings? Note, for example, that Richard Rorty classified him as a panpsychist.[35] However, a strength of his metaphysics is, I think, that it grounds the attribution of mentality to animals. Thus Donald Griffin, in his influential book *Animal Thinking*, mentioned Whitehead's metaphysics, and classified it as a kind of "panpsychism."[36] Accordingly, to sharpen the problem, let us restrict it as follows: how, in particular, can such concepts hold of (actual occasions of) material bodies?

To make this last question more concrete, let us consider a familiar sort of case from physics: the motion of an arrow just as it leaves a bowstring. Its motion results (let us assume) from the combination of three causal factors: the motion imparted by the bowstring, the resistance of the air, and the force of gravity. (Cf. the mathematical concept of the vector sum of forces.) This combining together of causal factors might be construed as a sort of process of integration (or synthesis). However, it does not (seem to) involve any valuation, nor does it (seem to) involve any subjective aim. Instead, it is interpreted by conventional physics as being purely mechanical.

How is it interpreted by Whitehead's metaphysics? *Process and Reality* also contains an account of the process whereby actual occasions of a material body arise from their causal pasts. That account too is complex, and cannot be summarized here. Accordingly, I can only attempt an answer to this question that is very incomplete.

The event of the arrow leaving the bowstring is a complex of actual occasions. For simplicity, let us focus on one such actual occasion *M*, and view the three causal factors from *M*'s subjective point of view. Physical actions are transmitted from actual occasion to actual occasion by means of physical prehensions. Roughly speaking, the physical action of the bowstring is transmitted by means of physical prehensions to *M*, as are the resistance of the surrounding air and the gravitational action of the earth. Consequently, *M* has to bring these physical prehensions together, *M* has to integrate (or synthesize) them in the right way. Thus we encounter concretely the problem of Whitehead's (alleged) panpsychism: how do *M*'s physical prehensions involve valuation?; how can *M*'s integration of them be guided by a subjective aim?

In discussing such "inorganic actual occasions," Whitehead sometimes used the word "negligible."[37] Let me rephrase (and simplify) an example. In comparison with the physical actions "which they receive and transmit," the valuations and subjective aims of such occasions "are individually negligible."[38] "The inorganic occasions are merely what the causal past allows them to be."[39] Thus the valuations involved in *M*'s physical prehensions are negligible, and so is *M*'s subjective aim.

How are we to understand this term "negligible"? A familiar idea from the special theory of relativity is that the mass of a body increases as its velocity increases. For instance, the mass of a spaceship moving at 93,000 miles per second (i.e., about half the speed of light) is about 1.15 times its mass at rest. However, when the velocity of a body is very small in comparison with the speed of light, its increase in mass is negligible. For example, the mass of an automobile moving at 90 miles per hour is only about 1.000000000000018 times its mass at rest. In general, the "relativities" (e.g., of mass or length or time) in the theory of relativity hold of some events noticeably, and of others negligibly. In light of such cases from science and mathematics, I suspect that Whitehead might have answered the above question as follows: analogously, the teleological concepts in the metaphysics in *Process and Reality* hold of some actual occasions noticeably (e.g., occasions of human minds), and of others negligibly (e.g., occasions of material bodies).

Let me summarize this analogy in a single sentence. Just as (according to relativity theory) Newtonian mechanics is approximately correct when velocities are sufficiently small, so (according to Whitehead's metaphysics) the mechanistic explanations of conventional physics are approximately correct when actual occasions are sufficiently rudimentary. Accordingly, I think that Whitehead should be classified as a panpsychist only if that term is used in a very general sense.

But why did he want such generalized teleological concepts to hold of nonsentient matter even negligibly? In contrast to Descartes's mind–body dualism, Whitehead's metaphysics shares with modern materialism the view that there is just one "stuff." But there is this crucial difference: whereas the orthodox materialist wants to explain mind in terms of a matter that is devoid of subjectivity, Whitehead wanted to explain mind in terms of a "stuff" (i.e., actual occasions) that is *not* devoid of subjectivity (in a suitably generalized sense). Which sort of explanation is better? Our ignorance of the fundamental nature of matter (e.g., are quarks composed of superstrings?) is enough to warrant the following contention: the sort of explanation preferred by Whitehead should not be dogmatically rejected. In doing metaphysics, there is value in exploring diverse alternatives, no matter how speculative.[40]

Thus Whitehead "naturalized" the mind. The stream of actual occasions constituting a human mind is included in streams of actual occasions constituting a brain. I have postponed the following question: are mind occasions themselves brain occasions? In contrast to modern materialism, Lucretius, an ancient materialist, maintained (in Book III of *De Rerum Natura*) that the mind is composed of atoms that are intermingled with the atoms composing the body. Similarly, Whitehead speculated that a human mind is constituted by a linear series of actual occasions that are intermingled with actual occasions of a brain: "This route of presiding occasions [i.e., the occasions of the mind] probably wanders from part to part of the brain, dissociated from the physical material atoms."[41] Because of subsequent developments in biology, his speculation might seem fantastic. I want to stress that his neo-Lucretian speculation is not entailed by his general conception of actual occasion. And that conception is compatible with a variety of accounts of the relation between mind and brain (including, arguably, a sort of identity theory).

Having emphasized one of Searle's four features of the mind, let me discuss very briefly the other three – consciousness, intentionality, and mental causation – in order to indicate further the relevance of *Process and Reality* for the philosophy of mind. First, "In general, consciousness is negligible"; i.e., only (actual occasions) of higher organisms are conscious.[42] There is a complex "account [of consciousness that] agrees with the plain facts of our conscious experience."[43] Second, the conception of prehension includes a sort of "aboutness" that is broadly similar to the factor of "aboutness" in the idea of intentionality. Note that, in addition to physical prehensions, there are prehensions that are about "propositions" (i.e., "propositional prehensions"); cf. the intentionality of "propositional attitudes" (e.g., "S believes that p"). Third, each occasion of my mind physically prehends immediately past brain occasions. Conversely, each occasion of my mind is physically prehended by immediately future brain occasions. The idea of mental causation is grounded on the causal transmission of mental activity by means of physical prehensions from mind occasions to brain occasions.

In conclusion, in providing an introduction to Whitehead's metaphysics in this chapter, I have concentrated on a few subjects, and omitted many others – for example, his causal theory of perception (which includes the perception of causation), his conception of God in terms of the idea of process, and his Platonic theory of universals.[44] Moreover, his metaphysics is formulated as a labyrinthine system of categories, most of which have not even been mentioned. My hope is that this limited introduction will encourage readers to explore Whitehead's metaphysics further.

It should now be quite evident that his metaphysics is extraordinarily revisionary, not just because it incorporates concepts derived from the theory of relativity, but also because it incorporates teleological concepts derived from human experience. It is so revisionary that it is most likely false, or so it would seem. Why, then, read Whitehead? Speaking for myself, one reason that I have for reading him is a reason that I have for reading Descartes or Lucretius or Strawson or Searle – to find stimulation in developing my own ideas – a reason that reflects the title (and spirit) of another of his books, *Adventures of Ideas*.[45]

Notes

1 Originally published in 1929, the preferred edition is Alfred North Whitehead, *Process and Reality: An Essay in Cosmology*, corrected edn., ed. D. Griffin and D. Sherburne

(New York: The Free Press, 1978). Whitehead's later work is also part of the stream of European philosophy. He acknowledged the influence of many philosophers – e.g., Plato, Descartes, Locke, and Bergson. As background for reading *Process and Reality*, I would especially recommend the following books: Plato's *Timaeus*, Locke's *Essay Concerning Human Understanding*, and James's *Essays in Radical Empiricism*.

2 John Searle, *Minds, Brains and Science* (Cambridge, MA: Harvard University Press, 1984), p. 17.

3 Whitehead, *Process and Reality*, p. xii.

4 Ibid., pp. 20–8.

5 The theory of relativity is central to three of his earlier books (which were written in London): *An Enquiry Concerning the Principles of Natural Knowledge* (1919), *The Concept of Nature* (1920), and *The Principle of Relativity, With Applications to Physical Science* (1922). *Process and Reality* develops and transforms ideas from those earlier books. As background for reading it, I would also recommend the reading of a work on relativity theory – e.g., J. R. Lucas and P. E. Hodgson, *Spacetime and Electromagnetism: An Essay on the Philosophy of the Special Theory of Relativity* (Oxford: Clarendon Press, 1990).

6 For a fuller (and somewhat different) statement of my interpretation, see my *Whitehead's Ontology* (Albany: SUNY Press, 1972). Additionally, see my "Whitehead's Category of Nexūs of Actual Entities," *Process Studies*, 29 (2000): 16–42; and "The Time of Whitehead's Concrescence," *Process Studies*, 30 (2001): 3–21.

7 For a different interpretation of his metaphysics, see Jorge Luis Nobo, *Whitehead's Metaphysics of Extension and Solidarity* (Albany: SUNY Press, 1986). For a study of the text of *Process and Reality* that distinguishes different compositional layers, see Lewis S. Ford, *The Emergence of Whitehead's Metaphysics* (Albany: SUNY Press, 1984). For a discussion of the historical context, see George R. Lucas, Jr., *The Rehabilitation of Whitehead: An Analytical and Historical Assessment of Process Philosophy* (Albany: SUNY Press, 1989). Whitehead's philosophy and the philosophy and theology of Charles Hartshorne are the primary sources of process theology. Some interpreters of Whitehead's metaphysics approach it from the standpoint of process theology. For such an approach in an introductory work, see Thomas E. Hosinski, *Stubborn Fact and Creative Advance: An Introduction to the Metaphysics of Alfred North Whitehead* (Lanham, Maryland: Rowman & Littlefield, 1993). A journal with a special focus on Whitehead is *Process Studies*. Each issue usually contains reviews and brief summaries of books and articles about his thought.

8 Searle, *Minds, Brains and Science*, p. 16.

9 Whitehead, *Process and Reality*, p. 160.

10 See ch. 9, "The Stream of Thought," in the first volume of James's *Principles of Psychology*.

11 René Descartes, *Meditations on First Philosophy*, in *Descartes: Selected Philosophical Writings*, tr. J. Cottingham et al. (Cambridge: Cambridge University Press, 1988), p. 24. Page references are to the Adam and Tannery edition.

12 Whitehead, *Process and Reality*, p. 81. As Whitehead noted (ibid., p. 158), this is Santayana's term. See George Santayana, *Scepticism and Animal Faith* (New York: Dover Publications, 1955), pp. 15ff.

13 James Joyce, *Ulysses*, 1st American ed. (New York: Random House, 1934), p. 748.

14 The two mathematical terms are from his first book, *A Treatise on Universal Algebra* (1898). Although Whitehead the mathematician is best known for his work in mathematical logic, his other mathematical writings are not without importance. Universal algebra, a current field of mathematics, derives its name from the above book. See Garrett Birkhoff, "Lattices and their Applications," in K. A. Baker and R. Wille, eds., *Lattice Theory and its Applications* (Lemgo, Germany: Heldermann Verlag, 1995), p. 19.
15 Descartes, *Meditations*, p. 49.
16 Whitehead, *Process and Reality*, p. 208.
17 Ibid., p. 29.
18 P. F. Strawson, *Individuals: An Essay in Descriptive Metaphysics* (London: Methuen, 1959), p. 9.
19 Ibid., p. 11.
20 Whitehead, *Process and Reality*, p. 160.
21 For a lucid explanation of that interpretation, see the chapter "Four-Dimensional Space-Time" in Jeremy Bernstein, *Einstein* (New York: The Viking Press, 1973).
22 Willard Van Orman Quine, *Word and Object* (Cambridge, MA: MIT Press, 1960), p. 172.
23 Robert Geroch, *General Relativity from A to B* (Chicago: University of Chicago Press, 1978). The quotations in this paragraph are from pp. 3–4.
24 Alternatively, in light of Abraham Robinson's Nonstandard Analysis, a minimal event might occupy an infinitesimal region of space-time. See my "Whitehead's Actual Occasions and the New Infinitesimals," *Transactions of the Charles S. Peirce Society*, 25 (1989): 29–39.
25 Whitehead, *Process and Reality*, p. 73.
26 David Bohm, *The Special Theory of Relativity* (London and New York: Routledge, 1996), p. 183.
27 Ibid., p. 184.
28 Ibid., p. 174.
29 This and the following six paragraphs draw upon ibid., pp. 131, 133, 150, 156, and 174.
30 For this example, see Geroch, *General Relativity from A to B*, p. 29.
31 Whitehead, *Process and Reality*, p. 123.
32 Ibid., p. 65. Additionally, see my "Time and Strict Partial Order," *American Philosophical Quarterly*, 37 (2000): 373–87.
33 Whitehead, *Process and Reality*, pp. 34–5.
34 Ibid., pp. 240–1.
35 Richard Rorty, *Philosophy and the Mirror of Nature* (Princeton, NJ: Princeton University Press, 1980), p. 113.
36 Donald R. Griffin, *Animal Thinking* (Cambridge, MA: Harvard University Press, 1984), p. 29.
37 Whitehead, *Process and Reality*, p. 177.
38 Ibid., p. 47.
39 Ibid., p. 177.
40 For a recent discussion of the mind–body problem from the standpoint of process philosophy (with emphasis on Whitehead), see David Ray Griffin, *Unsnarling the*

World-Knot: Consciousness, Freedom, and the Mind–Body Problem (Berkeley: University of California Press, 1998).

41 Whitehead, *Process and Reality*, p. 109.

42 Ibid., p. 308.

43 Ibid., p. 267.

44 For instance, see my "Does Whitehead's Metaphysics Contain an Ethics?" *Transactions of the Charles S. Peirce Society*, 37 (2001): 515–36.

45 There is no space in this chapter to discuss Whitehead's numerous remarks about the history of ideas. One much-quoted example is: "The safest general characterization of the European philosophical tradition is that it consists of a series of footnotes to Plato" (*Process and Reality*, p. 39). In addition to *Adventures of Ideas* (1933) and *Process and Reality* (1929), such remarks are found in *Science and the Modern World* (1925), with its criticism of the mechanistic world-view inaugurated by the scientific revolution of the sixteenth and seventeenth centuries. Together these books form a kind of trilogy.

Suggested reading

Gare, Arran, "Speculative Metaphysics and the Future of Philosophy: The Contemporary Relevance of Whitehead's Defence of Speculative Metaphysics," *Australasian Journal of Philosophy*, 77 (1999): 127–45.

Haack, Susan, "Descriptive and Revisionary Metaphysics," *Philosophical Studies*, 35 (1979): 361–71. Reprinted in S. Laurence and C. Macdonald, eds., *Contemporary Readings in the Foundations of Metaphysics* (Oxford: Blackwell Publishers, 1998).

Kraus, Elizabeth M., *The Metaphysics of Experience: A Companion to Whitehead's Process and Reality*, 2nd edn. (New York: Fordham University Press, 1998).

Lowe, Victor, *Alfred North Whitehead: The Man and His Work*, 2 vols. (Baltimore, MD: The Johns Hopkins Press, 1985 and 1990). Contains a detailed biography of Whitehead.

Rescher, Nicholas, *Process Metaphysics: An Introduction to Process Philosophy* (Albany: SUNY Press, 1996).

Schilpp, Paul Arthur, ed., *The Philosophy of Alfred North Whitehead*, 2nd edn. (New York: Tudor Publishing Co., 1951). Contains a bibliography of Whitehead's writings.

Simons, Peter, "Metaphysical Statements: A Lesson from Whitehead," *Erkenntnis*, 48 (1998): 377–93.

Whitehead, Alfred North, *Adventures of Ideas* (New York: The Free Press, 1985 [1933]).

——*Process and Reality: An Essay in Cosmology*, corrected edn., ed. D. Griffin and D. Sherburne (New York: The Free Press, 1978 [1929]).

——*Science and the Modern World* (New York: The Free Press, 1997 [1925]).

Chapter 14

C. I. Lewis, 1883–1964

Sandra B. Rosenthal

Biographical Note

C. I. Lewis was born in Stoneham, Massachusetts, and was associated with Harvard for most of his life. In both personal style and political leanings he was a conservative New England citizen. As an undergraduate, he studied with James, Royce, and Santayana, receiving a B.A. from Harvard in 1905. This was followed by a brief period of high-school teaching in Quincy, Massachusetts, and a few terms as an English instructor at the University of Colorado. While there, Lewis married a New England woman, Mabel Maxwell Graves, who encouraged him throughout his career. She strengthened his determination to return to Harvard and complete his graduate degree, which he received in 1910. The following year he served as an assistant at Harvard as the result of a job shortage, but the next year he began teaching at the University of California, Berkeley, where he became an associate professor. In 1920 Lewis returned to Harvard, first as a visiting lecturer and then as an assistant professor. In 1924 he was promoted to tenured associate professor, and the following year became a full professor. In 1945 Lewis was elected to the Edgar Peirce professorship, and he remained at Harvard throughout the rest of his career, retiring in 1953. He died in Menlo Park, California.

For all the classical pragmatists, purposive human behavior partially shapes the manner in which indeterminately rich nature enters our experience as the coherent, meaningful experience of things. Such a process calls for an a priori element within experience which regulates in advance the contours of this entry. Yet, with the exception of C. I. Lewis, a pragmatic reconstruction of an a priori element within experience is lacking in pragmatist thought. Moreover, although Lewis refers to his novel doctrine as a pragmatic a priori, it not only by and large has not been used to shed light on the other pragmatists,[1] but is in fact one source of the general perception that Lewis does not quite fit in with these others. His focus on the a priori highlights a concern with epistemic issues that distances him from the other pragmatists who are both less involved in his so-called abstract epistemic approach and display little interest in the a priori. For this reason, taking his concept of the a priori as the point of departure for exploring the pulse of classical American pragmatism that permeates his thought may strike some as strange. However, it can serve to highlight central features not just of Lewis's pragmatism, but of classical American pragmatism in general.

The epistemology to which the other classical pragmatists object is one to which Lewis objects as well, for pragmatism rejects all remnants of Cartesian philosophy and the resultant epistemology which begins with a subject–object split. They maintain that Cartesian epistemology illicitly detaches the subject from the "external world" and then tries to prove its existence, attempting to put together again that which it never should have pulled asunder. But a fundamental epistemological focus on existence can open meanings to the fullness and richness of their epistemic depth at the ground level of lived experience. At this level, the examination of the pre-reflective epistemic substrate for knowledge is inextricably intertwined with an explication of the structure and process of the concrete existence of the knower. Thus Lewis, supposedly the most "epistemically" oriented of the pragmatists, understands knowing always "within the context of being."[2] To see the depths of this rootedness of knowing in the ongoing organism-environment transactions constitutive of concrete human existence, the place to begin is with Lewis's most abstract concern – his work with symbolic systems and the distinctively pragmatic understanding of the a priori to which this led him.

The A Priori

Lewis's concept of the a priori occupies a unique position in the debate concerning the nature of a priori knowledge and the very possibility of an analytic–synthetic distinction. Drawing from a fundamentally Kantian scheme made responsive to the insights of American pragmatism and adapted to fit the needs of contemporary logic, Lewis established an a priori which is coextensive with the analytic, yet cannot be said to be empirically vacuous. It both arises from experience and has possible reference to experience. This unique doctrine of the pragmatic a priori emerged during his study of logic. His work in logic, combined with a healthy respect for Kantian epistemology, a long exposure to Roycean idealism, and an appreciation of certain basic tenets of classical American pragmatism, produced the context from which the pragmatic a priori, the vital core of Lewis's conceptual pragmatism, took shape.

Lewis spent many years studying logic, disturbed by two sorts of problem.[3] The first set of problems arose from the paradoxes of the extensional logic of Whitehead and Russell's *Principia Mathematica*. This "material implication" deviated strikingly from the ordinary sense of implication. According to it, a false proposition implies any proposition, while a true proposition is implied by any proposition. The problem, Lewis maintained, was that the logic of propositions formulated in *Principia* is an extensional one, while ordinary deductive inference depends upon the meanings of the propositions used, and hence is rooted in intensional relations. This led Lewis to develop a system of strict implication in symbolic logic, and carried him beyond logic into the field of epistemology and the development of a detailed theory of meaning and analyticity.

A second issue, arising from the possibility of an alternative to the logic of material implication, led to his interest in various alternative logics, such as many-valued logics and so-called "queer" logics. Thus Lewis was led to his second task – that of understanding the criteria for deciding which possible logistic systems contain the principles which state the truth about valid inference. Two points became clear to him. First, internal consistency is not sufficient to determine a truth which is independent of initial logical assumptions. Second, every process of reasoning within a logical system itself contains an extra-logical element, for any particular conclusion presented as *the* conclusion is selected from an indefinite number of valid inferences. The guiding fact in both cases is purpose or interest. In this way Lewis arrived at the conclusion that the inferences chosen within a logical system, as well as the original choice of a logical system, answer to criteria best called pragmatic. That is, we choose that which works in answering our interests and needs.

In this way, also, he was carried beyond logic to the development of a theory of knowledge asserting the free creation of and pragmatic selection among various possible conceptual schemes as tools for interpreting experience. Indeed, he recognized from the start of his logical investigations the more general issues into which he would be drawn, and thus set his plans "to argue from exactly determined facts of the behavior of symbolic systems to conclusions of more general problems."[4] Lewis holds that the behavior of symbolic systems operates in the same way as the behavior of the human mind: there is nothing in them that we have not put in ourselves, but they teach us the meaning of our commitments. A priori truth is independent of experience because it is purely analytic of our conceptual meanings. The line between the a priori and the a posteriori coincides with the divisions between the conceptual and the empirical, between the contributions of mind and what is given in experience, between the analytic and the synthetic.

Moreover, not only is our choice of an analytic, a priori conceptual scheme conditioned by experience – in that it is based on pragmatic considerations operative in the light of past experience – but the logic which the conceptual schemes apply and by which they are interrelated is itself based on pragmatic considerations and hence is, in the last analysis, conditioned by experience. Lewis's pragmatic interests reach this more fundamental level through his attempts to understand the foundation of valid ordinary inference. Logical relationships represent implications of our accepted definitions in accordance with consistent thinking. And, if the law of non-contradiction is the ultimate ground of the validity of logical principles, then what is its own ground of validity?[5] As the canon of deductive inference and logical laws, such as that of excluded middle and the very necessity of consistency itself, Lewis grounds logic in his pragmatism, which reaches down into the very core of his thought.

Humans are basically acting beings. Meanings the mind entertains, the logic that explicates such meanings, and mind itself emerge from behavioral responses to the environment in which humans find themselves. Our ways of behaving which are made explicit in our accepted logic are those ways that have worked, and thus lasted because they work. The principle of consistency upon which the "if-then" of ordinary inference is based in decision-making, and to which only some formal logics correctly apply, is a pragmatic imperative that must be adhered to if thought and action themselves are not to be stultified. The nature of logical necessity arises from the experiential necessity of inference.[6] The final ground for the imperative of consistency ultimately lies in the purposive, anticipatory nature of experience. As Lewis summarizes, "Practical consistency cannot be reduced to or defined in terms of merely logical consistency. But logical consistency can be considered as simply one species of practical consistency."[7] Though Lewis's logical concerns begin at the level of abstract conceptual systems, they in fact work downward to the point from which Dewey's own pragmatic understanding of logic begins its ascent. The above point was phrased simply by Dewey when he said that "the practical character of necessity is teleological." Or, as he states concerning the basic "patterns" of human thought, "rationality as an abstract conception is precisely the generalized idea of the means consequence relation as such." The serial relations of logic are rooted in the conditions of life itself; they are "prefigured in organic life."[8]

Although the above discussion should clearly indicate that Lewis's understanding of meaning and analyticity cuts beneath the level of linguistic conventionalism, philosophers' continuing assimilation of his claims to the framework of linguistic analysis demands a more explicit discussion of this aspect of his position. Analytic truths, for Lewis, state relations not merely between linguistic meanings, but also between sense meanings. The view that the a priori is coextensive with the analytic but dependent upon linguistic conventions fails to justify the epistemic function of the a priori. Contrary to this conventionalist view, the analyticity of linguistic meaning is determined by the fixed intensional relationships of sense meanings.[9] To separate linguistic meaning from the sense meaning it conveys is to engage in a process of abstraction, for these two aspects are supplementary, not alternative, and "separable by abstraction rather than separated."[10] The abstraction of language from the sense meaning it expresses can be useful for some purposes of analysis, but Lewis considers it disastrous for philosophical theory when one makes the distinction absolute and posits linguistic meaning as the focal point for investigations.

The Rejection of Phenomenalism

Lewis's focus on sense meaning is in large part responsible for another popular interpretation of his position, one which again serves to distance him from classical American pragmatism: he is viewed as positing a phenomenalistic reductionism that views meanings as reducible to the sense data out of which they are built.[11] But though meaning is derivative from the sensuous, and though meanings themselves can be termed sensuous insofar as they refer to experience, even meaning in its sensory aspect cannot be reduced to the content of experience. For Lewis, the sensuous aspect of meaning provides, literally, the "sense" or principle or form by which humans interpret and organize the sensory aspect of experience. Meaning incorporates a response which, as an interpretive principle, enters into the very character of what is grasped; thus the meaning of any thing is irreducible to any data as existing apart from the character of the response. It is only within the context of such an interpretive principle that the sensory comes to awareness.

This interactive unity of knower and known emerges from the interactive unity of organism-environment at a primordial level of experience. Lewis pragmatically views meanings in the biological context of habits or attitudes of response.[12] There is an inseparable relationship between the human biological organism bound to a natural environment and the perceiver who partially constitutes a world. From the contexts of organic activity and behavioral environment there emerge irreducible meanings that allow a world of objects to come to conscious awareness. Such meanings are irreducible to physical causal conditions or psychological acts and processes, yet they emerge from the biological – when the biological is properly understood – because the content of human perception is inseparable from the structure of human behavior within its natural setting. The phenomenological significance of habit is that such habits, dispositions, or tendencies are immediately experienced and pervade the very tone and structure of immediately grasped content. Thus Lewis can state that he is not advocating phenomenalism, but rather is presenting a "phenomenology of the perceptual."[13]

Lewis points out that there is a generally unnoticed complexity to sense meaning.[14] An implicit sense meaning is a disposition or habit by which humans interact with the environment In contrast, an explicit sense meaning is a schema or criterion in the mind by which one grasps the presence of something to which a particular type of response is required in order to obtain the desired result.[15] As specifying types, the schema, with its possible images or aspects, is general as opposed to the particulars grasped by it.[16] While the specific empirical content of experience is best understood as one particular among many, the schema for the application of a living meaning or habit to experience is best understood as the one which determines the many.

Indeed, the importance of the content of the schematic structure lies in the way in which it comes into being. Such a structure represents an aspect of the dispositional structural order that regulates it, and that governs the possible transformations from one schematic aspect to another. Meaning as dispositional is a rule for the production of schematic aspects as the conditions for possible verifying instances. The living meaning virtually contains the conditions for its verification. Such conditions are not collections of actual or possible verifying instances, but rather consist of the relational generality of schematic aspects that set the conditions of recognition for what will count as verifying instances. The disposition or habit, that is, the "living meaning," is possible to inspect through its particular applications, but impossible to exhaustively examine, since it can never be reduced to any series of such applications. What follows is that though a meaning is never fully inspected, any aspect of it can be examined. The fundamental concept of Lewis's notion of analyticity, then, is not synonymy but, rather, containment.

Both Lewis's theory of meaning and his notion of the test schema reveal that his theory of analyticity is basically one of inclusion or containment, not synonymy. Through the logic of the functioning of sense meaning as dispositional, Lewis can offer a solution to the problem of containment, for it clarifies how one discovers that some quality or character not explicit in a definition is nevertheless essential to the meaning in question. C. S. Peirce likewise finds the answer in the distinction between the concrete disposition or habit as the rule of organization and the awareness of the schematic aspects of that which is organized by the rule, thus his statement that the living meaning "virtually contains" these aspects.[17] If that which a meaning generates or contains is too frequently inapplicable, it can change through the formation of new habits that creatively fixate inductively accumulated experiences in new ways.[18] But what we have then is a new meaning, or a new rule, for the generation of verification conditions, which now necessarily contains at least partially different schematic possibilities. Though the same words may be used, the meanings attached to them are different.[19] Analytic truths, then, state relations between sense meanings and not merely between linguistic meanings. Lewis's entire understanding of meaning, analyticity, and the a priori clearly undercuts the conventionalist position that analytic truth expresses nothing beyond what is or can be determined by the language system that embodies it. Although he holds that there are conventional elements in the choice of symbols, in the assignment of the symbols to the meanings, and in the choice of the meanings to be considered, Lewis insists that the interrelation of the meanings is neither linguistic nor arbitrary.

Moreover, though the relation between meanings is statable apart from any particular instance of fact, the meanings are built up in the light of past experience and chosen for pragmatic reasons. A priori truth as legislative emerges within the context of purposive attitudes of interpretation drawn from the context of past experience. As Lewis summarizes this point:

> What is a priori is prior to experience in almost the same sense that purpose is. Purposes are not dictated by the content of the given; they are our own. Yet purposes must take their shape and have their realization in terms of experience. . . . In somewhat the same fashion what is a priori and of the mind is prior [to present experience] yet in another sense not altogether independent of experience in general.[20]

For Lewis, then, concepts are a priori rules, rooted in dispositional tendencies, which legislate ways in which experience can be interpreted – and a priori truths explicate the implicational relations contained within and among them. Genetically, these rules arise though the cumulative effect of past experience and the creative synthesis or fixation,[21] within the ongoing course of experience, of dispositionally organized relationships among possible experiences. But, at any point in the experiential process, the dispositional meaning logically contains all that it has creatively synthesized or "fixated" or, conversely, all that it now has the power or potential to generate.[22] Such intensionally grounded analytic relationships emerging from purposive activity pervade all levels of experience, from the most rudimentary expectations of prereflective experience to sophisticated scientific knowledge and the development of abstract formal systems. Important meaning structures may be difficult to capture by tracing which concepts are included in an explicit articulation of a relationship. But explicit articulation of the analysis of a concept is ultimately an attempt to capture what has been implicitly operative in the structure of our purposive activity, a structure that contains the schematic forms of its applicability.

The Given in Experience

Interpreters of Lewis's position are led to the phenomenalist camp not only because of his focus on sense meanings but also through his concern with the given element in experience. Perhaps no one aspect of Lewis's philosophy has been subject to more frequent and diverse attacks than his concept of the given element in experience. He expressed an ongoing frustration that his understanding of the given had been so misinterpreted over the years, stressing that the point he was trying to make was so obvious that he wondered how anyone could contest it. If there is nothing given, there would be no content for thought, nor could there be success or failure in action, and prediction would be incomprehensible. His emphasis on the given, as he himself stresses, is not a foundationalist or phenomenalist concern about data from which we build up a world of objects, but a pragmatic concern with the way we verify our beliefs. The failure to understand Lewis's pragmatic reconstruction of experience leads to persistent interpretations of his position as that of sense data phenomenalism, a position which he emphatically denied.[23]

As noted above, one of the most distinctive and crucial aspects of pragmatism is the understanding of experience as an interaction or transaction between organism and environment. Experience is that rich, ongoing transactional unity between organism and environment, and only within the context of meanings that reflect such an interactional unity does what is given emerge for conscious awareness. Transactional unity is more than a postulate of abstract thought, for it has epistemic or phenomenological dimensions. That which inexplicably intrudes into experience is not bare datum, but, rather, evidences itself as the over-againstness of a thick world "there" for our activity. If experience is an interactional unity of our responses and the ontologically real, then the nature of experience reflects both the responses we bring and the pervasive textures of that independent reality or surrounding natural environment. In such an interactional unity both poles are manifest: the ontological otherness onto which experience opens, and active organism within whose purposive activity it emerges.

What appears within experience is also the independently real; there is no ontological gap between appearance and reality. Further, it simultaneously appears "to me" and reflects my intentional or interactional link with the externally real. What appears within experience, then, opens in one direction toward the structures of the independently real and in the other direction toward the structures of our mode of grasping the independently real. Or, in other terms, what appears within experience is a function of both in interaction and thus "mirrors" neither exactly, though it reflects characteristics of each. The pervasive textures of experience, which are exemplified in every experience, are at the same time indications of the pervasive textures of the independent universe which, in every experience, gives itself for our responses and which provides the touchstone for the workability of our meanings. There is an elusive coerciveness at the basis of our selectivity in organizing experience that cannot be selected at will, but rather must be acknowledged by any selective organization that is to be workable.

Those who focus on the aspect of alternative conceptual schemes in Lewis's philosophy as the basis for viewing him as an analytic philosopher have at times noted a "nonconformity" in his thought: certain fundamental principles – such as the if-then order of causal relationships and the processive order of time – are not partially determined by alternative conceptual schemes but, rather, are necessary for the very possibility of the applicability of any conceptual scheme to experience. This awareness of such a coerciveness at the basis of meaning selection has led both to claims of problems in Lewis's "analytic" position and to the assertion that such fundamental principles, which are categorial in the sense of being illustrated in every possible experience, imply a heritage from Kant of a fixed, unalterable a priori necessity of the mind.[24] However, this "problem" from the framework of analytic conventionalism cannot be solved by bringing in the baggage of Kantian fixed categories of the mind, for, in addition to contradicting Lewis's explicit and emphatic rejection of such fixed, necessary categories of the mind, it ignores a critically important aspect of Lewis's position toward which this element of coerciveness, when properly located, directly points. Such coerciveness does not close us within the phenomenal, forever cut off from the noumenal by necessities of mind, but rather throws us outward toward the features of the ontologically real – and in so doing negates conventionalist claims. Failure to recognize this interactional "reflecting," and as a result to substitute for it a mirroring either of the ontologically real alone or of our selective activity alone, leads to the self-defeating alternatives of traditional realism or idealism, realism or antirealism, foundationalism or anti-foundationalism, objectivism or relativism. Lewis captures the import of this interactional unity: "It may be that between a sufficiently critical idealism and a sufficiently critical realism there are no issues save false issues which arise from the insidious fallacies of a copy theory of knowledge."[25]

This move beyond the alternatives of idealism or traditional realism is reflected in Lewis's emphatic overwhelming rejection of the set of alternatives that have shaped philosophy since Descartes, namely, "(1) knowledge is not relative to the mind, or (2) the content of knowledge is not the real, or (3) the real is dependent on mind."[26] Realists accept our knowledge of an independent reality by rejecting the view that knowledge is relative to the mind. Idealists, accepting the relativity of knowledge to the mind, accept the unqualified dependence of reality on mind. Kant and phenomenalists in general, in accepting the relativity of knowledge to the mind as well as the dependence of the phenomenal object on the mind, accept the conclusion that we cannot know the real in itself.[27] Lewis holds at once that the content of knowledge is the ontologically real, that the ontologically real has an independence from the mind, and yet that the content of knowledge is partially dependent upon the knowing mind. As he well indicates, rejecting one or the other of the above alternatives stems from a failure to once and for all reject the presuppositions of a spectator theory of knowledge.

The various aspects of reality may be known or unknown at any particular time, but reality itself is eminently knowable and becomes known, though always from the perspective of an interpretive net. Thus Lewis compares facts to a landscape: "A landscape is a terrain, but a terrain as seeable by an eye. And a fact is a state of affairs, but a state of affairs as knowable by a mind."[28] Peirce makes this point with a similar kind of distinction between events or occurrences and facts. While an occurrence is a concrete slice or slab of the universe in all its infinite detailed richness, a fact is a slab of the universe as related to abstractive interpretive activity.[29]

Temporality and Process

Lewis's brief but crucial discussions of temporality and the processive nature of the universe are a key factor in understanding his philosophy, but these discussions are usually ignored by his interpreters. The passage to process metaphysics can be found in his claim that the "absolutely given" as independent of noetic activity is a "Bergsonian duration."[30] He writes: "The absolutely given is a specious present fading into the past and growing into the future with no genuine boundaries. The breaking of this up . . . marks already the activity of an interested mind." While an individual object depends upon interpretive activity, the potentiality of thus appearing is in the independently existing reality itself,[31] and this potentiality is not the potentiality of ideal archetypes or substantive features in any sense, but rather is the potentiality inherent in "modes of persistence" or "continuities." For Lewis, the object as an experienced particular has a generality which "overflows" its lines of demarcation,[32] not because the universe is amorphous or ephemeral, but because it has the indefinite richness of a dense, opaque, thick, changing process. An object as an experienced particular is an abstracted portion of a concrete continuum of events. In a similar way, Peirce characterizes reality – before the conceptual cuts by which we grasp it – as a continuum which "swims in indeterminacy."[33]

The role of dispositional meaning in transforming the processive universe into a context of meaningfully structured objects is evinced in Dewey's assertion that "structure is constancy of means, of things used for consequences, not of things taken by themselves absolutely."[34] Further, the "isolation of structure from the changes whose stable ordering it is, renders it mysterious – something that is metaphysical in the popular sense of the word, a kind of ghostly queerness." As George Herbert Mead states of the universe at the "boundary" of experience or the "outer edge" of our purposive activity, "At the future edge of experience, things pass, their characters change and they go to pieces."[35] For all the pragmatists, the structures of objectivities grasped by the knowing mind do not reach a reality more ultimate than the temporally extended anticipatory interactions of concrete experience, but, rather, there is a lived-through grasp of our openness to a temporally developing universe as the very foundation for the emergence within experience of meaningful structure.

Lewis's distinctively pragmatic reconstruction of the a priori, which contours the manner in which a processive universe enters experience as the meaningful world of things, is inextricably woven into his subtly complex understanding of a temporally founded noetic creativity, rooted in purposive biological activity and constitutive of the nature of experience as experimental. This a priori element in experience, which regulates in advance the possibility of the emergence within experience of meaningful structure or of facts and objects of particular types, is rooted in the concreteness of human behavior and arises from, is made possible by, and is replaceable or alterable within the finite temporal structure of such behavior. In this way it makes possible a perspectival grasp of an independent processive universe, providing the vehicle by which we render determinate within our experience the inherent indeterminacy of an unfolding temporal universe with its indefinite richness of possibilities and potentialities that reach throughout past, present, and future. In so doing, it also serves as a focal point for capturing the spirit of classical American pragmatism that permeates Lewis's philosophy, thereby helping to secure his place as a major figure in this tradition.

Notes

1 I have explored the implicit development of an a priori in Peirce's philosophy in *Charles Peirce's Pragmatic Pluralism* (Albany: SUNY Press, 1994), ch. 2, and I have focused on the importance of Lewis's concept of the a priori for pragmatism in general in my *Speculative Pragmatism* (Amherst: The University of Massachusetts Press, 1986; paperback edn. Peru, IL: Open Court Publishing Co., 1990), ch. 3.

2 See C. I. Lewis, appendix D to *Mind and the World Order* (New York: Dover Publications, 1956), and introduction to *An Analysis of Knowledge and Valuation* (La Salle, IL: Open Court, 1962).
3 The following problems are most concisely summarized by Lewis in "Logic and Pragmatism," in the *Collected Papers of Clarence Irving Lewis*, ed. John D. Goheen and John L. Mothershead, Jr. (Stanford, CA: Stanford University Press, 1970).
4 "Logic and Pragmatism," p. 6.
5 Asher Moore, in "Lewis's Theory of the A Priori," argues that the principle of noncontradiction is synthetic a priori in Lewis's position, and shows with startling clarity its far-reaching implications that wreak havoc with Lewis's position concerning logical relationships. See Paul A. Schilpp, ed., *The Philosophy of C. I. Lewis*, Library of Living Philosophers Series (La Salle, IL: Open Court, 1968), pp. 155–99.
6 C. I. Lewis, *Our Social Inheritance* (Bloomington: Indiana University Press, 1957), p. 101.
7 John Lang, ed., *Values and Imperatives Studies in Ethics* (Stanford, CA: Stanford University Press, 1969), p. 122.
8 John Dewey, "The Superstition of Necessity," in *The Early Works*, vol. 4, pp. 30, 33.
9 For Lewis, "meaning cannot be literally put into words or exhibited by exhibiting words and the relations of words." *An Analysis of Knowledge and Valuation*, p. 140.
10 Ibid., p. 33.
11 This phenomenalistic interpretation can be seen throughout *The Philosophy of C. I. Lewis.*
12 As Lewis states, a meaning is "a sort of purposive attitude": *Mind and the World Order*, p. 228.
13 C. I. Lewis, "Autobiography," in the *Collected Papers of Clarence Irving Lewis*, p. 18.
14 Lewis, *An Analysis of Knowledge and Valuation*, p. 134.
15 Although Lewis usually speaks of sense meaning as a precise, explicit schema, sense meaning is, for Lewis, intensional or conceptual meaning, and this he frequently identifies as a disposition or habit. He clarifies this dual aspect of sense meaning when he observes that a "sense meaning when precise and explicit is a schema." Ibid.
16 Lewis's position can perhaps best be clarified by taking the term "image" or "schema-image" as "aspect." For example, one may say, quite correctly, that an ocean presents a turbulent image or aspect.
17 C. S. Peirce, *Collected Papers of Charles Sanders Peirce*, ed. Charles Hartshorne and Paul Weiss (Cambridge, MA: Belknap Press, 1960), 4.233. For a detailed support of this claim, see my *Charles Peirce's Pragmatic Pluralism*, ch. 2.
18 The ambiguity of William James's principles falls into focus within the context of the above discussion. James holds that there is a coerciveness among necessary and eternal relations which the mind finds between certain of its ideal conceptions, and that they form a determinate system independent of the order of frequency in which experience may have associated the conception's originals in time and space. So far as some of nature's realities fit this network, "we can make a priori propositions concerning natural fact." Yet he also indicates that our regulative principles are themselves conditioned by the experiences they serve to organize. James holds at times that there is a sharp distinction between the way in which we justify the a priori truths of logic and mathematics and the a posteriori truths of physics. Yet there are places where James comes close to maintaining that physical and mathematical theories are alike not only in being "spontaneous variations"

but also in being "rational propositions." What seems implicit here is not an ambiguous vacillation but a development toward a view that physical truths contain an a priori element, although for physical truths, such an a priori element both arises within the matrix of experience and must be found workable within the context of experience. William James, *The Principles of Psychology*, II, pp. 1215–70.

19 *Mind and the World Order*, p. 235.
20 Ibid., p. 24.
21 Peirce's use of the term "abduction" is most appropriate here.
22 Though the meanings change, the words used to designate them may remain the same; thus Peirce holds that "what is inconceivable today may become conceivable tomorrow." *Collected Papers of Charles Sanders Peirce*, 8.191; 2.29.
23 See Lewis, "An Analysis of Knowledge and Valuation," and "Replies to My Critics," in *The Philosophy of C. I. Lewis*. The "frequent and diverse attacks" mentioned in the article can also be found in *The Philosophy of C. I. Lewis*.
24 Lewis White Beck, "The Kantianism of Lewis," in *The Philosophy of C. I. Lewis*, pp. 274–84.
25 *Mind and the World Order*, p. 194.
26 Ibid., p. 154.
27 Ibid. Although Kantian philosophy is considered the beginning of "the rejection of the spectator," Kant himself was not immune to some of its presuppositions; in attempting to justify the absoluteness of the Newtonian or Modern World View in some sense, Kant was still caught up in the problems emerging from the absolutizing of scientific content based on an inadequate understanding of scientific method.
28 Lewis, "Replies to My Critics," p. 660.
29 Charles Peirce, The Microfilm Edition of the Peirce Papers, Houghton Library, Harvard University, MS 647, p. 8.
30 *Mind and the World Order*, p. 58. By the term "specious present" Lewis does not mean a false present but rather a spread-out present.
31 "Realism or Phenomenalism," in the *Collected Papers of Clarence Irving Lewis*, pp. 341, 346.
32 "A Pragmatic Conception of the A Priori," in the *Collected Papers of Clarence Irving Lewis*, p. 232.
33 Peirce, *Collected Papers*, 1.171–2.
34 Dewey, *Experience and Nature* (Carbondale, IL: Southern Illinois University Press, 1981), pp. 64–5.
35 George Herbert Mead, *Philosophy of the Act*, ed. Charles Morris (Chicago: University of Chicago Press, 1938), p. 34.

Suggested reading

Primary sources

Mind and the World Order (New York: Dover Publications, 1929).
The Ground and Nature of the Right (New York: Columbia University Press, 1955).
Our Social Inheritance (Bloomington: Indiana University Press, 1957).
Symbolic Logic, with C. H. Langford (New York: Dover Publications, 1959).

An Analysis of Knowledge and Valuation (La Salle, IL: Open Court, 1962).
Values and Imperatives, ed. John Lange (Stanford, CA: Stanford University Press, 1969).
Collected Papers of Clarence Irving Lewis, ed. John D. Goheen and John L. Mothershead, Jr. (Stanford, CA: Stanford University Press, 1970).

Secondary sources

Ducasse, C. J., "C. I. Lewis's Analysis of Knowledge and Valuation," *Philosophical Review*, 57 (1948): 260–80.
Firth, R. and R. B. Brandt, et al., "Commemorative Symposium on C. I. Lewis," *Journal of Philosophy*, 61 (1964): 545–70.
Henley, Paul, "Lewis's Analysis of Knowledge and Valuation," *Journal of Philosophy*, 45 (1948): 524–32.
Rosenthal, Sandra, *The Pragmatic A Priori: A Study in Epistemology of C. I. Lewis* (St. Louis, MO: Warren H. Green, 1976).
—— *Speculative Pragmatism* (Amherst, MA: The University of Massachusetts, 1986).
Schilpp, Paul A., ed., *The Philosophy of C. I. Lewis*, The Library of Living Philosophers (La Salle, IL: Open Court, 1968).

Chapter 15

Susanne K. Langer, 1895–1985

Richard E. Hart

Intellectual Biography

Susanne K. Langer (1895–1985) was born in New York City and received her doctoral degree in philosophy from Radcliffe College. Early on she taught at Radcliffe and Columbia College, concluding her teaching career with a distinguished tenure at Connecticut College from 1954 to 1962. In between, she held visiting appointments at the University of Delaware, New York University, The New School, the University of Washington, Northwestern University, the Ohio State University, and the University of Michigan. By any measure of academic achievement, hers was an exceptionally distinguished career in philosophy, with regard to both teaching and scholarship. Yet, surprisingly, her voluminous written work, pioneering and evocative in many respects, has been fairly neglected in professional circles. Some possible reasons for this unhappy circumstance will be offered at the end.

Langer possessed a towering, expansive intellect, unquestionably the equal of any original or systematic philosopher of her time. She was a consistent "pluralist" in terms of her interests and contributions within and outside the borders of philosophy. Within philosophy she made major contributions to a diverse array of sub-fields, ranging from symbolic logic (one of the earliest classroom texts was her *An Introduction to Symbolic Logic* (1937)) to symbolism and semiotics, to aesthetics, philosophy of mind, and a fundamental re-envisioning of the nature and practice of philosophy. She is best known for her highly influential work, *Philosophy In A New Key: A Study In The Symbolism of Reason, Rite and Art* (1942), one of the largest selling paperbacks in the history of the Harvard University Press. Her most important works in aesthetics were *Feeling and Form: A Theory of Art Developed From "Philosophy In A New Key"* (1953), *Problems of Art* (1957), and *Reflections on Art* (ed. 1958). Her first book was on the nature of philosophy itself, *The Practice of Philosophy* (1930). Additionally, she published

Philosophical Sketches (1962), and the capstone of her life's work, *Mind: An Essay on Human Feeling* in 3 volumes (1967, 1972, 1982), the final volume of which appearing when Langer was 87 years of age.

Langer brought to her philosophical work a broad, democratic spirit of intellectual inquiry that she sought to relate, in a compelling manner, to the expansive intelligibility of all human experience. She considered the philosophical tradition to be generally confused, often misguided, and filled with numerous dead-ends. Every doctrine within the tradition, she contended, was refuted by several others, every conception of philosophy challenged by radically different orientations. Philosophy, for Langer, had always been either too broad in its sweep or too narrow. So how could it progress? She set out to rectify the situation through (somewhat ironically) narrowing the method or technique of philosophical analysis while substantially broadening the experiential reach of the philosopher's grasp. Scholars who have taken serious interest in her work argue over whether her agenda succeeded.

In the 1930s Langer seemed to favor "logical" or "analytic" methods and techniques of philosophical inquiry, rooted in the materials of the natural sciences and concentrated chiefly on the clarification of terms and the conceptual frameworks in which all our propositions are made. But, simultaneously, she also reacted against the predominant and misguided "scientism" of her day as a way of establishing a base for her own unique insights. A telling passage from *New Key* points to her move from "scientism" and "analysis" to a philosophical focus on "meaning" and "symbolization":

> A philosophy that knows only deductive and inductive logic as reason, and classes all other human functions as "emotive," irrational, and animalian, can see only regression to a prodigal state in the present passionate and unscientific ideologies . . . But a theory of mind whose keynote is the symbolic function, whose problem is the morphology of significance is not obliged to draw that bifurcating line between science and folly.[1]

While retaining the "analytic" technique and method, utilizing logic for analysis of concepts and corrections of errors, Langer struggled valiantly to posit a new guiding principle that would ultimately redefine philosophy and prescribe an amended procedure for engaging in the practice. That working basis and ultimate aim (the new principle) was to be the pursuit of meaning, and the understanding of symbol in relation to all human mentality, action, and creation. Her total dedication to this modified task for philosophy is reflected in her claim that "[t]he continual pursuit of meanings – wider, clearer, more negotiable, more articulate meanings – is philosophy."[2] This turn of thought proved to be both liberating and constraining. On the one hand, she successfully identified and articulated a fuller, richer realm of human experience and valuing, as compared to the self-imposed narrowness of "scientism." Yet, on the other, the pursuit of meaning for Langer seemed to entail specific reflections on the "meanings of our words" and the implications of our statements. "[S]he quite literally means that the focus of philosophical enquiry is to be on *words* rather than *things* or *actions* or *beliefs*."[3]

Since philosophy for Langer deals with symbols, and can never penetrate through to reality, it must focus itself on a consideration of words and meanings separate from facts, standing between man and reality. While human life is "an intricate fabric of reason and rite, of knowledge and religion, prose and poetry, fact and dream,"[4] all of which we need to take into our philosophical work, philosophy as discipline remains a critique of working concepts and symbols in all aspects of life. Conceptual analysis of science and scientific progress, along with contemporary theory of knowledge, thus represented for Langer the exemplars of philosophical work in her time. This amply demonstrates a deep and perhaps not fully realized split in Langer's thought – her astonishing openness to experience, with man's basic need for symbolization at its core, coupled with a narrow conception of philosophy as the analysis and improvement of our stock of explanatory concepts. As corroboration, consider two basic points in Langer: (1) her acceptance of the notion that intellectual advance is best represented in scientific progress, and (2) her impassioned argument that philosophy needed a "new key," a new generative idea, one that "changes the questions of philosophy."[5] This, of course, became manifest in her desire to turn from simple facts and science-based knowledge to meaning and language – that is, to symbolism. For Langer, the vast sweep and expanse of symbols, understood as intellectual constructs, allowed her to appreciate and incorporate the broad horizons of experience in her work. Her writings in aesthetics, to be discussed shortly, are a powerful example of just such a "key change."

Influences

Wittgenstein of the *Tractatus* and her teacher, A. N. Whitehead, were clear influences on Langer's thought. Like Whitehead, Langer was a systematic philosopher. To illustrate, philosopher Beth J. Singer has written that Langer "developed a structure of mutually supportive concepts and principles which she progressively analyzed, elaborated and illustrated."[6] Langer herself contended that all of her works were interconnected, the later books based on the earlier ones. *Feeling and Form*, her general aesthetic theory, grew out of symbolism as developed in *Philosophy In A New Key*, and everything she wrote was preparatory to and evolving toward her final study, *Mind: An Essay On Human Feeling*.

Perhaps the most profound influence, however, on the formation of Langer's philosophy was the neo-Kantian Ernst Cassirer. His monumental work, *Philosophy of Symbolic Forms* (3 vols., 1923–9) helped her get a fruitful grasp on what she frequently called the "unlogicized" areas of life: myth, ritual, and art. She and Cassirer insisted that these non-scientific areas of human life and experience, nonetheless, had an intellectual character and were, therefore, proper subjects for philosophy. Cassirer proposed a new way of seeing the arts in relation to other aspects of human culture, while Langer sought to retain and extend the vision of "logical philosophy" by including such non-scientific areas within the orbit of intellectual activity. Symbols, in whatever realm, had to be seen as properly intellectual in character and not simply reducible to immediate sense perception or emotive response. "[T]hey are symbols of what transcends the present. Far from being 'signals' of immediately present objects, they mediate meanings that are beyond the here and now."[7] Art and language, thus, function similarly and belong in the same category.

Cassirer systematically modified and broadened Kant's categories of the understanding (substance, causality) and forms of intuition (space, time) in order to focus on the language and symbol systems we employ in thinking and talking about the world around us. These symbol systems actually determine what the world will be for us rather than simply mirroring the world. Thus it is that the great symbolic forms (in art, for example) create a world ("our" world) and reveal to us our own human powers rather than some fundamental reality "out there." For Cassirer and Langer, man literally inhabits a "symbolic universe," a theme epitomized by art though by no means confined solely to it.

Langer's early attachment to Cassirer's theory of semiotics (or symbolism) also grew out of her passion for symbolic logic. She was convinced that symbolic logic had the capacity for clarifying numerous semantic confusions that bedeviled the general intellect and professional philosophy, thus helping to straighten out numerous pathetic muddles of philosophic thought in her day. On her view, formal logic would, conceptually, lead to the advancement of philosophy. Her second book was in fact a textbook, *An Introduction To Symbolic Logic* (1937). In the Preface she re-emphasized the notion of "system" and introduced another Cassirer-influenced concept of "form." Her text promoted logic as "system, its progress from the specific to the general, from the general to the abstract . . . its treatment of logic as a science of forms."[8] Her preoccupation with "form" (as a complement to symbol) extended to all areas of human pursuit and inquiry, from "form" in logic and science, myth and culture, to "form" in music. Thus, symbol and form were two grounding notions indispensable to Langer's thought from the earliest days. In these respects, her early work on symbolic logic prefigures similar, later developments in her aesthetics, as we shall now see.

Art and Aesthetics

Langer, though undeniably influenced by logical positivism, became far more than simply a positivistic logician inclined toward science. She was thoroughly grounded in a wide variety of arts, and in the middle stage of her career sought to move the notions of symbol and form beyond logic and science and apply them, in novel ways, to the arts and aesthetic experience. To most critics and interpreters, it is in the realm of aesthetics that Langer made her greatest and most lasting contributions.

Her first major step in this direction was to articulate a critical distinction between two different kinds of symbol, "discursive" (as found in science and logic), and "expressive" or "presentational" (as found in the arts). This would further suggest different modes of "truth" in the various forms of inquiry and creation, even different types of "knowledge" realized through different systems of signs – knowledge in the sciences and philosophy, and knowledge in religion, myth, and poetry. Though different in character and function, all were, in a sense, constructs of the intellect and could be apprehended through the intellect.

The basic distinction between types of symbols, truth, and knowledge provided important pieces of the architecture of her general aesthetics. She related the concepts first to music (in *New Key*), and this led to further theorizing about the relation between "feeling" and the arts. The creation of a work of art involves the idealization of experience and feeling, and objectification of that which is important in experience. In terms of musical meaning, for example, Langer claimed that "The tonal structure we call 'music' bears a close logical similarity to the forms of human feeling."[9] Music is an analogue of emotive life in general, not an expression or evocation of particular emotions in a personal sense. Art neither imitates nor produces specific feelings, but rather presents the "form of feeling." Art thus symbolizes the very structure of psychic process by exhibiting its generic features. For Langer, "all works of art are purely perceptible forms that seem to embody some sort of feeling."[10] In *Feeling and Form* (which evolved directly from *Philosophy in a New Key*) Langer extends the concept of art as symbol to all other basic art forms. Every art work, regardless of medium, is a presentational symbol (bearing its own sense of knowledge and truth), an expressive form created for perception through sense or imagination, and finally an "appearance" or "semblance." Art, as expressive form, is not the same thing as an art object. Nor is it something abstract or abstracted, but rather it "appears," enfolded by meaning. As "semblance," a work of art, says Langer, creates a realm of aesthetic illusion distinct from experiential reality, for example, the illusion of dance through gesture or the illusion of time through music. Aesthetic forms exist only in that they are perceived through sense or imagination. Art, thus, becomes a "merely virtual object" in the sense of illusion, rather than a "thing" in the realm of space and time. Every work of art creates a sense of "otherness" from reality. Each art has a special and unique semblance-character – painting as virtual space rather than actual space as lived, music as virtual time rather than what we call real time. Says Singer, "The idea that what is presented or exhibited in art is 'virtual' rather than actual is the main theme of Langer's analysis of each of the arts in *Feeling And Form*."[11]

Thus, an assembly of metaphysical and epistemological dualisms come together to form the basis of Langer's unique aesthetic theory – art as presentational rather than discursive symbol; art as symbolic representation of generic psychic process rather than immediate feeling; art as semblance or illusion rather than object; art as an imaginary virtual realm of reality rather than actual reality. Concomitantly, for Langer the appreciation of a work of art requires mental shifts that parallel these underlying metaphysical dualisms. Notes on a sheet become music, colors on a canvas a painting, words on a page a poem only insofar as the perceiver adopts a contemplative "intellectual" grasp of the idealized artistic import of the structure of the work as a whole, which amounts to fully apprehending its virtual or semblance existence. The aesthetic aspect of our experience, rooted in intellectual comprehension, thus lives its own life.

Professional Neglect

Given the sheer magnitude and originality of Langer's work it is reasonable to ask why she has been undervalued as a philosopher, even virtually ignored for periods of time. For sure, Langer's philosophy cannot really be grasped piecemeal. In order to appreciate its significance, the whole of her interconnected system must be studied patiently, with an extremely open mind and with a reasonable degree of interdisciplinary sophistication. Langer readily infused her writings with material from the social sciences, art, cultural studies, religion, and myth, and moved about within such realms with an ease and mastery most readers are scarcely up to. For instance, in her 3-volume capstone, *Mind*, she offers detailed, well-documented accounts of the evolution of human culture and mentality, along with comparative studies of other animal species and their mentalities. While thoroughly integrative and original, many philosophers may regard this beyond the boundaries of philosophy per se, and thus have little patience for it.

Arguably, her overall perspective may come across as inaccessible and confusing, possibly due to the conflicting tendencies alluded to earlier in this chapter: her broad appreciation of human experience yet surprisingly narrow conception of the work of philosophy. Moreover, some philosophers today are thoroughly intolerant of what they consider worn-out metaphysical and epistemological dualisms stemming from the tradition of Descartes, examples of which we noted as at least implicit in Langer. The fact is that Langer was something of a rebel. She did not publicly align herself with any dominant philosophical tradition or school of thought of her time. Contrarily, she intended, at least, to challenge philosophy to rethink its nature and expand its boundaries. While influenced by positivism, she at times referred to it as the least interesting of all philosophical doctrines growing out of science. In sum, Langer's challenge to herself was astonishingly large and ambitious, a matter not always appreciated by those with more modest abilities and goals. Beatrice Nelson has written: "Langer embraced the twin currents of logical, scientific philosophy and of transcendental, idealist, or aesthetic philosophy and sought to discern philosophy's new direction in their comingling."[12] Whether this could ever be possible, or fully realized in a satisfactory manner, is open to legitimate question.

It must also be recalled that Susanne Langer was a woman, indeed, a divorced woman, working in a male-dominated field during her time. By all accounts, she was supremely self-assured and forthright, and was apparently not one to suffer fools lightly. Given our present milieu, with its focus on the contributions of women philosophers and renewed interest in the work of previous women, we can only hope this neglect will be corrected. Her intellectual mastery and originality was the equal of any twentieth-century philosopher, her grasp of arts and culture the envy of anyone who cares about such matters. As John J. McDermott has remarked, "Regretfully and comparatively neglected in our time, the cast of reflection offered by Susanne K. Langer has yet to be fully explored."[13]

Notes

1 Susanne K. Langer, *Philosophy In A New Key* (Cambridge, MA: Harvard University Press, 1942; 3rd edn. 1957), pp. 292–3.
2 Ibid., p. 293.
3 James Campbell, "Langer's Understanding of Philosophy," *Transactions of the Charles S. Peirce Society*, 33/1 (Winter 1997), p. 136.
4 Langer, *Philosophy In A New Key*, p. 45
5 Ibid., p. xiii.
6 Beth J. Singer, "Susanne K. Langer," unpublished paper presented to Society of Philosophers in America, American Philosophical Association, Eastern Division Meeting, December 29, 2000, p. 5.
7 Richard M. Liddy, "Susanne K. Langer's Philosophy of Mind," *Transactions of the Charles S. Peirce Society*, 33/1 (Winter 1997), p. 151.
8 *An Introduction to Symbolic Logic* (New York: Dover Publications, 1937), p. 11.
9 *Feeling and Form* (London: Routledge and Kegan Paul, 1953), p. 27.
10 *Philosophical Sketches* (Baltimore, MD: Johns Hopkins University Press, 1962), p. 85.
11 Singer, "Susanne K. Langer," p. 8.
12 Beatrice K. Nelson, "Langer's Concept of 'Symbol' – Making Connections Through Ambiguity," *The Journal of Speculative Philosophy*, New Series, 8/4 (1994), p. 278.
13 John J. McDermott, "Symposium on Susanne K. Langer: A Foreword," *Transactions of the Charles S. Peirce Society*, 33/1 (Winter 1997), p. 132.

Suggested reading

Primary sources

The Practice of Philosophy (New York: Henry Holt, 1930).
An Introduction to Symbolic Logic (New York: Dover Publications, 1937).
Feeling and Form (New York: Charles Scribner's Sons, 1953).
Philosophy in a New Key: A Study in the Symbolism of Reason Rite and Art, 3rd edn. (Cambridge: Harvard University Press, 1957).
Problems of Art (New York: Charles Scribner's Sons, 1957).

Philosophical Sketches (Baltimore, MD: Johns Hopkins University Press, 1962).
Mind: An Essay On Human Feeling (Baltimore, MD: Johns Hopkins University Press, 1967–82).

Secondary sources

Colapietro, Vincent, "Symbols and the Evolution of Mind: Susanne Langer's Final Bequest to Semiotics," *Semiotics* (1998).
Dryden, Donald, "Whitehead's Influence on Susanne Langer's Conception of Living Form," *Process Studies*, 26/1–2 (Spring–Summer 1997).
Gill, Jerry H., "Langer, Language and Art," *International Philosophical Quarterly*, vol. 34, 4/136 (December 1994).
Kuklick, Bruce, *The Rise of American Philosophy* (New Haven, CT: Yale University Press, 1977).
Nelson, Beatrice K., "Langer's Concept of 'Symbol' – Making Connections Through Ambiguity," *The Journal of Speculative Philosophy*, New Series, 8/4 (1994).
"Symposium on Susanne K. Langer," *Transactions of the Charles S. Peirce Society*, 33/1 (Winter 1997).

Chapter 16

Willard Van Orman Quine, 1908–2000

Peter T. Manicas

Introduction

Perhaps no contemporary American philosopher has had greater influence than W. V. O. Quine. Working solidly within the Anglo-American "analytic" tradition that was initiated by Bertrand Russell and developed in Vienna positivism, he made substantial contributions to his first love, mathematical logic – contributions that pale in comparison with the influence of his work in general philosophy, marked by his seminal 1951 "Two Dogmas of Empiricism."[1] This essay advanced theses, developed into arguments that eventually culminated in his 1990 book *The Pursuit of Truth*.[2] These arguments had remarkable consequences: they powerfully assisted in what became a frontal attack on some of the main claims of the dominant logical empiricist epistemology and philosophy of science, stimulating new forms of what might be called "pragmatism" and anti-realism in the philosophy of science.[3] They spawned both materialist and reliabilist versions of naturalistic epistemology.[4] And even more directly, Quine's arguments inspired an American version of post-modernism which, in turn, seemed to converge with Continental post-structuralist semiotics and the denial of what Derrida called "the metaphysics of presence."[5] Finally, these theses became central to the currently very fashionable, if too often uncritically held, idea that the world is a human creation.

Two Dogmas of Empiricism

What were the dogmas of the famous "Two Dogmas" essay and what did Quine offer in replacement of them? I quote him:

> Modern empiricism has been conditioned in large part by two dogmas. One is a belief in some fundamental cleavage between truths which are *analytic*, or grounded in

> meanings independently of matters of fact, and truths which are *synthetic*, or grounded in fact. The other dogma is *reductionism*: the belief that each meaningful statement is equivalent to some logical construct upon terms which refer to immediate experience.[6]

Since it permitted modern empiricism to expunge necessity from nature and confine it to language, the analytic/synthetic distinction was the center of logical empiricism ("logical positivism," "positivism").[7] Putting aside formally true sentences (e.g., p or not-p), the truth of analytic statements is guaranteed by meaning, where meaning (or intension) is sharply distinguished from "extension," (reference), defined as "the class of all entities of which a general term is true." For example "creature with a heart" and "creature with kidneys" are unlike in meaning even if they are alike in extension.

For Quine "extension" is a perfectly clear idea, but meaning is not. As he notes, "meaning is what essence becomes when it is divorced from the object of reference and wedded to the word." Meanings are presumably "meant entities" ("intentions," as Brentano had it).[8] Worse, the notion of analyticity requires that we have a clear idea of synonymy, or sameness of meaning. But, insists Quine, we do not.

Quine considers alternative routes to solving the problem – definition, perhaps. But, except where one is stipulating, "let us take F to mean G," definition presupposes synonymy. Similar problems beset the idea that two terms are synonymous if they are interchangeable *salva veritate* (without a change in the truth value of the sentence). If we assert: "Necessarily all and only bachelors are unmarried men," we beg the central question, since "necessarily" is presumed to apply only to analytic statements. If our language does *not* contain modal words like "necessarily" (and other words that do not behave extensionally), then interchangeability guarantees *extensional equivalence* – the truth is preserved, but it cannot guarantee *cognitive synonymy*, sameness of meaning. Similarly, we can construct semantical rules for a language that make them analytic in that language but, unfortunately, this sheds no light on analyticity. As Quine notes, "We understand what expressions the rules attribute analytic to, but we do not understand what the rules attribute to those expressions."[9]

Perhaps the solution is to be found in the second dogma: in general terms, "the verification theory of meaning." This idea is often attributed to Peirce; it is certainly a central pillar in the dominating logical empiricism. On this view, "the meaning of a statement is the method of empirically confirming or infirming it."[10] It is hard to overstate the influence of this doctrine, especially as regards still very widely held notions of science. Presumably, the difference between making reference to photons or quantum jumps is very different from making reference to gods or witches, or else there is nothing to the "objectivity" of science. Presumably, the empirical meaning of "photon" is guaranteed by the ability to confirm or disconfirm hypotheses that make reference to them. But seeing that this requirement was not directly satisfied – one tests theory by deductively elaborating and testing the empirical consequences of theory – empiricists were led, in a story not to be told here, to a series of moves by Carnap, Hempel, and others (e.g., partial interpretation, correspondence rules) to find a satisfactory way to link theory and experience, finally acknowledging that one could not draw an absolute boundary between the theoretical and the observational.[11] Nonetheless, the verifiability principle remains (despite gestures in the direction of Quine) part of the lore of hypothesis, theory, and "operational definition" for social scientists who seek to emulate the methods of "hard science." More important, perhaps, the verification theory of meaning has been the main weapon against beliefs whose meanings seemed not to answer to the test: sentences that are metaphysical, ethical, political, and aesthetic. "Value judgments," on this view, are not "cognitively meaningful," that is, they are neither true nor false.[12]

The verification theory then implies that "statements are synonymous if and only if they are alike in point of method of empirical confirmation or infirmation." So indeed the two dogmas collapse into one. But this raises a new problem, namely, what is "the nature of the relation between the statement and the experiences which contribute to or detract from its confirmation?" It would seem that truth "depends upon both language and extralinguistic fact," so that one is tempted to suppose that "the truth of a statement is somehow analyzable into a linguistic component and a factual component."[13] But can this be analysis be carried out?

Quine notices that Carnap's first efforts at what Quine calls "radical reductionism" not only failed, but failed in principle. Regardless of whether the statement was to be translated (reduced) into a statement about "sense data as sensory events" or "sense data as sensory qualities," in the artificial language which Carnap employed, talk about physical objects could not be reduced (on Quine's account, Carnap's language was "parsimonious," even if "empiricists there are who would boggle at such prodigality"). But he observes, even with the abandonment of this austere (procrustean?) program, "the dogma of reduction survives in the supposition that each statement, taken in isolation from its fellows, can admit of confirmation or infirmation at all."[14]

This was indeed the master insight: "Empiricism without dogmas" could proceed:

> The totality of our so-called knowledge or beliefs, from the most casual matters of geography and history to the profoundest laws of atomic physics or even of pure mathematics and logic, is a man-made fabric which impinges on experience only along the edges. Or, to change the figure, total science is like a field of force whose boundary conditions are experiences. . . . Reevaluation of some statements entails reevaluation of others, because of their logical interconnections – the logical laws being in turn simply further statements of the system, certain further elements of the field. . . . But the total field is so underdetermined by its boundary conditions, experience, that there is much latitude of choice as to what statements to reevaluate in the light any single experience. No particular experiences are linked with any particular statements in the interior of the field, except indirectly through considerations of equilibrium affecting the field as a whole.[15]

This vision of knowledge as "holistic" both caught the imagination of philosophers and provoked Quine's subsequent research program. Notice here that, as regards the quoted text, it is unclear, first, whether Quine had in mind belief and/or meaning as a "fabric" and, second, whether *all* belief (or meaning) was underdetermined by experience (or whether, as with Pierre Duhem, his concern was only with scientific theories as they were then generally understood). That is, were there many fields or one large field (perhaps common sense?) with subfields interspersed?[16]

Pragmatism and Naturalism

Quine's "pragmatism" was present in the "Two Dogmas" in his account of physical objects. He wrote:

> As an empiricist I continue to think of the conceptual scheme of science as a tool, ultimately for predicting future experience in the light of past experience. Physical objects are conceptually imported into the situation as convenient intermediaries – not by definition in terms of experience, but simply as irreducible posits comparable, epistemologically, to the gods of Homer. For my part I do, qua lay physicist, believe in physical objects and not in Homer's gods; and I consider it a scientific error to believe otherwise. But in point of epistemological footing the physical objects and the gods enter our conceptions only as cultural posits. The myth of physical objects is superior to most in that it has proved more efficacious than other myths as a device for working a manageable structure into the flux of experience.[17]

But the essay left another set of tensions that, I think, seem unresolved and perhaps also give readers ample room for interpretation – and misinterpretation. One tension, a seemingly technical one, regards physical objects and especially their status in Quine's empiricism and theory of language; another is the question of relativism. Suppose we agree that "the myth of physical objects is superior . . . as a device for working a manageable structure into the flux of experience," what rules out other "myths" that seem to help cultures work "manageable structures into the flux of *their* experience"? What about explanations that appeal to God's will? Who, more generally, is the "our" in "our culture" and why should "science" be privileged epistemologically?

Indeterminacy of Translation

Quine's 1968 John Dewey Lectures, titled "Ontological Relativity," offer the most direct answers to the key doctrines of his later writings, and the now famous

Quinean themes: (1) "the inscrutability of reference," and (2) "the indeterminacy of translation."

The first lecture begins with a statement of some strong connections to Dewey. Quine notes that he is "bound to Dewey by the naturalism that dominated his last three decades," and shares with Dewey that "knowledge, mind and meaning are part of the same world that they have to do with, and that they are to be studied in the same empirical spirit that animates natural science." Moreover, "meanings are, first and foremost, meanings of language;" and, critically, "language is a social art which we all acquire on the evidence solely of other's people's overt behavior under publicly recognizable circumstances." As Dewey had insisted, "Meaning . . . is not a psychic existence; it is primarily a property of behavior."[18]

So far, Quine and Dewey are naturalists; as such, both stand clearly opposed to various "mentalistic" conceptions of meaning, well characterized by Quine:

> Uncritical semantics is the myth of a museum in which the exhibits are meanings and the words are labels. To switch languages is to switch labels. . . . Now the naturalist's primary objection to this view is not an objection to meanings on account of their being mental entities, though that could be objection enough. The primary objection persists even if we take the labeled exhibits not as mental ideas but as Platonic ideas or even as the denoted concrete objects. Semantics is vitiated by a pernicious mentalism as long as we regard a man's semantics as somehow determinant in his mind beyond what might be implicit in his dispositions to overt behavior. It is the very facts about meaning, not the entities meant, that must be construed in terms of behavior.[19]

Putting aside for the moment the troublesome notion of "behavior" (and whether intentional objects, "the entities meant," are dispensable), we see that once we are committed to a behavioral view of meaning, that is, "we give up assurance of determinacy." Indeed, when we do this, we see not only that there are some indeterminate cases, but that indeterminacy is pervasive – Quine's famous "indeterminacy of translation."

What is the gist of the argument and what are the consequences? The argument begins with a famous artificial example of "Gavagai," introduced in his 1960 *Word and Object*. We are to imagine a field linguist seeking a translation for the native word, "Gavagai." There is no vocabulary or manual since it is just his job to create one. All he has is the behavior of natives. Now, it is a fact that "a whole rabbit is present, when and only when an undetached part of a rabbit is present; also when and only when a temporal stage of a rabbit is present" (meaning by this last, there are definite space and time coordinates for his location). Ostension (pointing) will not suffice since there will be no behavioral difference to be discerned in the speaker's assent to "gavagai": it might, accordingly, mean "rabbit," *or* "undetached rabbit part," *or* "rabbit stage." This is Quine's famous "inscrutability of reference."[20]

It may be supposed that there is a non-ostensive means available once our linguist has developed a grammar for the language, a grammar that includes decisions on plural endings, the "is" of identity, etc. Eventually, by abstraction, he gets a system for translating. Then, "insofar as the native sentences and the thus associated English ones seem to match up in respect to appropriate occasions of use, the linguist feels confirmed in these hypotheses of translation – what I call analytical hypotheses." Quine notes that this route is both "laudable in practice and the best we can hope for," but it does not allow us to settle the indeterminacy. It does not because of the holistic character of meaning: there is no reason to believe that there isn't another, or perhaps aren't several other translation manuals, that are wholly consistent with all the behavioral data.[21]

But if this were not sufficiently provocative, Quine argues that it can also be shown that "radical translation begins at home," and that inscrutability of reference pervades the home language itself. Our usual "domestic rule" of translation is "homophonic": we equate the same string of phonemes in our own mouths with similar strings in others. But we all employ "a principle of charity," construing "a neighbor's word heterophonically now and then if thereby we see our way to making his message less absurd."[22] Indeed, things are even worse, for the "inscrutability of reference is not the inscrutability of fact: there is no fact of the matter. But if there is really no fact of the matter, then the inscrutability of reference can be brought even closer to home than the neighbor's case; we can apply it to ourselves." Quine balks:

> We seem to be maneuvering ourselves into the absurd position that there is no difference on any terms, interlinguistic or intralinguistic, objective or subjective, between referring to rabbits and referring to rabbit parts or stages; or referring to formulas and their Gödel numbers. Surely this is absurd, for it would imply that there is no difference between the rabbit and each of its parts or stage. . . . Reference would now seem to become nonsense not just in radical translation but at home.[23]

Quine asserts that the answer is readily at hand: "reference is nonsense except relative to a coordinate system." It is nonsense to ask absolutely whether the terms "rabbit," or "rabbit part" "really refer respectively to rabbits, rabbit parts . . . We can only ask this relative to some background language."[24] Quine knows, of course, that this threatens a regress, indeed, an infinite regress. *Practically speaking*, to be sure, the regress ends with our "home language": "by acquiescing in our mother tongue and taking words at face value."[25] *Philosophically speaking*, this would seem to be a disappointing result, one which, in his subsequent writings, Quine tried valiantly to remedy. In *Theories and Things* (1981), reference became relative to a "translation manual," but the problem remained. In his 1990 *The Pursuit of Truth* we read: "If we choose as our manual of translation the identity transformation [which pairs off each term off with itself], thus, taking the home language at face value, the relativity is resolved."[26] It is hard to see how this differs from "acquiescing in our mother tongue."

Barry Stroud has argued that we can admit that "there is no place for an internal 'museum' of meanings," that speakers of a language do have knowledge which enables them to respond appropriately to the sayings of others, and that the only evidence for this is behavioral.[27] But he insists that the behavior in question "must be described using intensional terms: like 'says that p', 'believes that p', and so on."[28] Sentences that contain them behave intensionally, that is, they fail to satisfy the conditions of extensionality (above, note 5). In the famous example, "Tom believes that Cicero denounced Cataline," substituting "Tully" for "Cicero" (who is one and the same person) does not preserve the truth of the compound, since Tom may not know or believe that they are one and the same.

Canonical Notation

In *Word and Object*, Quine noted that the "Brentano thesis of the irreducibility of intensional idioms is of a piece with the thesis of the indeterminacy of translations." One then could accept the Brentano thesis "either as showing the indispensability of intentional idioms and the importance of an autonomous science of intention [as per Husserl] or as showing the baselessness of intentional idioms and the emptiness of a science of intention."[29] Although, indeed, intentional idioms may well be "practically indispensable," Quine chooses the latter – and his reasons are of some importance. They help us to see how his commitment to the Russellian task of clarification with the use of formal methods remains critical to his general philosophy. And they help us also to clarify Quine's naturalism.

Admitting intensional idioms into the language requires, for Quine, "a bifurcation in "canonical notation."[30] Although elaborating what Quine believes creates this problem would take us deep into arguments in logical theory,[31] the main point is clear enough. The predicate calculus with identity (substantially, a truncated version of Russell and Whitehead's *Principia Mathematica*) is a demonstrably powerful tool for analysis and clarification. "Reducing to canonical form," then, is simply the translation of ordinary English into the most economical schema in the extensional language of the predicate calculus.

Two points are additionally critical: First, "on the whole the canonical systems of logical notation are best seen not as complete notations for discourse on special subjects [for example, physical theory], *but as partial notations for discourse on all subjects*." Second, "*A maxim of shallow analysis prevails: expose no more logical structure than seems useful for the deduction or other inquiry at hand*."[32] Indeed, "the quest of a simplest, clearest overall pattern of canonical notation is not to be distinguished from a quest of ultimate categories, a limning of the most general traits of reality."[33]

These philosophical prepossessions both enabled and constrained Quine's inquiry. For example, through the use of "canonical schema," he was able to resolve rigorously existence questions: "to be is to be the value of a variable."

"Existence is what existential quantification expresses. There are things of kind F if and only if (Ex)Fx."[34] Accordingly, we can determine if there are classes or numbers or wombats by seeing if these putative objects must occur as the bound variables of quantifiers. Of course, to say that "there are things of kind F if and only if (Ex)Fx" is "as unhelpful as it is undebateable, since [by recursion to "the home language"] it is how one explains the symbolic notation of quantification to begin with." On the other hand, "the fact is that it is unreasonable to ask for explication of existence in simpler terms."[35] Simplest, perhaps, but the metaphysician in many of us may want more.

But the inquiry is also constrained: Intensional idioms do not behave extensionally, but he insists that their exclusion is not a disaster. Since "we are limning the true and ultimate structure of reality, the canonical schema for us is the austere scheme that knows no quotation but direct quotation and no propositional attitudes but only the physical constitution and behavior of organisms."[36] It is not for the sake of logicians that large chunks of the analysis in *Word and Object* and in "Ontological Relativity" (as in many of Quine's essays), require "translating" ordinary notions into the constructed language of the predicate calculus or why he can so easily move from ordinary examples to similar examples in mathematical theory, e.g., the difference between a formula and a Gödel number.[37] On the other hand, if one is interested in humans and in *human* language, as presumably part of the natural world, then why confine matters to "the physical constitution and behavior of organisms"?

Naturalistic Epistemology

The foregoing suggests that Quine's naturalism at least waffles toward a materialism and a reductive one at that. The connection to the foregoing discussion of language and method is easily seen in his brief, but also very influential "Epistemology Naturalized."[38] Quine asserts that "epistemology is concerned with the foundations of science."[39] Grant that the effort to "ground" science explains the epistemological problem in its modern form, and putting aside current connotations of "foundations," most writers would say that epistemology is concerned with knowledge, including, of course, the knowledge which presumably is produced by the practices of the sciences. Quine has persistently run the two ideas together, a consequence of ambiguity regarding the application of his holism. Drawing then on questions familiar to inquiry into the foundations of mathematics, he notes that there are two linked sorts of inquiry, "conceptual studies," concerned with meaning, and "doctrinal studies," concerned with truth. On the doctrinal side, Quine sees little progress from where Hume left us. On the conceptual side, however, progress has been made.[40]

In his efforts to accomplish Russell's program, that is, "to account for the external world as a logical construct of sense data," Carnap provided the most successful effort on the conceptual side of the project.[41] Of course, he failed, but even had he succeeded, he would not have solved the doctrinal problem. Carnap was seeking a "rational reconstruction," and "any construction of a physical universe in terms of sense experience, logic, and set theory would have been seen as satisfactory if it made the physicalist discourse come out right." But "if Carnap had successfully carried out such a construction . . . how could he have told whether it was the right one?"[42] As Quine insists, every language (natural or artificial) has materials to settle questions of reference, existence, and truth. But why choose any one, if there are potentially others?

Quine's response to this dilemma, odd as it may seem, takes him straight to naturalistic epistemology as he conceives it. He asserts:

> But why all this creative reconstruction, all this make believe? The stimulation of sensory receptors is all the evidence anybody has had to go on, ultimately, in arriving at his picture of the world. Why not see how this construction really proceeds? Why not settle for psychology? Such a surrender of the epistemological burden to psychology is a move that was disallowed in earlier times as circular reasoning. If the epistemologist's goal is validation of the grounds of empirical science, he defeats his purpose by using psychology or other empirical science as the validation. However such scruples against circularity have little point once we have stopped dreaming of deducing theories from observation.[43]

It is hard to see here, as in Quine's earlier treatment of relativist regress, how abandoning the "dream of deducing theories from observation" undermines scruples against circularity. In any case, to pick up on his argument, given the failure of the empiricist program to *translate* science into "logic, observation terms and set theory," and "to settle for a kind of reduction that does not eliminate, is to renounce the last remaining advantage that we supposed rational reconstruction to have over straight psychology."[44]

Quine and Dewey are both naturalists in the ways that Quine identified in the Dewey Lectures, but there are naturalisms and there are naturalisms. I have already noted problems regarding description of behavior in terms of intentions. As there are naturalisms and there are naturalisms, there are psychologies and there are psychologies. A problem symmetrical to the problem of describing behavior arises as regards all the "evidence" we have.

Carnapian austerity was evident in *Word and Object*, where Quine insisted that "it was important to think of what prompts the native's assent to 'Gavagai' as stimulations not rabbits." He spoke of "visual stimulations" in terms of patterns of "chromatic irradiation of the eye."[45] This was not quite adequate however. "Better," he noted, "to take as the relevant stimulations not momentary irradiation patterns, but evolving radiation patterns of all durations up to some convenient limit or *modulus*."[46] Indeed, why not rabbits – keeping in mind that even if what we mean by "rabbit" is not what our native might mean by "Gavagai." Wouldn't a psychologist seek to explain how we see, if not a rabbit, perhaps a physical object or an animal that is furry, four-legged, etc.? Plainly the force of "see" is at issue here, but there is no consensus in the psychology of perception on this.[47]

But however these causal questions get answered, if we are to have an epistemology (and not merely a psychology), we somehow need to get to evaluative or normative issues. One obvious way to do this is to show (non-circularly) that science does generate truths, and that, accordingly, if we better understood it, we could abstract and generalize those features that make it successful. Many people have read Dewey as holding to some such view. But it is clear enough in any case that Dewey's most persistent effort in this direction was his little read (and understood) *Logic: The Theory of Inquiry* which both disavowed the pursuit of truth, replacing it with "warranted assertability," and which wholly rejected the then dominant logical empiricist conception of both logic and science.[48] Or one might simply *assume* the practices of the several sciences and then use them to seek an understanding of how humans arrive at the beliefs they have. But unless we can say what counts as true belief (and why) it is hardly clear that the project is *epistemology*. For reasons already noted, Quine is less than clear on some of these critical issues.

In "Epistemology Naturalized," after telling us that "epistemology, or something like it, simply falls into place as a chapter of psychology and hence of natural science," Quine offers that this means that it studies "a natural phenomenon, viz., a physical human subject." "This human subject is accorded a certain experimentally controlled input – certain patterns of irradiation in assorted frequencies, for instance – and in the fullness of time the subject delivers as output a description of the three-dimensional external world and its history." We do this, he says, for "somewhat the same reasons that prompted epistemology; namely in order to see how evidence relates to theory, and in what ways one's theory of nature transcends any available evidence."[49]

Even as a purely scientific project, what is quite obviously omitted in this remarkable research program is any reference whatsoever to the intentional and social features of knowledge. It would not be denied that humans, wherever they are found, relate symmetrically to the external world, that "reality" is the source of all our primitive sensory inputs.[50] But it would surely seem that getting to concepts and to belief requires more than a neurophysiological psychology. And on the side of epistemology, it is likely the case that all groups generate languages. But on Quine's own arguments, there is no reason to believe that these languages all converge into one which is isomorphous to what is real, and which, accordingly, "get it right."

The Objectivity of Science

Chapter 1 of *The Pursuit of Truth* is entitled "Evidence." "Evidence" is a term of logic in just the sense that evidence counts for (or against) some belief – even if, to be sure, the logical empiricist's dream of an "inductive logic" remains entirely unsatisfied. Empiricism requires that belief be grounded in "observation sentences." As Quine notes, "The observation sentence is the means of verbalizing the prediction that checks a theory," and "an observation sentence is an occasion sentence [which may be true on some occasions and false on others] on which speakers of the language can agree out-right on witnessing the occasion." There is still the causal problem of getting from "stimulations" to "observation sentences." Further (and as an unacknowledged part of this problem), there is the question of the "theory-ladenness" of observation. On this issue, Quine sees no real difficulties. "There is a sense . . . in which [observation sentences] are all theory-laden, even the most primitive ones, and there is a sense in which none is, even the most professional ones." The "primitive ones," e.g., "Rabbit" or "The salt dissolved in the water" need to be seen "holophrastically," that is, as whole expressions. Then, "as conditioned to stimulatory situations, the sentence is theory-free; seen analytically, word by word, it is theory-laden." But the same is true of the very sophisticated observation sentences assented to by special communities. "What qualifies them . . . is still their holophrastic association with fixed ranges of sensory stimulation, however that association be acquired."[51]

Nor, as above, is holism a problem. It remains the case that "the test of a hypothesis . . . hinges on a logical relation of implication," but this is two-sided. "On the one side, the theoretical, we have the backlog of accepted theory plus the hypothesis. This combination does the implying. On the other side, the observational, we have an implied generality that the experimenter can directly test, directly challenge." "A generality that is compounded of observables in this way – 'whenever this, that' – is what I call an *observation categorical.*" Holism shows that "the falsity of the observation categorical does not conclusively refute the hypothesis." "Over-logicizing" (*sic*) we are asked to consider a set of truths which jointly imply the false categorical. We rescind the one "which seems most suspect, heeding a maxim of minimum mutilation." Having "diffused" the implication, we now track down the sets of sentences that imply our newly rescinded beliefs until consistency has been restored.[52]

On its face, the foregoing suggests, first, that Quine's interest is in saving *science* against the widespread and frequently injudicious attacks on its "objectivity" and, second, that in point of fact, he has not himself strayed very far from the "received view." Taken together, if true, this is, of course, paradoxical. It was precisely the task of the logical empiricists to provide a "foundation" for science (and like Quine, they always had in mind physical science, and particularly physics). Quine needs no foundation, but even given his refutation of analyticity and the verifiability theory of meaning, his conception of science has a definite logical empiricist cast. In the end, Rorty may be more correct in judging that, despite his best efforts to the contrary, Quine has not fully appreciated the revolutionary impact of his work.[53] For Rorty, of course, we are "at home" in our language; and "our" civilization has developed modern science. For him, at least, that is all that can be or needs to be said.[54]

Notes

1 In Quine, *From a Logical Point of View*, 2nd edn., revised (New York: Harper Torchbooks, 1961).

2 W. V. O. Quine, *The Pursuit of Truth* (Cambridge, MA: Harvard University Press, 1990).

3 As for example, in Larry Laudan, *Science and Relativism* (Chicago: University of Chicago Press, 1990) and Bas Van Fraasen, *Laws and Symmetry* (Oxford: Oxford University Press, 1989). Strictly speaking, the "classical" pragmatists, beginning with C. S. Peirce, had no philosophy of science in the modern sense; but what they had to say about science is nevertheless a long way from what current "pragmatists" have to say. For some discussion, see my "Pragmatic Philosophy of Science and the Charge of Scientism," *Transactions of the Charles. S. Peirce Society*, 24/2 (Spring 1988) and "John Dewey and American Social Science," in Larry Hickman, ed., *Reading Dewey* (Bloomington: University of Indiana Press, 1998).

4 For examples of both, see Hilary Kornblith, ed., *Naturalizing Epistemology* (Cambridge, MA: MIT Press, 1985).

5 See the writings of Richard Rorty, especially *Consequences of Pragmatism* (Minneapolis: University of Minnesota Press, 1982).

6 Quine, *From a Logical Point of View*, p. 20.

7 "Empiricism" because it was a development of British empiricism from George Berkeley, and "logical" because it was committed to using the tools of Russell and Whitehead's *Principia Mathematica*. Also termed "positivism" following the usage of Comte, the inventor of the term. A positivist rejects metaphysics as no part of science. Scientific explanations (in contrast to metaphysical or theological explanations) depend only upon "laws," rendered as "invariable relations of association and resemblance." This last, a Humean conception of causality, and a deductivist notion of explanation remain key features of most accounts of science.

8 As regards meaning, older accounts contrasted "extension" (also denotation), or what terms are true of, and "intension" (or connotation). Quine collapses into "intension," "intention" which involve mental states and sometimes psychic objects, and/or what Russell called "propositional attitudes," e.g., "believes," "knows." "Intension," accordingly, is a wider concept than "intention." See Joseph Margolis's very brief and useful *Philosophy of Psychology* (Englewood Cliffs, NJ: Prentice Hall, 1984).

The notion of an extensional language is critical for all of Quine's work. A language is extensional only if (a) any two predicates which agree extensionally (that is, are true of the same objects) are interchangeable *salva veritate*, (b) for its compound sentences, the truth value is a function wholly of the truth values of the components (i.e., the "connective is truth-functional"), and (c), for the components of a compound, (a) is satisfied. In modern logic, the predicate calculus is extensional. All natural languages have a host of terms that do not behave extensionally. In addition to verbs expressing propositional attitudes, modal words, like "necessarily," and "possibly," and verbs like "causes" do not satisfy the foregoing definition of extensionality.

9 *From a Logical Point of View*, p. 33.

10 Ibid., p. 37.

11 As almost everyone now says, facts are theory-laden. A very good discussion both of Quine's role and of the efforts to repair the damage to "the received view" is found

in Frederick Suppes' introduction to his edited volume, *The Structure of Scientific Theories*, 2nd edn. (Urbana, IL: University of Illinois Press, 1977). Suppes also summarizes alternatives, beginning with Stephen Toulmin's *The Philosophy of Science: An Introduction* (London: Hutchinson, 1953) and including Hanson, Popper, Kuhn, and others. Notably absent is the radical redrawing of the central issues in the work of Rom Harré, *The Principles of Scientific Thinking* (Chicago: University of Chicago Press, 1970). In this book, Harré challenged "deductivism" and, in later writings, Humean causality.

12 The most readable statement remains A. J. Ayer's *Language, Truth and Logic* (New York: Dover Publications, 1952). First published in 1936, the Dover edition contains Ayer's valuable new introduction. In it, Ayer noticed that the theory did not provide a general theory of meaning since it did not "cover the case of sentences which did not express any propositions at all," that is, sentences, like "God is dead," which in the terms of the verification theory, had no truth value whatsoever.

13 *From a Logical Point of View*, pp. 37, 38, 36.

14 Ibid., pp. 40, 41.

15 Ibid., pp. 42f.

16 This (ambiguous?) holism is sometimes referred to as the Duhem-Quine thesis. Pierre Duhem, arguing from "conventionalist" premises, maintained that isolated hypotheses are not severally verifiable by experience. Symmetrically, theory is "underdetermined by observations." The idea is found also in Mary Hesse's network model of theories. Hesse notes in *The Structure of Scientific Inference* that "Quine seems to obscure unnecessarily the radical character of his own position by conceding too much to more traditional accounts" (Berkeley: University of California Press, 1974, p. 27). There is also a relation to Kuhnian incommensurability. One way to state the difference would be to say that Quine tends to remain with a verifiability theory, but in contrast to the received view, it is holistic. On most readings, at least, Kuhn is more radical.

17 *From a Logical Point of View*, p. 44.

18 W. V. O. Quine, "Ontological Relativity," *Journal of Philosophy*, 65/7 (April 4, 1968) and reprinted in *Ontological Relativity and Other Essays* (New York: Columbia University Press, 1969).

19 Ibid., p. 186.

20 W. V. O. Quine, *Word and Object* (Cambridge, MA: MIT Press, 1960), especially section 12.

21 *Ontological Relativity and Other Essays*, p. 190.

22 Ibid., p. 199. This idea is now also very well established in the literature, but in terms of the "indexical" character of utterances. See especially the Wittgensteinian influenced work of Garfinkel and ethnomethodology.

23 Ibid., p. 200.

24 Ibid.

25 Ibid., p. 201.

26 *The Pursuit of Truth*, p. 52.

27 Here the appropriate comparison is to "classic" American naturalism, in G. H. Mead, *Mind, Self and Society* (Chicago: University of Chicago Press, 1967) and John Dewey, *Experience and Nature, The Later Works, 1925–1953*, vol. 1 (Carbondale, IL: Southern Illinois University Press, 1981). For some discussion, see several of the essays in John Ryder, ed., *American Philosophical Naturalism in the Twentieth Century*

(Amherst, MA: Prometheus Books, 1994), including my "Nature and Culture." Although this cannot be pursued here, the critical move in Mead and Dewey is not to deny that intentions figure in communication, but to argue that meaning cannot be explained in terms of intentions (psychic or otherwise). For example, if someone is to be taken as making a request, as James Tiles (in his clear exposition of Mead/Dewey) writes: "he has to be taken to have responded to the object not as a stimulus but from the point of view of the [other]. And what establishes the possibility of thus adopting the standpoint of the other is the recognition of the regularity of the relationship between gesture and completed act" (*Dewey* (London and New York: Routledge and Kegan Paul, 1988), p. 49). Mead called his behaviorism "social" for very good reasons.

28 Barry Stroud, "Quine on Exile and Acquiescence," in Paolo Leonardi and Marco Santambrogio, eds., *On Quine: New Essays* (Cambridge: Cambridge University Press, 1995), p. 49.

29 Quine, *Word and Object* (Cambridge, MA: MIT Press, 1960) p. 221.

30 Ibid.

31 See "Reference and Modality," in Quine, *From a Logical Point of View.*

32 *Word and Object*, p. 160; italics added.

33 Ibid., p. 161.

34 Quine, "Existence and Quantification," in *Ontological Relativity and Other Essays,* p. 97.

35 Ibid.

36 *Word and Object*, p. 221.

37 In "Ontological Relativity," Quine asks us to picture ourselves "at home in our language, with all its predicates and auxiliary devices. This vocabulary includes 'rabbit', 'rabbit part', 'rabbit stage', 'formula', 'number', 'ox', 'cattle'; also the two-place predicates of identify and difference, and other logical particles" (p. 200). This is not *my* language, to be sure, since my language contains, in addition to the so-called "propositional attitudes," words like "necessarily," and "causes." This last is worth mention: "Putting salt in water causes it to dissolve" becomes "If salt is put in water, it dissolves." "If-then" is truth-functional, but there is no way to "reduce" "causes" in the ordinary sense to "canonical form." Most philosophers are content with this, since, having already accepted a Humean conception of causality as constant conjunction "If p, then q" suffices. Of course, this leaves the problem of counterfactuals and thus the analysis of dispositions handicapped; worse, cause in a realist sense is expunged from science!

38 In Quine, *Ontological Relativity and Other Essays.*

39 Ibid., p. 69.

40 Ibid., p. 72.

41 In Carnap, *Der logische Aufbau der Welt* (Hamburg: F. Meiner, 1961).

42 *Ontological Relativity and Other Essays*, p. 75.

43 Ibid.

44 Ibid., pp. 76, 78.

45 *Word and Object*, p. 31.

46 Ibid., p. 32. It is this sort of argument which makes Quine the background inspiration for the "scientistic" naturalistic epistemologies of S. Stich's "no-belief" theory and the "eliminative materialism" of Patricia and Paul Churchland. For discussion, see

Susan Haack, *Evidence and Inquiry* (Oxford: Basil Blackwell, 1995), ch. 8. As she summarizes matters, "what is on offer is, on the one hand, evidence which, it is claimed, shows that the sciences of cognition can provide explanations of action without positing beliefs, desires, etc.; and, on the other, in-principle arguments allegedly showing that this is no accident, since the ontological bona fides of intentional states are at best doubtful" (p. 159).

47 I have in mind here the continuing argument between Gibsonians who hold to a version of what is called "direct perception" against "representationalist" views. See M. T. Turvey, R. E. Shaw, E. S. Reed, and W. M. Mace, "Ecological Laws of Perceiving and Acting: in Reply to Fodor and Pylyshyn," *Cognition*, 9 (1981).

48 John Dewey, *Logic: The Theory of Inquiry, Later Works, 1925–1953*, vol. 12 (Carbondale, IL: Southern Illinois University Press, 1986). See Thomas Burke, *Dewey's New Logic: A Reply to Russell* (Chicago: University of Chicago Press, 1994). Among the many treasures of Burke's account are his Deweyan criticisms of representational and computational models of cognition and his defense of an "ecological psychology" as inspired by Gibson.

49 *Ontological Relativity and Other Essays*, pp. 82f.

50 This is a critical but always ignored feature of the work of the *bête noir* of "analytic epistemologists," naturalistic or otherwise, of the so-called "strong programme in the sociology of knowledge." See P. T. Manicas and A. Rosenberg, "Naturalism, Epistemological Individualism and the 'Strong Programme' in Sociology of Knowledge," *Journal for the Theory of Social Behavior*, 15 (1985).

51 *Pursuit of Truth*, pp. 4, 8.

52 Ibid., pp. 8, 9f, 14f.

53 See especially Rorty's "The World Well Lost," in *Consequences of Pragmatism* (Minneapolis: University of Minnesota Press, 1982).

54 The concluding paragraph of *Pursuit of Truth* reads: "What the indeterminacy of translation shows is that notion of propositions as sentence meanings is untenable. What the empirical under-determination of global science shows is that there are various defensible ways of conceiving the world" (p. 102).

Suggested reading

Primary sources

From a Logical Point of View (Cambridge, MA: Harvard University Press, 1953; 1980).
World and Object (Cambridge, MA: MIT Press, 1960).
Ontological Relativity and Other Essays (New York: Columbia University Press, 1969).
The Roots of Reference (La Salle, IL: Open Court, 1974).
The Ways of Paradox and Other Essays (Cambridge, MA: Harvard University Press; rev. and enlarged edn. 1976).
Theories and Things (Cambridge, MA: Harvard University Press, 1981).
The Time of My Life (Cambridge, MA: MIT Press, 1985).
Pursuit of Truth (Cambridge, MA: Harvard University Press, 1990; rev. edn. 1992).
"Two Dogmas in Retrospect," *Canadian Journal of Philosophy*, 21 (1991): 265–74.
From Stimulus to Science (Cambridge, MA: Harvard University Press, 1995).

Secondary sources

Barrett, R. and R. Gibson, eds., *Perspectives on Quine* (Oxford: Basil Blackwell, 1990).

Davidson, D. and J. Hintikka, eds., *Words and Objections: Essays on the Work of W. V. Quine* (Dordrecht: D. Reidel, 1969).

Gibson, R. F., *The Philosophy of W. V. Quine: An Expository Essay* (Tampa: University Press of Florida, 1982).

—— *Enlightened Empiricism: An Examination of W. V. Quine's Theory of Knowledge* (Tampa: University Press of Florida, 1988).

—— *The Cambridge Companion to Quine* (Cambridge: Cambridge University Press, 2003).

Hahn, L. and P. Schilpp, eds., *The Philosophy of W. V. Quine* (La Salle, IL: Open Court, 1986; expanded edn. 1998).

Hookway, C., *Quine: Language, Experience and Reality* (Oxford: Polity, 1988).

Leonardi, P. and M. Santambrogio, eds., *On Quine* (Cambridge: Cambridge University Press, 1995).

Orenstein, A., *Willard Van Orman Quine* (Boston: Twayne, 1977).

Quine, W. V. O., R. F. Gibson, and R. B. Barrett, eds., *Perspectives on Quine* (Oxford: Blackwell Publishers, 1990).

Chapter 17

Alain L. Locke, 1885–1954

Leonard Harris

Introduction: Background and Early Career

Alain L. Locke played many roles in his life: cultural critic, editor, author, mentor, educator, patron of the arts, and philosopher. Locke was born in Philadelphia, Pennsylvania, the son of Mary H. Locke, a teacher in Camden, New Jersey who attended the Felix Adler Ethical Society. Locke's father, Pliny I. Locke, was a graduate of Howard University's Law School (1872), and worked for the Freedmen's Bureau and the Freedmen's Bank. Locke was among the first African American graduates of the prestigious Central High School, Philadelphia; he was the first African American to win a scholastic competition to become a Rhodes Scholar at Oxford University (Hertford College, Oxford, 1907–10; University of Berlin, 1910–11), and the first African American Ph.D. from Harvard University's Department of Philosophy (1918).

Locke's short essays, "Cosmopolitanism" (1908), "Oxford Contrasts" (1909), and "The American Temperament" (1911), written while a Rhodes Scholar, tell the story of his aversion to racial essentialism, whether in the form of European racialism or black *kitsch*. Locke's cosmopolitanism was a part of his lived experience in Europe, exemplified by his experiences with racial prejudice and his relationship with future luminaries such as Pixley K. I. Seme, creator of organizations that became the African National Congress in South Africa, and Horace M. Kallen, future cultural pluralist and later a noted Zionist.

In many ways Locke's 1918 doctoral dissertation, "The Problem of Classification in the Theory of Value," prefigured his future theoretical contributions to value theory. His dissertation was completed under the direction of Ralph B. Perry, who later wrote the definitive biography of the pragmatist William James. Locke argued that values perpetually undergo transvaluation. Categorizing painting, for example, as potentially beautiful, rather than associating beauty with a formal proof in symbolic logic, is a way of categorizing the object of beauty that is not intrinsic to the object. Transvaluation for Locke makes it possible to associate beauty with proofs in symbolic logic. Locke's work in axiology was coterminous with the development of his pragmatism. He considered the relationship between our daily world of practice and our world of value creation as tied together such that values existed in a living connection to activity. Locke arrived at his views through a review and critique of authors he found informative, especially Christian Freiherr von Enrenfels, Alexius Meinong, Franz Brentano, and Wilbur Urban.

While an instructor at Howard University, prior to completing his doctoral dissertation, Locke presented a series of lectures, sponsored by the then nascent National Association for the Advancement of Colored People (NAACP), in Washington, DC in 1916. These lectures were collected in an anthology, *Race Contacts and Interracial Relations* (1992). Locke was denied the opportunity to teach a course on race relations at Howard University because the then white administration in the arts did not consider the topic of race relations academically warranted. Consequently, the NAACP sponsored Locke's presentation. One reason for sponsoring Locke was that, as a baccalaureate graduate of Harvard University, a doctoral candidate in philosophy, and the first black Rhodes Scholar, he was among the most highly accomplished intellectuals in the black community. Locke argued that race did not determine culture and that race was not a biologically determined category. He contended that race was strictly socially defined and thereby constantly changing. Racialized groups for Locke were warranted in organizing themselves as socially shaped cultural groups, of which their racialization was a cultural feature, in order to defeat racism and to promote their cultural goods. Race consciousness, whether functionally beneficial as a way for groups to sustain cohesion and promote their unique cultural goods or as a vicious source of prejudice, was considered by Locke as relatively permanent. However, contrary to the then most noted anthropologist of race, Franz Boas, and the tendency of the most noted sociologist and political activist of the time, W. E. B. Du Bois, Locke rejected the link between blood and racial genius and blood and culture. Race was a non-natural category. He tended to sustain the Darwinian picture of groups competing for scarce resources, where race was one way to form cohesion to maximized offspring chances, but he rejected the social Darwinian justification of racism, namely, that whatever race dominated surely was ipso facto evidence of their inherent superior cognitive ability. Racism for Locke was a function of practice – groups usurping undue material and status resources through an array of relationships.

Locke's value theory, developed in its nascent stage as early as his doctoral dissertation in 1918, and his exploration of the nature of racial ontology, introduced in his formative period, yet highly controversial and provocative, in his 1916 lectures, are the foundations for his unique version of pragmatism: critical pragmatism. Critical pragmatism promotes a deep-seated commitment to transforming a world, too often filled with racial hatred and prejudice, through intellectual engagement in ways that do not rely on what he considered the enemies of cross cultural communication – absolutism, metaphysics, and treating existing social groups, including any particular race or nation, as a natural creation rather than as the vagary of human manufacture. Rather than promoting ethics of absolutist principles, cultural uniformity, or a realism of aesthetics that contended that there are beauty-making properties tied to unchanging creations, Locke's critical pragmatism promoted aesthetic pluralism whereby beauty-making properties are considered subject to transvaluation. Neither an approach of reasoned judgments to convince the racists and those suffering from self-deprecation, often favored by liberals, nor the imposition of propaganda, often favored by absolutists, are genuine sources of aesthetic change. Racist images, like all other images, change for Locke through grand shifts, leaps, breaks, disjunctions, and rifts – transposition, transvaluation, transfiguring.

It was the Bahá'í faith that, in the 1920s, Locke found most spiritually satisfying. Unlike all other classical American pragmatists, such as John Dewey or Jane Addams, who were fundamentally Christian or Christian in the kinds of religious sensibilities they expressed, Locke attended Bahá'í firesides, titularly joined but never consistently practiced Bahá'í religious doctrine. Nonetheless, he wrote for the Bahá'í *World*, considered religious pluralism (the view that all religions provide a contribution to our understanding of spiritual possibilities) far more appealing than religious dogmatism, traveled to Haifa, a religious center for the Bahá'í, found the Bahá'í moral requirement of racial amity appealing and maintained a lifelong respect for the Bahá'í faith.

The Harlem Renaissance

Locke can be seen as one of the first "Renaissance" men of the modern age because he is best known for the crucial role he played in the Harlem Renaissance (1919–35), when his edited anthology *The New Negro* (1925) served as the anchor of an innovative collection of literary and art works that inaugurated the Renaissance. Harlem, a community in Manhattan, New York, was often identified as the center of a national cultural movement that attacked the popular definition of *humanitas* – particularly, activists attacked the categorization of humanity into racial kinds and their arrangement into hierarchies; attacked the way the black was treated as an inferior subject, incapable of creating aesthetically pleasing works, and as a living embodiment of the ugly encased in a biologically determined and unchanging racial category. From his position as a professor of philosophy at Howard University in Washington, DC, Locke was the most influential intellectual associate of an entire generation of artists, writers, and scholars, including authors in the anthology, *The New Negro*: Langston Hughes, Claude McKay, Countee Cullen, Zora Neale Hurston, Montgomery Gregory, Albert C. Barnes, Jessie Fauset, Arthur A. Schomburg, James W. Johnson, Robert R. Moton, Kelly Miller, and Ralph Bunche. *The New Negro* also included illustrations by Winold Reiss and Aaron Douglas, as well as songs, a copy of an anti-slavery pamphlet cover, and African sculptures. The "Introduction" to *The New Negro* announced the existence of a generation of black activists who rejected the stereotypes associated with Negroes as poor imitators of white artistic creators and self-effacing minstrel musicians; rejected scholarship that was deferential to the way white racialists perpetuated the myth that black poverty was self-induced, and that white racist expropriation of black wealth through pillage and theft were non-existent. Authors in Locke's *The New Negro* portrayed blacks as responsible, creative, complex, and honorable agents. *The New Negro* poets, playwrights, artists, sculptors, and essayists avoided romanticizing African people as primitives, emotionally uncontrolled and lacking virtues. For different reasons, Houston A. Baker, Jr., in *Modernism and the Harlem Renaissance*, and George Hutchinson, in *The Harlem Renaissance in Black and White*, concur that the classical heritage which the vast majority of Renaissance authors hoped to recover was not a pristine African culture nor a vision of the pure emotive primitive. Locke was concerned to make apparent those features of African American culture that existed historically, which were either nascent in the artistic production of the victimized black or openly expressed but ignored.

Locke's expressionism – namely, that the aesthetic dimension arises from experience and is often an expression or reflection of feelings and needs intricate to cultural realities – motivated his argument that black folk culture was a source of sophisticated and universally valuable aesthetic products. Locke rejected the traditional distinction between folk art and high art in which high art was the product of independent intellects uninfluenced by folk culture. High culture, for Locke, best existed as an expression of the sophisticated results of select folk expressions. The Renaissance for Locke was not a recovery of the classical, nor a return to a pristine past, but a recovery and creation of the universalizable within the past and present folk.

Locke's expressionism existed in conjunction with his advocacy theory approach. The project of aesthetic appreciation and creation, for Locke, in its best manifestation existed as a function of promoting human uplift. It was not the disinterested, dispassionate, unconnected, third-person observer of artistic form, structure, idiom, and theme that determined the beautiful. Rather, it was such formalistic features in living relationship to content, context, function, expression, experience and contribution to human uplift that represented the best traditions of artistic creation. For Locke, artistic expression is invariably tied to the existence of some community, although likely a matter of individual creation. Commitment to a community's uplift or expressing some feature of a peculiar history is compatible with the creating of universally valuable art. In one sense, valuation is always tied to transvaluation and transposition. Thus, his view of indeterminacy in language translation, the sociality of language and the fluidity of possible meanings undergirded his approach to community and identity.

Locke favored moderate cosmopolitanism and democratic socialism, contrary to an approach to community that promoted racial nationalism advocated by the nationalist Marcus Garvey, leader of the Universal Negro Improvement

Association, or that of class analysis of Marxist-influenced socialist activists such as Hubert H. Harrison. Locke's approach is best exemplified by his anthology, *When Peoples Meet: A Study in Race and Culture Contacts* (1942), co-edited with Bernard J. Stern, published by the Progressive Education Association and drawn from a series of lectures under the organizational leadership of Ruth Benedict. Locke and Stern collected papers that helped establish that communities are constantly in formation and that cross cultural contact transforms the valuations each community considers unique to its own heritage. The dream of ethnic or racial authenticity and relative autonomy for the editors was a misguided dream, just as the dream of anarchists, communists, or radical cosmopolitans who favor the negation of all boundaries are defeated by our need to be in communities of close association, associations that need not become egregious forms of separatism.

Locke's approach to pedagogy was enlivened by his cosmopolitan approach to community and values: Cultural education in the arts creates alternative, non-racist, xenophobic, ethnocentric values and ways of viewing persons as full agents. It does so because artistic appreciation involves reformation of perception, whereas appeal to analysis, reasoned argumentation, and dialogue (literal mindedness) or propaganda (which relies on maintaining rigid categories and uses the same assumptions about reality as its object), all fail to accomplish a substantively new arena of thought. Locke, as the President of the American Association for Adult Education (in 1945), introduced cultural education as a central feature of adult education. He edited a series, the *Brown Booklets*, that provided historical accounts of African American life and accomplishment. And as a tireless promoter of young artists and literature, he authored annual reviews of African American literature for the journal *Opportunity*. The world of artistic creation, however, was as much involved in promoting stereotypes and demeaning images as the world of propaganda and literal argumentation. Locke was not oblivious to the problems of using progressive over-generalizations, such as stylized-honored motifs of black achievers or romantic presentations of black culture as a culture enlivened by a desire for human uplift without the terrors of inter-racial class exploitation. However, for Locke, there is a propensity for the ennobling to win out over the degrading. The object of degradation will, over time, surmount the ill effects of self or other deprecation. The agents of demeaning stereotypes and those that valorize the pain inflicted on others are likely to change, not as a function of what is arguably unwarranted, but as a function of what is unlikely to satisfy across cultural borders.

Locke's faith in art as ennobling and providing alternative perceptions was often criticized as romantic. W. E. B. Du Bois, the leading political and intellectual head of liberal and progressive activists during the Renaissance, criticized Locke for promoting art for its own sake and expecting alternative perspectives to be a substantive source for social change. Although Locke never claimed that cultural changes were the sole, primary, or fundamental causal agent for social change, he consistently maintained that altered perspectives through the arts were a crucial factor for the possibility of change. His rejection of folk culture as itself high culture, that is, the anarchist view that all cultural products are inherently equal, and his maintaining the distinction between high and low art, although within the context of advocacy art, was criticized by such artists as Zora Neale Hurston and Claude McKay as being elitist and as maintaining the stifling view that African American artists had a moral responsibility to engage in racial uplift. Locke has also been criticized, especially by more contemporary authors, for occasionally treating racial groups as ethnic groups, for blurring the distinction between the two, and for occasionally treating race as a stable category or conflating racial identity and cultural productions. His use of such terms as "race geniuses" or "race gift" to depict an author or artistic contribution arguably shows that Locke was not completely free of thinking in terms of racial categories as categories defining kinds and contributions. Locke knowingly used romantic images of blacks on more than one occasion. He thereby used ennobling stereotypes to fight demeaning stereotypes, facing the reality that stereotyping necessarily subordinates important individual distinctions and treats persons invariably as members of an undifferentiated group. This ameliorative use of stereotypes reflects his pragmatic theory of valuation, a theory that requires the continual re-evaluation of categories used to picture reality. Locke's theory of valuation, his advocacy aesthetics, his insistence on moral imperatives as a necessary condition for the possibility of a moral community, his pedagogy of discipline and cultural integration, and his views of community as an evolving democratic experiment, all form a unique chapter of American pragmatism.

Contemporary Interpretations of Locke's Legacy

Judith M. Green's *Deep Democracy: Community, Diversity, and Transformation* (2000) is contemporary reformation and advancement of Locke's view of democracy and cosmopolitanism; Jason D. Hill's *Becoming a Cosmopolitan: What It Means to Be a Human Being in the New Millennium* (2000) supports Locke's desire for unity, yet, as a radical cosmopolitan who prefers the end of all ethnic, racial, and communal boundaries, Hill criticizes Locke's moderate cosmopolitanism. Mark Helbling's *The One and the Many* (1999) defends and interprets Locke's formative role in the literary creations of the Renaissance in conjunction with Melville Herskovits, Roger Fry, and Albert C. Barnes. Houston A. Baker, Jr.'s *Modernism and the Harlem Renaissance* (1987) defends Locke's commitment to a modernist aesthetic, that is, an aesthetic that preferred controlled literary structures, forms, and design used to advance middle-class social objectives. African American literature on this account fails to promote racial pride – virtues such as constraint, frugality, and marriage justifiably receive less praise or recognition. Baker's *Blues Ideology and Afro-American Literature: A Vernacular Theory* (1987), and Richard Powell's *The Blues Aesthetic: Black Culture and Modernism* (1989), provide additional reasons to consider commitment to racial uplift and literary forms compatible. In addition, Arnold Rampersad's *The Harlem Renaissance*

Revaluation (1989) and his introduction to Locke's *The New Negro* explore the contemporary relevance and historical debates regarding literary criticism during the Renaissance. Jane Duran's *Worlds of Knowing* (2001) uncovers and explores the aesthetic assumptions and principles that make for a defensible epistemology and aesthetic sensibility in Locke's approach to culture. *The Critical Pragmatism of Alain Locke* (1999) is an edited anthology of original articles evaluating Locke's theory of value, aesthetics, cosmopolitan community, and education, as well as the paradoxes and critiques of Locke's philosophy. Authors include Nancy Fraser, Sally J. Scholz, Richard Shusterman, Greg Moses, Charles Molesworth, Kenneth W. Stikkers, Talmadge C. Guy, Segun Gbadegesin, Stephen L. Thompson, Paul Weithman, and Beth J. Singer.

Suggested reading

Primary sources

"Cosmopolitanism," *The Oxford Cosmopolitan*, 1/1 (1908): 15–16.

"Oxford Contrasts," *Independent*, 67 (July 1909): 139–42.

"The American Temperament," *North American Review*, 194 (August 1911).

The Negro in America (Chicago, IL: American Library Association, 1933).

Report on Negro Adult Education Projects, dated March 15, 1934. Writings by Locke folder (Moorland-Spingarn Manuscript Collection, Howard University, Washington, DC).

Negro Art – Past and Present (Washington, DC: Associates in Negro Folk Education, 1936).

The Negro and his Music (Washington, DC: Associates in Negro Folk Education, 1936).

Minority Group Strategy Unpublished seminar presentation dated February 17, 1941. Alain Locke papers, Writings by Locke folder (Moorland-Spingarn Research Center, Howard University, Washington, DC).

Locke, Alain and R. M. Mclver, eds., *Group Relations and Group Antagonisms* (New York: Harper Brothers, 1944).

"The Minority Side of Intercultural Education." Final draft of paper published in N. D. Myers, ed., *Education for Cultural Unity*, Alain Locke papers, Writings by Locke folder (Moorland-Spingarn Research Center, Howard University, Washington DC, 1945).

Locke, Alain, and Bernhard J. Stern, eds., *When Peoples Meet: A Study in Race and Culture Contacts* (New York: Hinds, Hayden & Eldredge, 1946).

The Reflections on a Modern Renaissance Man, ed. Russell J. Linnemann (Baton Rouge: Louisiana State University Press, 1982).

The Critical Temper of Alain Locke: A Selection of His Essays on Art and Culture, ed. Jeffrey C. Stewart (New York: Garland Publishers, 1983).

The Philosophy of Alain Locke: Harlem Renaissance and Beyond, ed. Leonard Harris (Philadelphia: Temple University Press, 1989).

The New Negro, with an introduction by Arnold Rampersad (New York: Atheneum, & Maxwell Macmillan International, 1992).

Race Contacts and Interracial Relations, ed. Jeffrey C. Stewart (Washington, DC: Howard University Press, 1992).

Secondary sources

Baker, Houston A., *Modernism and the Harlem Renaissance* (Chicago: University of Chicago Press, 1987).

—— *Blues Ideology and Afro-American Literature: A Vernacular Theory* (Chicago: University of Chicago Press, 1984).

Buck, Christopher, "Alain Locke: *Bahá'í* Philosopher," *Bahá'í Studies Review*, 10 (2001): 7–50.

Davis, Arthur P., *From the Dark Tower: Afro-American Writers, 1900–1960* (Washington, DC: Howard University Press, 1974).

Du Bois, W. E. B., *Black Folk: Then and Now: An Essay in the History and Sociology of the Negro Race* (New York: Octagon Books, 1970).

Duran, Jane, *Worlds of Knowing* (New York: Routledge, 2001).

Gatewood, Willard B., *Aristocrats of Color: The Black Elite, 1880–1920* (Bloomington: Indiana University Press, 1990).

Green, Judith M., *Deep Democracy: Community, Diversity, and Transformation* (New York: Rowman & Littlefield, 2000).

Harris, Leonard, *The Critical Pragmatism of Alain Locke* (New York: Rowman & Littlefield, 1999).

Hay, Samuel A., *American Theatre: A Historical and Critical Analysis* (New York: Cambridge University Press, 1994).

Helbling, Mark, *The Harlem Renaissance: The One and the Many* (London: Greenwood Press, 1999).

Hill, Jason D., *Becoming a Cosmopolitan: What It Means to Be a Human Being in the New Millennium* (New York: Rowman & Littlefield, 2000).

Huggins, Nathan, *Harlem Renaissance* (New York: Oxford University Press, 1971).

Hutchinson, George, *The Harlem Renaissance in Black and White* (Cambridge, MA: Harvard University Press, 1995).

Linneman, Russell J., ed., *Alain Locke: Reflections on a Modern Renaissance Man* (Baton Rouge: Louisiana State University Press, 1982).

Powell, Richard, *The Blues Aesthetic: Black Culture and Modernism* (Washington, DC: Washington Project for the Arts, 1989).

Rampersad, Arnold, *The Harlem Renaissance Revaluation* (New York and London: Garland Publishing Inc., 1989).

Watson, Steven, *The Harlem Renaissance: Hub of African-American Culture, 1920–1930* (New York: Pantheon, 1995).

Chapter 18

Justus Buchler, 1914–1991

Kathleen Wallace

Justus Buchler developed an original metaphysical system – articulated in five books, published between 1951 and 1979 – which drew inspiration from the classical American philosophers as well as from other sources in the history of philosophy, most notably, Aristotle, Spinoza, Hume, and Hegel.

Justus Buchler was born in New York City in 1914, the eldest of three children. He attended the College of the City of New York where he earned a B.S.S. (1934) and then Columbia University where he studied philosophy, earning an M.A. (1935) and a Ph.D. (1938). He published his first article, "Note on Proust" (1934), while still an undergraduate. He studied under Morris R. Cohen and Yervant Krikorian, as well as Abraham Edel. At Columbia, Buchler wrote an M.A. thesis on Locke under F. J. E. Woodbridge. Buchler continued his studies for the Ph.D. at Columbia, writing a dissertation under Ernest Nagel, with whom he originally studied logic. The dissertation became a classic in Peirce studies and was published in 1939 as *Charles Peirce's Empiricism*. Buchler's professional career was established with a 1942 full-time appointment at Columbia. He worked closely with John Herman Randall, Jr., with whom he formed a deep intellectual and professional relationship. Buchler participated in the Contemporary Civilization (CC) program of Columbia College from 1942 until 1960. By his own estimation, CC was the greatest source of intellectual stimulation of his life. Buchler become Professor of Philosophy in 1956 and in 1959 Johnsonian Professor of Philosophy. As a member of the Columbia philosophy department, he was active in the editorship of *The Journal of Philosophy*, serving as Book Editor for many years. Up until 1951 and the publication of the first of his systematic works, *Toward A General Theory of Human Judgment* (TGT), Buchler wrote many trenchant reviews himself.

In addition to heading the CC program from 1950 to 1956, Buchler chaired the philosophy department at Columbia during the 1960s. In 1954, while still Administrative Head of CC, he wrote "Reconstruction in the Liberal Arts," a history of the development of the CC program for *A History of Columbia College on Morningside*. He wrote several articles on education, including "Liberal Arts and General Education," "What is a Discussion?" and "On the Problem of Liberal Education." Buchler was opposed to McCarthyism, and was active in the American Civil Liberties Union (ACLU). In 1971, Buchler left Columbia to become Distinguished Professor of Philosophy at the State University of New York at Stony Brook, where he offered courses in both the Ph.D. and M.A. programs. In 1973 he was awarded the Butler Silver Medal by Columbia University. Buchler suffered a serious stroke in March 1979; he retired in 1981. He died in Chambersburg, Pennsylvania, on March 19, 1991 at the age of 76. Buchler was married to the philosopher, Evelyn Shirk.

Metaphysics

Buchler characterized his work as a "metaphysics of natural complexes"; many commentators have called it "ordinal ontology."[1] Historically, metaphysical systems have been built around many different basic concepts, for example, "being," "substance," "object," "entity," and "existent." In Buchler's system, "natural complex" is the basic concept; that is, it is the generic term of identification for whatever is: existents and concepts, fictions, laws, dreams, individuals and societies, similarities, possibilities and actualities. Some philosophers regard the task of metaphysics as one of distinguishing the real from the unreal or merely apparent. Quine, for example, argues for the exclusion of "possible entities" from ontology.[2] Another approach regards metaphysics as providing a taxonomy of kinds or realms of being. For Santayana, the fundamental kinds or "realms" of being are "essence," "matter," "truth," and "spirit." Yet another approach views metaphysics as providing the one true description of the world, a kind of summation of the results of "finished science" (although if science is never finished, neither is metaphysics). This last approach sometimes leads to a denial of the reality of "middle-sized material objects," such as tables, chairs, houses – the objects that we take for granted. It is argued that while the table or the floorboards of the house appear to be solid, physics tells us that they are not really solid at all, because there are immense distances between the nuclei of the atoms making up the wood.[3] In a metaphysics of natural complexes such as Buchler's, there is no *ontological* distinction between the real and unreal; "middle-size material objects" (the table, chair, and house) are as real as the atomic reality described by physics.[4]

In the wake of logical positivism, some contemporary philosophers abjure "speculative" metaphysics. Postmodern philosophers argue that metaphysics obliterates differences by subsuming everything into one comprehensive picture of reality (surely a fault of a view which "obliterates" the reality of "middle-sized material objects"). Rather than seeing generalization as a matter of obliteration, though, Buchler sees it as conceptual orientation.[5] "First principles" in a Buchlerian approach are the pervasive principles or categories that describe any being or natural complex – the table, chair, or house qua "middle-sized material objects" and qua objects as studied by physics. Each reflects an aspect (what Buchler will call an "ordinal location") of the complex; each is equally real. The interpretation of the table, chair, or house as natural complex is not really the truth about the complex that is the explanation of physics; it is the most general interpretation. The virtue of such a metaphysical interpretation is that it provides a framework for locating differences and commonalities, for acknowledging and conceptualizing the complexity of whatever is. In Buchler's approach, the task of metaphysics is to conceptualize the reality of a complex's locations, not to insist that only one (aspect or location) is the really real one.

In addition, Buchler conceives of metaphysics as distinct from ontology.

> The term "metaphysics" is not analogous to the terms "aesthetics," "epistemology," "ethics," etc. It is not a subject-matter area in the same sense. It is one of the functions of philosophy. . . . The metaphysical function is to frame "the most fundamental and general concepts of a given subject-matter." . . . It is not the breadth of the subject-matter that distinguishes metaphysics, but the breadth of the complexes discriminated in a particular subject matter.[6]

Thus, the metaphysics of natural complexes articulates categories with which to interpret the broadest subject matter – ontology or "being in general."[7] Buchler also develops a metaphysics of human process, that is, categories with which to interpret a less broad subject matter, human process (more colloquially, "human nature"). The former comprehends the latter: a human *being* (qua *being*) is a *natural complex*; a *human* being (qua *human*) is a *proceptive process*.[8] A proceptive process is a natural complex, but not all natural complexes are human beings.

Buchler's view has been characterized as "naturalistic," but caution should be exercised here. "Nature" is often contrasted with the "divine" or the "supernatural." "Naturalism" in contemporary thought frequently connotes dependence on or derivation from science.[9] For Buchler, following leads from Dewey and Randall, naturalism neither has a meaningful contrasting term nor suggests that the divine is banished from metaphysical discourse and reality. Rather, nature is all-encompassing; it includes the divine, the world as studied by science, *and* the worlds of numbers and of fiction.[10] This represents both Jamesian (whatever is is pluralistic and inexhaustible) and Spinozistic (whatever is includes – rather than is a manifestation of – the divine) commitments. The use of the term "natural" in "natural complex" is intended to signify the rejection of the "supernatural," the "non-natural," the "artificial" and so on, as *ontological* categories, *not* to signify the unreality of the beings that are usually so classified, *not* to signify that only what science studies is real.[11]

Metaphysics of Natural Complexes

Affirming the equal reality of whatever is Buchler's ontology is guided by a principle of ontological parity[12] as opposed to a principle of ontological priority (an affirmation of degrees of reality, that some beings are more real than others). Thus, for example, Aristotle seems to have conceptualized being as substance (*ousia*); substance is the most real, relations are less or dependently real. Some philosophers have thought that God had the highest degree of reality and that creation (nature and the human) consisted in grades of reality – some, such as the human, higher than others, but all inferior to the reality of God. Others distinguish between fact and fiction, denying reality to the latter. Some philosophers are realists about universals, others insist that only individuals are real. Still others insist that "being" or ontology has to do with existence and existing entities.[13] With ontological parity, the divine, substances, relations, facts, fictions, existing entities, values, individuals, universals, possibilities, actualities, to wit, whatever is is equally real. All are natural complexes.[14]

Commitment to a principle of ontological parity entails the rejection of reductive ontologies, for example, materialism (everything is nothing but matter) or nominalism (only particulars are real).[15] A principle of ontological parity entails that no one kind of being is paradigmatic of reality. Parity is the beginning; additional categories are needed to conceptualize what a being is, that it is, how a being is different from and similar to other beings, and how beings and their ramifications are demarcated from one another. Substance ontologies conceptualize the whatness of a being as a substance with essential (and accidental) properties. Ordinal metaphysics conceptualizes the whatness of a being (a *complex*) as an interrelation of ordinal locations or traits; some traits are actualities, some possibilities. More formally, the metaphysics of natural complexes consists of six major categories which fall into three groups: (1) prevalence and alescence (the technical vocabulary for saying *that* a complex is); (2) ordinality and relation (the categories for talking about *what* a complex is); (3) possibility and actuality (categories that conceptualize the boundaries of a complex).

Consider an ordinary ("middle-sized material") object such as a house. Some traditional metaphysical views might categorize the house as a spatio-temporal substance, physical object, or existing entity, and treat its social, legal, and historical relations as secondary or "extrinsic" to it. There might be good empirical reasons for us, as a matter of common sense, to think of "the house" as an entity. However, on Buchler's view, the house *is* its relations, or "ordinal locations"; even the house thought of as an entity is so in virtue of specific kinds of relations or ordinal locations. The metaphysics of natural complexes conceptualizes the house as a complex of relations, similarities and differences, possibilities and actualities, and signals that a being is not something prior to or independent of its traits.

In ordinal terms, a house, qua physical object, *prevails* in spatio-temporal sets of relations or orders (which can be understood in common-sense, atomic, and quantum respects). The same house, qua legal and social entity, is owned, has an assessed value, a market value, and so on: the house prevails in social, economic, and legal contexts or orders (e.g., of zoning rules, ownership rules, market relations, etc.). The concept of order is intended to represent the complexity of traits.[16] The house *is* its traits insofar as it prevails in the orders that it does. At the same time, the house is also an order; it locates complexes (minimally, its own traits). Every trait (ordinal location) of the house is real: physical size is as real as atomic structure or legal status, color is as real as the possibility-of-being-sold. The house is a relational complex of all its traits in their unique interrelatedness ("intersection") constituting this "it" as distinct from another.[17]

Suppose Jane is selling the house and Emily is buying it. The category of *alescence* expresses the idea that a complex is altering its location in (or to or from) an order.[18] Thus, the house may be alescent in relation both to Emily and to Jane; when the sale is completed, the house prevails in the order of Emily as owner. Buchler adopts the category of alescence over more standard terminology, such as "becoming," because the latter tends to be too restrictive in scope. It works reasonably well for capturing physical and biological processes of change over time – an embryo becomes a fetus, a fetus becomes an infant, and so on – but the term "becoming" would not capture the altering-being of a developing mathematical proof or of a paradigm shift in scientific theory. While the term "alescence" is unfamiliar, the intent here is to introduce a concept that (a) will allow for greater precision of the metaphysical point than the more common-sense terminology "is altering" or "is becoming" and (b) will not obscure the insight of ontological parity, namely, that "becoming" is just as real as "being."[19] The sale is a complex, as real as the house as physical object; the developing proof is as real as the completed one.

Now consider the house as an object of perception. Ever since Locke, philosophers have often distinguished between primary and secondary qualities, the latter defined as "observer-dependent" and thus not really of or "in" the object. Some have argued that primary qualities, too, are "observer-dependent" and, therefore, that what is really true about the house cannot be known. On the Buchlerian conceptualization of the *ontological* issues involved in perception, the house prevails as smaller in the order of vision than the size in which it prevails in the spatio-temporal order; the order of human binocular vision is no less an order or location of the house than are the spatio-temporal, legal, and social orders. The philosophical convention is to say that the house *appears* smaller, but is not *really* smaller – that the visual "appearance" of the house is not really the house, but is a third "thing," a representation. Ordinal ontology would not deny the obvious, namely, that in human vision a retinal image is produced. But on this view, perception is understood as a relational complex, for example, house-in-perceptual-relation-to-observer or conversely, observer-in-perceptual-relation-to-house. The starting assumption here, contra Kant, is that perception is not determined solely by mental categories, but, qua ordinally located, is a relation between perceiver and perceived. The retinal image is a constituent of this overall relational complex and is as real as the object of which it is an image. Since every relation is reciprocal (although not necessarily symmetrical), the house is also a constituent (trait) of the retinal image. The house prevails in the visual order no less than it prevails in the spatio-temporal order. In a visual order the house has some traits that it may not have in a spatio-temporal order, and vice versa. It also has traits in a legal order that it may have in neither a spatio-temporal nor a visual order. Each of these locations is a constituent of (or, one could say that each ordinal location constitutes real traits of) the house.

Philosophers worry about allowing for the reality of illusions, hallucinations, and so on. The worry seems to be that if perceptions are real and if illusions are a product of the same sensory apparatus as perceptions, then we cannot tell the difference between them. In ordinal ontology, perceptions, illusions, and hallucinations may share some locations (e.g., location in the order of the sensory apparatus) but not all. We might not be able to tell the difference between perception, hallucination, and illusion solely on the basis of the sense experiences (from within the order of the sensory apparatus), or from the first person perspective alone. But, unlike hallucination, the constituents of a perception involve inter- and intra-perceptually accessible ordinal locations. Perceptual validation is possible through intersubjective duplication and confirmation or through reiterated perceptions and actions by the perceiver. Perceptual validation of the house is validation of the house as it really is in the order of perception. It is possible for two different perceptions of the same object, for example, the house, both to be "really" about the house. For example, in relation to color-blind perception the house is gray, and in relation to (humanly) normal-color-sighted perception the house is red. When we say that the house is "really" red, we are affirming the priority of the order of normal-color-sightedness in human experience (its utility, typically greater scope, and so on). However, what ordinal ontology affirms is that the *house-in-the-order-of-color-blind-perception* is really gray.[20]

A hallucination, on the other hand, is not located in an order which is plurally accessible and, hence, would not be able to be validated as a perception, however much it may feel like a perception to the hallucinator. (Of course, the hallucination is still real – qua product of say a drug- or other physiologically-induced state of the sensory apparatus, not qua perception.) A full analysis of validity requires further work in epistemology, philosophy of perception, and philosophical psychology. What ordinal ontology does say is that such analyses are helped neither by consigning hallucinations and illusions to the dustbin of non-reality nor by a narrowly mentalistic or psychologistic view of perception.[21] The ontological principle at stake here is that relation is always reciprocal, although not necessarily symmetrical; reciprocity does not entail symmetry. For example, a passer-by's perception of a house may be a fleeting and perhaps unimportant trait of the house (house-is / was-seen-by-passer-by-at-time-t), even though, for the passer-by the perception of that house may be strongly evocative of associations, important, say, to a psychotherapeutic process. The house and the passer-by would be reciprocally, but not symmetrically related. Similarly, as a resident of New York City I am a trivial and "dispensable" trait of the city (New York City would still be recognizably the same complex with or without my residence, even though in principal it would be (very slightly) different), while at the same time my residing in New York City may be strongly determinant of me. The ontological claim has two parts. One is that a relation, a location, is reciprocal, that is, mutually determining of trait(s), although not always symmetrical (not symmetrically determining). The second is that even trivial, unimportant, or fleeting traits are still traits and just as really (albeit weakly relevant) constituents of the respective complex(es) as are important (strongly relevant) ones.

Now consider *possibility.* Possibility is an extension or continuation of a complex. For example, in putting her house up for sale, Jane initiated the prevailing of a new possibility, namely, the possibility of a shift in ownership of the house. The possibility extends or redefines the boundaries of the house in legal and economic orders. The prevailing of the possibility does the redefining in what Buchler calls *natural definition* – "the kind of definition in which any natural complex sets limits to another, inherently demarcates the boundaries between it and another."[22] Prior to the house being put on the market, Jane's actual ownership defined a boundary of the house, but now the possibility that it may be sold extends (redefines) that boundary. Buchler is seeking to conceptualize two fundamental aspects of what is: (1) the reality of possibility and actuality, and (2) the notion of a complex having boundaries, however indefinite they may be or uncertain we may be of what they are.

Possibilities are defined in terms of what is actualizable in a complex; actualities and possibilities, including logical possibilities, are complexes and are ordinally located. Many philosophers understand logical possibility as "whatever is conceivable without contradiction." A typical example suggests that it is "logically possible" that the morning star and the evening star are not the same planet Venus. In an ordinal ontology, on the contrary, it would be a contradiction to assert that, in the order of the planetary system, Venus is not both the morning star and the evening star. An alleged logical possibility that Venus is not both involves a tacit stripping and adding of traits to the planetary system (the order) in which Venus is located, while retaining conventional modes of reference; an alleged absence of contradiction is based on a tacit abandonment of the order which would exclude such a possibility. Buchler's claim is that contradiction is always ordinal, located by the orders of the complex as much as by the order of logic. On an ordinal view the following would be consistent: (1) the planetary system of our galaxy could have been different such that the planet known as Venus could have had a different orbital relation to earth, could have had a twin planet, and so on; (2) in the evolution of the universe, what will be possible for Venus is different from what is possible for Venus in its current location; (3) in an order of thought experiments, it is possible to imagine a planet "just like" Venus in a planetary system "just like" ours except that its orbital relation to a planet imagined to be "just like" earth is one in which it is not both the morning and the evening star. But these are different from saying that it is a ("logical") possibility of Venus as it is ordinally located. According to a metaphysics of natural complexes, the notion of "logical possibility" is – no less than "empirical" or "real" possibility – a matter of ordinal location.[23]

The typical philosophic approach to the "problem of universals" exemplifies such concerns as worry about the reference of universal terms or doubt about the reality of universal "entities" in contrast to the reality of "existing individuals."[24] In the metaphysics of natural complexes, universals are real but not "entities." They are, however, understood as possibilities of a distinctive kind. "A universal [is] the possibility of different complexes having traits that are similar in a given respect" (MNC, p. 180). Thus, three-sided figures actualize the possibility of being similar in triangularity. As a possibility, "triangularity" is actualizable, but it need not be actualized. Some might say "*perfect* triangularity" is never actualized. It need not have actual instances for it to prevail as a possibility. It might constitute the ideal possibility to which actual three-sided figures similarly approximate (a kind of actualization). Its reality qua possibility is independent from its actualization, although not from (other) actualities altogether. For example, triangularity has actual traits and is located as a possibility in actual (e.g., geometric, mathematical) orders.

Let us summarize the ontological interpretation of the house according to the metaphysics of natural complexes. In *ontological* terms, a house is to be understood as a natural complex that prevails and is alescent in orders – it is a complex of traits, some of which are actualities and some of which are possibilities. The house as physical object ("middle-size" and "atomic") and the house as owned by Emily are each really the house. The exact boundary of a complex in ontological terms may be indefinite, even if for all empirical purposes its boundaries are well recognized and well defined. This does not lead to the claim that every complex is related to every other complex, for there is no single order in which all complexes are located.[25] Nor does it exclude individuals: individuals are a kind of natural complex, but not the fundamental building blocks of reality, and not more real or more actual than universals and societies.[26]

Metaphysics of Human Process

Ontologically, human beings are a kind of natural complex, but to understand them qua human, Buchler develops more specific categories.[27] Human beings are individuals distinguished by two features: (1) the kind of process which defines their way of being in the world, *proception,* and (2) the ways in which they judge or discriminate.

Buchler introduces the categories of *proception* and *judgment* in order to make a fresh start in conceptualizing the nature of human experience. The term "experience," while not replaceable in ordinary language and communication, carries too many assumptions with it to do the work of a metaphysical category.[28] "Rationality," too, has similar drawbacks, as a metaphysical category. The notion of judgment in Buchler's system includes, but is broader than, what is typically taken to be (rational) judgment.

For Buchler, more typical philosophical views that understand experience in terms of sensation and perception, or human beings in terms of rationality or mind and body, leave too much unexplained. Buchler argues that communication, for example, is a fundamental dimension of human process, but one which is not sufficiently explained either by the categories of sensation and perception or as a function of language or reason (even though any of these may enter into or be conditions for communication). Moreover, communication is both social *and* reflexive, that is, an individual communicates with others and herself. Descartes's skeptical cogitations are a rationally expressed form of reflexive communication;[29] the athlete's repeated modulations of her movements as she masters a particular skill are also instances of reflexive communication in action rather than in language. Buchler's point is that it would be impossible to adequately understand human experience (process) without recognizing communication as one of its fundamental dimensions. His analysis is inspired in part by Roycean and Peircean insights into the nature of communication, meaning, and sign theory.

In addition to communication, proception is characterized in terms of assimilation and manipulation, compulsion, convention, perspective, and validation. Perception, a species of proception, involves manipulation and assimilation: a perceiver sees as a duck a figure that can also be seen as a rabbit. The perception is a product of both assimilation (of the data of the drawing) and manipulation (the perceiver's visual interpretation or mental image). Perception, as a species of proception, is not determined *merely* by the perceiver's sensible nature, but is ordinally located. (Recall the earlier example of color perception.) All experience – all proception – has both recipient (assimilative) and agential (manipulative) dimensions to it, even though one or the other may be dominant in any given instance.

Proception and *judgment* are always ordinal, that is, they take place in a framework that is broader than the individual herself. Distinctively human orders are called perspectives; perspective is a species of order. Perspective is not merely a psychological or mental context (although it can be). Recalling our earlier example of the house, the legal and economic orders could be called perspectives. From the perspective of a family's history, the house is the nub of family gatherings and constellations of memories; in a visual perspective, the house is red; from the perspective of physics, the house is an atomic structure. Proceptive processes and judgments are always in or from perspectives; there is no perspectiveless perspective in human experience, no "view from nowhere."[30]

The second main category of Buchler's metaphysics of human process is *judgment.* Buchler's aim here is twofold: (1) to broaden the category of judgment to include the full scope of human judicative discrimination, and (2) to conceptualize judgment in ordinal or perspectival terms. Judgment is not merely a function of reason or the mind, but of the whole individual. Any judgment in particular is located in and articulates aspects of specific perspectives. There are three modes of judgment – assertive, active, and exhibitive. These are functional distinctions and any judgment may fulfill all three functions.

Judgment, for Buchler, is not merely "propositional," "linguistic," or "rational," but rather is the broader function of appraising, discriminating, or producing. "Judgment is a selection, discrimination or combination of (natural) characters, rendered proceptively available" (TGT, p. 51). Thus, an artist's painting is a product or judgment; so, too, is a decorative arrangement of flowers. An economist's prediction of rising interest rates is a judgment, just as is a meteorologist's forecast and the taking of an umbrella on one's way out the door. The buying of a house is a judgment, as is the calculation of one's cash flow in light of a mortgage of a particular value. Of these examples, some are not propositions or assertions, but actions or arrangings, yet all are discriminative and, hence, what Buchler would call "judicative." The artist's painting and the flower arrangement are exhibitive judgments or products. The economist's and meteorologist's predictions are assertive judgments, while the taking of the umbrella is an active judgment. In the latter case, the action of taking the umbrella is itself a judgment that it might rain.[31] The act of buying a house is a (economic, personal, lifestyle, aesthetic) judgment just as much as an individual decision about whether one can afford it is. Rejecting a particular house is also a judgment, even when one can't fully explain in linguistic or "rational" terms why it is that one is rejecting it. Through judgment, the individual transcends herself (TGT, p. 53); that is, she transcends her proceptive individuality and leaves a mark of herself in the world. As a product, judgment may be fleeting or inconsequential or it may be widely consequential. An arrangement of cut flowers may last only a few days, but while it does, it both adds something to the world and reflects something of the individual(s) who produced it (who judged exhibitively). An economist's prediction may have extensive influence in the world (financially, socially, and so on), or it may be dismissed. In the former, the causal scope of the prediction is great, in the latter, virtually nil, but in either it is still a judgment. The *act* of casting a vote and not just the decision to do so is a judgment. Insofar as every judgment is located in a perspective, it is a candidate for communicative effect and meaning – reflexively for the individual, socially between individuals, or both.

Typically, philosophers have thought of judgment more narrowly as "assertive judgment," and have focused their concerns with validation on the meaning, verification, truth value, and justification of assertive judgments. Scientific method aims to establish the non-falsifiability of a scientific hypothesis. A demonstrative proof of a mathematical theorem aims to establish the truth of that theorem. These are, of course, instances of validation. They are not, however, the only kinds of validation, nor are they paradigmatic for validation in general. For if judgment is broader than assertive judgment, then validation may aim at other values than truth.

For any of the three modes of judgment, validation involves a reflexive assenting to a judgment or product as a relative finality (as not requiring further manipulation). For example, the judges' scoring of a gymnast's execution of a double pike validates in an assertive mode the gymnast's judgment in both its active and exhibitive modes (its correctness qua action and its grace – an exhibitive dimension of the judgment). Validation need not be in the assertive mode. For example, a basketball team's victory – the victory, qua upshot of active judgments by the players – may validate the coach's choices (judgments) in making player substitutions.

Validation of assertive judgments typically involves the capacity to duplicate or re-enact the production of the judgment – for example, validation in science requires the repeatability of experimental conditions and results. Validation of exhibitive judgments – a work of art, for example – may not involve such re-enactment, not even for the artist herself. Thus, exhibitive validation of a musical composition may consist in the way the phrases interact with one another (e.g., harmonically or emotionally complement, are dissonant with, juxtapose, amplify). A musical composition or series of compositions might also be of great consequence in the development of a method or style of composition. Here the composition may be validated as an active judgment, that is, as a judgment with extensive or temporally crucial efficacy with respect to future musical judgments.

One aim of the Buchlerian theory of judgment is to free it from psychologistic, rationalistic, and narrowly epistemological associations. Judgment is a pervasive feature of human process (proception); what philosophers have typically taken to be judgments (e.g., rational assertions or decisions) are a species of a much broader phenomenon. Buchler's theory of judgment is designed to enable recognition and interpretation of the full range of judicative production – the athlete's and the artist's, as much as the scientist's and the philosopher's – without reducing each to one mode (typically the assertive) or regarding those of the athlete and the artist as inferior qua judgments.

Buchler develops a theory of poetry, a distinctive kind of exhibitive judgment, in his last book, *The Main of Light*. Building from or inspired by the categorial structure developed by Buchler, others have worked on issues in ethical theory, and on the implications of Buchler's work for philosophical theology, the idea of modernity, temporality, education, and logic, to name just some of the areas currently being researched.[32]

Notes

1 See Beth Singer's *Ordinal Naturalism: An Introduction to the Philosophy of Justus Buchler* (Lewisburg, PA: Bucknell University Press, 1983) and Stephen J. Ross's *Transition to an Ordinal Metaphysics* (Albany: SUNY Press, 1980). "Ordinal" connotes, in non-technical terminology, "positionality in a context or relation." It should not be interpreted in a mathematical sense or as implying hierarchy or orderliness.

2 W. V. O. Quine, *From A Logical Point of View*, rev. edn. (Cambridge, MA: Harvard University Press, 1961), ch. 1.

3 For example, see Wilfrid Sellars, *Science, Perception, and Reality* (New York: Humanities Press, 1963).

4 Hilary Putnam argues for this as well, although his "internal" or "pragmatic" realism differs from Buchler's metaphysics of natural complexes in its underlying origins (in epistemology and philosophy of language, more than in frankly ontological problems) and in the kind of conceptual orientation it offers. See among his many writings *Realism and Reason: Philosophical Papers*, vol. 3 (Cambridge: Cambridge University Press, 1983) and *The Many Faces of Realism* (La Salle, IL: Open Court, 1987).

5 For development of this notion, see Kathleen Wallace, "Metaphysics and Validation," in Thomas Rockmore and Beth J. Singer, eds., *Antifoundationalism: Old and New* (Philadephia: Temple University Press, 1991).

6 Justus Buchler, "Reply to Greenlee: Philosophy and Exhibitive Judgment," in *Metaphysics of Natural Complexes* (New York: Columbia University Press, 1966; 2nd expanded edn. Albany: SUNY Press, 1990), p. 207. Hereafter referred to as MNC; pagination refers to 2nd expanded edn.

7 For Aristotle, "metaphysics" covered the study of the first principles of logic and causation, of the nature of the divine and of being qua being. "Metaphysics" has become associated with the last, as logicians, philosophers of science and scientists, and theologians investigate the former. The eighteenth-century philosopher Christian Wolff, following Clauvergius (1647), used the term "ontology" rather than "metaphysics" for the study of entities or being in general. See Christian Wolff, *Philosophia prima sive ontologia* (Francofurti: Prostat in Officina Libraria Rengeriana, 1730). See also Jorge J. E. Gracia, "Christian Wolff on Individuation," *History of Philosophy Quarterly*, 10/2 (April 1993): 147–64.

8 We will discuss the notion of *proception* below.

9 See Yervant Krikorian, ed., *Naturalism and the Human Spirit* (New York: Columbia University Press, 1944). Similarly, by "naturalized epistemology," Quine means to suggest that epistemology should be "contained in natural science, as a chapter of psychology." See W. V. O. Quine, "Naturalized Epistemology," in *Ontological Relativity and Other Essays* (New York: Columbia University Press, 1969), p. 83. According to Putnam, "metaphysical realism" is "*natural* metaphysics," by which he means materialism. It represents a commitment to "scientism," viz. that physics approximates to a sketch of the one true theory of the "furniture of the world." See Hilary Putnam, "Why There Isn't a Ready-Made World," in *Realism and Reason: Philosophical Papers*, vol. 3 (Cambridge, MA: Cambridge University Press, 1983). Putnam rejects metaphysical realism for "internal or pragmatic realism," but it is the linking of "natural" with "science" that is of interest to us here.

10 As we will see, Buchler's metaphysical category is "order," rather than "world."

11 On naturalism, nature, and "natural complex," see Justus Buchler, *The Main of Light* (New York: Oxford University Press, 1974), pp. 103–4; hereafter, referred to as ML. See also MNC, pp. 6, 200, 260–81. See also Sidney Gelber, "Radical Naturalism," *The Journal of Philosophy*, 61/5 (February 1959): 193–9; (reprinted in *Nature's Perspectives*); Kathleen Wallace, introduction to *Metaphysics of Natural Complexes*, 2nd edn., MNC, pp. xvii–xxix.

12 This principle was clearly anticipated by John Herman Randall, Jr., *Nature and Historical Experience* (New York: Columbia University Press, 1958), p. 131.

13 "To *exist*, to be an *entity*, to have *ontological status* are the same." Gustav Bergmann, *Realism: A Critique of Brentano and Meinong* (Madison: University of Wisconsin Press, 1967).

14 See MNC, pp. 31–51 for an extended defense of the principle against contending claims of degrees of reality.

15 These are just two of the most well-known types of reductive ontologies.

16 "Order" and "ordinality" connote positionality, not hierarchy or orderliness. See also note 1 above.

17 The identifiability of the complex as the complex that it is and no other is captured by the concept of *contour*, or *gross integrity* (see MNC, pp. 22, 215–23, and Appendix II).

18 I have simplified the concept for ease of assimilation of one of the more unfamiliar aspects of the categorial structure. See MNC, ch. 2 and pp. 290–5.

19 See MNC, pp. 76–8. Sometimes philosophers need to rid themselves of the weight of traditional associations that accompany familiar terminology. For example, Alfred North Whitehead introduced the category of "prehension" into philosophic thinking; Spinoza gave new meaning to the concepts of "attribute" and "mode"; Leibniz adopted "monad" as a philosophic category; Peirce introduced "pragmatism" and then "pragmaticism." Without such linguistic freedom, philosophic thought would be stultified.

20 In other words, the house conceptualized as natural complex has traits in given respects. When it is conceptualized as an entity with certain "intrinsic" properties, perceptual traits become something extrinsic.

21 Regarding other types of delusion, even, say, mass delusions, or just plain differing interpretations of the same facts, the ontological claim that they are real would not entail that they are valid *in particular purported respect(s)*. Just as the grayness of the house would not be valid if the claim were that the pigmentation of the house paint is gray, some interpretation may not be valid in a given respect. With interpretation of scientific data and other more complicated data, evidential and other methodic standards of the pertinent mode of inquiry come into play as well. What the Buchlerian approach does say is that as far as *ontology* goes, the issue is to identify the ordinal locations of the interpretation. The correctness of any one interpretation depends on both the features of the complex(es) in the relevant respect(s) as well as relevant evidential criteria (which themselves may be subject to examination and revision).

22 "Reply to Anton: Against 'Proper' Ontology," in MNC, p. 206. The passage continues: "[N]atural definition leads us to infinite ramifications of the actual and the possible. . . . That kind of natural definition which I call prefinition, wherein a complex defines the *extension* or *continuation* of its contour, is what we mean by a possibility." On *natural definition*, see MNC, pp. 161–70.

23 On logical possibilities, see MNC, pp. 134–42. See also Phil Weiss, "Possibility: Three Recent Ontologies," *International Philosophical Quarterly*, 20/2 (June 1980): 199–219, reprinted in *Nature's Perspectives*, pp. 145–69; Kathleen Wallace, "Ordinal Possibility: A Metaphysical Concept," in Armen Marsoobian, Kathleen Wallace, and Robert S. Corrington, eds., *Nature's Perspectives* (Albany: SUNY Press, 1991), pp. 171–87, and "Weiss/Wallace Discussion: Possibility and Metaphysics," in *Nature's Perspectives*, pp. 189–99.

24 For example, see Bob Hale, "Introduction to Abstracta: Properties, Numbers, and Propositions," in Steven D. Hales, ed., *Metaphysics: Contemporary Readings* (Belmont, CA: Wadsworth, 1999), pp. 197–206. See also Terence Parsons, "Referring to Nonexistent Objects," *Theory and Decision*, 11 (1979): 95–110.

25 See "On the Concept of 'the World'" (OCW), in MNC.

26 A metaphysics of individuals or of individuality would be less broad than the metaphysics of natural complexes and, in Buchler's view, not general enough to do the work of general ontology. For an alternative view, see Jorge J. E. Gracia, *Individuality: An Essay on the Foundations of Metaphysics* (Albany: SUNY Press, 1988).

27 These categories are developed primarily in *Toward a General Theory of Human Judgment* (New York: Columbia University Press, 1951; 2nd rev. edn., Dover Publications, 1979) and *Nature and Judgment* (New York: Columbia University Press, 1955). Hereafter, these publications are referred to as TGT and NJ, respectively.

28 See Buchler's illuminating analysis of the concept of "experience" in the introduction to TGT. It is for *philosophic* purposes that Buchler recommends moving beyond experience.

29 On Descartes, see TGT, pp. 70f. and *The Concept of Method* (New York: Columbia University Press, 1961), pp. 69–86; hereafter referred to as CM.

30 The phrase comes from Thomas Nagel, *The View From Nowhere* (New York: Oxford University Press, 1986).

31 These categorizations are based on what seems to be the primary functional mode of the judgment, but other modes may be in play in any given case as well.

32 For ethical theory, see for example, Beth J. Singer, *Operative Rights* (Albany: SUNY Press, 1998) and *Pragmatism, Rights and Democracy* (New York: Fordham University Press, 1999); Kathleen Wallace, "Reconstructing Judgment: Emotion and Moral Judgment," *Hypatia: A Journal of Feminist Philosophy*, 8/3 (Summer 1993): 61–83; and Michael J. McGandy, "The Ethical Import of Justus Buchler's Notion of Query," *Journal of Speculative Philosophy*, 11/3 (1997): 203–24. See also Justus Buchler, "Russell and the Principles of Ethics," in Paul Arthur Schilpp, ed., *The Philosophy of Bertrand Russell* (Evanston, IL: Northwestern University Press, 1944). For philosophical theology, see Peter Hare and John Ryder, "Buchler's Ordinal Metaphysics and Process Theology," *Process Studies*, 10/3–4 (Fall–Winter 1980): 120–9; Robert S. Corrington, "Finitude and Transcendence in the Thought of Justus Buchler," *The Southern Journal of Philosophy*, 25/4 (Winter 1987): 445–59, and "Horizons and Contours: Toward an Ordinal Phenomenology," *Metaphilosophy*, 22/3 (July 1991): 179–89, and *Nature and Spirit: An Essay in Ecstatic Naturalism* (New York: Fordham University Press, 1992). Regarding the idea of modernity, see Lawrence E. Cahoone, "Buchler and Habermas on Modernity," *The Southern Journal of Philosophy*, 27/4 (Winter 1989): 461–77, and "The Plurality of Philosophical Ends," *Metaphilosophy*, 26/3 (1995): 220–9. Regarding temporality, see Gary Calore, "Temporality and Radical Naturalism," Ph.D. Dissertation, Bryn Mawr College, 1986, DE586–17151. For issues related to education, see James J. Norman, "Some Implications of Justus Buchler's Thought for a Philosophy of Education," Ph.D. Dissertation, Rutgers University, Department of Education, 1986, DES86–13876; and Kathleen Wallace, "General Education and the Modern University," *Liberal Education*, 69/3 (Fall 1983): 257–68. See also some of Buchler's own work in this area: "The Liberal Arts and General Education," *The Journal of Higher Education* (April 1952); "Reconstruction in the Liberal Arts," in Buchler, et al., *A History of Columbia College on Morningside* (New York: Columbia University Press, 1954); "What is a Discussion?" *The Journal of Higher Education* (October 1954). Regarding logic, see Jon Gold,

"Complexity, Ordinality and Logic," Ph.D. Dissertation, SUNY at Stony Brook, 1981, DDJ81–27109.

Suggested reading

Primary sources

"Russell and the Principles of Ethics," in Paul Arthur Schilpp, ed., *The Philosophy of Bertrand Russell* (Evanston, IL: Northwestern University Press, 1944).

Toward a General Theory of Human Judgment (New York: Columbia University Press, 1951; 2nd, rev. edn. New York: Dover Publications, 1979).

"The Liberal Arts and General Education," *The Journal of Higher Education* (April 1952).

"Reconstruction in the Liberal Arts," in Buchler, et al., *A History of Columbia College on Morningside* (New York: Columbia University Press, 1954).

"What is a Discussion?" *The Journal of Higher Education* (October 1954).

Nature and Judgment (New York: Columbia University Press, 1955).

The Concept of Method (New York: Columbia University Press, 1961).

Metaphysics of Natural Complexes (New York: Columbia University Press, 1966; 2nd expanded edn., Albany: SUNY Press, 1990).

"On a Strain of Arbitrariness in Whitehead's System," *The Journal of Philosophy*, 66/19 (1969): pp. 589–601. Reprinted with small emendations in Lewis S. Ford and George L. Kline, eds., *Explorations in Whitehead's Philosophy* (New York: Fordham University Press, 1983), pp. 280–94.

The Main of Light (New York: Oxford University Press, 1974).

The Southern Journal of Philosophy, 14/1 (1976), ed. Beth J. Singer and Joseph Grassi. A special issue of the journal devoted to Buchler's work; consists of articles by critics and Buchler's replies. Several of Buchler's replies are reprinted in MNC (1990).

"On the Concept of 'the World'," *The Review of Metaphysics*, 31/4 (June 1978): 555–79. Reprinted in MNC (1990); all references herein will refer to the MNC pagination.

"Probing the Idea of Nature," *Process Studies*, 8/3 (Fall 1978): 157–68. Reprinted in MNC (1990); all references herein will refer to the MNC pagination.

Secondary sources

Cahoone, Lawrence E., "Buchler and Habermas on Modernity," *The Southern Journal of Philosophy*, 27/4 (Winter 1989): 461–77.

——"The Plurality of Philosophical Ends," *Metaphilosophy*, 26/3 (1995): 220–9.

Corrington, Robert S., "Finitude and Transcendence in the Thought of Justus Buchler," *The Southern Journal of Philosophy*, 25/4 (Winter 1987): 445–59.

——"Horizons and Contours: Toward an Ordinal Phenomenology," *Metaphilosophy*, 22/3 (July 1991): 179–89.

——*Nature and Spirit: An Essay in Ecstatic Naturalism* (New York: Fordham University Press, 1992).

Garrett, Roland, "The Limits of Generalization in Metaphysics: The Case of Justus Buchler," *The Southern Journal of Philosophy*, 27/1 (Spring 1989): 1–28; analysis of ontological parity and ordinality, brief comparison with Quine.

Greenlee, Douglas, "Particulars and Ontological Parity," *Metaphilosophy*, 5/3 (July 1974): 216–31.

Hare, Peter and John Ryder, "Buchler's Ordinal Metaphysics and Process Theology," *Process Studies*, 10/3–4 (Fall–Winter 1980): 120-9.

Journal of Philosophy, 61/5 (February 1959); issue devoted to articles on Buchler's work.

Marsoobian, Armen, Kathleen Wallace, and Robert S. Corrington, eds., *Nature's Perspectives: Prospects for Ordinal Metaphysics* (Albany: SUNY Press, 1991); contains a complete bibliography of secondary literature on Buchler's work through 1991.

McGandy, Michael J., "The Ethical Import of Justus Buchler's Notion of Query," *Journal of Speculative Philosophy*, 11:3 (1997): 203–24.

Norman, James J., "Some Implications of Justus Buchler's Thought for a Philosophy of Education," Ph.D. Dissertation, Rutgers University, Department of Education, 1986. DES86–13876.

Singer, Beth J., *Ordinal Naturalism: An Introduction to the Philosophy of Justus Buchler* (Lewisburg, PA: Bucknell University Press, 1983); provides comprehensive overview of the system and contains a complete bibliography of Buchler's work.

——*Operative Rights* (Albany: SUNY Press, 1998).

——*Pragmatism, Rights and Democracy* (New York: Fordham University Press, 1999).

Wallace, Kathleen, "General Education and the Modern University," *Liberal Education*, 69/3 (Fall 1983): 257–68.

——"Reconstructing Judgment: Emotion and Moral Judgment," in *Hypatia: A Journal of Feminist Philosophy*, 8/3 (Summer 1993): 61–83.

Part III

Major Themes in American Philosophy

Chapter 19

Community and Democracy

James Campbell

The story of America is the story of communities. While this is no doubt true of all societies, the story of America is further the story of democracy, of free and equal membership in communities. This powerful story is at the core of America's self-image; and, while it is far from true, this story of democratic community is not simply an instance of self-deception. It has played a powerful role in what success has been attained; and, because it contains valuable insights and suggestions, it can help guide us toward future advancement.

From our studies beginning with the earliest days of European settlements in America, we recognize the importance of community to the settlers' lives. First of all, those who came to America were community builders who could not have succeeded otherwise. Further, the question of what it is to be an American could never have been far from the surface of discussion in a society that has always seen itself to be engaged in an ongoing process of self-creation. In addition, whatever model of human perfection has filled their vision, Americans have stressed that it is the community that provides the emotional and moral place where individuals can approximate it. And, at the many times like the present, when there has been uneasiness about the direction of American society, the solution has always been seen as a reformation of the community.

One important locus of this communal story is the "Mayflower Compact," the Pilgrims' statement of communal purpose formulated as they rode at anchor off Cape Cod in 1620. In this covenant, the signers accepted the political necessity of establishing a framework of laws and offices, and pledged their obedience for the general good of their fragile project. Another statement of the importance of community was made by John Winthrop aboard the *Arabella* 10 years later, when he maintained that the 'city upon a hill' that the Puritans hoped to build would be able to flourish only with a communal focus that caused them to labor and suffer together, to rejoice and to mourn in common. Many other similar statements of this communal focus could be cited; let me list just one more. Moving westward, and closer to our own time, we find a statement of the community spirit in the contract signed in May of 1849 by the members of the Green and Jersey Company assembled at St. Joseph, Missouri, as they were about to set out for California by wagon train. The company members agreed that "in view of the long and difficult journey before us, [we] are satisfied that our own interests require for the purpose of safety, convenience, good feeling, and what is of utmost importance, the prevention of unnecessary delay, the adoption of strict rules and regulations to govern us during our passage." In light of this recognition, they pledged "that we will abide by all the rules and regulations that may be made by a vote of a majority of the company, for its regulations during our passage; [and] that we will manfully assist and uphold any authorized officer in his exertions to strictly enforce all such rules and regulations as may be made." Further, should any members of the company be unable to go on, "we pledge ourselves never to desert them, but from our own resources and means to support and assist them to get through to Sutter's Fort, and in fact, we pledge ourselves to stand by each other, under any justifiable circumstance to the death."[1]

We now recognize that this community of westerners, like the other communities that we have considered and the many more that we could have considered, surely demonstrated a blindness to the prior settlers of the continent and an underdeveloped sense of the important value of equality. But these communities did demonstrate as well a fundamental understanding of the human individual as rooted in a social existence of values and goals and a powerful recognition of the necessity for cooperation to deal with the exigencies of a shared destiny. In this chapter, I want to discuss the presentation of this spirit of communal democracy in the thinking of the classical American philosophers.

Community as the Sharing of Experiences and Values

The importance of community in American history has been reflected in the history of American philosophy, especially since this philosophical tradition became self-conscious about a century ago. Two of the most important figures from this 'classical' period in American philosophy – Josiah Royce and John Dewey – saw community as an essential element in any attempt to understand humans and their world, and as a central piece of any attempt to better human experience. Royce maintained that we need to make community the central component of our social philosophy. Its centrality was based on his recognition of the vital role that community plays in our understanding of ourselves and our neighbors, and in any efforts to overcome the isolation of individual existence. He writes that "we are saved through the community," because community functions as a concrete and living focus for the loyalty that is at the core of our humanity. Without such a communal focus, human individuals have no meaning for their lives. As he puts it, "[t]he detached individual is an essentially lost being."[2] Similarly, Dewey writes that our political structures were built upon communal foundations, democracy being "the idea of community life itself." Historically, our polities developed out of genuine community life in small towns and villages. In the intervening years, however, we have lost touch with our communal roots. We have forgotten the importance of our communities as places where all adult persons benefit from the values that the groups sustain and share responsibility for collective activities. Dewey continues that, if we do not come to realize the significance of local communities, we will not be able to maintain our democracy. He phrases the point as follows: "Unless local communal life can be restored, the public cannot adequately resolve its most urgent problem: to find and identify itself."[3]

Deciding just what is to count as a community is not a simple matter. The indicators of community to which Royce and Dewey point are at least three. The first two are in some sense objective: geographical locality and permanence, factors that result in human association and shared activity. The third indicator, which goes beyond interaction, is more subjective and emotional: a conscious identification with and affection for the group and its members. Dewey denies the possibility of community unless there is such recognition of other members. He writes: "To have the same ideas about things which others have, to be like-minded with them, and thus to be really members of a social group, is therefore to attach the same meanings to things and to acts which others attach. Otherwise, there is no common understanding, and no community life." Central to this common understanding within a community is the sharing of values. There must thus be a central core of common felt values that are articulated within the lives of the members of the community. In a community, Dewey writes, each individual "feels its success as his success, its failure as his failure"; and for individuals living in such a group, " 'we' is as inevitable as 'I'."[4] Royce's formulation of this point runs parallel to Dewey's, requiring the conscious identification of the community's work with our lives. People form a community, Royce writes, "when they not only cooperate, but accompany this cooperation with that ideal extension of the lives of individuals whereby each cooperating member says: 'This activity which we perform together, this work of ours, its past, its future, its sequence, its order, its sense – all these enter into my life, and are the life of my own self writ large'."[5]

Both Dewey and Royce believed that the topic of community, and even the term itself (and its many synonyms) contain a fundamental ambiguity. On the one hand, in our discussions we refer descriptively to all sorts of communities. On the other, we refer eulogistically to what we might, following Royce, characterize as "the Great Community," a sort of ideal state to which our present communities should ever aspire. Descriptively, community for Royce and Dewey means a minimal level of association requiring a conscious common identity and common events and practices; yet, for both, community holds out the promise of an ideal state, to be sought even if never to be reached because of the complexities of human association (Dewey) or the weaknesses of human nature (Royce). They use terms like "community" in either a eulogistic or descriptive sense, depending on what type of human association they are emphasizing at any given time. Dewey writes: "The terms society, community, are thus ambiguous. They have both a eulogistic or normative sense, and a descriptive sense; a meaning *de jure* and a meaning *de facto*." Dewey believed that social philosophers focus for the most part on the eulogistic meaning, emphasizing such social goods as "praiseworthy community of purpose and welfare, loyalty to public ends, [and] mutuality of sympathy." Besides this eulogistic or honorific sense of association, replete with loyalty and sympathy and hope, there remains the simple descriptive meaning of community *de facto*. At this level, we are not describing any "great" community, but "a plurality of societies, good and bad." Here we find garden clubs and reading groups with their shared values; we find as well "[m]en banded together in a criminal conspiracy, business aggregations that prey upon the public while serving it, [and] political machines held together by the interest of plunder."[6] On this same point of misdirected loyalty, Royce notes that "[a] robber band, a family engaged in a murderous feud, a pirate crew, a savage tribe, a Highland robber clan of the old days – these might constitute causes to which somebody has been, or is, profoundly loyal."[7]

Building upon this duality of the concept of community, Dewey developed criteria for evaluating communities, for separating the narrow and the harmful from the good. The criteria to which he points are two: "How numerous and varied are the interests which are consciously shared? How full and free is the interplay with other forms of association?" In any social group whatever, he continues, "we find some interest held in common, and we find a certain amount of interaction and cooperative intercourse with other groups." But, if we focus upon a criminal band, for example, "we find that the ties which consciously hold the members together are few in number, reducible almost to a common interest in plunder; and that they are of such a nature as to isolate the group from other groups with respect to give and take of the values of life." Thus, while a criminal band or a pirate crew consequently can be seen as a community, it remains a weak or incomplete one because it possesses few of the potential qualities of a rich community. Internally, its common interests are limited in number and narrow in breadth; externally, its interplay with other forms of association remain negligible. Still, even such an antisocial community is not a completely worthless group: "each of these organizations, no matter how opposed to the interests of other groups, has something of the praiseworthy qualities of 'Society' which hold it together." We find in an antisocial community like a criminal band such values as "honor" and "fraternal feeling" and "intense loyalty."[8] To the extent that it demonstrates the traits of vibrant community, it is good; but, because it demonstrates them in such a narrow fashion, it is a weak and narrow community.

Royce presented similar evaluative criteria for community in a discussion of the importance of expanding our loyalties in the face of the 1914–18 war, the humanitarian horror of his last years. He writes that "if ever relief is to come to humanity's great woe of combat, it will come not merely through a cessation of hate and a prevalence of love for individual men, but through the growth of some higher type of loyalty, which shall absorb the men of the future so that the service of the community of all mankind will at last become their great obsession." In other words, the exclusively inward-looking loyalty of the nation-state that had led inexorably to this conflagration had to be replaced with the broader outlook that incorporated the supernational perspective of all humankind. This larger vision Royce characterizes not as loyalty to one's country but as "loyalty to loyalty"; and he calls upon each of us to "so choose your cause and so serve it, that, by reason of your choice and of your service, there shall be more loyalty in the world rather than less. And, in fact, so choose and so serve your individual cause as to secure thereby the greatest possible increase in loyalty amongst men. More briefly: *In choosing and in serving the cause to which you are to be loyal, be, in any case, loyal to loyalty.*"[9]

Any consideration of the nature and role of community in human life must include as well a consideration of the individuals, the selves who create and sustain and benefit from the community. The reason why the nature and role of community is so important to our understanding of human well-being is simply that humans who live in vibrant communities live better lives. Human individuals are inherently social, creatures for whom community is natural; and they need good groups to become better humans. Humans do not live together like books on a shelf or bricks in a wall; they are living organisms who need a supportive social environment. Selves take nourishment from the give and take with others who share their social places. We develop our humanity, our individuality, in the midst of community living.

The self is not present at the birth of the individual. Rather, it emerges over time, developing in the course of living communally with other individuals. Individuals grow to a sense of self-consciousness *through* the communities in which they live, not simply *in* them. For both Royce and Dewey, we should not attempt to understand selves in terms of either separateness from others or faithfulness to some pre-set trajectory. Their analysis emphasizes the emergence of the self within the social context. Emergent selves are social through and through, growing within and because of their communal life, developing in a situation of shared living. "Everything which is distinctively human is learned, not native," Dewey writes. "To learn to be human," he continues, "is to develop through the give-and-take of communication an effective sense of being an individually distinctive member of a community; one who understands and appreciates its beliefs, desires and methods, and who contributes to a further conversion of organic powers into human resources and values." Moreover, this process of individual development is one that "is never finished."[10] Ongoing participation in a community is essential to a fulfilled human existence because this participation makes possible a more diversified and enriching experience for all members.

True individuality is thus a cluster of abilities developed over time and through interaction, not an original essence that grows from within as long as the person is not deflected from his or her "true" path. Such individuality, Dewey continues, is not private but social. "No man and no mind was ever emancipated merely by being left alone," he writes. "Liberty is that secure release and fulfillment of personal potentialities which take place only in rich and manifold association with others." In particular, the values that we incorporate as developing individuals – *our* values – come from this life within a community. As Dewey writes: "An assembly is formed within our breast which discusses and appraises proposed and performed acts. The community without becomes a forum and tribunal within." As growing and developing selves, we absorb enemies and friends, taboos and goals, as they are presented to us by our group. The way our group does things, he continues, becomes the proper way: "[w]hat is strange or foreign . . . tends to be morally forbidden and intellectually suspect." These socially derived values are less restraints upon us than reinforcers within our selves. These socially derived values are, for good or ill, at the core of who we are. Of course, we are not replicants of some unbending collective persona, because we live in social situations that are themselves complex and changing; and we come to understand that it is at times necessary for us to react in various ways against the community, to separate out what we see as its "prejudices" from its legitimate values. This is how we come to recognize that the values held by the criminal band or the pirate crew are inadequate. We come to recognize that one of our ongoing requirements is to focus human concern upon the overarching ideal of cooperation and community, and foster what Dewey calls "the miracle of shared life and shared experience."[11]

Democracy as the Practices of Community

The understanding of democracy that is primary in classical American philosophy is built upon this understanding of community. Democracy's defense of equality is grounded in the equal worth of each person within a community. Its defense of freedom is grounded in the liberty each must have to find and develop his or her proper contribution. And the procedural values of democracy – which Dewey lists as "mutual respect, mutual toleration, give and take, the pooling of experiences" – are grounded in community and its cooperative efforts to seek the common good. We have been drawn together in community to solve our problems; but it is the togetherness and the resultant shared values themselves, not the various solutions, that prove to be the primary results. In this regard, Dewey writes, "[d]emocracy is the faith that the process of experience is more important than any special result attained." He thus calls for a greater appreciation of the process of interactive success and failure in which we live our lives, and writes that democracy is "the sole way of living which believes wholeheartedly in the process of experience as end and as means."[12] In our attempts to build and further democratic community, the process of developing shared activity and values held in common is what matters. We need to foster the kind of long-term focus that sees beyond particular issues to the cultivation of dialogue and ongoing cooperation. Following this interpretation of democracy, we can see how it can be understood as a moral ideal and not just a group of institutional procedures or organizational machinery.

We test democracy as a way of life by interactive living. Dewey writes that "if democracy has a moral and ideal meaning, it is that a social return be demanded from all and that opportunity for development of distinctive capacities be afforded all." Democracy, because of this emphasis upon engagement in social life, is not a method that appeals to some senses of efficiency. It is, rather, "the road which places the greatest burden of responsibility upon the greatest number of human beings." The level of work necessary to fulfill one's responsibilities in a democracy makes citizens active participants in communal life. "The key-note of democracy as a way of life may be expressed," he continues, "as the necessity for the participation of every mature human being in formation of the values that regulate the living of men together."[13] Without the chance to participate in social processes of all sorts, individuals will not grow fully. As Dewey writes, "human nature is developed only when its elements take part in directing things which are common, things for the sake of which men and women form groups – families, industrial companies, governments, churches, scientific associations, and so on." When an individual is to be a "spectator" rather than a "participant," that person will assume the attitude of "a man in a prison cell watching the rain out of the window; it is all the same to him." Consequently, he holds up to us the goal of developing "the particular kind of social direction fitted to a democratic society – the direction which comes from heightened emotional appreciation of common interests and from an understanding of social responsibilities," a direction that can be gained "only by experimental and personal participation in the conduct of common affairs."[14]

Democracy as a way of life is an element in the whole spectrum of human life. Keeping this large scope of democracy in mind, we can briefly consider two particular manifestations: the political and the economic. As Dewey writes, "the supreme test of all political institutions and industrial arrangements shall be the contribution they make to the all-around growth of every member of society." Other manifestations of democracy, such as the artistic and the medical and the religious, can be imagined; the meaning of educational democracy will be considered briefly below. In the political realm narrowly construed, Dewey writes that democracy denotes "a mode of government, a specified practice in selecting officials and regulating their conduct as officials." What is special about this mode of government is that it "does not esteem the well-being of one individual or class above that of another; [it is] a system of laws and administration which ranks the happiness and interests of all as upon the same plane, and before whose law and administration all individuals are alike, or equal."[15] In furtherance of these goals many procedures have been developed with which we are familiar: universal suffrage, frequent elections, the trio of initiative, referendum, and recall, regulations about funding, and so on. The political aspect of democracy includes as well attempts to develop and then to integrate the work of experts in our attempts to solve our social problems.

The economic aspect of democracy is, in the contemporary world, no less important than the political. In particular, economic changes that have occurred since the time of the foundation of our political frameworks have rendered these frameworks to a large extent irrelevant. As Dewey writes, "economic developments which could not possibly have been anticipated when our political forms took shape have created confusion and uncertainty in the working of the agencies of popular government." In the modern world, where so many people have only a minimal level of control over the conditions of their own subsistence, he continues, "it is a problem of the future of democracy, of how political democracy can be made secure if there is economic insecurity and economic dependence of great sections of the population." As a response, he advocated the democratic management of our economic system, if necessary as extensive as "the socialization of all natural resources and natural monopolies, of ground rent, and of basic industries." Related to the democratic aspects of industrial management, a full sense of the economic element of democracy would also require that the kinds of employment available to workers bring meaning in their lives and involve them as participants in productive decisions. Dewey writes that each should be able "to see within his daily work all there is in it of large and human significance,"[16] a comment about the actual ordering of the work process and about the corresponding educational arrangements.

Fundamental to this account of community as essential to democracy is the conception of democracy as a cooperative inquiry. Both of these terms are equally important. Dewey emphasized that the process of living in a democratic community requires a recognition on our part that political life "is essentially a cooperative undertaking, one which rests upon persuasion, upon ability to convince and be convinced by reason." As he continues, "the heart and final guarantee of democracy is in free gatherings of neighbors on the street corner to discuss back and forth what is read in uncensored news of the day, and in gatherings of friends in the living rooms of houses and apartments to converse freely with one another." Such communal interactions have as their aim more than being social diversions: their goal is to help advance the community. Dewey believed that we can achieve, through "back-and-forth give-and-take discussion," a public opinion that can rise above tradition and cut through appearance. Democracy requires, in addition to "sympathetic regard for the intelligence and personality of others," the additional step "of scientific inquiry into facts and testing of ideas."[17]

To form public opinion that is more than just opinion, it is necessary to isolate what matters from the sea of information in which we are increasingly awash, and to do this requires ongoing cooperative inquiry. He writes, for example, "I am a great believer in the power of public opinion. In this country nothing stands against it. But to act, it must exist." And, more importantly for Dewey, "[t]o act wisely, it must be intelligently formed." For public opinion "[t]o be intelligently formed, it must be the result of deliberate inquiry and discussion." He believed that modern society had finally developed an adequate method for social reconstruction, a method "of cooperative and experimental science which expresses the method of intelligence." This "method" is better understood as a *mentality* for approaching and dealing with problems than as a *protocol* for setting out in advance our responses to possible conditions. As such, it offers no predetermined path of reform, no claim that individual reformers can be made irrelevant, and no guarantees of ultimate success. What sets this method off from other possible methods – like following custom or authority – is that its justificatory process is grounded in the requirement of participation in and acceptance by a vibrant citizenry. Dewey's point is that through publicity and reflection we can learn from our social mistakes. Equally important to effective democracy is the nature of the relationships among the citizens. "Democracy must begin at home, and its home is the neighborly community."[18]

This understanding of democracy, although prominent in classic American philosophy, does not find an equivalent place in America's traditional political practices. For it to become prominent, fundamental reconstruction would be necessary. Dewey and Royce were not deterred here because they believed that democracy, as it had worked itself out in the American past, had been largely an accidental good rather than one consciously built. The plurality of religious perspectives had forced the recognition of individual conscience; the growth of science and technology had given rise to industrial centers and had expanded transportation and communication. Whatever our theoreticians might have said about democracy, it was our frontier society, with its decentralized and unobtrusive government, that left most life-decisions to individuals themselves, and most problem solutions to the creative responses of local communities. When it began to become clear toward the end of the nineteenth century that this frontier society was gone, the beginnings of many attempts to redress problems were undertaken; but none was granted any absolute status. Each was a temporary fix or a partial patch; and all sorts of new attempts to revitalize our democratic life remain viable possibilities if they respect communal values. Dewey writes that we need to "re-create by deliberate and determined endeavor" the kind of democratic life that in earlier times was "largely the product of a fortunate combination of men and circumstances." The first step, he believed, was to recognize that democracy cannot be confined to a consideration of political machinery. Democracy must be grounded in community, in the belief that "every human being, independent of the quantity or range of his personal endowment, has the right to equal opportunity with every other person for development of whatever gifts he has."[19] Central to this faith is the role of education to enable all individuals to contribute to the extent of their powers.

Education as the Means to Democratic Community

Although the child is born in organic association with others, each must still learn how to become a member of the community. Education is the means. Through the process of education, Dewey writes, "the individual gradually comes to share in the intellectual and moral resources which humanity has succeeded in getting together." By means of education, each becomes "an inheritor of the funded capital of civilization." Through the educational process of shared living, each grows from an initial focus on personal actions and feelings to be able to value and pursue the common good. Moreover, this individual growth has a social equivalent. As Dewey writes, "the unsolved problem of democracy is the construction of an education which will develop that kind of individuality which is intelligently alive to the common life and sensitively loyal to its common maintenance."[20]

Dewey understood the social situation in America to be full of possibilities, many of which were not as yet even recognized. Thus, he understood that a rich and effective democracy would be something approached only in the future. But he saw education as the key element in creating this democracy because full democracy is impossible without liberating the mind. As he writes, education is "the most far-reaching and the most fundamental way of correcting social evils and meeting social issues." Just as the individual is plastic, so too is society, shaping itself and its future with every significant choice. Dewey describes this educational point as follows: "Since the young at a given time will at some later date compose the society of that period, the latter's nature will largely turn upon the direction children's activities were given at an earlier period." It is consequently our duty to attempt to shape the experiences of the young "so that instead of reproducing current habits, better habits shall be formed, and thus the future adult society be an improvement on their own."[21]

The intimate connection that Dewey saw between democracy and education can be demonstrated further in such passages as the following: "Democracy has to be born anew every generation, and education is its midwife." Moreover, vibrant democracy itself is an educational principle because it fosters growth through ongoing involvement with the problems of society. "Full education," he continues, "comes only when there is a responsible share on the part of each person, in proportion to capacity, in shaping the aims and policies of the social groups to which he belongs."[22] His mention of "capacity" here should not be seen to imply a commitment on his part to some system for ranking citizens. It is, rather, a claim that in a democracy citizens must receive an education sufficient to enable them to function as adequate critics of social proposals.

This emphasis on the possibilities of education ought not to suggest that improvement is in any sense guaranteed; and Dewey emphasized, as much as anyone else did, the practical limits in the educational process. Schools do not work in a vacuum, but rather in a complex web of institutions and social arrangements, of prejudices and values, that influence the shaping of minds. Still, Dewey sees educational reform as the essential means to break free from the unthinking reproduction of outdated institutions. As he writes: "while the school is not a sufficient condition, it is a necessary condition of forming the understanding and the dispositions that are required to maintain a genuinely changed social order."[23]

The role of the school and of education generally in democratic social reconstruction has two distinguishable aspects. The first of these aspects is to help students become better problem-solvers in the new and difficult situations of their world, to help them learn how to think for themselves rather than to fill them with whatever information we now believe they will need in later life. Rather than graduating students "possessed *merely* of vast stores of information or high degrees of skill in specialized branches," Dewey writes, our goal as educators should be to produce students with "that attitude of mind which is conducive to good judgment in any department of affairs in which the pupils are placed." The ultimate goal of education is thus to produce adults capable of "sound judgment," people who are able "to pass judgments *pertinently* and *discriminatingly*" on the problems of human living. This focus of education on fostering judgment rather than on imparting information is part of Dewey's overall emphasis on wisdom as a moral term related to evaluation, to the criticism of the choices by which we are building our future world. The attempt to foster the power of judgment will require that we abandon our historical reluctance to criticize aspects of our collective past that has resulted in the simple-minded promulgation of the *status quo*. "If our public-school system merely turns out efficient industrial fodder and citizenship fodder in a state controlled by pecuniary industry," he writes, we are not building good citizens. In its place, we must attempt to give the students "some unified sense of the kind of world in which they live, the directions in which it is moving, and the part they have to play in it."[24] In this way, we can help students to make more sense of their lives at present and to develop a more ordered entry into the future.

The second aspect of education and schooling in democratic social reconstruction is the importance of helping students learn to live more cooperatively: to listen to each other so that they can better recognize the problems that are developing and work together to achieve the sorts of response that cannot be effected individually. Educators thus play a central role in the ongoing process of socializing the student; and, if they resist the temptation to foster the narrow loyalty to our past and its values that Royce rejected, they can broaden the student's sense of living in a world among others. Dewey expands this point as follows: "Education should create an interest in all persons in furthering the general good, so that they will find their own happiness realized in what they can do to improve the conditions of others."[25] In this way, the importance of social purpose as a determining factor in activities of future citizens will grow, and we will be more likely to attain the broader possibilities with which our social situation has presented us. Moreover, the future effectiveness of the social criticisms of moral prophets – like Thoreau and Gandhi and King – in influencing the directions of the larger community will be increased by efforts based in the schools to prepare an audience for such critical insights.

Education can help the students become better able to recognize values and more conscious of the nature of possibilities of social progress. Students can grow in the "ability to judge men and measures wisely and to take a determining part in making as well as obeying laws." And they can develop the ability "to take their own active part in aggressive participation in bringing about a new social order." This is possible, however, only in the context of an education that conceives its task as the furtherance of communal life. Part of this emphasis can be accomplished through the widespread dissemination of the conclusions of social inquiries, and the sharing of knowledge in a democracy requires the abandonment of our purely individualistic notion of intelligence. "Knowledge cooped up in a private consciousness is a myth, and knowledge of social phenomena is peculiarly dependent upon dissemination, for only by distribution can such knowledge be either obtained or tested."[26] The knowledge that our society possesses has been gained through the cooperative efforts of human beings living together. For democracy as cooperative inquiry to succeed, there must be communal interaction over the broad range and through the ongoing processes of shared living.

While the school is an information-transmitting place, a place where the complex array of necessary material is sorted into something thought to be manageable by the young, it is more importantly a place where values are cultivated. It is the business of schools, Dewey writes, "to deepen and extend" the students' sense of the values found in their home life. The cultivation of such values as cooperation, fairness, and respect is what he has in mind – not values like blind obedience or unquestioning loyalty to our past – and these values cannot be well cultivated through authoritarian moralistic inculcation. On the contrary, these values are more successfully developed in the processes of social living. As Dewey writes, "the best and deepest moral training is precisely that which one gets through having to enter into proper relations with others in a unity of work and thought."[27] The young can most successfully learn the meaning of democratic life through the process of cooperative activity a school that attempts to recreate the life of the larger community and fosters its shared goods.

Dewey believed that students' abilities to participate and evaluate can be fostered by democratic school procedures. Conversely, schools in which the decisions are made for students, in which the individual and collective responsibility of the young to determine courses of action is not deliberately developed, will not foster an inquiring democratic citizenry. A democratic school thus does not divorce the ends of socialization from the means of its attainment: to improve students' skills for social life, we must engage them in social life. Dewey maintains that we must thus attempt to create in our schools "a projection in type of the society we should like to realize, and by forming minds in accord with it gradually modify the larger and more recalcitrant features of adult society." If we provide our young with an education in a school organized along the lines of the "principle of shared activity," we can hope for a very different overall impact from that of an isolating school in which all work is private. We are far more likely to succeed in developing the sorts of shared meanings that would make fuller democratic community life possible if we can make each individual "a sharer or partner in the associated activity so that he feels its success as his success, its failure as his failure."[28]

Dewey's emphasis upon the relationship between democracy and education is not just a point about schooling, but rather about the ongoing education of engaged citizens. Education, he writes, "is a process of living and not a preparation for future living." Our pupils, at whatever level, are alive, not getting ready to live. Conversely, education is not a segment of life that we should hope to get beyond. In any life that is not stagnant, education remains ongoing. All of life is, or at least should be, a process of educational growth. We are ever learning, revising, evaluating, reconstructing. Only when life is understood in this way can it follow that, as Dewey notes, "education must be conceived as a continuing reconstruction of experience . . . the process and the goal of education are one and the same thing." As members of communities, we are ever encountering new individuals and new situations. As citizens, we will continue to confront new problems. We will not be able to deal with any of this novelty if we cannot grow, if we have not incorporated the habits of openness and adaptability. Future judgments will have to be made in the future, out of elements of intermediate solutions that are themselves not yet known. Because of our need for ongoing evaluation and criticism, he emphasized the need to foster ongoing inquiry. "The most important attitude that can be formed," he writes, "is that of desire to go on learning."[29]

Dewey saw the possibilities inherent in human existence to justify a belief in meliorism based upon faith. By faith he means a willingness to try, to take a chance; and he had faith that our experience would continue to contain possibilities for solving the problems that we were to face. From his standpoint, no situation is ever hopeless. Each situation is transitional, containing undeveloped possibilities that if properly cultivated might be realized. For Dewey, this kind of faith is a tendency toward action rooted in what he calls "the dumb pluck of the animal."[30] Without such a faith, we could not act in the face of uncertainty. We live in an evolving world, a world without guarantees; and we need an experimental philosophy that will guide us as we move onward. There are, as William James recognized, "cases where a fact cannot come at all unless a preliminary faith exists in its coming";[31] and, with regard to our social problems, this point is extremely important. Because what we have or have not done involves us in the development of our problems, we can influence how well we address these ills by our actions. Our efforts are thus both definitely necessary and possibly efficacious.

This faith in the possibilities of democratic community is recognized upon careful examination to be nested in other faiths. There is, first of all, in Dewey's words, a "faith in the capacities of human nature," justifiable because there are distinctive qualities in each normal human person and, if these qualities are given the proper means of self-development, "each individual has something to contribute." There is also a faith in the possibilities of education as a way to free the minds of present and future political participants. This faith in individuals and "in the capacity of human beings for intelligent judgment and action if proper conditions are furnished"[32] underlies democracy as the means to the development of the capacities of individual members of society. If we can develop cooperative problem-solvers of the sort discussed above, Dewey felt that we can legitimately have faith in our future possibilities.

While this faith is admittedly without any guarantees of success, it is still more than a vague hope that these individuals will somehow happen upon adequate answers. Dewey's faith is a faith in the adequacy of our responses when we operate in cooperative associations. He had faith in democracy because he believed "in the power of pooled and cooperative experience" to solve our problems. This faith in democracy is thus related to faith in science as a widely used method of problem-solving; and, rejecting any distinction between realms of nature and of history, this faith in democracy is bolstered by "what the method of experimental and cooperative intelligence has already accomplished in subduing to potential human use the energies of physical nature." The whole of this faith is reducible, Dewey writes, to "faith in the capacity of the intelligence of the common man to respond with commonsense to the free play of facts and ideas which are secured by effective guarantees of free inquiry, free assembly, and free communication."[33] His belief is that future problems will be able to be solved if they are approached in an intelligent and cooperative fashion by average people.

For our part, the recognition that such a faith is essential to successful social life commits us to long-term endeavors to foster democratic community: to build through our educational system a wise citizenry both self-critical and concerned with social issues, and to foster through our political institutions an involved citizenry that can both learn from and contribute to the common life. Over the years, Dewey writes, we have learned that "every generation has to accomplish democracy over again for itself; that its very nature, its essence, is something that cannot be handed on from one person or one generation to another, but has to be worked out in terms of needs, problems and conditions of the social life of which, as the years go by, we are a part."[34] He believed that to have any hope for success as a society we must further develop democratic community; and both this goal and the indicated means Dewey shared with Royce.

Democratic Community as an Ideal

We have been considering the interrelation of three fundamental themes – community, democracy, and education – in classical American philosophy. We have focused upon the thought of Josiah Royce and John Dewey because they offered the most developed analysis of these themes. As a summary of their overlapping views, I would suggest the following. Human existence takes place within natural and social processes that find their meaning in experience. It is the richness of the lives of individuals that provides the worth of existence. By means of its deliberate attempts at education, a society tries to develop individuals who have internalized its value system and who will then work to carry these values forward. All value systems contain conflicting elements; and, at times, individuals come to challenge parts of these inherited value systems using as their tools other parts of the system. When the resulting conflicts are resolved through intelligent and cooperative interactions that recognize the contributions of all the participants, the reconstructions advance morality. Democracy thus has moral significance and is grounded in a faith that it could both resolve our problems and advance communitarian values at the same time.

In the years that have passed since the highpoint of classical American philosophy, we have come to realize, better than its representatives like Royce and Dewey were able to, that much of the ideal vision of communal democracy that they presented failed to connect with their realities. Our situation may now be worse than theirs was, or we may simply be more skeptical at present; but based on this less laudatory interpretation of American practices, our contemporary world is one that is leery of any use of the term "community" in the singular, doubtful about any moral potential for democracy, and skeptical about the power of education to bring about democratic community. Our reality has thrown into question the story of democratic community on which so much of American history has fed; and with these doubts have come hesitancy regarding the work of Royce and Dewey. These doubts cannot be ignored; but, on the other hand, they do not automatically invalidate the ideal. The power that this ideal still has can be seen in the fact that, when we criticize our current situation, we frequently use an ideal of communal democracy much like the one that Royce and Dewey developed as our pattern.

Notes

1 Daniel J. Boorstin, *The Americans*, 3 vols. (New York: Random House, 1958–73), vol. 3, p. 66.

2 *The Hope of the Great Community* (New York: Macmillan, 1916), pp. 130, 46.

3 *The Public and Its Problems*, repr. in *The Later Works of John Dewey, 1925–1953* (hereafter *LW*), 17 vols., ed. Jo Ann Boydston (Carbondale: Southern Illinois University Press, 1981–90), vol. 2, pp. 328, 370.

4 *Democracy and Education*, repr. in *The Middle Works of John Dewey, 1899–1924* (hereafter *MW*), 15 vols., ed. Jo Ann Boydston (Carbondale: Southern Illinois University Press, 1976–83), vol. 9, pp. 35, 18; *The Public and Its Problems*, p. 330.

5 *The Problem of Christianity* (Chicago: University of Chicago Press, 1968 [1913]), p. 263.

6 Dewey, *Democracy and Education*, p. 88.

7 *The Philosophy of Loyalty* (New York: Macmillan, 1908), p. 108.

8 Dewey, *Democracy and Education*, p. 88.

9 *War and Insurance* (New York: Macmillan, 1914), p. 24; *The Philosophy of Loyalty*, p. 121.

10 *The Public and Its Problems*, pp. 331–2.

11 Ibid., pp. 340, 329; *Human Nature and Conduct: An Introduction to Social Psychology*, repr. in *MW*, vol. 14, p. 216; *Democracy and Education*, p. 21; *Reconstruction in Philosophy*, repr. in *MW*, vol. 12, p. 201.

12 "Democracy and Education in the World of Today," repr. in *LW*, vol. 13, p. 303; "Creative Democracy – The Task Before Us," repr. in *LW*, vol. 14, p. 229.

13 *Democracy and Education*, p. 129; *Freedom and Culture*, repr. in *LW*, vol. 13, p. 154; "Democracy and Educational Administration," repr. in *LW*, vol. 11, p. 217.

14 *Reconstruction in Philosophy*, pp. 199–200; *Democracy and Education*, p. 131; "Education and Social Direction," repr. in *MW*, vol. 11, p. 57.

15 *Reconstruction in Philosophy*, p. 186; *The Public and Its Problems*, p. 286; "The Need of an Industrial Education in an Industrial Democracy," repr. in *MW*, vol. 10, p. 137.

16 *Freedom and Culture*, p. 107; "Democracy and Education in the World of Today," p. 300; "No Half-Way House for America," repr. in *LW*, vol. 9, pp. 289–90; *The School and Society*, repr. in *MW*, vol. 1, p. 16.

17 "Organization in American Education," repr. in *MW*, vol. 10, p. 404; "Creative Democracy," 227; "The One-World of Hitler's National Socialism," repr. in *MW*, vol. 8, p. 443; *Ethics* (with James H. Tufts), repr. in *LW*, vol. 7, p. 329.

18 "Introductory Address to the American Association of University Professors," repr. in *MW*, vol. 8, p. 100; *Liberalism and Social Action*, repr. in *LW*, vol. 11, p. 58; *The Public and Its Problems*, p. 368.

19 "Creative Democracy," pp. 225–7.

20 "My Pedagogic Creed," repr. in *The Early Works of John Dewey, 1882–1898* (hereafter *EW*), 5 vols., ed. Jo Ann Boydston (Carbondale: Southern Illinois University Press, 1969–72), vol. 5, p. 84; "Education and Social Direction," p. 57.

21 "Philosophy and Education," repr. in *LW*, vol. 5, p. 297; *Democracy and Education*, pp. 46, 85.

22 "The Need of an Industrial Education," p. 139; *Reconstruction in Philosophy*, p. 199.

23 "Education and Social Change," repr. in *LW*, vol. 11, p. 414.

24 *How We Think: A Restatement of the Relation of Reflective Thinking to the Educative Process*, repr. in *LW*, vol. 8, p. 211; *Individualism: Old and New*, repr. in *LW*, vol. 5, p. 102; "The Need for Orientation," repr. in *LW*, vol. 11, p. 164.

25 (with Tufts), *Ethics*, p. 243.

26 Dewey, *Democracy and Education*, p. 127; "Education and the Social Order," repr. in *LW*, vol. 9, p. 182; *The Public and Its Problems*, p. 345.

27 "My Pedagogic Creed," pp. 87–8.

28 *Democracy and Education*, pp. 326, 18.

29 "My Pedagogic Creed," pp. 87, 91; *Experience and Education*, repr. in *LW*, vol. 13, p. 29.

30 *Human Nature and Conduct*, p. 200.

31 William James, *The Will to Believe and Other Essays in Popular Philosophy*, ed. Frederick H. Burkhardt (Cambridge, MA: Harvard University Press, 1979 [1897]), p. 29.

32 "Democracy and Educational Administration," pp. 219–20; "Creative Democracy," p. 227.

33 "Democracy and Educational Administration," pp. 219; *Liberalism and Social Action*, p. 64; "Creative Democracy," p. 227.

34 "Democracy and Education in the World Today," p. 299.

Suggested reading

Ahlstrom, Sidney, *A Religious History of the American People* (New Haven, CT: Yale University Press, 1972).

Berry, Wendell, *The Unsettling of America: Culture and Agriculture* (San Francisco: Sierra Club Books, 1977).

Boorstin, Daniel J., *The Americans*, 3 vols. (New York: Random House, 1958–73).

Campbell, James, *The Community Reconstructs: The Meaning of Pragmatic Social Thought* (Urbana: University of Illinois Press, 1992).

Dewey, John, *The Early Works of John Dewey, 1882–1898* [*EW*], 5 vols., ed. Jo Ann Boydston (Carbondale: Southern Illinois University Press, 1969–72).

—— *The Middle Works of John Dewey, 1899–1924* [*MW*], 15 vols., ed. Jo Ann Boydston (Carbondale: Southern Illinois University Press, 1976–83).

—— *The Later Works of John Dewey, 1925–1953* [*LW*], 17 vols., ed. Jo Ann Boydston (Carbondale: Southern Illinois University Press, 1981–90).

—— *Democracy and Education* [1916], repr. in *MW*, vol. 9.

—— *Human Nature and Conduct: An Introduction to Social Psychology* [1922], repr. in *MW*, vol. 14.

—— *The Public and Its Problems* [1927], repr. in *LW*, vol. 2, pp. 233–372.

—— *Individualism: Old and New* [1930], repr. in *LW*, vol. 5, pp. 41–123.

—— *A Common Faith* [1934], repr. in *LW*, vol. 9, pp. 1–58.

—— *Liberalism and Social Action* [1935], repr. in *LW*, vol. 11, pp. 1–65.

—— "Creative Democracy – The Task Before Us" [1939], repr. in *LW*, vol. 14, pp. 224–30.

Goodman, Percival, and Paul Goodman, *Communitas: Means of Livelihood and Ways of Life* (New York: Columbia University Press, 1990 [1947]).

James, William, *The Will to Believe and Other Essays in Popular Philosophy*, ed. Frederick H. Burkhardt (Cambridge, MA: Harvard University Press, 1979 [1897]).

Manicas, Peter T., *The Death of the State* (New York: Capricorn, 1974).

McDermott, John J., *Streams of Experience: Reflections on the History and Philosophy of American Culture* (Amherst: University of Massachusetts Press, 1986).

Mead, George Herbert, *Mind, Self and Society from the Standpoint of a Social Behaviorist*, ed. Charles W. Morris (Chicago: University of Chicago Press, 1934).

Pearce, Roy Harvey, ed., *Colonial American Writing*, 2nd edn. (New York: Holt, Rinehart and Winston, 1969).

Royce, Josiah, *The Philosophy of Loyalty* (New York: Macmillan, 1908).

—— *The Problem of Christianity* (Chicago: University of Chicago Press, 1968 [1913]).

—— *War and Insurance* (New York: Macmillan, 1914).

—— *The Hope of the Great Community* (New York: Macmillan, 1916).

Smith, John E., *Royce's Social Infinite: The Community of Interpretation* (New York: Liberal Arts Press, 1950).

—— *America's Philosophical Vision* (Chicago: University of Chicago Press, 1992).

Sullivan, William M., *Reconstructing Public Philosophy* (Berkeley: University of California Press, 1982).

Tinder, Glenn, *Community: Reflections on a Tragic Ideal* (Baton Rouge: Louisiana State University Press, 1980).

Tufts, James Hayden, *The Real Business of Living* (New York: Henry Holt, 1918).

Wilson, Raymond Jackson, *In Quest of Community: Social Philosophy in the United States, 1860–1920* (New York: Wiley, 1968).

Chapter 20

Knowledge and Action: American Epistemology

Scott L. Pratt

In 1917, John Dewey and several of his colleagues published *Creative Intelligence: Essays in the Pragmatic Attitude*, a collaborative volume designed to reconstruct philosophy along new lines. At the heart of the first article, Dewey takes to task the "industry of epistemology" that had come to function as the main business of philosophy.

> The problem of knowledge as conceived in the industry of epistemology is the problem of knowledge in general – of the possibility, extent, and validity of knowledge in general. What does this "in general" mean? In ordinary life there are problems a-plenty of knowledge in particular; every conclusion we try to reach, theoretical or practical, affords such a problem. But there is no problem of knowledge in general.[1]

The work of philosophy had gone wrong because it failed to take seriously the idea that knowledge is not some exclusive relation between a knower and an object of knowledge, but rather a matter of ongoing complex interactions among particular knowers and things. Questions of knowledge, seen from this angle, are bound to distinctive problems, situations, and disciplines. For some recent philosophers, this apparent denunciation of the work of philosophy marked the beginning of an American movement away from the practice of philosophy as an attempt to answer questions and toward philosophy as a kind of critical therapy bent on overthrowing the convictions it had spent centuries establishing.[2] This interpretation of Dewey's position in *Creative Intelligence* was helpful in some quarters, especially among those who found logical positivism and its successor theories of language and knowledge constraining and disconnected from the dominant problems of the age. At the same time, the view of American philosophy as primarily therapeutic in its approach has had the disadvantage of directing attention away from the importance of epistemology in the American tradition. Beginning with the idea that knowledge is a kind of interaction, theories of knowledge have been central in American philosophy as a way to understand the interactions between people and their environments and as a resource with which to imagine and assess future action. Epistemology, from this perspective, can be viewed as one of the central projects of American thought, and the resulting treatments of knowledge can provide key insights into the diverse strands of theory that make up the American philosophical tradition.

In *Creative Intelligence*, Dewey and his colleagues, in fact, do not reject theorizing knowledge, but rather reject a philosophical attitude that had come to dominate American academic philosophy at the turn of the nineteenth century. The contrast, as Dewey puts it, is between a philosophical tradition that tries to understand knowledge in terms of certainty and another tradition that saw knowledge as a methodological matter whose "foundations" are not found in antecedent principles but in the situations in which knowledge is produced. The conflict of attitudes, in a sense, can be seen as a conflict in what one expects to serve as the foundation of knowledge. The dominant philosophical tradition began with the expectation that if there is knowledge, there will be some fixed and unchanging foundation that can guarantee its certainty. The tradition advocated by Dewey begins with the expectation that if there is knowledge, it will be the product of a process of interaction and its "foundations" will be in the situation itself, changing as circumstances change. Certainty, for this tradition, is replaced by what Dewey called "security," and what might now be called "reliability," where claims about the world are produced relative to the resources available, are routinely tested, and are revisable when they are no longer supported by successful use.[3] To borrow William James's famous phrase, knowledge is "what works," where working is not merely a kind of wish fulfillment, but rather is a matter of the interaction of things within a situation, conditioned by interests as well as by material conditions, history, and culture. Certainty marks the expectation that knowledge will "work" regardless of circumstances. Security marks the expectation that knowledge is developed in particular contexts and, while it is likely that it will work in new and similar circumstances, such knowledge is also always open to revision or replacement.

Both the dominant tradition and the American alternative represented in *Creative Intelligence* adopt central expectations for what counts as knowledge and what counts as "real." The tradition that seeks certainty expects "real" things to be independent of particular instances of knowing in order that they can serve as sure foundations for the knowledge that describes them. On this view, human experience at its best is understood as a form of knowledge certain in its relations to the objects that already make up the world. The alternative tradition, represented by Dewey and his colleagues, expects that knowledge and the "real" thing known emerge together in the process of knowing. Dewey's "postulate of immediate empiricism" makes this explicit: "things are what they are experienced as."[4] Contrary to the dominant tradition, knowledge is best understood as a mode of experience where to know something about the world is to know something "real," but not something independent from the complex process of experiencing. The "essences" of things rather than being givens before experience are always a matter of the relations in which they are engaged. As a result, the connection between knowing and being leads to a fundamental ontological pluralism: things are at least as diverse as there are ways of knowing. While the "epistemology industry" began with the expectation that fixed and unchanging "reals" ground knowledge, Dewey and his colleagues were committed to the idea that interactions formed a limited foundation of knowledge and serve as the starting point for new knowledge and new being.

The same attitude that opens the discussion of epistemology with the expectation that knowledge is grounded in interactions will also be an attitude that recognizes continuity between knowledge and action. This does not imply that theories of knowledge committed to an ideal of certainty have no concern with the implications of knowledge for action, but rather that such implications are secondary and by definition separate from the concern about what makes something knowledge. The alternative approach within the American tradition is one which expects that as part of an interaction between knowers and their environments, knowledge is already both a consequence of action and, to the extent it serves to settle problems and dispose knowers toward their environments, also leads to action. Once the process of knowing is located within an environment, it becomes subject to all the interests and desires that characterize human relations with each other and their world and so knowing is recognized as a part of the process of seeking goods and responding to crises. Knowledge engaged from this perspective is no longer "reason" of the sort manufactured by the epistemology industry but "intelligence," reason aware of itself as a process of interaction. In *Creative Intelligence*, Dewey raises this connection between knowledge and action to nearly biblical proportions: "Faith in the power of intelligence to imagine a future which is the projection of the desirable in the present, and to invent instrumentalities of its realization, is our salvation."[5] In effect, by beginning with a commitment to the idea that knowledge is a matter of interaction, knowledge becomes a bridge between human interests and the world that channels and facilitates action even as it provides a route by which the consequences of action return to the knower and lead to new knowledge and future action.

There are two consequences of approaching the American philosophical tradition as one involving an epistemology framed around a principle of interaction. First, questions of knowledge in this tradition can be seen as questions distinct from those raised in the "epistemology industry." As Dewey concludes, the alternative philosophy should not be viewed as "a device for dealing with the problems of philosophers," but rather as "a method, cultivated by philosophers," for responding to the problems of human society.[6] Second, once viewed as a method to deal with the experienced problems of human beings in their environments, it is also possible to see the American philosophical tradition as work done by a much wider range of theorists. When people examine the processes of knowledge and the kinds of interaction that characterize its production, they are not speculating about transcendent categories or inaccessible essences, but rather the ways in which knowledge and objects emerge in human experience. Such questions gain urgency when the investigations respond to the experience that something has gone wrong in the process, where knowledge seems to fail and in so doing undermines the possibility of new experience. If, in the American tradition, theorizing knowledge in response to social crises counts as the practice of philosophy, then the tradition, grounded in the principle of interaction, consists of more than a few professional philosophers. Instead, American philosophy becomes a broad field of thinkers whose work can be seen as a contribution not only to the literature of philosophy but also to the quality and character of human lives. In this brief introduction to epistemology in American philosophy, I will suggest the outlines of this broad tradition as organized over a common commitment to the idea that knowledge is a process of interaction between knowers and their environments.

Eighteenth-Century Beginnings: Cadwallader Colden and Benjamin Franklin

Even before Immanuel Kant published his own critique and response to the philosophical tradition that demanded a real and transcendent world in order to account for knowledge, the American philosopher Cadwallader Colden (1688–1776) both published a series of critiques of the dominant forms of European philosophy and proposed his own alternative. At the heart of his approach is a formulation of the principle of interaction: "We have no knowledge of substances, or of any being, or of any thing, abstracted from the action of that thing or being. All our knowledge of things consists in the perception of the power, or force, or property, or manner of acting of that thing."[7] For Colden, the epistemological principle was to be viewed as the guiding ontological principle as well: "Every thing, that we know, is an agent, or has a power of acting: for as we know nothing of any thing but its action, and the effects of that action, the moment any thing ceases to act it must be annihilated as to us: we can have no kind of idea of its existence."[8] As a critique of European philosophy, Colden anticipated the problems of the empiricism of John Locke that led to the skepticism of David Hume and the phenomenology of Kant. Locke argued that knowledge was dependent upon the ideas of sense caused by independent objects and, while one could not directly access the things in themselves, the process of sensation was reliable enough to supply knowledge of what things really are. Hume recognized the potential for radical doubt in Locke's system by observing that one could never have an impression of causation itself and so ideas of causation were at best the product of constant conjunction of events in a knower's experience. While they may be reliable, they could never be certain. Skepticism about causation necessarily undermines Locke's presumed connection between things in themselves and human knowledge of them. Colden, like Hume, realized this potential for skepticism in empiricism. But unlike Hume, Colden set aside concern about independent being and instead reconstructed the idea of knowledge around a notion of interaction. Here objects of knowledge, like knowers themselves, are agents whose actions are their essences. Skepticism of the Humean sort is unnecessary because sense perception is not the passive reception of impressions but an active engagement, like a dialogue, framed by experiment and the expectation that things to be known are agents in their own right. When Kant attempted to solve the problems generated by Hume, he also proposed a kind of interactive conception of knowledge where the categories of reason interacted through experience with the noumenal world to produce human knowledge. Colden went further, however, and rejected considerations of the noumenal world as irrelevant to both knowledge and being and focused on what happens in the interaction between knowers and their environments. From this perspective, Colden saw knowledge as an ongoing process, subject to changing circumstances and the changing actions of the agents who were part of the process. Colden, like Dewey and his colleagues more than a century later, thus gave up the certainty that Kant sought to preserve, even as he set aside Hume's skepticism.

The practical temper of Colden's work helped set the stage for the work of Benjamin Franklin (1706–90). Although Colden was largely written out of the history of American thought in the wake of the American Revolution – he remained a Loyalist until his death in 1776 – his work was nevertheless well known by most American intellectuals of his day, including Franklin. Although Franklin's senior, Colden apparently recognized Franklin's intelligence and encouraged his interest in scientific inquiry. Not long after they met by chance while traveling, Colden sent Franklin the first edition of his work, *An Explication of the Causes of Action in Matter*, in which he set out an early form of the principle of interaction. Not long afterward, Franklin, who had long had an interest in experimental science inspired in part by Newton's *Optics*, began to do his own experiments on the phenomena of electricity. In the context of this work, Franklin developed a theory of electricity that ended in the principle of interaction. "The electrical matter," Franklin says, "consists of particles extremely subtile," "subtile" enough that electricity's status as matter was unimportant. What was important was what electricity does in the process of being known. It is, he observed, something that permeates "common matter, even the densest metal, with such ease and freedom as not to receive any perceptible resistance." Should anyone doubt the conclusion, or wish to know the action of electricity first hand, "a shock from an electrified large glass jar, taken through his own body, will probably convince him."[9] What something is, for Franklin, is a matter of how it acts and its action is all that can be known. Franklin makes the point explicitly when he discusses the apparent reasons that lightning rods attract lightning. He concludes:

> Nor is it of much Importance, to know the Manner in which Nature executes her Laws; 'tis enough, if we know the Laws themselves. 'Tis of real Use to know, that China left in the Air unsupported, will fall and break; but *how* it comes to fall, and *why* it breaks, are Matters of Speculation. 'Tis a pleasure indeed to know them, but we can preserve our China without it.[10]

Colden and Franklin's focus on processes of interaction as central to knowledge and its implications for action become a starting point for two related American approaches to questions of knowledge. For one, the application of the principle of interaction to scientific inquiry set a direction for the American scientific community whose work came to be centered on the need for practical knowledge.[11] This was not the view that science was only to be understood as a kind of practical problem-solving, but rather the idea that science would begin and end in the interactions between human beings and their world. When scientific inquiry yielded repeatable results, they became a resource for solving other problems and for making new opportunities. The principles of electricity, for example, were not sought in order to solve the problem of house fires caused by lightning strikes; rather, the principles gained in investigation of the environment inhabited by human beings led to conclusions that could help solve a serious problem of human existence in that environment. In this case, the principle of interaction does not limit knowledge to things immediately useful, but begins with the idea that knowledge is grounded in processes of interaction. The view that Franklin applied to science applied also to his wider conception of human society. What matters in human society, at least as it was developing in the Americas, was not one's rank, what one "was," but how one acted in the context of their community. As he put it in a letter of advice to European immigrants planning to cross the Atlantic, America is a place "where people do not enquire concerning a Stranger, *What is he?* But *What can he do?*"[12]

The second strand of epistemology that emerged from the emphasis on interaction took up knowledge in the context of culture. At work already in the background of Colden and Franklin's work was the recognition that American society was growing in a context of a rich cultural pluralism. Both Colden and Franklin recognized an extreme form of this pluralism in their work mediating conflicts across the border between Native and European America. Colden's earliest career was as a surveyor for the Royal Province of New York, in which capacity he spent months at a time along the provincial border with the Haudenosaunee (Iroquois Confederacy). In the course of his work, the Mohawk people adopted him and later, during his long term as Lieutenant Governor of New York, he continued to serve as an advocate for Native people in their relations with the British government. The principle of interaction itself as it emerges in Colden's time may in part have been a product of his work with the Haudenosaunee. In an environment where communication was limited by language and culture differences, the Haudenosaunee developed a process of diplomacy that was framed by formal interaction and reliance on the actions of those involved in negotiations. Along the border, one is understood by what one does.[13] The approach to diplomacy was an application of a pervasive approach to knowledge and ontology in Haudenosaunee culture. Here, both knowledge and being were dependent upon processes of self-expression and the concept of "*orenda*," sometimes translated as "power" and sometimes as "song" or "voice."[14] Like Colden's principle of interaction, the concept of *orenda* recognized objects as agents and their interactions as the means by which they are and are known. When Colden began his scientific and philosophical work in the 1740s, it was in the wake of his significant experience with the Haudenosaunee and the publication of his first major work, *A History of the Five Nations* (1727), the first English-language history of the Iroquois Confederacy. Even here, in this early work, Colden notices the role of interaction in a way that anticipates Franklin's advice to prospective immigrants: "Their Leaders and Captains . . . obtain their Authority, by the general Opinion of their Courage and Conduct, and lose it by a failure in those Virtues."[15] Authority is not a matter of who one is, but what one does.

Franklin likewise participated in negotiations along the border between the Pennsylvania and the Delaware and Haudenosaunee peoples. In addition to serving as a representative in several diplomatic negotiations, Franklin wrote a number of important essays on Native culture and Native/European relations. At work in the practical experience of both Colden and Franklin was the idea that knowledge across sharp differences could best be understood in the interactions themselves. When Franklin began his work as a founder of the European American republic in North America, it was in the wake of his work with Native people as a diplomat and his impassioned defense of Native rights after the massacre of a Native community at Lancaster in 1763.[16] When Franklin finally came to write about the need to establish a new society in America, it was in a way that sought to preserve the differences of state and culture, while emphasizing the possibility of unity through shared actions. Here the principle of interaction provided a way to take up questions of knowledge in the context of interaction between diverse peoples that affirmed their differences and also directed attention to what was shared: interactions framed by political borders, different material cultures, and common interests. For Franklin, the flourishing of a unified American society turned on the interactions among "real" differences.

Transcendentalism: Ralph Waldo Emerson and Lydia Maria Child

The transcendental philosophers who followed Colden and Franklin at the beginning of the nineteenth century at times seem to give up the earlier interest in interaction in favor of a view of knowledge and meaning that is understood in terms of unity and transcendence. Ralph Waldo Emerson (1803–82), the recognized leader of the movement, observed: "Intellect separates the fact considered from you, from all local and personal reference, and discerns it as if it existed for its own sake."[17] At the same time, the principle of interaction remains central to the possibility of this "transcendent" point of view. "Everything real is self-existent," but even so, he continues, "As I am, so shall I associate, and so shall I act; Caesar's history will paint Caesar. Jesus acted so, because he thought so."[18] In his call for a distinctively American literature and philosophy, Emerson explicitly binds thought and action together in the claim that it is only through one's actions in relation to one's context, one's society and environment, that they will become fully themselves. "Character is higher than intellect. This is the function. Living is the functionary."[19] Rather than seeking self in some unity outside experience, selves come to be in action guided by the knowledge that emerges within experience.

While Emerson's work provides a well-recognized starting point for American philosophy, perhaps more important for its development was the work of Lydia Maria Child (1802–80). Child, often mentioned among the earliest members of the transcendental movement, was born in 1802 and grew up along the border between the small European settlements of the new state of Maine and the well-established territories of the Abenaki and Penobscot nations. Although she received little more than a year of formal schooling, she read widely and in 1824 published her first novel, *Hobomok*, a historical novel about a young English settler, Mary Conant. At the center of the story is the tension between English and Native American culture and the ways in which the futures of both peoples depended upon the ways in which cross-cultural interaction was carried out. For Child, the knowledge relevant to sustaining communities in a culturally plural context is first a matter of particular interactions. Here, no general principles will do, only those that are concretely responsive to circumstances as they develop. In a collection of essays published in 1845, *Letters from New York*, Child presents this conception of knowing through metaphors of place: "I always see much," she says, "*within* a landscape."[20] Knowledge, what she finds within a landscape, can promote further interaction as it engages shared interests that emerge within the situation even as such knowledge always remains bound to particular perspectives defined by cultural traditions, language, religion, and gender. Like Colden and Franklin, Child affirms the centrality of interaction for the process of knowing and she indirectly acknowledges her relation to the tradition in a letter on "animal magnetism" that examines the character of interactions between living organisms. She observes: "The most learned have no knowledge what electricity *is*; they can only tell *what* it does, not *how* it does it."[21] The principle of interaction applies to broader issues of knowing as well. "Assuredly, we are all, in some degree, the creatures of outward circumstance; but this in nowise disturbs the scale of moral responsibility, or prevents equality of happiness." What we do, she concludes, is what matters: "Our responsibility consists in the *use* we make of our possessions, not on their *extent*. Salvation comes to all through obedience to the light they have, be it much or little."[22] The resulting differences, generated by the particularities of circumstance, lead to a kind of irreducible pluralism of knowledge. "Words being of truth, are divided into many dialects, and nations cannot understand each other's speech; and so it is with the opinions and doctrines of mankind." Unity, or at least the potential for shared action, emerges in interaction among different peoples and places. "But the affections are everywhere the same; and music, being their voice, is a universal medium between human hearts."[23] It is in the context of associated action, where affections are generated, that shared understanding emerges and new possibilities develop. Writing about the contact between Native and

European American differences, Child observes both the consequences and value of difference: "The *same* influences cannot be brought to bear upon them; for *their* Past is not *our* Past; and of course never can be. But let ours mingle with theirs, and you will find the result variety, without inferiority. They will be flutes on different notes, and so harmonize the better."[24]

Child's work, though rarely viewed as part of the American philosophical tradition, nevertheless provided resources for at least two other more practical political movements in the middle and late nineteenth century: abolitionism and feminism. Child's focus on interaction and its basic presumption of pluralism provided an excellent ground for an argument against slavery. Even as slavery was justified by the belief that African people were necessarily inferior to Europeans, the principle of interaction demanded that consideration focus on how people emerged in action. When taken up from this perspective, it becomes clear that there are no grounds for the claim that Africans are inferior, but rather that they are as capable as whites when given the opportunity. In this light, African peoples are not a separate "species," as some argued, but are at once part of humanity and a distinctive group characterized by history, morphology, and circumstance. Child makes this case in detail in her 1833 treatise, *An Appeal on Behalf of that Class of Americans Called Africans.* While Child's argument was well received by many abolitionists, its consequences for the world after slavery were less acceptable. For most abolitionists the end of slavery would mark the beginning of a process of assimilation in which people marked as different by skin and culture would vanish into a single nation of Americans. Child's approach to the question based on the principle of interaction rejected this future. Even as interaction undermined the idea of essential inferiority, it also sustained the idea that deep differences in knowledge and culture were likely and beneficial. In simplest terms, interaction, the source of knowledge and the direction for new action, involves a fundamentally diverse world of agents to participate in the process. To eliminate diversity would militate against the possibility of new knowledge and action. Rather than undermining differences, American society after slavery should be one in which differences flourish but where prejudice, the expectation of necessary superiority and inferiority, is eliminated.[25]

Child applied a similar analysis to the status of Native Americans, siding with Native leaders such as Sagoyewatha (Red Jacket) and John Ross in their calls to preserve traditional Native lands and national autonomy. Similarly, in her discussions of the status of women, Child argued against the developing suffrage movement and its claim for the sameness of men and women, and argued that circumstances made for differences, including differences of knowledge, but not differences of value. At each stage of the development of her treatment of knowledge as interaction, Child also presented a methodology for engaging interactions in a way that could show how particular knowledge emerged from problematic situations. The resulting narrative approach provided a new strategy for others in North America who sought to undermine the established philosophical quests for certainty. Later writers, including Louisa May Alcott (1832–88), Charlotte Perkins

Gilman (1860–1935), Anna Julia Cooper (1858–1964), and Jane Addams (1860–1935), all reflect a conception of knowledge committed to the principle of interaction and framed by a narrative strategy like Child's that is grounded in concrete situations or places.

The Rise of Pragmatism: Peirce, James, and Dewey

When Darwin's theory of evolution broke into the intellectual life of North America in 1859, it reached a philosophical tradition already disposed to take seriously the interactions of organisms and environments and the expectation that interactions will result in change. As Dewey noted years later, the impact of Darwin was to provide both empirical grounds for rejecting the idea of fixed essences and a conceptual scheme for understanding change. At Harvard in the years following the Civil War, a number of young philosophers met together as the now famous "Metaphysical Club," which provided a forum for discussing philosophical questions and the implications of evolution for the perspectives of European philosophy.[26] Among the participants were C. S. Peirce (1839–1914) and William James (1842–1910). Both men (and most of the other members of the group) were well grounded in the American philosophical tradition as it had developed. Peirce's father, Benjamin, was a renowned mathematician and an associate of the leaders of the transcendental movement. James's father, Henry James, Sr., was among the leading theorists of transcendentalism and the younger James knew most of the principals in the movement, including Emerson, Bronson Alcott (Louisa May Alcott's father), and probably Lydia Maria Child. In an important way, the longstanding commitments to the principle of interaction in epistemology and ontology were already present when the Metaphysical Club met to discuss Darwin.

It is not surprising that in the years following the Harvard discussions, Peirce published two papers explicitly establishing a version of the principle of interaction as what came to be called "the pragmatic maxim." Recalling Colden's principle, Peirce proposed that knowledge of a thing amounts to a conception of what it will do: "Consider what effects, which might conceivably have practical bearings, we conceive of the object of our conception to have. Then, our conception of these effects is the whole of our conception of the object."[27] Interaction, again, forms the starting point for knowledge and, as in Colden's case, Peirce also binds truth and reality to the process that begins in inquiry framed by the pragmatic maxim. "The opinion which is fated to be ultimately agreed to by all who investigate, is what we mean by the truth, and the object represented in this opinion is the real."[28] In 1898, William James identified Peirce's principle as the key to a philosophical method that could dissolve the problems of abstract philosophy and direct human attention to the problems of life. In light of the pragmatic maxim, "the whole function of philosophy ought to be to find out what definite difference [a claim] will make to you and me, at definite instants of our life, if this world-formula or that world-formula be the one which is true."[29]

When Dewey came to adopt pragmatism as the name for his work, he did so as already committed to the importance of interaction. While Peirce framed one version of interaction in his response to evolution and James used the principle as a conceptual framework for both his philosophical method and his theory of consciousness, Dewey reconstructed the principle as the key component in his own theory of knowledge, the theory of inquiry. For Dewey, the process of knowing begins in the interaction between organism and environment as the quality of the interaction changes from stable and secure to unstable and indeterminate in its outcomes. Organisms respond to such instability with efforts to change the circumstances enough to reestablish the quality of security in their interaction. Dewey makes explicit the implication of the principle of interaction as it reconstitutes the process of knowing as a response to the problems people actually experience: "The function of reflective thought is, therefore, to transform a situation in which there is experienced obscurity, doubt, conflict, disturbance of some sort, into a situation that is clear, coherent, settled and harmonious."[30] Human beings interact with an environment both biologically and in ways framed by the developments of culture, including the presence of meaningful symbols. With the addition of language to the process, the response to indeterminate situations becomes one of inquiry, using language as a way to frame and experiment within the situation in search of alternative ways of restoring security. Interaction here becomes intimately bound up with language and the possibility of engaging things as objects that are related to a constellation of other things through meaning. The theory of inquiry provides a way to understand the ways in which meaning emerges in language and the ways in which inquirers can structure their engagements with indeterminate situations, but it does so by preserving the basic commitment to the idea that the knowledge produced through inquiry is nevertheless the product of interaction.

Interaction in Practice: Jane Addams and W. E. B. Du Bois

Pragmatism's development in the early twentieth century became widely influential in the field of philosophy, but formal discussions were, in a sense, a minor part of the tradition's impact on society. Even as Peirce, James, and Dewey brought the principle of interaction into systematic discussion, people such as Jane Addams (1860–1935) and W. E. B. Du Bois (1868–1963) recast the principle in terms more akin to those of Child's concrete responses to the social crises of the years before the Civil War. Addams, best known for her social work at Hull House in Chicago, developed a distinctive conception of knowledge in her attempts to respond to the landscape of economic oppression, immigration, racism, and sexism that characterized the experience of many in American cities at the turn of the nineteenth century. Influenced by the Social Gospel Movement and the work of the European settlement movement inspired by Arnold Toynbee and Leo Tolstoy, and by the work of American women writers, including Child, Harriet Beecher Stowe, Louisa May Alcott, and others, Addams adopted a philosophical approach parallel to that of James and Dewey.[31] Just as Child had framed her conception of knowledge within narrative structures bounded by place, Addams began with a kind of "domestic analysis," which examined social crises in terms relative to those affected. For Addams, response to social problems could only be successful when based on knowledge of the circumstances. Such knowledge could not be acquired from outside the situation, but could be developed from within from the perspective of those most affected and most harmed. Such knowledge would not take the form of truths that could stand independent of their context and so needed to be engaged in a way that preserved their connections to the context from which they emerged. The result was that Addams used a kind of narrative investigation that engaged the circumstances and sought resources to address the problems by talking to the people of the immigrant communities that surrounded Hull House and by representing their accounts in ways that could direct transformation of the situation.

Behind Addams's discussions in her works on social change, including *Ethics and Social Democracy* (1907) and *Newer Ideals of Peace* (1911), her theory of knowledge was based on the expectation that while interactions produce knowledge, the knowledge needed for social reform demands a particular process of interaction: memory. In her study, *The Long Road of Woman's Memory*, Addams argues that memory has two functions, "first, its important role in interpreting and appeasing life for the individual, and second its activity as a selective agency in social reorganization."[32] Knowledge in the form of memory gains its force, its ability to affect circumstances, in its ability to reconstruct the past. Because knowledge and ontology are bound together through the principle of interaction, memory is not a matter of claims standing in relation to antecedent facts or objects, but, rather, memory begins from present interaction and traces out ways to understand how things came to be, what opportunities were taken and missed, and what possibilities remain. Rather than reinforcing an oppressive circumstance, memory has the function of finding power in the past which can be brought to bear on present circumstances in order to transform them – what Addams calls "the sifting and reconciling power inherent in Memory itself."[33] For Addams, such a reconstructive power is not independent of knowers, but is part of how people interact with their environments conditioned by histories, material circumstances, and their own bodies. Memory understood in this way is not a universal process equally accessible to all, but rather a process activated and cultivated by those most disempowered. After recounting the narrative of one of the women who visited Hull House, Addams makes the importance of embodied and situated interaction clear: "The experience of my friend bore testimony that in spite of all their difficulties and handicaps, something of social value is forced out of the very situation itself among that vast multitude of women whose oppression through the centuries has typified a sense of helpless and intolerable wrongs."[34] Social transformation depends upon the possibility of "something of social value," the memory of those whose experience is of a society that is constantly unstable and perilous. While Peirce, James, and Dewey give voice to a theoretical epistemology, Addams gives the same principles a practical shape in the lives of women in the slums of Chicago.

Du Bois, a student of James's, who began his work informed by the theorists of abolition and reconstruction whose work in part emerged from the traditions of Child, Franklin, and Colden, began, as did Addams, with the idea that epistemology was a radical business. As Addams's conception of situated knowledge was the key to power and social transformation for women, Du Bois saw embodied knowledge as the ground for the double purpose of achieving racial equality and maintaining cultural difference. In *The Souls of Black Folk*, Du Bois sets out the fundamental tension of the color line in America, not as a matter of racial essences but as a complex product of historical prejudice, morphological differences, and concrete action. As he puts it in his autobiography, *Dusk of Dawn*, in the end, "the black man is a person who must ride 'Jim Crow' in Georgia."[35] At the same time, even as interaction produced the color line, it is also a source of distinctive knowledge that can serve as a resource for transforming society. "We [African Americans] have the chance here to teach industrial and cultural democracy to a world that bitterly needs it."[36] In his 1920 collection of essays, *Darkwater*, Du Bois provides a sustained examination of the nature and application of knowledge in a racialized world. He begins his essay, "The Souls of White Folk," with an assessment of the epistemological position in which he finds himself. "Of [white folk] I am singularly clairvoyant. I see in and through them. I view them from unusual points of vantage. Not as a foreigner do I come, for I am native, not foreign, bone of their thought and flesh of their language."[37] Such knowledge, like that of the women of Hull House, is not a product of a transcendent viewpoint nor an independent set of facts, but emerges with the reality of race and oppression in North America. As such, it both marks a perilous situation and the possibility of its transformation. Later in the volume, he applies his racialized theory of knowledge to an analysis of democracy. What prevents democracy is the disenfranchisement of people based on the practices, policies, and expectations of the society that marks some as worthy of exclusion. In order to correct the problems of exclusion, however, it is not enough simply to declare that the excluded part of the whole requires the fully established practices of democracy. "Democracy alone," he says, "is the method of showing the whole experience of the race for the benefit of the future and if democracy tries to exclude women or Negroes or the poor or any class because of innate characteristics which do not interfere with intelligence, then that democracy cripples itself and belies its name."[38] Just as Addams argues for the importance of women's knowledge, Du Bois argues for the power of racial knowledge, the knowledge that comes from economic exclusion, and the knowledge of the oppression endured by women of color. The transformations that would follow the freeing of racial knowledge would not, however, lead directly to the end of racial or cultural difference. On the contrary, a truly democratic society will be marked by the flourishing of diverse groups and their interaction. Here, the past, and the distinctive places, practices, characters, interests, and knowledges born of the struggle, will serve as a constant source of strength to sustain and renew the character of the society as a whole.

The Challenge of Logical Positivism: Quine and Contemporary Voices

American epistemology of the first third of the twentieth century was soon called into question by new work closely related to the tradition Dewey criticized in *Creative Intelligence.* In particular, the rise of logical positivism brought a new temper to American philosophical discourse. Interaction-framed theories of knowledge reached an apex in the 1930s with the publication of Dewey's *Logic: The Theory of Inquiry* (1938), but the work did not find a wide audience, in part because it focused on a reconstruction of Aristotelian logic without attending to developments in modern symbolic logic. The new empiricisms of Bertrand Russell, Ludwig Wittgenstein, and A. J. Ayer once again approached knowledge as dependent upon independent facts and systems of truth-preserving logical rules.[39] The approach provided a philosophical viewpoint especially well connected to the interests of those who wanted to apply the methods of science to other disciplines using formal systems of mathematics and logical inference. At first viewed as allies of those schooled in the American tradition, the logical positivists soon became the dominant voice in American academic philosophy, sustained in part by the promise of a philosophical system that could restore certainty to knowledge.[40]

At the heart of the empiricist project was a commitment to the neo-Kantian distinction between analytic and synthetic statements. The former are statements that are true independent of any particular facts and the latter are those grounded in matters of fact. Implicit in both is the further claim that no statement can stand alone, but, as knowledge, must be reducible to terms that refer to "immediate experience." Synthetic statements guaranteed by experienced facts could be joined with other such true statements in a comprehensive system of knowledge held together by the necessarily true relations implied by analytic statements. The resulting approach appeared to make it possible to answer questions of knowledge "in general" even as it identified the means of guaranteeing certainty. In this context, W. V. O. Quine (1908–2000), a student of Alfred North Whitehead at Harvard, challenged the new empiricisms by arguing that their foundations could not hold.

In his well-known 1952 paper, "The Two Dogmas of Empiricism," Quine argued that it is not possible to make a clear distinction between analytic and synthetic statements since their meanings are always relative to a particular language. As a result, the meaning of an analytic statement depends upon synthetic statements about the particular language just as synthetic statements depend upon analytic statements of true relations within the language used. From this perspective no purely analytic or synthetic statements are possible. Further, since statements cannot be reduced to these categories and so are isolated from the larger system of a language, the claim that all statements can be reduced to terms that refer to immediate experience must also fail. The problem, he argued, was that the empiricists had come to focus on the meanings of statements when they should have focused on systems of language and associated practices that are grounded in broad shared experience. "The unit of empirical significance," he concluded, "is the whole of science."[41] Like the pragmatists before him, Quine came to believe that knowledge does not begin with the grasp of independent facts or states of affairs, but in an interaction already conditioned by a structure of beliefs and practices.[42] Here things are what they are in the interaction that leads to knowledge. Ontology then becomes a matter of how things are encountered within the system of the beliefs and practices that frame the process of knowing. As such, there is no fixed ontology, only conceptions of what things are as they have emerged in practice. When alternative ontologies appear, it is not a matter of finding out which is "better" relative to "the objects themselves," but rather which is better relative to the conceptual schemes available. The principle of interaction, now formalized within a conception of science, marks the point of contact between the results of past investigation and the presence of a changing world of experience.[43]

By recalling the principle of interaction as a starting point for theories of knowledge, Quine's work became fertile ground for a number of new approaches to knowledge that are related by degrees to the philosophical tradition that began with Cadwallader Colden in the eighteenth century. Richard Rorty, for example, using Quine's critiques as a beginning, offers his own systematic critique of the tradition challenged by Dewey. *Philosophy and the Mirror of Nature* (1979) draws together a version of Dewey's conception of knowledge and the critical philosophies of Wittgenstein's later work and of Martin Heidegger to attack the idea that philosophy is a form of knowledge at all. Instead, he argues, philosophy is best seen as a process of critical engagement that can "keep the conversation going."[44]

Feminist philosopher Lynn Hankinson Nelson focuses on Quine's holism and its implications for knowing as the work of an "epistemological community." Such communities are not narrow, independent disciplines that stand apart from wider concerns, but rather are necessarily interconnected and as such both constrain transformative work on behalf of women and make it possible. Using Quine's holistic approach to meaning and the resulting focus on systems of knowledge ("webs of belief," as he calls them), Nelson recalls the epistemology of Addams whose conception of memory connects social reorganization to the resources of the established community and, through the vital perspective of women, to social needs and new possibilities.[45]

Cornel West has similarly acknowledged Quine's importance in clearing the way for a resurgence of the American philosophical tradition, but, unlike Nelson, West explicitly calls on Du Bois and Dewey as the starting point for the constructive aspect of his work.[46] West illustrates his connections with the American philosophical tradition in the epigrams that introduce his first book, *Prophesy*

Deliverance! The first, from Dewey's essay in *Creative Intelligence*, recalls the centrality of the principle of interaction to philosophy. "I believe that philosophy in America will be lost," Dewey declares, ". . . unless it can somehow bring to consciousness America's own needs and its own implicit principle of successful action." The quotation from Dewey is paired with a second quotation from Ralph Ellison's *Invisible Man*: "We create a race by creating ourselves and then to our great astonishment we will have created something far more important: We will have created a culture."[47] Together, the two statements reassert the possibility of real change in the world as a matter of interaction, framed by circumstances but bound to a vision of social reconstruction. West calls his version of this tradition "Prophetic Pragmatism."[48] Like Rorty's therapeutic philosophy, prophetic pragmatism stands as a critical methodology undermining the philosophical attitude committed to the idea of certainty and its attendant exclusions. It is also an epistemological philosophy, theorizing the kinds of knowledge that play a role in transformation. The African American tradition in particular brings a way of knowing that stands outside and in tension with the dominant approach and so provides hope for change. Prophetic pragmatism is also an activist philosophy, like those of Addams and Du Bois, that identifies problems and provides means for recognizing and responding to circumstances through the knowledge of those most harmed.

Framed in terms of the principle of interaction, epistemology in American philosophy becomes a crucial part of a wider effort to respond to the problems and possibilities of American society. The resulting view of the American tradition both dramatically expands what counts as philosophy and broadens the range of resources available for new philosophical projects. By recovering the history of American philosophy in this way, the landscape of American thought is also transformed, so that, like the landscape itself, it can begin to display its richness and its potential for sustaining a diverse and flourishing society in the twenty-first century.

Notes

1 John Dewey, "The Need for a Recovery of Philosophy" (1917), repr. in *The Middle Works, 1899–1924* (hereafter *MW*), ed. Jo Ann Boydston, vol. 10 (Carbondale: Southern Illinois University Press, 1980), p. 23.

2 See for example Richard Rorty, *Consequences of Pragmatism* (Minneapolis: University of Minnesota Press, 1982).

3 See John Dewey, *The Quest for Certainty* (1929), repr. in *The Later Works, 1925–1953* (hereafter *LW*), ed. Jo Ann Boydston, vol. 4 (Carbondale: Southern Illinois University Press, 1984), ch. 1.

4 John Dewey, "The Postulate of Immediate Experience" (1905), repr. in *MW*, vol. 3 (Carbondale: Southern Illinois University Press, 1977), p. 162.

5 Dewey, "The Need for a Recovery," p. 48.

6 Ibid, p. 46.

7 In Paul Russell Anderson and Max Harold Fisch, eds., *Philosophy in America* (New York: D. Appleton-Century Company, 1939), p. 102.

8 Ibid.

9 *The Writings of Benjamin Franklin*, vol. 2 (1907), collected and ed. Albert Henry Smyth (New York: Haskell House Publishers, Ltd., 1970), p. 427.

10 Ibid., pp. 434–5.

11 See I. Bernard Cohen, *Benjamin Franklin's Science* (Cambridge, MA: Harvard University Press, 1990).

12 *The Writings of Benjamin Franklin*. vol. 8, p. 606. See also James Campbell, *Recovering Benjamin Franklin: An Exploration of a Life of Science and Service* (Chicago: Open Court, 1999).

13 See Francis Jennings, William N. Fenton, Mary A. Druke, and David R. Miller, eds., *The History and Culture of Iroquois Diplomacy* (Syracuse, NY: Syracuse University Press, 1985).

14 See J. N. B. Hewitt, "Orenda and a Definition of Religion," *American Anthropologist*, 4 (1902): 33–46, and Scott L. Pratt, "Ceremony and Rationality in the Haudenosaunee Tradition," in Cynthia Willett, ed., *Theorizing Multiculturalism: A Guide to the Current Debate* (Oxford: Blackwell Publishing, 1998), pp. 401–21.

15 Cadwallader Colden, *History of the Five Indian Nations* (New York: Allerton Book Co., 1922), vol. I.

16 See "A Narrative of the Late Massacres in Lancaster County," in *The Writings of Benjamin Franklin*, vol. 4, pp. 289–314.

17 Ralph Waldo Emerson, *The Works of Ralph Waldo Emerson* (Boston: Houghton, Mifflin, 1883), vol. 2, p. 304.

18 Ibid., p. 316.

19 Ibid., vol. 1, p. 99.

20 Lydia Maria Child, *Letters from New York*, ed. Bruce Mills (Athens and London: The University of Georgia Press, 1998), p. 16.

21 Ibid., p. 159.

22 Ibid., p. 160.

23 Lydia Maria Child, *Letters from New York*, 2nd series (New York: C. S. Francis & Co., 1845), p. 115.

24 Child, *Letters from New York*, ed. Bruce Mills, p. 163.

25 See ibid.

26 See Philip P. Wiener, *Evolution and the Founders of Pragmatism* (Cambridge, MA: Harvard University Press, 1949) and Bruce Kuklick, *The Rise of American Philosophy* (New Haven, CT: Yale University Press, 1977).

27 Charles Sanders Peirce, *The Essential Peirce*, vol. 1, ed. Nathan Houser and Christian Kloesel (Bloomington and Indianapolis: Indiana University Press, 1992), p. 132.

28 Ibid., p. 139.

29 William James, *Writings, 1878–1899* (New York: Library of America, 1992), p. 1081.

30 John Dewey, *How We Think* (1933), repr. in *LW*, vol. 8 (1986), p. 195.

31 See Jane Addams, *Twenty Years at Hull House* (New York: Signet Classic, 1981).

32 Jane Addams, *Long Road of Woman's Memory* (New York: Henry Holt, 1916), p. xiii.

33 Ibid., p. 23.

34 Ibid., p. 112.

35 W. E. B. Du Bois, *Writings* (New York: Library of America, 1986), p. 666.

36 Ibid., pp. 714–15.

37 W. E. B. Du Bois, *Darkwater* (Mineola, NY: Dover Publications, 1999), p. 17.

38 Ibid., p. 84.

39 See Bertrand Russell, *Logic and Knowledge* (London: Unwin Hyman, 1956); Ludwig Wittgenstein, *Wittgenstein's Tractatus*, tr. Daniel Kolak (Mountain View, CA: Mayfield Publishing, 1998); and A. J. Ayer, *Language, Truth and Logic* (New York: Dover Publications, 1952).

40 Ronald N. Giere, "From Wissenschaftliche Philosophie to Philosophy of Science," in *Minnesota Studies in the Philosophy of Science*, XVI (Minneapolis: University of Minnesota Press, 1996).

41 W. V. O. Quine, *From a Logical Point of View* (Cambridge, MA: Harvard University Press, 1980), p. 42.

42 See "Epistemology Naturalized," in W. V. O. Quine, *Ontological Relativity and Other Essays* (New York: Columbia University Press, 1969).

43 See Quine, "On What There Is," in *From a Logical Point of View*, and "Ontological Relativity," in *Ontological Relativity and Other Essays.*

44 Richard Rorty, *Philosophy and the Mirror of Nature* (Princeton, NJ: Princeton University Press, 1979), p. 377. See also his *Contingency, Irony, and Solidarity* (Cambridge: Cambridge University Press, 1989).

45 See Lynn Hankinson Nelson, *Who Knows? From Quine to a Feminist Empiricism* (Philadelphia: Temple University Press, 1990).

46 See Cornel West, *Keeping Faith* (New York: Routledge, 1993), pp. 125ff.

47 In Cornel West, *Prophesy Deliverance!* (Philadelphia: Westminster Press, 1982), p. 13.

48 See West, *The American Evasion of Philosophy* (Madison: University of Wisconsin Press, 1989), ch. 6.

Suggested reading

Addams, Jane, *The Long Road of Woman's Memory* (New York: Macmillan, 1916).

Child, Lydia Maria, *Letters from New York*, 2nd series, letters XII and XIII (New York: C. S. Francis & Co., 1845).

Colden, Cadwallader, "The Principles of Action in Matter," in Paul Russell Anderson and Max Harold Fisch, eds., *Philosophy in America* (New York: D. Appleton-Century Company, 1939).

Dewey, John, "The Need for a Recovery of Philosophy," in *Creative Intelligence: Essays in the Pragmatic Attitude* (New York: Henry Holt, 1917).

—— *The Quest for Certainty*, chs. 9 and 10, repr. in *The Later Works, 1925–1953*, ed. Jo Ann Boydston, vol. 4 (Carbondale: Southern Illinois University Press, 1984).

Du Bois, W. E. B., *Darkwater* (Mineola, NY: Dover Publications, 1999).

Emerson, Ralph Waldo, "Intellect," in *Essays*, 1st series (Boston: Houghton Mifflin & Company, 1883).

Franklin, Benjamin, "Opinions and Conjectures, concerning the Properties and Effects of the Electrical Matter, arising from Experiments and Observations, made at Philadelphia, 1749," in *The Writings of Benjamin Franklin*, vol. 2, ed. Albert Henry Smyth (New York: Haskell House Publishers, Ltd., 1970).

James, William, "Philosophical Conceptions and Practical Results," in *Writings, 1878–1899* (New York: Library of America, 1992).

Nelson, Lynn Hankinson, *Who Knows? From Quine to a Feminist Empiricism* (Philadelphia: Temple University Press, 1990).

Peirce, Charles Sanders, "The Fixation of Belief and How to Make Our Ideas Clear," in Nathan Houser and Christian Kloesel, eds., *The Essential Peirce*, vol. 1 (Bloomington and Indianapolis: Indiana University Press, 1992).

Quine, Willard V. O., "Ontological Relativity and Epistemology Naturalized," in *Ontological Relativism and Other Essays* (New York: Columbia University Press, 1969).

Rorty, Richard, *Philosophy and the Mirror of Nature* (Princeton, NJ: Princeton University Press, 1979).

West, Cornel, *The American Evasion of Philosophy* (Madison: University of Wisconsin Press, 1989).

Chapter 21

Religion

William D. Dean

If in philosophy there is an "American grain," its center is, in part, religious. Religious thought has germinated much that is indigenous to American philosophy and much that differentiates that philosophy from, for example, most European philosophy.

That center matured between the early 1870s and the mid-1930s – from one of Charles Sanders Peirce's presentations to The Metaphysical Club in Cambridge, Massachusetts to John Dewey's Terry Lectures at Yale, issuing in *A Common Faith*. Just as the original genius of a theoretical physicist often ripens early in his or her career, so the genius of America's religious thought ripened during the relatively young and "classical" period in the career of American philosophy.

Of course, just as no theoretical physicist can mature without scientific education, America's religious thought could not have matured if it had not had something to build on. In the eighteenth century Jonathan Edwards had introduced a new, empirical interpretation of religious experience and Benjamin Franklin virtually reinforced the new, American pragmatic and inventive style of thinking, even about religion. Such thinkers, in turn, depended on a relatively common and distinctively American religious attitude. And this attitude, in turn, flowed from two influences important in the American experience: (1) the mix of environmental and historical factors that composed the American circumstance; and (2) biblical religious traditions proliferated for centuries by church organs – publishing organs, vocal organs, and brass organs. Like future physicists lying on hillsides gazing at the stars, America's future religious thinkers sat on church pews and studied in church-founded colleges. However, by the middle and late twentieth century, most American philosophers, theologians, and religious thinkers were ignoring the American tradition of religious thought.

Commenting on the predicament of American theology, which is much like that of American philosophy of religion, historical theologian Joseph Haroutunian once said:

> It is doubtful that there is a prospect for American theology at all without a new knowledge of the history of theology in this country. America may not have produced an Augustine or a Schleiermacher, but its hope of producing theologians who shall do more than live off the European mind has little chance of being realized unless the history of theology in America is studied, not as a tributary of European theology, but, for all its derivative character, as an expression of American experience.[1]

In this chapter, I will take Haroutunian's point and apply it to American religious thought, the philosophy of religion in particular. I will begin by commenting on qualities of American experience that seem to have stimulated classical American philosophy and religious thought, and then will turn to the classical American philosophers. In this brief sketch, I have omitted much, particularly the peculiarly Calvinistic tone of American religious thought, properly emphasized by Bruce Kuklick in *Churchmen and Philosophers*, and the traditionalism of the newly important Society of Christian Philosophers.

Religious Thought as American

To root American religious thought in the American experience can appear wrong, for the very idea of "the American experience" seems to be precluded by America's unparalleled ethnic diversity and cultural plurality. How could Americans carry in their very different heads any semblance of a common structure of experience? Further, it can be said that American thought cannot be distinctive, when (except for Native American thought) it depends so heavily on non-American thought, especially on Western European thought.

However, without denying the validity of these objections, it can be argued that American commonality and distinctiveness are like spices in a stew, flavoring but not replacing the plurality and provenance of the ingredients. American commonality derives in part from American diversity, which exceeds that of any nation in history. Unexpectedly, diversity is more a foundation on which the American consensus rests than an obstacle to its realization. If Americans had not been so different in religion, class, and national origin, those who interpreted the Declaration of Independence and the Constitution would not have required themselves to honor that difference so vigorously by offering specifically American guarantees of freedom and equality. These guarantees were only extended when the Immigration Act of 1965 officially welcomed non-Europeans as it once had welcomed Europeans, and the civil rights and feminist movements lifted people of color and women to candidacy for equal treatment as the earlier guarantees had once lifted white males to that same candidacy. Thus, American commonality is built on, not precluded by, differences in genes and geographical origins. Multiculturalism, properly understood, is an argument for rather than against a common American culture.

But this is only half the story. Plurality and diversity are themselves products of a fact even more elementary than American identity: immigration. All Americans have recently come from somewhere else – even the Native Americans, who were brutally uprooted from their own lands and cultures and forced to immigrate into what certainly felt like another country. Even today, America has a percentage of first-generation immigrants that approaches that of any period in its history.

The immigration experience has made Americans different from most others. Most other people have a definite sense of what is ancient, and find themselves in local histories and within genealogies that reach into a boundless past, and they can point to houses of worship, ruins, and landmarks that are focal points, often the birthplaces of their belief and their identity. Lacking this, Americans are inclined to see themselves as more the inventors than the inheritors of tradition. Americans have tended to refer to some other country as "the old country," while their own country seems new, sometimes redundantly, maddeningly, and trivially new.

All of this makes Americans an uprooted people, a nation of displaced persons. Add to this the fact that most Americans have systematically and tragically deprived other Americans of the freedom by which they might have coped with their displacement. Americans need, for this and other reasons, what must be called a religious opportunity to be forgiven, as well as to be creative – a God, or something like a God, who forgives and redeems people as well as promotes their creativity.

During the years when classical American religious thought was developed, American intellectual leaders began to come to terms with their actual plight and to seize their religious identity. But in subsequent years, they neglected their own psychology and, as a result, enfeebled their religious thought, and America with it.

Three Elements of American Religious Thought

Among the classical American philosophers, the most important were Charles Sanders Peirce, William James, and John Dewey, together with the honorary classical American philosopher Alfred North Whitehead. Most of their work shared at least three important elements: (1) pragmatism, (2) a radical empiricism, and (3) constructivism. Most of those elements grew out of the Americans' experience of displacement and most affected American religious thought.

Pragmatism

As a people uprooted from an Old Country, thrust in a New World that was experienced as a cultural, if not a natural, wilderness, Americans lacked the intellectual poise of people who were guided by an assured past. For others, a present belief felt reliable because it reflected a hallowed and still-relevant tradition, even though it moved partially beyond that tradition. The Americans lacked such intimate connection with a distant and authoritative past, so they needed a different kind of guide to reliable belief. Pragmatism was not itself that guide, but it gave a method for being guided.

Pragmatism offered a way to be guided by the future rather than the past. Pragmatism tested beliefs by examining their consequences – or, more accurately, what happened when the beliefs in question were acted on. As it looked to future consequences rather than to past causes, pragmatism was a nurse to a historically shallow people who stumbled through the present, relying largely on its wits. It certified beliefs that floated like clouds above the past, asking only that they be able to cast a shadow on the future. The pragmatists argued that a belief is meaningful if its adoption changes the future and that a belief is true if its adoption improves the future. With the passage of time, pragmatism developed until, in the writings of the classical American philosophers, it evaluated, without constituting, an explicit philosophy of religion.

Pragmatism could not ground a philosophy of religion because it offered little more than a technical and bloodless test for a belief's meaningfulness and truth. But while religious people want to know that a religious belief is meaningful and true, they want to know more than that. They want a living reality to which they can relate. Pragmatism at its most ambitious might suggest that a belief works because it is connected to something real, but pragmatism itself provides no evidence of that reality. For all pragmatism knows, the belief could be just a lucky idea, having no more behind it than a lottery ticket has. For pragmatism, what counts is the results of believing, not the past or present basis or origin of the belief. For pragmatism, what reality the belief might (or might not) refer to is either completely irrelevant or a total mystery. While most Americans may not be metaphysically curious, and while most may be able to live with partial mysteries, they and all other Western religious people want a reality to which they can relate. Pragmatism provides hardly a clue to such a reality.

Radical empiricism

The second shared element of classical American philosophers of religion provided at least a clue, as it offered a possible way to know religious realities. This was an empiricist way of knowing, but an unusual empiricist way of knowing because it involved perception that was not sense perception. Through this elemental, radical (or root) form of perception, people were said to receive intimations or adumbrations of moral, aesthetic, and religious realities (including God or some equivalent to God). The American philosophers of religion described radical perception variously – as bodily, physical, non-conscious, emotional, vague – but always as unclear and indistinct. They regarded such perception as the fecund source for the perception of the five senses. As the sense perceptions abstracted from this source, they left much of it behind, including what was morally, aesthetically, and religiously crucial. The classical philosophers gave different names to their epistemologies: Peirce called it "instinct"; James called it "radical empiricism"; Dewey called it "immediate empiricism"; Whitehead called it an awareness of "causal efficacy." With their several varieties of religious empiricism, the classical philosophers of religion were able to do what they could not do as pragmatists: to say how religious experience could refer to a reality.

The Americans had a particularly acute need for religious perception because, lacking deep historical roots, they found it more difficult to relate to God through ancient institutions and religious traditions. Uprooted, thrown at first onto natural and then cultural frontiers, Americans needed a rough, ready, and direct form of religious knowledge. It is not surprising, then, that Americans tapped into religious reality through the highly emotional revival meetings so characteristic of the First and Second Great Awakenings. Always risking and often inviting the charge that this experience was vulgar, fallacious, even a threat to an open society, many Americans, especially the lower classes, nevertheless made it their form of religious piety. In this, they anticipated radical empiricism.

But also knowing that their radical perception was the source of religious error, if not fanaticism, American religious thinkers then invoked their distinctive means of certification, the pragmatic test of meaning and truth. Pragmatism now had a thoroughly religious use. It was the means of criticizing claims to religious knowledge. If religious knowledge, when acted on, had no apparent consequences, then it could be forgotten as meaningless. If religious knowledge had deleterious consequences, it could be rejected as meaningful but false. If it had real and favorable consequences, it could be accepted as true.

Constructivism

The third element in much classical American philosophy of religion was, particularly in the typically tradition-based world of religion, unexpected and remarkable. This was the belief that people could help construct, or add to, the realities to which they related. Unblessed with a strong sense of cultural continuity, Americans sometimes met unforeseen demands not by revisiting tradition but by inventing solutions that to their cousins in Old Worlds could seem ad hoc and modern to a fault. Not content always with new ways to interpret settled truths, some of the classical philosophers tended to argue that new interpretations could, themselves, help to create new truths. Hence, James would famously argue that faith in a fact can help create a fact. With the possible exception of Friedrich Nietzsche, European thinkers were to wait long decades, until the postmodern upheavals of the late twentieth century, to embark on a similar course – and then they seldom saw how this related to religious thought.

These three elements – pragmatism, radical empiricism, and constructivism – not only recur in the classical American philosophy of religion, they help comprise a distinctly American body of religious thought. I will sketch the presence of these elements in a few American philosophers of religion, and then conclude with comments on why this distinctive and ingenious body of thought is now waning.

A Brief History

Bending as far as he did to adjust to the new American circumstance, Jonathan Edwards (1703–58) could have been the seminal, the great classical American religious thinker, at least until the middle of the twentieth century. But Edwards was not that, nor was he anything approximating the Augustine of American philosophers of religion. To explain why, despite his enormous importance as a father to the classical American philosophers of religion, he fell short in this respect is one way to emphasize the fuller range of the ideas that made the classical philosophers truly classical.

Young Edwards read the philosopher John Locke and, with the enthusiasm natural to an intellectual prodigy, he carried Locke's empiricism further than had empiricism's great founder. Locke's *An Essay Concerning Human Understanding* (1689) sought to replace Descartes' theory that people should ground knowledge in ideas innate to the human mind with the theory that people should ground knowledge in perceptions of the five senses. Young Edwards adopted Locke's new epistemology, agreeing that the deliverances of the senses provided a more reliable source of knowledge. But Edwards added to Locke's five senses a "sense of the heart," whereby one can sense the aesthetic and spiritual qualities of the external world and, particularly, one can sense "being in general" (or, God). Just as "there is a difference between having a rational judgment that honey is sweet, and having a sense of its sweetness," Edwards said, there is a difference "between having an opinion, that God is holy and gracious, and having a sense of the loveliness and beauty of that holiness and grace."[2]

While American historian Perry Miller rightly calls Edwards's radical empiricism "a mighty American precedent," Edwards did not offer a precedent for two other distinctively American elements in religious thought. First, the sense of the heart would one day appear to be vague and highly fallible, needing evaluation by something more certain than Edwards's Calvinist theology. Out of this need grew the test of ideas provided by pragmatism. Second, by the end of the nineteenth century people would insist that religious thought grow in ways commensurate with the growth of society, making Edwards's contentment with a richer experience of firmly settled theological verities seem inadequate. Out of this need grew the idea that faith could help construct new religious truth.

After more than a century, Charles Sanders Peirce and William James were prepared to add to Edwards's accomplishment.

It was Peirce (1839–1914) who formally initiated the pragmatic test of the meaning of a belief. Together with James, Peirce hosted periodic meetings of what "half-ironically, half-defiantly" was called "The Metaphysical Club." In 1872 Peirce presented to this small group a paper on pragmatism and it was received, said Peirce, with "uncalled-for kindness." It was expanded and published as two papers in *Popular Science Monthly* in 1877 and 1878, and then immediately published in France.

Peirce developed what he believed was a scientific analysis "of hard words and of abstract concepts" to ferret out their clear meanings.[3] His method was, he believed, like the methods used in science, and his lofty objective was to find the scientific rules whereby civilization could learn "how to give birth to those vital and procreative ideas which multiply . . . advancing civilization and making the dignity of man." Such discovery had been waylaid by the imposition of false beliefs by authoritative bodies like the church or state, by people's clinging to old ways of thinking, and by the unwarranted trust in innate (a priori) ideas. For example, people were led by churches to believe that the wine in the sacrament was Christ's blood. Peirce rebelled, arguing that we can mean nothing "by wine but what has certain effects, direct or indirect, upon our senses; and to talk of something as having all the sensible characters of wine, yet being in reality blood, is senseless jargon." Peirce summarized by saying, "Our idea of anything *is* our idea of its sensible effects."[4] Here was a method that would abandon the false certifications of ideas provided by authorities, habits, and a priori ideas, and bring needed clarity, for example, to Edwards's language about "the loveliness and beauty of that holiness and grace." His pragmatism alone could not, however, "give birth to those vital and procreative ideas" religion needed or discover the realities that gave the ideas meaning.

Peirce would find these ideas with his version of radical empiricism. Admittedly, believing in God is meaningful on pragmatic grounds. Just as we infer the meaning of a great thinker when we observe the change of conduct continually found in those who follow that thinker, we can infer the meaning of God when we observe the change of conduct of people who come to believe in God. In short, we test the meaning of the belief in God by looking at what happens to people who hold that belief. But this pragmatic test shows only the meaningfulness of the belief in God, not the reality that God is. Although God cannot be known precisely and atheists properly rebel against such precision, God can be known, Peirce claimed. Just as scientists can sometimes know the cosmic order instinctually, without being able to define it conceptually, people can sometimes know God instinctively. By instinct, Peirce meant not some biological drive, but a vague sensibility for things not detected by the five senses.

But instinct is highly fallible, so that pragmatism – looking at the consequences of holding beliefs – is needed to certify which senses of God are true. Accordingly, pragmatism tests, but also needs and appeals to, instinct. In fact, pragmatism's argument "is as nothing, the merest nothing, in comparison to its force as an appeal to one's own instinct, which is to argument what substance is to shadow, what bed-rock is to the built foundations of a cathedral."[5] Peirce sometimes called this instinct "common sense," with the emphasis on "sense," making this the counterpart to Edwards's sense of the heart.

But what is God for Peirce? For Peirce, God is the creative power and purpose behind all that is, just as for Edwards, God, when not acting as judge, is the creator of the natural world.

Unexpectedly, Peirce and Edwards concur in one more way. The instinctual awareness of the personally severe C. S. Peirce was opened up by a playful exploration of the uncanny ways in which the world holds together, a play that Peirce called "musement."[6] The sense of the heart for the Calvinistic Edwards was opened up by the experience of natural beauty. Both approaches were unexpectedly aesthetic.

With a typical quirkiness, William James (1842–1910) granted to theological truth both less and more than did Edwards and Peirce. With a religious detachment alien to Edwards and to the later Peirce, he closes his 1899 *The Varieties of Religious Experience* by clinically observing that the God of the people he analyzes is supernatural, never bothering to note that such a supernatural reality makes little sense in his own naturalistic philosophy. But his 1908 *A Pluralistic Universe* describes a nature wild, fluid, and mysterious enough both to violate the structured worlds of Edwards and Peirce and to make room for a God that is not supernatural but that is clearly superhuman and alive. The later feat was possible largely because James set his radical empiricism and his pragmatism in a world that was not only evolving but evolving with the assistance of humans who contributed to its evolution through constructing truth based on faith.

James's labeled both his world-view and his empiricism "radical empiricism." In both cases, it refers to the subterranean antecedents to the clear phenomena discerned above ground by the five senses. More than anything else, these antecedents are relations. James postulates that the world consists of many physical facts rather than one grand set of ideas; but, while James denies idealism's ideas, his is not a positivistic world limited to separate material things. Added to atomic things are the relations between things, forming a world that is relationally connected as well as a plural. These relations, both conjunctive and disjunctive, are imperceptible to the five senses. But people perceive them, nevertheless; and that perception is just another relation, this time between the self and its world. If and when a perception of a relation becomes conscious, it is a foggy "thatness" rather than a clear "whatness." This perception mediates moral and aesthetic value, allowing us to know love and hatred, disparity and complementarity.

The perception of relations is also the source of religious experience. When empiricism is restricted to the five senses, offering only atomic facts that you can measure, atheism may be the only honest conclusion. But, as Luther said, it is only when you despair of earning knowledge that you inherit a deeper truth. If you open yourself again to experience, James said, can you see atheism "give way to a theism now seen to follow directly from that experience more widely taken."

According to James, with radical empiricism we are acquainted with a reality continuous with our "tenderer parts," "a *more*," "an invisible spiritual environment from which help comes." This "more" is what James meant by "God."[7]

Like Peirce, James was quite aware that religious perception, as well as other perceptions of radical empiricism's wider world, is not only vague but highly disputable and fallible. To cope with this uncertainty, James applied the pragmatic method he had already appropriated from Peirce, but which he used now to test truth as well as meaning. It was natural, then, for James to say, "On pragmatistic principles, if the hypothesis of God works satisfactorily in the widest sense of the term, it is true."[8] To amplify, if adopting a God hypothesis yields consequences that are different from other hypotheses, then the God hypothesis is meaningful. But if adopting that hypothesis also yields consequences that "in the long run and on the whole"[9] are satisfactory, then it is true.

James never explained very well what he meant by "satisfactory," but implicit in it is the idea that truth evolves, partly through the human construction of truth, for what is satisfactory for one generation may not be so for a later generation. Truth evolves because it is set in an evolving world where everything changes along with the environment (and occasionally changes in ways not demanded by environmental change). Accordingly, truth about God also evolves; and when it does so in a way that enhances life in a new environment, it is satisfactory. But for the truth about God to change, truth must be constructed, partly by humans.

In religious matters, the evolution of truth was not anticipated by Edwards the Calvinist minister, whose God was absolute, or by Peirce the mathematician, whose God, like all real things, was grounded in unchanging reason. For them, because God is eternally the same, truth about God could do no more than indicate an unchanging reality, and therefore could not truly change.

But for James, God is not absolute or unchanging but historical, living in time and within an environment. As only a part of an environment, God is finite and lacks infinite power.[10] If God's aim is to promote satisfaction (salvation), and if God is finite and, therefore, sometimes unable simply to ensure satisfaction, then humans might "help God." Through their own initiative, people can enlarge those environmental conditions that make human satisfaction more likely. That is, if the God hypothesis is to continue to be true, in the sense that accepting it leads to satisfaction, people must help *make* that hypothesis true, and do this by doing what they can to make the environment more conducive to satisfaction.[11] Thus, James argued that religious "faith in a fact can help create the fact," and by that refers to action based on trusted possibilities rather than to wishful thinking based on nothing. (Similarly, faith in a possible friendship can help make that friendship actual through causing one to trust and build on friendship opportunities.[12]) In all this, humans help construct truth, including the truth of God.

Although John Dewey (1859–1952) was born and raised in Vermont, he was the first of these American philosophers of religion to live outside New England, teaching in Michigan, Chicago, and New York. His more peripatetic career, coupled with his initial philosophical idealism, which emphasized wholes rather than particulars, may have contributed to his one, great advance over his American predecessors: to formulate an American philosophy of religion for societies rather than for individuals. And here Dewey, so often seen as secular to the point of atheism, was more religiously orthodox than Edwards, James, or Peirce. Western religious traditions – whether biblical religion, Christianity, Judaism, or Islam – spoke more about the salvation of societies (Israel, the Church, and the Jewish and Muslim peoples) than about the salvation of individuals.

Dewey's speculations about radical empiricism, constructivism, and pragmatism were guided by a central, largely Darwinian vision. For Dewey, a society can be threatened much like a species is threatened, particularly when it falls out of harmony with its environment. Then, a society's task is to change itself or its environment, until it replaces maladjustment with a new adjustment between itself and its environment.

Accordingly, Dewey sought to overthrow religious attitudes appropriate to the society and the environment of an earlier era, and to replace them with attitudes appropriate to the contemporary social realities. He continually maintained that this adjustment could not be accomplished piecemeal, by tampering with societies alone or environments alone, until they better fit each other. Instead, the adjustment came in terms of a larger view of the universe, a sense of the whole. This produced a canopy under which society or environment found their respective and coordinated roles. Further, although this view was introduced by those who imagined it, it was possible only because something greater than human imagination was involved.

Present thinkers found that their ideals were shaped by inherited ideals that Dewey called "the mysterious totality of being the imagination calls the universe."[13] This totality formed a living tradition, or convention, that became active and alive, perhaps even took on a life of its own, and worked partly to convey old overarching ideals and partly to prompt new imaginings of new ideals. To elaborate, God comes as a "heritage of values we have received," and operates as "the unity of all ideal ends arousing us to desire and actions."[14] This heritage impacts the imagination, presenting the past and spurring the imagination to introduce needed novelty. In short, God is the living tradition that stimulates the spiritual leaders of a society to develop a new, more adequate view of the universe, one that will reconcile inherited beliefs, society's new practices, and the environment's new conditions. To all intents and purposes, the living tradition functioned in the society as a God is commonly thought to function, contributing to the survival and growth of a changing society in a changing environment.

The constructivist implications of Dewey's philosophy of religion are obvious. When religiousness works as it should, it translates the urgings of the divine ideal and uses them to orient a society's spiritual particular "sense of the whole."[15] While the divine heritage may prompt the imagination, it is the imagination that must reflect on "the hard stuff of the world of physical and social experience" and then move beyond the hard stuff, beyond past religion, and provide the ideas that enlarge the sense of the whole. Thereby, religious persons engage in constructive activity, as they set forth ideals that never existed before.[16]

With this new, broader view of things, religiousness that works "as the directing criteria and as the shaping purposes"[17] that orient all of a society's more particular practices (everything from its arts to its engineering). Although Dewey belabored the point, it is obvious that for him both God and religiousness are meaningful and true for pragmatic reasons – because they literally save societies headed for extinction.

Dewey called his version of radical empiricism "immediate empiricism."[18] Beneath conscious knowledge, Dewey said, lies an immediate experience that is far broader than knowledge; for Dewey, as for James, it provides a vague or unconscious sense of *that*, from which is distilled the more discriminating knowledge of a precise *what*. It is through such immediate perception that the sense of the whole is discerned and then constructively altered. And, of course, this enlarged sense of the whole goes to work. When, for example, art provides a hypothesis that unifies some aspect of the world, it derives that hypothesis from a religious sense of the world's new unity.

Dewey and James left basically unresolved the apparent tension between constructivism and radical empiricism. Constructivism emphasizes innovation when it has people constructing truths where no truths existed before; radical empiricism emphasizes replication when it has people deriving ideas from the experienced world. If religious understanding depends on inventions that go beyond what is received from the past, that is one thing. If it depends on intimations of the sacred through a radical perception of the past, that is another thing. These may not be mutually contradictory; in fact, they may be complementary. But neither Dewey nor James explicitly reconciled them.

Alfred North Whitehead (1861–1947) did reconcile constructivism and radical empiricism as part of his general enlargement of American philosophy of religion. While his general world-view was formed before he arrived in America from England at the age of 63, his philosophy of religion can, nevertheless, be identified as partly American for at least three reasons: it was written after he immigrated to America, it was influenced by the Americans James and Dewey,[19] and its major impact on American religious thought arose largely from its good fit with American experience.

Whitehead's greatest contribution as a religious thinker was to give to American philosophy of religion its first full-blown metaphysics, derived partly from physics and mathematics. This, in turn, enabled him to amplify pragmatism, radical empiricism, and constructivism in specific ways.

The revolutionary character of Whitehead's metaphysics is implicit in the way he reconciled radical empiricism and constructivism. He did not accomplish that by simple addition: either by allowing empiricism's past world to determine things up to a point and then giving constructivism's innovation its day; or by adding present subjective interpretation to objective knowledge of the past. In Whitehead's relational universe, there was no strict determination, nor objectivity, nor sheer innovation, nor pure subjectivity, nor the strictly past, nor the strictly present.

He revised these terms by setting them in the relativity theory of physics, arguing that nothing exists at a unique point in space and time. The definition of the past is fixed partly by the one who defines it, so that the location and time of a past event is defined both by the event itself and by the observer – so that the past is different from observer to observer. It is not the case that the past is what it is and that the present interpreter simply interprets it. The present and the past exist only because and as they are interrelated to each other as two, mutually dependent ends of the same pole. All present entities are composed of the past, and the past is real only as it is utilized in the present, so that the past and the present are inseparable.[20]

From this it follows that the past known by radical perception and the present augmented by construction are not only coherently related to each other, but are mutually dependent. Radical empiricism speaks of the rawest, purist possible contact with the past as it supposedly is. But the radical perceiver, as a perceiver, is at the same time always to some small extent a constructor of the past, so that the past cannot be raw and pure but is always partly constituted in various ways by various perceivers.

Whitehead's reconciliation of radical empiricism and construction, as well as his pragmatism, emphasized the historicity of religion. According to Whitehead's metaphysics, the self is restlessly in pursuit of aesthetically richer forms of experience. The self did not invent that restlessness; rather, it came through God's influence on the self by way of religious history or by way of the radical perception of God in the immediate historical past, or by both. Thereby, radical perception is one way of experiencing God's action in history. But beyond this, as the self serves the creative purposes of God, it does so not by leaving history to serve an eternal and divine ideal, but through present historical decisions that help construct the past. Religious people are made (empirically) by history and they (constructively) make history. According to Whitehead's pragmatism, ideas about God are tested in and by history. Ironically, just as Dewey described the sociality at the center of Western religions, Whitehead described the historicism at the center of Western religions.

Whitehead's principal reason for introducing a concept of God was to explain why the world evolves. At odds with the world's growing dissipation of aesthetic order (as described, for example, by the Second Law of Thermodynamics) is a simultaneous trend in living systems toward increasing aesthetic order.[21] Believing that evolution must have a reason, and that that any reason is rooted in a fact, Whitehead called that fact "God." First of all then, God provides the world with a lure, urging it toward growth in aesthetic complexity (greater contrast within unity).

Whitehead went on speculatively to extend his first thoughts about God, until in *Process and Reality* he arrived at a concept of God that more completely filled the gaps in his cosmology. There, in what might best be seen as a *gedankenexperiment* (an experiment in thought), he applied his concept of relations to God. God as active (the primordial nature of God) gives the world its enduring order and its potentialities for construction. God as passive (the consequent nature of God) receives from the world its historical accomplishments, enabling God subsequently to "know" enough about the past to know what potentialities should be offered to the world at any given moment. In effect, these were elaborate ways of explaining how God could lure the world to evolve.[22]

Charles Hartshorne (1897–2000) worked largely within the frameworks provided by Peirce and Whitehead, and was their most noted successor in the American philosophy of religion. He called Whitehead's primordial nature of God the absolute nature and Whitehead's consequent nature the relative nature. He developed and extended Whitehead's dual-natured God in original and so far incontrovertible ways, both contradicting and developing many of the conclusions of the classical Christian concept of God.[23] He argued that, if God is truly related to the world, receiving from as well as giving to it, God cannot be entirely absolute, living independently and self-sufficiently. Nor can God be unaffected by the world's mistakes and calamities, nor unchanging, nor omnipotent, nor omniscient. At the same time, without the absolute order God embodies and provides, the world would have no order, not even the order within which relativity works. Hartshorne made the rational analysis of God's absoluteness the most important tool in his philosophy of religion, devoting parts of three books to defending Anselm's "ontological argument" and editing a third book on Anselm.

Henry Nelson Wieman (1884–1975), an equally important but less noted exponent of Whitehead's concept of God, analyzed Whitehead's primordial nature of God in a very different way. Rather than use reason to understand God, Wieman used empirical investigation to discover and extend the creativity that God gives the world, finally identifying God with that creativity. This carried Wieman into the study of nature and society, bringing him eventually closer to John Dewey than to Whitehead.

However, despite their importance to students of American philosophy of religion, Hartshorne and Wieman were more derivative than their predecessors, so that it can be said that the major advances in the American philosophy of religion ended with Whitehead.

The Waning of American Philosophy of Religion

This distinctively American philosophy of religion did not die, but lived on, particularly in the forms of process theology, as the principal topic of study for the

Highlands Institute for American Religious and Philosophical Thought, and as the most important theological element in the burgeoning discussing of science and religion. Nevertheless, in the remaining decades of the twentieth century the American philosophy of religion did not grow in ways commensurate with its original importance. In fact, while organized religion in America held its own, the distinctively American philosophy of religion significantly waned.

Any effort to explain the recent waning of the American philosophy of religion is speculative. I offer two explanations: (1) American philosophers of religion failed to recognize and respond philosophically to the tragic element of the American experience; (2) American philosophers eventually rejected radical empiricism (and other accounts of religious experience) as too metaphysical or as false appeals to objective truth, leaving pragmatism and constructivism without their companion leg and unable to make an American philosophy of religion stand up.

The most vivid illustration of the neglect of the tragic element of the American experience can be found in the criticism Reinhold Niebuhr (1892–1971) directed at John Dewey. By the 1930s, informed by the Social Gospel and by socialism, Christian social ethicist Niebuhr had seen the misery of the poor, the plight of the laboring classes, and the venality of capitalism, but had also grown increasingly skeptical of liberal solutions to those problems. Perched in New York's Union Theological Seminary, Niebuhr looked across the street at Dewey's Columbia University, and called Dewey's program naive. This was not a shout across a wide canyon separating the pious and the profane, but a critique by one left-wing, ethical, American pragmatist of another. The problem with Dewey's approach was not that it was ill-intended, but that it was impractical, informed by a pathetic trust in the human capacity for reform and failing to see the obstacles thrown up by the selfishness, greed, and hypocrisy of all parties to all problems. Niebuhr offered no obvious solutions, but only modest procedures for mitigating damage through balancing the egocentrism of one faction against that of another.[24] As it turned out, Niebuhr's pessimism made much better sense of the ensuing Depression and the Second World War than Dewey's more optimistic expectations. The high hopes of Dewey's approach were largely abandoned by the 1950s, and no one stepped forward to give the American philosophy of religion the needed realistic, Niebuhrian revision.

Since the Second World War, Niebuhr's pessimism has been starkly confirmed, in ways he did not fully anticipate, through the evidence provided by racism, sexism, and homophobia – as well as new concerns about environmental disaster and weapons of mass destruction. New critics of these ills were rewriting the American experience, arguing that America's unusual diversity of immigrants was not only a blessing that gave social energy, but a curse that brought hatred, arrogance, indifference, and exploitation. Others argued that America's great wilderness and its religious intentions brought more than religious naturalism and a desire to save a fallen world, but also opportunities to exploit nature and to threaten the world with nuclear weapons.

In short, the meaning of America had taken on a tragic nuance, and this should have but did not fundamentally change America's distinctive philosophy of religion. Its typical emphasis on creativity, where God was more the creator who made people better than the redeemer who saved people from wretchedness, was simply not adequate to a world abounding in social evil. Those who sustained this philosophy of religion on through the twentieth century were, to some extent, wrong-footing the new history and losing balance. It did not help that their philosophical heroes were economically comfortable, straight, white males of European extraction whose philosophical foundations were laid prior to their experience of war and who had not lived in a time or place to experience ecological disaster.

The second reason for the waning of the American philosophy of religion was provided by a new skepticism about radical empiricism and other theories of religious experience. Some critics attacked radical empiricism for what they mistakenly believed was its objectivism. Others dismissed radical empiricism as an irrelevant attempt to prove religious truth by a theory of how we know (epistemology), nonchalantly admitting that ideas usually come by way of accident, blind imagination, or political self-interest – and that, in any case, how they come makes no difference. This made philosophers of religion mere clerks who checked out the social consequences of religious hypotheses, usually with negative results.

Without radical empiricism or other grounds for defending religious experience, American philosophers of religion had to live without their equivalent to what medieval and Reformation thinkers had meant by "faith seeking understanding." With religious experience, American religious thinkers could begin their work with a religious commitment, and proceed to build their philosophies constructively and to test them pragmatically. Without religious experience, philosophers of religion were accused of begging the question and called upon to prove their ideas from scratch, without introducing assumptions – a task impossible for any discipline. With religious experience, philosophers could plausibly assert that religious truth could not be fully plumbed by the examination of consequences alone; without it, the philosophy of religion was just flimsy thinking about vague outcomes. By the end of the twentieth century, language about a "more" (James), "a good not our own" (Wieman), uncanny grounds for a sense of "Peace" (Whitehead), or "the mysterious totality of being the imagination calls the universe" (Dewey) sounded like the musings of old men.

Today, many American philosophers of religion, like many theologians, earn their spurs by demonstrating their high regard for other academic movements – in secular philosophy, in the sciences, in cultural and literary theory, and in movements for social change, to name a few. On the whole, such scholars are bereft of any religious truth that is independent and irreducible to other academic disciplines. These philosophers of religion are sometimes given a place at other academic tables, and become decent second-rate exponents of other academic disciplines. But, since they have nothing original or distinctive to offer, they may be occasionally used but seldom are they truly heard.

Notes

1 Joseph Haroutunian, "Theology and American Experience," *Dialog* 4 (1965): 176.
2 Jonathan Edwards, *The Nature of True Virtue* (Ann Arbor: The University of Michigan Press, 1984), p. 24; "A Divine and Supernatural Light," in *Jonathan Edwards: Basic Writings*, ed. Ola Elizabeth Winslow (New York: New American Library, 1978), p. 129.
3 Charles Sanders Peirce, "Pragmatism in Retrospect: A Last Formulation," in *Philosophical Writings of Peirce*, ed. Justus Buchler (New York: Dover Publications, Inc., 1955), pp. 269–71.
4 "How to Make Our Ideas Clear," in *Collected Papers of Charles Sanders Peirce*, 6 vols., ed. Charles Hartshorne and Paul Weiss (Cambridge, MA: The Belknap Press, 1978; henceforth *Papers*), vol. 5, pp. 257–8, 264, 258.
5 Peirce, "My Belief in God," in *Papers*, vol. 6, pp. 340–7.
6 "A Neglected Argument for the Reality of God," in *Papers*, vol. 6, pp. 311–39.
7 William James, *A Pluralistic Universe* (Cambridge, MA: Harvard University Press, 1977), pp. 138–41.
8 *Pragmatism* (Cambridge, MA: Harvard University Press, 1975), p. 143.
9 Ibid., p. 106.
10 James, *Pluralistic Universe*, p. 144.
11 William James, *The Will to Believe and Other Essays in Popular Philosophy* (Cambridge, MA: Harvard University Press, 1979), p. 55. See also *Pragmatism*, pp. 137–8.
12 James, *Will to Believe*, pp. 29, 28. See also *Pragmatism*, pp. 137–8.
13 John Dewey, *A Common Faith* (New Haven, CT: Yale University Press, 1952), p. 85.
14 Ibid., pp. 87, 42.
15 John Dewey, *Art as Experience* (New York: Capricorn Books, 1958), pp. 193–5.
16 Dewey, *Common Faith*, p. 49.
17 Ibid., p. 85.
18 See John Dewey, "The Postulate of Immediate Empiricism," in *The Influence of Darwin on Philosophy: And Other Essays in Contemporary Thought* (New York: Holt, Rinehart and Winston, 1938), pp. 226–41.
19 Alfred North Whitehead, *Process and Reality: An Essay in Cosmology*, ed. David Ray Griffin and Donald W. Sherburne (New York: The Free Press, 1979), p. xii.
20 Alfred North Whitehead, *Science and the Modern World* (New York: The Free Press, 1967), pp. 113–22.
21 Alfred North Whitehead, *The Function of Reason* (Boston: Beacon Press, 1959), ch. 1.
22 Whitehead, *Process and Reality*, pp. 342–51.
23 Charles Hartshorne, *The Divine Relativity: A Social Conception of God* (New Haven, CT: Yale University Press, 1964); *Omnipotence and Other Theological Mistakes* (Albany, NY: SUNY Press, 1984), ch. 1.
24 Robert B. Westbrook, *John Dewey and American Democracy* (Ithaca: Cornell University Press, 1991); Arthur Schlesinger, Jr., "Reinhold Niebuhr's Role in American Political Thought and Life," in Charles W. Kegley and Robert W. Bretall, eds., *Reinhold Niebuhr: His Religious, Social, and Political Thought* (New York: The Macmillan Co., 1956).

Suggested reading

Primary sources

Dewey, John, *Art as Experience* (New York: Capricorn Books, 1958).
——*A Common Faith* (New Haven, CT: Yale University Press, 1952).
Edwards, Jonathan, *Jonathan Edwards: Basic Writings*, ed. Ola Elizabeth Winslow (New York: New American Library, 1878).
——*The Nature of True Virtue* (Ann Arbor: The University of Michigan Press, 1984).
Hartshorne, Charles, *Anselm's Discovery: A Re-examination of the Ontological Proof for God's Existence* (La Salle, IL: Open Court, 1965).
——*The Divine Relativity: A Social Conception of God* (New Haven: Yale University Press, 1964).
——*Omnipotence and Other Theological Mistakes* (Albany, NY: SUNY Press, 1984).
James, William, *A Pluralistic Universe* (Cambridge, MA: Harvard University Press, 1977).
——*Pragmatism* (Cambridge, MA: Harvard University Press, 1975).
——*The Varieties of Religious Experience* (Cambridge, MA: Harvard University Press, 1985).
——*The Will to Believe and Other Essays in Popular Philosophy* (Cambridge, MA: Harvard University Press, 1979).
Niebuhr, Reinhold, *Moral Man and Immoral Society* (New York: Charles Scribner's Sons, 1960).
Peirce, Charles Sanders, *Collected Papers of Charles Sanders Peirce*, 6 vols., ed. Charles Hartshorne and Paul Weiss (Cambridge, MA: The Belknap Press, 1978).
——*Philosophical Writings of Peirce*, ed. Justus Buchler (New York: Dover Publications, Inc., 1955).
Whitehead, Alfred North, *The Function of Reason* (Boston: Beacon Press, 1959).
——*Process and Reality: An Essay in Cosmology*, ed. David Ray Griffin and Donald W. Sherburne (New York: The Free Press, 1979).
——*Science and the Modern World* (New York: The Free Press, 1967).
Wieman, Henry Nelson, *The Source of Human Good* (Atlanta, GA: Scholars Press, 1995).

Secondary sources

Brown, Delwin, Ralph E. James, Jr., and Gene Reeves, eds., *Process Philosophy and Christian Thought* (Indianapolis: The Bobbs-Merrill Company, Inc., 1971).
Dean, William, *American Religious Empiricism* (Albany, NY: SUNY Press, 1986).
Delattre, Roland André, *Jonathan Edwards: Beauty and Sensibility in the Thought of Jonathan Edwards* (New Haven, CT: Yale University Press, 1968).
Kucklick, Bruce, *Churchmen and Philosophers: From Jonathan Edwards to John Dewey* (New Haven, CT: Yale University Press, 1995).
Levinson, Henry Samuel, *The Religious Investigations of William James* (Chapel Hill: University of North Carolina Press, 1981).

Miller, Perry, *Jonathan Edwards* (Amherst: University of Massachusetts Press, 1981).

Raposa, Michael L., *Peirce's Philosophy of Religion* (Bloomington: Indiana University Press, 1989).

Westbrook, Robert B., *John Dewey and American Democracy* (Ithaca, NY: Cornell University Press, 1991).

Chapter 22

Education

Nicholas C. Burbules, Bryan Warnick, Timothy McDonough, and Scott Johnston

Overview

The thought of American philosophers, as for any nation, is too eclectic to be summarized in a simple manner. Nor is American culture in general homogeneous enough to be captured in stereotypes. Still, it is useful for the purposes of this chapter to highlight some philosophical themes that do seem quintessentially "American," and which can be seen in the work of several major American philosophers. We describe these themes in terms of tensions: competing values or imperatives that are not easily reconciled. In our view, one of the major characteristics of American philosophy is in working within these sorts of tensions, sometimes trying overtly to reconcile them, sometimes tending toward one pole or another of these dialectics.

Our overall claim is that *education* is a recurring theme for many American philosophers, even those who are not professional philosophers of education, because education is an activity wherein these tensions are thought to be reconcilable. Education in both its informal processes and its formal institutions has always been given responsibility for addressing broader social challenges – often, we would argue, to an unrealistic extent. In the American philosophical context, education is frequently proposed as the answer to dilemmas that may in fact be unsolvable. This is not an approach that will yield timeless verities:

> [American] philosophy no longer was to be understood as a purely theoretical quest for eternal truths or knowledge of an ultimate and unchanging reality. Its job was no longer to analyze experience into the real and unreal, the substantial and the insubstantial. Instead it must be practical, critical, and reconstructive; it must aim at the successful transformation or amelioration of the experienced problems which call forth and intrinsically situate it, and its success must be measured in terms of this goal.[1]

The first of these tensions emerges from the origins of the American nation itself: a country founded on land whose history was not its own, an invented country – self-invented, in fact – which was regarded by its first citizens as an unbesmirched haven, virgin territory (although of course it had been long inhabited by others). This idea of a nation as a bold experiment, beginning *sui generis* and governed by a consciously designed Constitution that was regarded as a demonstration proof derived from a new political theory, runs deep in the American self-concept. This idea has encouraged an aggressive, risk-taking attitude, a sense of destiny and unlimited potential. Correspondingly, American thought has been perpetually dynamic, evolving, and forward-looking. The experimental attitude is manifested in a pervasive attitude of pragmatism (small "p"), a "can-do" ethos that regards every challenge as an opportunity, every problem as potentially solvable, every crisis as an occasion to learn, to grow in strength and understanding.[2]

At the same time, this self-conception is cut off from any longer sense of history, any thick sense of origins. No other country in the world measures itself from such a specific date of birth. No other country would build an entire theory of law and jurisprudence around the concept of its Founders' "original intent" (and then be fundamentally undecided about what that intent actually was). This lack of deep roots, this sense of perpetual self-invention, gives the American sensibility an ambivalent relation to the past: while broadly British and Eurocentric, the orphaned United States is always searching for its parents or, more precisely, continually adopting new ones and then abandoning them as it keeps rewriting the narrative of where it came from. In the context of philosophy, and in philosophical views on education, this has produced an uneasy relation to "Great Books," on the one hand searching for intellectual and cultural origins in resources that seem classic and enduring (for a nation which recognizes that it is not), and on the other hand suspecting, even denigrating, the need to shackle its restless energies of creativity and ambition to something past-regarding, especially to a past that is in some sense derivative, not truly its own. Education is a primary domain in which this tension has been manifested.

A second tension concerns the location of the American nation itself: founded on an expansive territory that (while already occupied by people) was largely undeveloped, almost limitless in this scope and resources. The encounter with Nature in its rawest form, the sense of unbridled horizons, reinforced the American spirit of unlimited possibility, giving it both symbolic and material reinforcement. This romance with Nature, with a land of perpetual discovery and almost endless variety, rested in uneasy tension, however, with the ambitious and utilitarian ethos that drove this country from one coastline to the other, and now into the boundless frontier of space itself, always seeking awesome beauty *and* economic benefit; pursuing scientific knowledge through exploration *and* racing to occupy and establish proprietary domain; driven by the most intrepid and courageous curiosity *and* manifesting the most boorish self-indulgence (carving initials on the red rock spires of the southwest, or playing golf on the moon). These twin imperatives – bravery and relentless curiosity on the one hand, and a presumptuous, even arrogant, desire for expansion and domain on the other – characterize aspects of American cultural and intellectual life as well: a romanticization of the authentic, the natural, alongside a bold, audacious aspiration for the new. In education, too, this spirit is manifested in perpetual reforms and reinventions; continual tinkering aimed at the perfection of the learner and the society, but always also striving to unleash a natural talent and freedom that the actual institutionalized forms of education are frequently seen as threatening.

A third tension arises from the coincidence of the emergence of the American nation with the rise of industrialism and the development of an evolutionary understanding of the natural and social worlds. This context has given the American mindset not only an exaggerated sense of confidence in science and technology (a faith that can be amply substantiated by pointing to the amazing growth and prosperity of this nation), but also a view of itself as the product of an evolutionary process, a society that believes that its hardiness and ingenuity have *earned* it the benefits it has received.[3] Just as evolution rewards the most nimble and quickly adapting species, so has the United States regarded itself as benefiting from its "natural" advantages over other nations; and just as a species picked out from its competitors as the most deserving is therefore advantaged in reproducing itself, so too does the United States assume that its ideas and inventions, which have served it so well, are destined to benefit the rest of the world. This sense of American specialness, most vividly expressed in the doctrine of Manifest Destiny, can be partly seen as the hubris of a nation that has never suffered crushing defeat or occupation, whose memory is not long enough to appreciate the inevitable cycles of dominance and failure over centuries.[4] But it is also a manifestation of an optimistic belief in science, progress, and meritocracy – one that can be supported to a significant extent by the overall national experience (though certainly not by all of its members).

In philosophy this frequently gives American thought a robustness, a confidence in taking on all problems without diffidence or hesitation. Scientific investigation, in the general sense of inquiry and experimentation, is trusted to dissolve the antinomies of traditional doubts and dilemmas; a sensible, skeptical attitude confronts even the most intractable problems as just another challenge to overcome. The post-Darwinian philosophies of America stress process, not transcendent aims; and emphasize progress, not revolution. Such views of epistemology, ethics, and education are perfectly wedded to the meliorist institutions of a liberal democracy.

The fourth tension grows out of the unique character of the United States as an immigrant nation. Almost from its beginnings, the nation saw itself challenged by the task of forging a common national identity, despite its divisions into states, regions, and increasingly multiple ethnic, racial, and religious subcommunities. Hence from the very beginning American thought has wrestled in a special way with the competing values of particularism and universalism: respecting diversity while also trying to define, and then to defend, a shared set of values and a patriotic ethos. Certainly, schools have been a primary locus in which these competing imperatives have played themselves out, sometimes tending more in one direction, sometimes more in the other. Pluralism is seen simultaneously as one of the greatest resources of the nation, and as one of its perennial problems; it is both a point of pride, and a point of tremendous frustration, intolerance, and sometimes even violent conflict.

These four themes can obviously be seen to overlap in many ways: the American attempts to define and redefine its origins, its attitudes toward nature, its faith in science and progress, and its problems with pluralism are perennial and interrelated tensions that can never be finally settled. They are indeed the sorts of question that are struggled with, not "answered." And they mesh closely with an activity like education, directed at the aims of growth and development, but at the same time perpetually adapting and questioning itself.

In this chapter we have selected four exemplary American philosophers, all of whom have addressed education directly, but who otherwise represent quite different philosophical outlooks: Ralph Waldo Emerson, John Dewey, Richard Rorty, and Martha Nussbaum.[5] In each of these cases we see them struggling with the tensions described above – in different ways, to be sure, and to different results. In this respect we find them quintessentially American in character, with each exhibiting in his or her own way the genius and the hubris of the American attitude. For these authors, and for American thought generally, education is thought to provide a way of navigating these tensions, advancing the process of national self-formation at the same time that it provides an opportunity for individual flourishing. Education is an institution that perfectly exemplifies the American faith in natural potential and self-advancement; in constructing and transmitting a tradition and at the same time continually promising to surpass it; in unbridled scientific inquiry and technological innovation; and in promoting a putatively common culture and national spirit, while also bringing together, and purportedly celebrating, the distinct and diverse influences that have shaped an immigrant nation: "Conceived as they were at the apogee of the Enlightenment, the principles on which the United States was founded included the efficacy of education and the perfectibility of man.[6] Because education, mandatory for American youth, is regarded as a domain of self-determination, merit, and freely chosen directions of inquiry, it seems to reconcile perfectly the American beliefs in freedom, on the one hand, and destiny, on the other – in education one makes one's own way, but in doing so one also advances the nation's mission.[7]

Ralph Waldo Emerson

"Let me remind the reader that I am only an experimenter," writes Ralph Waldo Emerson. "I unsettle all things. No facts are to me sacred; none are profane; I simply experiment, an endless seeker with no Past at my back."[8] The subject of Emerson's experimentation is the development of human powers. He aims at understanding the potential of the individual mind and the forces that increase its capacities. The questions that drive Emerson, then, are educational questions. Sin consists in a stationary mind, a mind that does not continually change and develop, a mind that seeks "foolish consistency" rather than bold adventure. Emerson's philosophy both speaks of the growing mind, and exemplifies it: his thought was in constant flux, and he was not afraid to announce when reading a sermon that he no longer believed the sentence he had just read.[9]

Education is the constant struggle to add new powers to the formlessness existing in each individual mind. It is a process both of bringing out the potential that lies within the learner's soul, and of taking the learner back toward the soul, which is the infinite source of human power.[10] The soul is both the cause and product of education. It is the object of life, and reveals the proper aim of education:

> The great object of Education should be commensurate with the object of life. It should be a moral one; to teach self-trust: to inspire the youthful man with an interest in himself; with a curiosity touching his own nature; to acquaint him with the resources of his mind, and to teach him that there is all his strength, and to inflame him with a piety towards the Great Mind in which he lives.[11]

How does one know human potential? Past heroes and geniuses are "representative men"; they exemplify the potential power within the soul. In a uniquely American voice, Emerson describes Plato as the "great average man," and his goal in discussing Shakespeare is that we may see "the Shakespeare in us." The question of how to develop these powers, exemplified in genius, is *the* problem that drives Emerson's thought. Emerson sees the world through an educational lens.

This lens focuses Emerson's thought in different ways. Under the educational gaze, for example, the first principle of his discussion of friendship becomes *truth*:

> A friend is a person with whom I may be sincere. Before him I may think aloud. . . . Almost every man we meet requires some civility, requires to be humoured; – he has some talent, some whim of religion or philanthropy in his head that is not to be questioned, and so spoils all conversation with him. But a friend is a sane man who exercises not my ingenuity, but me.[12]

The sincere differences that are had between friends provoke struggle and mental exercise. Emerson writes, "The only joy I have in his being mine, is that the *not mine* is *mine*. It turns the stomach, it blots the daylight, where I looked for manly utterance, or at least a manly resistance, to find a mush of concession. Better be a nettle in the side of your friend than his echo."[13] The not-me, in friendly disagreement, becomes a thorn that requires exertion of the intellect. Thus, Emerson's discussion of friendship revolves around its pedagogical possibilities.

For Emerson, education is as broad as the human experience – every acquaintance, action, and aggravation is a force for change. Emerson places the major influences on the mind into three categories of experience: nature, action, and books (when used properly). The complete person embraces all three influences. Commonly, however, people are forbidden to be whole; in their specialization they have "suffered amputation" and "strut about so many walking monsters, – a good finger, a neck, a stomach, an elbow, but never a man."[14] The three influences that reverse this amputation constitute major themes of Emerson's thought: Nature, action, and books.

For Emerson, "Nature" is the earliest and most important school of the mind. Nature is defined both as "[A]ll which distinguishes as the NOT ME, that is, both nature and art, all other men and my own body," and, in a less philosophically precise but more common-sense definition, as the "essences unchanged by man; space, the air, the river, the leaf."[15] Emerson, like Heraclitus and the Stoics, saw the natural world as infused with rationality, the human mind forming part of this broader whole. The rational ordering of the world's natural flux instructs the mind: "Space, time, society, labor, climate, food, locomotion, the animals, the mechanical forces, give us sincerest lessons, day by day, whose meaning is unlimited. They educate both the Understanding and Reason."[16] Nature educates by informing our language and providing ways to express what would otherwise remain inexpressible. For example, the experience of nature allows the mind to structure the world of morality: "All things are moral," writes Emerson, "and in their boundless changes have an unceasing reference to spiritual nature."[17] He constructs a genealogy of morals and argues that, by relying on metaphor and analogy, spiritual and moral language is linked to the experience of material reality:

> *Right* means *straight*; *wrong* means *twisted*. *Spirit* primarily means *wind*; *transgression*, the crossing of a *line*; *supercilious*, the *raising of the eyebrow*. We say the *heart* to express emotion, the *head* to denote thought; and *thought* and *emotion* are words borrowed from sensible things, and now appropriated to spiritual nature. . . . [These metaphors] are not the dreams of a few poets, here and there, but man is an analogist, and studies relations in all objects. He is placed in the centre of beings, and the ray of relation passes from every other being to him.[18]

The experience of the mind in the natural world serves as the basis for metaphors used to structure the spiritual and the ethical world. "Who can guess," writes Emerson, "how much firmness the sea-beaten rock has taught the fisherman? how much tranquility has been reflected to man from the azure sky?"[19] And since all human beings experience nature, this provides a basis for a moral common ground.[20]

Nature not only enriches language, but develops the discrimination of the mind: "Our dealing with sensible objects is," he writes, "a constant exercise in the necessary lessons of difference, of likeness, of order, of being and seeming, of progressive arrangements; of ascent from particular to general; of combination to one end of the manifold forces."[21] While the experience of nature educates the senses, human artifacts can stunt their growth. The clock and the compass, for example, hinder us from astronomy. Nature demands a heightened use of the senses; it teaches one to see, to hear, to feel, to taste, to perceive, to classify, to test one's powers to discern. The technological world, conversely, is *obvious* – one does not even need to step outside to determine tomorrow's weather, one is simply presented with the weather forecast. Thus, natural science sharpens the discrimination: "Cities," writes Emerson, "give not the human senses room enough."[22]

Action is the next educational category. Action leads to experience. Acting in the world plugs us into the world's rational processes. Since the world mirrors mind, acting in the world teaches us about our own minds. The wider the variety of actions, the greater the realm of experience, and the more developed become human powers: "Drudgery, calamity, exasperation, want, are instructors in eloquence and wisdom. The true scholar grudges every opportunity of action passed by, as loss of power. It is the raw product out of which the intellect moulds her splendid products."[23] Action allows for experience that gives our language life and synchronizes the mind to the ebb and flow of the world's undulations. Furthermore, as with the later pragmatists, action allows us to test our theories, to see what "we may call truth," and what needs revision.[24] All action is instructive, especially manual labor: "I ask not for the great, the remote, the romantic . . . I embrace the common, I explore and sit at the feet of the familiar, the low."[25] Hence, Emerson, at his most American, develops his "democracy of experience." Even mundane tasks are full of pedagogical power. All people have access to the educational opportunities of experience and may have an "original relation to the universe."[26]

We engage present experience through action and past experience through books. Books, however, become noxious if they devalue the present experience and discourage action: "Books are for the scholar's idle times. When he can read God directly, the hour is too short to be wasted in other men's transcripts."[27] For Emerson, it is the act of thought that is sacred, not the record of thought. Books present the thinking of others and make us forget that we also are thinkers: "Meek young men grow up in libraries, believing it their duty to accept the views which Cicero, Locke, which Bacon had given; forgetful that Cicero, Locke, and Bacon were only young men in libraries when they wrote these books."[28] Books are for inspiration. They reveal another's thoughts, and must urge us to develop our own power.

Emerson's later thought emphasizes the limitations of learning through individual experience, and he comes to recognize that all experience is mediated experience – a realization that he deeply mourns. We do not experience the world directly: "We have no means of correcting these colored and distorting lenses which we are," he writes, "or of computing the amount of their errors."[29] Instead, and tragically, the force of the world cannot fully reach us: "We live amid surfaces, and the true art of life is to skate well on them."[30] Still, hope exists in poetry. More than anything else, poetry allows the seeker to go beyond the surface of things to the depths of nature and the soul.[31]

Emerson's ideal of the engaged mind is manifest, he says, in the boys of New England, the "masters of the playground and street,"[32] who constantly roam and experiment. These boys, when left to explore the world, seem to crave new experience and learning, and others seem pleased to teach them. Their activities demonstrate that learning and teaching are natural impulses: "The whole theory of the school is on the nurse's or mother's knee. The child is as hot to learn as the mother is to impart. There is mutual delight."[33] Such happy situations exemplify the "natural college." But with organization and the attempt to expedite education, difficulties begin. Students become bored; teachers become "departmental, routinary, [and] military."[34] The only education which can transform the real into the ideal is one based on the methods of love: "the secret of education lies in respecting people."[35] This route is surely more difficult and has "immense claims on the time, the thoughts, on the life of the teacher."[36] Instructing through a degrading power, conversely, is seductive since, "in this world of hurry and distraction, who can wait for the returns of reason and the conquest of the self; in the uncertainty too whether it will ever come?"[37] Yet the fact remains: the truly educative path goes uphill.

Although Emerson was engaged in educational institutions at almost every level – as a classroom teacher, a dedicated administrator of common schools, a college board member – and although he knew major educational reformers such as Bronson Alcott and Charles Eliot, he confesses ignorance concerning which educational reforms to suggest. He advises teachers to "smuggle in a little contraband wit, fancy, imagination, thought" and to make the schoolroom "like the world" – full of action, nature, and (sometimes) books. In the end, however, the individual, the semigod, surpasses all reform. An educator needs be an endless seeker.

John Dewey

For Dewey, education determines the capacity of humans to reason and know. It is not simply that education enhances and draws out natural features of intelligence, but that education establishes the practices of inquiry by which individuals in specific historical societies generate the meaningful structures through which their world is known.

Dewey challenges modern philosophers to overcome the debilitating distinction between theoretical inquiry and practical activity that was a mark of the philosophical discourse dominant at the beginning of the twentieth century. Modern philosophy, especially as filtered into the American context, was concerned predominantly with grasping reality as it exists independent of the conditions of interaction between the knower and the known. Dewey described "modern thought" in the following manner:

> [I]t retains the substance of the classic disparagement of the practical in contrast with the theoretical, although formulating it in somewhat different language: to the effect that knowledge deals with objective reality as it is in itself, while in what is "practi-

> cal," objective reality is altered and cognitively distorted by subjective factors of want, emotion and striving.[38]

Establishing law-like, a priori, or universal accounts of the conditions of reality in accord with which human actions could be judged correct or true was the goal of the modern philosophers opposed by Dewey.

Contrarily, according to Dewey, our theoretical understanding of reality is itself a product of specific relations between the knowing subject and the known object. Theoretical understandings, or the significance of our ideas, can only be understood as derived through practical engagement with the world:

> [M]eanings are what they are in themselves and are related to one another by means of acts of taking and manipulating – an art of discourse. They possess intellectual import and enter fruitfully into scientific method only because they are selected, employed, separated and combined by acts extraneous to them, acts which are as existential and causative as those concerned in the experimental use of apparatus and other physical things.[39]

Dewey sees our ideas as objects subject to the same sort of modification and perspectival understanding as those things we normally take to be the proper objects of scientific study. For Dewey, our concepts are to be regarded as human artifacts, subject to the creative energies and practical concerns of those who use them.

The appropriateness or truthfulness of ideas is to be measured not by the extent to which they correspond to some ultimate reality, but by the degree to which they permit the resolution of practical problems. This was one of the main tenets of the pragmatic tradition in which Dewey participated, a view articulated by C. S. Peirce, Josiah Royce, and William James before him. Pragmatism argues for a conception of knowledge that is local and temporal, subject to amendment as the situational conditions change presenting the particular community of inquirers/interpreters with new and different problems to solve. Knowledge, for Dewey and the pragmatists, is communicative and social, conceived as specific to a community of inquirers:

> [Mind] consists in the habits of understanding, which are set up in using objects in correspondence with others, whether by way of cooperation and assistance or rivalry and competition. Mind as a concrete thing is precisely the power to understand things in terms of the use made of them; a socialized mind is the power to understand them in terms of the use to which they are turned in joint or shared situations.[40]

Dewey refers to knowledge as "mind" to signify its living and vital qualities. Such active knowing is the collective product of the communicative relations within a community of inquirers. As such, it has a motive force of its own and grows or degenerates depending upon the quality of relations within its sustaining environment.

Insofar as knowledge is particular to a community at a certain time and place, it is not merely available as such to the perceptive neophyte or uninitiated foreigner. The individual relying solely upon his or her own individual natural faculties of cognition cannot arrive at a knowledge of the world in accord with that shared internally within a community. Reality is not simply a field of objects whose simple relations are available to any perceiving and reasoning individual. The individual has to be introduced to the community's developed understanding and the currently legitimate norms by which that society derives its knowledge. Inquiry is conceived as a practical art by Dewey, one in which its practitioners require an education in order to become competent participants in the ongoing process of knowing.

The type of communal knowing (i.e., the type of education, communication, and inquiry) which Dewey propounds throughout his works on education is that type particularly suited to a society exhibiting basic forms of democratic association accompanied by a development of scientific rationality. His work in this area was designed to be a practical and relevant critique of practices exhibited within his own community and society. He explicitly criticizes forms of knowledge retaining vestigial norms from periods of earlier, primarily aristocratic and feudal, societies. Insofar as a community proclaims democratic principles and enjoys scientific progress, and yet limits inquiry in accord with aristocratic or guild-based norms, Dewey argues that the development of knowledge is therein constrained from responding to problems as they arise in the sociohistorical circumstance. In such cases a problematic gap is established between practical knowledge and theoretical-institutional knowledge.

In democracy relative to its aristocratic forerunners, inquiry advances as communicative relations are broadened, permitting the society to respond to evolving social conditions in a more critical, self-adjusting, and pluralistic fashion.[41] For Dewey, the vitality of a democracy depends on how it balances two conflicting imperatives: "How numerous and varied are the interests that are consciously shared? How full and free is the interplay with other forms of association?"[42] Democratic education as an instruction for inquiry promotes communication across the diverse and complex sectors of society, encourages the sharing of a wide variety of interests, and radically increases the possibility of establishing shared purpose. It enables members of society to further expand their collective knowledge and respond positively in the face of future challenges, questions and problems.

Dewey argues for a type of education which enhances citizens' capacities to offer a creative critique of dominant forms of knowing in a pluralistic arena of shared inquiry; his goal is to promote the progressive growth of society in a democratic and rational direction. Hence, free debate and sharing of diverse interests and ideas are essential to the vitality of a community. Knowledge must be explicitly understood by all participants in inquiry as fallible, and always subject to critique and reformulation. Furthermore, if knowledge is to contribute to the greatest good for the greatest number of participants in the community, the practices of inquiry by which that knowledge is generated must be widely participatory; that is, it must be open and responsive to the needs of all segments of the community. In order for democratic inquiry to be so practiced, it is necessary that as many members of the community as possible learn the methods of inquiry which permit their participation in the resolution of the problems facing them as a community. This is the chief task of education.

Education for all forms of society is, for Dewey, a means of inculcating in new members the dominant modes of communication and inquiry in order to assure a generational reproduction and development of that society. Education is thus the means by which the methods that permit the exchange of interests and ideas, which is constitutive of a community, can be historically secured. In a complex society, education serves the purpose of "simplifying and ordering the factors of the disposition it is wished to develop; purifying and idealizing the existing social customs; creating a wider and better balanced environment than that by which the young would likely, if left to themselves, be influenced."[43] Education provides direction and control of the impulses and interests that provide the personal motive force of young learners' own exploration. This schooling permits them to advance their knowledge in a manner consistent throughout the population, thus contributing to the development of social capacities for inquiry in a continuum, i.e., in line with the achievements of the past, in accord with the norms of the present, and directed toward future accomplishments.

The role of philosophy in society is at least partially fulfilled by informing educational practitioners of the proper, effective, and vital methods of inquiry in which to instruct future members of the society. Practices of inquiry and the working relations of society are not only mutually supporting, but the type of inquiry engaged in actually determines the character of society. It is through inquiry practices that a society meets its challenges and shapes its future. Philosophy is that branch of inquiry which reflects on the processes of inquiry in order to critique and adjust them so that they will be appropriate for dealing with the problems arising within the developing social context. As a philosopher Dewey is concerned with critically reflecting upon the methods of inquiry engaged in within his society so as to adjust existing practices to meet the democratic-scientific aims of that society. Educating citizens to adopt the methods of inquiry which best meet their aims and solve their emergent problems assures the progressive growth of their society toward the fulfillment of its own goals and potential.

Knowledge as held by a community and produced in communal practices of inquiry requires that the citizens be properly schooled, that is, raised in the norms of inquiry of that community. In a twentieth-century democratic society, or any derivation thereof, the public must be pragmatically schooled, if knowledge is to be attained that is conducive to its further growth. That means that the capacities of individuals must be developed to allow them to recognize problems in their environment, to observe phenomena relevant to the problematic situation, to develop hypotheses based upon past knowledge and their own insights, to test those hypotheses, and to share their findings with others:[44]

> [S]cientific method is the only authentic means at our command for getting at the significance of our everyday experiences of the world in which we live. It means that scientific method provides a working pattern of the way in which and the conditions under which experiences are used to lead ever onward and outward.[45]

Dewey regards this method as the best means to assure that ideas are understood as hypothetical and always subject to further testing and critique; thus any advance in the community of inquirers' knowledge was effectively an enhancement of their capacity to generate and test further ideas to answer future questions.

Instructing the members of a community in a specific method of inquiry might seem indoctrinatory, but Dewey was, as a student and product of his society, very much an individualist. The method he championed relied upon the creative power of the individual to challenge existing practices in order to improve the responsiveness of society to emergent conditions. The democratic underpinnings of the society in which Dewey practices his philosophical reflections permitted this normative instruction in practices of inquiry to allow for the creativity of the individual to play a constructive part. The scientific method, which Dewey explicitly articulates, contains within itself the grounds for its own progressive development to meet future demands of an always-changing society. It remains the role of future philosophers to articulate and enhance methods of inquiry and education appropriate to meeting the challenges of their society.

Richard Rorty

One way to start thinking about Richard Rorty is in his reaction to this core ideal of inquiry and its "scientific" status. Much of Rorty's fame rests on a few seemingly scandalous theses regarding society's lack of need for the expressly *philosophical*, if by philosophical one means metaphysical, transcendental, necessary, or absolute. And Rorty is by no means shy about expressing his opinions on the state of the discipline of philosophy. His penchant for deliberately occasioning controversy through certain rhetorical postures is well known. But in the final analysis his themes are not that different from his pragmatic predecessors, most notably Dewey.

What is less well known about Rorty (though certainly not to educators) are his pronouncements, consistent with his overall thinking about the point and purpose of philosophy, on education and schooling. So it seems appropriate here to focus on some of the statements he has made on this topic. In what follows, we shall briefly discuss his chief themes relating to philosophy and to metaphysics, epistemology, and political theory in particular, followed by an outline of his thoughts on the subject of education, and concluding with a brief look at how Rorty has been taken up by educators.

With the publication of *Philosophy and the Mirror of Nature*, Rorty seemingly burst upon the scene a fully formed thinker. In actuality, he had been gathering together his random thoughts on a critique of Cartesian epistemology and metaphysics for some time. In the 1960s and early 1970s, he seemed the consummate analytic philosopher. His early topics included such themes as incorrigibility and the mental. But he became discouraged with what he saw as a behind-the-scenes pretension to claim ultimate truths about linguistic and logical discoveries. Then, in the early 1970s he began on a new trend of thinking that ultimately formed the background material for his now-famous *Philosophy and the Mirror of Nature* (1979).[46]

The thesis of that book was Rorty's argument that the quest for knowledge, central to Cartesian and post-Cartesian (Enlightenment and post-Enlightenment) philosophy, is a dead-end. It is so because such a quest invariably occasions a transcendental turn to a claim that "this is the way the world really is," which we have no business making. The alternative is a radical historicization of knowledge. When we historicize the world, Rorty thinks, we immediately fall back onto the proper basis for making knowledge claims: the social, the cultural, and the linguistic. Rorty's heroes in this work are Dewey, Heidegger, and Wittgenstein; heroes because they help us to see through the illusion of transcendentally based knowledge claims and, thereby, lead us back to human concerns.

In his following work, *Consequences of Pragmatism* (1982),[47] Rorty played up the pragmatic side of the knowledge-as-historical-and-cultural argument. This collection of essays, mostly written in the 1970s, represented the early evidence of Rorty's break from analytic philosophy. The essays were written in the easy, engaging style that was to win Rorty many fans and seal his reputation as a public intellectual. The central epistemological thesis of his earlier work is repeated here. What is notable with this work is his self-stated affinity with the "first wave" of pragmatism (notably, James and, especially, Dewey), together with a now-famous address to the American Philosophical Association, Western Division, in which he traced the history of, and justified, the split between analytic and continental traditions in American philosophy programs.

In *Contingency, Irony, and Solidarity* (1989)[48] Rorty treated us to his beginning thoughts on social and political concerns. It was this work, most of all, which raised the attention and concern of educators, no doubt because of Rorty's pronouncements on liberal democracy. In this work, Rorty carved out two sorts of selves: a private self, which is responsive to strongly poetic narratives, and a public self, which must be concerned with building and maintaining a strong democratic order. The first self is romantic, the second pragmatic. Most important for Rorty is the caution not to mistake the *selbstbildung* of the former with the *volksbildung* of the latter. This is what is meant by the now-famous tag, "liberal ironist." We cannot propel our private self-edification into the public sphere.

Rorty's several statements on education are scattered throughout his work, and do not constitute a self-conscious project or theme; rather, they are an extension of his thinking on social and political matters. Rorty characteristically sees little role for philosophy in education if by philosophy what is meant is a search for the absolute. This is of a piece with his thinking on the role of philosophy in politics. As philosophy, shorn of its transcendental pretensions, has the social function of helping society get out from under the rug of transcendental thinking, so philosophy of education, if it is to have any use at all, ought to do the same. A rhetorical function for philosophy is thus put forth by Rorty: to persuade others to quell the transcendental urge. Similar to his talk of private and public selves, Rorty sees education as encompassing two very different roles. The first is education for private self-edification. The second is education for socialization. The former is the responsibility of the individual and has no public goal whatsoever. The latter is the responsibility of society, and is manifest in the schooling that society provides for children from kindergarten through high school.

In dealing with the social and political concerns of American schooling, Rorty has more to offer. He suggests that elementary and secondary schools should be in the business of *persuasion*. Teachers should be rhetoricians for a certain history: the history of liberal, democratic society and the attendant rise of, and struggles to maintain, freedom and the social responsibility that freedom entails. The content of such an education is to promote the best that our Western culture has to offer. In this respect, his view is similar to E. D. Hirsch's, whom Rorty admires. The "Great Books" approach appeals to Rorty, not surprisingly, as he was a product of just such an approach while an undergraduate at the University of Chicago.

Rorty's vision certainly is not a utopian one, and he has no truck with providing an education wrapped up in jingoism. Yet he does claim to be a patriot, and he insists that the overarching narrative taught should be one of progressive improvement in pursuing and achieving the goals of liberal democracy. Thus he sees little place in elementary and secondary schooling for the Marxist and postcolonialist-driven narratives of resistance and subversion. Rorty considers the challenge posed by competing narratives (for example, that of the teacher as opposed to that of parents or of other social institutions) as disruptive and confusing. He does, however, see the need for these alternative readings of society at the level of higher education. Not only does he hope that most (if not all) citizens attend higher education, but that they benefit from the sort of social criticism that colleges and universities do best. Rorty sees this as a necessary adjunct in the quest for further freedoms and the reduction of harms.

Rorty's work has generated a great deal of writing on the part of educators, though most of those taking Rorty up in print have been critical of his ideas. A number of them have objected to Rorty's call for philosophers to abandon metaphysics. Others have criticized his notion of the "liberal ironist." Still others have chided him for his sometimes negative pronouncements on revered educator/philosophers, notably Dewey. One scholar has emerged, though, as an especially sensitive and thoughtful reader of Rorty, even if, in the last analysis, he cannot be a disciple: René Vincente Arcilla. Arcilla, like many educators, takes

Rorty's pronouncements on the end of philosophy-as-we-know-it as entirely too dogmatic. In his book, *For the Love of Perfection: Richard Rorty and Liberal Education*,[49] Arcilla treads a middle path insofar as he accepts Rorty's critique of metaphysics as a positive science, while questioning (and ultimately rejecting) Rorty's dismissal of a public place for such notions as moral and social perfection.

Martha Nussbaum

Martha Nussbaum's book *Cultivating Humanity* (1997)[50] is a forceful exposition and defense of liberal education, emphasizing values of Socratic reason and cosmopolitanism that are grounded in the classical origins of the Western tradition itself. Nussbaum argues for the centrality of the study of non-Western cultures, of underrepresented racial and ethnic groups, of women, and of the varieties of human sexuality, all as part of a truly cosmopolitan, pluralistic liberal education. The capacity of students to appreciate the experiences and perspectives of those different from themselves is intrinsic to the breadth and inclusiveness of outlook that she identifies with the liberally educated person.

Focusing on the context of higher education, Nussbaum praises the educational virtues that Socrates so highly valued: those of challenging superficial and conventional beliefs, upsetting the complacency of settling for conformity with what is familiar and safe, and insisting that the unexamined life is not worth living. Yet for Nussbaum,

> We must therefore construct a liberal education that is not only Socratic, emphasizing critical thought and respectful judgment, but also pluralistic, imparting an understanding of the histories and contributions of groups with whom we interact, both within our nation and in the increasingly international sphere of business and politics. If we cannot teach our students everything they will need to know to be good citizens, we may at least teach them what they do not know and how they may inquire. We can acquaint them with some rudiments about the major non-Western cultures and minority groups within our own. We can show them how to inquire into the history and variety of gender and sexuality. Above all, we can teach them how to argue, rigorously and critically, so that they can call their minds their own.[51]

American education must articulate a conception of itself that defends the standards of reason, while remaining open to new points of view; that preserves the intellectual traditions and canons that define US culture, while consciously broadening the curriculum to expose students to traditions which diverge from their own and which, in their difference, may confront students with an awareness of their own parochialism; that remains respectful and tolerant of many points of view without lapsing into relativism; and, in short, that manages to prepare students simultaneously to be citizens of US society, and cosmopolitans, "citizens of the world." In *Cultivating Humanity* Nussbaum also touches on several of the major issues that trouble contemporary US universities: the "Great Books" debates; the tensions between promoting free speech and discouraging hate speech on campus; the proper role of proliferating Ethnic Studies areas; the call for requiring courses in non-Western studies as part of a liberal education; and the degree to which campuses have been in the past, and frequently remain, inhospitable places for racial minorities, for women, and for homosexuals.

The educational virtues that Nussbaum highlights – Socratic reason and a respect for diversity – are, in her view, the essential qualities of democratic citizenship. It is important to see that what Nussbaum means by the democratic underpinnings of "Socratic reason" is actually an amalgam of a range of notions, some taken from Socrates, some from the Greek and Roman Stoics, some from Madison and the American tradition of deliberative democracy, along with other sources. On the issue of cosmopolitanism, Nussbaum draws from classical authors including Diogenes and Seneca, and on to contemporary sources, characterizing cosmopolitanism as a view of persons as simultaneously citizens of two communities: their own local and particularistic group, and humanity generally. Liberally educated persons must be able to appreciate the distinctive character of each sphere, and the responsibilities appropriate to each. In order for this to happen, students must be exposed to the histories, cultures, literature, and mores of different world societies and should, according to Nussbaum, learn about at least one of these societies in considerable depth, including its language. The educational benefits of doing so are both to foster a respect for diversity and to learn to see what seems natural or neutral about one's own history, culture, literature, language, and mores from a more encompassing and reflective vantage point.

Yet her implicit belief in the existence of universal values and human characteristics entails that the main reason for studying people who are different from us is so that, ultimately, we can find out that we are all basically the same.[52] There is little examination of the kinds of tensions, if not contradictions, between the principles she advocates. For example, Nussbaum says that "comparative critical study, by removing the false air of naturalness and inevitability that surrounds our practices, can make our society a more truly reasonable one. . . . For attaining membership in the world entails *a willingness to doubt the goodness of one's own way*."[53] But she sees no friction between this position and statements such as:

> We have not produced truly free citizens in the Socratic sense unless we have produced people who can reason for themselves and argue well, who understand the difference between a logically valid and logically invalid argument. . . . [P]articipants in such arguments should gradually take on the ability to distinguish . . . what is parochial from *what may be commended as a norm for others*, what is arbitrary and unjustified from what may be justified by reasoned argument.[54]

In all of this we return to the narrow conception of philosophy that drives Nussbaum's argument. She equates philosophy with the defense of Socratic reason, and fails to consider that this mode of analysis may not provide the universal discourse for resolving disagreements even *within* American society, let alone on a global scale. And we ought to reflect upon who would be left out of the universalism she advocates.

One example, by way of illustrating this point. Nussbaum notes, quite forthrightly and with sincere concern, that "In twenty years of teaching in departments of philosophy and classics I have taught only two black graduate students and have had no black colleagues . . . very few black students take nonrequired courses in philosophy."[55] She puzzles over this, considering (and rejecting) the view of the Committee on Blacks in the American Philosophical Association that this may partly be due to required courses in formal logic that "black students do not feel comfortable with."[56] But having rejected this explanation for why so few African-American students choose philosophy as a field (an explanation provided by qualified African-Americans *within* the field of philosophy), she remains silent on any alternative explanation. Now, on Nussbaum's own account, this should be an urgent, pressing issue: If it is true that philosophy of the sort practiced in philosophy departments is uncongenial to the outlook, concerns, and thought processes of African-American students (or any other significant group in society), then this constitutes a serious impediment to the kind of cosmopolitanism she wants to promote. Why *are* these students so severely underrepresented in the field? At what point does a consistent pattern of selection, and the rationale provided for those choices *by the persons making them*, need to be taken seriously as counterevidence to the assumption that "Logical reasoning . . . comes naturally to human beings"?[57] Nussbaum takes any doubts along these lines as expressing the racist idea that "black students cannot think logically."[58] But perhaps the onus of the debate is not on African-American students, but on what many philosophers think it means to "think logically," or on the assumption that this method represents the only valid basis for arguing and adjudicating different views about truth and value, or on the possibility that the putatively universal truths explored in philosophy departments may not in fact speak to the felt concerns of many individuals and groups. One need not be a "relativist" to think that.

Conclusion

This chapter has tried to show how much of philosophical thought in America has exemplified, and struggled with, tensions that are very much part of the broader American character: an ambivalent relation to the past; a restless energy for making fresh starts and creating ideas anew; an implicit faith in a certain native character and authenticity that are potentially threatened by institutionalized forms of social organization; a faith in science, evolutionary change, and process-oriented prescriptions for reform; a privileging of freedom, merit, and self-determination; and a perpetual struggle with the competing values of pluralism and cultural or political unity. These ideas and attitudes, and the unresolved tensions within and among them, have given philosophy in America an ongoing set of problematics that can be seen in philosophical work as otherwise diverse as, for example, Quine and Davidson's post-analytic rebellion; the pragmatism of James and Dewey; American feminist philosophy; the liberal and communitarian debates of Rawls, Michael Sandel, Alasdair MacIntyre, and others; and the various receptions of and reactions to postmodernism or poststructuralism on this side of the Atlantic. It can be seen even more dramatically in the audacious work of Rorty, Stanley Cavell, and others who have taken it upon themselves to question and reconfigure the entire project of "philosophy." In all of this, we have suggested, philosophy in America manifests its character as a distinctively *American* style of philosophy.

The four authors chosen for review here show different ways of coping with these tensions; but their particular use for us is in showing how education has frequently played a central role in philosophical attempts to balance or reconcile those tensions. Education, whether in organized, institutionalized contexts or not, seems inherently hopeful and forward-looking; it emphasizes potential and possibility; it is intrinsically meliorative and reformist. It perfectly blends the American faiths in progress, merit, and self-determination. But as can also be seen by the thought of these exemplary philosophers, such pronouncements about education also tend to bring out a certain naive idealism – even from philosophers who on other matters are relentlessly discerning, skeptical, and down-to-earth. Perhaps it is good to be so: after all, if one cannot be hopeful and forward-looking about education, why bother at all? Yet for many of us who work as philosophers of education, where education is the *primary* subject of philosophical reflection and questioning, education appears as a much more ambivalent and contested notion; an endeavor that creates as many ethical and epistemological problems as it solves. From this perspective, education is not a *solution* to these kinds of tensions, but simply another arena in which they need to be debated.

Notes

1 John J. Stuhr, "Classical American Philosophy," in *Pragmatism and Classical American Philosophy*, 2nd edn. (New York: Oxford University Press, 2000), p. 3.

2 Ibid., p. 4; see also Giovanna Borradori, *The American Philosopher* (Chicago: University of Chicago Press, 1994); John Rajchman, "Philosophy in American," in John Rajchman and Cornel West, eds., *Post-Analytic Philosophy* (New York: Columbia University Press, 1985); and Cornel West, *The American Evasion of Philosophy: A Genealogy of Pragmatism* (Madison: University of Wisconsin Press, 1989).

3 Daniel J. Wilson, *Science, Community and the Transformation of American Philosophy, 1860–1930* (Chicago: University of Chicago Press, 1990), pp. 1–4; see also Max H. Fisch, "The Classic Period in American Philosophy," in Fisch, ed., *Classic American Philosophers* (New York: Fordham University Press, 1996), pp. 10–17; and Paul F. Boller, Jr., *American Thought in Transition: The Impact of Evolutionary Naturalism, 1865–1900* (Chicago: Rand, McNally and Company, 1969), p. ix.

4 Of course, the Civil War was an excruciating trauma for the nation. But even in this instance most of the devastation was limited: over 60 percent of the war was waged within the state of Virginia. And the scars of defeat, obviously, were borne disproportionately within some regions of the country and not in others.
5 It is provocative to consider that these four figures have also been among the most active and visible public intellectuals among American philosophy – and perhaps as a consequence each has also been contested in some circles as being a "true" philosopher. Yet even among more mainstream professional philosophers (C. I. Lewis, W. V. O. Quine, Donald Davidson, Thomas Kuhn, John Rawls, and others), many of these same tensions can be discerned; yet none of them, to our knowledge, has addressed educational issues to any significant extent (see Wilson, *Science, Community and the Transformation of American Philosophy*, pp. 4–6 and 150–79, on the professionalization of American philosophy).
6 Peter Caws, ed., *Two Centuries of Philosophy in America* (London: Blackwell, 1980), p. 4.
7 John E. Smith, *The Spirit of American Philosophy* (Albany: SUNY Press, 1983), pp. 132–4.
8 "Circles," in L. Ziff, ed., *Ralph Waldo Emerson: Selected Essays* (New York: Penguin Books, 1982), p. 236.
9 E. Wagenknecht, *Ralph Waldo Emerson: Portrait of a Balanced Soul* (New York: Oxford University Press, 1974), p. 36.
10 B. Helm, "Emerson *Agonistes*: Education as Struggle and Process," *Educational Theory*, 42/2 (1992): 165–80.
11 R. W. Emerson, "Education," in *Emerson's Complete Works*, vol. X (Boston: Houghton, Mifflin, and Company, 1895), p. 134.
12 "Friendship," in *Essays and Poems* (London: Everyman, 1992), pp. 99–100.
13 Ibid., pp. 102–3.
14 "The American Scholar," in L. Ziff, ed., *Ralph Waldo Emerson: Selected Essays* (New York: Penguin Books, 1982), p. 84.
15 "Nature," in Ziff, ed., *Ralph Waldo Emerson*, p. 36.
16 Ibid., p. 55.
17 Ibid., p. 58.
18 Ibid., pp. 48, 50.
19 Ibid., p. 59.
20 "Education," p. 130.
21 "Nature," p. 55.
22 "Nature," (2) in *Essays and Poems* (London: Everyman, 1992), p. 261.
23 "The American Scholar," p. 92.
24 "Education," p. 132.
25 "The American Scholar," p. 102.
26 "Nature," p. 35.
27 "The American Scholar," p. 89.
28 Ibid., p. 88.
29 "Experience," in Ziff, ed., *Ralph Waldo Emerson*, p. 304.
30 Ibid., p. 294.
31 "Education," p. 133.
32 Ibid., p. 137.

33 Ibid., p. 146.
34 Ibid., p. 148.
35 Ibid., p. 141.
36 Ibid., p. 151.
37 Ibid., pp. 151–2.
38 *Experience and Nature* (Chicago: Open Court, 1929), p. 28.
39 Ibid., p. 308.
40 *Democracy and Education* (New York: The Free Press, 1944 [1919]), p. 3.
41 Ibid., pp. 86–8.
42 Ibid., p. 96.
43 Ibid., p. 22.
44 Ibid., 150; John Dewey, *Experience and Education* (New York: Touchstone, 1938), p. 69.
45 *Experience and Education*, p. 88.
46 *Philosophy and the Mirror of Nature* (Princeton, NJ: Princeton University Press, 1979).
47 *Consequences of Pragmatism* (Minneapolis: University of Minnesota Press, 1982).
48 *Contingency, Irony, and Solidarity* (Cambridge: Cambridge University Press, 1989).
49 René Vincente Arcilla, *For the Love of Perfection: Richard Rorty and Liberal Education* (New York: Routledge, 1995).
50 *Cultivating Humanity: A Classical Defense of Reform in Liberal Education* (Cambridge, MA: Harvard University Press, 1997). The material in this section is adapted from a longer review essay of *Cultivating Humanity* (see Nicholas C. Burbules, "Essay Review of Martha Nussbaum, *Cultivating Humanity: A Classical Defense of Reform in Liberal Education*," *Harvard Educational Review*, 69/4 (1999): 456–66).
51 *Cultivating Humanity*, p. 295.
52 Martha Nussbaum, "In Defense of Universal Values," in *Women and Human Development: The Capabilities Approach* (New York: Cambridge University Press, 2000).
53 *Cultivating Humanity*, pp, 55, 62; italics added.
54 Ibid., p. 36, 62; italics adeed.
55 Ibid., p. 152.
56 Ibid., p. 177.
57 Ibid., p. 36.
58 Ibid., p. 177.

Suggested reading

Burbules, Nicholas C., "Continuity and Diversity in Philosophy of Education," in *Educational Theory*, 41/3 (1991): 257–63.

Chambliss, J. J., "History of Philosophy of Education," in J. J. Chambliss, ed., *Philosophy of Education: An Encyclopedia* (New York: Garland Publishing, 1996), pp. 461–72.

Ericson, David, "Philosophical Issues in Education," in Marvin Alkin, ed., *Encyclopedia of Educational Research* (New York: Macmillan, 1992), pp. 1002–7.

Maloney, Karen E., "Philosophy of Education: Definitions of the Field, 1942–1982," in *Educational Studies*, 16/3 (1985): 235–58.

Phillips, D. C., "Philosophy of Education: Historical Overview," in T. Husen and T. Neville Postlethwaite, eds., *The International Encyclopedia of Education*, 2nd edn. (Oxford: Pergamon Press, 1994), 4447–56.

Chapter 23

Art and the Aesthetic

Armen T. Marsoobian

Art and aesthetic experience play a central role in the human condition and as such are of prime importance to American philosophers' attempts to make sense of that condition. Of the philosophers from the classic period in American philosophy, two stand out for their contributions to the field of aesthetics: George Santayana and John Dewey. While most other philosophers in this period had significant things to say about the arts, Santayana and Dewey were the only ones to write whole works on the topic, the former writing two volumes, *The Sense of Beauty* (1896) and *Reason in Art* (1905), the latter writing *Art as Experience* (1934). Besides these books, both wrote numerous essays and reviews on topics in the fine arts and literature. Santayana at one time was better known for his novelistic and poetic skills than he was for his technical philosophy, while Dewey wrote poetry unbeknownst to his philosophical colleagues.[1] Of the remaining classical figures, Charles S. Peirce must be mentioned, not for any extensive or sustained treatment of art on his part, but for the fecundity of his semiotic theory for future analyses of art by philosophers in the latter half of the twentieth century.[2] By the time of Dewey's death in 1952 a dramatic shift had begun in the philosophical treatment of artworks. The increasing specialization within the discipline and the linguistic turn of much of its practitioners led to a narrowing of concerns. But our story begins a generation earlier than that of the classic period philosophers. For it is with Ralph Waldo Emerson that many of the sustaining themes in American aesthetics were first established.

Ralph Waldo Emerson: Art as the Commonplace

Ralph Waldo Emerson (1803–82), the transcendentalist philosopher, essayist, and poet, took many of his themes from the German and British romantic traditions and gave them a unique formulation that would reverberate in his philosophical heirs through the century ahead. Emerson had traveled to England both early and late in his career, having met such important figures in British romanticism as Coleridge and Carlyle. This was a milieu in which post-Kantian idealism dominated aesthetic thought. It was common to talk of mind, spirit, or soul as inhabiting the natural world. Emerson's idealism is manifested in his claims about art and aesthetic creation. He begins his 1841 essay "Art" with these words: "Because the soul is progressive, it never quite repeats itself, but in every act attempts the production of a new and fairer whole. This appears in works both of the useful and the fine arts." Art, he goes on to say, does not imitate nature but captures the "expression of nature." In the same essay he continues: "Thus in our fine arts, not imitation, but creation is the aim. In landscapes, the painter should give the suggestion of a fairer creation than we know. The details, the prose of nature he should omit, and give us only the spirit and splendor."[3] Emerson adamantly rejects any conception of art that treats it as naive mimesis.

Emerson often speaks of the artist as a conduit for a higher intelligence: "the artist's pen and chisel seems to have been held and guided by a gigantic hand to inscribe a line in the history of the human race."[4] The beauty in nature and the beauty of art derive from the same source. This source is the fount of creativity that runs through both the human and the non-human world. Emerson identifies this source by many names, often referring to it as the "Soul," or an "Aboriginal Power," and in the above referenced essay he invokes "Art" with a capital "A" to capture this notion. He describes this power as follows:

> The reference of all production at last to an Aboriginal Power, explains the traits common to all works of the highest art, – that they are universally intelligible; that they restore to us the simplest states of mind; and are religious. Since what skill is therein shown is the reappearance of the original soul, a jet of pure light, it should produce a similar impression to that made by natural objects. In happy hours, nature appears to us one with art; art perfected, – the work of genius.[5]

If nature is art perfected, then artists in creating works of art are attempting to capture or express something intrinsic to themselves. Artistic creation is the expression of human character. "The artist will find in his work an outlet for his proper character."[6] For Emersonian idealism there is no contradiction in the claim that art expresses nature while at the same time expressing human character. Art is intelligible to us the spectator because we see "the deepest and simplest attributes of our nature" manifested in these works. For Emerson, artists do not primarily respond to the history of art and art-making. Emerson may well have been puzzled by the fashionable twentieth-century notion that the subject matter of art is art itself. Art, for Emerson, was not self-referential; its models were "life, household life, and the sweet and smart of personal relations, of beating hearts, and meeting eyes, of poverty, and necessity, and hope, and fear."[7]

The creation of art is not a passive event. Emerson saw the role of the arts as central to the project of human self-creation. This notion held true from his early works through his final writings. Art was to serve a unique educative goal. One does not study art merely for the sake of art appreciation. Art is neither created nor experienced for its own sake. The grand European tour in which the upper-class gentlemen and ladies of the yet to come Gilded Age experienced the great art of Rome, Paris, and London would be a phenomenon easily ridiculed by Emerson. One does not study art in order to learn the new or the unfamiliar. Great historical and mythological paintings and sculptures do not in themselves hold great moral lessons for us. Emerson writes of his own experience:

> I remember, when in my younger days, I had heard the wonders of Italian painting, I fancied the great paintings would be great strangers; some surprising combination of color and form; a foreign wonder, barbaric pearl and gold. . . . When at last I came to Rome, and saw with eyes the pictures, I found that genius left to novices the gay and fantastic and ostentatious, and itself pierced directly to the simple and true; that it was familiar and sincere; that it was the old, eternal fact that I had met already in so many forms, – unto which I had lived; that it was plain *you and me* I knew so well, – had left at home in so many conversations. . . . I saw again in the Academmia at Naples, in the chambers of sculpture, and yet again when I came to Rome, and to the paintings of Raphael, Angelo, Sacchi, Titian, and Leonardo da Vinci. . . . It had travelled by my side: that which I had fancied I had left in Boston, was here in the Vatican, and again at Milan, and at Paris, and made all travelling ridiculous as a treadmill. I now require this of all pictures, that they domesticate me, not that they dazzle me. Pictues must not be too picturesque.[8]

The claim that pictures must not be too picturesque is consistent with Emerson's sustained and highly influential cultural criticism, a criticism that was to serve as a model for Friedrich Nietzsche in the years ahead. Art loses touch with its true resources in the human when it becomes overly preoccupied with technique and surface brilliance. Art that is produced purely for show or extravagance is an art that has not achieved maturity. Art will remain immature "if it is not practical and moral, if it do not stand in connection with the conscience, if it do not make the poor and uncultivated feel that it addresses them with a voice of lofty cheer."[9]

Emerson is clearly providing a normative conception of art. He is presenting a diagnosis for the moral ills of humankind while identifying its tell-tale symptoms in the products of art. His essay is peppered with such remarks as: "The fountains of invention and beauty in modern society are all but dried up." "Art is poor and low."[10] A clear symptom of these ills is the perversion of beauty. Emerson contends that when humans are dissatisfied by their moral self-image, "they flee to art, and convey their better sense in an oratorio, a statue, or a picture." As a result the practical and everyday becomes devoid of beauty. By divorcing beauty from the useful and placing it primarily in the domain of fine art, we demean and degrade aesthetic beauty. If pleasure and enjoyment find their only source in aesthetic beauty, then art becomes a form of "escapism" from the practical and everyday. For Emerson the resulting art will manifest a "sickly beauty":

> This division of beauty from use, the laws of nature do not permit. As soon as beauty is sought not from religion and love, but for pleasure, it degrades the seeker. High beauty is no longer attainable by him in canvas or in stone, in sound, or in lyrical construction; an effeminate prudent, sickly beauty, which is not beauty, is all that can be formed.[11]

The cure for this disease is to live life as art. Life should be a work of art or a performance piece, but a performance neither in the style of Oscar Wilde nor that of Karen Finley. Emerson warns against the danger of long-established artistic forms whose inherent fixity stifles the soul. Such fixity leads to the stagnation of habit and routine that plagued both the art and the political culture of his day. Art that harkens back to the artistic forms of older generations is a dead art. "True art is never fixed, but always flowing. The sweetest music is not in the oratorio, but in the human voice when it speaks from its instant life, tones of tenderness, truth, or courage." In transposing aesthetic and literary categories to the human individual, Emerson provides a striking re-imagining of human possibilities: "All works of art should not be detached, but extempore performances. A great man is a new statue in every attitude and action. . . . Life may be lyric or epic, as well as a poem or a romance."[12] Beauty will thus be restored to the commonplace and the practical. "Beauty must come back to the useful arts, and the distinction between the fine and the useful arts be forgotten." Everyday experience would be an enhanced aesthetic experience. The distinction between instrumental and aesthetic use no longer holds. The artistic instinct in all humans would thus "find beauty and holiness in new and necessary facts, in the field and roadside, in the shop and mill."[13]

The theme that art is an enhanced experience of the commonplace is one that Dewey takes up almost 100 years later in *Art as Experience.* Art for art's sake is not to be countenanced. The idea that fine art is divorced from the everyday and only can be truly experienced when one "suspends" oneself from one's practical, utilitarian concerns, is an idea rejected by Emerson, Dewey, and contemporary pragmatic thought about the arts.[14] What Dewey later calls "*an* experience" finds its roots here in the Emersonian ideal of Art with a capital "A." For Dewey "*an* experience" is a more naturalized and biologically based notion, but functions as a normative ideal much in the same fashion as Emersonian Art.

George Santayana: Beauty as the Objectification of Pleasure

Before further examining Dewey's theory of aesthetic experience, we must first take up the work of George Santayana (1863–1952). With the publication of his book *The Sense of Beauty: Being the Outlines of Aesthetic Theory* in 1896, Santayana clearly established himself as an important and original thinker when it came to art and aesthetics. He completed the book after teaching courses in aesthetics as a junior professor at Harvard College in the years preceding. While he soon came to reject many of the claims he made in this book, the originality and simplicity of the book's major thesis assured it a place in the canon of aesthetic theory. This thesis is captured in the closing lines of the first chapter of the book: "Thus beauty is constituted by the objectification of pleasure. It is pleasure objectified."[15]

Santayana had reached this thesis by employing what he calls "a psychological method" for approaching the subject of aesthetics. This method is one that is distinct from either the actual employment of aesthetic judgments (i.e., the "praise" or appreciation of artworks) or the historical-anthropological explanation of art and the diversity of its products and processes (i.e., what Santayana refers to as the "philosophy of art"). The "nature and elements of our aesthetic judgment" will be the focus of his inquiry: "[The psychological method] deals with moral and aesthetic judgments as phenomena of mind and products of mental evolution. The problem here is to understand the origin and conditions of these feelings and their relation to the rest of our economy."[16] By systematically focusing on the nature of aesthetic judgment, Santayana's book demarcated a theoretical space that was soon to become the philosophical specialization known as aesthetics. This was a distinctly twentieth-century outlook. In the nineteenth century the aesthetic and moral sensibilities were often discussed and highly prized as distinctly human characteristics, ones that separated human beings from the rest of the animal world. While much was written about the importance of the aesthetic sensibility, little scientific or analytical attention was paid to it. For Santayana, all human value, whether aesthetic or moral, derives from the satisfaction of desires and as such is common to many other creatures. There is no sharp demarcation between the human and the non-human. Thus Santayana's early analysis of aesthetics fits nicely with his more mature philosophical naturalism. Whether other non-human creatures have values is hard to say, but the processes we find in human valuation are continuous throughout much of the natural world.

Santayana claims that values per se are not found in the world. Values require the presence of human consciousness – not just an intellectual consciousness but an emotional consciousness. If human beings are conceived as merely intellectual observers of the world, "every event would then be noted, its relations would be observed, its recurrence might be expected; but all this would happen without a shadow of desire, of pleasure, or of regret." The emotional life is at the core of the aesthetic and moral life, for without it "all value and excellence would be gone." Thus Santayana concludes: "So that for the existence of good in any form it is not merely consciousness but emotional consciousness that is needed. Observation will not do, appreciation is required."[17] Beauty is a species of the good – that is, of value.

Unlike the British empiricist tradition where the senses are often portrayed as passive capacities (faculties) that receive sensations, Santayana claims that the aesthetic sense is an active capacity which responds to sense perception.[18] This active capacity is what Santayana will call "objectification." Rudimentary sense perception, besides providing cognitive data, oftentimes results in pleasures and pains. The smooth, cold touch of one's hand against a polished piece of marble may give one pleasurable sensations, but for Santayana this is insufficient for the occurrence of aesthetic pleasure. These physical pleasures call attention to some part or organ of the body. He writes:

> Aesthetic pleasures have physical conditions, they depend on the activity of the eye and the ear, of the memory and the other ideational functions of the brain. But we do not connect those pleasures with their seats . . . the ideas with which aesthetic pleasures are associated are not the ideas of their bodily causes.[19]

Objectification of pleasure requires that our sense organs be "transparent," thus allowing our attention to be carried directly to some external object. This capacity, or what he sometimes calls "artifice of thought," is the basis for many of the distinctions we find in modern philosophy's model of the world. Our sensations are organized and ordered by our mind and projected into the world. The secondary qualities are the stuff to be organized, what is out there in the world, that is, the primary qualities (e.g., extension) are taken as the given. Santayana relies on "current theories of perception" to explain this "psychological phenomenon, viz., the transformation of an element of sensation into the quality of a thing": "External objects usually affect various senses at once, the impressions of which are thereby associated." Through repetition and the associations of memory, these impressions merge and unify into a single precept. "But this precept, once formed, is clearly different from those particular experiences out of which it grew. It is permanent, they are variable." These constructions of mind come to stand for reality, while their materials are deemed merely appearance.[20]

In a similar fashion we come to understand beauty as in the object, viz., as a quality of the thing. Our emotion and feelings operate on a similar model to that of sense perception described above. Yet in our emotional life we recognize the boundaries of this objectification. The inclusion of the emotional element in what Santayana refers to as "the intermediate realm of vulgar day" has for the most part been exercised. This is the world of mechanical science in which our ideas of things are composed of "exclusively perceptual elements." Yet objectified emotion and feeling still hold sway in religion and art. There is a curious sense in which Santayana sees art and religion as representing our failure to understand how our own psychology works. These realms represent the work of the remnants of a primitive and "mythological habit of thought." The sense of beauty is a "survival" of an archaic and primitive mind:

> Beauty is an emotional element, a pleasure of ours, which nevertheless we regard as a quality of things. . . . It is a survival of a tendency originally universal to make every effect of a thing upon us a constituent of its conceived nature. The scientific idea of a thing is a great abstraction from the mass of perceptions and reactions which the thing produces; the aesthetic idea is less abstract, since it retains the emotional reaction, the pleasure of perception, as an integral part of the conceived thing.[21]

Most other pleasures, those of a non-aesthetic kind, we recognize as effects of objects and associate them with particular sense organs. Oddly then, beauty is the result of a peculiar failure on our part.

Much of Santayana's analysis that follows the setting forth of this bold thesis regarding the sense of beauty entails the fleshing out of the constituents and processes of objectification. The variety of sense impressions constitutive of an aesthetic experience may each individually provide pleasure, but without a "constructive imagination" they fail to cohere and provide the synthesis necessary for the emergence of beauty. Form is what we call this synthesis:

> The synthesis, then, which constitutes form is an activity of the mind; the unity arises consciously, and is an insight into the relation of sensible elements separately perceived. It differs from sensation in the consciousness of the synthesis, and from expression in the homogeneity of the elements, and in their common presence to sense.[22]

Santayana provides numerous detailed descriptions and analyses of the varieties of form in the visual arts, the language arts and in natural landscapes. The final process of the imagination which completes Santayana's exploration of objectification is labeled by him "expression." This is a process by which we bring a certain meaning and tone from other experiences to a new experience:

> The hushed reverberations of these associated feelings continue in the brain, and by modifying our present reaction, colour the image upon which our attention is fixed. The quality thus acquired by objects through association is what we call their expression. Whereas in form or material there is one object with its emotional effect, in expression there are two, and the emotional effect belongs to the character of the second or suggested one.[23]

Santayana's nuanced insights into aesthetic expression are too numerous to capture in a mere summary such as this. John Dewey, nearly 40 years later in the opening pages of *Art as Experience*, highlights the importance of this insight into the "hushed reverberations" of associated feelings when he lays out his conception of lived experience.[24] Whether one accepts or rejects Santayana's overall thesis, reading *The Sense of Beauty* provides a gold-mine of aesthetic insights and challenges, besides being in itself an aesthetic pleasure to read.

In the intervening years between the publication of *The Sense of Beauty* in 1896 and *Reason in Art* in 1905 there was significant transformation in Santayana's outlook on the prospects for a science of aesthetics.[25] The biologism of writers such as Hippolyte Taine (1828–93) helped to deepen Santayana's naturalism. He had come to believe that the literary psychology that formed the method of his earlier work was rootless and neglected the transitory and fleeting nature of aesthetic experience. In 1904 he had published a short article in *The Philosophical Review* entitled "What is Aesthetics?"[26] In this article Santayana abandons the notion that aesthetics can be a separate field of inquiry. What seems at first as a critique of the soon to be dominant aesthetics of Benedetto Croce turns out to be a subtle critique of his own earlier work:

> The truth is that the group of activities we can call aesthetic is a motley one, created by certain historic and literary accidents. Wherever consciousness becomes at all imaginative and finds flattering unction in its *phantasmagoria*, or whenever a work, for whatever purpose constructed, happens to have notable intrinsic values for perception, we utter the word "aesthetic"; but these occasions are miscellaneous, and there is no single agency in nature, no specific organ in sense, and no separable task in spirit, to which aesthetic quality can be attributed. Aesthetic experience is so broad and so incidental, it is spread so thin over all life, that like life itself it opens out for reflection into divergent vistas.[27]

There is no isolatable subject matter for the science of aesthetics to study and investigate. The aesthetic is so inextricably bound up with sensuous and rational interests that to speak of it in isolation is to trivialize it:

> Aesthetic good is accordingly no separable value; it is not realizable by itself in a set of objects not otherwise interesting. Anything which is to entertain the imagination must first have exercised the senses; it must first have stimulated some animal reaction, engaged attention, and intertwined itself in the vital process; and later this aesthetic good, with animal and sensuous values imbedded in it and making its very substance, must be swallowed up in a rational life; for reason will immediately feel itself called upon to synthesize those imaginative activities with whatever else is valuable.[28]

Aesthetics is neither a part of psychology nor a distinct philosophical discipline. Either approach does "violence to the structure of things. The lines of cleavage in human history and art do not isolate any such block of experience as aesthetics is supposed to describe." In lieu of an aesthetic science, we have what Santayana calls "the art and function of criticism."[29] Santayana spent the next half-century actively engaged in such criticism and produced a wealth of material on the fine, literary, and performing arts.

Sanatayana's realization of the above insight served to motivate his work in the years following the publication of *The Sense of Beauty.* The publication in 1905 of the five volumes of his *The Life of Reason; or The Phases of Human Progress* was the fruit of his endeavor to make sense of this complexity of the human in the natural world. He begins his analysis in *Reason in Art* by employing the term "art" in the broad sense of making, or what the Greeks called *techne*. "Art is action which transcending the body makes the world a more congenial stimulus to the soul. All art is therefore useful and practical." The moral dimension is omnipresent for Santayana. The ultimate end of art is human happiness: "If art is that element in the Life of Reason which consists in modifying its environment the better to attain its end, art may be expected to subserve all parts of the human ideal, to increase man's comfort, knowledge, and delight."[30] Yet this is a happiness that is often fleeting. It would be hard to summarize the argument of *Reason in Art*, but a pervasive feature of Santayana's characterization of aesthetic value and aesthetic experience is its accidental and transitory nature. Accidental not for the individual per se but accidental in the evolutionary development of the life of reason in the material world.

The vital and naturalistically embedded nature of aesthetic experience is also recognized by John Dewey in his work *Art as Experience*. Both Santayana and Dewey share a naturalistic perspective on these ideal products of human endeavor, yet it is also their naturalism that seems to divide them.[31] The thoroughgoing naturalism of Santayana recognizes that the "vital harmonies" of aesthetic experience are momentary and fleeting. For Dewey, his meliorism colors his naturalism. The human project is to make aesthetic experience ever more pervasive in our lives.

John Dewey: The Centrality of Aesthetic Experience

Unlike Santayana, John Dewey (1859–1952) began his philosophical investigations of art and the aesthetic relatively late in his career. Though the importance of the fine arts and crafts was recognized by him as central to his educational theory, it was not until the mid-1920s that he began any systematic treatment of the processes and products of the fine arts. His growing friendship with the art collector Albert C. Barnes, who had taken a course with him at Columbia University in the academic year 1917–18, helped to solidify his interests in the visual arts, especially painting. He published a series of essays in the 1920s, one of which appeared in the *Journal of the Barnes Foundation*.[32] Barnes had an excellent collection of French art housed in his school in Merion, Pennsylvania. Dewey also took a tour of European art museums with Barnes in 1925 and established a number of contacts with collectors, artists, and painters, including Leo Stein and Henri Matisse. In 1925 Dewey delivered his Carus Lectures, which appeared that year as *Experience and Nature*. *Experience and Nature* is arguably Dewey's most important philosophical work. Undoubtedly, it would have been a significantly different work if Dewey had not been as absorbed in the fine arts during this especially fecund period in his intellectual development. It is not just that a chapter of this book is devoted to art, but the whole metaphysical analysis of experience is shaped by his insights into aesthetic experience. Dewey's intellectual journey culminated in his 1931 William James Lectures at Harvard University that were to serve as the basis of his seminal work *Art as Experience* (1934).

In chapter 9, entitled "Experience, Nature and Art," the penultimate chapter of *Experience and Nature*, Dewey brings together many of the themes of the previous chapters. His particular concern is to demonstrate the limitations of many of the distinctions common to both philosophical and everyday discussions of science and the arts. He contends that, beginning with the ancient Greeks, there has been a tendency to disparage the practical, so-called "menial" arts, in contradistinction to the theoretical activities of reason or science. Theoretical activity was contemplation and not practice. This prejudice has been carried over into the modern day but in a slightly altered form: "Modern thought . . . combines exaltation of science with eulogistic appreciation of art, especially of fine and creative art."[33] Unlike the Greeks, who saw the commonalities between the fine arts and the practical industrial arts, our modern age emphasizes their differences. What results, according to Dewey, is an "esoteric" notion of fine art. Art and the aesthetic are evermore isolated from activities and practices of the everyday. This is a view that he will later call the "museum view" of art.

For Dewey the lesson to be learned from the success of modern science is that theory is not akin to the Greek notion of contemplation; rather, theory is productive and as such is infused in practice when such practice is elevated above mere routine. Dewey would like us to cut through all the unhelpful distinctions that inhabit our intellectual landscape:

> It would then be seen that science is an art, that art is practice, and that the only distinction worth drawing is not between practice and theory, but between those modes of practice that are not intelligent, not inherently and immediately enjoyable, and those which are full of enjoyed meanings. . . . Thus would disappear the separations that trouble present thinking: division of everything into nature *and* experience, of experience into practice *and* theory, art *and* science, of art into useful *and* fine, menial *and* free.[34]

Dewey places his examination of the fine arts within this broader project. Instead of dualisms, he provides a naturalistic account that stresses the continuities between the biological, the psychological, the social, and the intellectual. Art in this most generic sense plays a pivotal role in the naturalistic metaphysics of experience that Dewey lays out in the pages of *Experience and Nature*. This is made clear in the following summary that Dewey gives of his book's argument:

> Thus the issue involved in experience as art in its pregnant sense and in art as processes and materials of nature continued by direction into achieved and enjoyed meanings, sums up in itself all the issues which have been previously considered. Thought, intelligence, science is the intentional direction of natural events to meanings capable of immediate possession and enjoyment; this direction – which is operative art – is itself a natural event in which nature otherwise partial and incomplete comes fully to itself. . . . The doings and sufferings that form experience are, in the degree in which experience is intelligent or charged with meanings, a union of the precarious, novel, irregular with the settled, assured and uniform – a union which also defines the artistic and the esthetic. For wherever there is art the contingent and ongoing no longer work at cross purposes with the formal and recurrent but commingle in harmony.[35]

This commingling in harmony is what Dewey, in *Art as Experience*, will call "*an* experience." While the theme of *Art as Experience* is more explicitly focused upon fine art and aesthetic experience, this notion of "*an* experience" is fundamental for understanding the metaphysical project of *Experience and Nature*. The two books, possibly along with his later book *Logic: The Theory of Inquiry* (1938), provide the core of Dewey's philosophical naturalism.

In *Experience and Nature* Dewey makes a number of references to what we would consider today to be theories of aesthetics or art. These include some veiled criticisms of Croce's theory of art as the expression of emotion and Clive Bell and Roger Fry's theories of aesthetic form.[36] All of these are taken up in much greater detail in *Art as Experience*. This book had a significant impact on theorizing about the arts for next 30 or so odd years. Its crucial third chapter, "Having an Experience," was anthologized in every significant textbook published in philosophical aesthetics for the reminder of the century. With the rise of analytic aesthetics in the 1950s Dewey's experiential approach fell out of fashion, but in the last decade there has been a significant revival of interest in his aesthetics. This has in part been the result of a renewed interest in pragmatism in general.

In *Art as Experience* Dewey provides a far-ranging analysis of many issues central to philosophical aesthetics. Such issues as the definition of a work of art, the nature of expression, the relation of form and content, the role of appreciation and criticism are all examined from the perspective of his reconstructed conception of experience. To understand what this perspective is and the key role that "*an* experience" plays in it, we must first lay out what this notion of experience is not. Dewey denies that he is employing the term in the manner often found in the British empiricist tradition. For Dewey, traditional empiricism provides much too subjectivist an approach. Experience is not something "had" in the mind but is the interaction of the human organism with its environment, an interaction that has reached a particular level of organization. This is what Dewey means when he writes in *Experience and Nature* that "experience is *of* as well as *in* nature." Eschewing any opening for dualisms that place experience as some sort of veil between us and nature, he continues:

> It is not experience which is experienced, but nature – stones, plants, animals, diseases, health, temperature, electricity, and so on. Things interacting in certain ways *are* experience; they are what is experienced. Linked in certain other ways with another natural object – the human organism – they are *how* things are experienced as well. Experience thus reaches down into nature; it has depth.[37]

Though years later he came to see the limitations involved in retaining a traditional term such as "experience," for it created much misunderstanding among careless or unsympathetic readers, he believed at this stage that his reconstructed notion could do much work.[38] He even retained the term "empiricism" and dubbed his philosophical method "either empirical naturalism or naturalistic empiricism."[39]

This method of experience is pervasive throughout Dewey's treatment of art in *Art as Experience*. He views his own treatment of art and the aesthetic as much more than simply an exploration of art that employs the insights he has gleaned from his empirical naturalism. In an important sense, the project of *Experience and Nature* could not be completed until aesthetic experience was more fully probed in *Art as Experience*. In a chapter near the end of this book, entitled "The Challenge to Philosophy," Dewey writes: "To esthetic experience, then, the philosopher must go to understand what experience is." For it is aesthetic experience which is experience in its "integrity . . . freed from the forces that impede and confuse its development as experience; freed, that is, from factors that subordinate an experience as it is directly had to something beyond itself."[40] What Dewey had learned about the arts in the preceding decade was now seen as a challenge and a test of the adequacy of his naturalism. The practices of the arts, that is, the content of artistic practice and appreciation, was to shape and test his more general theory, his metaphysics of experience. This was the standard by which his book was to be judged:

> While the theory of esthetics put forth by a philosopher is incidentally a test of the capacity of its author to have the experience that is the subject-matter of his analysis, it is also much more than that. It is a test of the capacity of the system he puts forth to grasp the nature of experience itself. There is no test that so surely reveals the one-sidedness of a philosophy as its treatment of art and esthetic experience.[41]

Whether Dewey has met his own test is not a question that can be decided in these pages.[42] What is certain is the positive reception his book received in non-philosophical circles and the more recent revival of interest in his work by a number of philosophically trained aestheticians.[43]

In the opening chapter of *Art as Experience*, entitled "The Live Creature," Dewey suggests that in order to understand the meaning of artistic products we must first take a "detour" through "the ordinary forces and conditions of experience that we do not usually regard as esthetic." His aim of "going back to experience of the common or mill run of things" is "to discover the esthetic quality such experience possesses." For it is his claim that what he calls the "work of art," as distinguished from the "art work or product," is an intensification of the aesthetic quality that lies dormant in much of our "normal" or everyday experience. The art work, for example, the poem, painting, or song, will issue from the work of art. Appreciation of artworks also works in a like manner. The implication is that there is nothing alien, mysterious, or other-worldly about artistic creation. Dewey contends that the "full meaning of ordinary experience is expressed" in our experience of art.[44]

The opening chapters of *Art as Experience* trace the "biological commonplaces" that lie at the root of aesthetic experience, the chief of which Dewey identifies as the continual attempt of the organism to reach an equilibrium between itself and its environment. Humans, along with all "live creatures," are forever trying to establish a balance or harmony with their environments. Without such equilibrium there is no growth:

> For only when an organism shares in the ordered relations of its environment does it secure the stability essential to living. And when the participation comes after a phase of disruption and conflict, it bears within itself the germs of a consummation akin to the esthetic.[45]

It is these germs of a consummation that Dewey explores in the crucial chapter of *Art as Experience* entitled "Having an Experience." Whether it is at the more complex level of ordinary experience or that of an aesthetic experience with an artwork, the generic traits of "*an* experience" are key to understanding what may justifiably be called Dewey's notion of life as art. Dewey claims that the traits of completeness, uniqueness, and qualitative unity characterize *an* experience. The live creature in constant interaction with its environment, in a constant tension of doing and undergoing, has moments of fulfillment. In an often quoted passage Dewey writes:

> [W]e have *an* experience when the material experienced runs its course to fulfillment. Then and then only is it integrated within and demarcated in the general stream of experience from other experiences. A piece of work is finished in a way that is satisfactory; a problem receives its solution; a game is played through; a situation, whether that of eating a meal, playing a game of chess, carrying on a conversation, writing a book, or taking part in a political campaign, is so rounded out that its close is a consummation and not a cessation. Such an experience is a whole and carries with it its own individualizing quality and self-sufficiency. It is *an* experience.[46]

The examples Dewey has chosen are of varying temporal durations and characters. None of these is necessarily aesthetic in the sense of a fine art sense of the aesthetic. Yet they are all aesthetic in the generic sense Dewey wishes to employ. All these experiences have an emotional element that he calls their "esthetic quality," a quality that "rounds out an experience into completeness and unity."[47] When experience fails to achieve such consummations, we say that the experience was "anesthetic" or "non-esthetic." The aesthetic and the anesthetic are on a continuum. For Dewey the aesthetic is a matter of degrees not kinds. Every experience has in some rudimentary sense the traits of the aesthetic. The task of social intelligence is to make the aesthetic more available in all our doings and makings. From the workplace to the classroom Dewey proposes ways in which to create space for having *an* experience.

The above task is also true of the fine and performing arts. The pages of *Art as Experience* are rich with suggestions as to how we may enhance our lives through *an* experience with the arts. Dewey also reserves sharp criticism for the theories and attitudes about art that are hindrances to having such experiences. He often refers to these as the "esoteric theories of art." Highly subjectivist views of expression as well as overly formalist approaches to art come under Dewey's critical scrutiny. One could not effectively summarize all of Dewey's valuable insights in these matters, but by way of illustration, we can examine his criticisms of aesthetic formalism, in particular the notion of significant form as proposed by Clive Bell and defended by Roger Fry.

Significant form and the theory from which it emerges are illustrative of the modernist rejection of traditional representationalist theories of art. The formalists claim that aesthetic value derives solely from the significant form in a work of art. Clive Bell, in his work *Art*, gives the following definition: "When I speak of significant form, I mean a combination of lines and colors (counting white and black as colors) that moves me esthetically." He further claims that significant form is the "one quality common to all works of visual art."[48] In a later formulation Bell extends this notion to include the literary arts and hints at its universality to all the arts.[49] Significant form then is "the essential quality of a work of art, the quality that distinguishes works of art from all other classes of objects."[50] Roger Fry, in his work *Transformations*, maintains that the truly aesthetic emotion is not "about objects or persons or events." In a very un-Deweyan fashion Fry claims that "When we are in the picture gallery we are employing faculties in a manner so distinct from that in which we employed them on the way there, that it is no exaggeration to say we are doing a quite different thing." He thus concludes that it "is not impossible to draw a fairly sharp dividing line between our mental disposition in the case of esthetic responses and that of the responses of ordinary life."[51]

Dewey himself sees the value of the formalist position to lie in its explanative force in dealing with artistic appreciation and creation, especially in the visual arts. Dewey approvingly quotes Roger Fry to the effect that "ordinary seeing" is primarily in the service of representation, while "aesthetic vision" in painting is not. Employing Fry's own words, Dewey claims that there is a "harmony" and "rhythm" in aesthetic seeing that leads to a unique kind of focused attention: "Certain relations of line become for him full of meaning; he apprehends them no longer curiously but passionately, and these lines begin to be so stressed and stand out so clearly from the rest that he sees them more distinctly than he did at first." The same enhancement of vision is true for colors. The goal is not the representation of objects: "In such a creative vision, the objects as such tend to disappear, to lose their separate unities and to take their place as so many bits in the mosaic of vision."[52] For Dewey, art is not at its core a simple-minded mimesis nor does it communicate through some form of "correct descriptive statement."[53] But the shortcoming in the formalist view lies in the inferences it draws once representation is rejected. Typical of one such unacceptable inference for Dewey is Clive Bell's restriction of aesthetic appreciation to form alone. Bell, in discussing what he calls "descriptive painting," claims that such paintings "do not move us aesthetically . . . they are not works of art." Such representational works "leave untouched our aesthetic emotions because *it is not their forms* but the ideas or information suggested or conveyed by their forms that affect us."[54] Bell takes his rejection of representationalism to an extreme by claiming that the representative content in a work of art is irrelevant. He contends that "to appreciate a work of art we need bring with us nothing from life, no knowledge of its ideas and affairs, no familiarity with its emotions." Art, according to Bell, "transports us from the world of man's activity to a world of aesthetic exaltation."[55] Dewey categorically rejects the kind of separation that Bell advocates for aesthetic appreciation. Such a view leads to what Dewey has often deemed a "completely esoteric theory of art."[56]

Dewey's criticism of formalism hinges on the important distinctions he draws between his notion of aesthetic form and that of significant form. He contends that the formalist appreciation of significant form rests upon a totally ahistorical notion of experience. For Dewey, the having of experience cannot be treated as a discreet here and now event. Such ahistorical discreteness smacks of the empiricist tradition he is attempting to overturn. Aesthetic form is not the "exclusive result of the lines and colors" but "a function of what is in the scene in its interaction with what the beholder brings with him." For Dewey, the aesthetic emotion that is stirred by aesthetic form is not divorced from the emotional life of the artist or the audience. His analyses always stress the continuities in experience:

> Some subtle affinity with the current of his own experience as a live creature causes lines and colors to arrange themselves in one pattern and rhythm rather than another. The passionateness that marks observation goes with the development of the new form – it is the distinctly esthetic emotion that has been spoken of. But it is not independent of some prior emotion that has stirred in the artist's experience.[57]

There is for Dewey no state of pristine seeing. Aesthetic sensibility is a complex affair, involving more than the seeing of lines and colors in terms of their formal relationships within a painting.

The central chapters of *Art as Experience* further develop Dewey's important notion of aesthetic form. The unified perception that is integral to *an* experience occurs when we experience an artwork (or any object or event) with no external or extrinsic end in view. At times it appears that Dewey is claiming that the degree of unity or completeness of an artwork, or, more correctly, of our experience of an artwork, depends upon our heightened ability to minimize the external demands on our attention. Dewey employs the example of people on a ferry crossing the Hudson River into New York City to illustrate his point. Each passenger is seeing the city skyline but with a different purpose in mind. Some see particular buildings as landmarks in order to calculate the length of time remaining in the journey ahead, others see the expanse of buildings from the perspective of their interest in real estate and land values, while still others who are journeying for the first time across the river "are bewildered by the multiplicity of objects spread out to view." In contrast, Dewey portrays aesthetic seeing in the following manner: "Finally the scene formed by the buildings may be looked at as colored and lighted volumes in relation to one another, to the sky and to the river. He is now seeing esthetically, as a painter might see." This vision is concerned with "a perceptual whole" that is "constituted by related parts." No one aspect in this scene is singled out for some external end. When buildings are seen "pictorially," their values and qualities as seen "are modified by the other parts of the whole scene, and in turn these modify the value, as perceived, of every other part of the whole." Dewey concludes that "there is now form in the artistic sense."[58] What Dewey appears to be describing is a highly integrated sort of perception. Every aspect of the scene is related to and modifies every other aspect of the scene. Such a view comes suspiciously close to a view of organic unity – a view that he is sometimes at pains to reject. Dewey needs to walk a fine line between stressing the need for a more focused and mindful experience with art and the dangers of once again isolating art from our everyday routines and activities. His ultimate goal, as we have seen, is to bring the same, what we could legitimately label "reconstructed," sense of aesthetic sensibility and engagement with artworks to the world of our more mundane activities. The goal is to live life as art but in the uniquely Deweyan sense of art. Thus Dewey's concept of aesthetic form captures this goal:

> In a word, form is not found exclusively in objects labeled works of art. Wherever perception has not been blunted and perverted, there is an inevitable tendency to arrange events and objects with reference to the demands of complete and unified perception. Form is a character of every experience that is *an* experience. Art in its specific sense enacts more deliberately and fully the conditions that effect this unity. *Form may then be defined as the operation of forces that carry the experience of an event, object, scene, and situation to its own integral fulfillment.* The connection of form with substance is thus inherent, not imposed from without. It marks the matter of an experience that is carried to consummation.[59]

Living life as art requires that all our experiences obtain aesthetic form to some degree. This may be a Herculean project, but it is one that Dewey was unwilling to shirk.

The success of Dewey's project is not one that is easy to judge. *Art as Experience* received many highly favorable reviews from both philosophers and non-philosophers alike. Dewey himself was especially pleased by its reception among artists. By the time of its 1987 publication in the Southern Illinois University Press critical edition of his Later Works, *Art as Experience* had remained in print for well over 50 years, having sold more than 135,000 copies. For a rather theoretically challenging and sometimes intellectually dense work, this is a remarkable accomplishment.

Defining Art: Monroe C. Beardsley and George Dickie

In the 20-odd years between the writing of *Art as Experience* and Dewey's death in 1952, the philosophical climate in America had changed markedly. The rise of logical positivism and its migration from Europe into the academic life of American universities in the pre-war and war years signaled important changes for the practice of philosophical aesthetics. Positivism, along with the growing influence of Ludwig Wittgenstein, led to a reframing of many of the questions explored by philosophically trained aestheticians. What later came to be called "analytic aesthetics" was in the ascendancy.

The details of this transformation cannot be our concern in this chapter. Marking out some of the general differences of approach and interest will be useful for appreciating the motivations for the renewed interest in Deweyan aesthetics toward the end of the twentieth century. The following characterization is necessarily overly generalized, and important and compelling exceptions can be found to the broad-brushed portrait painted here. (Monroe C. Beardsley (1915–85) and Susanne K. Langer in particular stand out. See the separate treatment of Langer's aesthetic theory in chapter 15 of this volume.) But what stands out in the period of the 1940s through the 1970s is a marked disinterest in global approaches to art and aesthetic phenomena. The professionalization of the discipline of philosophy led to increasing emphases upon article-length arguments that could easily be summarized, or in some cases formalized, and thus refuted in similarly article-length arguments that appeared in the pages of professional journals. The range of topics and concerns found in a work such as *Art as Experience* were rare in this period. Very important work of an analytical nature was done on a host of issues and problems that had long bedeviled writing about the arts, but little was done to put these insights together in works of significant scope. The legitimacy of any such broadly synthetic approach to the role of art and the aesthetic was questioned by some. In a much debated 1941 article in *Mind*, entitled "The Dreariness of Aesthetics," J. A. Passmore chides aesthetics' penchant for global generalizations and recommends "an intensive special study of the separate arts, carried out with no undue respect for anyone's 'aesthetic experiences,' but much respect for real differences between the works of art themselves."[60] Respecting differences need not lead to philosophic myopia, but such a tendency was clearly evident in some of the work produced in this period.

Among the range of topics explored by American philosophical aesthetics in the last half of the twentieth century, the following will briefly be remarked upon to close out this chapter: (1) the aesthetic attitude and experience; (2) definitions of art; (3) representation; (4) interpretation. We will then close with some remarks concerning the naturalistic and pragmatic alternatives that have been present all along during this period but have of late experienced a renascence.

In an influential article in 1964, the American philosopher of art George Dickie (1926–) argued that the existence of a distinct realm of aesthetic experience was a myth. He rejected the idea prevalent in the history of aesthetic theory that there is a unique aesthetic faculty such as taste. Unlike Dewey, who sees the seeds of the aesthetic within ordinary perception, Dickie argues that there is no principled distinction between aesthetic perception and ordinary perception. In one reading of this claim, Dewey could be said to agree, for there is no distinction in kind between the two, just in degree. But Dickie is making a stronger claim. Aesthetic perception is not a heightened form of ordinary perception. Properties such as completeness or qualitative unity that marked the having of *an* experience for Dewey are of little merit in helping us distinguish what is unique to the aesthetic. Though Dickie, for the most part, does not address Dewey directly, choosing instead to direct his analytical counter-examples against Edward Bullough's "psychical-distance" theory along with its contemporary variant, Jerome Stolnitz's theory of "disinterested attention," and Monroe Beardsley's concept of aesthetic experience, these refutations could just as easily pertain to Dewey.[61] For Dickie, the disinterestedness that is claimed to mark aesthetic perception is not a feature of how we attend to the artwork itself, but is a reflection of the motives of the spectator. Recalling our earlier example of the ferry passengers, Dickie would claim that the passenger looking at the New York City skyline simply in terms of real estate values is not attending to the visual field at all. If one accepts the premise that the skyline is a work of art, then there is only one way to attend to it, though there may well be different levels of sophistication or connoisseurship at play.

Dickie's attack on the myth of aesthetic experience became clearer in a 1965 article in which he directly challenges Monroe Beardsley's and, by extension, Dewey's conception of aesthetic experience.[62] Beardsley had put forth a conception of aesthetic experience in his earlier book *Aesthetics: Problems in the Philosophy of Criticism* (1958), a book that was, in many ways, indebted to John Dewey. He restates his position in a later article:

> I propose to say that a person is having an aesthetic experience during a particular stretch of time if and only if the greater part of his mental activity during that time is united and made pleasurable by being tied to the form and qualities of a sensuously presented or imaginatively intended object on which his primary attention is concentrated.[63]

Beardsley, while wanting to distinguish himself from the "more cryptic passages in *Art as Experience* where Dewey proposes to identify the work of art with an experience," does provide a spirited defense of the concept of aesthetic experience.[64] Dickie claims that aesthetic experience is a myth because there is no coherent sense in which the predicate "unified" can be applied to experience. Unity, as we have seen, is a fundamental trait of Dewey's (and Beardsley's) concept of aesthetic experience. Dickie contends that the seeing of a unified visual pattern or the hearing of a sound pattern *as* unified are unjustifiably transferred to the whole of the experience undergone, thus leading to the mistaken inference that the experience itself is unified. We may be moved and aroused by an artwork, but there is no unity, coherence, or completeness to the sequence of affects the work may have on us. Dickie attributes "this error in Dewey to the lingering malign influence of German idealism, which made such expressions as 'the unity of experience' seem to mean something."[65] Yet for Beardsley such expressions do have meaning. The key traits of aesthetic experience, which he has identified as coherence, completeness, and unity, are demonstrated by Beardsley to be perfectly intelligible when applied to the effects of art upon an audience. He claims, for example, that the effects of hearing a musical composition may lead to a coherent experience: "In describing coherence of experience (relying, obviously, on John Dewey), I wrote that 'one thing leads to another; continuity of development, without gaps or dead spaces, cumulation of energy toward a climax, are present to an unusual degree.'"[66] Dickie had contended that these descriptions intelligently could *only* apply to the perceived musical composition as such and not to the whole experience. Beardsley shows that they do make sense in describing the feelings we have while hearing a musical composition:

> A feeling, for example, may vary in intensity over a certain stretch of time, and it may change by gentle degrees or abruptly; or it may be interrupted by quite opposed or irrelevant feelings; it may fluctuate in a random way. . . . It seems to me that the terms "continuity" and "discontinuity" apply quite clearly to such sequences, and continuity makes for coherence, in affects as well as in objects.[67]

In a similar fashion Beardsley goes on to demonstrate the weaknesses in Dickie's arguments for the unintelligibility of completeness and unity as the distinguishing traits of aesthetic experience. Thus he concludes that "our experiences of works of art, and especially our experiences of good works of art, are in fact generally of a high order of unity."[68] Despite the fact that Beardsley was a highly respected aesthetician and taught many students during his career, his was a rather lonely voice in the defense of aesthetic experience during this period.

During this period of the 1950s and '60s, another central concern of philosophical aesthetics was the definition of art. Earlier generations often raised the question "what is art?" but in this period the focus shifted to questions such as "what per se is a definition or are definitions themselves possible?" Ludwig Wittgenstein's *Philosophical Investigations* had appeared in 1953. Neo-Wittgensteinian arguments to the effect that art was an open concept seemed persuasive to a great many philosophers. An open concept is a concept for which there is no necessary condition or set of conditions in order for something to be an instance of that concept. Morris Weitz, in his often-anthologized 1956 article "The Role of Theory in Aesthetics," argued for this position and further claimed that there was an effective alternative to the standard necessary condition type of definition, the family-resemblance method based upon Wittgenstein's famous discussion of games.[69] The family-resemblance class of artworks is generated by an object's resemblance to previously established works of art. In addition, an object being an artifact is not a condition for its candidacy as an artwork. According to Weitz the family-resemblance approach is the only way we could be assured that our concept of art could encompass the creativity and originality manifested in new works of art.

Dickie objects to Weitz's denial of artifactuality and to his employment of the notion of family resemblance definitions. He contends that Weitz conflates classificatory and evaluative statements regarding works of art. For example, Weitz cited statements such as "That driftwood is a work of art" to buttress his claim that artworks need not be artifacts. Yet Dickie points out that such statements are primarily evaluative. Dickie also rejected the family-resemblance approach to distinguishing art from non-art. First, it leads to an infinite regress. Second, family resemblance ultimately rests on the idea of resemblance and since everything resembles everything else in some respect, we would be forced to count everything as art. Dickie himself proposes an alternative definition of art, one that does recognize jointly necessary conditions: "A work of art in the classificatory sense is (1) an artifact (2) a set of the aspects of which has had conferred upon it the status of candidate for appreciation by some person or persons acting on behalf of a certain social institution (the artworld)."[70] This definition, what came to be called the "institutional theory of art," generated much discussion and controversy in the 1970s and '80s. Dickie later came to revise it by substituting a looser term, "artworld public," for the status conferring authority of what he had earlier called the "social institution" of the artworld.[71] Passmore's phrase, "the dreariness of aesthetics," may well have taken on new meaning if he were to reflect upon the countless pages written during this period on the topic of defining art.

Nelson Goodman on Reference and Arthur C. Danto on Interpretation

The term "artworld" was appropriated by Dickie from Arthur C. Danto's (1924–) 1964 article "The Artworld."[72] Danto and Nelson Goodman (1906–98) were considered by many to be the two leading aestheticians from the early 1970s through the 1990s. Holding chairs in philosophy at the home institutions of Dewey and Santayana, Columbia and Harvard respectively, their writings reflect marked differences in interest and style. Danto wears many hats, being a painter and the art critic for *The Nation* among them. Goodman was a formidable logician, who wrote extensively on issues in epistemology, science, and language. Danto, the better stylist, writes with wit and a rich sense of the history of the fine and literary arts. Goodman wrote in a more technical and formalized vocabulary. Danto is more comfortable in the visual arts, especially painting. Goodman was director of an art gallery, an avid art collector, a collaborator in multidisciplinary performance pieces, and an outspoken advocate for arts education. Both have argued, albeit in different ways, that representation is a necessary condition for art.

Beginning with his book, *Languages of Art: An Approach to a Theory of Symbols* (1968), Goodman developed a complex theory of symbols, one that could do justice to the representationalism he believed was inherent to the fine and performing arts. While acknowledging familiarity with the symbol theory of such philosophers as C. S. Peirce, Ernst Cassirer, Charles Morris, and Susanne Langer, Goodman explicitly defers from identifying any agreements or disagreements he may have with these and any other philosophers for fear that these would distract from the analysis at hand.[73] With regard to Peirce, it is clear that there is a fundamental disagreement between them about the nature of signs. Symbols are dyadic for Goodman: "A symbol system consists of a symbol scheme correlated with a field of reference."[74] Peirce maintains a triadic concept of sign. For him, a sign has meaning only if it is translatable by another sign, its interpretant. Reference for Peirce is ultimately determined by interpretation.[75]

For Goodman the notion of reference, which lies at the heart of representation, is a more complex affair than the simple linguistic sort of denotation of which we are familiar. Denotation is only one of a number of species of reference and has itself a variety of subspecies. Reference is Goodman's most generic term for what he calls "all sorts of symbolizations, all cases of *standing for*." Denotation is reserved "for the application of a word or picture or other label to one or many things."[76] Among the many subspecies of denotation which pertain to art, Goodman has identified: (1) verbal denotation (e.g., words, phrases, or predicates); (2) notation (e.g., musical scores, dance notation); (3) pictorial denotation (e.g., depiction or representation by drawing, painting, sculpture, photograph, film, etc.).

Much of the initial criticism directed against Goodman's work focused upon the third mentioned subspecies, pictorial denotation. Goodman has argued that for a symbol (i.e., a painting, drawing, or sculpture) to represent or depict an object, it must participate in a conventional symbol system similar to that of verbal language. The possible resemblance of the symbol to its object has nothing to do with it being a representation of that object. What determines the referential relationship becomes a matter of the conventions in the symbol system. Symbol systems themselves vary, often greatly. They are characterized by what Goodman calls degrees of syntactical and semantic density. Further, he introduces a notion of "repleteness" (i.e., a form of relevant interconnectedness) to distinguish artistic representation from other forms of representation.

For Goodman reference is primary. This can readily be seen in his handling of the traditionally non-representational arts such as absolute music or abstract painting. Goodman introduces the concept of exemplification (i.e., another key species of reference) to encompass these forms. Exemplification "runs in the opposite direction" from denotation:

> Exemplification is selective, obtaining only between the symbol and some but not others of the labels denoting it or properties possessed by it. Exemplification is not mere possession of a feature but requires also reference to that feature. . . . Exemplification is thus a certain subrelation of the converse of denotation, distinguished through a return reference *to* denoter by denoted.[77]

The properties (or labels) that a symbol possesses may not all be among the so-called "literal properties" of that symbol. A symbol may have "metaphorical properties," for example, a symphony may be tragic, a painting powerful. When such metaphorical properties are exemplified we have yet another sub-variety of reference called "expression." The traditional non-representational art forms are often expressive in this sense. Such artworks express their metaphorical properties. Goodman can thus have expression while still retaining reference.

In arguing against traditional theories of "pure" or non-representational art, Goodman writes: "Plainly not all the countless features of the work matter (not, for example, the painting's weighing four pounds . . .) but only those qualities and relationships of color or sound, those spatial and temporal patterns, and so on that the work exemplifies and thus selectively refers to."[78] All exemplification *is selective*. Not all the properties of the symbol are of equal relevance for the artistic symbol. Often the features that are selected in this self-referential process vary for any given symbol. Just as we may have ambiguity of reference in a language system, so may we have ambiguity of exemplification in the arts. Yet what, if anything, controls the selection of the properties of the symbol that are exemplified? Symbols, in Goodman's scheme, require reference to be the symbols that they are, but what requires the reference to be the kind of reference that it is?

Goodman's system does not provide a ready answer to these questions. Arthur C. Danto takes up these questions in his highly influential 1981 book, *The Transfiguration of the Commonplace*. Danto proposes a different way of talking about representation, or what he prefers to call "aboutness." He employs some very clever and entertaining examples to convey his point. Tying together Wittgenstein's puzzles about the identity of indiscernibles and the controversies surrounding Marcel Duchamp's ready-mades, Danto suggests that the differences between two visually indistinguishable objects, one of which is an artwork and the other a "mere real thing," rests upon the former having the property of "aboutness." Duchamp's urinal was "transfigured" into an artwork known as *Fountain* by the fact that it was about, for instance, modernism's break with representationalism. A commercially bought and used urinal is not "about" anything. The genus of an artwork is identified by the property of "aboutness." But other objects that are not artworks have this property – for instance, simple traffic signs. A difference is added to this genus: "The thesis is that works of art, in categorical contrast with mere representations, use the means of representation in a way that is not exhaustively specified when one has exhaustively specified what is being represented."[79] So when we approach an artwork with understanding, we must be able to talk not only about its content but about the way the work expresses something about that content. This process of understanding is interpretation. In a later book, *The Philosophical Disenfranchisement of Art*, Danto writes: "An object is an artwork *at all* only in relation to an interpretation."[80] Interpretation is the agency by which quite commonplace objects can be raised or "transfigured" to the level of art.[81] Even primarily referential works (e.g., portraits) are "never merely referential." They have what Danto calls a "semi-opacity," that is, they present a content. An object is meaningful as an artwork only when we see the interrelation between the "what" (the content) and the "how" (the mode of presentation) of the work. Ultimately, for Danto, this is the work of interpretation.

Justus Buchler: Art as Exhibitive Judgment

The models of meaning that both Goodman and Danto were operating with were primarily based upon how meaning is engendered in language. A radically different approach to meaning had been earlier developed by one of Danto's colleagues at Columbia University. Justus Buchler (1914–91) (see chapter 18 in this volume) had not taken the so-called "linguistic turn" of many in his profession in the 1950s and '60s. His approach to meaning was based upon his deep-seated and thoroughgoing naturalism. He proposed a general theory of human judgment or utterance that attempted to overcome the difficulties of semantically based theories of meaning by broadening our understanding of communication. Language was not to serve as the model for human communication. Buchler contends that if we treat all human utterance broadly conceived as falling under three general functional types – that is, as assertions, contrivances, and actions – we avoid the paradoxes of artworks being meaningful but not about any easily specifiable content. In a Deweyan-like sense, Buchler is shifting the focus to the issue of *how* humans produce, that is, to the character of human production.

Buchler contends that "every product is a judgment." What he means is that every product is at bottom a stance adopted toward the world. Man naturally and continuously discriminates and selects from the complexes that make up his world. Judgment, in this sense, is inevitable, ubiquitous, and never fully isolatable into discrete events. Most importantly for Buchler, judgment is never exclusively identified with mental activity or consciousness.

> [Man] judges continuously, through what he includes and excludes, preserves and destroys, is inclined to and adverse to; through what he makes and fails to make, through the ways he acts and refrains from acting, through what he believes and disavows. His attributes, and hence his commitments, are his whether he is aware of them or not.[82]

To fully appreciate this insight into the judicative nature of human production, it must be emphasized that judging is not primarily a discrete mental act preceding or subsequent to other forms of behavior. We do not necessarily judge first, in the sense of formulating a course of action, and then act. The action, the doing itself, is a form of judgment. Thus the artist in the act of making is judging; so too, albeit in a different sense, is the spectator in the act of appreciation. The emphasis and ultimately the basis for distinguishing the three modes of judgment (i.e., active, assertive, and exhibitive) rests upon the way in which the judging occurs. Buchler writes: "To say that a man judges, for example, through what he makes, does not mean that he makes after he has discriminated and selected and become committed. It means that his making what he makes *is the way* he has discriminated and selected and become committed."[83]

For Buchler, active, exhibitive, and assertive judgment do not mark structural but, rather, functional differences. A given product may function in more than one mode. This is an important consideration for resolving some of the difficulties raised by borderline cases between art and non-art. Summarizing the important functional differences between these modes Buchler writes:

> (1) When we can be said to predicate, state, or affirm, by the use of words or by any other means; when the underlying direction is to achieve or support belief; when it is relevant to cite evidence in behalf of our product, we produce in the mode of assertive judgment, we judge assertively. (2) When we can be said to do or to act; when the underlying direction is toward effecting a result; when "bringing about" is the central trait attributable to our product, we produce in the mode of active judgment, we judge actively. (3) When we contrive or make, in so far as the contrivance rather than its role in action is what dominates and is of underlying concern; when the process of shaping and the product as shaped is central, we produce in the mode of exhibitive judgment, we judge exhibitively. On the methodic level, where (minimally) purposiveness and intention belong to judgments, assertive judgment is exemplified by science, or more generally, inquiry . . . ; active judgment, by deliberate conduct morally assessable; exhibitive judgment, by art.[84]

On Buchler's view no product is intrinsically active, assertive, or exhibitive. The judicative function is determined by the communicative context. For a literary work the communicative context typically does not call for interpretation in terms of truth and falsity. The artwork does not primarily aim to compel or support belief, although this does not rule out its possible role in the expression or inculcation of beliefs. For example, Harriet Beecher Stowe's *Uncle Tom's Cabin* may serve to support certain beliefs about abolition, but in the artistic context the latter is incidental to exhibitive confrontation. In the literary context the work offers itself to interpretation and appraisal as an arrangement or constellation of materials; in literature it may do so through the use either of conventional or devised linguistic signs and through the use of such signs in conventional or non-conventional ways. As an exhibitive judgment its communicative effect is neither more nor less direct than that of language used assertively.

Buchler's modes of judgment do not privilege one form of communication over another. Semantically based theories of meaning, while recognizing the role of the active and exhibitive dimensions of communication, tend to subordinate their judicative and cognitive value to that of the assertive. This leads, as Buchler says to "the false implication . . . that the work of art always conforms to the model of a dumb-show-pointing to one-knows-not-what [representational theories], or to the model of total-sensory-affective involvement [expression theories] – both wholly noncommittal."[85] For Buchler, a product functions meaningfully if it initiates the articulation of some perspective within which it is located. The phrase "articulation of perspective" is more generic than interpretation. Articulation may take place in any of the three modes of judgment. The perspective that is articulated is the communicative context. This context varies in scope for each particular instance of communication. There is an indeterminate number of perspectives in which an artwork may function articulatively. This permits us to claim that an artwork has meaning in non-artistic orders of judgment. A Freudian interpretation would thus be meaningful, but not in the same manner as that found in the exhibitive order of artworks. In the latter order, articulation takes the form of either the *production* or the *discovery* of other elements within the perspective. Judgments, for Buchler, are thus ramified and ramifiable.

The ramification of judgment is synonymous with the increased availability of its order for assimilation and manipulation. Within the order of artworks, ramified judgment may take the form of the artistic influence of one artwork upon another, or one school or style of artistic invention upon other schools, styles, or individual artists. Alternatively, the communicative effect might take the form of the ramified judgments of the spectator or audience.

The Buchlerian insight that articulation of perspective may be in any of the three modes of judgment, either singly or in combination, generalizes the notion of interpretation. The meaning of an artwork is not primarily or solely a function of reference. Meaning in the arts is no longer limited to a model of "messages" or "themes," whether in the form of a predicate or a property, to be conveyed or denoted by the artwork. Meaning is not fixed – either by the artist or the critic. Yet this does not mean that any meaning at all is possible. The artwork has determinate traits that enter into – that is, communicate with – viewers, other artworks, and even whole artistic movements. These communicative contexts provide the *meanings* of an artwork.

Unfortunately, during most of his career, Buchler was swimming against the linguistic tide in many areas of philosophy, especially aesthetic theory. The current climate has shifted, if only incrementally, toward more pluralistic and pragmatic concerns in aesthetics. Philosophers such as Richard Rorty, Richard Shusterman, Stanley Cavell, and Arnold Berleant have shifted the focus back to many of the themes found in the writings of Emerson, Santayana, and Dewey. The impact of feminist and Continental writing has also had a major impact on philosophical aesthetics and its professional organs. Such a diverse and rich ferment of ideas and perspectives can only serve to reinvigorate American philosophical aesthetics in the years ahead.

Notes

1 *The Complete Poems of George Santayana*, ed. William G. Holzberger (Lewisburg, PA: Bucknell University Press, 1979); George Santayana, *The Last Puritan, A Memoir in the Form of a Novel* (New York: Charles Scribner's Sons, 1936); John Dewey, *The Poems of John Dewey*, ed. Jo Ann Boydston (Carbondale, IL: Southern Illinois University Press, 1977).

2 See the following for a collection of essays on Peircean aesthetics: Herman Parret, ed., *Peirce and Value Theory: On Peircean Ethics and Aesthetics* (Amsterdam: John Benjamins Publishing, 1994). Also the following articles are of interest in this regard: Armen T. Marsoobian, "Saying, Singing, or Semiotics: 'Prima la Musica e Poi le Parole' Revisited," *Journal of Aesthetics and Art Criticism* 54/3 (Summer 1996): 269–77; Carl R. Hausman, "Insights in the Arts," *Journal of Aesthetics and Art Criticism* 45 (Winter 1986): 163–73. For book-length studies, see: Douglas R. Anderson, *Creativity and the Philosophy of C. S. Peirce* (Dordrecht: M. Nijhoff, 1987) and Carl R. Hausman, *Metaphor and Art: Interactionism and Reference in the Verbal and Nonverbal Arts* (Cambridge: Cambridge University Press, 1989).
3 Ralph Waldo Emerson, "Art," in *The Essays of Ralph Waldo Emerson* (Cambridge, MA: Harvard University Press, 1987), p. 209.
4 Ibid., p. 210.
5 Ibid., p. 213.
6 Ibid., p. 214.
7 Ibid., pp. 213–14.
8 Ibid., pp. 214–15.
9 Ibid., p. 215.
10 Ibid., p. 217.
11 Ibid.
12 Ibid., pp. 216–17.
13 Ibid., p. 218.
14 See Richard Shusterman, *Pragmatist Aesthetics: Living Beauty, Rethinking Art*, 2nd edn. (Lanham, MD: Rowman & Littlefield, 2000).
15 *The Sense of Beauty: Being the Outlines of Aesthetic Theory*, in *The Works of George Santayana*, vol. 2, ed. William G. Holzberger and Herman J. Saatkamp, Jr. (Cambridge, MA: MIT Press, 1988), p. 35.
16 Ibid., p. 7.
17 Ibid., p. 15.
18 Arthur Danto unravels Santayana's debt to and "satiric" criticism of British empiricism in his introduction to *The Sense of Beauty*. Santayana's Schopenhauerean influences are also ably identified.
19 *The Sense of Beauty*, pp. 25–6.
20 Ibid., pp. 30–1.
21 Ibid., p. 32.
22 Ibid., p. 64.
23 Ibid., pp. 121–2.
24 John Dewey, *Art as Experience* (New York: Minton, Balch & Co., 1934), p. 18.
25 *The Life of Reason; or The Phases of Human progress*, 5 vols. Vol. 4: *Reason in Art* (New York: Charles Scribner's Sons, 1905).
26 "What is Aesthetics?" *The Philosophical Review*, 13/3 (1904): 320–7. Reprinted in Justus Buchler and Benjamin Schwartz, eds., *Obiter Scripta* (New York: Charles Scribner's Sons, 1936).
27 Ibid., pp. 32–3.
28 Ibid., pp. 35–6.
29 Ibid., p. 36.
30 *Reason in Art*, pp. 15–17.

31 See their exchange in the pages of the *Journal of Philosophy*: George Santayana, "Dewey's Naturalistic Metaphysics," 22/25 (December 3, 1925) and John Dewey, "Half-Hearted Naturalism," 24/3 (February 3, 1927). Michael Eldridge treats this controversy in chapter 4 of this volume.
32 "Qualitative Thought," *Symposium*, 1 (January 1930): 5–32; "Affective Thought in Logic and Painting," *Journal of the Barnes Foundation*, 2 (April 1926): 3–9. Republished in *Philosophy and Civilization* (New York: Minton, Balch and Co., 1931), pp. 93–116 and pp. 117–25.
33 *Experience and Nature*, 2nd edn. (New York: Dover, 1958), p. 355.
34 Ibid., p. 358.
35 Ibid., pp. 358–9.
36 Ibid., pp. 388–9, 391–2.
37 *Experience and Nature*, p. 4a.
38 "Experience and Nature: A Re-Introduction," ed. Joseph Ratner, contained in *The Later Works, 1925–1953*, ed. Jo Ann Boydston (Carbondale, IL: Southern Illinois University Press, 1981).
39 *Experience and Nature*, p. 1a.
40 *Art as Experience*, p. 274.
41 Ibid.
42 For an analysis of some of the virtues and shortcomings of his approach to aesthetic experience, see my "Aesthetic Form Revisited: John Dewey's Metaphysics of Art," in Richard E. Hart and Douglas R. Anderson, eds., *Philosophy in Experience: American Philosophy in Transition* (New York: Fordham University Press, 1997), pp. 195–221. Also of value is Philip W. Jackson's *John Dewey and the Lessons of Art* (New Haven, CT: Yale University Press, 1998).
43 See Shusterman, *Pragmatist Aesthetics: Living Beauty*; Thomas Alexander, *John Dewey's Theory of Art, Experience, and Nature* (Albany: State University of New York Press, 1987); and Arnold Berleant, *Art and Engagement* (Philadelphia: Temple University Press, 1991).
44 *Art as Experience*, pp. 11–13.
45 Ibid., p. 15.
46 Ibid., p. 35.
47 Ibid., p. 41.
48 Clive Bell, *Art* (New York: Frederick A. Stokes, 1913), pp. 20, 18.
49 See his *Proust* (London: L. & V. Woolf, 1928), p. 67.
50 *Art*, p. 17.
51 Roger Fry, *Transformations: Critical and Speculative Essays on Art* (London: Chatto & Windus), pp. 5, 6.
52 Roger Fry, quoted by Dewey, *Art as Experience*, pp. 86–7.
53 Ibid., p. 85.
54 *Art*, p. 22.
55 Ibid., p. 27.
56 *Art as Experience*, p. 88.
57 Ibid., pp. 88–9.
58 Ibid., pp. 135–6.
59 Ibid., p. 137.
60 J. A. Passmore, "The Dreariness of Aesthetics," *Mind*, 60 (1951): p. 60.

61 See George Dickie, *Introduction to Aesthetics: An Analytical Approach* (New York: Oxford University Press, 1997), pp. 28–34, 145–7.

62 George Dickie, "Beardsley's Phantom Aesthetic Experience," *The Journal of Philosophy*, 62 (1965): 129–36.

63 Monroe C. Beardsley, "Aesthetic Experience Regained," in Michael J. Wreen and Donald M. Callen, eds., *The Aesthetic Point of View: Selected Essays* (Ithaca, NY: Cornell University Press, 1982), p. 81. Originally published in *The Journal of Aesthetics and Art Criticism*, 28 (1969): 3–11.

64 Ibid., p. 78.

65 Ibid., p. 83.

66 Ibid., p. 84.

67 Ibid., pp. 84–5.

68 Ibid., p. 87.

69 Morris Weitz, "The Role of Theory in Aesthetics," repr. in Joseph Margolis, ed., *Philosophy Looks at the Arts*, 3rd edn. (Philadelphia: Temple University Press, 1987).

70 George Dickie, *Art and the Aesthetic* (Ithaca, NY: Cornell University Press, 1974), p. 34.

71 George Dickie, *The Art Circle* (New York: Haven Publications, 1984), passim.

72 Arthur C. Danto, "The Artworld," *Journal of Philosophy*, 61 (1964): 571–84.

73 Nelson Goodman, *The Language of Art: An Approach to a Theory of Symbols*, 2nd edn. (Indianapolis, IN: Hackett Publishing, 1976), pp. xii–xiii.

74 Ibid., p. 143.

75 Unlike Goodman, for Charles Sanders Peirce "sign" is the generic term and "symbol" is a type of sign. Peirce maintained that every sign involves a triadic relation between a physical object or quality (the material thing taken as a sign), something which it denotes or refers to (its object), and another sign which it is said to "mean" or "connote" (its interpretant). Though many of the details of Peirce's general theory of signs are open to differing interpretations, it is clear that "sign" is a relational and functional notion. The sign relation requires not a particular class of things, but an object functioning significatively. To function significatively, that is, to have meaning, a sign must be translatable, be interpretable by another sign, its interpretant. The sign–object relation (reference) is conditioned upon the sign–interpretant relation (interpretation). The sign–interpretant relation, to use Peirce's language, provides the "ground of representation." This determining relation is a rule of interpretation. Rules needn't be formal or presented in propositional form. They are sign-conventions which take the form of habits, varying in strength and alterability. They provide the standpoint, the perspective for interpretation. All interpretation is thus selective or abstractive. Features of the sign (or, to use Goodman's terms, labels of the symbol) are necessarily included or excluded in relation to this standpoint. All representation involves the selection and discrimination of specific properties by means of an interpretation. The object (referent) is thus related to a sign by the interpretant.

76 Nelson Goodman, *Of Mind and Other Matters* (Cambridge, MA: Harvard University Press, 1984), p. 55.

77 Ibid., p. 59.

78 Ibid., pp. 59–60.
79 Arthur C. Danto, *The Transfiguration of the Commonplace* (Cambridge, MA: Harvard University Press, 1981), pp. 147–8.
80 *The Philosophical Disenfranchisement of Art* (New York: Columbia University Press, 1986), p. 144.
81 Ibid., p. 78.
82 Justus Buchler, *The Main of Light: On the Concept of Poetry* (New York: Oxford University Press, 1974), p. 92.
83 Ibid., p. 94.
84 Ibid., pp. 97–8.
85 Ibid., p. 100.

Suggested reading

Primary sources

Beardsley, Monroe C., *Aesthetics: Problems in the Philosophy of Criticism* (Indianapolis, IN: Hackett Publishing, 1981 [1958]).
Buchler, Justus, *The Main of Light: On the Concept of Poetry* (New York: Oxford University Press, 1974).
Danto, Arthur C., *The Transfiguration of the Commonplace* (Cambridge, MA: Harvard University Press, 1981).
Dewey, John, *Art as Experience* (1934) in *The Later Works, 1925–1953*, vol. 10, ed. Jo Ann Boydston (Carbondale, IL: Southern Illinois University Press, 1987).
Emerson, Ralph Waldo, *The Essays of Ralph Waldo Emerson* (Cambridge, MA: Harvard University Press, 1987). Contains *Essays: First Series* and *Essays: Second Series.* Numerous other editions of Emerson's essays are in print.
Goodman, Nelson, *The Language of Art: An Approach to a Theory of Symbols*, 2nd edn. (Indianapolis, IN: Hackett Publishing, 1976).
Santayana, George, *The Sense of Beauty: Being the Outlines of Aesthetic Theory*, in *The Works of George Santayana*, vol. 2, ed. William G. Holzberger and Herman J. Saatkamp, Jr. (Cambridge, MA: The MIT Press, 1988).
——*Interpretations of Poetry and Religion* (New York: Charles Scribner's Sons, 1911).
——*Obiter Scripta*, ed. Justus Buchler and Benjamin Schwartz (New York: Charles Scribner's Sons, 1936).
——*Reason in Art*, vol. 4 of *The Life of Reason; or The Phases of Human Progress*, 5 vols. (New York: Charles Scribner's Sons, 1905). *The Life of Reason* is available in various editions.

Secondary sources

Alexander, Thomas, *John Dewey's Theory of Art, Experience, and Nature* (Albany: State University of New York Press, 1987).
Cavell, Stanley, *Conditions Handsome and Unhandsome: The Constitution of Emersonian Perfectionism*, Carus Lecture, 1988 (Chicago: University of Chicago Press, 1990).

Danto, Arthur C., "Introduction" to George Santayana, *The Sense of Beauty: Being the Outlines of Aesthetic Theory*, in *The Works of George Santayana*, vol. 2, ed. William G. Holzberger and Herman J. Saatkamp, Jr. (Cambridge, MA: The MIT Press, 1988).

Jackson, Philip W., *John Dewey and the Lessons of Art* (New Haven, CT: Yale University Press, 1998).

Shusterman, Richard, *Pragmatist Aesthetics: Living Beauty, Rethinking Art*, 2nd edn. (Lanham, MD: Rowman & Littlefield, 2000).

Epilogue: Editors' Note

John McDermott's "The Renascence of Classical American Philosophy" – which follows – was published in 1986. In it, McDermott offers a brief account of the place of the study of classical American philosophy in American universities, as well as a survey of the availability of primary works by the major figures in the tradition. It is suitable that this piece appear in this context, because it has been McDermott more than any other single person who has been responsible for maintaining the viability and availability of the classical American philosophical tradition through the several decades during which, as he indicates here, there was little room for its study in American departments of philosophy.

Nevertheless, in the more than 15 years since this essay was first published a number of things have changed – for the better we are pleased to be able to say. First, the Society for the Advancement of American Philosophy continues to be active, and its membership has nearly doubled since 1986. This in turn means that there are considerably more specialists in the history of philosophy who are offering courses to their undergraduates and graduate students in classical American philosophy and in the contemporary developments within the tradition. Second, additional avenues for the publication of studies in the American tradition have appeared, one of which is the re-established *Journal of Speculative Philosophy*, which is currently published by the Department of Philosophy at Pennsylvania State University. Another important development in the publication of work in the tradition has been the establishment at Vanderbilt University Press of the Library of American Philosophy series, and a similar series has been established at Fordham University Press. Third, serious interest in classical American philosophy has since the mid-1980s extended beyond the borders of the United States. The works of classical American philosophers are appearing in new translations around the world, from China to Russia and many nations in between. In the same spirit, there is growing interest in the classical American tradition in such places as Central and Eastern Europe, where, in 2000, the Central European Pragmatist Forum was founded to promote study in the field and to foster communications between specialists in America and in that part of the world.

Fourth, there has been increased interest in classical American philosophy, especially pragmatism, primarily through the influence of Richard Rorty and what is sometimes referred to as neo-pragmatism. Fifth, there has been in recent years growing interest and work in figures in the American tradition who had been largely overlooked earlier. The chapters in this volume speak to that point, with essays on figures such as W. E. B. Du Bois, Alain Locke, Jane Addams, Susanne Langer, and Justus Buchler.

And finally, the publication of primary works by the major figures in the American tradition has continued. Several of the collections to which McDermott refers as in progress have now been completed. This is the case with the collected works of Dewey and the James editions. Also, as general editor, McDermott has finished the 12-volume critical edition of the *Correspondence of William James* published by the University of Virginia Press. The Santayana edition is continuing, and the Peirce Project at Indiana University-Purdue University Indianapolis is continuing to publish volumes of Peirce's work. The list of primary works made available since 1986 is too long to provide here, but the suggested readings lists at the end of each of the chapters of this volume will give the reader a sense of the extent of the work ongoing in the field, as well as directions in which to look to develop a richer appreciation of the wealth of philosophical insight that lies in the American philosophical tradition, classical and contemporary.

Epilogue: The Renascence of Classical American Philosophy

John J. McDermott

> *I believe that philosophy in America will be lost between chewing a historic cud long since reduced to woody fiber, or an apologetics for lost causes (lost to natural science), or a scholastic, schematic formalism, unless it can somehow bring to consciousness America's own needs and its own implicit principle of successful action.*
>
> Dewey, "The Need for a Recovery of Philosophy"

Descriptive terms such as German philosophy, French philosophy, and American philosophy carry with them some intrinsic difficulties. Some commentators object to this national adjectival approach to philosophy as necessarily narrowing or even chauvinistic. From their perspective, philosophy has universal significance and should not be identified with the cultural life of a single people, region, or historical period. On behalf of this position, it must be agreed that efforts to confine philosophy to the interests and language of a single cultural tradition are inevitably procrustean and even counter to the longstanding mission of philosophical inquiry to seek the truth however and wherever that journey takes us. Consequently, no philosophical position is to be ruled out of consideration simply because its origins are antique or because it proceeds from a tradition and a language different from the one native to the philosopher in question.

The above strictures are to be taken as a caveat to those who believe that philosophic inquiry can be restricted by historical, linguistic, or even naturalistic confines. This is a method which is at best reductionistic and at worst propagandistic. These strictures, however, do not preclude the significance of the historical and cultural contextuality which attends all philosophical activity. The history of philosophy over and again attests to the presence of a historical matrix from which the philosophers formulate their version of the world, a version as culturally idiosyncratic as it is profound. Can one conceive of Plato and Aristotle as other than Greek philosophers? of Anselm as other than a medieval monk? of Descartes as other than a protégé of the new mathematics and science of the seventeenth century? of Hegel as other than a realization of German *Systemphilosophie*? The point here is not that these philosophers are reduced to their cultural contexts, or even that their respective contexts are able to account for the distinctive quality of their work. Rather, our intention is to indicate that the great philosophers proceed from their inherited linguistic, cultural, and historical settings in a way that enables them to feed off those settings and yet transcend them. It is both a paradox and a truism that those thinkers who attempt to ignore their inherited setting and thereby issue "universal" truths, *ab ovo*, inevitably find their work to be of significance to very few. With creative and seminal philosophers, their own cultural setting accounts for the origin of their work. It does not, however, account for its extensive influence. That influence is due, rather, to their ability to understand and transform their situation in a way which has distinctive meaning for world culture. In that vein, for example, Aristotle, Augustine, Leibniz, and Marx take their place alongside Lao Tzu, Buddha, and Jesus as profound articulators of their own experience as well as harbingers of the possible experiences of others in distant cultures.

The above comments are a backdrop to an examination of the thorny question of the relationship between American philosophy and philosophy in America. A full-scale analysis of this relationship would require nothing less than a focused survey of the history of American culture, a project far outdistancing the scope of [this chapter]. Nonetheless, some clarifying remarks are in order. The prepossessing character of America on the world scene tends to cloud from view the fact that for more than a century and a half America was a colony of England. Furthermore, given geographical range, America most often followed the cultural proprieties of Spain and France as well as those of England. In short, with regard to the affairs of high culture, the arts, literature, and philosophy, American achievements were thought to be second-hand. Whatever may have been the actual aesthetic achievements of American vernacular culture during the colonial period, the fact remains that American self-consciousness as to the worth of its cultural activities was dependent on evaluation from abroad.

The first public salvo against this cultural self-denigration was the prophetic utterance of Emerson in his preface to his essay "Nature": "The foregoing generations beheld God and nature face to face; we, through their eyes. Why should not we also enjoy an original relation to the universe?"[1]

Partially in response to the call of Emerson and others of his time, and partially in response to the explosive implications of the publication of Darwin's *The Origin of Species*, American thought in the last decades of the nineteenth century took the direction of originality. Led by Chauncey Wright (1830–75) and the young Charles Sanders Peirce (1839–1914), the distinctive interests and persuasions of American philosophy began to develop. If previous centuries had shown America to be derivative (an arguable contention), the last four decades of the nineteenth century revealed American intellectual and philosophical thought to be both original and substantial in influence. Indeed, no less than "Charles Darwin is reported to have observed that there were enough brilliant minds at the American

Cambridge in the 1860s to furnish all the universities of England."[2] In quick succession, each with a distinctive flair and contribution, American philosophy of that period was graced with the appearance of William James (1842–1910), Josiah Royce (1855–1916), John Dewey (1859–1952), George Herbert Mead (1863–1931), and George Santayana (1863–1952), as well as other, less well-known thinkers such as C. H. Howison (1834–1916), W. T. Harris (1835–1909), and Thomas Davidson (1840–1900). This period came to be known as the golden age of American philosophy or, more modestly, as the classical age. Whatever nomenclature one wishes to append to this period, there is no doubt as to its unusual importance in the history of American culture nor, above all, to its singular importance in the history of American philosophy.

This is not to say, of course, that significant philosophers and philosophical developments did not take place after the classical period. A "second generation" of important philosophers was led by C. I. Lewis (1883–1964), Brand Blanshard (1892–1987), and the coming in 1924 of Alfred North Whitehead (1861–1947) to Harvard University.[3]

Appropriately, it was Harvard that extended the invitation to Whitehead, for although John Dewey was an extremely notable exception, the entire classical period, from Peirce to Whitehead, was dominated by Harvard, either on behalf of its teachers or on behalf of its graduate students of philosophy, many of whom became the premier teachers of the succeeding generation.[4] This contention is not in any way to be taken as a denigration of the important philosophical work found at the University of Chicago at the turn of the century or the subsequent significance of Columbia University's development of pragmatic and historical naturalism which flourished in the second, third, and fourth decades of this century – traditions largely due to the influence of John Dewey. Rather, it is simply a matter of fact that Harvard had the edge.

After the Second World War, the philosophical situation in America took on a very different cast. The political upheaval in continental Europe caused many outstanding philosophers to emigrate to the United States. During the decade of the 1930s, America received Herbert Feigl, Herbert Marcuse, Rudolph Carnap, Carl Hempel, Hans Reichenbach, and Alfred Tarski, among others. Further, as is well known, the war forced Bertrand Russell to stay in America from 1938 until 1944. As a result of these events, the positivism of the Vienna Circle, sophisticated Hegelian-Marxism of the Frankfurt School, and the Russellian approach to philosophy all gained a foothold on the American scene. After the Second World War, these influences were joined by the flood of writings from France and Germany on behalf of phenomenology and existentialism. Many American students once again returned to England for their philosophical education and brought back the early messages of logical empiricism, ordinary language, and linguistic analysis – varieties of what came to be known subsequently by the generic term "analytic philosophy."

From 1950 until 1965, the student of philosophy in America, a term now used advisedly, was confronted with a bewildering array of philosophical materials from

Europe. Although the emphasis differed depending on the individual university and graduate program, American philosophy students at that time were reading Wittgenstein, Ryle, Ayer, Austin, the above-mentioned thinkers from the Vienna Circle, Kierkegaard, Nietzsche, Camus, Sartre, Husserl, Heidegger, Marcel, or Merleau-Ponty. The professionally oriented graduate schools were often characterized more by the technical accompaniment of logic than by that of languages. Increasingly, argumentation superseded interpretation as the proper mode of philosophical discourse, whether found verbally or as written in the learned journals. Whatever else one wants to say about this development of philosophy in America after the war, it remains incontrovertible that interest in classical American philosophy had all but disappeared from the academic philosophical scene.

From one point of view, the comparative neglect of classical American philosophy after the Second World War is baffling. Surely, no other major Western culture would so completely abandon its own philosophical tradition. Can one think of French philosophy without constant, even if critical, recourse to Descartes? Can one similarly think of German philosophy without relation to Kant or British philosophy without relation to Hume? (As a general response, the answer would be no!) Yet from another point of view, the neglect is understandable, even if lamentable. America, again by tradition, has prided itself on being ever open to novelty, be it ideas or things. Less praiseworthy, but also endemic to American culture, has been its susceptibility to the belief that native culture is inferior to that spawned elsewhere. This proceeds from a complex historical dialectic between a peculiar American version of the oriental doctrine of "face" and a longstanding sense of cultural inferiority, the latter healed apparently only by periodically imported European wisdom. As with other remarks made above, these contentions also deserve extensive commentary, but they too would take us beyond the mandate of the present [chapter].

Lest the reader doubt the neglected status of classical American philosophy in the 1960s, I offer some autobiographical comments. When I set out in 1965 to prepare a comprehensive edition of the works of William James, the publication scene was revealing. I found multiple paperback editions of the popular writings of James in print: *The Varieties of Religious Experience*, *Pragmatism*, and *The Will to Believe and Other Essays in Popular Philosophy.* They were casually "introduced," if introduced at all, and poorly printed. James's major philosophical writings, such as *Essays in Radical Empiricism* and *A Pluralistic Universe*, were out of print and difficult to obtain. In response to this situation, I published *The Writings of William James* (New York: Random House, 1967; Chicago: University of Chicago Press, 1977), which included a complete text of *Pragmatism* and a complete text of Ralph Barton Perry's 1943 edition of *Essays in Radical Empiricism* and *A Pluralistic Universe.* Appended to this volume was an updated and corrected version of Ralph Barton Perry's "Annotated Bibliography of the Writings of William James."

The response to this volume was revealing. A consensus revealed surprise at the range of James's interests, fascination with the comparative contemporaneity of his thought, and, significantly, an acknowledgment of his technical philosophical virtuosity. Soon after this publication of James's writings, other editions appeared: some claimed James for phenomenology (Bruce Wilshire, *William James: The Essential Writings* (New York: Harper and Row, 1971)) and others pointed to his catholicity of interests, philosophical as well as literary (Andrew J. Reck, ed., *Introduction to William James* (Bloomington: Indiana University Press, 1967); John K. Roth, ed., *The Moral Equivalent of War and Other Essays* (New York: Harper and Row, 1971); Gay Wilson Allen, ed., *A William James Reader* (Boston: Houghton Mifflin, 1972)).

A similar situation existed when I began to prepare a comprehensive edition of the writings of Josiah Royce. Virtually all of his works were out of print, and the few to escape that fate were published without introduction and without scholarly apparatus. Royce was still regarded by many as a throwback to the German idealists. He was thought to be a derivative thinker, and there was little acknowledgment of the extensive development in his thought or of the range of his interests. In 1968, prodded by the editorial wisdom of Morris Philipson, the University of Chicago Press set out to present the works of Royce in a comprehensive format. The first volume was an edition of Royce's *The Problem of Christianity*, published originally in 1913. The Chicago edition of this work has a perceptive and detailed introduction by John E. Smith. In 1969, the Chicago series was continued by the publication of *The Basic Writings of Josiah Royce*, in two volumes, which I edited. Included in these volumes was "An Annotated Bibliography of the Published Works of Josiah Royce," by Ignas Skrupskelis. As with the earlier mentioned response to the James volume, so too here did the reviewers stress their surprise at the variety of Royce's writings, especially with regard to his work in social philosophy and American history and religion. The fourth volume of this series was published in 1974, entitled *The Letters of Josiah Royce*, edited by John Clendenning. The fifth and final volume, a biography of Royce by Clendenning, is now in preparation at the University of Wisconsin Press. At this writing, the Chicago series is the most substantial version of Royce now in print. There are no present plans, unfortunately, for a collected and critical edition of his writings. This is especially to be regretted because the Royce archives at Harvard University contain a considerable amount of unpublished papers, notably on logic, which merit wider public attention.

In the late 1960s, John Dewey's writings were better represented than those of James or Royce. The standard comprehensive edition was that of Joseph Ratner, *Intelligence in the Modern World* (New York: Modern Library, 1939), but it had the defect of presenting many excerpted materials and following themes designated as significant by the editor rather than by Dewey himself. In 1960, Richard Bernstein edited a helpful collection of Dewey's essays, *On Experience, Nature and Freedom* (Indianapolis: Bobbs (Liberal Arts), 1960). All but one of these essays, however, were confined to Dewey's work after 1930. Another coherent collection of Dewey's writings was to be found in *John Dewey on Education,* edited by Reginald Archambault (New York: Modern Library, 1964). At this time, most of Dewey's original books were still in print, even if only in paperback editions. An attempt to provide a minimally comprehensive edition of Dewey's writings can be found in my two-volume edition, *The Philosophy of John Dewey* (Chicago: University of Chicago Press, 1981).

The upshot of these developments with regard to the works of James, Royce, and Dewey is that an effort was made to provide competent and comprehensive editions of their works and to overcome the haphazard and casual presentations of their major writings. These efforts, at least in the case of Dewey and James, acted as a creative backdrop to a major breakthrough on the American philosophical scene. For the first time, national funding was provided for a collected critical edition of the writings of philosophers. The first venture, largely supported by the National Endowment for the Humanities, was that devoted to the works of John Dewey. Originated by the Center for Dewey Studies of Southern Illinois University at Carbondale, and partially supported by a grant from the John Dewey Foundation and from Mr. Corliss Lamont, the entire project is edited by Jo Ann Boydston. The first 5 volumes are published as *The Early Works, 1882–1898.* They include Dewey's early essays, his writings on Leibniz, psychology, and ethics, and his periodic and episodic pieces during that period. The next group of volumes are referred to as *The Middle Works, 1899–1924.* All 15 volumes projected for this period have been published, containing Dewey's classic writings on education, his many journal articles and book reviews of that time, and his important work of 1903, *Studies in Logical Theory. The Later Works, 1925–1953*, is projected as having 16 volumes. As of this writing, 7 volumes have been published, including the very important text of *Experience and Nature.* To this will be added an index and other important editorial information. Some 10 volumes of correspondence await confirmation as to actual publication. Of the volumes published thus far, it can be said that they are characterized by helpful introductions, accurately emended texts, and impeccable editorial supervision by Ms. Boydston. When this massive project is completed, even serious students of Dewey will be awed anew at his prodigious output, his learning, and above all his extraordinary ability to sustain intellectual quality over such an extensive span of time and work.

Between the publication of *The Early Works* and the initial volumes of *The Middle Works*, the National Endowment for the Humanities funded a second proposal for a collected, critical edition of the writings of a major classical American philosopher, William James. Founded by Frederick Burkhardt and John J. McDermott, and sponsored by the American Council of Learned Societies, this edition, inclusive of unpublished writings, is projected to be 16 volumes. The general editor is Frederick Burkhardt and the textual editor is Fredson Bowers. The publisher is Harvard University Press. The introductions to these James volumes are much more extensive than those found in the Dewey edition, and take as their task to provide the genesis of the text, its major contentions, and an analysis of the critical response to the text over the years of its existence. The James edition has not been published in chronological order, although when finished it can be read that way. Thus far, 13 volumes have been published, comprising a 3-

volume edition of *The Principles of Psychology* and 10 other titles. As with the Dewey volumes, this edition of James establishes an exact text, inclusive of James's emendations, subsequent to the first printing. In the James volumes, an added feature is the work of Ignas Skrupskelis, who has traced every reference or allusion made by James to its original source. The result is a veritable map to the panoply of persons and issues which laced the European and American intellectual scenes of the late nineteenth and early twentieth centuries. The collected critical editions of James and Dewey, when completed, will provide the student of American philosophy with a vast amount of philosophical and cultural material from which to assess their significance as thinkers. Provided also will be a rich context for the understanding of almost a century of vibrant philosophical activity. Although not as technically proficient or nearly as complete, the Chicago series of Royce volumes adds a still further enriching context for understanding that period in American and European cultural history.

I turn now to the last three thinkers of the classical period, C. S. Peirce, George Santayana, and George H. Mead. The story of Peirce's inability to publish most of his writings during his lifetime is now a depressing biographical chapter in any history of American philosophy. After his death in 1914, many boxes of his papers were sold to Harvard University, where they languished for years, uncatalogued and unsung. Due to the efforts of two young philosophers then at Harvard University, Charles Hartshorne and Paul Weiss, six volumes of these papers were published between 1931 and 1935.[5] In 1958, this series was brought to a completion by the publication of the seventh and eighth volumes under the editorial supervision of Arthur W. Burks. Before and during this time, several smaller anthologies of Peirce's writings were published: *Chance, Love and Logic*, ed. Morris R. Cohen (New York: Harcourt, Brace and Co., 1923); *The Philosophy of Peirce*, ed. Justus Buchler (London: Routledge and Kegan Paul, 1940); *Charles S. Peirce, Essays in the Philosophy of Science*, ed. Vincent Tomas (New York: Liberal Arts Press, 1957); *Charles S. Peirce, Values in a Universe of Chance*, ed. Philip P. Wiener (New York: Doubleday, 1958). A much later collection of *The Essential Writings of Peirce* was edited by Edward C. Moore (New York: Harper and Row, 1972).

The collected papers of Peirce, however, did not exhaust the treasure trove of his writings. This was made clear with the publication of Richard Robin's *Annotated Catalogue of the Papers of C. S. Peirce* (Amherst: University of Massachusetts Press, 1967). Robin's catalogue made clear that the *Collected Papers*, although a magnificent endeavor in its time, fell short in scope and in editorial organization. It came, then, as very welcome news when the National Endowment for the Humanities announced its funding support of the publication of a collected and critical edition of Peirce's works. This edition, to be prepared chronologically, will be under the supervision of the distinguished Peirce scholar Max H. Fisch. When completed and joined with the edition of Peirce's mathematical writings edited by Carolyn Eisele, we shall have extant virtually all of Peirce's work, arranged and edited in the best tradition of scholarship. At present, two volumes have been published by Indiana University Press, taking Peirce's writings from 1857 until 1871, inclusive of biographical material by Max Fisch.

With regard to the work of George Santayana, a similar program is under way. Santayana's writings have been periodically reprinted in paperback editions, and two volumes have been devoted to his unpublished writings; these are *Santayana: Animal Faith and Spiritual Life*, ed. John Lachs (New York: Appleton-Century-Crofts, 1967), and *Physical Order and Moral Liberty*, ed. John Lachs and Shirley Lachs (Nashville: Vanderbilt University Press, 1969). Other collections of Santayana's essays have appeared, and it can be said that a high proportion of his works are available in one form or another. Yet, as with the other classical American philosophers, his reputation has suffered from the unavailability of a comprehensive edition of his writings. This situation has been rectified by a grant from the National Endowment for the Humanities on behalf of the editor, Herman Saatkamp, Jr., to publish a critical edition of the writings of George Santayana, to be published by the MIT Press.

The last thinker under direct consideration is George H. Mead. A colleague of John Dewey for ten years at the University of Chicago, Mead remained there after Dewey's departure. A profound teacher, he published comparatively little in his lifetime. After his death, many of his manuscripts and lectures were published, including *The Philosophy of the Present* (Chicago: Open Court, 1932); *Mind, Self and Society* (Chicago: University of Chicago Press, 1934); *Movements of Thought in the Nineteenth Century* (Chicago: University of Chicago Press, 1936); and *The Philosophy of the Act* (Chicago: University of Chicago Press, 1938). These volumes are still in print and have been supplemented by the publication of Andrew J. Reck's edition of most of Mead's previously published essays under the title of *Selected Writings* (Indianapolis: Bobbs-Merrill, 1964). A bibliography of Mead's writings, including details about his unpublished work, can be found in David Miller's authoritative study, *George Herbert Mead – Self, Language and the World* (Austin: University of Texas Press, 1973). Miller has also published *The Individual and the Social Self: Unpublished Work of George Herbert Mead* (Chicago: University of Chicago Press, 1982).

In addition to the extraordinary developments in the area of scholarly editions of the writings of the classical American philosophers, the last ten years have also witnessed the publication of important works in the area of secondary literature. The two standard works in the history of American philosophy have been by Herbert Schneider, 1946, and by Joseph Blau, 1952. In 1977, there appeared an impressive two-volume study entitled *A History of Philosophy in America* (New York: G. P. Putnam's Sons, 1977). Written by Elizabeth Flower and Murray Murphey, it is thorough and philosophically sophisticated. Its range is from the Puritans to C. I. Lewis, and it has taken its place as the standard history of American philosophy, despite its title, which announces "Philosophy in America."

In the last decade, two important biographies have been published: Gay Wilson Allen's *William James* (New York: Viking Press, 1967), and *The Life and Mind of John Dewey* (Carbondale: Southern Illinois University Press, 1973), by George

Dykhuizen. As mentioned earlier, a biography of Royce by John Clendenning is in progress, and so too is one of Whitehead by Victor Lowe, *Alfred North Whitehead: The Man and His Work*, vol. I (Baltimore: The Johns Hopkins University Press, 1985). Of note also in this regard is the recent publication of *The Poems of John Dewey*, edited by Jo Ann Boydston (Carbondale: Southern Illinois University Press, 1977). As with all of Ms. Boydston's editing, this volume is a model of scholarship, and her introduction provides a lucid account of the circumstances surrounding Dewey's writing of poetry and an accompanying perspective on a heretofore little known aspect of Dewey's life.

Commentaries on the American philosophers have also increased both in quantity and quality. As a further testament to the renascence of American philosophy, in 1974 the Society for the Advancement of American Philosophy was founded. Now in its twelfth year, the Society has more than 600 active members and meets four times a year. The quarterly journal, *Transactions of the Charles S. Peirce Society*, has widened its focus to become "A Quarterly Journal in American Philosophy." This renewal of interest, coupled with the publication of collected critical editions of the classic American philosophers, should considerably enhance the quality of work in American philosophy. Assuming that the editions are published as planned, the year 1990 should bring us over 100 volumes of superbly edited works in American philosophy.

Aside from the sheer aesthetic and editorial importance of these events, what significance accrues for the study of philosophy in the widest sense of that term? First, it gives to those who are teaching and writing philosophy in America a local touchstone from which to understand essential dimensions of contemporary philosophy. The work of contemporary philosophers as diverse as W. V. O. Quine, Nelson Goodman, Wilfrid Sellars, Richard Rorty, and Hilary Putnam is inseparable from the influences of the earlier classical American period.

Second, European philosophers are used to working from a tradition which is characterized not only by brilliance but by girth. In the past, American philosophy was represented by isolated works, leaving the enormous scope of each major thinker hidden from view. The publication of the respective collected works will present an imposing and coherent body of materials from which to proceed. In short, the tradition of classical American philosophy will take its public place among the other great and warranted philosophical traditions of the past. This will give a new generation, whatever its geographical location, an opportunity to evaluate the continuing worth of American philosophy.

Finally, quite aside from the importance of the renewed availability of the works of the American philosophers, we stress here the intrinsic importance of the works themselves. The American philosophers address themselves, at one time or another, to virtually every significant philosophical theme, most often in a language which is accessible and rich. Their disputes, insights, and failings constitute one of the truly creative philosophical clusterings in the history of philosophy. Their work is seminal for our work, and the general admonition of Santayana is still to the point: those of us who forget the past will be condemned to relive it.

Such a reliving would be done in ignorance, which is certainly an unforgivable condition for philosophers.

Notes

1 Ralph Waldo Emerson, "Nature," in *The Complete Works of Ralph Waldo Emerson*, vol. 1 (Boston: Houghton Mifflin, 1903–4), p. 3.

2 Philip P. Wiener, *Evolution and the Founders of Pragmatism* (Cambridge, MA: Harvard University Press, 1949), p. v. For a detailed consideration of this period, see Ralph Barton Perry, *The Thought and Character of William James*, 2 vols. (Boston: Little, Brown and Co., 1935).

3 For a discussion of the major American philosophers after the classical period, see Andrew J. Reck, *Recent American Philosophy* (New York: Pantheon Books, 1964) and *The New American Philosophers* (Baton Rouge: Louisiana State University Press, 1968).

4 For a brilliant, provocative, and contentious evaluation of the central importance of the Harvard philosophy department during this period, see Bruce Kuklick, *The Rise of American Philosophy – Cambridge, Massachusetts, 1860–1930* (New Haven, CT: Yale University Press, 1977).

5 The fascinating story of how this Peirce project came to be is retold in later interviews with Richard Bernstein, given by Hartshorne and Weiss. See "Recollections of Editing the Peirce Papers," *Transactions of the Charles S. Peirce Society*, 6 (1970): 149–88 (ed. Richard Bernstein).

Index